WHY WAR?

MAKING SENSE OF CONSCIOUSNESS AND SELF

"One Is the All"

Mario Rendón

IPBOOKS.net
International Psychoanalytic Books

International Psychoanalytic Books (IPBooks)
New York • http://www.IPBooks.net

To Diane, Adán, and Renata

In memory of Karen Horney, and all those who struggle to recover
their lost voice in psychoanalysis

TABLE OF CONTENTS

"Of the Nature and State of Man, With Respect to Society"

EPISTLE III: ARGUMENT (of Pope's book *Essay on Man*)

I. The whole Universe one system of Society. Nothing made wholly for itself, nor yet wholly for another. The happiness of animals mutual.

II. Reason or Instinct operates alike to the good of each individual. Reason or Instinct operates also to Society in all animals.

III. How far Society carried by Instinct; how much farther by reason.

IV. Of that which is called the state of nature. Reason instructed by Instinct in the invention of the arts; and in the forms of Society.

V. Origin of political societies; origin of Monarchy; patriarchal government.

VI. Origin of true Religion and Government, from the same principle of Love; origin of Superstition and Tyranny, from the same principle of Fear. The influence of Self-love operating to the social and public good. Restoration of true Religion and Government on their first principle. Mixed government. Various forms of each, and the true end of all."

Alexander Pope (1733) Essay On Man.1

---

1   Pope, A. (1733) *Epistle III. An Essay on Man.* In: Epistles to a Friend. London. Printed for J. Wilford. Online in Poets' Corner. Bookshelf. Alexander Pope. Accessed from <http://www.theotherpages.org/poems/pope-e3.html> on 2016-06-10.

PREFACE

"Thus God and Nature link'd the gen'ral frame,
And bade Self-love and Social be the same."

Pope[2]

The argument of Pope could be the argument of this book. It is remarkable that he wrote it in 1733, foretelling so many modern themes: that the total set of interrelations of the universe must include society (Hegel); that everything stands in relationship to everything else (Darwin); that happiness and love are reciprocal (Freud); that reason is a continuation of instinct (Darwin); that instinct produces social institutions (Veblen), that patriarchy had a historical origin as did religion, and that therefore unlike material imperatives they are reversible (Morgan, Meszaros); that governments based on love and those based on fear are antipodes (Marx); and that true self-love results in public good (Adam Smith). These are all themes of this book, based on the Spinozist principle that God and Nature are one, and therefore God is only the good sense of nature, its awesome intelligence of which humanity partakes. This shows how old the fundamental ideas of this book are. Our lack of action is not due to lack of ideas.

The title of the book expresses its main thesis. Freud got close to answering the question but his ideology blurred his vision to the dialectical nature of instinct: to the effect that altruism, the phenomenon that so productively puzzled Darwin, is his Eros, the feminine instinct. Thanatos, its opposite unrestrained, manifests itself in constant war today. This is based in the Freud-Einstein correspondence after, in 1931, the Institute for Intellectual Cooperation invited Ein-

2   Pope, A. (1733) Epistle III. An Essay on Man. In: Epistles to a Friend. London. Printed for J. Wilford. Online in Poets' Corner. Bookshelf. Alexander Pope. Accessed from <http://www.theotherpages.org/poems/pope-e3.html> on 2016-06-10.

stein to a cross-disciplinary exchange of ideas about politics and peace with a thinker of his choosing. Einstein chose Freud and asked hum *Why War?* within the parameters of might and right that Freud, interestingly, substituted for violence and right. Einstein was hoping for a psychological explanation and Freud answered only partially and rather hopelessly through his instinctual construct of-Thanatos but rather unilaterally and mechanically.[3] Freud did not see his contradiction: that his whole theory of culture was based on sublimation, and therefore the question "why is war?" an exception to sublimation? This book endeavors to answer this question by placing history on the psychoanalytic couch in the first part - by interpreting its trauma that repressed altruism. A deeply traumatized animal species, we ourselves inflicted the trauma when we abandoned the morality of evolution,[4] and compromised our inherent moral uprightness.

This work stems from dissatisfaction with the practice of psychoanalysis, from its compartmentalization that disconnects it from other sciences, and the logical conclusion that its object cannot be narrowed to "the unconscious." The urgent study of consciousness, long neglected by him, was the course Freud was taking at the end of his life with his focus on anthropology and particularly his critique of religion and culture. Consciousness is the psychological isomorph of culture. Karen Horney and the culturalists continued that search but did not pursue it to its final conclusion. Applied to *ideology* the actual consciousness of the actual self psychoanalysis is a critical effort endeavoring to find the real consciousness of the real self. In an attempt to return to a morality of evolution psychoanalysis must start with the natural phenomenon *instinct* (animal intelligence) because as we stem from animal species, consciousness stems from instinct.

In its human version, however, it is not instinct but *instinctual disposition* Freud's *drive* instinct exceptionally transformed by

---

3   The Einstein-Freud Correspondence (1931-1932). Accessed from <http://www.public.asu.edu/~jmlynch/273/documents/FreudEinstein.pdf> on 2015-04-10.
4   Horney, K. (1950). "A Morality of Evolution." Introduction to: *Neurosis and Human Growth*. New York. Norton. Pp. 13-15.

history and culture, that concerns us. We observe this miraculous transformation in every newborn, as it takes place in the hands of a tending mother. Listening to history with the "third ear," we can also observe it phylogenetically. This is the task of this book.

There are many possible points of departure in this task, and we may as well choose the cultural phenomenon of the Bible, its explanation of origins, and reinterpret its metaphor. The pivotal question posed by the snake in Genesis is about why we are kept from wisdom, the awesome good sense of nature. The snake addresses the question to Eve, who has the natural predisposition to wisdom as the one who naturally selects. This arouses doubt and desire in Eve, her sin but also the fundament of culture. In the Spinozist equation, the word it turns out that Natural Wisdom had to be represented as God in its latest manifestation, Logos, hitherto unspoken.

The snake is probably the most loaded symbol in mythology, originally feminine in many cultures throughout the world, in some identified with the rainbow and water, but later appropriated by the patriarch as Phallus, the symbol of power. Its capacity to alternatively represent one and zero is probably the source of its unequaled ambiguity of fact and negation, being and nothingness. This is the reason I have chosen Ouroboros as a symbol of the dialectic. The original sin was Envy where our human alienation starts, Eve's being unaware that it was she who was the latest expression of Wisdom. Our tragedy has been all about God-like wisdom, consciousness reified starting with the apple in paradise. We will see, in Chris Knight's chapter, how Eve went on to invent a culture, only to be again reified by a patriarchal coup.

The expulsion from paradise is another metaphor that Otto Rank believed to be the trauma of birth. In our version it is the trauma not of vaginal birth as much as it is of its analogue the *separation trauma* that took an unpredicted lengthy course adding to the biological cost of the species. After innumerable millions of years of maternal steering of the species, maternal dependence that I arbitrarily compress to two hundred thousand years of anatomical modernity, from the long transition from apehood to modern *Homo sapiens* a violent separation took place, leading to slavery and patriarchy. It is the trauma of the son's deposing and killing his mother, the tragedy of Orestes before Oedipus.

This trauma did not produce culture that had been already fully developed by mothers, along evolutionary adaptations that I refer to as *first order mediations,* in sync with nature. Although it significantly augmented productivity and accumulation, and although it concomitantly accelerated consciousness, it took place through the inversion of the previous matriarchal mediations with nature to a second-order category based on sex and class hierarchy, on slavery and patriarchal command. This was the unnatural attempt to objectify human subjects *en masse.* The natural balance of mutually constraining sexuation, two opposite but equal instinctual dispositions, male and female, gave place to a hegemonic patriarchal hierarchy. The original equalizing Mother Right was subverted through a political coup that deposed ruling mothers replacing them by their sons who then transformed into patriarchs through identification, enslaving all others, all that were not in the class of propertied patriarch.

The first part of the book is about the original matriarchal culture, leading to the primal trauma of its overthrow. It focuses on evidence presented reiteratively to academia throughout the years and from different scientific perspectives, coming for the most part from male researchers before feminism took the matter into its own hands. This evidence has been reiteratively rejected under the pretext of proof: show me one society without fathers or husbands. This evidence has been recently presented by Hua Cai; and the response is dead silence. The second part of the book deals with the effects of the trauma of separation on consciousness and the self. Here Hegel's and George Herbert Mead's theories are the guides respectively.

Evolutionarily, an effort is made to emphasize the continuity of nature-history that legitimates human science and that was first proposed by Spinoza as a monist alternative to Descartes' dead-end duality. Hegel picked up the Spinozist thread. Psychoanalysis is a particularly fit instrument for this task because it focuses on the repressed in science, the ideologically discredited, repudiated or ignored. Psychoanalysis uniquely uses this material to reconstruct the whole of human science. In this regard it is no coincidence that psychoanalysis, along with matriarchal anthropology, recapitulation theory, and Marxism, have all been discredited but remain quite symptomatic. Compared to other sciences, psychoanalysis has the advantage of working with a *subjectivity* that all other sciences avoid, and that makes it an art also.[5] Because the terminology of the various rather specialized domains is not always familiar to the reader, I have included a glossary at the end explaining the sense in which I use some terms.

The critical psychoanalytical stand of the author is a bequest of Karen Horney's deconstructive attitude towards Freud. With George Herbert Mead, Lev Vygotsky, and A.N. Leontiev, an alternative critical psychology is also sketched, indispensable for the new century. Istvan Meszaros' constant argument in defense of Marxism as best science *vis à vis* the repeated onslaughts of reifying capitalist ideology is endorsed and the backbone of this book. Finally, Thorstein Veblen, Robert Briffault's and Chris Knight's courageous stand in their scientific and political communities inspires emulation. The debt to many feminist women is too huge to list; some of it will be seen interspersed in the text.

Southbury, Tuesday, March 6, 18

---

5   Sullivan, H.S. (1970). *The Psychiatric Interview*. New York. Norton.

INTRODUCTION AND SUMMARY

" 'Co-muni-cation' is giving gifts (from the Latin munus--gift) together. It is how we form the 'co-mu-ni-ty.' "

Genevieve Vaughan[6]

"The radically different worldview that we need now is not the worldview of the gift economy as practiced by Indigenous peoples only, but a worldview that recognizes and derives from the gift economy both in Indigenous societies and, though hidden and mis-named, inside Patriarchal Capitalism itself; we might even say, inside every human being.

In 1484 The Papal Bull of Innocent VIII was published, marking the beginning of the Inquisition, during which, by some estimates as many as 9,000,000 witches, most of whom were women, were killed over a period of 250 years. It is perhaps not coincidental that these two genocides, of Native Americans and of European women, happened simultaneously."

Genevieve Vaughan.[7]

---

6   Vaughan, G. (1997). *For-Giving: A Feminist Criticism of Exchange. Austin*, Texas. Plainview Press in collaboration with the Foundation for a Compassionate Society. Ch. 1., P. 15. Free download from < http://www.gift-economy.com/forgiving.html> on 2016-03-21.

7   Vaughan, G. (2007). "Introduction: A Radically Different Worldview is Possible." In: Vaughan, G. Ed. (2007). *Women and the Gift Economy. A Radically Different Worldview is Possible.* Toronto, Canada. Innana Publications and Education Inc. Accessed from < http://gift-economy.com/wordpress/wp-content/uploads/2013/08/womenand-thegifteconomy.pdf> on 2016-02-09.

"I think women are foolish to pretend they are equal to men, they are far superior and always have been."

William Golding[8]

---

8   William Golding made this comment about the superiority of women in an introduction to an unabridged audiobook version of "Lord of the Flies." The quote was taken from an explanation from Golding about why "Lord of the Flies" was a story about little boys and not little girls. Accessed from <https://www.truthorfiction.com/sir-william-goldings-words-wisdom-women/> on 2016-09-15.

THE RESTORATION OF WOMEN'S RIGHTS,
A MARKER OF SOCIAL EVOLUTION

> " According to Marx, the class including the 'class for itself' is necessarily tied to pre-history. Consequently, the idea of a conscious collective totalization on a class basis, notwithstanding the qualitative differences between the contending classes, is and remains a problematical concept."

Meszaros, *Beyond Capital*[9]

1. The Issue of Equality

Before social class became a concept in the human mind as described by Plato in his *Republic,* the real phenomenon (property-determined hierarchical segments in the collective mode of relations) had already taken place in Greece and around it. This is the historical phenomenon in which social value is largely determined by property. Before there was social class, however, there was another form we can call "natural class": this is the non-hierarchical natural division of labor between female and male of the species through which the female selects mates, fit males successful in their fights for access. Natural class thus dictates the division of labor for reproduction. It is equal in that both components equally belong to the same species, but opposite morphologically, because of their opposed sexual characteristics.

I will argue throughout this book that in general the capacity to fight is a masculine bias in the human species, and that to discriminate, and select, a feminine one. In other words the *might and right* that Einstein referred to in his correspondence with Freud about

---

9   Meszaros, I. (1995). *Beyond Capital. Towards a Theory of Transition.* London. The Merlin Press. Online in Scribd. Accessed from <104011633-Beyond-Capital-To-wards-a-Theory-of-Transition.pdf> on 2015-07-19.

war,[10] although shared concepts, are differently titrated in both natural classes of the species. I also argue that their historical form of relation is determined by their naturally designed reciprocal constraint capacity. The corollary is that this requires two sex-determined instinctual dispositions.

The distinction between *natural* and *historical* is important because unlike the first, being the result of human mediation, the second is reversible. Unable to see this Freud could not possibly be optimistic in his response to Einstein.

Evolutionarily all evidence seems to indicate that the original and default class, the class that generates others, is the female class, in its function of reproductive mothering. Unlike in politics, where equality is a goal, biologically equality is not the rule or desirable. Our differences are so obvious that any concept of equality easily finds overwhelming evidence to the contrary, both genetically and morphologically. We could live in harmony if we were to acknowledge our natural design based on variation, difference and complementarity, spiritual diversity included. Sexually, the issue is not equality but parity based on the mutual recognition of our essential constraining alterity.

Living without war could thus be accomplished through the leveling acknowledgment of our natural differences: foremost sex, but also skin color, environmental determinations, and spiritual beliefs. Evolutionarily, sex introduced alterity within sameness, otherness within the same species, the first step toward a dialectic of consciousness: sameness in alterity. Sexuation for the first time introduces in some natural species two opposite classes indispensable to each other for their perpetuation.

In its present form, abstract equality possible only in the eyes of God, is a mystifying historical construct. It is used to conceal the overriding of the natural design of equal reciprocal constraint that

10 Einstein, A, and Freud, S. (1931-2)."The Einstein-Freud Correspondence." Online in Arizona State University. Accessed from <www.public.asu.edu/~jmlynch/273/documents/FreudEinstein.pdf> on 2016-11-07

produces the natural balance of the species. Darwin did not confirm identity anywhere in nature but instead variation, one thing leading to another. We are all born genomically not only different but unique, and particular conditions and activity will determine our outcomes. We are designed for an average expectable environment[11] that unfortunately, through our capacity to mediate, we have radically transformed into unpredictable and even dangerous.

The abstract notion of human equality is a vestige of the Platonic idealism that historically made Christianity a successful historical revolution by declaring all humans equal in the eyes of God. As an abstraction, equality can be shared in fantasy only. The Malthusian[12] and Nietzschean[13] morality of voracious and insatiable individualism promoted by the ruling class are based on the identification with the aggressor.

Political equality on the other hand, the desirable goal, is equality in the fulfillment of needs that may be different from one individual to another according to natural and historical determinations. It is universal attainment of human rights.

In this regard the suffix "archy," has two meanings: "… It means "beginning" as well as "domination." Therefore, we can translate "matriarchy" accurately as "the mothers from the beginning," and also as "when mothers dominated."[14] We need not be shy about the

---

11   Hartmann, H. (1958) *Ego psychology and the problem of adaptation.* Trans. David Rapaport. New York : International Universities Press. Journal of the American Psychoanalytic Association., Monograph series, no. 1. Online in Questia. Accessed from <https://www.questia.com/read/10945256/ego-psychology-and-the-problem-of-adaptation> on 2015-11-01.

12   Malthus, T. (1798). *An Essay On The Principle Of Population, As It Affects The Future Improvement Of Society With Remarks On The Speculations Of Mr. Godwin, M. Condorcet, And Other Writers.* London, Printed For J. Johnson, In St. Paul's Church-Yard. Online in Project Gutenberg. Accessed from <http://www.gutenberg.org/files/4239/4239-h/4239-h.htm> on 2015-11-01.

13   Nietzsche, F. (1887). *The Genealogy Of Morals.* Trans. Horace B. Samuel. New York. Boni And Liveright Publishers. Online in the Internet Archive. Accessed from <http://www.archive.org/stream/genealogyofmoral00nietuoft/genealogyofmoral00nietuoft_djvu.txt> on 2015-11-01.

14   goettner-abendroth, h. (no date). "Matriarchal Society and the Gift Paradigm." Accessed from <http://www.gift-economy.com/womenand/womenand_matriarchal.ht-

latter meaning, or try to suppress it for political correctness. We must recognize, however, that patriarchy is characterized by domination in a way matriarchy was not, judging by the present evidence. The original social leadership of mothers, if it was exercised through giving rather than exploitation, could not have been an analogue of patriarchy.

2. The Status of Women in the Nineteenth Century

There is plenty of evidence amassed to illustrate the incredible exploitation of women since they were transformed into "not-men," something that happened historically against the logic of evolution ten thousand years ago at the most. Through a political coup imposed by their sons, and perhaps even with their own initial acquiescence, mothers, who had introduced culture in sync with nature's boundaries, ended up being their sons' slaves. They lost the natural command of their groups, their positions as strategists of the species, priestesses, and group leaders. Mothers had jumpstarted human society by organizing and leading their large consanguineous *gentes or clans,* extended families the societies of their day. The inventors of social rules, institutions and morality were subjugated as mere productive and reproductive objects, even their generative capacity's being controlled by husbands and fathers. This was accomplished by reverting the incipient natural complementarity of the new species, based on altruism, back to the oppressive hierarchy of force of the food chain. Patriarchy is an unsuccessful attempt to historically regress to a pre-human morality; the struggle is still going on.

That this must have been the most traumatic episode to the blossoming coherence, the sprouting consciousness of humans, is documented by the universality of myths dealing with the slaying of dragons and the like. These myths were created to discourage the emerging form of power, the feared dragon of female solidarity, or

---

ml#top> on 2015-08-03.

any form of authority not held by the personifications of the patri-arch.[15] The return of the dragon indicates the fear that matriarchy may return. It is also the post-traumatic intrusion of the repressed trauma.

Slavery is the only possible form to assure hormonally predis-posed alpha males that their might is superior to mother right. At the same time, if there is anything a regular son would wants to repress as immoral, it is harm to his own mother. The only alterna-tive to repression that symptomatically does not work is bad faith. This transvaluation represents the world inverted, reality converted into fantasy, oppression legitimized by God, and so on. This became idealism and religion but, because it goes against the natural grain of consciousness, its good sense, it suffered the fate of the return of the repressed. Individual alienation is thus paired with periodic social unrest.

The groundbreaking nineteenth century book of August Bebel, *Women in the Past, Present and Future*,[16] dramatically documents the extent of the women's fall with the facts available at the time. It also points out that no historical movement of importance has taken place in which women have not played a prominent part as combat-ants and martyrs, a fact generally scantly acknowledged in patriar-chal historiography. No matter how silenced and subdued women have never lost their voice or their instinct. Their historical handicap has invigorated them like the Hegelian slave, with women's remain-ing the reservoir of hope for the species. Their voice's being true, comes not from any supernatural or abstract beings but from their natural, life-loving instinct.

The nineteenth century represents the dawn of feminine renais-

---

15   Knight, C. (2012). *World-historic defeat of women.* Chris Knight of the Radical An-thropology Group examines myths about a supposed "primitive matriarchy." Workers Weekly. Issue 910. 19 April 2012.
16   Bebel, A. (1910). *Women and Socialism.* Trans. Meta L. Stern. New York. Socialist Literature Co. (Orig. Pub. 1879). Online in Marxists Internet Archive (MIA). Ac-cessed from <https://www.marxists.org/archive/bebel/1879/woman-socialism/index. htm?utm_source=lasindias.info> on 2015-03-13.

sance. Although it is unfortunate that many women have had to become personifications of capital in order to succeed, identified with
their aggressor, this shows their capacity to be equal to men in men's
own territory. In the nineteenth century, however, women entered
the limelight of history in civil society : Queen Victoria, Jane Aus-
ten, Marie Curie, Florence Nightingale, Maria Montessori, George
Sand, and Jane Ellen Harrison, to mention only some of the most
notorious. These are among many who were able to use their voices
to contribute in their respective fields. Less fortunate women pro-
tested in code, symptomatically, and those are the hysterics that
taught Freud how to listen, and decode.[17] Not only culture and language, but code and enigma, were invented by women.

In the same century, and without hyperbole, Karl Marx and Friedrich Engels pointed out how the bourgeois patriarch saw his wife
as just another instrument of production. Bourgeois marriage, with
its *raison d'être* of property and inheritance, was for them a "system
of prostitution public and private." [18]Yet they did not pay their due
to women as authors of society, as first economists of the gift, and as
inventors of all first-order social mediations. Political economy, by
definition dealing with civil society, was not perspicacious enough
to give full credit to mothers for the first form of human economy.

However, the particular relevance of feminine agency and feminine struggle, and what makes it dangerous to patriarchy and capitalism, is that the society of the future Marx and Engels came up
with by studying the laws of history socialism has its precedent in
matriarchy. This scientific fact cannot be fully brought into relief,
however, until the original missing piece of history is fully restored
into the historical narrative in a psychoanalytic fashion. It must be

17   Breuer, J., and Freud, S. (1893). *Studies on Hysteria.* Trans. James Strachey. New
     York. Basic Books. Online in The Internet Archive. Accessed from <https://archive.
     org/details/studiesonhysteri037649mbp> on 2015-11-01.
18   Marx, K. and Engels, F. (1969). "Proletarians and Communists." In: Manifesto of the
     Communist Party. Chapter II. Pp. 98-137. Trans: Samuel Moore in cooperation with
     Frederick Engels. Marx/Engels Selected Works, Vol. One. Moscow. USSR. Progress
     Publishers, (Orig. Pub. 1848). Online in MIA. Accessed from <https://www.marxists.
     org/archive/marx/works/1848/communist-manifesto/ch02.htm> on 2015-02-08.

recovered from disavowed memory, from repression, to make the human species' biography whole.

3. The Psychoanalytical Evidence in favor of Matriarchy

The psychoanalytic view holds that if matriarchy had just been forgotten *bona fide* in the brain fog of the primitive mind, it would be just one more undisturbing accident. However, the fact that its symptom historically returns in the form of social and academic unrest means that the memory is active and that the mechanisms of its repression are failing. The memory of the trauma is alive. This means that to stop the symptom the memory has to be worked through via scientific analysis. Spoken, analyzed and reintegrated into the scientific narrative, it will cease to disturb. Social unrest almost unequivocally has to do with issues of equality or of antagonistic perception even though these are often alienated or distorted as nationalism, racism or religious intolerance.. Academic unrest is illustrated by the recurrent proposition, and evidence, even if fragmentary, of matriarchal origins in the human sciences.

Psychoanalysis has proven a need for individuals to be consciously complete : that is, to arrive at a satisfactory explanation that is total and inclusive. Successively, myth, religion, philosophy, and finally science have all had their historical moment in that explanation. Psychoanalysis belongs in the scientific present, but it actively conserves past forms. Applied psychoanalysis would allow history to speak for itself by reintegrating what had been repressed. The basic conflict[19] is the antagonistic opposition of ideology and science.

The unconscious traumatic memory of the patriarchal coup attempts to return and be acknowledged. Evidence will be presented from evolutionary science, from anthropology, linguistics, psychology, political economy, and even forensics. It started with ethnology and, fragmentarily, meaning pieces missing that for the most part

---

19   Horney, K. (1945). *Our Inner Conflicts*. Chapter Two. The Basic Conflict. New York. Norton. Online in Internet Archive. Ac-cessed from <https://archive.org/details/OurInnerConflicts> on 2017-05-10.

were later found. These are expressed in terms like matrilineality, matrilocality, matronymic kinship forms and identity, and matriarchal customs, rituals, and myths. Even today these are all present in various degrees in societies across the world as anyone interested can verify. Add to these facts the vehemence of the rejection and the acrimony the debate has taken at times, and it is not difficult to conclude that there is a scientific problem.

The collective trauma of the enslavement of women, and others after them, split the human consciousness and created an artificial dichotomy of competing ideologies instead of consciousness. What was natural sexual dialectic became class antagonism, often illustrated by hierarchical binaries. The basic problem is that split human consciousness, or ideology, can not match natural good sense and therefore will occasion unrest and clash. We are repressively kept within the margin of an abstract "democracy" that does not match the real facts, when real democracy is evidently possible. The result is the most serious ecological damage to our own instinctual dispositions that dictate the form our behavior takes. We have lost the capacity to identify the aggressor that is ourselves within our own split species, and instead we must identify with our aggressor to survive. Baruch Spinoza was the first to be puzzled by this.

The first political coup in human history was also the first detour from the morality of evolution. It was not mythical but real, and it is largely conserved, coded in myths for which Feuerbach gave us the simple analytical key: to decode them, simply invert them. Feuerbach's earliest call to invert religion into its anthropology has reached only a few specialists in the field. Religion remains the most potent vehicle of human alienation. Freud used the method to contribute to the understanding of dreams, symptoms, myths, and even social institutions such as religion, but in the narrow field of science. The most substantial inversion of human alienation, accomplished by Marx, remains largely out of reach, discredited and repressed in mainstream academia.

Women's agency is, however, in ascendance and their contribution is likely to correct the bias of patriarchal science. It came to a peak with the suffragettes and has continued subsequently in its several waves of feminism and in academia with the accruing work of female intellectuals. Women's agency brings back the possibility of an alternative society based on the substantial equality of universal need-fulfillment.

Psychoanalytically, it is thus important to consider the female instinctual disposition as a balancing buffer to the patriarchal excess the world is experiencing. Going back to true balancing reciprocity, as it was designed by evolution, is necessary to achieve the evolutionary equilibrium of *Homo sapiens*.

4. Psychoanalytic Neurobiology

Only the mother offers her body as the sanctuary for each newcomer in the human species, and at her own cost. Only the mother is handicapped by the discomfort of pregnancy and delivery. It is the mother who, from her own metabolism, through the umbilical cord provides the aliment, protein, defenses, and all other ingredients necessary to painstakingly build the edifice of the human body with her own protein. She exclusively provides the energy, force, muscle and blood, for a painful delivery, and continues to hold, shelter, protect, and encourage the successful resolution of parasitic, symbiotic, and conflictive dependence and individuation. She invests her time, energy, and resources, toward the successful maturity of her newborn.

Neurobiology has shown us that the mother switches on every single human sense, kinesthesia, tactility, position, skin pressure and thermal sensation, pain and comfort, smell, taste, audition, and all other human indispensables such as safety, sense of trust, sense of plenitude, of waste, of beauty, of good and bad, right and wrong, and so on.

She puts nipple to mouth together simultaneously with words that soothe and indicate safety in a basically hostile world for a premature infant. She speaks to her infant before s/he is ready to understand words to create the need for language and communication. Most importantly, she intuitively imprints humanity in her newborn when she synchronizes her retinal fovea with that of her infant at the optimal distance of her breast. She starts the processes of recognition and desire, the first subject in constant search for its "object." These are the most important ingredients of human socialization, the first order mediations of human identity. She acknowledges, measures, tends, provides, and takes; she is the proxy regulator of the premature human until learning has made self-regulation possible.[20]

By the time the father, developmentally, socially, and meaningfully arrives in the child's consciousness, all the necessary first order mediations have been put in place emotionally and cognitively for the child to transitions to the new environment of civil society, the domain of the father. Here, Freud was correct in placing the Oedipus Complex years after birth.

5. The Symptomatic Woman and Psychoanalysis

The subversive protest of women could, for centuries, only be expressed in code, in symptoms,i.e., the language of the unconscious. Since the *paterfamilias,* fathers and husbands, were the "owners" of their bodies and lives, it was too dangerous to speak clearly. Casualties of the long and surreptitious gender war had been reported for a long time before Freud, as attested by the history of hysteria. Going back to Plato and Hippocrates, the diagnosis of an obstructive animal in the uterus, the imaginary replica of the dragon of feminine power as the wandering womb in the body of the woman, was a belief that practically held until Breuer and Freud. Then, with the help of a number of Viennese women patients, these two pioneers started to decode what ultimately turned out to be a political message into

---

20   Schore, A. (1994). *Affect Regulation and the Origins of the Self. The Neurobiology of Emotional Development.* Hillsdale, N.J. Lawrence Erlbaum Associates. Online in Questia. Accessed from <http://www.questia.com/read/57185676/affect-regulation-and-the-origin-of-the-self-the> on 2013-03-07.

medical terms. Women invented code and, although they did not get recognition in the academic literature, they taught Freud and Breuer to decode.

Freud's "unconscious" is the metaphor for the outcome of repression, the wasteland of human agency. Although he explicitly used political repression as his model, Freud was unable to completely elucidate the political phenomenon of women's being seen as not completely human. It took well into the latter part of the twentieth century for the mystery of neurosis to be deciphered in full, as alienating self-idealization, by Karen Horney,[21] as "problems in living" by Harry Stack Sullivan,[22] and as protest by Thomas Szasz.[23] Hysteria did disappear from the psychiatric nosology[24] as soon as it was itself decoded as the voice of protest and the symbol of oppression, particularly of women.

French existentialists Jean Paul Sartre and Simone de Beauvoir presented alternative formulations to the unconscious of Freud from the standpoint of philosophy. Sartre considered an unconscious within consciousness an ontological impossibility. Instead, he thought, Freud may have provided an alibi for *bad faith*. The unconscious construct allowed people to remain unaccountable for their alienating and surrendering deviant behavior, and Freud's patients knew what was in their so-called unconscious, although they pretended not to know.[25] Bad faith, according to Sartre caused the surrender of human subjectivity and human agency and their subordination to a social role, a reified coercive social prescription.

De Beauvoir saw it differently and more illuminatingly. Instead of the additional blow of bad faith, she saw the second sex as robbed

21   Horney, K. (1950). *Neurosis and Human Growth.* New York. Norton.
22   Sullivan, H.S. (1953). *The Interpersonal Theory of Psychiatry.* Ed. Helen Swick Perry and Mary Ladd Gawel. New York. Norton.
23   Szasz, T. (1974). *The Myth of Mental Illness.* New York. Harper Perennial.
24   DSM-III. (1980). Diagnostic and Statistical Manual of Mental Disorders. Third iteration. Arlington, VA. American Psychiatric Association.
25   Sartre, J.P. (1992). *Being and Nothingness.* New York. Washington Square Press. (Orig. Pub. 1943). Online in Scribd. Accessed from <http://www.scribd.com/doc/10268925/Sartre-Being-and-Nothingness#scribd> on 2015-11-02.

of its transcendence, agency and voice, of its full subjectivity, by the patriarchy. Women were thus left to survive only with what they could keep alive internally, their *immanence*. Expressive *transcendence*, clear voice, was forcefully monopolized by men.[26]

It remained to be seen that Sartre was adopting the patriarchal perspective. He is correct to point out the master's bad faith that in the slave is the unconscious.

We have witnessed, since the dawn of the eighteenth century, how women have progressively left the narrow enclave of the bourgeois family where they were imprisoned for too long. They have growingly enlisted themselves in all areas of civil society, including material and spiritual production, as well as government and even the military. In spite of this, they have been unable to achieve the political parity needed for a society designed for balance.

6. Matriarchy and the Production of Life: The Evolutionary Evidence

For the production of human life, evolution did load the dice toward females, and at a high price for them. Pregnancy, birthing, tending, teaching and giving, from your body and mind, are instinctual predispositions of the female of the species. More "productive" conquest, possession, expending, wasting, and territoriality are the predispositions of males. The incentive for females is altruism, moral satisfaction; for males it is material self-enhancement and more chances for reproduction. Women are more prone to focusing on relations and collaboration, while men are more inclined to compete and achieve. The operation of these two dispositions is determined by natural conditions, both sexes being endowed with both instinctual proclivities to be expressed according to environmental circumstances and both internal and external regulation. These two instinctual dispositions are clearly opposites and reciprocally constraining,

---

26 De Beauvoir, S. (2011). *The Second Sex.* New York. Random House. Online in MIA. Accessed from <https://www.marxists.org/reference/subject/ethics/de-beauvoir/2nd-sex/index.htm> on 2015-11-02.

to achieve an appropriate balance at any time.

In environments of abundance and relative safety, such as those that usually characterize sedentary, settled, and agricultural families, the female disposition is bound to manifest itself based on giving and sharing. Under opposite conditions of scarcity and threat, probably more common in nomadic and hunting groups, it is the male instinctual disposition that will probably express itself more predominantly in the group and its organization. It is logically possible that opposite forms of leadership would take place according to these natural circumstances. The governing issue is natural conditions for access to resources; while matriarchs led a society based on the universal fulfillment of needs, patriarchs on the contrary focused on saving for a rainy day. Institutionalized and magnified, the latter trend developed the capacity, through excessive accumulation by few, to paradoxically produce scarcity for the most. This is the case today in capitalism.

This differential sex-bound life principle has determined the way humans have related in society during different historical epochs. After gradually emerging from the original war of the food chain through collaboration and incipient culture, it was possible after two hundred thousand years to settle in sedentary agricultural societies, mostly about twenty thousand years ago in different areas of the continents. Subsistence's being guaranteed in a relatively peaceful and abundant environment allowed for hearth-based, harmonious gens (group) life to develop and thrive, driven by female instinctual predisposition of universal-need fulfillment. The ensuing probably man-created predatory environments, leading to the scarcity of nomadic conditions associated with climate changes, must have regressed neighboring groups thus, the intraspecies reinstatement of the previous strategy of the food chain, that consitutes war. This is described by Merlin Stone and Marija Gimbutas, among others, around the Mediterranean and in Europe. The harmony, cooperation and mutual tending that had prevailed in the settled agricultural societies gave place to competition, strife and self-concern in the second.

To address this problem, civil society was implemented as a second-order institution modeled on the gens, but based on a legal social contract to mediate diverse interests rather that the natural moral code that prevailed in matriarchy. It thus produced a governing patriarchal state that appeared along with the patriarchally established new, class-based division of labor in settled city states and nations. Skills development and technology allowed for an increase in productivity, and slave labor accelerated accumulation and private property for patriarchs who became citizens.

The historical upset leading to male hegemony must have come as a result of very paradoxical conditions. Material accumulation, that had started domestically, led to progressive exchange with surrounding communities instead of exclusive use in the gens. Exchange and property rather than shared use became the new form of economic relation, more in tandem with the male disposition. Subsequently, all previous cultural forms of organization implemented by females were inverted in order to erase their memory.

7. What is instinct?

Psychologically in humans, instinctual disposition is the bridge between nature and culture and it is rooted in natural instinct. In organisms, instinct is the expression of natural sense wherefrom consciousness emerges. This was Darwin's position.[27] Instincts are thus unconscious behaviors for the most part sublated or overriden by consciousness to become habits; and they are no exception to the logic of dialectics in that they oppose each other first externally and are subsequently internalized, to achieve, through mutual self constraint, a transient equilibrium. The same way agonist muscular motion needs reciprocal inhibition of the antagonist, a male instinct

---

27   Darwin, C. (1912). *The origin of species by means of natural selection, or the preservation of favoured races in the struggle for life.* Ch. 8. Instinct. New York: Hurst and Co. Darwin Online. Accessed from <http://darwin-online.org.uk/converted/pdf/1912_Origin_F518.pdf> on 2016-05-28.

is constrained by its opposite the female. In the hemispherically disconnected brain after surgery or lesions in the *corpus callosum*, agonistic dyspraxia occurs. There is for example an automatic execution of opposite motor commands by one hand when the patient is asked to perform movements with the other, the alien-hand syndrome. Here the hands compete and the non-dominant one does it unconsciously. This shows that the hemispheres of the brain have opposite, inhibitory functionality. In diagonistic dyspraxia, one hand directly opposes and interferes with the other.[28] This hemispheric mutuality of self-constraint may help us understand dominance as imbalance, the lack of inhibition of one side of the brain.

Regarding instinct, biologists have mapped out two polar strategies of reproductive natural selection, and others in between. Given unpredictable and highly predatory environmental conditions, organisms tend to reproduce fast, in high numbers, and at a lower cost per unit, *i.e.*, like rabbits. The strategy is technically designated as *r* for rate. On the opposite side, when environmental conditions are relatively stable, peaceful, and friendly, organisms then turn to reproduce through a contrasting strategy: slowly, in low numbers and at high investment costs. In the latter the paradigm is the protracted pregnancy and further prematurity of humans. This strategy is called *K* for constant and for capacity in German.[29]

The sexuation of the human species, coming from a natural reciprocal division of labor and necessary for collaboration, includes both instinctual strategies in a complementary fashion. Males speedily produce high numbers of low cost and easily disposable sperm cells. Females slowly produce comparatively few and costlier ova, only one maturing at a time through a hormonal and morphological cycle. These two different evolutionary strategies, instincts paired and reciprocal, not only determine a) the sexual division of labor

---

28 Akelaitis, Andrew J. (1945). "Studies on the corpus callosum: IV. Diagonistic dyspraxia in epileptics following partial and complete section of the corpus callosum". American Journal of Psychiatry 101 (5): 594–9.
29 Pianka, E.R. (1970). "On r and K selection". American Naturalist 104: 592–597. Accessed from <http://www.zo.utexas.edu/courses/THOC/rK.pdf> on 2015-03-14.

based on sexual instinct, but also b) opposite instinctual dispositions with morphological variations and behavioral differences between male and female. Freud, constrained by patriarchal ideology but also by the status of science, could only see one human instinct, libido, that he arbitrarily assigned to the male, although he always puzzled about the duality of instinct.

Females tend to seek for, and thrive in, stable, peaceful, and predictable environments; males are programmed to deal with riskier ones. In human society, the first opportunity of an agricultural and sedentary environment institutionalized the maternal consanguine first-order gens made it a custom. The gens or clan evolved to be transformed into the second-order patriarchal family that, now over-institutionalized, has overstayed its welcome. The change from gens to bourgeois family did not take place suddenly, but in a series of successive forms described by Morgan in his *Ancient Society*. As this happened, the second order patriarchal organization external to the gens, civil society, also developed changing characteristics in successive stages of the state, grossly slavist, feudal, and capitalist. Women were, throughout the patriarchal stage, confined to home arrest. From home, they continued their struggle while maintaining in their families elements of the old culture of the clan, such as a family economy geared to an equal fulfillment of needs.

It should mean something that ontogenetically, the default embryonic morphology in humans is female. During the intrauterine period, the human embryo detours in the male direction through the effect of a testosterone surge on the developing nerve cells; if that does not happen the fetal body remains in the female default position.[30] Once the differentiation of the sexual organs is achieved, the next step is the differentiation of the brain, under the influence of various contending male and female sex hormones on its developing cells. The permanent changes that result have organizing effects, and later, during puberty, brain circuits that developed in the womb

30   Swaab, D. F., Chung, W. C., Kruijver, F. P., Hofman, M. A., & Hestiantoro, A. (2003). "Sex differences in the hypothalamus in the different stages of human life." Neurobiology of Aging. Vol. 24. Supplement 1. Pp. S1–S16.

are reactivated by sex hormones.[31] Gender role (adjudicated social-ly), gender identity (the personal conviction), sexual orientation (be-havioral choice), and sex differences in cognition, tending, and ag-gressive behavior, as well as spatial and language organization, are all genetically programmed in this way. These very complex vari-ables are not quite replicable in other animal species as yet; when they have been, they have been found quite contradictory.

Differentiation of the genitals takes place in the first two months of pregnancy, while the sexual differentiation of the brain starts in the second half of pregnancy, creating a developmental gap that is still not well understood. Genital and brain configuration follow different time patterns and are therefore subject to different devel-opmental conditions. Studies have shown patterns of sex-atypical cerebral dimorphism in homosexual subjects, closer to the opposite sex. How sexual orientation, gender identity, and behavioral profile are processed in the brain are questions that remain largely unan-swered.[32] It is well established however that the fact that the brain continues to grow and develop after birth, gives it an opportunity to be shaped not exclusively genetically, but in dialectical interaction with its social environment.

Two connected but somewhat differently organized cerebral hemispheres, which could be analogues of sexual duality, may somehow have represented a regulatory attempt to mediate two dis-paraging instincts. This area of study is quite young. The best stud-ied multicellular organism, *Caenorhabditis elegans,* is a non-par-asitic small rod-like and bacteria-fed worm of temperate climates whose whole genome was the first to be deciphered. It does not have yet a respiratory or circulatory system but it does have a nervous

---

31   Phoenix, C. H., Goy, R. W., Gerall, A. A., & Young, W. C. (1959). "Organizing action of prenatally administered testosterone propionate on the tissues mediating mating behaviour in the female guinea pig. Endocrinology. Vol. 65, Pp. 369–382.

32   Savic, I. Garcia-Falgueras, A. Swaab, D.F. (2010). "Sexual differentiation of the hu-man brain in relation to gender identity and sexual orientation." *Progress in Brain Re-search.* Vol. 186. Pp. 41-62. Accessed from <https://teoriaevolutiva.files.wordpress.com/2014/02/sexual-differenciation-of-the-human-brain-in-relation-to-gender-iden-tity.pdf> on 2015-07-16.

system. The overwhelming majority of this species is female and hermaphrodite, males being only one in a thousand. The males have specialized tails with a needle-like structure for mating. Insemination by the male more than triplicates the amount of fertilized egg, showing a quantitative advantage to separate sexual reciprocity. Females in this species have two, XX, chromosomes, while males have only one (X0). Here we see a simple model of an organism that shows biological preeminence of females but also the advantage of oppositional duality. They have a selective sexuality with two choices, hermaphrodite and heterosexual, the male intervention's having quantitative reproductive utility possibly controlled by external conditions. Their early morphological differentiation includes a nervous system already, with around 300 neurons and 75.000 synapses.[33]

Fish have the most remarkable reproductive diversity. As species they may be unisexual, hermaphroditic, or heterosexual. They self-fertilize, group-spawn, or broadcast gametes in the water with no further obligation; they zealously guard nests and can even breed internal embryos.[34] It seems as if evolution rolled and rolled the dice in search perhaps of the most cost-effective reproductive option according to its varying conditions. With sexuation came sexual anatomic differentiation and behavioral duality, expressed in complementary mating systems. The social and behavioral derivatives of these natural determinations came to be regulated by the brain through the conditioning introduction of social mediations. These mediations were contingent upon instinctual releases and inhibitions that discriminate self-species from other species. Social discrimination initially based on morphological expression introduced a new selective give-and-take, a new discriminatory complexity, that eventually made growing coherence necessary. Consciousness is thus the

---

33 See Wikipedia. *"Caenorhabditis elegans."* Accessed from <https://en.wikipedia.org/wiki/Caenorhabditis_elegans> on 2015,07-18.

34 DeWoody, J.A. and Avise, J.C. (). "Genetic Perspectives on the Natural History of Fish Mating Systems. Journal of Heredity. Volume 92, Issue 2. Pp. 167-172. Online in Oxford Journals. Accessed from <http://jhered.oxfordjournals.org/content/92/2/167.full.pdf> on 2015-07-18.

reflective virtual outcome of this compounded material complexity captured by a nervous system. The self is the control organ, the regulatory organ of consciousness.

A dual natural instinct in a species has the obvious advantage of allowing for better adaptation to changing conditions of safety and scarcity through the adaptive preferential development of habits based on one instinct or the other. Chris Knight explains how this was the case in early human society that turned around this sexual duality cyclically and collaboratively. Early female solidarity controlled sexual access by introducing the mediatory contingency of family-feeding. Sexual behavior and productivity were then regulated along the female-synchronized conditions of the moon cycle and menstruation. This was probably a time when there was no brain dominance such as we have today. By repressing the expression of the female instinct and by creating artificial scarcity and insecurity through wasteful capitalist accumulation, patriarchs may have, hypothetically, lateralized the brain by hardwiring only their instinctual disposition.

No one would argue that the destructive war model of our present day society, linked to capitalist overvaluation of competition and force over collaboration and dialogue, brings the species closer to the food chain. Instead, it appears to be the design of *Homo sapiens* within an evolutionary morality of dialectical mutual constraint. To compound the historical paradox, globalization is making one the plurality of nations that up to now have appeared as a mosaic. It could be concluded from this that, with the world unified and totalized, we need a return to a family type of governance.

Inherently opposite natural instincts, harmonized by the brain's and by consciousness and self-regulatory capacities, are designed to adaptively balance the response to conditions both natural or social. Regulatory capacity is enhanced by the unique human capacity to mediate, to transform conditions and create historical needs. Lack of balance helps us understand our present condition of unnecessary constant war, parallel with constant wasteful accumulation of resources by individuals at the expense of others, the production of artificial scarcity. Patriarchal mediations have selectively corrupted the natural design of human consciousness to reflect a species, not individual, reality. What is the reality of the dominant class is presented as universal reality when the opposite is called for: universal reality ought to apply to the ruling class.

Patriarchal mediations are fetishistic, as Marx showed in his analysis of the commodity and capital, in that they displace the transformative and creative power of the species onto human objectifications, alien objects that appear to hold power over humans, such as capital, corporation, market, profit, wealth, the voice of money, *etc. Corpore, vox,* and *manu,* are symbolic projections of the human body into mystifying objectifications arising from the exploitative exchange of commodities. This has led historically to abstract incorporation instead of sensuality, money instead of *speech*, and market instead of self-regulation.

8. The First Inklings that there was a Matriarchal Epoch

Matriarchal means large groups of people in relatively small family-like gentes, all related by blood, and steered by the adaptive instinct and skills of their natural producers, mothers, who introduced the first order of cultural mediations through struggle and compromises with nature. Matriarchy does not mean the analogue of patriarchal domination, but a different type of cooperative organization based on skill, perhaps with the one exception that confirms the rule, the Amazons. The Amazons tried to beat patriarchs at their own game but failed.

There are references in the written historical record to the fact that societies ruled by women lived in Asia Minor. Diodorus of Sicily, in the first-century B.C.E, author of the first Universal History, wrote about Amazons who lived in Turkey, the Black Sea and Ukraine, and held the supreme power and royal authority in their societies. They were the authors of laws, their queens assigning tasks such as wool-spinning and other domestic duties to men. The right of succession went to the queen's daughter, and men were oppressed, male children being even tortured and handicapped to reduce their fitness.[35] This may represent the initial effort of women to resist surging patriarchal domination by identifying with the patriarch and adopting the patriarchal strategy alien to them.

Herodotus, the father of history, in the fifth-century B.C.E., reports matrilineality — female pedigree and matronymic identity — among the Lycians in the same area.[36] Mentioned in ancient literature as holding the same views are Nicholas of Damascus who lived in the first century B.C.E., and Heraclides Ponticus in the fourth-century B.C.E., both quoted by Bachofen.[37]

Ethnological studies of religion and myth, that started with the Swiss jurist Johann Bachofen, had a pervasive influence in early anthropology and have recently been revived by feminists. They conclusively prove the existence of early goddesses, and moon and underworld cults, that were the original template for the later heliocentric and masculine gods of patriarchal monotheism. Their polytheistic nature was a reflection of matriarchal parity that did not exclude males, even in the form of gods. During the Stone Age, many people carried small religious amulets for self protection, portable female statuettes.[38] This finding, replicated many times over in widely different areas of the world from Japan to Latin America, goes well beyond the realm of religious or historical speculation, its meaning being rather self-evidently that fetishes or amulets are symbols of religious power and female provenance. Mythical god-

35 Diodorus Siculus. (60-30 BCE). *The Library of History.* published in Vol. II of the Loeb Classical Library edition, 1935. §45 ff. Accessed from <http://penelope.uchicago.edu/Thayer/E/Roman/Texts/Diodorus_Siculus/2B*.html#note26> on 2015-02-26.
36 Herodotus (484-425 BCE). *The History of Herodotus,* Vol. 1. §173. Trans: G. C. Macaulay. Online in Project Gutenberg. Ac-cessed from <http://www.gutenberg.org/files/2707/2707-h/2707-h.htm> on 2015-02-26.
37 Bachofen, J.J. (1967). Myth, Religion, and Mother Right: Selected Writings of J.J. Bachofen. Trans. Ralph Manheim. P. 122. Princeton N.J. Princeton University Press.
38 See Wikipedia: Venus Figurines for references at <https://en.wikipedia.org/wiki/Venus_figurines#cite_note-14> accessed on 2015-02-26.

desses, matronymic kinship and denomination, female rule and succession that caused the war of Troy, and gave rise to legends such as the Amazons, are the small bone fragments that, properly arranged, help put together the skeleton of matriarchy.

All societies that have been discovered in the world, without exception, are religious; and this simply proves not that God exists but that religion was the earliest form of culture: alienated child-like magical cognition and explanation. After Ludwig Feuerbach religion can be understood as the key to the earliest anthropology, an inverted consciousness, through idealization, of a difficult life, soothed through imagination. After Moses Hess[39] and misquoted Karl Marx,[40] religion is also a powerful collective painkiller still in use. Religion remains for many a moral alternative to a corrupted science.

9. The Hard Evidence for a Matriarchal Society in its Traits

Joseph Francois Lafitau was a French Jesuit missionary assigned to the Canadian territory as late as the eighteenth century. Fur commerce with the French had displaced some member tribes of the New York Iroquois Federation to the mouth of the St Lawrence River, where Lafitau met and settled among them. Not by design, but

---

39   Wigoder, G. Ed. (1994). New Encyclopedia of Zionism and Israel. Plainsboro, N.J. Associated University Press.

40   Opposite to the trite opium stereotype Marx also has to say this: "Religion is, indeed, the self-consciousness and self-esteem of man who has either not yet won through to himself, or has already lost himself again. But man is no abstract being squatting outside the world. Man is the world of man – state, society. This state and this society produce religion, which is an inverted consciousness of the world, because they are an inverted world. Religion is the general theory of this world, its encyclopedic compendium, its logic in popular form, its spiritual point d'honneur, its enthusiasm, its moral sanction, its solemn complement, and its universal basis of consolation and justification. It is the fantastic realization of the human essence since the human essence has not acquired any true reality. The struggle against religion is, therefore, indirectly the struggle against that world whose spiritual aroma is religion." Marx, K. (1844). *A Contribution to the Critique of Hegel's Philosophy of Right. Introduction.* Online in MIA. Accessed from <https://www.marxists.org/archive/marx/works/1843/critique-hpr/intro.htm> on 2015-11-04.

endowed with a natural scientific curiosity, he realized he was in the midst of an immense ethnological mine. While doing his religious job, he was able to also document his anthropological observations for posterity and even make other scientific discoveries. All this happened a hundred years before the word "ethnology" itself would come into use. His book *Customs of the American Savages*[41] appeared in 1724, an impeccable model of ethnographic fieldwork and comparative anthropology for the time. Lafitau produced evidence for the first time, of what might have looked before like merely historical inference, or speculation based on myth: a society organized with the full input of women, material, spiritual, and political, at all levels. He describes not a leisure class of wealthy mothers driving men to spin, but women as the uppermost productive element in their societies, at the same time farmers, domestic workers, and social leaders. This he explicitly contrasted with predominantly idle men who defined themselves as designed for higher purposes, such as war.

The characteristics of the society described by Lafitau that interest us are, first of all, their long-houses and communal group living. Long-houses varied in size according to the number of families living in them, up to 200, matrilineal, matrilocal, consanguine, not at all centered on "deciduous" husbands, and mother-run if not exclusively, men's being in charge of external affairs. After their marriage, which was of monogamous type but transient and dissolvable at the will of either partner, husbands moved from their mothers' longhouses into those of their wives. In anthropology this is called matrilocality. The eldest women in the longhouses were in charge.

Chiefs of tribes were males appointed, evaluated and dismissed democratically, at the behest of the councils of mothers. Declaration

41 Lafitau, J.F. (1974). Customs of the American Indians Compared with the Customs of Primitive Times. 2 vols. Trans. William Fenton and Elizabeth Moore. (Orig. Pub. 1724). 2 Vol. Online in The Publications of the Champlain Society. Accessed from <http://link.library.utoronto.ca/champlain/DigObj.cfm?Id-no=9_96849&Lang=eng&Page=0113&Size=3&query=lafitau&searchtype=Fulltext&startrow=1&Limit=All> on 2014-07-28.

of war had to be approved by the mother's councils before being put to larger assemblies for consideration.

Lafitau's findings were fully independently replicated by New York attorney and founder of American Anthropology Lewis H. Morgan, a century and a half later. Morgan was an adoptee son of the Seneca tribe of the Iroquois and, like Lafitau, introduced totally novel research methodologies. He mailed family and kinship questionnaires throughout countries in the world for comparative purposes. His book *Ancient Society*,[42] published in 1877, is not only an independent scientific replication of Lafitau's findings on matriarchy, but also of Karl Marx's historical materialism as acknowledged by Marx himself. Inspired by Darwin, it reconstructs the development of the human family and of the political state in human history, subordinating them to the development of the material forces of production, technology.

Frederick Engels, in *The Origins of the Family, Private Property and the State*, using Marx's notes, built upon and fully endorsed Morgan's theory of evolutionary family and history of the state.[43] Morgan is the socialist skeleton in North America's closet, one of the reasons matriarchal theory is so dutifully repressed along with Marx's name.

10. Evidence from Other Perspectives

Coming from totally different perspectives, a number of people have found historical data confirmatory of the matriarchal theory of

---

42   Morgan, L.H. (1944). *Ancient Society Or Researches in the Lines of Human Progress from Savagery through Barbarism to Civi-lization.* (Orig. Pub. 1944). Online Edition in Marxists Internet Archive is reproduced from the "First Indian Edition (1944), published by BHARTI LIBRARY, Booksellers & Publishers, 145, Cornwallis Street, Calcutta. Composed by Tariq Sharif, "WATERMARK", Gujranwala, Pakistan. Accessed from   http://www.marxists.org/reference/archive/morgan-lewis/ancient-society/   on 2012-09-14.

43   Engels, F. (2000). *The Origin of the Family, Private Property and the State.* Trans. Alick West. Marx/Engels Selected Works, Volume Three. Online Version: Marx/Engels Internet Archive (marxists.org). Accessed from http://www.marxists.org/archive/marx/works/1884/origin-family/index.htm on 2012-09-14.

origins. A Swiss jurist and philologist contemporary of Morgan, with whom he corresponded, also developed a theory of social evolution emerging from an original matriarchy. Johann Jakob Bachofen's *Mother Right*[44] traced human beginnings to a primal animal horde with promiscuous sexuality, proven if only by the historical need for its regulation through taboos. He called this phase *hetaerism*. From this original transitional group, women built the first organized society following their matriarchal instinct. All this is expressed religiously, in the narratives and transformations of feminine deities. Bachofen's religious method of explanation preceded Feuerbach's.

Demeter was the prototype, the first goddess, and the first laws were consequently matriarchal, especially the incest taboo leading to exogamy. That first social formation transitioned, with the collaboration of women, into a second stage of organized society Bachofen called *Dionysian* after its male-God transitional prototype. This was a hybrid male- and female-ruled society that eventually (Dionysus being replaced by Apollo) metamorphosed into a fully patriarchal form, *Apollonian*. I must reiterate here that religion and mythology are representations of the earliest human forms of culture and consciousness; they are real anthropology. Of all theorists of matriarchy, Bachofen has been the most influential in the human sciences, in spite of being attacked for its mythical base and religious explanation.

Robert Graves, an English poet, novelist, critic, etymologist, and forensic classicist of the twentieth-century, continued Bachofen's line of thinking that he linked to James George Frazer's study of religion. In *The White Goddess*,[45] Graves proposes that poetic worship of a condensed moon-earth, birth-love-and-death goddess, under many names and perspectives, pervasively took place in the original wide expanses of the Mediterranean and Europe, at a time when the calendars of social activities were lunar, and synchronous

---

44 Bachofen, J.J. (1967). *Myth, Religion, and Mother Right:* Selected Writings. Ibid.
45 Graves, R. (1948). *White Goddess. A Historical Grammar of Poetic Myth.* London. Faber and Faber Limited. Accessed from <http://72.52.202.216/~fenderse/The-White-Goddess.pdf> on 2015-08-03.

with female menstrual cycles. A shift to patriarchy is reflected in the later solar calendar brought to prevail along with the worship of a corresponding masculine solar deity. Graves takes Frazer to task for not having, in his famous *The Golden Bough*,[46] revealed the secret that Christianity is only a sub-version, almost to the letter, of those ancient matriarchal practices. Grave's work, of course, has been discredited, and placed in the footnotes of "paganism."

Graves' rather esoteric approach is fully complemented, scientifically, by the first woman to enter the polemic from official anthropology: Marija Gimbutas, whose recent work[47] brings together ethnography, religion and linguistics, to bear on the proof of matriarchy. She argues that peacefully settled and established Mediterranean agrarian matriarchal societies in Europe were violently overrun by Russian nomadic patriarchs, the Kurgans.

Of course we must keep in mind that all human races originated in Black Africa, that it is in Africa that the roots of culture must be sought to properly link them to other forms and to the rest of civilization. The latest well-known evidence is archaeological, but historian Diodorus[48] already, before our current era, had placed Egypt as the cradle of humanity. This is a viewpoint that Africanist anthropologists such as Cheikh Anta Diop[49] are, not without the expected academic resistance, trying to bring to the debate. The original matriarchates I am talking about were for the most part Black societies.

---

46 Frazer, J.G. (2003). *The Golden Bow. A Study of Magic and Religion.* Online in Project Gutenberg [EBook #3623]. 1922 Abridged edition. Accessed from http://www.gutenberg.org/files/3623/3623-h/3623-h.htm on 2016-02-29.

47 Gimbutas, Marija (1970), "Proto-Indo-European Culture: The Kurgan Culture during the Fifth, Fourth, and Third Millennia B.C." In: Cardona, G., Hoenigswald, H. M., Senn, A. *Indo-European and Indo-Europeans: Papers Presented at the Third Indo-European Conference at the University of Pennsylvania,* Philadelphia: University of Pennsylvania Press, pp. 155–197.

48 Diodorus Siculus. (60-30 BCE). *The Library of History.* published in Vol. II of the Loeb Classical Library edition, 1935. §45 ff. Accessed from <http://penelope.uchicago.edu/Thayer/E/Roman/Texts/Diodorus_Siculus/2B*.html#note26> on 2015-02-26.

49 Diop, C.A. (1991). *Civilization or Barbarism. An Authentic Anthropology.* Trans. Yaa-Lengi Meema Ngemi. Chicago, Illinois. Lawrence Hill Books. (Orig. Pub. 1981). Online in Scribd. Accessed from <https://www.scribd.com/book/161307695/Civilization-or-Barbarism-An-Authentic-Anthropology> on 2015-02-26.

11. The Debate Continues: Further Evidence

The pervasive influence of Darwin in all the human sciences came to be felt sooner or later, and that included Freud as we know. From the same perspective, American economist, sociologist, and leader of the Institutional Economics Movement, Thorstein Veblen, was the first to propose a theory of social evolution based on male-female instinctual transformations resulting in social institutions. Influenced also by William James, Veblen posited that human activity can never exceed the scope of its instinctive dispositions or natural proclivities, which is the same as saying that the base always determines the superstructure, or that good sense will ultimately defeat sophistry. Instinct in the form of disposition or attitude, transformed into habit, is the base of consciousness that, in turn, is the superstructure of instinct. Instincts alone imprint their marks of purpose and efficiency, of pleasure and pain, in human conduct. Instinct theory, says Veblen, is more applicable to social institutions, including economy, than it is to individual psychology, the area where it has been almost exclusively tried. Institutions are only the result of habits and conventions conditioned upon a material environment, piggybacked on basic instincts. Human development teleologically combines characteristic elementary instinctual drives. The best outline of this theory is in Veblen's book *The Instinct of Workmanship and the State of the Industrial Arts*, published in 1914.[50] Female instinct plays a central role in it.

Interestingly, in a sort of re-enactment, what happened to matriarchal anthropology was what originally happened to matriarchy itself. While original nineteenth-century anthropology was for the most part matriarchal, it was successfully inverted to its patriarchal form with a stroke of the pen. Edvard Westermarck, a Finnish philosopher and sociologist student of exogamy and the incest taboo, simply took us back from Lafitau, Bachofen, Morgan, Frazer, Mc-

---

50   Veblen, T. (1918). The Instinct of Workmanship. And the State of the Industrial Arts. New York. B.W. Huebsch. (Orig. Pub. 1914). Online in Internet Archive. Accessed from <https://ia700406.us.archive.org/30/items/instinctofworkma00vebl/instinctof-workma00vebl.pdf> on 2014-11-30.

Lennan, Tylor, and Engels to the original theory that places the holy bourgeois family as the only historical type. The title of his main work spills the beans: *The History of the Human Marriage,* published in 1925.[51] Malinowsky followed suit,[52] and never was such pablum so well received by a discipline calling itself science. The concept that family and state had developmental, evolution-like sequences as a research hypothesis disappeared, evolution was shelved, and a here-and-now orientation came to prevail in the human sciences that became anti-historical.

Westermarck easily conquered patriarchal academia but he also inadvertently invigorated the debate with evolutionary theory. Darwin, in his *On the Origin of Species,* had reported females in evolution exerting the central function of selection. However, for ideological reasons, Darwin had to couch his observation in patriarchal terms: he said that sexual selection is the struggle between males for access to females, instead of simply saying that females select fitness-tested males is the same thing, which it is not. The evolutionary agency is subliminally displaced from the female to the male through simple inverted ranking. This minor detail may have precluded Darwin's being placed in the Hall of Science, and softened his impact by lubricating his entrance into mainstream patriarchal science through diminished resistance, compared to Marx for example and to some extent to Freud.

In any case, sexuated reproduction is designed to sublate, to supersede, to conserve in its synthesis the biological strengths of the participants. It augments fitness in the offspring, particularly within the K-strategy that produces costly specimens with complex brains and consciousness, as is the case in humans.

51 Westermarck, E. (1891). *The History of Human Marriage.* London. Macmillan. Online in Internet Archive. Accessed from <https://archive.org/details/historyhumanmar05westgoog> on 2015-03-14.

52 Briffault, R. and Malinowsky, B. (1956). Marriage, Past and Present: A Debate between Robert Briffault and Bronislaw Mali-nowski. Ed. M. F. Ashley Montagu. Boston: Porter Sargent Publisher. P. 30-1. Online in Questia. Accessed from <https://www.questia.com/read/28518901/marriage-past-and-present-a-debate-between-robert> on 2015-01-18.

To counter Westermarck and Malinowsky, after Veblen came Robert Briffault, the French surgeon, social anthropologist and novelist, who seized on evolutionary theory for his encyclopedic tsunami that he entitled *Mothers,* [53]directed at Westermarck and his acolyte. There is no known species in the animal kingdom, says Briffault, in which the male designs the evolutionary strategy. It is the natural role, the instinct, of the female, to determine the best adaptive conditions for her brood, the mother in the human species. Briffault presented his theory in three large volumes containing all inclusive evidence from fossils and scientific journals to hearsay and commonsense observation. Although Briffault is largely ignored in anthropology, his *Briffault Law* is quite popular. It states that the female, not the male, determines all the conditions of the animal family, and that where the female can derive no benefit from association with the male, no such association takes place. This re-statement of the Darwinian law of selection brings us to what is to follow, the recent synthesis of Chris Knight that brings anthropology, Marxist sociology and human activity as praxis, together.

12. Enter Chris Knight

In the human sciences, there is no question that the deepest influence today is the work of Darwin; it is a test kin disciplines must pass. Hegel's, Darwin's, Marx's and Freud's constitute the quartet of critical modern grand narratives in science. Darwin has been largely endorsed by academia, Freud reluctantly in the arts and hermeneutics, and Hegel and Marx in political commonsense. Chris Knight returns, starting from the critique of sociobiology, to the thorny issue of origins. Westermarck's rewarding "meme" is countered by an alternative, critical one, that does not lead to mainstream or the dollar sign.

---

53   Briffault, R. (1927). *The mothers: a study of the origins of the sentiments.* 3 Vol. New York. The Macmillan Company. Online in Hathi Trust Digital Library. Accessed from <http://babel.hathitrust.org/cgi/pt?id=mdp.39015009106751;view=1up;seq=10>   on 2013-06-17

To the most recent challenge to the old matriarchal theory, so-ciobiology, Knight has responded with his *Blood Relations. Menstruation and the Origins of Culture* published in 1991.[54] According to it, the ingredients women used to invent culture are a) first of all *solidarity*, which happens to also be the case in Freud's *Totem and Taboo*,[55] except between brothers, b) the natural phenomenon of menstruation, *synchronized* with a purpose: menstrual production of blood turned simultaneous and universal as a "no access" sign to include the alpha male, c) female *management* of envied blood-events, blood-power and blood-relations, and d) *conditioning* sex to productivity through the adage "no meat, no sex," the first rule and e) sublimation, subordination of the instinct of sex to the habit of work. In this original process, women invented the crucial human sign *No!* that has evolved all the way to Hegelian negation in philosophy, and to triggering crucial alternative neurotransmitter pathways in neuro-biology having to do with socialization. Knight's work, for the first time, offers a coherent theory of the origins of human culture that is highly fact-based and internally highly consistent.

Here it is also pertinent to mention as a crowning of the historical record the most recent and purest evidence of matriarchy recently discovered by anthropologist Hua Cai in Southern China, an answer to the perennial anthropological "show me." The Na are a society that lacks the social roles "father" or "husband." This group has resisted, although not without being partially diversified, the Chinese States' repeated attempts to turn it into the considered universal and normative mainstream bourgeois family.[56]

In a revolution without violence, blood being used constructive-

54   Knight, C. (1991). *Blood Relations. Menstruation and the Origins of Culture.* New York and London. Yale University Press.
55   Freud, S. (1919). Totem And Taboo Resemblances Between The Psychic Lives Of Savages And Neurotics. Authorized English Translation, with Introduction By A. A. Brill. London. George Routledge & Sons, Limited. (1912-3). Online in Project Gutenberg. Accessed from <http://www.gutenberg.org/files/41214/41214-h/41214-h.htm> on 2015-08-03.
56   Cai, H. (2001). *Society Without Fathers or Husbands. The Na of China.* Trans. Asti Hustvedt. New York. Zone Books.

48

ly for the first time, women were able to resolve the hypothetical problem of random sexual predation. The selfish instinct of males was subdued and sublimated through collective, female-designed rhythms of sexual strikes linked to their natural lunar cycle, alternating with collective equalitarian sexual satisfaction contingent on contributing to the feeding of the gens.

13. Where is the Women's Voice in all this?

The issue of matriarchy was until recently almost exclusively in men's hands, because men had appropriated to themselves the voice of science, having taken control of all forms of production invented by women. I will not pay the proverbial token to the women's voluminous recent contributions. They have gained popularity and I am not even faintly qualified to represent them fairly. Women have never been passive for an historical second. They have continued their subversive philosophy of giving and tending even in highly institutionalized bourgeois patriarchal families, and by now have substantially contributed to all fields of civil society, including the production of science.

Psychologically, however, it is necessary to mention Simone de Beauvoir, who measured up to Sartre and Freud's mainstream views of *bad faith* and *unconscious* respectively, in a way that makes it possible to allocate them along social class. Women having been in the class of the repressed, having had their voices muted through the political institutionalization of repression, were although deprived of *transcendence* resilient enough to save *immanence* as the real core of consciousness.[57] Women and the rest of the oppressed could express themselves only through a muted code, the symptomatic compromise Freud faced. Repressed people must develop an *unconscious* if they want to survive their repression; this is the destiny of the slave. The master does not face this problem because he sets the

57   de Beauvoir, S. (1972). *The Second Sex*. Ch. 2. Psychology. Trans. by H M Parshley, London. Penguin. (Orig. Pub. 1949). Online in MIA. Accessed from <https://www.marxists.org/reference/subject/ethics/de-beauvoir/2nd-sex/> on 2015-07-23.

norms of transcendence. This means he can, without an unconscious but in *bad faith*, ideologically alter consciousness in order to transcend ideologically.

The full design of consciousness was, however, with both full capacities in both sexes. Historical patriarchy altered the design in order to produce self-serving ideology. This is how it was able to institute the expression of the male instinctual disposition as the overriding one, at the price of sacrificing the natural design of balance and bipolar equilibrium.

Through the perspective of the patriarch, Sartre could see male bad faith where de Beauvoir was seeing lack of transcendence and Freud, also patriarchally, the generalized unconscious.

14. Conclusion

It is not the anatomical insignia but the instinctual disposition each one of us actively titrates, starting from a natural bias and others' previous concoctions, that constitutes our character our set of attitudes. Independent of sex, we have the freedom to steer our proclivities, which nature designed but culture historically transformed. Two opposite instincts are ingrained in both male and female brains that are first socially conditioned, and subsequently self-determined. This is how some men can be the personification of maternal dispositions and vice versa.

Our dialectical conscious structure is maintained by a dual brain with dual functions, and plasticity that in its form and function records the natural and social history of the species. Each brain hemisphere can stand as a backup for the other, but each alone cannot achieve full human totality. Dominance reflects historical preferences and choices. Inclusiveness, holism and a return to balanced self-constraining instinctual morality of evolution are needed to integrate what de Beauvoir called our "the other": our second sex and its healthy constraining instinctual function.

The four conditions of matriarchal origins-linearity or identity, locality or form of relational inclusion, property or form of relational objectivization, and, most important for the skeptics, rule or form of political ascendancy-have been produced as evidence for a matriarchal origin of society, from various scientific, religious and secular perspectives. The monolith of matriarchy continues to emerge, to return from the repressed, with ever-clearer contours, particularly with the activity and solidarity of feminism. This completes the puzzle of the origins of consciousness that will also permit us to elucidate its aims. As somebody said, the measure of how far we can see into the future (alternatives) is how far we can see into the past (historical facts).

The full restoration of womanhood to existential, including economic and political parity, that also entails the restoration of the rights of all "others," is the marker of the arrival of consciousness back to itself. As Hegel would say, it is the snake biting its self-confirming tail (ouroboros) recovered from its long alienation in patriarchal ideology. Consciousness could then look like coming from a balanced brain without dominance, without ecological imbalance.

IMPLICATIONS FOR CONSCIOUSNESS

1. What is Consciousness

Consciousness is the individual and collective representation of the universe, mediated by skill, language and culture. As such it can be monolithic as it probably was in matriarchy, and as science endeavors to make it. However, because patriarchy splits societies into antagonistic classes, consciousness can only be class consciousness. Class consciousness is ideology, narrowly transformed consciousness in the service of class interests. Consciousness serves the coherent activity of individuals and groups and therefore their interests, universally. "Consciousness can never be anything else than conscious existence, and the existence of men is their actual life-process. If in all ideology men and their circumstances appear upside-down as in a *camera obscura,* this phenomenon arises just as much from their historical life-process as the inversion of objects on the retina does from their physical life-process."[58]

Consciousness is embedded in theory; and theory, the reflection of the grammar of nature, is distorted by ideology. It is contended here that what nature contributed to the species was good sense, from which consciousness was constructed. Good sense, being natural, cannot be destroyed, but it is ideologically transformed in commonsense. Commonsense can be corrected back to good sense through the ideology of a universal class, the human family, the species. Good sense remains the arbiter when it comes to contending ideologies' competing for hegemony. This is what allows the universal class of women and workers to come together with a liberating ideology.

Consciousness strives for universality, and as such includes

---

58   Marx, K.(1845). *The German Ideology.* [4. The Essence of the Materialist Conception of History. Social Being and Social Con-sciousness]. Part I: Feuerbach. Opposition of the Materialist and Idealist Outlook. A. Idealism and Materialism. Online in MIA. Accessed from <https://www.marxists.org/archive/marx/works/1845/german-ideology/ch01a.htm> on 2917-05-15.

the relative notion of substantive equality. Consciousness cannot be equal, because each human individual has a different perspective, life experience, under different conditions. It is the accrual of perspectives that constitutes collective consciousness. Good sense starts with protoplasmic irritability and its journey to consciousness requires a modular nervous system with parallel and serial processes that illustrate the highest form of complexity.[59] Consciousness and personal theory, are emergent, non-reducible, phenomena of the brain.

In collective experiences common sense prevails over its more developed forms, prompting students of group psychology, including Freud, to infer that this type of collective behavior is a regression.[60] Since a great deal of common sense may be good sense, it is the function of a universal science to distill the latter in practice.

Consciousness, like all other properties of matter and energy, is an adaptive strategy of evolution that gives humans the capacity to truthfully reflect the world and use it operationally to its advantage. Truth starts from the perception of phenomena through the senses, good sense. It becomes truth as it is explained by historical reason, the grammar of consciousness that itself reflects the grammar of reality. In its most developed form, this is science. However, the explanation of origins of the universe in a Big Bang, for example, must be critically examined in the light of its expansionist historical context. More grammatically correct, more reasonable, would be an alternating theory of expansion and contraction.[61]

There have been two prevalent methods to explore the grammar of nature. The first was dialectical, a method geared to the study of motion that most resembles the natural phenomenon. The second,

59 Leise E M. (1990). "Modular construction of nervous systems: a basic principle of design for invertebrates and vertebrates." Brain Res Brain Res Rev. 15(1):1-23.

60 Freud, S. (2011) Group Psychology and the Analysis of the Ego. Trans. James Strachey. Project Gutenberg [EBook #35877]. Accessed from <http://www.gutenberg. org/catalog/world/readfile?fk_files=2083370> on 2012-05-21. (Orig. Pub. 1921).

61 Gurzadyan, V.G., and Penrose R. (2010). "Concentric circles in WMAP data may provide evidence of violent pre-Big-Bang activity." Online in Cornell University Library, Astrophysics. Accessed from <http://arxiv.org/pdf/1011.3706v1.pdf> on 2015-11-06.

formal logic, takes the form of objects at rest, analytically separated from their real totalities. Formal logic was introduces by patriarchy and it gave birth to idealism, an ideologically distorted form of philosophy that unfortunately still prevails. Hegel recovered the dialectical method for philosophy, that he was compelled to, while studying the complexity of consciousness in the *Phenomenology*. A central premise of the Hegelian dialectic is negation, the backbone of the logic of motion. In the constant succession of natural and historical phenomena, each event denies, supersedes the preceding one, and is in turn denied, replaced by the next.

Yet, the best explanation of the universe starts from a Big Bang, ashes being transformed into the large physical elements of the cosmos, stars, planets and galaxies and perhaps even universes. Matter grew and accrued physically and through chemical reactions. Planet Earth fulfilled certain conditions, such as optimal distance from the sun and atmosphere with optimal concentration of oxygen and other elements, thus creating appropriate atmosphere and climate conditions for the production of life, and upon it consciousness.[62] Life and consciousness are evolution's two main qualitative jumps or punctuations, revolutions alternating with slow quantitative change. It would appear that consciousness was a goal, perhaps economic, of natural evolution. Consciousness is the game-changer that has transformed evolution into human history to the extent we can talk about a concept such as anthropocene.

Chemistry, physics, and allied sciences can best explain archaic evolutionary phenomena. In a dialectic of randomness and teleology chemical and physical events appear to be random until science discovers their sense or lawful direction. The most complex the energetic exchanges of chemistry, the more selective they seem to become, including variables in their operations.

Forces such as expansion and gravity in physics dialectically

---

62   Cruz, M., and Coontz, R, "Alien Worlds Galore." Introduction To Special Issue. Science 3 May 2013: Vol. 340 no. 6132 p. 565. Accessed from <http://www.sciencemag.org/content/340/6132/565> on 2015-11-06.

struggle for hegemony and reach compromise, such as planets' orbiting. In the domains of physics and chemistry, natural sense began to appear, coherently, with the development of human consciousness. Carbon compounds and the ingredients of proteins evolved to produce organicity, and life, and correspondingly with life biochemistry, neurotransmitters and consciousness, To produce consciousness life must struggle with entropy.

The two original giants are *destruction* as in the Big Bang, and *production*, that insurgently manages to tilt the balance to functional complexity, life and consciousness. Production moves away from chaotic entropy toward coherent complexity and lawfulness. Darwin and Mendel have given us the first sketch of the long evolution of life. Today we are at the crucial crossroads of understanding a consciousness that holds the destiny of our life as a species. To survive we must overcome our alienation, our thinking ourselves other than we truthfully are as a species.

Consciousness was first historically understood as God, which is the good sense or *telos* of nature. With humanity came the new adaptive capacity to *produce virtually*, that is incurring the least energetic expenditure. Consciousness can produce an object virtually, in the mind, before it transforms it in reality through its objectification. Species other than human for the most part must adapt through slow morphological change. The enhanced human productive capacity based on consciousness spends minimal energy even if it was evolutionarily costly itself.

Consciousness is thus the most advanced form of natural adaptation that allows nature to transform itself with minimal morphological change, operating with forms only, virtually, at a minimal energetic cost. It requires, however, a very evolutionarily costly central nervous system that developed over millennia through trial and error, nature's throwing the dice until the "bingo" of the human species. By being able to represent itself in the emergent phenomenon of consciousness, nature largely sidesteps its own process of evolution in favor of history. The historical agency resides in the species universality, its collaborative dependency and collective unity. Our task is to re-appropriate consciousness from ideology.

2. Internalization and Externalization

Although internalization is more concretely visible in organisms that survive by ingesting aliment, particularly other organisms, the trend can be traced back to chemistry. A theory of the origins of cells is that one organism internalized another as its organelle (nucleus for example) and this is similar to the mechanism of the food chain. A fundamental mechanism of biological evolution is internalization where supersession or sublation can be seen to materially take place. The internalizing party that we can call proto-subject takes advantage of the advancement in complexity achieved by the internalized object. Here the subject is an open system whose energy is provided by its object. If in chemical reactions mutual destruction was necessary, one party, the subject, survives as organism. This metabolic process of internalization could have started as early as with RNA that advanced to produced protective membranes in the form of boundaries and organs. External boundaries are amongst the most typical characteristics of organisms and they already imply some degree of autonomy, protection, and self-control. Internalization was one of the processes that guided evolution throughout its phase of life, some proto-subjects expanding their complexity at the expense of others in the food chain. With structural complexity and functionality grew coherence the precursor of consciousness. Of course with internal metabolism also came the production and external disposition of waste.

Consciousness turns the cycle around, and although it needs external energetic fuel in the form of blood, glucose and oxygen, its peculiar function is to externalize itself in the form of objectification. The most complex organisms including humans developed specialized neural receptors to capture forms even at a distance, having the capacity to operate with forms only, and respond to the originating objects adaptively by modifying them or their environment. Evolutionarily, species gradually developed the capacity to respond to perceived forms through their senses, to enhance their adaptability to living conditions. In other words, advanced organisms have the capacity to produce virtually, therefore reducing the cost of production and saving energy to enhance they productive repertoire. One way they can do this is by anticipating because they have learned from previous experience stored in memory. Through anticipatory planning, they can conserve and avoid unnecessary destruction. This new property eventually makes trial-and-error unnecessary. Learning, virtual conservation of past forms and their grammar in memories of earlier events, is the highest, most economic adaptive capacity in the evolution of consciousness.

Consciousness also makes possible materially production through the internal combination, classification, and generalization of memorized forms of prior experience adapted to new circumstances. It is not far-fetched to conclude from this that, teleologically, the avoidance of wasteful destruction, and the consequent conservation of energy, may be a goal, if not *the* goal, of evolution. This allows further investment in complexity and heterogeneity, what Darwin called "variation for better chances at adaptation." From an energy-expenditure point of view, consciousness is the least costly form of productive operation. As I have already pointed out, this capacity has been achieved through the costliest evolutionary investment, *Homo sapiens,* and particularly its nervous system. This presents a huge paradox when we consider the present degree of waste that today is prompting a warning response from nature in climate change. It also makes us pause to think about the waste involved in mutual destruction and war.

3. Coherence, Contradiction and Compromise

If natural good sense is the particular direction of natural events, changing, from one form to another through negation, coherence the next step, takes into consideration the way phenomena *recip-rocally* establish harmony through specific forms of contradiction, struggle, and compromise. This determines what we can call objects' *goodness of fit,*[63] besides their epistemological differentiation into classes that for example, operate according to properties, characterize physical, chemical, and molecular domains of understanding, and are guided by different principles and laws. In Hegel's this corresponds to the first syllogism, moving from sense-certainty to law and understanding. [64]The Spinozist monist duality matter-sense moves forward long before our understanding takes place. Males inseminated females long before paternity was fathomed. The evolutionary, and historical, capacity to understand, came much later than the material event; before full understanding there was sense-certainty and perception. I have called coherence the mediatory step between sense and consciousness, and coherence occurs in many forms.

In chemical reactions, for example, coherence requires the understanding of new levels of phenomena such as conditions, structural and functional requirements, *etc.* At the same time, at this new level, destruction may be lowered by understanding mediations such as buffering, enzymes, etc. With the notion of *conservation*, an organic phenomenon such as the food chain can be understood from the perspective of fulfilling the need for ecological balance in totality. Here conditions enter to play their role. Animal coherence expands to provide complex relational alternatives, such as mating, fighting or flying, which require intelligent judgment and choice.

63   The goodness of fit of a statistical model describes how well it fits a set of observations. In psychology "goodness of fit" was a concept introduced in developmental theory by Stella Chess and Alexander Thomas to measure mother-child temperamental com-patibility. See for example: Chess, S. and Thomas, A. (1996). *Temperament in Clinical Practice*. London and New York. The Guil-ford Press.
64   Hegel, G.W.F. (1807). "– A –Consciousness. III. Force and the Understanding –The World of Appearance and the Supersensible World." In: *The Phenomenology of Mind*. From Harper Torchbooks' edition of the Phenomenology, from University of Idaho, Department of Philosophy by Jean McIntire. Online in MIA, Hegel by Hypertext. Accessed from <https://www.marxists.org/reference/archive/hegel/works/ph/phac.htm> on 2015-07-11.

This is where contradiction and its resolution are relevant because the acknowledgment of possibilities, perspectives, and choices require it.

The end of the syllogism is type of compromise or synthesis that depends on the struggle and negotiation of the contending phenomena in order to achieve a less destructive direction in favor of a more economic one. The task of understanding is to reach this level of coherence.

4. Consciousness, Self-Consciousness and Totalization

Consciousness supersedes natural coherence, and it is what some ancient Greek philosophers called *logos,* that meant *ground,* originally; [65]others saw it rather differently. Manifest in words, consciousness for them was God: "In the beginning was the Word, and the Word was with God,[66] and the Word was God." The sense of the ground has been found to have a logical lawfulness perceptible through regularities relationally identifiable by means of words, a new level of struggle and compromise. Consciousness expands the coherent representation of the world by going beyond its phenomenal ground, its appearance, and revealing its essence: all of its previous developmental, historical forms. The only undesirable side effect is excess of human imagination, which historically led to still extant philosophical idealism.

Because it manifests itself individually before it becomes consensual, coherence becomes consciousness, accruing from many standpoints of individually experienced reality- initially a very limited, sense-based perspective. Coherence is already a limited synthesis of perspectives, a composite of dimensions leading to full object-and-context representation. The understanding of physics and chemistry is perspectival, and the same is the case for all sciences.

---

65   Wikipedia. "Logos." Accessed from <https://en.wikipedia.org/wiki/Logos> on 2015-07-29.

66   John 1:1English Standard Version (ESV). Accessed from <https://www.biblegateway.com/passage/?search=John+1%3A1&version=ESV> on 2015-07-29.

Only the synthesis of all perspectives can approach the understanding of the whole, universal object in its awesome complexity that no individual can grasp alone. Collectively, by consensually joining perspectives, it is possible to dialectically arrive at the truth. When this happens, culture adopts the consensus and institutionalizes it to be used as *reality testing* that unifies groups and discourages outliers. Variation in perspective is augmented by skill and reified in social class.

I find in the *hologram* the best metaphor to understand consciousness.[67] Laser beams, organized in parallel form, when focused and deployed upon an object reproduce it in all its dimensions, thus producing a stereoscopic virtual image. The image is then objectified in space as a replica of the object. Additionally, the image can be reproduced totally from any of its parts, as in cloning. This is a good description of consciousness and its recursive quality that can reconstruct totality starting from any of its parts, Holographic representation rests on the combination of three properties: coherence, interference and diffraction.[68] The equivalents of these in consciousness are coherence, contradiction, and compromise; and here we meet the Hegelian syllogism again.

The backbone of reciprocal activity in human relationships — the specific energy Freud called "libido"—[69] is the constant reverberating mirroring of consciousness irremediably attached to its object. Melanie Klein advanced this notion in the understanding of transference. Her notion of *imago,* which is the relational synchronization with the internal prototype, helps us understand transference as an intersubjective phenomenon, reciprocal and reverberational. Along the same tradition, libido was properly redefined by Fairbairn

---

67   Wikipedia. "Holonomic Brain Theory. Accessed from <https://en.wikipedia.org/wiki/Holonomic_brain_theory> on 2016-05-28.

68   Stroke, G. W. (1966). An Introduction to Coherent Optics and Holography. New York and London. Academic Press. Accessed from <http://tocs.ulb.tu-darmstadt.de/46920919.pdf> on 2015-03-16.

69   Freud, S. (1963). "Libido Theory." In: *General Psychological Theory: Papers on Metapsychology.* New York. Touchstone, Simon and Schuster, Inc.(Orig. Pub. 1923).

as *object-seeking tendency*.[70] This is the inescapable need of consciousness to always be attached to an object. Like coherence, consciousness cannot exist by itself; it is a relationship.

"Mind" is the figurative container of consciousness, and both mind and consciousness are emergent properties of the brain; they cannot be reduced to the brain or to any of its parts. Consciousness is the metabolic activity contained in the mind that mirrors the material metabolism of nature and human society, ultimately nature relating to itself. The self-regulation of consciousness in the individual self is a replica of the way the collective regulates itself through culture.

Only in humans does consciousness take the form of self-consciousness. In evolutionary terms, self-consciousness is a new punctuation, a new qualitative jump in the same chain that started from natural sense. Self-consciousness is the culmination of the process leading to subjectivity, consciousness of consciousness or metaconsciousness.

Self-consciousness makes it possible to combine conscious perspectives (conscious partial representations) that are inherent in the different conditions of individuality, besides the particularity of class. Self-consciousness through a synthetic procedure *totalizes,* *i.e.* fits every piece of information within one total puzzle. In this fashion it temporarily closes the circle of understanding within a historical paradigm. Myth, religion, philosophy, and science have been successive historical paradigms for totalization. Through them, self-consciousness has achieved its total dimension. Every new stage offers a new form of explanation that promises to better achieve truth through their particular method, going from belief through reason, to experiment and proof.

Collective human activity, the universal ensemble of social relations, connects individuals through their cultural groups. Cultural groups converge in one process of human civilization, the ultimate

---

70   Fairbairn, W.R.D., (1952). Psychoanalytic Studies of the Personality. London: Routledge and Kegan Paul, 1981.

totality.

The drive for universality of consciousness requires a common language and shared values. Although the world, because it functions dialectically, would never be uniform, the antagonisms of the future can be reduced by abolishing class antagonisms that lead to war and waste, by planning and by ranking human needs for their fulfillment. This would allow consciousness to return to its roots, natural sense that has been lost with the split of class society and the corruption of consciousness into ideologies.

In view of changing conditions, consciousness necessarily has to endlessly go back and forth from perceptual verification to knowledge. The method used by consciousness is syllogistic in the Hegelian sense, re-shuffling the three cards of individuality, particularity, and universality. Hegel came up with fifteen basic forms of syllogistic combinations in which each one of the three terms is used to mediate the other two.[71]

In humans the dual sexual instinct introduces a more nuanced perception of reality and its current conditions that includes its unique constraining morality. Both instinctual dispositions, male and female, built in all human individuals independent of sex, can be cultivated differently according to conditions. Natural sexual disposition has been greatly modified historically through human mediation. Opposite perspectives are determined by natural and historical parameters. The characteristic function of cultures is to totalize; and cultures do it differently according to their degree of advancement. The founder of sociology, Auguste Comte proposed three stages, theological, metaphysical, and positivist, that he claimed could classify all societies.[72] This is close to the present classification of

71 Hegel, G.F.W. (1969) "Hegel's Science of Logic." Science of Logic. The Doctrine of the Notion. Section One: Subjectivity. Chapter 3. The Syllogism. Trans. by A. V. Miller. Sydney. Allen & Unwin. (Orig. Pub. 1812). Online in Marxists Internet Archive. Hegel by Hypertext. Accessed from <http://www.marxists.org/reference/archive/hegel/works/hl/hlobject.htm#HL3_729> on 2012-10-28

72 Comte, A. (1876). System of Positive Polity: Social Dynamics; or, The General Theory of Human Progress. Vol. 3. London. Longmans, Green and Co. (Orig. Pub. 1853) Online in Internet Archive. Accessed from <https://play.google.com/books/reader?id=y-

myth or religion, philosophy and science. The unifying process of civilization totalizes the fragmentary cultural processes by diffusion from one culture to another, struggle and compromise. This is more visible with the current acceleration of globalization. Since totality and universality are the aim of consciousness, it would seem that the present state of global connectivity fulfills the necessary material conditions for consciousness universality. The major obstacle to this is the fragmentation of ideologies.

What was sense in the physical and chemical worlds, and co-herence in organisms, evolves to become fitness in species, and in humans, consciousness. Consciousness, in turn, goes through a long history of development from protoplasmic irritability to sensation, perception, object-image and thought, to reasoned knowledge, and is simultaneously objectified in language, social institutions, and evolving technology. All these steps are linked coherently, devel-opmentally, and their coherence is captured differently in different scientific domains.

5. Sexuation and Consciousness

The effect of testosterone in organizing the brain and behavior has been observed in animals and humans although we don't know its full extent and many of the details. It seems that approaching behaviors and impulsivity in males may be so determined. If levels of hormones that rise during adolescence do so also during critical periods of brain development *in utero,* sexuation must determine consciousness. Transcendental consciousness we have called be-havior and self-consciousness identity, sameness in change. This sameness is dual, determined not only by species but also sexually, and is expressed in different behaviors that are culturally sanctioned, but that must also have a basic natural determination, instinctual and hormonal.

Biologically, with sexuation the reproductive relation becomes the unit of the species rather than the sexually halved individual. Opposites that epitomize instinctual opposition and complementary duality as differentials of sex did not only obviously affect reproductive behavior but also, in a more nuanced way, social behavior in general. This dialectical monist duality inherently requires some type of equilibrium as synthesis or compromise to be reached between the two sexual opposites. To the extent that such balance involves consciousness, and to the extent that both participants, male and female, have equal agency, this equilibrium can only be based on altruistic morality, empathy and full regard for the wellbeing of the other. This is a moral value that has been preached by religions since the Golden Rule.

This is more convincing if we consider that both participants in the sexual unit, although gendered and hormonally biased, have the same reproductive potential and the same dual instinctual structure. They both have the destructive capacity along with the productive one.

In view of these considerations, the politically institutionalized repression of one by the other, by force not by reason, logically disturbs the equilibrium that was the original design of the species and can lead to no other result than the one we are leaving: natural catastrophe based on immoral ecological tampering.

In spite of the fact that human embryos become anatomically and physiologically differentiated as sexual opposites *in utero* with the same as well as different potentialities, the result must be a universal potential for human growth. These crucial mother-child and brain-to-brain interactions that leave the imprint, the template for affect and social self-regulation, particularly through the right hemispheres of the brain,[73] are socially overriden by patriarchal culture that has created different needs. They were originally reciprocal,

73   Schore, A. (1994). *Affect Regulation and the Origins of the Self. The Neurobiology of Emotional Development.* P. 75ss. Hills-dale, N.J. Lawrence Erlbaum Associates. Online in Questia. Accessed from <http://www.questia.com/read/57185676/affect-regulation-and-the-origin-of-the-self-the> on 2013-03-07.

meaning activated from both ends, and reverberational, meaning a whole complex relational narrative. They become hierarchical in the preparation for civil society that Oedipus entails, loosing their balanced reciprocity.

The form of reciprocity entailed in sexuality determines form of consciousness and its cultural form affects all participants, not only the subordinate. Originally based on two mutually self-constraining instinctual dispositions, subject to conditions for adaptive capacity, they lose the latter in favor of unnatural, historical needs such as those created by capitalism. Unlike their natural counterparts, these spurious needs, are historical and reversible; they are not material imperatives. Even though they may appear as such.

The subjection of women has resulted in the unconstrained expression of the male instinct, resulting in the present state of war and destruction in so many ways.

The balancing purpose of sexuation and its reflection in consciousness and behavior consequently lost the adaptive purpose radically altered by forced patriarchy opening's a rift with nature. The resulting alienation makes us incapable of recognizing ourselves and our deformation because, our consciousness corrupted, the *status quo* appears natural.

6. Attachment, Consciousness, and Development

Because of evolutionary anatomical changes related to bipedalism that made delivery necessarily premature, the full reproductive production of *Homo sapiens* individuals requires a long period of dire dependence on others after birth. Because of the increase in productivity, this period of dependence has been culturally prolonged to include childhood and adolescence, the period of essential education that takes place first within the institution of the family, and subsequently mostly within the educational institutions of civil society. "Attachment" is the term we use to characterize the consequences of the earliest part of this period, particularly stemming from the particular form of relationship with the mother. Dependency, leaning on others for survival and identity confirmation, never ends, and mental health is characterized by an optimal degree of dependence and distance.

Initial attachment is first dyadic and anaclitic, mother-dependence for essential functions, and it has been institutionalized to loosely last from birth to the pre-school period. Mothers are biologically designed to be able to provide aliment to their children, aliment that they have partially metabolized within their own body first. Along with that, the mother provides for other needs of the child while the child is learning to cope with vital and social functions. Within the domain of the family, dependence normally then takes on a triadic form, with the psychological inclusion of the father and others, starting with the Oedipal period. Here the father and other members of the family and society are included within a separate social dynamic. Each type of relationship has its own form of attachment based on the prior attachment to the mother, and its own processing and therapeutic or noxious features. The diversification of relations to father, siblings, and others prepares the child for her or his entrance into civil society, which comes with different demands and etiquette. Institutionalized education has an important role, as it concerns entrance into civil society and being socialized and acculturated.

This material process of leaning, particularly during its earliest phases leading to separation and individuation, has deep psychological implications that have been researched by the school of Bowlby and Ainsworth under the name of attachment. Learning socialization requires flexibility in different social domains, different types of identification with others. Identification is the psychological isomorph of alimentation. Body image, for example, its early integration as ground of the self-image, takes place upon the internalized template of the maternal body, and the kinesthetic and sensory stimulation the mother provides. As the mother stimulates sensory receptors in her handling of the child, she switches on all sensory organs. The mother is the one who first handles the whole body, sensorily stimulating the mind of the infant and providing appropriate sensory aliment. Our first totalized "identity" is our body image, built from a replica of the mother's body, the mother acting not only as a mirror, but instrumentally as the first universal selfobject.

This is how human imprinting takes place, imprinting being the intuitive knowledge, and consequent behavior, that conveys we know we belong to our species.[74] We must consider that our first body image independent of sex is, mother-like, independent of sexual identity. In humans, the complex phenomenon of sexual homogamy (species-specific choice) is achieved in the triangular Oedipal situation.[75]

It is from the earliest interactions with our mother that we learn human activity: in other words all the first-order regulatory elements of a grammar and syntax of behavior and spirituality that, socially, shape our material activity. We learn what goes with what and what doesn't, particularly as it concerns visual and aural images in language, but also in how our senses concatenate with each other and how social regulation applies. Since birth, we also hear ourselves cry, and later speak, and therefore eventually made the connection of an "I" that speaks and designates itself as a separate object.

Interpersonal mirroring continues to be an essential phenomenon in consciousness and consciousness replicates it within itself. At first it is body *gestalt* that perceives its totality in others during a critical period of imprinting, selectively connecting to members of a species. Specialized mirroring neurons in the frontal cortex of the brain have been confirmed in primates and humans.[76] We mostly differentiate self from other as distance sense receptors such as

---

74   Spalding, D. A. (1872). On instinct. *Nature, 6,* 485-486.

75   Bereczkei, T., Gyuris, P., & Weisfeld, G. E. (2004). Sexual imprinting in human mate choice. *Proceedings of the Royal Society B: Biological Sciences, 271*(1544), 1129–1134. Accessed from http://doi.org/10.1098/rspb.2003.2672 on 2016-03-06.

76   Rizzolatti, Giacomo; Craighero, Laila (2004). "The mirror-neuron system."Annual Review of Neuroscience 27 (1): 169–192. Accessed from<http://www.kuleuven.be/mirrorneuronsystem/readinglist/Rizzolatti%20&%20Craighero%202004%20-%20The%20MNS%20-%20ARN.pdf> on 2016-01-12.

those involved in vision and audition, mature. As newborns we are not able to differentiate self from other, experiencing all as a hybrid undifferentiated protoplasm.

This brings us back to the contentious issue of mother origins and matriarchy. If the mother is universally the first individual strategic instrument in dealing with nature and society, and if the female is by and large the selecting strategist of sexuated species, it stands to reason that in the case of human origins ontogeny recapitulates phylogeny. If the father is a latecomer in the psychological formation of the individual, why is it that we can infer that that was also the case historically?

The very high cost of child development typically assumed by the mother is universal, the father being often totally absent. It is the mother who puts in place all first-order mediations naturally and socially necessary.

7. Consciousness, Speech and Language

Language in humans is objectification, intentional expression of meaning through the combination of arbitrary signs historically developed in particular societies. Language is transcendence that makes consciousness ponderable. We are ushered into a language at birth, into a cultural system full of symbols embodied in all sorts of meaningful objects and institutions that make language omnipresent.

Consciousness' expression through language is the externalization of meaningful human activity, agency, and purpose. Each generation adopts, uses and develops iconic and verbal signs, instruments inherited from previous generations. These signs are therefore historical condensations, units of meaningful human activity objectified ancestrally and consensually maintained and enhanced by each generation before they are endowed to the next. Signs are therefore for the most part already present in reality, embodied as cultural objects, when we come into the world. Their specific forms are fit for our senses, gradually being imprinted in our consciousness. Meaningful historical experience and personal narrative combine signs and grammatically connect them as consciousness, starting from the moment each one of us leaves the uterine environment. The particular form of totalization our family uses is conveyed in speech and iconic signs. Words are cultural organizers that organize each one of us until we may be able to partially override their inertia. Signs, expanded and organized as cultural objects, place us in the midst of a small universe of ready-made and compelling information that makes us human. We will irremediably leave our own greater of lesser mark in such a collective object by maintaining it, and perhaps even transforming it, even if passively; inaction is implicitly endorsement of the *status quo.* Culture and language make up a metabolic organism maintained by the collective activity of affine relationships and contending groups.

Linguistic images, such as words and cultural objects in their pervasiveness, constantly convey universality to us; we in turn through them make sense of changing reality. We close the circle of meaning through the thesaurus we inherited from our ancestors and with our *personal theory,* the particular form we ideologically understand to be reality. It is through those archaic universals and their derivatives that we understand the constant fluidity of our life situation. When we analyze we understand object properties; when we act upon the object we are guided by that understanding. The journey of self-guided historical experience and critical judgment that we can finally embark upon as autonomous, free beings is eminently relative, in that we develop as our social reality develops us. We may or may not be able to consciously, adaptively, move as reality moves. We are always in a chess-game of class-related political reciprocity that makes autonomy and independence more an illusion than reality.

Olfaction and taste signs are our first channels to reality and were also probably so phylogenetically. They are chemical senses and operate through pheromones, chemicals released by an animal to cause behavioral and physiological changes in another animal. These are vehicles for proximal relationships, requiring intimate contact and extreme dependence on the caretaker. Contact and thermal pressure and bodily signs originating in skin muscles and organs inform the nervous system about position, environmental conditions and safety in a way that requires relational proximity. As infants we are handled in ways that leave their mark on our attitude towards the world, in our sensuousness and sexuality. Visual and hearing signs coming from light and sound; sensory organs allow for more distant and abstract connectivity with objects, and for complex inter-subjectivity. The experience of early human dependence is gradually internalized as what illusorily appears as "identity," the ground of our human experience which is in fact alterity. Constant mirroring and the impact of the other in bodily experience are maternally coupled to speech sounds gradually integrated to become the form, the particular grammar, of behavior. These start with visual, foveal mother-child synchronizations, the initial vehicle of crucial human imprinting that leads to what Hegel called human *recognition,* the *sine qua non* of humans.[77]

It is language and its paradigmatic form, speech, that are the new relational tools of the species. Consciousness is dialectically internalized language in the most general sense; its autonomy, as reflected in the fact that deaf mutes are conscious, owes to the fact that speech is only a small part of language, the latter being omnipresent for the senses that require it. Before speech, there is iconic or imaginary consciousness.

Hearing ourselves cry at birth becomes the landmark of our dual consciousness, subjective and objective and of our self. Each one of us universally hears his/her cry at birth and, although we are it, we do not know we will be separate individuals. In this first act we simultaneously project and introject, thus expressing our potential

77   Schore, A. (1994). *Affect Regulation and the Origins of the Self. The Neurobiology of Emotional Development.* Hillsdale, N.J. Lawrence Erlbaum Associates. Online in Questia. Accessed from <http://www.questia.com/read/57185676/affect-regulation-and-the-origin-of-the-self-the> on 2013-03-07.

subjectivity and agency. From this beginning the mother assumes the role of proxy subject, piggybacking words and sound images onto other perceptual images. The mother produces consciousness collaboratively, by giving what she has, aliment and care upon which words are contingent. The monumental acceleration of speech and language in young children that could not occur mechanically, but is based on the genetic readiness and modularity of the brain has been a puzzle still not understood. Since language like air, is a universal medium, individuals can only borrow from it, only rarely making it. Individuality, therefore, as preferentially expressed in language, is only the expression of our universality, and the fact that our ancestors govern us.

Consciousness itself is an imponderable object, verifiable only through language; so is self, objectified only in agency and personality what we do in spite of what we may say.

8. Consciousness is Material, a Practical Tool

From the point of view of adaptation, human self-consciousness is a practical tool and its purpose is behavioral fitness. This means that consciousness guides appropriate behavior under varying natural and cultural conditions. We know behavior is appropriate because consciousness, particularly collectively, remains forever irrevocably subordinated to its natural sense, and although we may detour, sooner or later from it, the antagonism will be eventually manifest and correction attempted. Our species has come to be technologically very intelligent, but at the same time has lost the sense to correct its alienated course, to bring it back within the window provided by nature. No one can deny that our world today for the most part does not make sense.

Practically, in our relations with each other and with nature, our lack of coherence manifests itself in antagonism, commonsense corrupted by ideology. Nowhere is this clearer than in our political language and practice. Politicians constantly invoke democracy, but only as an abstract term, always to remain an "ought." If democracy is the rule of a society by its people in order to satisfy its needs, we are far from achieving it. Politicians invoke "freedom" to explain antagonism, freedom remaining abstract, applicable to only a few. Equality has turned out to be only an abstract birth-right; in practice, an abstract equal opportunity. The disadvantaged are blamed as victims of their lifestyle and free choices, *etc.* One's Zip code at birth, together with gender, skin color, and religion, place each newborn already in a hierarchical niche that many are unable to change.

Practice not ideological, but endowed with free truthful consciousness, was called *praxis* by the Greeks; and it is worthwhile to maintain the distinction, as Marx did. Praxis is moving from understanding and scientifically explaining the world by transforming it accordingly.[78] Theoretical brilliance can spin the truth in many directions if not constrained by good sense and coherence. The promise of science has been co-opted and corrupted by capital, which in the first place makes it largely inaccessible, compartmentalized, and therefore susceptible to ideological influence. This, unfortunately, prompts many to return to earlier forms of explanation, mainly religious.

Alienated consciousness, ideology, is a broken or corrupted instrument that can at best approximate but not accomplish the goals of optimal human adaptation. Its fraudulence started with the destruction of checks and balances as a result of the historical repression of the female instinct and the implementation of slavery. The restoration of consciousness would be a return to a non-alienated real self for all individuals equally. This would not be possible in a capitalist society that inherently fosters exploitation of some by others. For the typical psychoanalytic patient, however, the consciousness gained in the psychoanalytic process is usually only a return to baseline dominant ideology, equally shared by analyst and

---

78   Marx, K. (1969). *Theses on Feuerbach*. Thesis XI. Trans: W. Lough. (Written 1845, edited by Engels; Orig. Pub: 1888). Pro-gress Publishers, Moscow, USSR. Online in MIA. Accessed from <https://www.marxists.org/archive/marx/works/1845/theses/theses.htm> on 2015-11-10.

analysand, and always left intact. Psychoanalysis allows the alienated individual to fictitiously make sense of her or his biography, and to appropriate it as unique personal synthesis, as the ideologically alienated coherent totality of the self's totalization. As practiced today, psychoanalysis does not correct the deeper human alienation caused by ideology that pervades both family and civil society. Psychoanalysis for the most part focuses on the patriarchal family that is considered free of ideology. The scientific scope of psychoanalysis is quite narrow, as is that of every other compartmentalized human science in a class society.

The discontent of civilization is never addressed because it is mistakenly considered not to be intrapsychic. The mind is mistakenly also considered separate from society and government. Therefore, only applied psychoanalysis can critically enlighten our good sense through the analysis of institutions.

9. Structure and Function of Consciousness

Human consciousness is dual, self-reflective, and like a mirror designed to always, during sentience, be attached to the image of its object.[79] It can only be *consciousness of,* even if it is of its own content or operations. The difference between consciousness and mirroring is twofold. The mirror is passive and consciousness active. Additionally, although the mirror can mirror itself only in another mirror, consciousness, although it needs another mirror to jumpstart itself, develops the internal capacity to reflect itself. Consciousness classifies objects into words that are generalizations in nesting sequences of inclusion, according to objects' properties. It also logically combines concepts and words to express conditions and operations. It moves from sense to coherence, to culture and governance

---

79 James, W. (1904). "Does Consciousness Exist?" In: Classics in the History of Psychology. An internet resource developed by C.D. Green, York University. Toronto. Ontario. (Orig. Pub. in *Journal of Philosophy, Psychology, and Scientific Methods, 1*, 477-491. Accessed from < http://psychclassics.yorku.ca/James/consciousness.htm> on 2016-03-09.

internalized as forms of consciousness and self. It also starts with logical class categories such as useful and useless, or helpful and dangerous, good and bad, a moral function that has been located in the amygdala of the brain.[80] The first morality was that of evolution, then modified through cultural mediations.[81]

Key elements in the moral process are first the intersubjective *reciprocity,* the mutual recognition of individual activity as human. This starts with its debt to all other subjects' previous mediations, the ensemble of the social relations. Since it is an accruing property of the mind towards the better understanding of nature, consciousness keeps a record in its different forms including its objectification in culture. Reciprocally mirroring subject and object have different adaptive demands; they must negotiate through dialectical processes such as assimilation and accommodation. This is particularly true when it comes to the relationship between two active subjects that both demand recognition of their subjectivity. In order to relate, subjects must display their compromising properties, and they do this through attitudes that become communicational symbolic gestures[82] within a pre-established cultural pentagram.

Reciprocity leads to the key element of *morality*, the highest form of consciousness. Morality is based on altruism and empathy, the intersubjective capacity to reverberationally assume one's and the object's position alternatively or simultaneously and put them on par with one another. Morality manages the conflict between subjectivities through compromise, and one such form of attempt at compromise in civil society is the state, product of the so-called social contract. Religion historically became the repository of morality; and that is the reason for its strong attractiveness to humans. Human

---

80   LeDoux, J.E. (2008), Scholarpedia, 3(4):2698. Accessed from < http://www.scholarpedia.org/article/Amygdala> Accessed on 2016-03-09.

81   Horney, K. (1950). "A Morality of Evolution." In: *Neurosis and Human Growth.* New York. Norton.

82   Mead, G.H. (1934). *Mind Self and Society.* Section 23: Social Attitudes and the Physical World. (Edited by Charles W. Morris). Chicago: University of Chicago. Pp. 178-186. Online in Brock University. Accessed from < https://www.brocku.ca/MeadProject/Mead/pubs2/mindself/Mead_1934_23.html> on 2016-02-17.

relations have always been guided by the Golden Rule that characterizes human morality. Hegel discovered its patriarchal violation, in the master-slave historical dialectic,[83] the alienating breakdown of the Golden Rule that attempts to convert subjects into objects. Patriarchy introduced the use of others as means.

Collaboration is another key element that has historically made consciousness possible. Hegel's metaphor is an attempt to explain productive collaboration in the human process. An alternative is true collaboration, as expressed in the alternating metaphor of Vygotsky in human development, where the stronger in an exercise of true altruism does not exploit, but shares his strength with the other, weaker, or emerging subject. The matriarchal type of social organization preceding patriarchy applied this opposite, constructive paradigm, best expressed by Lev Vygotsky in his collaborative notion of the *zone of proximal development*.[84] In this model, the better-adapted subject, the mothering one for example, contributes to the development of the less fit. This is the way mothers produce subjectivity.

The final necessary element in consciousness is *self-organization*. Consciousness is its own organizer, its own master, and that determines its autonomy, its freedom, what we call the self in humans.

Structurally and functionally, therefore, we can define human consciousness as the dual, reciprocal, moral, collaborative self-organized activity, operating within an emergent virtual reality produced in the body, particularly the brain, that syllogistically and adaptively

---

83   Hegel, G.W.F. (1967). *Hegel's Phenomenology of Mind.* B. Self Consciousness. 3. Lord and Bondsman. From Harper & Row's Torchbooks' edition (1967) of the Phenomenology (1807), translated by J B Baillie (1910), from University of Idaho, Department of Philosophy, thanks to Jean McIntire. § numbers from the Baillie translation have been inserted into the text of the Baillie translation and linked to explanations by J N Findlay. Φ links to original German text: Phänemenologie des Geistes. Online in MIA. Accessed from <https://www.marxists.org/reference/archive/hegel/phindex.htm> on 2014-10-05.

84   Vygotsky, L. S. (1978). "Zone of Proximal Development: A New Approach." In: *Mind in society: The development of higher psychological processes.* Chapter 6. Interaction between learning and development. Cambridge, MA: Harvard University Press. Accessed from <http://www.cles.mlc.edu.tw/~cerntcu/099-curriculum/Edu_Psy/EP_03_New.pdf> on 2014-09-28.

reflects the world, with the purpose of energetic economy through anticipatory guidance and self-mediation, leading to optimal survival fitness in the human species.

Marx,[85] and particularly Freud.[86] saw consciousness as transferential, connected to others. Transference was first and foremost maternal. Sartre[87] and de Beauvoir[88] emphasized that consciousness is eminently teleological, and transcendental. Horney[89] introduced the notion of morality of evolution, and Locke,[90] Hegel[91] and James[92] believed consciousness to be moral and self-regulated.

85   "In a sort of way, it is with man as with commodities. Since he comes into the world neither with a looking glass in his hand, nor as a Fichtian philosopher, to whom "I am I" is sufficient, man first sees and recognises himself in other men. Peter only establishes his own identity as a man by first comparing himself with Paul as being of like kind. And thereby Paul, just as he stands in his Pauline personality, becomes to Peter the type of the *genus homo.*" Marx, K. (1887). *Capital.* Footnote 19. Section 4. Chapter 1. (Orig. Pub. 1867). Online in MIA. Accessed from < https://www.marxists.org/archive/marx/works/1867-c1/ch01.htm#19> on 2016-02-19.

86   Freud, S. (2010). "Transference." in: *A General Introduction to Psychoanalysis.* Trans. G. Stanley Hall. New York: Boni and Liveright, (Orig. Pub.1920). Online in bartleby.com. Accessed from <http://www.bartleby.com/283/27.html> on 2015-10-11.

87   Sartre, J.P. (1956). Being and Nothingness. A phenomenological essay on ontology. Trans. Hazel E. Barnes. New York. Philo-sophical Library. Online in Dominican House of Studies, Priory of the Immaculate Conception. Accessed from <http://www.dhspriory.org/kenny/PhilTexts/Sartre/BeingAndNothingness.pdf> 0n 2014-11-06.

88   de Beauvoir, S. (1972). The Second Sex. Trans. by H M Parshley, London. Penguin. (Orig. Pub. 1949). Online in MIA. Ac-cessed from <https://www.marxists.org/refer-ence/subject/ethics/de-beauvoir/2nd-sex/> on 2015-07-23.

89   Horney, K. (1950), *Neurosis and Human Growth.* Introduction. A morality of evo-lution. p. 13. Online in Internet Archive. Accessed from <https://archive.org/details/NeurosisAndHumanGrowth> on 2014-07-18.

90   Locke, J. (1690). An Essay Concerning Human Understanding. Online in En-lightenment. Accessed from <http://enlightenment.supersaturated.com/johnlocke/BOOKIIChapterXXVII.html> on 2015-09-24.

91   Hegel, G.W.F. (1807). *Phenomenology of Mind. B. Self-Consciousness.* From Harper Torchbooks' edition of the Phenomenology, from University of Idaho, Department of Philosophy by Jean McIntire. Online in MIA, Hegel by hypertext. Accessed from <https://www.marxists.org/reference/archive/hegel/works/ph/phconten.htm>   on 2015-04-11.

92   James, W. (1890). *The Principles of Psychology.* Chapter X. "The Consciousness of Self." In: Classics in the History of Psy-chology. An internet resource developed by C.D. Green. York University, Toronto, Ontario. Accessed from < http://psychclassics.asu.edu/James/Principles/prin10.htm > on 2016-03-09.

10. Civilization and its Discontents

Freud pointed out the conflict between individual self-expression and cultural repression as the cause of collective discontent. His narrow individualistic perspective, however, did not allow him to connect repression either to its historical beginnings with female repression and slavery, or synchronically to social class. He therefore could not see a viable solution, because he could not see far enough into the past to predict a future.

With climate change, the discontent has become rather pervasive restlessness. Social media allowed the Arab Spring and Occupy Wall Street to speedily spread throughout the world. The foreboding is so deep that it is as if nature has joined in. In their alienation, groups select various bones of contention, even though the deeper issues remain unclear to all. It is as if humanity were navigating with a broken compass in the middle of a sea storm, with no instrument to determine direction. We cannot avoid the analysis of ideology, the corruption of our consciousness by repression. To repair consciousness we must fight ideology with ideology, the difference being determined by the degree of ideological inclusiveness that today's good street sense defines as one versus ninety-nine percent. The quality of ideology must be measured by its inclusivity, by its representation of the most universal interests. Marx gave early warnings in his critique of capital, and of its corrupt ideology, even pointing out the ecological impact to no avail. His warnings are still to be heeded by the dominant mainstream that has used his theory to revamp capitalism and prolong its destructive life. Capitalism's biological and psychological roots, as alleged here, are in patriarchy, and restoring women to full parity in all domains could be the pivot to a new era. Mothers would not so flippantly send their children to war and would more likely use dialogue and compromise to solve problems. The good sense of men would join them.

In the present conditions, war has taken hold of economies and we produce for war, produce to destruction that appears to selectively propel some nations. Nations then relate on the presupposition that they could destroy each other in order for the mightier to impose its particular version of truth. All this must occur upon the premise of artificial scarcity that naturally creates fear and foreboding. Besides survival, the fear is one of social descent and loss of dignity through the ravages of poverty and illness that must be displayed as constant reminders. Saving and thriftiness, the replicas of capitalist accumulation, produce the ideological illusion that individuals have it in their power to push up their niche in the hierarchy. This balancing act is what keeps the middle class, the pivotal one, in place, while liberal policies such as austerity shift the laws of motion of resources to drift upwards, the inverted law of gravity of capital. Massive accumulation and technical advances such as robotization continue to surprise and even impress ideologically mystified peoples that have lost the compelling biological capacity to identify their aggressor. Again and again, most people participate in the narrow ritual of elections, the backbone of democracy. Democracy never arrives; but that does not mean its invocation loses its imaginary power. It remains alive as an "ought" to be reached in the unalterable future. Deceptive promises made by antagonistic parties, which alternate in power to maintain the game, are implemented and then reversed, leading to a standstill.

The species that was designed to override force as means, to substitute for it with intelligence, has regressed, through patriarchy, to the most primitive level of the food chain. An intraspecies application, through its conditioning, creates unrestrained competition for hierarchy and class individuality. This is after two hundred thousand years of successful matriarchal organization that have been foreclosed from memory. The result is reification, the regressive objectification of the species that started with slavery, today known as wage work.

The current approach to climate change is the best illustration of the harmful and paralyzing split of consciousness into ideologies. While scientific consensus, representing the interests of most, presents convincing evidence of global warming as a result of our mode of production, capital has the unlimited capacity to hire its own pseudo-science establishment, well-paid armies of prize-fighters, to respond with counter-facts, balance profit outlooks in any solution, and maintain the independent variable of a profit agenda. The form of the social structure that needs this type of diabolic dialectic is properly captured by good commonsense as one against ninety-nine percent, the model of capitalist equilibrium.

Syllogistically, we are stuck in a fetishized form of universally forced small-class particularity that has corrupted, alienated and reified consciousness, our compass. This is how we hope for profitable technology and artificial intelligence to eventually solve our problems instead of looking for our inner resources; in other words, hoping that more of the same, alienation and reified consciousness may be the homeopathic solution. Instead of God, the good sense of nature, the new fetish is capital, the invisible hand that benevolently operates in the market for the benefit of all. Corporations, social artifacts and projections of the human body, take precedence over our real bodies. They have the personhood and agency that most of us lack. The volume of the speech of money, the megaphone of the one percent, drowns the voice of collectivity. This is only possible thanks to the ideological corruption of human consciousness by all possible means of sophistry followed by, when necessary, forceful warring repression. This is the invisible war.

This must again be placed in the context of its ten-thousand-years legacy versus two hundred thousand years of matriarchy, when existence was based on the universal fulfillment of survival and social necessities by all. Democracy was then participatory universality, with the interests of all addressed while emerging from a merely natural state and entering the realm of progressive human development. The historical aberration started with slavery imposed on previously ruling women, and the creation of a civil society, an alternative to the gens, by men. Civil society then needed a state to mediate inevitable class differences. The oppression of women, and, after them, of the working class, became the ground of ideology, the corruption of consciousness.

The secret of alienating ideology, exposed among others by Hegel and Marx, Fromm and Horney, is this total inversion of the map of reality by a narrow self-interested particularistic class perspective today politically represented by powerful lobbying interest groups.

The result of this perverse collective alienation of individuals and whole societies manifests itself in many forms, from individual mental illnesses to universal war.

ABOUT THE SELF

1. Definition, Origins and Evolution

The expression of consciousness is accomplished only through the activity of an individual self even if it is in a group, and what we call *the self* is the organizing property of consciousness in an individual. Consciousness is constant activity during sentience; it must be organized for practical purposes that were originally adaptive. The self is to consciousness what the state is to culture; the mediator and organizer.

Being the product of a dual consciousness (animal and self-consciousness) and at the same time a compromise between two instinctual dispositions, masculine and feminine, the self is a compromise. *Animal consciousness* is activity based on instinctual disposition, close to what Freud called *It,* although perennially socially mediated by conditioning and learning. Conditioning is external mediation by others; learning leads to internal self-mediation.

Self-consciousness is the repository of all past learning based not only in individual experience but in the history of the species. It is human constraining activity based on species experience, and transmitted first from mother to child. This is closer to what Freud called *superego*. The two forms struggle to organize, giving shape to the final instrument consciousness executed by a self. Within that self, the first form of consciousness takes the form of "I," the second is "me." The fact that *I* is capitalized and not *me* represents a historical social class bias. As a repository not only of personal but of species experience, *me* is equally important to *I*, the *sapiens* part of *Homo*.

The self operates internally as a compromise somewhere between the two polarities of I and *me*. Because of political expediency or of dire need under duress, the self cannot come out and express itself naked. Culturally dressed as *person,* it must develop strategies and habits in order to be accepted and to belong. The Etruscans saw this for the first time, theirs being the notion of fixing masks to funeral ums, to give them a human appearance. The Sartrean social roles that we surrender to reinforce the Jungian archetypes. The natural design of two sexes endowed with two opposite instinctual dispositions to end up in a delicate balance that also includes inner ground and outer pull, thus providing the paradigmatic example of complexity.

This model resolves either or new issues in psychology by, dialectically, integrating opposites. The self, like consciousness, is structured in a syllogistic fashion, the synthesis of a prior struggle of opposites. The biographical root of the self is the *mirroring* of the maternal body that imprints as *body image.* Anatomy is not destiny. Destiny, Comte said, is our governance by the dead. Marx concurred and named our essence, *the ensemble of the social relations.* This is how, in the last instance nature, the species, prevails, rather than the individual. Men and women through their own circumstances and active self-mediations, both have the potential to cultivate and develop one instinctual disposition over the other, as we most clearly see today in sexual fluidity. They titrate these dispositions according to environmental conditions and cultural needs.

One of the main functions of the self is to *totalize.* This means to discriminate and synthesize, putting practically every sensation, every image, in its place in the total puzzle of the map of reality, closing the circle of understanding with a unified, total form. This way it conserves sameness in the midst of constant change. Totalization occurs through something like a personal theory that fits things and events together and gives them meaning, a combination of evolutionary good sense and historical consciousness. Patients come to psychoanalysis to correct unresolvable contradictions in their personal theory.

If consciousness is virtual representation, it must reflect the structure and metabolism of its society.[93] Individual consciousness and its collective analogue, cultural consciousness, are continuous but have become split according to class ideologies. The split of the self from real to idealized self is not an unsolvable mystery; it is the reflection of class ideology and class struggle.

Self is then guided not only by its inner structure and proclivity, but simultaneously by a teleological social activity that constantly places demands from others onto the self, and therefore require constant compromise. Degree of autonomy and range of choice are thus limited, as illustrated by the concepts of anxiety and defense. The self's individual form of agency selects, organizes, regulates and deploys its degree and form of consciousness. Actual consciousness is ideology, in its practice bound by natural necessities and by historical personal and social needs.

This dual human agent, under dual reciprocal control, determined by social relations and relations with nature, is the *subject* that —largely unconsciously according to Marx— has collectively made history. "Not only is the material of my activity given to me as a social product (as is even the language in which the thinker is active): my own existence is social activity, and therefore that which I make of myself, I make of myself for society and with the consciousness of myself as a social being."[94] "Society made me first and still coerces me in that I make myself for it," as de Beauvoir said,[95] and, Sartre added: "making myself upon the ruins of what they made of me,[96] which is exercising my limited degree of freedom of choice.

93   Mészáros, I. (2010-1). *Social Structure and Forms of Consciousness.* Two Volumes. New York. Monthly Review Press.

94   Marx, K. (1959). *Economic and Philosophic Manuscripts of 1844.* Private Property and Communism. Trans: Martin Mulligan. (3). VI. Moscow, Progress Publishers. (Orig. Pub. 1932). Online in MIA. Accessed from <https://www.marxists.org/archive/marx/works/1844/manuscripts/comm.htm> on 2015-01-13.

95   De Beauvoir, S. (1972). "Woman as Other." In: *The Second Sex.* Introduction. Trans: H M Parshley. East Rutherford, NJ. USA. Penguin. (Orig. Pub. 1949). Online in MIA. Accessed from <https://www.marxists.org/reference/subject/ethics/de-beauvoir/2nd-sex/index.htm> on 2016-02-19.

96   Sartre, J.P. (1946). "Existentialism Is a Humanism." In: Kaufman, W. Ed. (1989). *Existentialism from Dostoyevsky to Sartre.* Trans: Philip Mairet. Oklahoma City, OK,

I can only access that freedom through critical consciousness, which I can exercise only through the dialectic of my self by knowing my needs.

When working on his *Interpretation of Dreams* Freud saw this. He discovered that there are two registers, a dual thesaurus, two reservoirs for interpretation: the conventional one that can be found in dictionaries, and the idiosyncratic one, the individual one exclusively based on personal experience.[97]

Autonomy and freedom are the capacities of an individual or group to produce and implement its own form of self-governance, upon the premise that is impossible to escape material imperatives. We have to breath, eat, find shelter from the destructive phenomena of nature, and substantially conform to the norms of our cultural environment in order to successfully exist. Culture imposes on us ethical behavior and etiquette.

Self is *moral agency,* meaning self-regulated activity within natural and social constrains. Self-government is the internalization of government by others, starting with the mothering one, upon whose relational template self-regulation expands. To a large degree, most individuals continue to be governed by others for life. Psychoanalysis offers the opportunity that most people lack: it appropriates self, making it for itself.

Human agency, the evolutionary capacity to introduce self-serving mediations, is not merely reflexive or instinctual. Mediations start as cultural inhibitions, then accrue add-ons interposed between stimulus and response in a Pavlovian fashion: first as contingencies, and then as recombinations of reflexes and inhibitions Piaget illustrated this in his theory of intelligence. Contingently, combinatorial

USA. Meridian Publishing Company, (Orig. Pub. 1956). Online in MIA. Accessed from <https://www.marxists.org/reference/archive/sartre/works/exist/sartre.htm> on 2016-02-19.

97   Freud, S. (1913). *The Interpretation of Dreams.* Trans. A. A. Brill. (Orig. Pub. 1900). Originally publish in New York by Macmillan. Online in Classics in the History of Psychology. Accessed from <http://psychclassics.yorku.ca/Freud/Dreams/> on 2015-01-15.

learning leads to intelligence, consciousness, and self, and is based upon the anticipatory potential of the brain.

Tracking back the self therefore, takes us from human freedom to animal instinctual determination on the one hand, and to the total history of cultural mediations on the other. Freedom is always relative, conditioned and subordinated to the knowledge of need. It is constrained, not only by culture, but also by natural imperatives or necessities.

The same way consciousness is verifiable only as language, self can only be seen as person, with both susceptible to modification for political purposes. Following Mead, and Marx, the structure of the self/person consists in the relation of two parts, *I* and *me*.[98,99] In this regard *me* is the source of morality, the script, or analogue, of genome in the mind, the ensemble of social relations.

2. "I" Represents the Drive from Instinct to Agency

The ego has a long trajectory in philosophy and psychology. The Cartesian model has predominated in modern times, separating the mind from the body. The alternative, Spinozist model, more acceptable from a scientific viewpoint, is that mind and body are one and so are *I* and *me*, behavior and experience. This is the position of the Lev Vygotsky school and that of H. G. Mead in psychology. In this view, mind and behavior are not separate but one and the same, viewed from different perspectives. Human activity has its other side in consciousness the same way nature has it in sense: logos. *I* represents uniquely human activity, virtual, that results in objecti-

---

98   Mead, G.H. (1934). "The I and the Me." Part 3, number 5 In: *Mind, Self and Society from the Standpoint of a Social Behaviorist*. (Edited by Charles W. Morris). Chicago: University of Chicago. Online in A George H. Mead Source Page. Accessed from <https://www.brocku.ca/MeadProject/Mead/pubs2/mindself/Mead_1934_22.htm> on 2016-03-12.

99   Marx, K. (1938). *Theses on Feuerbach. 6.* In: *The German Ideology.* London. Lawrence and Wishart. (Written in 1845). Online version Marxists Internet Archive. Accessed from <http://www.marxists.org/archive/marx/works/1845/theses/index.htm> on 2012-09-09.

fication of a subject that simultaneously builds its subjectivity as it instrumentally transforms nature through labor. The *I* has prevailed in part because it is the most visible part of the self, the resulting phenomenon. *I* is agency that originally comes from a disposition that can be traced backwaard instinctually. By itself, however, it would not be different from animals' self-assertion. *I* is thus instinctual disposition, in itself binary, besides having been modified by something else: culture. *Sapiens* qualifies *homo* as its essence.

The container of *I*, the self, is both the premise and outcome of human activity, only possible as social activity precisely because it originated in the phenomenon of mirroring that it continues to require. Such mirroring is not passive, but a form of external regulation that in the first place served as template for the self in the internalization of the relationship with the mother. The self continues to grow through identification of one's activity with that of significant others in the constant process of reciprocal regulation. Mothers uniquely carry in their natural objectifying capacity the ability to produce and imprint humanity on their children. The first-order mediations that mothers introduce prepare their children for moral family life.

To begin to form the structure of a self, human activity in an individual, represented by the pronoun *I*, is the formal representation of itself grounded in animal instinct. Instinctual disposition is the previous species-stereotyped and environment-bound, immediate, animal relation to nature that humans eventually learn to mediate by introducing changes in the gap between stimulus and response. Freud also called it "drive," and philosophers, leading to Schopenhauer who influenced Freud, had called it "will."[100] Will is animal instinct compounded through deliberation; it is instinct humanized as activity, and it boils down to human agency, always countered by other human agency. Social animal activity that is metabolic, based on survival at the cost of destruction, becomes human when,

---

100 Schopenhauer, A. (2011-2). *The World as Will and Idea.* (1909, Sixth Edition). Online in Project Gutenberg. 3 Vols.

through consciousness, it places productiveness before destruction, morally. When it comes to dire survival there is no barrier to an *I* that is designed to strive for fitness.

3. *Me* is Inherited Morality, Attitude, and Gesture

Me is the particular form *I* takes in an individual, morally compounded and redirected by historical precedent. What the species has learned during its particular form of evolution is recorded in *me*. Human agency as *I* differs, from mere animal instinct, in that it has an opposite that always constrains it morally, the *me*. These two opposites constitute the essential dialectic of the self.

Part of *me* is what used to be religiously considered as conscience, and within the self the residue of God that was the soul. It is also what Marx, in his *Theses on Feuerbach*,[101] called the ensemble of social relations. The *I* of a moment is, dialectically, present in the *me* of the subsequent moment, said Mead,[102] indicating that the *me* stores experience for further use in the form of learning and memory. Freud's close equivalent is the superego, the part of the psyche that has to do with moral values.

The paradox of consciousness is that, being collective because it has been constructed by individuals for generations, it can reproduce itself only individually, although individuals can only do it socially. Culture constrains individual *I*'s through their *me*'s and vice versa; *me*'s expression is reciprocally constrained through the influence of *I*. *I* without *me* is animal behavioral randomness that responds to the environment without moral mediation. Me is the accrual of all past

---

101 Marx, K. (1969)." Theses on Feuerbach." Marx/Engels Selected Works, Volume One, p. 13 – 15. Trans: W. Lough. (Written: Spring of 1845, edited by Engels). Moscow, USSR. Progress Publishers, Online in MIA. Accessed from <https://www.marxists.org/archive/marx/works/1845/theses/theses.htm> on 2015-01-30.

102 Mead, G.H. (1934) "The 'I' and the 'me'", Section 22 in *Mind Self and Society from the Standpoint of a Social Behaviorist* (Ed. Charles W. Morris). Chicago: University of Chicago: Pp. 173-178. Online in A George H. Mead Source page. Accessed from <https://www.brocku.ca/MeadProject/Mead/pubs2/mindself/Mead_1934_22.html> on 2016-03-14.

and present mediations that are largely written in the form of the brain, in its morphological memory, resulting in human behavior. It is *me* that provides direction, sense and coherence. In its highest form, *me* is morality, and in its reciprocal, reverberational form, morality is unique to the human species. *Me* constantly matches present reality to previous ones, and determines the choice of the subject's attitude.

Attitude is the form we assume, our form of presentation, our readiness to approach the particular object. Attitude is determined in part by the object but also by our previous history accrued in personality and *me*. Attitude is demeanor and non-verbal communication. The notions of attitude and gesture were proposed first by George Mead.[103]

The particular form of agency of the *me* part of self is its repertoire power. All mediations historically introduced and accommodated in the original gap between stimulus and response, starting with the use of tools, have transformed animal into human behavior. *Me* is precisely the universal record of that learning process, involving all generations past and present. All those individuals' experiences, all that they individually and collectively learned that is significant to adaptation and evolution, has accrued and is represented in the *me* part of the self. *Me* is therefore the constant and ongoing record of human activity with all its trials, errors and corrections, conserved. This is part of the reason the hope of humanity is not in the individual *I*, the hero that most people expect in the form of a savior, but in the *me* that, conscious of its collective power, will ultimately correct its course back towards human universality, recovering its primacy over ideological individuality.

Me is by nature moral but it was repressed by patriarchy. It carries within itself the residue of evolutionary sense that Karen Horney

103 Mead, G.H. (1934). *Mind Self and Society from the Standpoint of a Social Behaviorist.* Part 1. Chapters 2 and 3. (Edited by Charles W. Morris). Chicago: University of Chicago. Pp. 8-18. Online in A George H. Mead Source page. Accessed from <https://www.brocku.ca/Mead-Project/Mead/pubs2/mindself/Mead_1934_toc.html> on 2016-03-14.

called morality of evolution. The breakdown of the self in neurosis has to do with the repression of the *me* that takes place ideologically and leads to what Horney called idealization of the self, leading to a hypertrophic *I*. This we see in narcissism. The real self would be the restoration of the balance between *I* and *me*, only possible if good sense and consciousness are restored.

Temperament also denotes the instinctual, characteristics of an individual as opposed to *character,* the biographical contribution according to conditions and circumstances. These are the two correlates of *I* and *me*. The human body and brain, as well as consciousness, are designed, to genetically constantly change an expectable range of varying conditions[104] to the real ones. Stress, if not optimally titrated, is harmful.

Only the synthesis of all individual perspectives can produce and maintain consciousness alive. This includes all perspectives, even the outliers, because consciousness itself is about the trespassing of boundaries. This is how radicals turn out to be prophets, because they have the capacity to see far beyond that of the average person that does not agree with them. God was the first historical synthesis, consciousness in the sense of nature, that Feuerbach translated into "species being," and Marx into human essence, the ensemble of social relations. In the individual this is *me*.

Neurosis, as Horney explained it, is the counterphobic compensatory god-like inflation of *me* that has been corrupted through idealization. Normally *me* is the constraining force that channels, gives good sense and morality, to what can be considered the instinctual randomness of *I* in the context of culture.

4. On Perspective

The particular configuration of the ensemble of the social relations in *me,* although a universal quality, is unique to each individual

---

104 Hartmann, H. (1958). *Ego psychology and the problem of adaptation.* Trans., David Rapaport. New York: International Universi-ties Press, Inc. (Orig. pub. 1939.)

because it comes in part from her or his unique natural pedigree, life experience and type of agency, what ecologists, and gestaltists, called *umwelt*,[105] environment, the personally unique, immediately experiential universe that includes not only social but physical, psychological and spiritual environments giving its particular idiosyncrasy to personal biography.

Environment is universal because all individuals are subject to its conditions. It is simultaneously unique because not all categories of environment overlap from individual to individual, some being idiosyncratic. How knowledge is limited by perspective is well illustrated by the Hindu fable poetically told in John Godfrey Saxe's poem about the blind men and the elephant.[106] Each participant wise man, being blind, experiences the elephant with full sense-certainty, but is limited by the lack of a total vision. With absolute certainty, each participant argues that the elephant is what he feels with his hands; a wall, a pillar, a rope, a fan, a branch, a pipe. They are all victims of their perspective. Only the total sum of their perspectives could render truth. This type of subjectivity is what science tries to overcome by consensual synthesis of sense-gathered information and reasoning. Ideology today claims to overcome the problem of subjective perspective or opinion through a fetishized "objectivity" that is undialectical in that it does not sublate, but rejects subjectivity.

Our individuality, with its limited horizon and sexual and cultural bias, limits our perspective. So does our social class, a particularity that distorts our perceptions through narrow interests, affecting what we call "reality testing." Only an ensemble of the totality of social relations can provide the true synthesis, by adding up the to-

---

105 von Uexkull, J. (1934). "A Stroll through the Worlds of Animals and Men. A Picture Book of Invisible Worlds." In: *Instinctive Behavior. The Development of a Modern Concept*. Editor and Translator: Claire H. Schiller. New York. International Universities Press. Accessed from < http://cspeech.ucd.ie/Fred/docs/vonUexkuell.pdf> on 2016-02-22.

106 Saxe, J.G. (1872) "The Blind Men and the Elephant." In: The poems of John Godfrey Saxe. Boston: J. Osgood. Accessed from <http://en.wikisource.org/wiki/The_poems_ of_John_Godfrey_Saxe/The_Blind_Men_and_the_Elephant> on 2015-03-06.

tality of perspectives, and the larger the ensemble the more truthful the blend. Consciousness strives for universality.

Since sexuality determines a natural class and perspective,[107] each human is biased by his or her instinctual disposition; s/he perceives the world from a sexuated, body that already presents with an instinctual attitude and gesture. To provide for optimal balance, however, both sexes are programmed with both sexual determinations and they are capable of substantively altering the bias through mediations that are personal and cultural. Sexuation is the foremost sameness in difference within a species. The two sexual dispositions, having different basic perspectives, are mutually constraining in their expression, not only externally but anticipatorily, internally.

I is drive and agency, activity and its destructive potential. *Me* on the other hand, is conservative and productive by nature. *Me* regulates and balances according to past experience. *Me* is the reservoir of sense, of direction, of morality going back to evolutionary consciousness matched with original good sense. This dual structure of the self is what gave consciousness its operating capacity, the syllogism. Individual sense only appears idiosyncratically, connected to the sense of the mother; it turns into consciousness by entering the full realm of culture.

5. Self was Person first: the Object of Others

The dramatics of the origins of self as governance can be understood by following Freud's reasoning in group psychology.[108] Each individual in a group ideally projected him or herself in the form of ego ideal for Freud, onto the screen of a skillful leader.

---

107 Firestone, S. (1970). *The Dialectic of Sex: The Case for Feminist Revolution.* Ch. 1. New York. Bantam Books. Accessed from <https://teoriaevolutiva.files.wordpress.com/2013/10/firestone-shulamith-dialectic-sex-case-feminist-revolution.pdf> on 2016-01-18.

108 Freud, S. (1922). *Group Psychology and the Analysis of the Ego.* Trans. James Strachey. London. The International Psychoana-lytic Press. Online in the Internet Archive. Accessed from <http://www.gutenberg.org/files/35877/35877-h/35877-h.htm> on 2015-01-14.

Collaboratively, a social role was thus created, an external niche to be occupied by the *person*, object of the projections. So to say, this was ideally voting, agreeing to follow one person as occupier of the new leader's social role. The leader agreed, and, subsequently, if not everyone, the majority of the members of the group identified with -thus subordinating themselves to that person. This completed the first circle of projective identification to create the role leader, and it is not difficult to see the same mechanism working to produce other social roles.

Was self first or person-first looks a chicken/egg problem but if selves created person, the problem is resolved. However, person indicates other-governance, governance by others, and therefore here the person had to be first, to be identified with, introjected as a symbol, and then behaviorally subordinated to. Historically, personhood was originally the exclusive attribute of few individuals in leadership social roles, and this may have been the situation in matriarchy, where the division of labor was limited. Because group projections were idealized, it is not difficult to see the closeness, if not identification, of God and leader that prevailed in earlier times. Psychological projections translated into material benefits for the leader, but also into limitations, a sort of imprisonment within the role that Freud emphasizes in his description.

Personhood as a result of projective identifications is the result of the same mechanism for every person, and it is maintained by constant recognition. Historically, the notion of person came first as the self was entangled in the soul. Although the mother was the original repository of idealizations and the original leader of the groups, with the advent of patriarchy there was a radical shift in social leadership and the father came to be idealized as the leader of both family and civil society. It was only with the disentanglement of the soul from theology that the self could be recognized.

The political aspect has changed since slavery, and with democracy personhood and selfhood have been democratized, carrying the side effect of narcissism. To be a sustained self-person needs constant recognition.[109] This is what leads to neurotic idealization and excessive self-objectification in paraphernalia and wealth in the present society. This give-and-take, essentially imitative, constitutes a "dialectic of personal growth," which is at the same time that of social organization. Society, genetically considered, is not a composition of separate individuals; on the contrary, the individuals are differentiations of a common social protoplasm. The conclusion is drawn that the individual is a "social outcome not a social unit." We are members one of another. The oppositions, conflicts, and antinomies of personal and social life are late developments that are sharpened with the rise of reflective and ethical thinking."[110]

The self was historically recorded first in the form of person, recognized from outside particularly in its own objectification as producer and proprietor. Person was originally a legal term for an individual free male with property and rights, a free citizen as opposed to a slave who didn't own even his life or body. Blood and consanguinity were not any longer enough, in the new complexity of paternal affiliations, one in which paternity could not be determined with the same certainty maternity had been.

With the rights of a person came the need for prescriptive ethics, the alternative for family morality. There was no need for ethics in communist matriarchy because, everything being communal, there was no private property and no trespassing. All production was destined for use and any surplus was given to whoever needed it in the

---

109 Hegel, G.W.F. (1807). "Self Consciousness. A: Independence and Dependence of Self-Consciousness: Lordship and Bondage." In: The Phenomenology of Mind. From Harper Torchbooks' edition of the Phenomenology, from University of Idaho, Department of Philosophy by Jean McIntire. Online in MIA, Hegel by Hypertext. Accessed from <https://www.marxists.org/reference/archive/hegel/works/ph/phprefac.htm> on 2015-07-11.

110 Baldwin, J.M. (1930). *Autobiography of James Mark Baldwin.* II. Genetic and social psychology: circular reaction, the socius, social heredity. In: *Classics in the History of Psychology.* An internet resource developed by Christopher D. Green. York University, Toronto, Ontario. First published in Murchison, Carl. (Ed.) (1930). *History of Psychology in Autobiography* (Vol. 1, pp. 1-30). Accessed from <http://psychclassics. yorku.ca/Baldwin/murchison.htm#f8> on 2016-03-15.

group. Every individual was then guided by a morality of evolution that consisted in group need-fulfillment.

Ethical rules became necessary with patriarchy, accumulation, social class, and slavery. The first slaves were women whose lives had been based on giving and domesticity, while establishing a human economy based on giving and tending and need fulfilling. Patriarchy came to be based on the pre-eminence of civil society and accumulation and exchange. Emphasis on identity and individuality came late, in civil society. Individuality became the patriarchal banner, historically resulting in tyrants, emperors, kings, masters and lords, who forcefully demanded recognition and even imposed it.

John Locke represents the new modern trend of representative political constitutionality, the parliamentary alternative that eventually led to what today is called democracy in the abstract. Locke famously argued the political debate with the deservedly well-unknown absolutist patriarch Robert Filmer. Locke correctly asserted that that property starts with one's own person and life.[111] The propertied moral self, the owner of a live body, ought to be legally recognized as person by others. External personhood was not enough, however. In order for the new democracy to work, each person must have an internal regulatory mechanism the analogue of the state. Self-regulation was the sine qua non of democracy, Locke thought.

The self was really born with Locke to mean the right to one's own body and life that makes all individuals uniformly propertied. This was translated as that 'we are all born equal.' Unfortunately today we know we are in fact not born equal except for body and life. That a return to gender parity is a marker of social development is something Marx hinted at.

The return to consciousness from ideology is the only way to, from the psychological standpoint, return to human baseline after the long detour of patriarchy leading to the present crossroads. Hu-

---

111 Locke, J. (1690). *Second Treatise on Civil Government*. Ch. 5. Sec. 27. Online in Constitution Society. Accessed from <http://www.constitution.org/jl/2ndtr05.htm> on 2015-03-06.

man baseline is the morality of evolution, the parity of gender, the balance of I and me, and consequently that of consciousness and good sense. The quality of consciousness can only be measured by its degree of inclusiveness, equality in difference, of human universality. This is the take home message of this book

PART ONE -MATRIARCHY IS SILENCED

"The gens has passed through successive stages of development in its transition from its archaic to its final form with the progress of mankind. These changes were limited in the main to two; firstly, changing descent from the female line, which was the archaic rule, as among the Iroquois, to the male line, which was the final rule, as among the Grecian and Roman gentes; and, secondly, changing the inheritance of the property of a deceased member of the gens from his gentiles, who took it in the archaic period, first to his agnatic kindred, and finally to his children. These changes, slight as they may seem, indicate very great changes of condition as well as a large degree of progressive development."

The gentile organization, originating in the period of savagery, enduring through the three sub-periods of barbarism, finally gave way, among the more advanced tribes, when they attained civilization—the requirements of which it was unable to meet. Among the Greeks and Romans political society supervened upon gentile society, but not until civilization had commenced. The township (and its equivalent, the city ward), with its fixed property, and the inhabitants it contained, organized as a body politic, became the unit and the basis of a new and radically different system of government."

L.H. Morgan[112]

---

112 Morgan, L.H. (2005). *Houses And House-Life Of The American Aborigines.* Chapter 1. The Gens. Project Gutenberg EBook #8112. Accessed from <http://www.gutenberg.org/files/8112/8112.txt> on 2016-08-04.

"This goddess was (Ashoret) the chief divinity of the Semites in their primitive matriarchal stage of organization. She was the analogue of the human matriarch, free in her love, the fruitful mother of the clan, and its leader in peace and war."

J. Hastings[113]

The statement that from the beginning of time oppression was the common lot of woman and the laborer must be emphasized even more forcibly with regard to woman. Woman was the first human being that tasted bondage, Woman was a slave; before the slave existed!

August Bebel[114]

113 Hastings, J.A. (1900). *A Dictionary of the Bible.* Edinburgh. T&T Clark. Quoted by Stone, M. (1976). *When God was a Woman.* New York. Barnes and Noble. P. 165.
114 Bebel, A. (1897). *Woman in the Past, Present, and Future.* San Francisco. G. B. Benham. Online in the Internet Archive. Ac-cessed from <https://archive.org/details/womaninpastpres00bebegoog> on 2014-11-03.

1.1 THE MYTH OF MATRIARCHY

"The men, who are idle in their villages, make their
indolence a mark of honor, giving it to be understood
that they are properly born only for great things, especially for warfare."

Joseph Francois Lafitau on the Iroquois.[115]

1.1.1 My Personal Myth

Myth, the first historical form of explanation, was well fit to the
infancy of humanity. Since then, it has continued its function of *totalizer*: When philosophy and science cannot go all the way in their
explanations, myth is always there to complement them. Totalization, closing the circle of understanding, is always necessary in the
final reality testing of existential here and now where everything
seems to be in its proper place. Unfinished representations of the
real are temporarily understood through the totalizing complementarity of myth, a good example being religion, God fulfilling the
function of *panchreston*, mythical closure for the yet unexplained.

Regarding matriarchy, there is enough objective reality behind
the scientific hypothesis, as we will see in the first part of this book.
There are many leads and fragments that can be followed and integrated together, in the way archeology and forensics do to build full
hypotheses and even theories. Mainstream anthropology has refused
to do this for matriarchy. If we place together matrilineality (ma-

---

115 Lafitau, J.F. (1974). *Customs of the American Indians Compared with the Customs
of Primitive Times. 2 vols.* Trans. William Fenton and Elizabeth Moore. (Orig.
Pub. 1724).Vol. 2. Ch. 3. P. 98. Online in The Publications of the Champlain Society. Accessed from <http://link.library.utoronto.ca/champlain/DigObj.cfm?Id-
no=9_96849&Lang=eng&Page=0113&Size=3&query=lafitau&searchtype=Fulltex-
t&startrow=1&Limit=All> on 2014-07-28.

ternal kinship and nominal identity), matrilocality -residence with the wife's family-, Goddess religion, and inheritance on the female side, it is not difficult to conjure up a theory of matriarchal right. The problem is that patriarchal advocates want to judge matriarchy by a society in which the exercise of power is an analogue of patriarchy. This is not possible because all consensus is that matriarchal societies were not hierarchical but egalitarian, exercising a type of right still based on females, mothers in particular, as evolutionary ushers. Believing that in this area anthropology lacks scientific imagination, I place all these reality pieces together to construct with them my myth of matriarchy with the available information that I have at hand.

Matriarchy, the first and lengthiest form of social organization continuous with apehood, is the necessary matrix of culture and, in the historical syllogism, the *thesis*. Ignoring matriarchy is equivalent to disavowing or foreclosing one's infancy, how one came to be. In fact, patriarchy, the antithesis of its predecessor, radically inverted and modified, repressed matriarchal culture so effectively, that not only common sense, but mainstream academia, knows nothing of such a thing. And yet it stands to reason, mainly on evolutionary grounds, that matriarchy is the first template of all social institutions. It must have introduced the *first-order mediations* (transitions from nature to history in a gentile organization) that later were inverted and replaced by patriarchal *second-order mediations* (civil society and its institutions). Matriarchal first-order mediations included the regulation of biological and instinctual activity; the concomitant regulation of productive labor according to the needs of the gens; the division of labor and its concomitant establishment of suitable exchanges; the planning, coordination and control of social activities according to natural cycles; the social allocation of resources to fight scarcity; and the creation and enactment of laws to regulate the global social activities balancing individual and collective rights.[116]

---

116 Meszaros, I (2008). *The Challenge and Burden of Historical Time*. New York. Monthly Review Press. P. 44.

Claiming cultural authorship and absolute original hegemony, patriarchy politically repressed and consciously silenced all the preceding history and manifestations of matriarchy. Matriarchy has persisted, although not in written documents, in myths and religious codes, and, most important in the domain of the family, in that it operates substantially on the bases of their members' needs. It is in this regard that the family is the live antipode of civil society. A counterphobic scientific silence about the subject, caused by the unconscious fear of the return of mother-ushering, has dominated patriarchal academia, and particularly the so-called human sciences. All descriptions of matriarchy depict a society without hierarchy, of giving and sharing, of equality and of internal peace, what we seem to fear.

But the repressed, as Freud unequivocally pointed out, constantly pushes to return; and that is what patriarchal history has confirmed: patriarchy can be summed up as the history of reiterated attempts for a return to a society of substantive equality, the life of the species characterized by the universal fulfillment of needs. Since human science finally was admitted into the Hall of Science with the Romantic Movement, a society of substantial equality is its utopia, the full reintegration of women and the repressed.

Of course our historical future is syllogistically determined by the past, and that is the reason for the unconscious fear of the hegemon. Each historical revolt, like a symptom improperly interpreted, has brought humanity a bit closer to its original synchronicity with nature's good sense, with the morality of evolution represented in substantive equality, sexual parity, and universal need fulfillment for the species.

In the final chapters of this part of the book we will see how the first human negation, the thesis of humanity, was implemented by females of the species. By saying no to their children, mothers invented culture, and they still reinvent it for each child everyday. A maternal *no* is eminently constructive and most often opposite to its paternal, "utilitarian" analogue.

Chris Knight from anthropology shows us how women could have invented culture by solidarily saying no, including to the predatory-at-will alpha male, to sexual access.[117] This seminal female invention included strategic social planning, and checks on compliance through feigning menstruation bodily art (natural colorants in non-menstruating females) and through synchronizing social rhythms with the moon cycles. Knight's book, and Hai Cua's that describes a society in China where fathers and husbands are not kin[118] are only the last in the mountain of evidence presented in favor of matriarchy so far. Although anthropology was originally for the most part matriarchal and evolutionary, in the nineteenth century it was rather forcefully turned patriarchal and static with a stroke of the pen.[119]

As much as we may take pride in our civilization's accomplishments, in our daily life we still largely operate guided by obsolete myths, some of them bad faith trying to circumvent science. Our sciences have indeed made large dents into pockets of reality, some of them deep and not all practical. When it comes to human science, however, we are even more embedded in myth, the number of gaps we still fill with speculation being huge. This is where ideologues find opportunity, the origins of society being a case in point. And yet, we will not know ourselves thoroughly until we are certain about our origins.

The landmarks in the human sciences worth keeping in mind regarding the present work start with logic in its mathematical form, with the pre-Socratics who showed math is derived from nature's

117 Knight, C. (1991). *Blood Relations. Menstruation and the Origins of Culture.* New Haven and London. Yale University Press.

118 Cai, H. (2001). *Society Without Fathers or Husbands. The Na of China.* Trans. Asti Hustvedt. New York. Zone Books.

119 Westermarck, E. (1894). *The History of Human Marriage.* Second Edition. New York and London. MacMillan. Online in Google eBooks. Accessed from <https://books.google.com/books?id=ZSoKAAAAIAAJ&pg=PA319&lpg=PA319&dq=The+home+is+kept+pure+from+incestuous+defilement&source=bl&ots=Lpe3h-r5GHx&sig=H1SpuJTxSW6wqPo-qtI-TYXA1BiU&hl=en&sa=X&ei=9PefVPX-2CMilNrujgZAC&ved=0CCcQ6AEwAw#v=onepage&q=The%20home%20is%20kept%20pure%20from%20incestuous%20defilement&f=false> on 2014-12-28.

form. Along the same lines, Aristotle provided us with the syllogism as the tool of the mind *par excellence* that Hegel later would make dialectical and historical. Unfortunately, logic infatuated with itself grew unrestrained, sometimes as a weed, in philosophical idealism from the Sophists to the Renaissance at the peak of patriarchy. The *Republic* of Plato was a map of class society then, Greek civil society, and simultaneously of its hierarchical mind. Spinoza in turn represents a huge step in identifying the two faces of the same object, God and nature, and is followed by the two British Bacons, Roger and Francis, who from very different vantage points demanded scientific proof thus inaugurating the modern scientific proof, era proper. Finally, the authors of the grand narratives, Hegel in philosophy, Darwin in biology, Comte and Marx in sociology, and Freud in psychology, have shown us that consciousness' drive is to totalize, a drive parallel to globalization and human universality. All of these inform the present work.

In sociology, the pioneers of political economy up to Marx introduced us to the anatomy of the unconscious heart of society. In turn the semiotic sciences, linguistics, hermeneutics, and psychoanalysis, greatly contributed to decoding the mysteries of meaning and communication. Then came evolutionary theory, holding its moment to the present after the great synthesis of Darwin and Mended, challenging and influencing the human sciences presently as sociobiology.

This chapter introduces what I call my myth in the hope of starting a controversial dialogue necessary for the transition to a new age after patriarchy and capitalism. It is highly inspired by Chris Knight, endorsing and largely paraphrasing his compelling and well-informed anthropological theory of origins. The concern with human origins symmetrically projects itself to the future, to the alternatives for a fully humanized and universal society. I see that society as the normal syllogistic completion, a synthesis of history of the two ages of matriarchy and patriarchy. It is based on the belief that if our future can only involve substantive human equality in the fulfillment of needs, equivalent to substantial freedom, there is already a historical precedent for it in matriarchal society. I see in my project as much of a myth as I see in the Big Bang theory that Einstein diplomatically qualified as a beautiful theory of creation.

By the time history-making was appropriated by human males it was in fact quite late in making history. Mothers had been making it for two hundred thousand years. Mediterranean patriarchs constitute the Oedipal period of human history after a long, painstaking infancy. Species female ushering goes back to the millions of years that bridged us with other hominids and even farther. Compare to this the scripturally based description decade of thousands of years of patriarchy. This gives us pause to think about the longevity of the species, and about the fact that, as Marx said, we may still be in the pre-historical phase. Psychoanalytically, the return of the repressed memory of matriarchy helps explain egalitarian revolutions and social unrest, without displacing economic factors that are co-determinative, the unconscious of society explained by Marx.

The first political *coup d'état,* the paradigm of repression, has been redacted from the books of history. It was the brutal enslavement of mothers, previous strategists and ushers of gentes, clans and tribes, by their sons. This was not Oedipus', but Orestes' story, as Bachofen already points out.[120] The demotion and degradation of women to the status of objects does not seem, logically, necessary for any survival reason, particularly after their lengthy natural hegemony. It was rather that males of the species wanted to get rid of constraints to the expression of their instinctual disposition to war and conquest. That women practiced an economy of gifts, that they did most of the daily labor in sedentary agricultural societies, the input of males being incidental and limited to defense, made possible their demotion without resistance. Increased productivity leading to accrual, excess accumulation, and exchange, besides the growing division of labor and the blossoming of civil society, gave

120 Bachofen, J. (1992). Myth, Religion and Mother Right. Preface by George Boas, introduction by Joseph Campbell, translated by Ralph Manheim. Princeton NJ: Princeton University Press. P. 116. (Orig. Pub.1967).

the opportunity to males.

Behind these material facts, psychologically, was the envy of motherhood, envy of how females reproduced the species, besides the way they handled blood. Blood was equivalent of life and of soul,[121] and it determined matronymic identity and its inherent human qualities of loyalty and solidarity. These are weighty determinants. It turned out that those qualities, the sources of envy, were all eventually susceptible to inversion by sons whose mothers to some extent colluded. This is how sons turned around blood-handling into war, gift into commodity, commonality of property into inheritance, evolutionary morality into law, and equality into hierarchy. To accomplish this, it was necessary to not only remove females from political power, but also deprive them as much as possible of voice and subjectivity.

Mothers did fight back in many ways, most ostensibly reflected in the stories of the legendary Amazons who identified with the aggressor and adopted the weapons and instinct of their adversaries. More durably, mothers have been able to preserve matriarchal values to the degree it is possible, in families that, as long as they are under their care, are guided by the communal principle of universal fulfillment of needs. The modern family is the vestigial organ that attests to the historical existence of primitive matriarchal communism. It is the family that has made possible the preservation of the evolutionary success of the human race, in that it struggles to survive as an opposite within the dialectic of family versus mighty civil society. Mothers have historically buffered, as much as they can, the selective destructiveness of patriarchs. They have done this through values such as indiscriminate universal home care, tending, morality, education, and, uppermost, giving.

Blood is thus the icon of women producing and of men destroying; it is the symbol of fertility and creativity, but also of annihila-

---

121 Alton, E. (no date), Ed.. "The Moon and Menstruation. A Taboo Subject. Selected Extracts of Robert Briffault's *The Mothers*" A Radical Anthropology Group Publication. London. University of East London. Accessed from <radicalanthropologygroup.org/sites/default/.../pub_the%20mothers.pdf> on 2015-08-02.

tion and destruction depending on whose hands it is in. However, it is important to keep in mind that both genders have the ability to cultivate one or the other instinctual disposition independent of sex, since critical and sensitive periods and habitual practice have the capacity to overturn instinctual proclivity. The patriarchal thirst for blood however does not seem satisfiable, for lack of natural constraint written in hormone balances and in the hemisphericity of the brain. In academia the ferocity of the suppression of a matriarchal theory of origins and its irk was revealed in the Briffault-Malinowsky debate,[122] and also in the reiterated demand for an impossible proof of a matriarchal analogue to of patriarchy.

Biologically, females have no choice but to select males for their culturally-disguised destructive capacity, in part because destructiveness is an archaic form of object relations going back to chemical reactions as we will see. Destruction is the nemesis of production, from plain chemistry to the food chain in evolution, but the blind force of the survival of the fittest is superseded in the human species by the capacity to group, collaborate, dialogue, and compromise. This amounts to producing consciously with minimal destructiveness. Although destruction is not by any means exclusive to males in the species, the evolutionary bias threw its dice in their favor.

Females did tame male random sexuality to produce culture instead, largely by regulating the aggressive take and universalizing access. But when their historical moment came, males re-inverted the trend through war. War for possession, disguised as humanitarian and often mingled with paranoid, anticipatory fear and the alibi of self-defense, came to prevail. Freud already identified hoarding money with fearful, constipating human waste.[123]

Money is the current historical version of the alienated fantasy

---

122 Montague, M.F.A. (1956). *Marriage, past and present: a debate between Robert Briffault and Bronislaw Malinowski.* Boston. Porter Sargent Publisher. Online in Archive Org. Accessed from <https://archive.org/details/marriagepastpres00brif> on 2016-01-18.
123 Freud, S. (1908). "Character and anal erotism." Standard Edition, Vol. 9. (pp 169-175)). London, Hogarth Press.

of perfection and omnipotence. In its reifying form that transforms humans, it is the closest to magic and the universal amulet. As a fiction reified in an object, it substitutes the real, collective subject, the magic of evolution. In its form of accumulation of capital, money is alienated productive human activity, largely metabolized into substantial waste, most blatantly in war economies. The effect of capital is seen in the impoverishment that goes with it, the human misery it engenders. As private reified potential idleness, it must rest on the collective activity of others, dead human labor, and necrophilia. Since labor is the expression of human subjectivity, the cult of dead labor in money is the most tragic form of human alienation.

This book destroys myths originated in repression, brings to life myths that were repressed because of their threat to the status quo, and builds myths that can serve as scaffold for future understanding. The ultimate goal is a better, more scientific and less mythical understanding of reality. Like dreams myths fall into place within the large puzzle of social reality.

1.1.2 The Wise Steps of Evolution

Nature operates dialectically based on the interaction of the two opposite forces of destruction and production. The paradigm of human reproduction is the mother who materially and spiritually, produces all children through painstaking and costly labor that patriarchy has for the most part failed to recognize as such in its political economy equation. Here it is proposed that labor started with maternal labor, the construction of each new member of the species, and their difficult delivery to the world, the template for all labor.

The Big Bang is only part of the eternal pulse of cosmic evolution, a self-reignition from a previous state of total entropy.[124] The

---

124 "The idea of entropy comes from a principle of thermodynamics dealing with energy. It usually refers to the idea that everything in the universe eventually moves from order to disorder, and entropy is the measurement of that change. The word entropy finds its roots in the Greek entropia, which means "a turning toward" or "transformation." The word was used to describe the measurement of disorder by the German

present expanding cycle of the universe thus started in the form of destructive fire, and before the Big Bang total entropy was the end of a previous cycle of contraction. The Big Bang fire produced ashes that became stars and planets, some still burning like our sun and the inner part of our earth. It is upon those ashes that constructive forces of evolution restored their subversive trend fourteen billion years ago. Life, the opposite of entropy, came to be seen right behind, only a billion years later.

Evolution is metabolic, constructive destruction or anabolic catabolism. Construction cannot take place without destruction, because energy and matter can only be transformed; they cannot be created or destroyed.[125] Evolution is a zero-sum game. If we are in an expansive phase of a universal cycle of expansion and contraction, this means that constructive forces such as life presently have the upper hand. This will eventually change back, and, what physicists call entropy, the regressive force to disorder, will eventually have its moment.

Fire is a chemical reaction and thus an original form of physical object relations. This chemical reaction was the first constructive destruction in the physical universe : both objects, the burning energy and the burned matter, perished to produce a new one, their ashes. The sciences of chemistry and physics deal with the most primitive forms of object relations.

Evolutionarily the biological food chain is a new upgraded form of object relations compared to mineral chemistry. It became necessary with the arrival of organisms into the process of evolution. The food chain is a less destructive form because only one of the objects

---

physicist Rudolph Clausius and appeared in English in 1868. A common example of entropy is that of ice melting in water. The resulting change from formed to free, from ordered to disordered increases the entropy." From: vocabulary.com. Entropy.

125 Clausius, R. (1817). *The Mechanical Theory of Heat, with its Applications to the Steam-Engine and to the Physical Properties of Bodies.* Ed. T. Archer Hirst. London. John van Woorst. Printed by Taylor and Francis. Online in Google eBooks. Accessed from <http://books.google.com/books?id=8LIEAAAAYAAJ&printsec=frontcover&dq=editions:PwR_Sbkwa8IC&hl=en&sa=X&ei=h6DgT5WnF46e8gSVvbynDQ&ved=0CDYQuwUwAA#v=onepage&q&f=false> on 2014-10-18.

perishes in the interaction between the two; the other, that will become the proto-subject, survives because it conserves its form at the expense of its victim.

After the food chain comes consciousness, as the third qualitative jump in object relations become necessary with the arrival of more complex, sensitive animals. Consciousness produces subjectivity, the property of producing with only forms, without destructive and slow adaptive morphological change in the producing subject. To produce, consciousness does not need to destroy its object because it can abstract and operate with the object's form. Animals differ from humans in that their consciousness is limited, bound to immediate reality, and organized without the huge human capacity to introduce historical mediations.[126]

The final qualitative jump is self-consciousness, uniquely human and paradoxically the least destructive. Self-consciousness can not only represent and anticipate objects and their properties; it can also anticipate operations and operations with operations, and therefore it can make the most complex plans. Self-consciousness is the most productive of evolutionary options in what respects conservation of energy, because it can anticipatorily produce with only forms.

Prior to consciousness, sexuation was required. Evolution did in sexuation titrate constructiveness and destructiveness differently. It did so by simultaneously making females the selective agent and the "re-productive" vehicle. Sexuation is inherently reproductive incompleteness, if we compare it with hermaphroditism, for example. There is an explicit requirement for inclusion of the other in order to self-reproduce, and it therefore enshrines the productive and non-destructive self-other relation, the collaborative social relation, as a natural necessity. The need to fill up gaps through otherness, in

---

126 Vygotsky, L. (1968). "The Problem of Consciousness." Collected Works of L. S. Vygotsky, Volume III, Part 1: Problems of the Theory and Methods of Psychology, Chapter 9: The Problem of Consciousness, pp 129-138. First Published: in The Psychology of Grammar, Moscow; (Written 1934). Online in MIA. Accessed from <https://www.marxists.org/archive/vygotsky/works/1934/problem-consciousness.htm> on 2015-08-02.

mediatory form, is also the essence of consciousness.

The reason for the early pluripotentiality of the human brain,[127] the seat of human consciousness, is prematurity as we know. The brain comes out of the oven before it is fully cooked, so to speak. This disadvantage is turned around to be opportunity, what allows the brain to develop within the reciprocal constraints of its environment. The brain, through the senses incorporates, and responds to, the stimulating form of its objects; it also builds up a parallel form or representation.

The wisdom of evolution, its constructive directionality, and its movement from sense to coherence to selectivity and finally to subjectivity (that started as a chemical reaction) is the process that goes from natural sense to consciousness.

1.1.3 The Instinctual Difference Between Men and Women

For reproduction women produce in their lifetime, serially, comparatively few ova, one of which usually matures for fertilization during a limited period of time on a monthly basis. Men produce simultaneously many spermatozoids and are always ready to impregnate and waste besides. To produce one spermatozoid is much less protein-costly than producing an egg. It is possible that a man can sire a thousand children during his lifetime[128] if he can access enough women, but a reproductive woman could not arrive at a hundred even producing more than one at a time. Yet the collective outcome is balanced, always close to sexual parity, one male to one female.[129] Here is an example of dialectical mutual constraint, through

127 Schore, A. (1994). Affect Regulation and the Origins of the Self. The Neurobiology of Emotional Development. Hillsdale, N.J. Lawrence Erlbaum Associates. Online in Questia. Accessed from <http://www.questia.com/read/57185676/affect-regulation-and-the-origin-of-the-self-the> on 2013-03-07.

128 Oberzaucher E, Grammer, K. (2014). The Case of Moulay Ismael - Fact or Fancy? PLoS ONE 9(2): e85292. doi:10.1371/journal.pone.0085292.

129 Fisher RA. (1930)."The genetical theory of natural selection". Oxford: Clarendon. Accessed from < https://archive.org/stream/geneticaltheoryo031631mbp/genetical-theoryo031631mbp_djvu.txt> on 2016-03-21.

quality and quantity, as competing fitness strategies. Females almost invariably, particularly in mammals, invest more in reproductive fitness and better outcome quality than do males. Bateman's principle[130] (that variability in reproductive success is greater in males than in females) explains why males tend more to be promiscuous and indiscriminate, while females tend more to be selective.[131] Any parental expenditure in time, energy, protein etc., benefits the offspring at a cost to the parents' ability to invest in other components of their own fitness. This is a particular form of sexual selection,[132] debatable as to how much of it is contingent predominantly on fitness conditions, due to determinants such as testosterone and dominance, or both.[133] The default chromosome of the species is female X, and the male determining one is Y. Absent the Y chromosome, the gonadal rudiment develops into ovaries. The ovaries produce estrogen, a hormone that enables the development of the female sexual characteristics. If the Y chromosome is present, testes form and secrete testosterone that morphologically masculinizes the fetus. Thus, the body has the female phenotype unless it is changed by the testosterone secreted by the fetal testes.[134]

These hard biological facts already determine a bias in the dichotomously sexuated human nature: men are more prone to spend, externalize, while women are more predisposed to preserve or in-

130 Bateman, A.J. (1948), "Intra-sexual selection in Drosophila", Heredity 2 (Pt. 3): 349–368. Accessed from <http://www.nature.com/hdy/journal/v2/n3/pdf/hdy194821a.pdf > on 2016-01-20.

131 Newcomer, S. D.; Zeh, J. A.; Zeh, D. W. (31 August 1999). "Genetic benefits enhance the reproductive success of polyandrous females". *Proceedings of the National Academy of Sciences* 96 (18): 10236–10241. Online in PNAS. Accessed from <http://www.pnas.org/content/96/18/10236> on 2016-03-20.

132 Trivers R. L., Willard D. E. (1973). Natural selection of parental ability to vary the sex ratio of offspring. Science, 179: 90–92. Accessed from <http://science.sciencemag.org/content/sci/179/4068/90.full.pdf> on 2016-01-20.

133 Grant, V.J. (2001). "The Maternal Dominance Hypothesis: Questioning Trivers and Willard." Evolutionary Psychology. vol. 1 no. 1. Accessed from <http://evp.sagepub.com/content/1/1/147470490300100106.full.pdf+html> on 2016-01-20.

134 Scott F. Gilbert, S.F. (2003). *Developmental Biology,* Sixth Edition. Sunderland, MA.Sinauer Associates, Inc. Accessed from http://www.ncbi.nlm.nih.gov/books/NBK9967/ on 2016-03-21.

ternalize. Advantages of human female's fitness are being better survivors, living on the average over five years longer than men, and having traits such as better pain tolerance and larger fat deposits for energetic survival. Women also use natural resources better, have better social and emotional intelligence, have an advantageous extra X chromosome that buffers X related mutations and linked illnesses, and, theoretically, it is possible for them to regress to reproducing without external genetic contribution, something impossible for males.[135,136] This differential natural endowment is part of the complementary coherence of the dual human instinctual disposition, where the female has both the evolutionary burden and advantage to assure the survival of the species.

Genetic and evolutionary sex differences go a long way to determine, besides the biological and environmental conditions, the relational proclivities, *i.e.*, attitudes-and-gestures,[137] of the sexes. Males are built to rather indiscriminately fertilize, but that is where their reproductive function often ends: witness modern single-parent families where not only the reproductive but the full load of raising children, falls to the woman and makes men incidental. Females are programmed not only to be selective as far as partners are concerned, but to stick with their progeny and fully provide for its development and growth. Instinctively, males can afford more impulsive activity and risk-taking, while women are geared to exercise more discriminative judgment and selective self-regulation.

---

135 Lazarus, C.N. (2011). ?Why Women Are the Superior Gender. In a Battle of the Sexes, Bet on the Women!" Think Well Blog. Psychology Today. Accessed from <https://www.psychologytoday.com/blog/think-well/201102/why-women-are-the-superior-gender> on 2016-01-20.

136 See for example: Virant-Klun, I., Cvjeticanin, B., et al. (2009). "Parthenogenetic Embryo-Like Structures in the Human Ovarian Surface Epithelium Cell Culture in Postmenopausal Women with No Naturally Present Follicles and Oocytes." Stem Cells and Development. January, Vol. 18, No. 1: 137-150.

137 Mead, G.H. (1934). "Wundt and the Concept of the Gesture", Section 7 in *Mind Self and Society from the Standpoint of a Social Behaviorist* (Ed. Charles W. Morris). Chicago: University of Chicago (1934): 42-51. Online in A George H. Mead source page. Accessed from <https://www.brocku.ca/MeadProject/Mead/pubs2/mindself/Mead_1934_07.html> on 2015-08-03.

Selection is a biological expression of the natural coherence that biases the sexes for a wider range of conditions, thus enhancing the whole species' adaptive capacity. It also calls in humans for ongoing reciprocal balancing, contingent on constantly, if at varying speeds, changing conditions. It would make sense that males as a group can afford to risk more, since they recover from loss relatively easily, as has traditionally happened after wars. This does not mean that females don't have the capacity to cultivate the same range of behaviors by the introduction of male cultural mediations. The same is true for males, as is illustrated by the present trend of sexual fluidity in younger populations. The natural bias, however, is basic and deep, based on instinct and sexual determination. Although Freud clearly struggled with the duality of instinct throughout his theory, in his several iterations he could not see an instinct in women except for lack of instinct, passivity, or at best, borrowed libido from males.[138]

Parturition and menses are visible phenomena that made women the handlers of human blood as opposed to men who had to resort to aggression, even envious self-aggression and war. It was mother's blood that determined all kinship relations long before the role of paternal insemination in reproduction was understood in history. It was always obvious who the mother was but not the father. To this day, some sixteen or so societies in South America believe in partible paternity -the idea that more than one father can contribute genetically to a child,[139] and the Na of China, who practice polygyny and polyandry, believe that men with their semen only water seeds that women alone germinate, men in fact doing a favor to women in

---

138 Freud, S. (1933). "Femininity." Lecture 3. in: *New Introductory Lectures on Psychoanalysis.* Online in Birdsville Independent School District. Accessed from <http://schools.birdvilleschools.net/cms/lib2/TX01000797/Centricity/Domain/1013/AP%20Psychology/Femininity.pdf> on 2016-01-19.

139 Beckerman, S., R. Lizarralde, et al. (2002) "The Barí partible paternity project: Phase 1." In *Cultures of Multiple Fathers: The theory and practice of partible paternity in South America.* Eds. S. Beckerman and P Valentine. Gainesville: University of Florida Press, pp. 27-41.

the sexual act. Needless to say, their permissive sexual behavior is associated with this belief.[140]

Mothers not only give birth but they typically raise every single child for a significant part of his or her life after the newborn transitions from parasitism to symbiosis. Mothers have to regulate every naturally impulsive child until the child learns self-regulation: how to exercise self-care and self-protection. Mother is the first regulator, external control, role model, and natural authority universally, independent of sex; it is the mother that carries the banner of universality. All fathers had mothers when mothers still didn't have acknowledgeable fathers, and the gift of mothers was to give to all, even at a high cost to themselves. This sublime characteristic was inverted in the myth of Pandora.

Along the same instinctual proclivity, some anthropologists and feminists in particular point out that the economic mode of female governance was based on giving.[141] Everyone in the family is still given to by Mother according to need, and every family in which this occurs is practicing communism. In historical matriarchy mothers used the resources of their gentes or clans to fulfill immediate needs of all their members, selectively and independent of their input. If males hunted, they were forbidden to eat from their own hunt, leaving it to females to cook and distribute usually excluding the hunter who could not eat of its own hunt. There were very few means of storage or accumulation particularly in nomadic groups that had to be on the move carrying their scant possessions, the fewer the better. Even later, fairly settled agricultural groups had to move once the soil was depleted, as there were no known fertilizers besides waste and manure. Storing and accumulating goods, and food practices such as salting, smoking and refrigerating, are late social technol-

---

140 Cai, H. (2001). *Society Without Fathers or Husbands. The Na of China.* Trans. Asti Hustvedt. New York. Zone Books.

141 Vaughan, G. (2000). "Gift Giving as the Female Principle vs. Patriarchal Capitalism." Presented at the Conference on the Female Principle, University of Texas at Arlington. The Gift Economy. Accessed from <http://www.gift-economy.com/articlesAndEssays/principleVsPatriarchal.html> on 2016-03-21.

ogies.

"There is no private property and there are no territorial claims. The people simply have usage rights on the soil they till, or the pastures their animals graze, for 'Mother Earth' cannot be owned or cut up in pieces. She gives the fruits of the fields and the animals to all people, and therefore the harvest and the flocks cannot be privately owned; instead they are shared equally. The women, and specifically the oldest women of the clan, the matriarchs, hold the most important goods in their hands, for they are responsible for the sustenance and the protection of all clan members. The women either work the land themselves or organize the work on the land and the fruits of the fields, and the milk of the flocks are given to them to hold and distribute equitably among the community. Matriarchal women are managers and administrators, who organize the economy not according to the profit principle, where an individual or a small group of people benefits; rather, the motivation behind their action is motherliness. The profit principle is an ego-centered principle, where individuals or a small minority take advantage of the majority of people. The principle, of motherliness is the opposite, where altruism reigns and the wellbeing of all is at the center of concerns. It is at the same time a spiritual principle which humans take from nature. Mother Nature cares for all beings, however different they may be. The same applies to the principle of motherliness: a good mother cares for all her children in spite of their diversity. Motherliness as an ethical principle pervades all areas of a matriarchal society, and this holds true for men as well. For example, among the Minangkabau in Sumatra, if a man desires to acquire status among his peers, or even to become a representative of the clan to the outside world, the criterion is: 'he must be like a good mother.'"[142]

Giving birth was of course a very significant event, and so was raising children and care-giving. Before paternity was known, there were mythical theories about fertility and conception, and most an-

<hr>

142 goettner-abendroth, h. (no date). "Matriarchal Society and the Gift Paradigm." Accessed from <http://www.gift-economy.com/womenand/womenand_matriarchal.html#top> on 2015-08-03.

cient deities were fertility goddesses. Blood was the first material object obviously connected with life and therefore translated into the first form of concrete spirit. Blood was the first soul that carried life within it. But bleeding was also the cause of death. The first symbol of blood as a bond was the totem —that in Algonquian means family mark— same blood.[143] Prohibitions to eat the totem came along with those of sexual restriction within your own gens; exogamy.[144,145]

Women created culture by transforming herd into organized gens, an original form of mother-led, largely extended, family or clan. The first cultural instrumental production of women was precisely to use blood as a sign; blood, hematite colorants and fruit dyes painted on the skin were the first cultural frustration, the original sign for NO ACCESS! to sex, as we will see in Knight's theory of origins. Collectively denying sexual access, women for the first time invented their own Lysistratean,[146] cultural solidarity.

These two original ingredients of culture, sex-negation and contingency and female solidarity, collectively coerced and mobilized males to help in a mother-run collaborative family fashion. Postponement of compelling sexual relations became subordinated to the contingency of feeding the family. That is how women got males to engage in a collaborative solidarity process. After the hunt males brought meat for women to share with everyone in the family, and they were rewarded sexually. This gave equal sexual opportunity to all males and females, not exclusive to the alpha male but also to

---

143 Merriam-Webster Online Dictionary and Webster's New World College Dictionary, Fourth Edition.

144 Knight, C. (1991). Blood Relations. Menstruation and the Origins of Culture. New York and London. Yale University Press.

145 Freud, S. (1919). *Totem And Taboo Resemblances Between The Psychic Lives Of Savages And Neurotics.* Authorized English Translation, with Introduction By A. A. Brill. London. George Routledge & Sons, Limited. (1912-3). Online in Project Gutenberg. Accessed from <http://www.gutenberg.org/files/41214/41214-h/41214-h.htm> on 2015-08-03.

146 Lysistrata is a comedy by Aristophanes. Originally performed in classical Athens in 411 BC, it is a comic account of one woman's extraordinary mission to end the Peloponnesian War.

less popular guys.

Creating solidarity, women created cooperation and transformed maternal altruism into social morality and ethics. They were also able to help transform and sublimate male aggression toward a constructive social purpose.[147]

1.1.4 The Patriarchal Coup

What Marx and Engels called tribal society and primitive communism were probably matriarchal stages, the transition to patriarchy's taking place in the second. "The man fights in the wars, goes hunting and fishing, procures the raw materials of food and the tools necessary for doing so. The woman looks after the house and the preparation of food and clothing, cooks, weaves, sews. They are each masters in their own sphere: the man in the forest, the woman in the house."[148] The Achilles heel of women's rule was probably their economic organization of the clan, which followed their instinctual proclivity; giving may not necessarily be the most efficient way to advance technology along the terms of the male penchants. As soon as they could, males would introduce the opposite trend, economic exchange. Mothers in the gens also demanded from and delegated to children, and sooner or later new developments in the hierarchical division of labor, such as commerce and civil exchange, are bound to make the young male more proficient than the mother in dealing with affairs not necessarily domestic but perhaps more productive. Better skills and specialization make productivity rise and also lead to accumulation and barter. This made necessary a new, more competitive form of economic relation; the male instinctual disposition's being prone to take the opportunity.

---

147 Knight, C. (1991). *Blood Relations. Menstruation and the Origins of Culture.* Introduction. P. 18. New Haven and London. Yale University Press.
148 Engels, F. (1968). *Origins of the Family, Private Property, and the State.* Ch. IX. Barbarism and Civilization. Trans. Alick West. Marx/Engels Selected Works, Volume Three. (Orig. Pub. 1884). Online in MIA. Accessed from < https://www.marxists.org/archive/marx/works/1884/origin-family/ch09.htm> on 2016-03-21.

Many societies have been described that have matriarchal traits, such as matrilineality and matrilocality. A glaring example of giving is the potlatch, a social gift-giving binge practice of the Pacific Northwest Indians and others. Potlatches were unsuccessfully banned by both the Canadian and United States federal governments; they went underground despite the risk of criminal punishment, so deeply rooted they were at the foundation of their cultures' economies. Since the practice was de-criminalized in the post-war years, the potlatch has re-emerged. In a potlatch wealth accumulation is given away to others in periodic orgiastic feasts, destruction of wealth sometimes also accompanying the gatherings. French sociologist Marcel Mauss and others reported the custom in anthropological circles.[149]

Forced by the change in the relations of production and also by instinctual proclivities, males the hunters and vicars of the external world also became the emissaries in social groups that were agglutinating and expanding through commercial and other forms of exchange. This made it logical that the economy would take a different form, geared to production for exchange rather than immediate use. This trend gradually grew to total commodity production that included the selling of labor force as a commodity. Exchange and commerce were obviously advantageous to both exchanging parties and it logically accelerated specialization and skill. It did not take too long for profit to show its ugly face, along with reinvestment, invention and technology.

Since women's labor was not commercially profitable at first sight, and remained governed by the old giving, it became invisible. Raising children and domestic work had always been *pro bono,* after all, and the success of men became more glaring as their creation. This is how civil society grew in complexity, totally out of the reach of women. These developments gave a bust to the phenomena of surplus and accumulation, and very early on started the capitalist thread

---

149 Mauss, M. (1966). *The Gift. Form and Functions of Exchange in Archaic Societies.* Trans. Ian Cunnison. London. Cohen and West Ltd. Online in the Internet Archive. Accessed from <https://archive.org/details/giftformsfunctio00maus> on 2015-08-03.

that chokes us today. They gave males their historical opportunity, because they became skillful and proficient at tasks new and alien to women. Then of course came private property of the means of production among which were included not only animals but women, children, and prisoners of war that, privatized, became property as the *paterfamilias*. This is how eventually capitalism started to develop its roots. The new institution of private property had inherent in it the quest for paternity, for inheritance, for virginity and monogamy, all leading at the beginning to what would become bourgeois type of family. A series of sexual exclusions through laws of incest and forms of kinship, characterized the evolution of the family.

These are the elements of the patriarchal coup, and the transition to the corresponding new form of social organization with the following characteristics: industry and commerce displaced the economic and social center of gravity of old societies from the internal gens to external civil society. Eventually, the state was formed under the aegis of propertied patriarchs, to regulate their conflicting interests through legal mediation. Gentes shrank into families to make room for civil society, and were placed in a subordinate role as the cells of reproduction of commanding civil society.

Babylonian, Egyptian, Persian, Greek and Roman societies in the West had an accelerated development under the new form of governance, not only in the areas of technology, productivity and commerce, but also politically, legislatively, and culturally. Law was the new morality of the civil society that granted states the exclusive monopoly on violence.

Religion, the original form of culture, along with later philosophy, art, politics and the military, all became the realm of a new, mediating middle class, pivotal and caught between the two opposite forms of ideology, ruling class, and rabble of producers. The ruling class got the advantage of producing and owning the material means of production and therefore became able to impose its ideology largely by hiring and buying its own ideological producers from within the middle class intelligentsia.

1.1.5 Implications for Consciousness and Self.

Consciousness' adaptive evolutionary function is to truthfully reflect reality. Consciousness has no choice unless transformed into ideology. Consciousness maps, records, and objectifies the ongoing historical development in a coherent narrative that becomes practical theories. It operates based, among other things, on the brain's functions of reflection, recognition, memory, imagination, and anticipation. These functions die with the brain and each individual, but culture as objectified collective memory allows them to survive in the form of transmissible folk verbal traditions and collective cultural institutions. Traditions are easily distorted by subjective influences, conditions and interests, but collectively memory, by turning itself into more durable objects, cultural artifacts that include language as a collective tool, and also social institutions material and spiritual, becomes a safeguard. Social institutions themselves change historically to reflect their changing material determinations, which are based on the form people relate to each other in the production and reproduction of their lives, including technology.

The whole historical process is morphologically recorded in the very form of the brain itself, evolution determining the form of the nervous system according to changing adaptive needs that go from deep reptilian structures concerned with survival basics, through successive layers leading to the advanced cortex of conscious *Homo sapiens.* Consciousness' originating threads appeared well before the human species and include all the earlier attempts, natural experiments, trials and errors leading to many other intelligent species that excel in partial forms of perception, representation, instinct and activity.

Pathognomonic to the human species is the development of self-consciousness, the self-unfolding of consciousness that develops as an organizing reflection of itself that replicates the moral organization of society, the meta-consciousness Hegel called self-consciousness. In the brain the latest evolutionary achievements are recorded in particular areas of the cortex such as the executive frontal area and language areas. In the human species, what we call the self is how consciousness regulates and governs itself through reciprocity. The highest regulatory function of consciousness is morality, a force that goes against all the long natural history of the food chain and before. Besides organizing consciousness through particular mediations between collective and individual priorities, scanning continuous incoming sensations and perceptions, the most important function of the self is to meaningfully integrate and morally organize, totalize, constantly in the here and now.

This means the self has to constantly logically place classified objects and events within the continuity of a past and a present narrative including its teleological anticipatory component that also looks at the future, within the huge manifold of reality, to constantly come up with a total and understandable, practical here and now. Totalization gives final form to the transiency of a mercurial reality of both subject and object. To totalize, human consciousness has used a successive number of logical, psychological and moral strategies that are built and developed as *knowledge*. These strategies are successively represented in historical forms such as totemism, mythology, religion, philosophy, and science. These are not just a sequence of dead bodies, but all continue to be alive and active part of the whole of a consciousness that, inclusive by nature, does not develop uniformly and that is not, and never will be, absolutely total. All those forms of totalization are temporary and perennial.

The patriarchal coup transformed all previous social constructs from their original form of-first order mediations based on the matriarchal instinct of producing, giving, and tending, all guided by a morality of evolution of the species in continuity with previous evolutionary forms, besides the relatively new element of social altruism. Forms of female expression and governance were abolished. The effects of this patriarchal shift to *second-order mediations* affected the course of the sense of evolution by introducing religious and idealistic explanations. Human beings started to be considered weak or less fit based on magnitudes of property rather than on their natural qualities. This has caused deep damage to the human evolutionary structure. The material damage now affects all humans, although to different degrees, with visible phenomena such as climate change, but also with less tangible ideological changes in consciousness and reason. The spiritual damage however, psychological and moral, equally affects all, through the corruption of inherent, self-critical consciousness and good moral sense in individuals. What we see in the species at large is the same form of universal alienation, independent of class, that internalizes as norm, as falsely adaptive a form of relation that excludes half of itself, women, in patriarchy, and extends to all others that are considered lesser, on the basis of lack of property. This is what common sense today calls ninety-nine percent. This form of not-total, not-universal imposed ideology cannot be adaptive for the species.

Syllogistically, what has happened is that the material and spiritual contribution of both halves, the sexes, to history, that naturally would have determined the motion and direction of the species based on their opposition as thesis and antithesis, female and male instinctual disposition, female and male consciousness mutually contributing to the unfolding synthesis of human civilization, has been artificially halved. This is equivalent to tying one wing in a flying bird. Materially we see the result in institutionalized poverty, competitiveness, lack of recognition, and empathy for human groups antagonistically considered others, and consequently war and destruction, all patriarchally imposed. Underlying this is the substitution of the first-order matriarchal giving mediations for the patriarchal ones of taking. Taking is hidden in exploitative labor and commercial practices, but more blatantly in wars.

The worse part, from a psychological viewpoint is the internalization of this state of affairs as natural, normal morality, evolutionarily adaptive and overriding good sense, because the balanced dialectic of human consciousness and natural good sense has been altered and corrupted.

From an evolutionary perspective, the worst consequence is the loss of the most basic animal capacity in evolution, the ability to identify the aggressor, often perceiving the aggressor as benefactor and allowing the aggressor, a patriarchal male élite, to govern the destiny of the species to its own grave. This is manifest in paralysis, in the inability of people to feel outrage, to revolt and remove the by now clear evolutionary obstacles that threaten the species' future. And often, when people rebel, they cannot see real causes of their distress and attribute it to religion, race, nationality, and other incidental causes.

Unfortunately, unless we change the material conditions of our societies, and the consequent capitalist hierarchical ideology through which we relate to each other, consciousness cannot be restored to its pristine instrumental form. Consciousness has been occupied by ideology. It cannot thus guide us according to a true morality of evolution wherein we, as subjects, can perceive the object, our society in a historical universe, as our collective objectification as a species. This amounts to ecological destruction in our own brains. A shift has to occur from the imposed ideology of the oppressor, to that of the victim with good evolutionary sense, before consciousness, and self, can be restored. The conscious morality of the victim, in its claim as present majoritarian and globalized form, is what Karen Horney called morality of evolution because it speaks in the interest of all, universally.

1.1.6 The Totalizing Instruments of Consciousness

Anthropologists have found not a single society without religion, although there are societies without an organized form of it, such as the small Pirahã of Brazil, who still believe in spirits.[150] Incidentally, they are also economically communist, socially leaderless, fight coercion at any cost, have very few kinship terms, no gods, and don't know numbers or grammatical recursion —which is logically repeating items in a self-similar way as in counting or embedding a

---

150 See "Pirahã" in Wikipedia. Accessed from <https://en.wikipedia.org/wiki/Pirahã_people> on 2016-01-20.

structure (sentence) within another to make a larger sentence.

Some, on the universality ground, have proposed that religion is a "natural" phenomenon, thus legitimizing its alienating form while leaving it unexplained. It is not religion, in fact, but the more comprehensive phenomenon of explanation peculiar to *Homo "sapiens,"* the knower species, that includes not only religion but also all other historical explanatory forms such as myth, philosophy and science. Religion, starting with various forms such as totemism and animism, is a phylogenetically infantile form of human explanation. It did not disappear with the appearance of its overriding successors, but still remains extant in its original form, and often ideologically unexplained, although the German philosopher Feuerbach scientifically explained it long ago as the first form of anthropology.[151]

Explanation is the logical totalized, that is, fit into a consensual existing paradigm organization of an ensemble of historical objects, properties and events. Explanation takes place according to the *gestalt* of an historical, contextual form of consciousness, and religion is only its earliest expression. Myths and gods made sense as central forms of explanation within their historical context, but they do not any more as they are out of that context. They do not make the same sense today than they did during their moment because their configurations can be explained by superseding better form of explanation, *i.e.*, philosophy or science. However, as we have seen, myth remains alive as a form of complementing other types of explanation for lack of a total understanding.

On the other hand, the fact that scientists such as Richard Dawkins and Daniel Dennett today plainly state that religion is irremediably opposed to science[152] or still in need of scientific anal-

---

151 Feuerbach, L. (1972). *The Essence of Christianity.* Trans: Introduction translated by Zawar Hanfi, remainder translated by George Eliot, 1854. Introduction from *The Fiery Brook,* remainder from *The Essence of Christianity* (Written: 1841). Online in MIA. Ac-cessed from <https://www.marxists.org/reference/archive/feuerbach/works/essence/index.htm> on 2015-02-26.

152 Dawkins, R. (1986). *The Blind Watchmaker.* New York. Norton. Accessed from <http://terebess.hu/keletkultinfo/The_Blind_Watchmaker.pdf> on 2016-01-20.

ysis[153] reflects their ignorance or neglect of the momentous work of philosophers who scientifically decoded religion as the inverted mapping of the real world into its wishful virtual image in order to cope with distress and provide explanation and succor, and with them hope, and morality, to early humans. Religion is anthropology since Hegel's disciple Feuerbach, and the roots of its explanation are in Spinoza.[154] The anthropological dimension, rather ambiguous in Spinoza, was explicitly formulated by Ludwig Feuerbach, and further developed by Marx and Engels. Patriarchal science tends to selectively ignore inconvenient historical facts.

Subjectivity has access to the property to explain, and this can be accomplished only through thinking individuals. Collectively, however, explanations have to become consensual, agreed upon by members of groups that come from different perspectives, and thus validated culturally as part of a totality within its paradigm. In the process, however, something may be both lost and emergently gained. Collectively, culture is what self is individually, the organizer, and in primitive groups its original form of explanation was religious. God is the good sense of nature and religion the first collective human organizer in the transition from an evolutionary to an historical form of human existence, God being the backbone of organized religion. God's is the ensemble of all the human virtues, assembled from individuals with a common moral good sense. The group projects and deposits its collective moral power into God, who then becomes its abstract inverted form, virtually projected into an abstract anthropomorph. Thus the affinity of God and self, and the frequent historical identification of God and leader: the first gods being in fact goddesses, because women were the first evolutionary

153 Dennett, D. (2006). *Breaking the Spell: Religion as a Natural Phenomenon.* New York. Viking Penguin. Accessed from <http://skepdic.ru/wp-content/uploads/2013/05/Daniel_C_Dennett_Breaking_the_Spell_Religion.pdf> on 2015-08-04.

154 Spinoza, de B. (1862). *Theological-Political Treaty.* London. Trubner & Co. Online in Wikisource. Accessed from < https://en.wikisource.org/wiki/Theologico-Political_Treatise_1862> on 2016-03-23.

leaders. [155,156]

An individual judgment does not go beyond opinion if it is not endorsed by the common sense of the group that embeds the individual. Institutionalized by groups, however, religion becomes an advanced and rather autonomous powerful social structure. In monotheistic religion, the unitary concept of God is the equivalent of a recursive person, all ego ideals condensed into one perfection, a projection of the discriminating, synthetic and anticipatory human mind and the awesome good sense of nature. In reality, the anthropomorphic individual God is the idealized version of a moral leader that the group needs to both project upon, identify with, and depend on for safety. Each individual contributes to it his/her own projected proxy. A godhead embodies the real power each individual has surrendered to her or him through projection, to then surrender to the moral constraints of the social contract.[157] Endorsed and enshrined by the collective through self-imposed ritualistic coercion, it represents for each individual personal and collective safety, the paradigm of group morality, and the necessary sublimation of instinctual dispositions. This can occur only by the group's endowment of its own force to the leader, as Freud correctly proposed in his explanation of group psychology. The ego ideal of Freud is an internalized blend of projected God, leader, and, vicariously, self, placed where instinctive *I* was.[158]

Religion as explanatory totalizing logic based on belief is histor-

155 Marija Gimbutas. *The Civilization of the Goddess. The World of Old Europe*. San Francisco: Harper, 1991.
156 Bachofen, J. (1992). *Myth, Religion and Mother Right*. Preface by George Boas, introduction by Joseph Campbell, translated by Ralph Manheim. Princeton NJ: Princeton University Press. (Orig. Pub.1967)
157 Freud, S. (1922). *Group Psychology and the Analysis of the Ego*. Trans. James Strachey. London. The International Psychoana-lytic Press. Online in the Internet Archive. Accessed from <http://www.gutenberg.org/files/35877/35877-h/35877-h.htm> on 2015-01-14.
158 Freud, S. (1922). *Group Psychology and the Analysis of the Ego*. Trans. James Strachey. London. The International Psychoan-alytic Press. Online in the Internet Archive. Accessed from <http://www.gutenberg.org/files/35877/35877-h/35877-h.htm> on 2015-01-14.

ically gradually superseded by philosophy that, by replacing belief with reason, as human judgment and logic develop, promises a better explanation. This results not necessarily in the abandonment of religion, but in the development of the capacity of an independent secularity and consequent freedom to operate. In philosophy, human logic was developed and reached its peak.[159]

In turn, philosophy and religion that still remain extant, are gradually being superseded by science that promises the displacement of the center of gravity of explanation from reason to proof and experiment, without discarding belief and reason, and promises also a more accurate explanation of totalities. All forms of explanation persist and their ultimate judge remains *good sense*.

In the abstract this historical process of supersessions is compelling, but in reality it is constrained by the division of society into economic classes that splits consciousness according to class interests. The dominant class is able to produce spurious explanations from hired middle-class intellectual prize-fighters, as has become clearer and clearer particularly in the present controversy of fossil fuels and climate change. Class interests that are far from universal, and often noxious, are spread through public relations campaigns and advertising in the mass media to influence and corrupt naïve minds. Particularistic class explanations are usually based on clinging to religious philosophical and instinctual spinning, based on the exploitation of emotion, fear, and desire. Not science, but often presented as pseudoscience, they are produced in bad faith to mystify. One result is the paradoxical contrast of luxury and scarcity we live in, and our contradictory political behavior whereby we vote for our oppressors and go on and on replacing them endlessly with the same, only with alternating labels. This loss of coherence, of good sense, in a context of human brilliant achievements in pockets of science, reflects our contradictory material reality.

The outcome of this mystifying process is societies that are in

---

159 See: Swindal, J. "Faith and Reason." Internet Encyclopedia of Philosophy. Accessed from <http://www.iep.utm.edu/faith-re/> on 2016-01-23.

distress, restless, and for the most part in pain and dysphoria because their material and spiritual needs are not fulfilled coherently, experiencing scarcity in the middle of abundance and wastefulness. Privately, individuals and collectively, groups, feel the malaise but cannot identify its causes properly because they have been mystified by spurious ideological theories leading to the belief that capitalistic conditions are natural. Worse yet, they have often introjected the mystifying mechanisms and processes and implemented by themselves their perpetuating process of mystification. Since their consciousness needs to explain and totalize through whatever frame of reference they have at hand, they resort to religion, nationality, ethnicity, or even race and gender to generate enemies and thus understand their own conundrums by blaming them. This is how presently religious fanaticism, pro-life versus pro-choice activism, racism, chauvinisms of different kinds, nationalism, and sexism are social manifestations that all express distress from narrow and misdirected perspectives. They misidentify other victims as their aggressor, and identify themselves with the aggressor to perpetuate the vicious cycle.

We have seen that our totalizing instruments are, in historical order, mythology and religion, philosophy, and science.

1.1.7 From Totemism to Science

Totemism was a "natural" religion, original and transitional, human collectivities leaning on a common symbol, the totem for their still hybrid, alienated identity. This identity was really alterity and even more, not self, but animal- or plant- based. This raises interesting epistemological questions, such as the possible inherent recognition of life as a form of consciousness. This is a time when humanity was unfolding from raw nature, and "inside" and "outside" were perhaps not as clearly differentiated in the mind as they later became. The social protoplasm did include its contextual natural analogue. The mind today conceives itself as the inside of itself, everything else's being excluded as objects outside, including even the mind when it applies its critical perspective to itself.

The totem is symbolically the first concrete metaphor to designate immediacy, necessary leaning on nature, and the birth of particularity, group-leaning only on a discrete part of nature as other groups do likewise. Self was originally the consanguine collective in the midst of other similarly structured groups. Self was a social protoplasm before it, through gender recognition, environment and group properties; and the division of labor became individuality. Its protoplasmic particularity is originally based on the exclusion of groups other than itself, determined through consanguinity and totem. Historically the phenomenon "individual," as well as the concept, emerged very slowly from the social protoplasm that was like a school of fish, or a herd of animals acting in unison; it became a recursive totality within concentric totalities. Individuality was the emerging new form of subjectivity that incorporated in its reflection of reality forms of social, protoplasmic organization. Institutions became revered as representatives of the same blood, the same social contract, emblem and form, and the same spirit. The new universality also started to emerge as a group exchanging materially with others objects or even connubial persons instead of war and cannibalism, and ritualizing, taming through magic and religion, their mutual narcissistic hostilities.

The perceptually required narrow notion of a particular world was then expanding to incorporate the difficult notion of variation in sameness; the recognition of other cultures with similar material and symbolic structures. The particular *Mitwelt* of the gestaltists[160] began to expand and strive for universality to a point where the "discovery" of other continents took place and next globalization and even the imagination of other planetary societies. Particularity thus spread in two opposite ways, individuality and universality, forming the Hegelian syllogism, the uppermost instrument of consciousness

---

160 Binswanger, Ludwig (1963). *Being-in-the-World: Selected Papers of Ludwig Binswanger.* New York: Basic Books.

and the conundrum of morality.

Today, for the most part, the patronymic name of an individual is what is vestigially left of the originally matriarchal, old totemic emblem. The last name continues to be the particularity of an individual, whose first name represents her or his individuality. Religious, political, professional and national affiliation are concentric particularities of civil society. They provide emergent identity elements that exclude their opposites as fiercely as families include. This is most visibly politically. These are the obstacles utopic human universality has to overcome. The quality of otherness of identity opposites easily becomes a threat when it comes to competing for resources considered scarce. This civil-society phenomenon unfortunately corroded the old family structure and objectified and repressed women and subsequently all others considered alien and inferior.

Mythology is largely a polytheistic form of magic or religious belief, an extension of totemism, that expands animistic qualities from the totem to other objects live and inert in an anthropomorphic fashion. As archaic form of explanation, mythology has become synonymous in some contexts with ideology. Behind its apparent universality, mythological thinking is a narrow perspective characterized by consensual self-centered projection. It represents largely an infatuation with the voluntaristic idea instead of the reality of the perceived external object. Monotheism historically becomes the true religious representation of universality, a unifying trend that makes what is varied appear similar through logical class inclusion. Contrary to what appears, properties of objects are more universal than the objects themselves. This is how human rights can clearly be more universal, if abstractly, than humans, and how being born equal is more universal than being equal. The original plurality of gods endowed with human properties found common denominators to organize classes of objects starting with human and divine. Notions such as gods and humans may have culturally displaced the natural classes of female and male, the first contrasting particulars.

A common denominator is a property that encompasses, unifies and totalizes natural variation and diversity in the immanent dialectic of the mind. In mythology, there is a shift from narrow totemic universality to the particularity of contrasting neighboring groups. Divine and secular are classes that arise on the same logical ground.

The opposite dynamic forces that constitute the idealized social role leader, the same that apply to imaginary God, individuality and universality, were originally studied by Freud in his group psychology.[161] The universal phenomenon is consensual projection of of each individual's power, ego ideal, onto one agreed-upon individual, the leader. Correspondingly, there is a reverse, simultaneous, individual, vicarious identification with the leader that provides group belonging and security. Melanie Klein's concept of *imago* is akin; it advances the description of the same phenomenon more dialectically as a reciprocal collusion or *projective identification*,[162] the collusion between the power-projector and its reflecting screen, the receiver of the projection, to individually enact the collective fantasy.

From totemism to mythology, explanatory forms become more complex because they take into consideration a wider segment of reality through processes of projection and analytic scatter, as well as introjection and synthetic assemblage. This is the ongoing dialectic of consciousness that Klein seems to have understood better than Freud, if we consider that our ongoing relations outside of the immediate family are based on the templates, first-order mediations, which the family and particularly the mother introduced, *imago*es for Klein. We move with growth into wider and wider ex-centric social circles; but our earlier relations leave an imprint that will determine our later perception. Our universe grows through here-and-now

---

161 Freud, S. (2011) *Group Psychology and the Analysis of the Ego.* Trans. James Stra-
    chey. Project Gutenberg [EBook #35877]. Accessed from <http://www.gutenberg.
    org/catalog/world/readfile?fk_files=2083370> on 2012-05-21. (Orig. Pub. 1921).
162 Klein, M. (1952), "Some Theoretical Conclusions Regarding The Emotional Life Of
    The Infant." In: *Envy and Gratitude and Other Works 1946-1963.* New York. Dela-
    corte (1975). P. 70. Accessed from <https://manhattanpsychoanalysis.com/wp-con-
    tent/uploads/readings/Attie_course/Klein_SomeTheoreticalConclusionsRegardingth-
    eEmotionalLifeoftheInfant.pdf> on 2015-08-05.

stations that includes new perceivable globalizations, and scientific panoramas that today go from quanta to plural universes. Klein gave us a clue to understand this as a form of recursion: "The interaction between the processes of introjection and projection, re-introjection and re-projection, determines ego-development."[163] Ego, however, is only one part of self, the analytical and destructive; the other part is me, compounded through human experience, the accruing ensemble of the social experience written in the form of the brain. Ultimately we each come to be from undifferentiated fragments, sensations and perceptions, and memories of Mother and *I* indistinguishable at first by the child. From those perceptual fragments, we gradually in our brain synthesize our self-image based on the template of the mother image, the first live mirror in front of us. From there we then grow to be able to correctly determine what is attributable to self and what is to others in a complex net of projective identifications. Failures in this process result in psychosis.

The initial psychological mechanism of projection accrued into the material object culture, originated historically by the first humans, through the totem reversed itself as a symbolic internalization of the totemic image, later appropriated as goddess, and finally as patriarchal God. Monotheism probably represents the first attempt at universality of this process: my God is everyone's God, that is, everyone that is correct. In the Greek cosmogony, for example, Chaos, the first notion of nothingness or a black hole, produces earth, darkness, night and the underworld, *etc.*, everything that came to be primal. Gaia hermaphroditically impregnated herself to produce son-gods that then she consorted with, to start reproduction of Titan-gods that will eventually mutate into a class of humans. Her early sons and daughters were born husbands and wives, and then generations, under the leadership of patriarchs, clashed to represent the conflicts of civil society. Titan and Olympian patriarchs soon take charge and invent war with each other, fathers and sons. Prometheus and his brother are charged with creating man.

---

163 Klein, M. (1952), "Some Theoretical Conclusions Regarding The Emotional Life Of The Infant." Ibid.

God-like personifications such as these ruled the world of mythology, and for archaic human groups that was the first form of
an anthropology not separated from the rest of their lives. Behind
these idealized personifications were real people, tyrants, emperors
and kings, and their families, and the events described as occurring in the divine world are based on real historical events transformed by imagination. The first form of alienation was totemism,
evolving into mythology and religion in the same fashion a child
goes through the Piagetian stages of intelligent understanding. The
visible hand and its labor were then only beginning to leave their
imprint in the brain. Spinoza saw God as the intelligence of nature,
and Feuerbach as the moral projection of the collective. Marx sees
it as the practical remedy for human misery, all three explanations
being far from antagonistic to each other. Freud correctly anchored
the symbolic and psychological phenomenon of monotheism to the
early imperial desires of Egyptian Kings, who saw for the first time
the possibility of one world under their rule.[164]

Philosophy, although at the end highly co-opted by the political
interests of class society buttressed by religion and its own idealism, was in spite of all able to supersede mythology and religion. It
shifted its method from faith to reason. The compellingness of ritual
and the characteristic beauty of myth were replaced by the more
rigorous method of syllogistic debate. The occupational hazard of
flight from reality spread epidemically, starting with the Sophists,
and lasted until the Renaissance. Reason had its historical moment
during this long period, but its original pre-Socratic dialectic, akin
to nature's method, was replaced by the analytic idealism of Plato
and then the added formal logic of Aristotle. This idealism of inertia
culminated in Kant and prompted the Romantics to rebellion. Hegel
then rescued the old dialectical thinking for modernity and made
it possible to understand the monism of Spinoza and the challenge

---

164 This is Freud's take in: Freud, S. (1939). *Moses and Monotheism*. Trans. Katherine
Jones. London. The Hogarth Press and the Institute of Psychoanalysis. P. 36. Online
in the Internet Archive. Accessed from <https://archive.org/details/mosesandmono-
thei032233mbp> on 2014-10-18.

of science, particularly human science, history and evolution. Although natural science had already shot its roots in Kepler, Newton, Copernicus, and the two Bacons, Roger and Francis, it was Hegel and his disciple Marx who fully opened the gates to human science from its previous philosophical containment. In terms of a thinking tool, Hegel brought back the syllogism to its dialectical form, a logic of motion and activity.

The syllogistic sublation method of Hegel, moving on through negation while conserving the constructive part of the thesis and antithesis, helps us understand that consciousness, in the last instance, cannot be created or destroyed, but only transformed; it leans on its past, on meta-consciousness and the *me* part of the self that is the other. This is how the historical method came to prevail in the human sciences with Hegel, Darwin, Marx, and Freud. It helps us understand that ideology is a transformation of consciousness that uses mythology, religion and philosophy, besides formal logic, the old methods, to work against the new methodology of science based on observation, proof and experiment. What once was symbiotic leaning on nature in totemism, the identity of self and totem, then went through a philosophical identity separation. "A cannot be B" in formal logic returns in science to a necessarily compromising dialectical method whereby B cannot be without emerging from A and negating it. The head of the serpent emerged from the tail; form emerged from amorphous protoplasm.

1.1.8 The Ouroboros

I illustrate the historical process, the process of human consciousness, in the cover of this book using the ancient Ouroboros icon, a serpent symbol that illustrates the merging of the beginning and the end, a totality that paradoxically is all contained by a boundary, a zero. This particular drawing is from the early alchemical text *The Chrysopoeia* (transmutation into gold) of Cleopatra, dating to 2nd century Alexandria. It contains the words *hen to pan*, "one is the all". Its black and white halves represent the duality of existence, the Western equivalent of the Taoist Yin-Yang symbol.[165]

The snake is probably the oldest matriarchal symbol of ritual, and of religion,[166] and of the natural compellingness of the need for explanation in human history. The serpent is ubiquitous in mythology, representing variously immortality, creation, protection, the underworld, water, wisdom, healing, and God.[167]

The historical narrative, and consequently consciousness, cannot be complete; the circle cannot be closed unless it puts together beginning and end. But knowing and explaining are asymptotic, and the circle is never closed. In the icon the lower part of the snake is white, indicating natural history, the history of the cosmos. The black upper half indicates human history, in my interpretation. The two colors also represent the knowledge of good and evil that leads to the peak of free consciousness, morality. Contrary to conventional interpretation the serpent was, in ancient societies, a widespread feminine icon, and a symbol of eternity[168] and of renovation, originally represented with some of the original goddesses such as in the Minoan snake goddess figurines. From a feminine icon, Freudian hermeneutics transformed it into a phallus, a symbol of power. The two polar forms straight and coiled have come to represent "on" and "off" in the age of electricity.

Hegel compared philosophy to a circle of circles,[169] which refers to the continuity, or each philosophical school's trying to to-

165 Wikipedia. "Ouoboros." Accessed from <https://en.wikipedia.org/wiki/Ouroboros> on 2016-03-26.
166 Coulson, S. D; Staurset, S. & Walker, N. (2011). "Ritualized Behavior in the Middle Stone Age: Evidence from Rhino Cave, Tsodilo Hills, Bostwana. *PaleoAnthropology.* ISSN 1545-0031. pp. 18-61
167 Wikepedia. "Snakes in Mythology." Accessed from < https://en.wikipedia.org/wiki/Snakes_in_mythology> on 216-03-26.
168 For Hegel the snake was symbol of eternity. See: Hegel, H.G.W. (1840-4). *Hegel's Lectures on the History of Philosophy. Introduction.* B. The Relation of Philosophy to Other Departments of Knowledge. Trans. Quentin Lauer and E.S. Haldane. (Orig. Pub. 1805-6). Online In MIA. Accessed from <https://www.marxists.org/reference/archive/hegel/works/hp/hpintrob2.htm> on 2016-03-26.
169 Hegel, G.W.F. (1830). *Encyclopaedia of the Philosophical Sciences (1830) Part One.*

talize from a particular historical perspective and being superseded by the next, but not extinguished. Hegel was the first philosopher to take philosophy as one single and continuous narrative instead of a bunch of separate schools. In fact, in Hegel allegorically the serpent arches itself to create interiority by bringing together its two ends, head and tail. Hegel thought he was the end of philosophy and in fact he was, in that he represents the sublated transition from philosophy to science and thus the end of classical philosophy.

Consciousness internalizes within itself the form of the world and constantly attempts to achieve its full representation as a totality. But, being carried by individuals, individual consciousness is condemned to always bond to a particular perspective and thus become fragmented. The totality of consciousness is thus only possible collectively. We have seen how internalization is a crucial mechanism to the whole process of evolution, until the use of projective reason that creates *telos*, anticipation, and the reversal of the previous internalizing trend. In this process, the nature of the self is to catch itself in its activity, to critically question, and correct itself again and again, socially. Consciousness grows as projection thanks to the ensemble of social relations that allows it to become objective, as culture.

The snake is an old matriarchal symbol,[170] so old it is reminiscent of our reptilian brain before mammalian life.[171] The superseding part of the brain, the early mammalian, was developed around nursing and maternal care while the third, cortical, has suffered the transition to patriarchal imbalance that has made it hemispherically dominant. "Mama" means mother, maternal determination. Patriarchy is thus a sort of unresolved antagonistic contradiction in evolution, its necessity being questionable. The mammalian brain, repressed and superseded by the cortical brain, brought about dominance of one hemisphere, biological evidence of the historical fact of the political

I. Introduction. § 15. Online in MIA. Accessed from < https://www.marxists.org/reference/archive/hegel/works/sl/slintro.htm> on 2016-03-25.

170 Knight, C. (1991). Blood Relations. *Menstruation and the Origins of Culture*. New Haven and London. Yale University Press. Online in Radical Anthropology Group. Accessed from <http://radicalanthropologygroup.org/sites/default/files/pdf/pub_chris_thesis.pdf> on 2016-01-25.

171 MacLean, P.D. (1985). "Brain evolution relating to family, play, and the separation call." Archives of General Psychiatry. Apr;42(4):405-17.

destruction of the balanced instinctual architecture of the species. This has had incalculable consequences.

The totem represents the original landmark of human evolution, the bifurcation from pure necessity to freedom. It was the first reflection of humans on their nature. From it *Homo sapiens* has advanced the reflective capacity through the successive supersessions of mythology, religion, philosophy and science, each one not eliminating but building upon its predecessor. This is in turn reflected in the morphology of the brain.

Syllogistically the human snake, Ouroboros, starts from the universal protoplasm of the matriarchal gens at the tail, represented in the ovum that develops beyond reptilian to erect forms, eventually to turn around upon itself its conscious head in search of its original tail. Universality that was at the origin and has been lost becomes an aim of the human species; and we have reached the objective landmark in globalization. This is equivalent to reaching the global gens or global family. What remains is to truly return to the old morality of the gens "from all according to capacity, to all according to needs."[172] This has been the philosophy of every mother's running a family in every epoch, since her organization of gens was alienated by patriarchy in civil society.

Teleologically, the metaphor of the serpent's biting its tail is humanity finding its synchronized, material and conscious, universality that was initially necessarily present in natural form. Species universality was lost through repression during the patriarchal epoch. Only a morality of evolution[173] will bring it back.

172 Marx, K. (1970). *Critique of the Gotha Programme.* Part 1. Marx/Engels Selected Works, Volume Three, p. 13-30. Moscow. Progress Publishers. (Written 1875, Orig. Pub. 1890). Online in MIA. Accessed from < https://www.marxists.org/archive/marx/works/1875/gotha/ch01.htm> on 2016-03-27.

173 Horney, K. (1950), *Neurosis and Human Growth.* Introduction. p. 13. Online in Internet Archive. Accessed from <https://archive.org/details/NeurosisAndHumanGrowth> on 2014-07-18.

1.2 THE OLD RESEARCH RECORD OF ORIGINS

"This is a rather curious position for any science —or any organized endeavor calling itself a science— to take. Science claims for itself a free and a full field, as far as its eyes can see and as far as its hands can reach. But where, except in certain schools of cultural anthropology, has science attempted to cut itself off from such an endeavor? Certainly not in astronomy, geology, or biology. Scientists unhesitatingly tackle such problems as the origin of galaxies, stars, planetary systems, and life in general in its many orders, genera, and species. If the origin of the earth some two billion years ago, or the origin of life untold millions of years ago, can be and is a proper problem for science, why not the origin of culture a mere million years ago?

The answer to this question by members of the Boas and the Functionalist schools is that this particular search for origins is futile; they cannot ever be found. As Margaret Mead has said flatly, it is a question "upon which there is not and cannot be any valid evidence." But we recall the wise words of Darwin on this point:

"It has often and confidently been asserted that man's origin can never be known; but ignorance more frequently begets confidence than does knowledge: it is those who know little, and not those who know much, who so positively assert that this or that problem will never be solved by science."

Leslie White[174]

---

174 While, L. (1959). *The Evolution of Culture: The Development of Civilization to the*

1.2.1 The Patriarchal Repression of its Matriarchal Origins

A record is an objectified extension of natural memory. The original capacity of the nervous system to record is a form of adaptation that has its origin in natural evolution. Civilization is the total record of humanity's objectifying itself, making nature reflect human activity. This is the same as saying that civilization is the total record of nature's recording itself, because humanity is only the conscious vanguard of natural evolution.

Growing consciousness deepens object understanding, which appears more complex the more the depth is achieved; complexity is behind the perceptual patina, phenomenology tells us. The narrative of civilization starts with some hard and some soft man-made objects. These are tools and words that in fact supplant each other, and that continue to expand with technologies, and upon them wordy agencies, institutions, and spiritual values: the virtual world of consciousness. Recording in evolution started way before full-fledged human consciousness. Self-selecting optimal conditions for chemical reactions are already a precedent of record. Cells in organisms becoming able to, under particular circumstances, adaptively conserve traces of their motions to facilitate or inhibit future ones, is a more complex form of recording. This form became the memory trace of a cellular sense or apprehension of its irritation or sensation. This evolutionary phenomenon was then developed all the way to the conscious specialization of the nervous system. In the brain, consciousness is produced, and stored in specialized areas as memory.

The externalized and objectively conserved durability of memory in cultural artifacts benefits future generations of the species, and greatly saves in cost, allowing for more efficient complexity along with better coherence. On the other hand, the artificial suppression

---

Fall of Rome. New York. McGraw-Hill. P. 71. Online in Questia. Accessed from <https://www.questia.com/read/8509592/the-evolution-of-culture-the-development-of-civilization> on 2015-01-19. The Darwin quotation is from *The Descent of Man*. Introduction.

or repression of memory, its alteration, is itself a cultural artifact that obviously constrains the totalizing capacity of consciousness and the full appraisal of nature. It therefore creates danger by defying the purpose of nature that in turn often responds with a symptom.

The symptom is a natural sign indicating that the expected process, painstakingly shaped and arrived at through trial and errors in evolution, has been violated. Human social symptoms, unlike individual ones, are usually manifested collectively as restlessness that moves up to upheavals and revolutions, and today pandemics, not only political but also medical and, particularly, psychiatric. Ideology itself is the disease of a narrow consciousness that rigidly imposes itself on all to represent only the interests of its originating group, not those of the whole. This is how ideology obstructs the dialectical flow of universal historical motion.

The active recording durability of biological human memory alone is limited by the narrow life span of each individual. Through the transformation of natural objects by labor, however, humans not only make objective the memory of their productive activity; the objects produced are a recording of that activity, as is the brain that is shaped in the process. Like institutions and culture, the form of the brain itself codifies in its form natural and social history.

Transformed through labor, natural objects incorporate the signature, and take the form, of their producers' will, becoming reminiscent of them. Conversely, producers see themselves with pride in their products. Produced objects to various extents project their authors beyond their own life span, and this is true for all cultural artifacts that are collective self objects.

Unfortunately, hard written language in the form of durable verbal narratives — the clearest, most lasting, economic and practical form of objectified consciousness and memory — came rather late in the historical process, and its capture of what happened before it did not necessarily reflect ancient reality with accuracy. Recorded mythology, poetic art and religious documents had been transmitted orally before they were recorded, and therefore became easily distorted by changing historical environments and by subjective inter-pretation. Reconstructing ancient history by putting together frag-mentary documents and verbal narratives lent itself to speculation and subjective distortion at the service of the interests of domination.

Archeologists and ethnologists have the hard task of deciphering and reconstructing cultural phenomena that had been recorded in very old societies before written language was available. They then had to decipher objects excavated from living quarters to get an idea of how ancient people lived and what their cultural practices were. The interpretation of these findings is of course subject to the pres-ent cultural biases, in particular those of the patriarchal academic mainstream of class societies. This is the reason why, since writ-ten history has for the most part taken place during the patriarchal epoch, the scientific assumption has been that human history has always been patriarchal. This can be understood in part by the fact that to be regarded by their peers, human scientists overwhelmingly need to build their theories in accordance with the politically correct ideological premises of their time. A critical mind is usually rarified in this context, as it pays the price of ostracism and ridicule, of dan-ger, and even loss of life, as was the case with the Inquisition and its various analogues.

Interestingly, the theory of matriarchy in academia unconscious-ly replicates matriarchy by enacting it: even though the first centu-ry of pioneer theorists in anthropology, the Nineteenth, was largely matriarchal, it was followed in the twentieth century by a cohort of strong patriarchalist repressive reactions that attempted to void the findings, often not with new facts but with speculation. The evolu-tionary method of the original explorers, a scientific plus since Spi-noza and Hegel, not to mention Darwin, was pejoratively devalued and replaced with so-called comparative, structural, functionalist methods as if they were opposed. They devalued history vehemently and criticized "grand narratives," attempts of the mind to integrate, universalize, and synthesize.

This is how, before the current feminist input, the discoverers of the science of humans became for the most part ignored, silenced or ostracized, or else relegated to footnotes. The origins debate in the human sciences has been acrimonious at times to an extent rare in the debates of the natural sciences.[175] The reason is not scientific, but ideological; and the emotional tone betrays the insecurity of the argument or its bad faith: matriarchal societies were generally described as egalitarian and communal, not a welcome precedent to a social organization based on hierarchy. Pseudoscience struggles to make social hierarchy appear as the natural phenomenon that, although present in the food chain, it is not in archaic human history. Hierarchy is precisely what evolutionarily humanity exited from. Malthusianism, Social Darwinism, and some trends in sociobiology are repeated attempts to legitimize patriarchal hierarchy as natural.

The importance of this issue is that the scientific acknowledgment of the evidence for matriarchy is obviously fundamental to the integrity, the wholesomeness, of human consciousness. Human history cannot be complete without a coherent narrative of its origins to permit projections into the future. Repressed, the issue of matriarchal origins therefore continues to return, and it will continue, like a symptom, until it is properly "worked through" by being integrated into the full narrative of human historical consciousness. The implications are dire for a future that must necessarily be modeled on substantial equality, if universality and true freedom are to be achieved.

The repressed matriarchal origins and their substantive equality will continue to return through the same mechanism that Freud discovered that makes symptoms return in individual patients. It will nag consciousness again and again until it is reintegrated in the puzzle of one history, natural and social. "Impressions — Freud said — which have been sunk into the id by repression, are virtually

---

175 Briffault, R. and Malinowsky, B. (1956). Marriage, Past and Present: A Debate between Robert Briffault and Bronislaw Mali-nowski. Ed. M. F. Ashley Montagu. Boston: Porter Sargent Publisher. Online in Questia. Accessed from <https://www.questia.com/read/28518901/marriage-past-and-present-a-debate-between-robert> on 2015-01-18.

immortal; after the passage of decades they behave as though they had just occurred"[176] Similar to thermodynamics in a closed system, the repressed is energy that cannot be created or destroyed, only symptomatically transformed.[177] Repression is an attempt to destroy that by nature is deemed to fail. All the repressed has to be worked through, reintegrated into the conscious narrative, and scientifically into the theory, of humanity.

The repression of the age of matriarchy is the first historical, collective, and political, form of repression as the repression, of women was the first political form. All subsequent forms of repression are modeled upon these.

In practical terms, this issue is at the heart of the quest for equality that humanity has been pursuing since slavery was imposed by violent means, domestic violence perhaps being the prototype. This huge historical repression of mother rule came along with the logical fashion of making all dialectical binaries hierarchical in value, starting with sex and gender, and ending in one versus ninety-nine percent.

1.2.2 Why the Scientific Record Must Start with Mythology

"So far our scholars have ignored this rich and well-documented tradition. They have concerned themselves solely with the eternally hopeless task of investigating "historical truth," taking no interest in a legend full of miraculous tales and impossibilities of all sorts, which forever excludes it from the realm of history. Either they disparage it or they say nothing at all. But to deny the historicity of a legend does not divest it of value. What cannot have happened was

---

176 Freud, S. (1933) [1932]). "The Dissection of the Psychical Personality." Vol. 22. Lecture XXXI in: New introductory lectures on psycho-analysis. Standard Edition, P. 74.

177 Clausius, R. (1817). *The Mechanical Theory of Heat, with its Applications to the Steam-Engine and to the Physical Properties of Bodies.* Ed. T. Archer Hirst. London. John van Woorst. Printed by Taylor and Francis. Online in Google eBooks. Accessed from <http://books.google.com/books?id=8LIEAAAAYAAJ&printsec=frontcover&dq=editions:PwR_Sbkwa8IC&hl=en&sa=X&ei=h6DgT5WnF46e8gSVvbynD-Q&ved=0CDYQuwUwAA#v=onepage&q&f=false> on 2014-10-18.

nonetheless thought. External truth is replaced by inner truth. Instead of facts, we find actions of the spirit. Banished from the realm of history, the Tanaquil tradition is a monument from the world of ideas. This ideal element suffices for our purposes. Not the historical events, but the ideas embodied in a tradition, form the object of our comparative study. Where the same complex of ideas produces analogous modes of expression, we are justified in assuming a close cultural connection. If we can also determine which of the similar myth cycles is closer to the basic idea and which one is further removed from it, we have determined which people perceived it from others. In an age when we consult comparative linguistics regarding the kinship between peoples, we can scarcely place less trust in a comparison of myths and ideas."[178] This is how Bachofen explains his method of investigation, and how he defends his original anthropological hermeneutics. He does not discard some historical artifacts, such as myths and legends, when he intends to reconstruct a historical period that was explained by them, because he believes they have a basis in reality. He includes all fragments in trying to put them together and so reconstructs a total historical reality through reasoning. Not only hard facts are susceptible to analysis and interpretation; not only what can be perceived by the senses, but also what can be accessed through reason.

Tanaquil is the legendary Etruscan prophet, the wife of Tarquinius Priscus, the fifth king of Rome. Tanaquil won the crown for her son in law Servius Tulius, recapitulating an early Asia Minor custom of mothers' being the grantors of monarchic power. This is a historical remnant of matriarchy before "Women were virtually household prisoners in fifth-century Athenian society in particular, as the legal orations of Lysias show, (see Chapter 11)[179] and this

---

178 Bachofen, J.J. (1992). "The Myth of Tanaquil." In. *Myth, Religion, and Mother Right. Selected Wriings of Bachofen.* Trans. Ralph Manheim, with a Preface by George Boas and an Introduction by Joseph Campbell. P. 213-214. Princeton, N.J. Princeton University Press.

179 Lysias. (2004). *The Orations of Lysias.* Online in Project Gutenberg. EBook #6969. (Written 388 BCE).

seems to have been the typical state of affairs from shortly before the time of Homer onward. There are many exceptions, however, in the Mycenaean world, most notably with Helen of Troy. Not only does her husband Menelaus carry on a ten-year war to retrieve her, but then, far from punishing her (as later Greek husbands of wayward wives were known to do, usually by death), he sits around placidly while she tells stories of her escapades to their guests! The reason that he had to fetch her back can only be a matter of succession: that the right to the throne of Sparta passed through her female blood-line, not his. Without Helen, Menelaus could not be king. This analysis is borne out by every detail known of the family: Helen is the queen even though she has two brothers, the famous twins Kastor and Polydeukes (Castor and Pollux in Latin), and her daughter Hermione, not one of Menelaus' sons, becomes the next ruler of Sparta after her death."[180]

If matriarchy, probably in various forms, is the first configuration of social organization pertaining to history prior to the written record, and if the prevalent form of explanation then was mythical, based on a different logic, a different grammar for the perception of reality, the first place to look for evidence of matriarchy is in mythology. Mythology is early history in sync with its own logic.

The existence of a supreme goddess is as much an indication of a matriarchal form of social organization as is that of male gods for patriarchy more recently, even though matriarchal goddesses did not exclude male gods, in the same way early mythology did not exclude animal or inanimate object-gods in totems. Preeminent goddesses have been described in many mythologies throughout the world, the more popular, and controversially attached to an extreme form of matriarchy, being the Amazons, warriors of Artemis, Goddess of the hunt and the Moon. This was a feminine society of conquerors and warriors that excluded males, and that appears in *The Iliad* and other Greek legends. They are said to have invaded Lycia, where

---

180 Wayland Barber, E. (1994). *Women's Work. The first 20,000 Years. Women, Cloth, and Society in Early Times.* Chapter 4. Footnote 4. P. 119. New York and London. W. W. Norton and Company.

Herodotus described matrilineality. They have also been described as being present in Northern Africa, Iran, Crete and Ukraine. They were described by Bertha Diner as the feminist wing of a young human race, whose other extreme wing was the stringent patriarchies that finally prevailed. In the Amazons women would have, for the first time, exercised their defense of a hegemonic history identifying with men's methods, to the not typically matriarchal extreme of excluding them.[181]

The transition from mythology to historiography must be considered a piece of a puzzle to be deciphered, rather than a hindrance to research. It is a difficult issue, as all transitions are, but even in the Greek pantheon Prometheus represents such a transition from the world of gods to that of humans. The fact that early human history was narrated mythologically is a logical fact similar to young children's explanations that challenge us to find their logic. Herodotus himself, in his effort to separate history from myth, presents a sample of such a transition.

1.2.3 From Early Historiography: Herodotus and Tacitus

The Amazons occur abundantly in Greek historiography, including the reports of senate discussions and the narratives of Gnaeus Pompeius Trogus, Pliny the Elder, Philostratus, Ammianus, Proccopius, and Diodorus Siculus.[182]

The first historian and father of history, Herodotus, is also the first to describe an important trait of a matriarchal society, matronymic identity. Writing about the Lycians of Anatolia, he described them as having "one singular custom in which they differ from every other nation in the world. They take the mother's and not the father's name. Ask a Lycian who he is, and he answers by giving his own name, that of his mother, and so on in the female line. More-

---

181 Diner, B. E. (1965). *Mothers and Amazons: The First Feminine History of Culture.* Trans. John Philip Lundin. New York: Julian Press,).
182 See "Amazons" in Wikipedia. Accessed from <http://en.wikipedia.org/wiki/Amazons#cite_ref-78> no 2015-01-06.

over, if a free woman marry a man who is a slave, their children are full citizens; but if a free man marry a foreign woman, or live with a concubine, even though he be the first person in the State, the children forfeit all the rights of citizenship."[183]

Herodotus also reported that the Sarmatians, Iranian nomadic tribes, were descendants of the Amazons, and that their wives observed their ancient maternal customs. No girl was allowed to wed till she had killed a man in battle. A group of Amazons is placed in southeastern Crimea who agreed to marry Scythian men. The Sarmatians fought along with the Scythians against Darius the Great in the fiftth century BC, and Hippocrates describes their women as having no right breasts.[184]

If Herodotus considers matriarchy to be an aberration, Tacitus much later, on the other hand, describes the Sitones, a matriarchy among the Teutons where women ruled. Here we have a less frequent characteristic of matriarchy, political rule. Thinking as a patriarch, Tacitus thinks of this type of social organization as a debasement worse than slavery, a historical regression.[185]

Instead of inciting mainstream academia to explore the fascinating issue of matriarchy, the mythical and ancient historiographical data is generally discarded as valueless, with the statement that most anthropologists and social scientists do not find it persuasive.

1.2.4 Early Anthropology Proper: Lafitau as Pioneer

The first, self-made modern ethnologist to propose matriarchy as an original form of social organization was French Jesuit missionary Joseph Francois Lafitau (1681-1746), who coined the term *gyneco-*

---

183 Rawlinson, G. (1858). *The History of Herodotus*. London. Vol. 1. John Murray, Albemarle St. P. 309.

184 Hippocrates. *Airs, Waters, Places*. Part 16 ff. Online in Perseus. Tufts University. Accessed from <http://perseus.uchicago.edu/perseus-cgi/citequery3.pl?dbname=Greek-Feb2011&query=Hipp.%20Aer.%2017&getid=2> on 2015-01-04.

185 Tacitus. *Germania*. Ch. 45. Online in UNRV. Accessed from <http://www.unrv.com/tacitus/tacitus-germania-12.php> on 2015-01-04.

cracy well before Bachofen, who is usually credited with it. Lafitau was also a published naturalist. A true pioneer in anthropology, if not its unrecognized founder, in the West, Lafitau was already doing independent fieldwork a century before the better-known pioneers, and for the first time introduced the comparative method.

From Canada, where he did his fieldwork with the Iroquois, he became conversant with the Indian civilizations of the American continent as well as with the existing historical record. On this basis he writes: "Gynecocracy, or women's rule, which was the basis of the Lycian [government], might well have been common formerly to almost all the primitive peoples of Greece, since it is quite wide-spread, as I have shown, [in speaking] of the Cantabrians, the people of Spain and those of Asia Minor. [It is found among almost all the people who migrated from there]. It may possibly even have come from the Amazons, whose empire is too vast in extent. It is likely enough that these women, some of whom settled in Lycia where they were vanquished by Bellerophon and then by the Greeks, tired at last of being always at war, and seeing their decadence and ruin at hand, finally compromised with their enemies, that they received them into the cities which they had built, keeping, on the one hand, the domain which they already had (in their possession) whether that of the fields which they were cultivating or the children which they were bringing up, and, on the other hand, they did honor to the men by combining some of the latter's customs with theirs and leaving them the care of affairs in such a way that the men would have only the honor and they themselves all the responsibility."[186] This seemingly naive and voluntaristic explanation is based on what Lafitau observed in the still alive matriarchy of the Iroquois. Women delegated their authority onto male chiefs for the purpose of civil society, a democratic form of government involving all and steered by proxy-warring men. An important fact on which Lafitau, without knowing it, agrees with Bachofen, is the historical influence of Asia

---

186 Lafitau, J.F. (1974). Ibid. Vol.1. p. 285. <http://link.library.utoronto.ca/champlain/DigObj.cfm?Idno=9_96848&lang=eng&Page=0428&Size=3&query=lafitau&-searchtype=Fulltext&startrow=1&Limit=All>

Minor on Greece and Rome, particularly as far as the historical remnants of matriarchy is concerned.

Lafitau continues: "Whatever the origin of the Iroquois and Huron may be, they have kept this form of government in its first simplicity for, besides this gynecocracy which is exactly the same as that of the Lycians, in which the care of affairs is in the men's hands only by way of procuration, all the villages govern themselves in the same way, by themselves, and as if they were independent of each other."[187] As the translators of Lafitau's work point out in their Introduction, his work, initially well received, then fell into the wide expanse of academic silence. Replication is one of fundamental requirements to validate findings in science, except when it comes to certain issues such as mother right, where replication invalidates.

I cannot find what is not clear in the observations of Lafitau. He describes Indigenous societies in America, the form of government of which was matriarchal, even though women delegated functions such as civil chiefdom to males that they could promote and demote according to their own performance evaluations. Women also had to approve declarations of war, even though males were the designated warriors. Had the Iroquois women been despots and warmongers to the exclusion of males, perhaps that would have made their matriarchy acceptable to patriarchal academia.

1.2.5 Bachofen, Renaissance Man and Human Scientist

The perspective of pioneer anthropologist, classicist, philologist, evolutionist, and jurisprudent Swiss John Jakob Bachofen (1815–1887) was as wide as his credentials. He based his theory on innumerable passages of ancient classical literature and on its own ethnological work that incidentally was maliciously ignored, but had later to be brought back to life.[188]

---

187 Lafitau, J.F. (1974). Ibid. Vol.1. p. 287. <http://link.library.utoronto.ca/champlain/ DigObj.cfm?Idno=9_96848&lang=eng&Page=0430&Size=3&query=lafitau&- searchtype=Fulltext&startrow=1&Limit=All>
188 Bachofen's "presence in the cultural life of the twentieth century and beyond is in

Bachofen proposed that the original form of social organization in human societies was based on what he called "Mother Right."[189] Doing for myth what Darwin did for species, Bachofen was led to the conclusion that humans first lived in a state of disorganized sexual promiscuity he called *hetaerism*. Its first guiding goddess was a Proto-Aphrodite under various names.

From hetaerism (temporary or continued sexual relations outside wedlock) women established the first coherent organization of society that was matriarchal, meaning produced and led by women. Descent could then only be determined in the female line, that is according to mother origin. Deities were women, and that was the case amongst all the peoples of antiquity including the Amazons, a rather late development in matriarchy, reactive to the patriarchal coup and to the enslavement of mothers. Since mother was the only parent known with certainty, women held the preeminent position of respect and honor in society, the foundation of the rule of *gynaecocracy,* the same term used by Lafitau. The transition to monogamy, after the transition to patriarchy, was a violation of a primitive religious law of universal female access. The early economic system in the matriarchal organization was communist, since there was no concept of private property. Hetaerism was thus followed by Mother Right or matriarchy. This all took place in an agricultural society with embryonic social organization, the dominant deity's being Demeter, a goddess of fertility.

Mother Right was then followed by a form of social organization transitional to patriarchy, somewhat regressive, and supported by women, although here is where the Amazons also appeared as the wing of protest. Dionysus was the representative god of this transi-

many cases more diffuse and harder to pin down than that of Freud, Marx or Nietzsche, and yet the idea that the ancient world was shaped by matriarchal societies very different from our own has proved remarkably persistent, despite its current lack of "respectability" in the mainstream of contemporary archeology." Davies, P. (2010). *Myth, matriarchy and modernity: Johann Jakob Bachofen in German culture, 1860-1945.* Berlin/New York. Walter de Gruyter GmbH & Co. KG.

189 Bachofen, J.J. (1992). *Myth, Religion, and Mother Right: Selected Writings.* Trans. Ralph Mannheim. Princeton N.J. Princeton University Press. Orig. Pub. 1861.

tional period. Finally, patriarchy was fully installed under the aegis of the Apollonian god, when males ushered in a radical inversion of all previous forms of social organization. All the first-order mediations mothers had introduced were for the most part transformed into their opposites, in order to represent male power. Our written history is all written as if the patriarchal second-order mediations had come as a natural order, and this historical distortion is the first act of repression of consciousness, political and psychological.

Bachofen's pioneer work did not have precedent, and his interpretation of historical facts is compelling and at the same time poetical. He relies on religion for his explanations, as is to be expected for his time and culture. He attributes the shift from matriarchy to patriarchy not to material conditions and political repression, but to religious changes that took place while we were entering the time of the Greeks. His legal and political interpretation of the myth of Orestes, however, based on his analysis of the Oresteia of Aeschylus,[190] is brilliant and compelling. Orestes is the thesis before the patriarchal Oedipus of Freud, the antithesis.[191]

The story of Orestes is the ancient representation of the early importance of female-based blood relations for Bachofen. Agamemnon, king of Mycenae, acquiesces to the sacrifice of his daughter Iphigenia, which in fact does not take place, but in response to which he is killed by his wife, the mother of Iphigenia and Orestes, Clytemnestra; Orestes avenges his father and kills Clytemnestra and he is then punished for that by the Erinyes, invisible accusatory female witnesses that with their deprecatory invectives drive him close to madness. When the case is brought to court, the blood relationship clearly takes precedence. Of the two murders, only Orestes' matricide is considered punishable, because it is considered a

190 Aeschylus. (1900). *The Oresteia of Aeschylus.* Translated and explained by C.W. Warr. London. George Allen. Online in Internet Archive. Accessed from <https://archive.org/stream/oresteiaofaeschy00aesciala#page/n7/mode/2up> on 2014-07-28.

191 Freud, S. (1913). *The Interpretation of Dreams.* Ch. 5. Trans. A. A. Brill (Orig. Pub. 1900). Originally publish in New York by Macmillan. Online in Classics in the History of Psychology. Accessed from <http://psychclassics.yorku.ca/Freud/Dreams/> on 2015-01-15.

blood-murder. Slaying of the mother-queen by her son is unprecedented, treasonous, and here highly symbolic because it represents the transition from the original sacredness of mother-blood to the new emerging secular patriarchal order.

Compared to the Freudian Oedipus, Bachofen's Orestes offers a more realistic blueprint for the configuration of the human mind. Those who enforce repression of the historical facts do so in bad faith. Those who from fear or ignorance accept the patriarchal distortion of reality are to suffer from unconscious repression and symptoms. Orestes represents the primitive "legal" repression of the original mother order.

1.2.6 The Iroquois Independently Revisited, and the American Brand of Marxism

Contemporary pen-pal of Bachofen, Scottish-American lawyer and pioneer Lewis Henry Morgan (1818-1881) wrote the classic of American anthropology *Ancient Society*,[192] that places him ahead of other European pioneers including Bachofen. Morgan, privileged as an insider by having been adopted by the Seneca tribe, scientifically replicated the findings of Lafitau. Since his early youth, Morgan was very conscious about the fact he was living in Iroquois expropriated land, Aurora in the Cayuga County. His grandfather, a Welsh New York pioneer, had bought land and settled there. Morgan from a very early age had a strong sympathy and identification with the aborigines. As it happened, the Iroquois were then in disgrace for having sided with France in the French-American war, and were being, if not openly dispossessed, cheated and pushed out of their land. Morgan was a pro-Iroquois activist as a youth, having with others

---

192 Morgan, L.H. (1944). *Ancient Society Or Researches in the Lines of Human Progress from Savagery through Barbarism to Civilization.* (Orig. Pub. 1877). Online Edition in Marxists Internet Archive is reproduced from the "First Indian Edition (1944), published by BHARTI LIBRARY, Booksellers & Publishers, 145, Cornwallis Street, Calcutta. Composed by Tariq Sharif, "WATERMARK", Gujranwala, Pakistan. Accessed from <http://www.marxists.org/reference/archive/morgan-lewis/ancient-society/> on 2012-09-14.

found a secret society that from its first appellation The Gordian Knot evolved to become The New Confederacy of the Iroquois. This youthful group was devoted to doing research on the Iroquois, who for centuries had lived in central and upstate New York. Beyond that, the group also intended to resurrect the spirit of the Iroquois, organizing itself on their tribal model, learning their language, and even performing initiation rites of "inindianation."[193] Morgan later had the opportunity to meet Iroquois individuals in person, and eventually provided them with legal services. This is how he was eventually adopted by the Seneca tribe of the Iroquois as their own son.

Morgan writes: "In treating the subject of the growth of the idea of government, the organization into gentes on the basis of kin naturally suggests itself as the archaic frame work of ancient society; but there is a still older and more archaic organization, that into classes on the basis of sex, which first demands attention. It will not be taken up because of its novelty in human experience, but for the higher reason that it seems to contain the germinal principle of the gens. If this inference is warranted by the facts, it will give to this organization into male and female classes, now found in full vitality among the Australian aborigines, an ancient prevalence as widespread, in the tribes of mankind, as the original organization into gentes."[194] He adds: "The organization into classes upon sex, and the subsequent higher organization into gentes upon kin, must be regarded as the results of great social movements worked out unconsciously through natural selection."[195] This is how Morgan untied the "Gordian knot" of the origin of the organization of humankind from sex-determined classes into kin-determined gentes (and later into property-based classes, Marx would add). The founder of anthropology in America thus replicated both the materialist principles of historical development of Marx, and, independently, the findings of Lafitau on the matter of egalitarian matriarchy amongst the Iroquois.

---

193 See "Lewis H. Morgan." in Wikipedia.
194 Morgan, L.H. (1944). Ibid. P.41.
195 Morgan, L.H. (1944). Ibid. P.41.

As a first paradigm of research methodology in the human sciences, Morgan was able to develop a whole theory of family and its evolution and to empirically confirm his hypothesis in the existence of group marriage in Hawaii and the Australasian islands. Besides, he confirmed the existence of even earlier logical forms of intersection of consanguinity and affinity in various parts of the world besides the ones he discovered while with the Iroquois. He arrived at his important conclusions based on exhaustive work conducted through questionnaires mailed to embassies and missionaries, comparing systems of kinship throughout the world. His first conclusion was that a natural class-based social organization on the bases of sex preceded any other form of social organization, the equivalent of the hetaerism of Bachofen. This scientific thread has been picked up most recently by Chris Knight, who demonstrates how women used sex to historically organize society.[196] This simply means that the first form of "classification" and of "class" in humans was sexual, a natural ground that was eventually replaced by gentes before patriarchal property-based classes.

Morgan's second conclusion is that in such form of primitive organization the family was first consanguine, blood-based. There were no rules against incest; and, on the contrary brothers and sisters were probably natural husbands and wives as some of the myths have it.[197] This was confirmed by comparing lawful systems of kinship or affinity with marriage rules prevailing at the time in different nations of the world. The system had historically evolved, through a series of steps or types of family, to gradually exclude larger groups of consanguine relatives from marriage and finally arrive at present monogamy.

The third conclusion, that makes Morgan the Marxist, is that the State and forms of government of societies likewise evolved historically as a superstructure following the development of the means

---

196 Knight, C. (1991). *Blood Relations. Menstruation and the Origins of Culture.* New Haven and London. Yale University Press.
197 A clear example is the Greek Pantheon with Gaia delivering son and daughters that were also husbands and wives.

of production of social groups. This is the part of Morgan's work that has been most condemned to silence and academic repression, particularly in his own land.

Morgan divides the development of society into three stages, Savagery, Barbarism and Civilization, with the form of both, family and state, paralleling their course. The Lower stage of Savagery corresponds to the Australopithecus period, and is the childhood of humanity. The original habitat of humans was then in tropical and subtropical areas, and humans were then partially tree-dwellers. Technologically, this is the age of the bow, of pottery and fire. The Middle Stage or Barbarism is that in which domestication of animals takes place, with agriculture, and metalworking; and, the Late Stage of Civilization has alphabet and writing. Human intelligence develops in parallel as technology accelerates. Bow and arrow are to savagery what the iron sword is to barbarism and firearms to civilization. All human society started from communist and matriarchal forms of organization.

Of course the agreement between Marx and Morgan did not help the cause of matriarchy; on the contrary, it made it more controversial, by highlighting the undesired elements of substantial equality and a communist economy, the nemesis of capitalism.

1.2.7 Morgan Replicates Marx, and Engels Endorses Morgan

Karl Marx read *Ancient* Society late in his life and he had it in the back burner for discussion within the framework of his encompassing theoretical system. Running short of time, he explicitly asked Engels to pursue the matter, which Engels did in his *Origin of the Family, Private Property and the State*, subtitled "in the light of the researches of Lewis H. Morgan."[198]

---

198 Engels, F. (2000). *The Origin of the Family, Private Property and the State.* Trans. Alick West. Marx/Engels Selected Works, Volume Three. Online Version: Marx/Engels Internet Archive (marxists.org). Accessed from <http://www.marxists.org/archive/marx/works/1884/origin-family/index.htm> on 2012-09-14.

Engels summarized and paid tribute to the work of Morgan, concluding that Morgan's theory was an independent scientific replication of historical materialism. He was dismayed, although perhaps not surprised, at the silent response of academia to Morgan's monumental findings. I will now quote at length.

"It is Morgan's great merit that he has discovered and reconstructed in its main lines this prehistoric basis of our written history, and that in the kinship groups of the North American Indians he has found the key to the most important and hitherto insoluble riddles of earliest Greek, Roman and German history. His book is not the work of a day. For nearly forty years he wrestled with his material, until he was completely master of it. But that also makes his book one of the few epoch-making works of our time."[199]

And further: "This rediscovery of the primitive matriarchal gens as the earlier stage of the patriarchal gens of civilized peoples has the same importance for anthropology as Darwin's theory of evolution has for biology and Marx's theory of surplus value for political economy. It enabled Morgan to outline for the first time a history of the family in which for the present, so far as the material now available permits, at least the classic stages of development in their main outlines are determined. That this opens a new epoch in the treatment of primitive history must be clear to everyone. The matriarchal gens has become the pivot on which the whole science turns; since its discovery, we know where to look and what to look for in our research, and how to arrange the results. And, consequently, since Morgan's book, progress in this field has been made at a far more rapid speed.

"Anthropologists, even in England, now generally appreciate, or rather appropriate, Morgan's discoveries. But hardly one of them has the honesty to admit that it is to Morgan that we owe this revolution in our ideas. In England they try to kill his book by silence, and dispose of its author with condescending praise for his earlier achievements; they niggle endlessly over details and remain obsti-

---

199 Engels, F. (2000). *The Origin of the Family*. Ibid. "Preface to the First Edition, 1884.

nately silent about his really great discoveries. The original edition of *Ancient Society* is out of print; in America there is no sale for such things; in England, it seems, the book was systematically suppressed, and the only edition of this epoch making work still circulating in the book trade is – the German translation.

"Why this reserve? It is difficult not to see in it a conspiracy of silence; for politeness' sake, our recognized anthropologists generally pack their writings with quotations and other tokens of camaraderie. Is it, perhaps, because Morgan is an American, and for the English anthropologists it goes sorely against the grain that, despite their highly creditable industry in collecting material, they should be dependent for their general points of view in the arrangement and grouping of this material, for their ideas in fact, on two foreigners of genius, Bachofen and Morgan? They might put up with the German – but the American? Every Englishman turns patriotic when he comes up against an American, and of this I saw highly entertaining instances in the United States. Moreover, McLennan was, so to speak, the officially appointed founder and leader of the English school of anthropology. It was almost a principle of anthropological etiquette to speak of his artificially constructed historical series – child-murder, polygyny, marriage by capture, matriarchal family – in tones only of profoundest respect. The slightest doubt in the existence of exogamous and endogamous 'tribes' of absolute mutual exclusiveness was considered rank heresy. Morgan had committed a kind of sacrilege in dissolving all these hallowed dogmas into thin air. Into the bargain, he had done it in such a way that it only needed saying to carry immediate conviction; so that the McLennanites, who had hitherto been helplessly reeling to and fro between exogamy and endogamy, could only beat their brows and exclaim: How could we be such fools as not to think of that for ourselves long ago?

"As if these crimes had not already left the official school with the option only of coldly ignoring him, Morgan filled the measure to overflowing by not merely criticizing civilization, the society of commodity production, the basic form of present-day society, in a manner reminiscent of Fourier, but also by speaking of a future transformation of this society in words which Karl Marx might have used. He had therefore amply merited McLennan's indignant reproach that 'the historical method is antipathetical to Mr. Morgan's mind,' and its echo as late as 1884 from Mr. Professor Giraud-Teulon of Geneva. In 1874 (*Origines de la Famille*) this same gentleman was still groping helplessly in the maze of the McLennanite exogamy, from which Morgan had to come and rescue him!"[200]

Replication, again, does not count here. It does not matter that Morgan independently replicated the theory of Marx, Lafitau and Bachofen, confirming its own scientific standing in the human sciences.

It becomes obvious that human history, from now on, in its widest horizon, consists of three epochs: matriarchy the thesis, patriarchy the antithesis, and whatever is to come next, perhaps socialism or a blend of fratriarchy and sorarchy. The future of our society will then be the synthesis and the promise of having learned. All in all, even with the theoretical differences, nineteenth-century anthropology was matriarchal. Not so for the next century.

I have not delved into other well-known anthropologists of the nineteenth century because they are not particularly relevant to the argument of this book, although they all take a matriarchal and evolutionary perspective in spite of their differences. Some of them will come up when discussing other issues.

---

200 Engels, F. (2000). *The Origin of the Family.* Ibid. Preface to the Fourth Edition, 1891.

1.3 MY READING OF VEBLEN: TRANSITION TO THE TWENTIETH CENTURY

1.3.1 Edvard Westermarck's Shift

If nineteenth-century human science was matriarchal and evolutionary, the twentieth brought with it the strongest reaction, spearheaded by a Finnish philosopher and pioneer of British sociology. Edvard Westermarck (1862–1939) had his first book, *The History of Human Marriage*, enthusiastically introduced by none other than Alfred R. Wallace. He became most famous for his "Westermarck effect" that postulates that people who grow up in close proximity to each other are sexually desensitized to each other. This is a voluntaristic notion based on observation of an advanced historical culture that does not represent our origins. It has no empirical evidence beyond such observation. Of course it makes the ideology of the unchanging patriarchal institution of marriage appear logical.

Instinct is kept at the basis of the argument, which gives it a certain natural legitimacy. "The home is kept pure from incestuous defilement neither by laws, nor by customs, nor by education, but by an instinct which under normal circumstances makes sexual love between the nearest kin a physical impossibility."[201] A physical impossibility, it needs to be added, that although frequently overridden by cases of incest of which only the minority end up in court, offers a logic legitimized by natural instinct. If sexual repulsion in the family was a natural given, the corollary is that there was no evolution

---

201 Westermarck, E. (1894). *The History of Human Marriage*. Second Edition. Ch. 15. Prohibition of marriage between kindred. P. 319. New York and London. MacMillan. Online in Google eBooks. Accessed from <https://books.google.com/books?id=ZSoKAAAAIAAJ&pg=PA319&lpg=PA319&dq=The+home+is+kept+pure+from+incestuous+defilement&source=bl&ots=Lpe3hr5GHx&sig=H1SpuJTxSW6wqPo-qtI-TYXA1BiU&hl=en&sa=X&ei=9PefVPX-2CMilNrujgZAC&ved=0CCcQ6AEwAw#v=onepage&q=The%20home%20is%20kept%20pure%20from%20incestuous%20defilement&f=false> on 2014-12-28.

in human sexual relations, created as they stand.

Westermarck adds: "A similar way of reasoning has also led me to the hypothesis that the family, consisting of father, mother, and children, existed already in primeval times and probably among our pre-human ancestors, owing to the offspring's need of care and protection and to the economic obstacles in the way of a permanent living in hordes; but this conclusion has a less solid foundation than the former one, because the necessity of paternal care is not so certain as that of maternal care. On the other hand, the causes, or hypothetical causes, to which marriage by capture, group-marriage, and mother-right may be traced are not such as to justify the belief in the universal prevalence of any of these customs at any stage of human civilization to say nothing of promiscuity, the existence of which as the exclusive form of the relations between the sexes, even among a single people, is extremely doubtful." Method here is "way or reasoning," evidence is "less solid," and causes in the opposite point of view "extremely doubtful."[202] On this precarious ground mainstream anthropology aligned, under the belief that the bourgeois family is the natural form, and an exception to evolution.

Protection by the father[203] is invoked in the argument to cement the role of the patriarchal male in the trans historical family, disregarding the fact that this is precisely such "protection" that has maimed the species: it has led us back to the barbarism we live out in the middle of so-called civilization, when we are protected from each other by means of war.

Only in the "lower races," women are "always more or less" in a state of dependence, and are transferred as objects from the possession of the father to that of the husband. Additionally, the Marxian belief that the level of development of a society can be measured by the status of its women, does not apply, judging by a review of

---

202 Westermarck, E. (1921). *The History of Human Marriage.* Volume: 1. 5th. Ed (rewritten). London. MacMillan. Ch. 1. The Origin of Marriage. Pp. 20-1. (Orig. Pub. 1901). Online in Questia. Accessed from <https://www.questia.com/read/10659049/the-history-of-human-marriage> on 2014-12-28.
203 Westermarck, E. (1921). *The History of Human* Marriage. Ibid. P.37.

history [204] This is the compromised mode of reasoning of Wester-marck well-fited to a patriarchal ideology. Thorstein Veblen, Robert Briffault, and most in the feminist research arena are of a different opinion.

Thorstein Veblen (1857-1929) was a Norwegian-American in-dependent economist, evolutionary theorist, and sociologist who lived the centennial transition in the United States. Veblen was a native of Wisconsin and did not have a successful academic career, because of his anti-capitalist views that were countered by a hos-tile gossipy focus on his personal life. Veblen however presents a most coherent theory of psychological evolution in the tradition of the classical evolutionists, Darwin, Romanes, and Spencer. He most uniquely and independently focuses on the effect of the economic structure of capitalism on human character, "human nature," deter-mined by capitalist social institutions.

Veblen describes the clear trends of the new American Society that do not fully adjust to the Protestant Ethics of his contemporary Weber,[205] the mainstream ideological antagonist of Marx. Being an economist by training, Veblen uniquely brings together mainstream economy and the Darwinian aspects of social selection, particularly as they impact on the human character. In this respect he precedes both Briffault and Freud in his effort to base human character on evolution, and specifically on instinct.

1.3.2 What Darwin Had to Say

Darwin's mistake in his sexual selection theory is not to have

---

204 Westermarck, E. (1924). *The Origin and Development of the Moral Ideas.* Volume 1. Chapter XXVI. "The subjection of Wives." Second Edition. London. MacMillan. Pp. 629 ff. (Orig. Pub. 1906. Online in Archive. org. Accessed from < https://archive.org/stream/theoriginanddeve01westuoft/theoriginanddeve01westuoft_djvu.txt> on 2016-04-02-28.

205 Weber, M. (1930). *The Protestant Ethic and the Spirit of Capitalism.* Trans: Talcott Parsons, Anthony Giddens. London & Boston. Unwin Hyman. (Orig. Pub. 1905). Online in MIA. Accessed from <http://www.marxists.org/reference/archive/weber/protestant-ethic/> on 2014-12-1.

seen clearly the pivotal role of females, as opposed to the incidental one of males, in evolution. Before evolutionary sexuation, the previous form of replication of organisms was through the production of rather identical copies as in fission, replication or self-cloning. Sexuation lead to the contradictory phenomenon of simultaneous difference and sameness (different sex, same species), a new cognitive complexity. This brought with it the checking advantage of meiotic recombination with chromosomal crossover, enhancing correction and variation in individual specimens, all leading towards a better species adaptation. The organismic default of evolution pre- and post-sexuation is the female of species, if only because of the obvious degree of *parental investment*. It is the female who selects partners, provides protein and nutrients from her body, and protects and teaches the each new organism after birth. Darwin saw this, but he was unable to override the prevailing patriarchal ideology in his conceptual framing when it came to explaining it. Instead of saying females select and build while males fight to be selected, he said males fight for access to preferred females. This inverts the species' sexual agency.

In *On the* Origin of *Species*[206] Darwin saw the purpose of sexuation, which that introduces the aesthetic element, along with the ethical one of object choice, subjective proto-consciousness. Sexual selection is an alternative to the prior utilitarian selfish and predetermined hermaphroditic self-replication or even more primitive mitosis. Trivers then said that "What governs the operation of sexual selection is the relative parental investment of the sexes in the offspring."[207] Contrary to most other species, both the aesthetic and ethical elements in humans are therefore adjudicated to the selective female. This evolutionary twist was probably necessary as a

---

206 Darwin, C. (1859). *On the Origin of Species*. (1st edition). London. John Murray. Chapter 4, page 88. Darwin Online. Accessed from <http://darwin-online.org.uk/content/frameset?viewtype=side&itemID=F373&pageseq=12> on 2015-01-16.

207 Trivers, R. L. (1972). "Parental Investment and Sexual Selection." In: Campbell, B. ed. Sexual Selection and the Descent of Man, 1871-1971. Chicago, Illinois. Aldine Publishing Company. Accessed from < http://www1.appstate.edu/~kms/classes/psy2664/Documents/trivers.pdf> on 2016-04-04.

prolegomenon to consciousness, because sexual selection and consciousness have the same underlying premise: lessening the role of destruction, and of waste, in the economy of evolutionary production, or in other words, better energetic adaptation.

Evolution accomplished this by shifting its model of fitness. If optimal adaptation in the food chain is based on the survival of the fittest, such fitness is based on evening mechanical harmony, based on force, of the organism with its environment. In humans, however, typical males in stress tend to rely more on force and competition than on intelligent reasoning. The case is the opposite for the female of the human species.[208] The selective power of females relies not on physical power, pitched against physical power but in more discriminating aesthetic and ethical considerations. This requires, for humanity, a different form of natural coherence, a survival-geared intelligence that is capable of discrimination and choice that, in turn, imply freedom.

The fact, then, is that with sexuation evolution introduced a totally different set of options in selective mechanisms. This does not mean that the older mechanism is obsolete; it is optimal for its conditions. The fact that we humans are still predominantly using it in all sorts of wars, is the best proof of its existence. This means that human history could ameliorate its highly destructive pattern significantly, by applying the intelligent form of selection historically repressed with the repression of women. Matriarchy was the failed attempt of evolution to apply the new model unscathed. The experiment failed because of the freedom and choices inherent in human consciousness, with its capacity to introduce its own mediations. The prolonged supersession of matriarchy by patriarchy was a historical regression that unfortunately impacted evolution in a negative way, as we well know today.

Darwin, instead of saying females select males based on their

---

208 Taylor, Shelley, E. Klein, Laura Cousino et al. (2000). "Biobehavioral responses to stress in females: Tend-and-befriend, not fight-or-flight". Psychological Review 107 (3): 411–29.

fighting adaptive quality for the species, turned the whole issue around, ideologically, simply by saying: males fight for access to females. This grammatical twist does away with the female agency by simply placing the emphasis on fighting rather than selecting, and placing the verb only on the side of males.

What Darwin did with a stroke of the pen was to rationalize patriarchal agency at the expense of the natural sexual female class. In this fashion, he provided good ammunition to the patriarchal-legitimation argument. His notions, however, of instinct as animal intelligence, and habit as a learned derivative, are crucial in the debate because they bridge nature and history.

1.3.3 Veblen on Evolution and Instinct

Veblen defines social evolution as "a process of selective adaptation of temperament and habits of thought under the stress of the circumstances of associated life. The adaptation of habits of thought is the growth of institutions. But along with the growth of institutions has gone a change of a more substantial character. Not only have the habits of men changed with the changing exigencies of the situation, but these changing exigencies have also brought about a correlative change in human nature."[209] This is a typical dialectical view, an analogue of Marx's, where reciprocal determination occurs between humans' transforming their environment through labor, and labor in turn transforming humans.[210]

Like Marx, whom he did not endorse explicitly, Veblen is a firm believer in the fact that society changes with the changing conditions of material life. This dialectic brings with it a process of selection that he sees in several ethnic types or ethnic elements. There

---

209 Veblen, T. (2013). "The Conservation of Archaic Traits." Ch. 9 in : *Theory of the Leisure Class*. Online in Project Gutenberg. eBook #833. Accessed from <http://www.gutenberg.org/files/833/833-h/833-h.htm - link2HCH0009> on 2014-11-30.

210 Fromm, E. (1961). *Marx's Concept of Man*. New York. Frederick Ungar Publishing. Online in MIA. Accessed from < https://www.marxists.org/archive/fromm/works/1961/man/index.htm> on 2016-04-04.

is a tendency in humans, according to Veblen, to revert to breeding according to old types of fixed human nature different from the present. This holds for several relatively stable ethnic types of mankind. These types have survived competition as variants of their original types. Ethnic variation is the result of selective processes' determining the course of cultures.[211] I believe what Marx calls social class, Veblen substitutes with "ethnic types," a Weberian maneuver.[212] Weber had diluted Marx through idealistic "types," and social "strata," and so does Veblen. What is paradoxically missing for an economist is the basic economic determination that seems to take second place to the ethnic classes. Ethnic types are cultural types and therefore superstructural.

That instincts and aptitudes are prime movers in the intelligence of nature is an evolutionary materialist viewpoint, compatible, however, with a scientific psychology. The presence of instinctual dispositions in the consciousness of humans indicates that there are material imperatives still determining the base of human behavior, with which consciousness must compromise. This was Freud's viewpoint. Veblen tells us that for mankind, as for the other higher animals, the life of the species is conditioned by the complement of instinctive proclivities and innate aptitudes. Not only is the continued life of the human race dependent upon the adequacy of these natural endowments, but its routine and the details of its life are also so determined.[213] This is a clear defense of the notion of instinct as a form of natural coherence and a material imperative operating as the ground of the psyche. In such a way, Veblen establishes a link not only with Darwin, Freud and Marx, but also provides a bridge

---

211 Veblen, T. (2013). "The Conservation of Archaic Traits." Ch. 9 in: *Theory of the Leisure Class*. Ibid.

212 Weber is the one who coined the notion of "ideal types." Weber, M. (1949). "Objectivity in Social Science and Social Policy" in The Methodology of the Social Sciences, E. A. Shils and H. A. Finch (ed. and trans.), New York: Free Press. (Orig. Pub.1904).

213 Veblen, T. (1914). *The Instinct of Workmanship. And the State of the Industrial Arts*. Introductory. P. 1. London. The Macmillan Company. Google Online in Internet Archive. Accessed from < https://archive.org/stream/instinctworkman00veblgoog/instinctworkman00veblgoog_djvu.txt> on 2014-11-30.

between classical and contemporary anthropology, connecting natural with social evolution.

Veblen's argument starts with the notion that the behavior of all animals that show directionality or selectivity is determined by those two complementary elements, instinct and aptitude, and behavior can never exceed the scope of these instinctive dispositions that produce its activity; "out of their working emerge not only the purpose and efficiency of life, but its substantial pleasures and pains as well."[214] In animal psychology, the word "instinct" has been superseded by more precise psychological and physiological concepts such as reflex and drive, gesture and attitude, this being particularly true in human psychology. But Veblen explicitly tells us that an inquiry into the nature and causes of the growth of institutions, his particular concern, does not demand such conceptual precision. "A genetic inquiry into institutions will address itself to the growth of habits and conventions, as conditioned by the material environment and by the innate and persistent propensities of human nature; and for these propensities, as they take effect in the give and take of cultural growth, no better designation than the timeworn 'instinct' is available."[215]

He also points out that although in the present context each of these propensities may be analyzed into simpler elements, it cannot be questioned that those simpler elements remain part of composite functional groups. Indeed, it is their particular concatenation that distinguishes the nature of man from that of the lower animals, which may share with him the more elementary traits.[216] Veblen's transformation of instincts is equivalent to what Briffault called instinctual dispositions. The concept is also close to what Freud meant by "sublimations."[217]

---

214 Veblen, T. (1918). *The Instinct of Workmanship.* Ibid. P. 1.
215 Veblen, T. (1918). *The Instinct of Workmanship.* Ibid. Pp. 2-3.
216 Veblen, T. (1918). *The Instinct of Workmanship.* Ibid. P. 3.
217 Freud, S. (1961) *Civilisation and Its Discontents.* Trans. James Strachey. London. Hogarth Press vol. XXI of the Standard Edi-tion. Pp. 79–80. (Orig. Pub. 1930). Free online version in Chrysoma Associates Limited. Publications Division - Electronic Books Library. Accessed from <http://www2.winchester.ac.uk/edstudies/courses/

Like Freud, Veblen points out that instincts differ from each other in that each has a characteristic purpose, an aim, and an object; Freud added a source. [218]Instincts for Veblen are thus teleological, and it could be considered that it is complexity that determines the transformation of instinct into consciousness, and habits, the transition from mere sense and coherence to practice that acts upon a widening and increasingly complex reality.

Instincts are different from the mechanical, anatomical or physiological, aptitudes that underlie them as well as from their actions, their distinctive feature being the particular character of their purpose. Instinct is different from tropismatic action, mere directional response of an organism to an external stimulus, because it already involves intelligent adaptive selectivity.[219] Instinct is a qualitative jump from prior and less complex natural coherence, and requires directionality represented in aim and object. The coherence of a tropism is externally determined; instinct is selectivity internally gathered.

In his discussion of instinct, Veblen reveals a grasp of the dialectical relation of instinct and consciousness. Although the pursuit of an objective end may be conscious, it is the instinct that makes it worthy of adaptation.[220] This represents a grounding of the superstructure of consciousness upon the base of a material imperative.

The ends and purposes of life remain first and foremost determined by man's instinctive proclivities; in this Veblen agrees with Freud. The ways and means of accomplishing goals are, however, a matter of individual intelligence. Humankind is guided by intelligence to a degree not approached by other animals, but its dependence on its instinctual endowment, the opposite, is no less abso-

level%20two%20sem%20two/Freud-Civil-Disc.pdf> on 2015-01-15.

218 Freud, S. (1905). Partial Impulses And Erogenous Zones. In: *Three Contributions to the Theory of Sex*. Trans. A. A. Brill. Nervous And Mental Disease Monograph Series No. 7. Second Edition. New York and Washington. Nervous And Mental Disease Publishing Co. Online in Project Gutenberg [EBook #14969]. Accessed from <http://www.gutenberg.org/files/14969/14969-h/14969-h.htm> on 2014-11-30.

219 Veblen, T. (1918). *The Instinct of Workmanship*. Ibid. Pp. 3-4.

220 Veblen, T. (1918). *The Instinct of Workmanship*. Ibid. P. 5.

lute. Instincts call for reflection and deliberation and they govern the choice of specific intelligent methods. Humans think and deliberate, but it is the human spirit, a specific species endowment of instinctive proclivities, that decides the path of their consciousness. Intelligence has a double determination; on the one hand is drive, on the other, it can only be deployed within the parameters of a conscious blueprint. The intelligence of Africans, long considered inferior by Europeans, is a different kind of adaptive intelligence for a different natural and social milieu, the best intelligence for their conditions of historical development.

Human life depends on instinctive proclivities mediated historically. The higher the degree of development of a community the more mediations have been interposed between instincts and their realization.[221] As it grows correspondingly, consciousness moves away from instinct and thus enlarges the gap between the two, making their dependency more and more difficult to perceive. While the illusion of separateness and autonomy grows, the dependence remains.

This is what Veblen has to say about the "ensemble of social relations": "This apparatus of ways and means available for the pursuit of whatever may be worth seeking is, substantially all, a matter of tradition out of the past, a legacy of habits of thought accumulated through the experience of past generations. So that the manner, and in a great degree the measure, in which the instinctive ends of life are worked out under any given cultural situation is somewhat closely conditioned by these elements of habit, which so fall into shape as an accepted scheme of life. The instinctive proclivities are essentially simple and look directly to the attainment of some concrete objective end; but in detail the ends so sought are many and diverse, and the ways and means by which they may be sought are similarly diverse and various, involving endless recourse to expedients, adaptations, and concessive adjustment between several pro-

---

221 Veblen, T. (1918). *The Instinct of Workmanship*. Ibid. Pp. 5-6.

clivities that are all sufficiently urgent."[222] This is saying that instinct has to rely, for its intelligent deployment, on the mediation of all the prior trial and errors, their outcomes, applied by all past generations, and from that what has been selected by our culture to be conserved in the form of institutions such as language, thought, consciousness, as well as prescriptions of "normal" reality testing and judgment.

Since Darwin, instinct has been opposed to habit. Habit for Veblen is what conventionally has evolved to become custom, prescription, etiquette, morality, becoming institutionalized in the process. Habit appears to acquire its own character and force different from instinct, the habitual ways being easy and obvious because they are universally sanctioned by social convention. They become what is right and proper, principles of conduct and political correctness. Habits can be said to be the common sense that guides everyday life. As such, they appear natural, as if they had been always the same.

This applies, for instance, to the metamorphosis that, through custom, has taken place regarding the acquisition and use of money. Most people are not conscious of the fact that the primary purpose of money was as a tool to facilitate the measure of exchange, substituting for previous complicated bartering. Money was invented, like any tool, for expediency and well-being, not for "having" it and obsessively accumulating it as a measure of social status. The immediacy of habit, besides the lure of the object money, historically inverted its meaning.

In many other areas of human conduct, immediate ends and means alone are conscious, and only upon reflection are their dispositional or instinctual roots discovered through analytical effort. There is no agreement among psychologists as to the number or scope of instincts; these issues become more important when it comes to understanding institutionalized social practices for Veblen.

Evolutionarily, instincts and aptitudes, that we can understand

---

222 Veblen, T. (1918). *The Instinct of Workmanship.* Ibid. Pp. 6-7.

as drives and their particular forms of applicability, are not to be confused with the attitudes or settled ways of G.H. Mead. According to Veblen, they may have all spread from an originally welded global ensemble.[223] They are unconsciously determined, similar to each other, and they exert their effect in the organism conjointly rather than in an isolated fashion. Veblen believes that on their basic physiological grounds human instincts ought not to be conceived as discrete and elementary. It is their interaction, blending, or even mutual interference and inhibition of each other that is usually manifested. This seems particularly true for the two central instinctive dispositions Veblen identifies as the "parental bent" and the "proclivity to construction or acquisition."[224] Although he did not do this, Veblen's instinctual duality can be easily parsed according to sex, the parental bent being a maternal function and the proclivity to construction (I would rather say destruction) or acquisition that of the male.

1.3.4 About "Human Nature"

Here is where Veblen becomes most relevant for us today, in view of the historical juncture we live *vis à vis* a nature, whose man-created latency we have pushed to the limit.[225] Veblen sees the sum of instinctive dispositions, propensities and sentiments, making up the spiritual nature of man, as the so-called "human nature." There may be wide departures from the norm, but if they are of no service to the species, they are selectively eliminated. The human nature animal being with moral wisdom, or *Homo sapiens,* the essence of *sapiens'* being its conscious morality—as I define it, prevails for the continuation of the species. If a culture adopts ways of life contrary to those under which it originated, thereby going against the foundation of its fitness, the group will eventually dwindle, says Ve-

---

223 Here Veblen (Ibid. p.9) quotes as his main source: Loeb, J. (1900). Comparative physiology of the brain and comparative psy-chology. New York: G.P. Putnam's Sons. "especially ch. xiii."

224 Veblen, T. (1918). *The Instinct of Workmanship.* Ibid. P. 11.

225 Meszaros, I. (2010-1). *Social Structure and Forms of Consciousness.* 2 vol. New York. Monthly Review Press.

blen. If this estimate is correct, it is possible that nature is already telling us that we must correct our ways or else. Capitalism's being our most immediate "way of life," and behind it the more-encompassing patriarchy, must be ended to go back into the natural path of the sense of evolution. The natural path of evolution is based on instinctual balance and reciprocal constraint. A new culture of equality, meaning full restitution of women's rights along with universal rights, is necessary as the next step in the series of cultures that constitute history. I believe Veblen's definition of human essence is not contradictory but rather complementary to Marx's ensemble of social relations.

In what Veblen calls the "hybrid mass of Western races," let's better say nations or ethnicities, he sees a competitive struggle for survival, in which shifting cultural demands and opportunities favor now one, now the other group. If instead of race we say gender, class, nationality, religion, ethnic or minority group, we can better understand Veblen, because race is a scientifically obsolete concept. Evolution seems to have allowed for historical patriarchy, to succeed, and within patriarchy capitalism. As the initial conditions of matriarchy were changed historically, those changes have consequences for the life and history of the species. Changes include the uncontrollable acceleration of unnatural conditions now antagonistic to nature and needing a radical realignment. Here Veblen's thinking is congruous with that of Marx, as far as it concerns the dialectical relationship between the categories of base and superstructure, forces and relations of production, and plainly mode of production and nature.[226]

The biological success of old adaptive capacities, let's say climatic fitness for example, shifted in humans to new forms such as spiritual fitness under the influence of cultural conditions that were themselves undergoing change. But the first form of fitness does not completely disappear in the process, although now it may be subject

226 Marx, K. (1859). *A Contribution to the Critique of Political Economy*. Trans: S.W. Ryazanskaya. Moscow. Progress Publishers. Online in MIA. Accessed from <https://www.marxists.org/archive/marx/works/1859/critique-pol-economy/> on 2015-08-09.

to different pressures through the feedback of natural adjustments. We must acknowledge that in the evolution of the human species, spiritual production has to a great extent modified the adaptive power of pure material production.[227] Spiritual production makes it easier to willfully detach from natural morality, by manipulating it to make the consequences less visible and more latent. Although the damage caused to nature in this process may be scientifically clear, the function of mystifying ideology is to provide finely rationalized alternative views. The rather transparent forms of corruption and immorality that prevail today are carefully framed to appear as nature or human nature, when they are in fact the opposite.

This is how spurious changes and maladaptations become spiritually entrained as habits, customs, and laws. These not only induce cascades of new habits of behavior, and of thought in communities; they come to determine principles of conduct that falsely appear natural. Original ranges of innate instinctual dispositions have been changed to adapt to created needs that are artificial and unnatural. The basic requirement for the groups' survival, then, their continued capacity to meet the material requirements of life, in other words their economic contribution to fitness, is flimsier and more perishable the more they have departed from their original form.

Our future as a civilization is thus bound up with the viability of our human stock and institutions, contingent on the new forms of spiritual fitness. The crucial question is: is the type of fitness presently imposed on us by our culture viable and conducive to survival?[228] Culture is a form of adaptation that can either enhance or reduce fitness, or else enhance a form at the expense of the other, unbalancing the whole, as happened with gender preference. Being more and more dependent on spiritual fitness, we must experience our world coherently, which is not the case today. The overwhelming incoherence of capitalism, as we see in the news every day, its destructiveness and wastefulness, is an ominous sign, and we sub-

---

227 Veblen, T. (1918). *The Instinct of Workmanship.* Ibid. P. 11.
228 Veblen, T. (1918). *The Instinct of Workmanship.* Ibid. Pp. 17-18.

liminally know it. Yet we seem dangerously slow in our change of direction, because ideology has dumbed our consciousness.

These Veblerian notions place the present world conflicts, largely compounded of contending institutional ideologies, in a very different perspective that is quite compatible with what I sketch in the present work, the backbone of which is the Horneyian notion of *a morality of evolution*. First of all, they question the notion of capitalism archaically imposed by a white race. This race eliminates a gender and substitutes a class, a European-ancestry patriarchal minority of the world. This group has managed to, through repression and war, gain the universal endorsement of similar national classes, patriarchal, hoarding, and hierarchical, élites of almost every other world group. The premises of this group, the only minority in the world, whether they are economic, political, or ideological, are presented not even as the best, but as the only alternative for humanity's future. What may have been adaptive at some historical juncture, *i.e.,* capitalism in its ascendant stage, is now clearly antithetical to a coherent adaptation of a human species overwhelmed by artificial scarcity and its consequences. These are all working against the species' human fitness. We are presently living the outcome of the historical rupture of a dialectical balance imposed by patriarchy. This is not what nature intended with its design of a dual and balanced instinctual dialectic.

The next logical, and practical, question is whether the key to the future of humanity is equality, starting from gender equality. This implies a return from destructive competition to constructive cooperation towards the universal satisfaction of the needs of all. If psychologically alienation is at the root of our species' ills, meaning by alienation the detouring from a morality of evolution, it would seem that the answer is evident. In Veblen's terms, the balance of two instincts that would exert checks and balances on each other has been disrupted; a return to it would logically be restorative.

Social institutions are in a dialectical relationship, of opposition says Veblen—with natural heredity, here taking a Freudian position.

Genetically, the basic ethnic type heredity is stable in its makeup. This means that instincts and traits are transmitted intact from the beginning of humanity, even though mutations may introduce rare variations. Institutions are the opposite; they are not grounded on natural continuity but on historical change, and therefore are incessantly transforming. This means, in the Marxist metaphor, that in its instinctual ground human nature remains much the same, while in its base and superstructure it constantly tends to change. In the present psychological schema, this oppositional duality corresponds to *sense* and *consciousness*.

1.3.5 Veblen on History

The initial phase in the life of all races has been called savagery, and from there institutional changes have changed the original form to the present process we call civilization. The early human cohorts would today be unable to survive our present conditions and vice versa; we would not last long under Stone Age life conditions, because our adaptational needs and skills have substantially changed and are unfit for them. No matter how much we have evolved in the direction of civilization, however, there persists a sentimental tendency for humans to look back into their earliest natural stages and life history. Someone said we can measure our capacity to foretell by the range of our vision into the past.

Hybrid forms have been the rule throughout the world evolutionarily after the phenomenon of meiosis became operational, phenotypes diverging widely from one another and from their parental types. This form of breeding makes it possible to create specimens with artificially selected characteristics that can be conserved as "pure lines"; this is *selective breeding* historically practiced by farmers for centuries before Darwin. Along the same premise, if the conditions of life of a community consistently favor a given type of hybrid, a selective trend is set in function that redirects the composite pure line in a desired direction. The opposite effect is achieved by intercrossing types; a cumulative trend to diverge from parental stocks is created. It is through these mechanisms that ethnic, national, and local types have emerged in the history of the world, according to Veblen. Although composite pure lines are provisionally stable, they break down under these sustained influences.

Hybrid populations by definition have a greater range of characteristics and higher variation than purebreds. A generic human type of spiritual endowment, let's say altruism or aggression, must be identifiable, however, in the same fashion zoologists identify common physical characteristics as they group species. Individual instinctive dispositions may vary in their presentation, but the basic innate complement of instincts is the same for the species, geared to the same adaptive ends. As it concerns original human nature, the inter-group variation of basic human nature could not be considerable. A slight bias, however, may come to have a decisive butterfly effect "when it works out cumulatively through a system of institutions. Such a system cumulatively carries the practice of generations, during which the life of the community has been dominated by the same bias, even if slight."[229] This is the power of institutionalization. Patriarchy and hierarchy for example, not slight biases by any stretch of the imagination, have had such an effect in human consciousness that they allow for ideology to take its place and appear natural. Their historical effect may have taken place through smaller desensitizing steps, or small biases. Veblen almost says this much in a footnote: "The all-pervading modern institution of private property appears to have been of such an origin, having cumulatively grown out of the self-regarding bias of men in their oversight of the community's material interests."[230] Private property could have been an adaptational tool in a previous form at some early historical point. From let's say personal instrument has, institutionally and spiritually, become human reification, the transfer of human power to capital.

---

229 Veblen, T. (1918). *The Instinct of Workmanship.* Ibid. P. 24.
230 Veblen, T. (1918). The Instinct of Workmanship. Ibid. P. 24.

Group differences regarding inherited spiritual traits are highly significant, because "in the last resort any race is at the mercy of its instincts. In the course of cultural growth most of those civilizations or peoples that have had a long history have from time to time been brought up against an imperative call to revise their scheme of institutions in the light of their native instincts, on pain of collapse or decay; and they have chosen variously, and for the most part blindly, to live or not to live, according as their instinctive bias has driven them."[231] This is equivalent to saying, with Marx,[232] and with Freud,[233] that peoples have, so far, made their history largely unconsciously. To make history consciously, then, would be our human goal for the future. This could be done by synchronizing consciousness and good sense, consciousness and balance of our two instinctual dispositions.

1.3.6 The Two Human Instincts: Parental Bent and Sense of Workmanship

Veblen does not explicitly parse his two instincts sexually, but they can, logically, fit the categories of female and male. In fact, every human individual can express either instinct because s/he has the infrastructure of both, although the natural bias toward one or the other is fairly clear. Our hormonal differences, for example, are not a qualitative but a quantitative matter, alterable through external pressures. The parental bent in Freudian terms is Eros and in Darwinian altruism. The sense of workmanship is Thanatos, food-chain survival-of-the fittest Darwinism, selfish transformation of nature.

---

231 Veblen, T. (1918). The Instinct of Workmanship. Ibid. Pp. 24-25.
232 Marx, K. (1937). *The Eighteenth Brumaire of Louis Bonaparte.* I. Trans. Saul K. Padover. Moscow. Progress Publishers. (Written: December 1851 - March 1852. Orig. Pub. 1852). Online in MIA. Accessed from <https://www.marxists.org/archive/marx/works/1852/18th-brumaire/index.htm> on 2014-11-29.
233 Freud, S. (2014). *A General Introduction to Psychoanalysis.* Eighteenth Lecture. General Theory of the Neuroses. Traumatic Fixation — The Unconscious. (Lectures originally delivered 1916-1917) Online in eBooks @ Adelaide. Accessed from < https://ebooks.adelaide.edu.au/f/freud/sigmund/general-introduction-to-psychoanalysis/chapter18.html> on 2016-04-10.

This instinctual combination is what propels human life through instinctual, *i.e.* hormonal, titration in both sexual diatheses, according to environmental conditions or circumstances. Genes express themselves according to conditions, not mechanically according to sex. With Marx, and Freud, Veblen considers transformational productivity, a sublimation of both instincts into labor, to be the uppermost human, survival-based characteristic. The parental bent is arbitrarily placed in second ranking by Veblen. Both instinctual dispositions have, however, much in common, including the same concrete objective ends, and the mutual furtherance of each by the other. This view diverges from Freud's.

"Parental Bent" (Eros or Altruism) is a notion Veblen acknowledges to have borrowed from McDougall.[234] Veblen defines it as "an instinctive disposition of much larger scope than a mere proclivity to the achievement of children... The parental solicitude in mankind has a much wider bearing than simply the welfare of one's own children."[235] This "wider bearing," sublimatory extension of the instinct, is evident in cultures where schemes of family, private property, and inheritance are different from ours. These are cultures that, for example, consider it morally unsustainable and inhuman for the current generation willfully to waste the resources of coming ones.

The "instinct of workmanship" or ''sense of workmanship," transforming productivity, is a concurrence of several ubiquitous instinctive aptitudes.[236] "The instinct of workmanship, no more than any other instinctive proclivity, is an isolable, discrete neural function; that does not, however, touch on the question of its status as a psychological element."[237] The instinct of workmanship is the instinct to transform, which is to destroy, in order to produce. Veblen narrows its meaning to industrial production, leaving aside other

---

234 McDougall, W. (1921) *An Introduction to Social Psychology.* Fourteenth Edition. Boston. John W. Luce & Co. Online in Internet Archive. Accessed from <https://archive.org/details/anintroductiont00macdgoog> on 2015-08-09

235 Veblen, T. (1918). The Instinct of Workmanship. Ibid. Pp. P. 26.

236 Veblen, T. (1918). The Instinct of Workmanship. Ibid. Pp. 27-28.

237 Veblen, T. (1918). The Instinct of Workmanship. Ibid. Veblen, T. (1918). The Instinct of Workmanship. Ibid. P. 29.

forms such as spiritual and artistic production. Productivity can be traced back to the basic coherence of nature as we have seen, but the parental bent or tending is foremost a characteristic of social species and is uppermost human.

1.3.7 The Persistent Instinctual Duality

In our present patriarchal environment, the facts of life, including biology, tend to be interpreted ideologically, through the lens of the male instinctual disposition, and Veblen is not an exception. His language is at times difficult, due to the pirouettes necessary to explain biological facts in an ideologically biased language. If we translate the instinct of workmanship into transformative productivity, labor, we can include in it the species' reproductive labor, the model of all production. The same goes for the parental bent; if we call it mothering, tending, or altruism, or the social instinct of Darwin, then things become clearer.

Veblen does want to give credit to women for their instinct and their historical contribution but he does it awkwardly and condescendingly because of the straightjacket of his ideologically determined language. The parental bent as equally sharing, for example, bears on the early growth of technology "when the common good of the group was still perforce the chief economic interest in the habitual view of all its members...(and)... Pecuniary competition had not yet become an institution, grounded in the ownership of goods."[238] These sentences give us a glimpse of the historical approach of Veblen. He tells us that distaste for waste, sensitivity to the feelings of workers and of animals and plants, fecundity, fertility, capacity to grow, and skill of care of crops and flocks, are all natural feminine endowments. "There is a magical congruity of great force as between womankind and the propagation of growing things."[239] The "parental" instinct places motherhood in the foreground in all that concerns the common good. Cultures based on tillage and cat-

238 Veblen, T. (1918). The Instinct of Workmanship. Ibid. P. 89.
239 Veblen, T. (1918`. The Instinct of Workmanship. Ibid. P. 93.

tle-breeding pair with motherhood as a central fact in the scheme of human history. In the agricultural phase, the parental bent and the sense of workmanship "worked together to bring the women into the chief place in the technological scheme..."[240]

Women thus exercised a leadership role in early industrial communities because of their technological expediency and moral sense. When the sense of community still prevailed, the natural produce on which the life of the group depended was substantially the contribution of women, as we can see in the descriptions of the life of the Iroquois. "And modern students, imbued with modern preconceptions of ownership and predaceous mastery, have even found themselves constrained by this evidence to discover a system of matriarchy and maternal ownership in these usages that antedate the institution of ownership."[241] The deities then were prevailingly goddesses of fertility and mothers of the people.[242] And subsequently: "With a change of base, from this early husbandry to a civilization in which the main habitual interest is of another kind, and in which the habitual outlook of men is less closely limited by the same anthropomorphic conceptions of nurture and growth, the goddesses begin to lose their preferential claim on men's regard and fall into place as adjuncts or consorts of male divinities."[243]

Veblen argues that matriarchal cultures were, as Rousseau would have it, peaceful, opposite to the Hobbesian ones crafted by the patriarchal hegemony. Peace, not war was "the habitual situation"[244] in matriarchy.

The largely unknown work *The Instinct of Workmanship* of Veblen represents a shift from the classical political economy paradigm that held hegemonic position in the social sciences in the nineteenth century, to the Darwinism of the twentieth. The cold war between the two paradigms is not over, the new sociobiology's taking the

---

240 Veblen, T. (1918). The Instinct of Workmanship. Ibid. P. 94.
241 Veblen, T. (1918). The Instinct of Workmanship. Ibid. P. 95-96.
242 Veblen, T. (1918). The Instinct of Workmanship. Ibid. Pp. 96-98.
243 . Veblen, T. (1918). The Instinct of Workmanship. Ibid. P. 99.
244 Veblen, T. (1918). The Instinct of Workmanship. Ibid. P. 101

explanatory hand at present, while political economy became high-ly technocratized and alien. Veblen was not fully welcomed in the mainstream of academia because of his highly independent, explic-itly materialist, views, close in many ways to a Marx he repudiated but whose influence he could not escape.

In his more popular book, *The Theory of the Leisure Class*,[245] Veblen more originally focuses on the new historical phenomenon of selfish *obsolescence* through disuse that historically contrasts with both the Protestant ethic and with the old custom of the pot-latch. Obsolescence is a new form of patriarchal waste, imposed by the ruling class as a desirable social way to show success. Here his analysis shifts more to social class, while retaining the evolutionary focus.

Most important is his conclusion that the standards of the lei-sure class have an effect not only upon the social structure but also upon the psychology of individuals. When such a point of view is made habitual as the general standard or norm of life, it shapes the character of the members of the society determining their habits of thought, aptitudes, and inclinations. This effect can be produced by a coercive, educational adaptation, influencing the habits of all indi-viduals and the selective elimination of the individuals considered unfit through those very standards.[246]

Here the central contribution of Veblen, in the present context, is the notion of a *dialectical duality of human instinct* and its histor-ical, institutional determinations.

---

245 Veblen, T. (2013). "The Conservation of Archaic Traits." Ch. 9 in: *Theory of the Lei-sure Class*. Ibid. Online in Project Guten-berg. eBook #833. Accessed from <http://www.gutenberg.org/files/833/833-h/833-h.htm#link2HCH0009> on 2014-11-30.
246 Veblen, T. (2013). "The Conservation of Archaic Traits." Ibid.

1.4 THE OVERWHELMING EVIDENCE FOR MOTHER RIGHT: MY READING OF BRIFFAULT

"We have no grounds for assuming that in this primitive state men were physically or mentally superior to women.*[247]

*Tacitus, for instance, states distinctly that among the Germans, who, in his time, had already reached a higher degree of civilization than the one under discussion, the women were by no means inferior to the men, either in size or strength."

Bebel[248]

To the evolutionist who goes beyond anthropological speculation, it cannot but appear notable that no trace of patriarchal organization is to be found in the animal world..."

Briffault[249]

1.4.1 Two Views of History

To read about the penuries of women throughout history, August Bebel's book of political history, *Woman in the Past, Present and Future*, quoted above is a good beginning; it was a product of the awakening of feminism in the nineteenth century. Along the same lines of Veblen's theory of instinct and institutions, Bebel points

247 Bebel, A. (1897). P. 1. *Woman in the Past, Present and Future*. San Francisco Publishing Co. G. B. Behnam. Online in the Internet Archive. Accessed from <https://archive.org/details/womaninpastpres00bebegoog> on 2015-01-17.
248 Bebel, A. (1897). *Woman in the Past, Present and Future.* Ibid. Footnote. P. 1.
249 Briffault, R. (1927). Ibid. Vol 1. Preface. P.v.

out that a continued social practice becomes a habit and gets to be perceived as natural. This is what happened with female servitude. "Servitude that lasts for hundreds of generations ends by becoming a habit. Inheritance and education teach both parties to regard it as a natural state."[250] Bebel's book is a must in terms of the historiography of institutions, particularly institutionalized exploitation and sexual exploitation, relating first to women, and extending to the majority independent of sex.

That women were the first slaves is documented also by recent anthropology.[251] The first written tablet signs describing slaves in Mesopotamia are from about 3,000 BC, and they refer to slave girls; the signs for slave male occur later.[252]

Bebel also points out the necessary restoration of women as equals in a socialist state of the future, only possible with the abolition of the current capitalist relations of production: that is, the private ownership of the means of production and the capitalist division of labor, particularly that between physical and spiritual labor. "In the new community woman is entirely independent, not even subjected to the appearance of supremacy or exploitation; she is a free being, the equal of man."[253]

The other side of the history of women, their continuous contribution and ascendance, is advanced by Robert Briffault who illustrates what we usually miss if we exclusively take the perspective of women's repression and victimization. Briffault illustrates the constant, pervasive and constructive presence of women in societies throughout history and around the world, and the power of women's constant silent insurgency. Briffault, however, does not write his book in response to Bebel but to Westermarck's *The History of*

250 Bebel, A. (1897). *Woman in the Past, Present and Future.* Ibid. P. 1.
251 Adams, R.M. (2005). *The Evolution of Urban Society: Early Mesopotamia and Pre-hispanic Mexico.* P. 95 ff. Chicago. Aldine. (Orig. Pub. 1966).
252 Harman, C. (2002). *A People's History of the World.* Ch. 3. "First Class Divisions." P. 22. London, Chicago and Sydney. Bookmarks.Online in digamo.free.fr/harman99. pdf. Accessed from <APEOPLE'SHXOFTHEWORLD.PDF.> on 2015-08-17.
253 Bebel, A. (1897). *Woman in the Past, Present and Future.* Ibid. P. 154.

Human Marriage,[254] to which Westermarck responded in turn.[255]

The acrimony about the issue of original marriage *vs.* herd promiscuity that spills from scientific anthropology to ideological antagonism and, of course, involves religion, is best illustrated in the public debate Briffault held with Bronislaw Malinowsky, who defended Westermarck's views, about the original issue. In it Briffault, not without sarcasm, states about marriage that "The criticism comes not from the East or from the West, from Bolshevists or from American misbehaviourists. It comes chiefly from the women of England. It is called forth by certain features of our marriage institutions which, while they make husband and wife one, seem to provide that the husband shall be that one. The subordinate position of the wife is indicated by her vow of obedience, by the legal and economic disabilities under which she labours, by her obligation to assume, not only her husband's name, but to set aside her very nationality and assume his."[256]

Here Briffault is an intellectual pugilist that leaves Malinowsky bruised at the end. He continues: "The patriarchal privileges which modern women are disposed to resent are founded in the last resort upon economic advantages. They are not founded upon the possession by men of superior physical force or superior brains, but in the possession of a superior banking account. The dependence of woman in patriarchal society is an economic dependence. That economic advantage of men is not necessarily the outcome of superior ingenuity, but is the result of the division of labour between the sexes. One

---

254 Westermarck, E. (1891). *The History of Human Marriage.* London, Macmillan. Online in the Internet Archive. Accessed from <https://archive.org/details/historyhumanmar05westgoog> on 2015-01-18.

255 Westermarck, E. (1934) "'*The Mothers,' A Rejoinder to Dr. Briffault,*" In: *Three Essays on Sex and Marriage,* Macmillan, London and New York. Pp. 163-335. See also: Westermarck, E. (1936). *The Future of Marriage in Western Civilization,* London and New York. Macmillan.

256 Briffault, R. and Malinowsky, B. (1956). *Marriage, Past and Present: A Debate between Robert Briffault and Bronislaw Mali-nowski.* Ed. M. F. Ashley Montagu. Boston: Porter Sargent Publisher. P. 30-1. Online in Internet Archive. Accessed from <https://ia600403.us.archive.org/28/items/marriagepastpres00brif/marriagepastpres-00brif.pdf> on 2015-01-18.

very definite reason why patriarchal society cannot be supposed to represent the primeval condition of the human race is that such an economic dependence of the women and economic monopoly of the men does not exist in the lower phases of culture. Far from the men possessing the advantage of a superior banking account, it is, on the contrary, the women who are the producers of every form of primitive wealth."[257]

Malinowsky in the debate represents Westermarck's viewpoint, along with the mainstream notion of the eternal institution of marriage. Briffault, on the other hand represents a theory of the evolution of economy, of power, of living and of sexual, and relational, arrangements. Yet, Briffault's life in the memory of anthropology has been short, his name for the most part falling into oblivion and silence. As is the case with all matriarchalists, his is a largely repressed theory in the mainstream, joining ranks with Lafitau, Bachofen, Morgan, Veblen etc..

1.4.2 "Instinctive Dispositions"

Briffault's *The Mothers* is a substantial opus of three volumes in which it is rare to find a paragraph without supporting references from the multiple fields of knowledge hard and soft — "the most wonderful treasure trove of very early references by travelers, priests, scientific observers and adventurers… from a Venetian who was sailing to unknown places and writing down his observations in 1590…" to "cutting-edge science of the day and scholarly references from The Journal of the Royal Anthropological Institute."[258] — collected in a lifetime and written at the end of his life. Robert Briffault (1876-1948) presents the overwhelming evidence for ma-

---

257 Briffault, R. and Malinowsky, B. (1956). *Marriage, Past and Present.* Ibid. P. 58

258 Alton, H. (2010) Ed. "The Moon And Menstruation: A Taboo Subject. Selected extracts from Robert Briffault's The Mothers." A Radical Anthropology Group Publication. Published by the Radical Anthropology Group, c/o Anthropology Programme Leader, School of Humanities and Social Sciences, 4-6 University Way, London E 16 2RD University of East London. Accessed from <http://www.radicalanthropologygroup.org/old/pub_the%20mothers.pdf> on 2014-10-20.

triarchy starting from up-to-date evolutionary anthropology. Hillary Alton from the Radical Anthropology Group tells the story of how a friend, upon his death, left her the book which turned out to be already an abridged version without references. She was intrigued and set out to look for the original, first in the British Library, where there was no trace of the three fat volumes. "To my great surprise it was not in the catalogue, even though it was a huge integrated one. This book really had sunk without trace."[259]

This is what a scathing book reviewer has to say: "In 1920 Professor Lowie stated in his book, *Primitive Society*,[260] that there was not a single theoretical problem on which modern anthropologists are so thoroughly in accord as that concerning the former and present non-existence of a 'matriarchate.' If this statement holds true, and I have no doubt that it does, then the present three volumes of Mr. Briffault do not tend to place him in the ranks of modern anthropologists. Mr. Briffault, in a manner similar to that of his precursors, came upon the idea of a former matriarchate as a convenient tool on which to hinge the idea of social evolution. The concept was, of course, assumed not only *a priori,* but even in contradiction to all known ethnographic facts. The author, in the quiet of his study, modestly proposed 'to draw up a list of the forms of the social instincts, and to investigate their origin.' Having progressed in his investigation to this extent, he discovered, to his surprise, that the social characters of the human mind are, one and all, traceable to the operation of instincts that are related to the functions of the female and not to those of the male."[261] In all this pablum, only the last sentence is true; and it remains so: to the extent we have been able to

---

259 Alton, H. (2010). "The Moon and Menstruation. (Ibid.).

260 Lowie, R.H. (1920). *Primitive Society.* New York. Boni And Liveright. Online in Questia. Accessed from <https://www.questia.com/read/4399132/primitive-society> on 2015-01-17.

261 Loeb, E. M. (1929). Book Reviews. Review of: The Mothers. Robert Briffault. New York: The MacMillan Co., 1927. 3 Vols. American Anthropologist. N. s., 31, 1929. P.146-152. Accessed from <http://onlinelibrary.wiley.com/store/10.1525/aa.1929.31.1.02a00150/asset/aa.1929.31.1.02a00150.pdf?v=1&t=i1hkhpaw&s=aeff-17cec6219936f5918ec15c78f954b7221782> on 2014-10-20.

survive the war on humanity declared by patriarchy since the onset of female slavery, it is only because the maternal social instincts have prevailed that we are still in the struggle.

Briffault's true anthropological misstep is to have challenged the dogma of patriarchy. "Human beings —Briffault says — are ultimately actuated by impulses, such as those towards nutrition and reproduction, which are common to all animals. They are also actuated, like animals, by more specialized *instinctive dispositions* (my italics)."[262] This paragraph brings us to the evolutionary crux of the matter, how is it that nature transitions from organismic reflex, the thesis, to more complex animal instinct, the antithesis, to mediated human consciousness, the synthesis.

What Veblen determined to be the two instincts of production and tending Briffault tells us are biologically traceable to the female of the species. She is the one who invests protein, consciousness and effort in the task of child-rearing that maintains the species. Historically, patriarchs suppressed the expression of the female instinctual disposition, producing a regression from the potential of full humanity back to the morality of the food chain. This species handicap left the expression of the male instinct unconstrained, creating the unbalance of war. The repression of universal love, cascading to that of empathy, of familiarity, of emotion, and even reason, spun to its opposite which is what we are living today, *Homo homini lupus*. The brave Afghani parliamentarian Malalai Joya puts it this way: society is like a bird, one wing being a man and the other a woman. "When one wing of a bird is injured or tied, can the bird fly?[263] Anthropology professor Shanshan Du uses a similar metaphor in the title of her book *Chopsticks Only Work in Pairs*.[264]

---

262 Briffault, R. (1927). *The mothers: a study of the origins of the sentiments. Vol.1.* Preface. p. 45. New York. The Macmillan Company. Online in Hathi Trust Digital Library. Accessed from <http://babel.hathitrust.org/cgi/pt?id=mdp.39015009106751;view=1u p;seq=10> on 2013-06-17.

263 Wikipedia. Malalai Joya. Accessed from <http://en.wikipedia.org/wiki/Malalai_ Joya> on 2015-01-18.

264 Du, S. (2003). *Chopsticks Come in Pairs.* New York. Columbia University Press.

The part of the female disposition repressed by the patriarch is the social instinct, altruism. It is the moral signature of the human species. The female of the species is the provider of life, *self-same production*, in its full sense of human life, because it is she who also builds the foundations of human consciousness in each individual as her child in the pre-Oedipal period. Mothers introduce all the first-order mediations that produce individual consciousness. The male instinctual disposition on the other side is geared to *transformative production*, production based on prior destruction.

These two dispositions originally attributable to the productive capacity of the female in nature must, with the appearance of the sexes, constantly be biased while simultaneously balancing themselves through reciprocity. They are a continuation of balanced destruction and production in evolution. Repressing the female altruistic disposition, as has been the case historically during patriarchy, injures one of the bird's wings. This must have been quite visible as the most painful trauma of humanity during early patriarchy and slavery; now repressed and made a habit, the damage is more difficult to discern.

The principle of *instinctive disposition* held by Veblen, Briffault, and also inherent in Freud's concepts of drive and sublimation, is crucial precisely because it is the bridge between natural and human history. Instinct is the animal intelligence that, mediated into drive, leads to consciousness. Freud struggled conceptually with the issue of instinct and how it is represented in consciousness. "The antithesis of conscious and unconscious is not applicable to instincts. An instinct can never become an object of consciousness— only the idea that represents the instinct can. Even in the unconscious, moreover, an instinct cannot be represented otherwise than by an idea. If the instinct did not attach itself to an idea or manifest itself as an affective state, we could know nothing about it."[265] It may be the affective state that mediates to make instinct an idea, emotions

---

265 Freud, S. (2001). "The Unconscious." The Standard Edition of the Complete Psychological Works of Sigmund Freud. Trans. James Strachey. Vintage. The Hogarth Press and the Institute of Psychoanalysis. Vol. 14: P.177. (Orig. Pub. 1915).

being a natural protolanguage. Freud provided a sketch of mediation as early as in his *Interpretation of Dreams* by showing the gap in the perceptual-motor reflex that allows for mediations to be introduced. Instinctive disposition is verifiable through attitudes and gestures, more deeply through affects, the same way consciousness is verifiable through language.

An instinctive disposition is a relational, reciprocal structure that can be partially understood through George Herbert Mead's concepts of *gesture*[266] (social activity) and *attitude*[267] (inevitable so-

---

266 This is how Mead explains gesture: "What is the basic mechanism whereby the social process goes on? It is the mechanism of gesture, which makes possible the appropriate responses to one another's behavior of the different individual organisms involved in the social process. Within any given social act, an adjustment is effected, by means of gestures, of the actions of one organism involved to the actions of another; the gestures are movements of the first organism which act as specific stimuli calling forth the (socially) appropriate responses of the second organism. The field of the operation of gestures is the field within which the rise and development of human intelligence has taken place through the process of the symbolization of experience which gesture--especially vocal gestures-have made possible. The specialization of the human animal within this field of the gesture has been responsible, ultimately, for the origin and growth of present human society and knowledge, with all the control over nature and over the human environment which science makes possible." Mead, G.H. (1934). "The Behavioristic Significance of Gesture." Section 3 in Mind Self and Society from the Standpoint of a Social Behaviorist (Edited by Charles W. Morris). Chicago: University of Chicago. P. 18. Note 1. Online in: A George H. Mead source page. Accessed from <https://www.brocku.ca/MeadProject/Mead/pubs2/mindself/Mead_1934_02.html> on 2014-09-26.

267 This is Mead's definition of attitude: "There is an organization of the various parts of the nervous system that are going to be responsible for acts, an organization which represents not only that which is immediately taking place, but also the later stages that are to take place. If one approaches a distant object he approaches it with reference to what he is going to do when he arrives there. If one is approaching a hammer he is muscularly all ready to seize the handle of the hammer. The later stages of the act are present in the early stages-not simply in the sense that they are all ready to go off, but in the sense that they serve to control the process itself. They determine how we are going to approach the object, and the steps in our early manipulation of it. We can recognize, then,, that the innervation of certain groups of cells in the central nervous system can already initiate in advance the later stages of the act. The act as a whole can be there determining the process." Mead, G.H. (1934). "The Behavioristic Significance of Attitudes" Section 2 in Mind Self and Society from the Standpoint of a Social Behaviorist (Edited by Charles W. Morris). Chicago: University of Chicago. P. 11. Online in: A George H. Mead source page. Accessed from <https://www.brocku.ca/MeadProject/Mead/pubs2/mindself/Mead_1934_02.html> on 2014-09-26.

cial embeddedness), the latter not to be confused with the aptitude (capacity) of Veblen. The dyad gesture-attitude is a dual, complementary disposition of subjects that makes possible their selves.

All humans, independent of sex, are endowed with both instinctual dispositions, only differently titrated. The historical phenomenon of *gender preference* has partially also biased their balance. From the original, natural classes male and female, historical circumstances shifted the notion of class to the present economic connotation. If the two forms of instinctual disposition were designed towards reciprocal constraint, artificially suppressing one in favor of the other inevitably creates an imbalance effect in the psyche. There is no way out of this conclusion because our mind and essence, consist only in the internalization of the total ensemble of social relations as they are, and not as they ought to be. Social relations internalized as consciousness are the human essence, or human nature. In polarized class society they become ideological, meaning split from each other and antagonistically opposed to one another. I propose that the hemispheric dominance of the brain must be related to the historical dominance of the patriarchal instinctual disposition after the primal coup that historically objectified women.

The result of the forceful repression of women since slavery was instituted, resulting in their hostile objectification, and in the unilateral expression of the male instinctual disposition, I propose, is precisely what has led to our present conflict with nature, the present ecological crisis. The healthily balanced complementarity of mutually self-regulating sexual relations has been substituted by an artificial gender hierarchy that has become social class. The consequence is omnipresent, if carefully disguised, class war constantly waged in many fronts, military war's being just one of them.

Good natural sense is thus confronted with destructive human intelligence. Animal instinct endeavors to balance a functional reciprocal correlation of morphology and environment. Its minimal expression in animals, including humans, is Mead's composite gesture-attitude. "The very nature of this conversation of gestures requires that the attitude of the other is changed through the attitude of the individual to the other's stimulus."[268] What humanity has arrived at today is the loss of this type of delicate but necessary empathic sense, the most basic layer of natural intelligence in species commonality. We experience this today as things' "not making sense." This is the bulk of our daily experience of absurdity, towards which we have become callous.

Marx said that "the relation of man to woman is the most natural relation of human being to human being."[269] The sexual relation in its most basic form reproduces the complementary duality gesture-attitude, a complex dialectic complementarity, that leads to

---

268 Darwin, C. (1859). "Instinct". Chapter 7 in *The Origin of Species by Means of Natural Selection or The Preservation of Fa-voured Races in the Struggle for Life*. London: John Murray: Pp. 234-263. Online in A Mead Project source page. Accessed from <https://www.brocku.ca/MeadProject/Darwin/1859_7.htmL> on 2-16-09-26.

269 The full quote from Marx is: "In the approach to *woman* as the *spoil* and handmaid of communal lust is expressed the infinite degradation in which man exists for himself, for the secret of this approach has its *unambiguous*, decisive, *plain* and undisguised expression in the relation of *man* to *woman* and in the manner in which the *direct* and *natural* species-relationship is conceived. The direct, natural, and necessary relation of person to person is the *relation of man to woman*. In this *natural* species-relationship man's relation to nature is immediately his relation to man, just as his relation to man is immediately his relation to nature – his own *natural* destination. In this relationship, therefore, is *sensuously manifested*, reduced to an observable *fact*, the extent to which the human essence has become nature to man, or to which nature to him has become the human essence of man. From this relationship one can therefore judge man's whole level of development. From the character of this relationship follows how much *man* as a *species-being*, as *man*, has come to be himself and to comprehend himself; the relation of man to woman is the *most natural* relation of human being to human being. It therefore reveals the extent to which man's *natural* behavior has become *human*, or the extent to which the *human* essence in him has become a *natural* essence – the extent to which his *human nature* has come to be *natural* to him. This relationship also reveals the extent to which man's *need* has become a *human* need; the extent to which, therefore, the *other* person as a person has become for him a need – the extent to which he in his individual existence is at the same time a social being." Marx, K. (1844). *Economic & Philosophic Manuscripts of 1844*. (Written: Between April and August 1844; Orig. Pub 1932). Moscow Progress Publishers, 1959; Translated: by Martin Milligan from the German text, revised Third Manuscript. [Private Property and Communism]. Online in MIA. Accessed from <https://www.marxists.org/archive/marx/works/download/pdf/Economic-Philosophic-Manuscripts-1844.pdf> on 2014-09-27.

reciprocity and reverberational collaboration. Gestures, including language, can converse because they are grounded in attitudes that shift under their own reciprocal influence.

Briffault's notion of instinctual disposition is the expression of a dual instinctual object-readiness, an attitude manifest in the character of the human animal, both participants endowed with the capacities of gesture and attitude, leading to a four-pronged dialectical complementarity. The unique, become spiritual, complementarity of human attitude and gesture is of a higher order than the animal's, however, because it entails a symmetrical and reverberational, formal and syntactic, reciprocity. This amounts to the complex and uniquely human phenomenon Hegel called recognition in the *Phenomenology*. Recognition is for the philosopher the psychological *sine qua non* of becoming human. It is lack of recognition that has led to the objectification of women depriving them of the transcendence of their subjectivity.

It is through our natural disposition, the non-hierarchical but complementary binary of gesture and attitude, in philosophical terms transcendence and immanence, that we relate to nature and to each other. How we relate to each other as individuals is largely written in our character structure and demeanor, starting with our gender.

Our species' instinctual disposition has been corrupted through the suppression of its duality. Libido is only masculine.[270] This is tantamount to making the bird fly with one wing.

1.4.3 The Forcefulness of Briffault's Argument

Briffault does not romanticize women, put them on a pedestal, or make them the agents of a hegemony that simply inverts the pa-

---

270 Freud reiterates this assertion many times throughout his work as early as starting with his letters to his friend Fliess. He provides his most detailed argument in: Freud, S. (1933). "Femininity." Lecture 33 in *New Introductory Lectures on Psychoanalysis*. Standard Edition, v. 22. pp. 136-157. London. ogarth Press.

triarchal one. The picture of women that emerges from Briffault's work is not the embellished and infantilized caricature we have for the most part become familiar with, or else the sacrosanct mother, but that of a female animal creature evolved on a par with the male.

During patriarchy, women have been coerced to express themselves substantially as the objects of the desire of men. In this way they have been subjected to paedomorphosis, that is physically reduced in their body mass average to infantile proportions. With this goes the pressure to think like children and to accept a diminished social role. This has been so habitual for so many centuries that it looks natural. Paedomorphosis serves the purpose of diminishing feminine power and agency, and in that way repressing women. The repercussion of this is not only practical for women, but a handicap to the collective subjectivity artificially masculinized through a universally halved instinctual expression from the point of view of the species. These practices become the aliment of the collective mind that takes their form. Normalizing repression as a habit has the effect of avoiding its emotional effects such as the expression of outrage. And yet, in spite of the amount and obvious high cost invested in repression, the immanent right side, the moral side of humanity does not totally succumb. Periodic social unrest and rebellion, unfortunately often mystified under the guise of racial, religious, or national antagonisms, naturally erupt, particularly as a result of economic pressures. The issue returns again and again because it is latent and, mystified, remains unsolved. A conflict not properly recognized, it constantly presses for appropriate expression and recognition.

Briffault explains why he shifted his scientific perspective from that of mainstream anthropology: "I had proposed to draw up a list of the forms of the social instincts, and to investigate their origin. I had not proceeded far before I discovered, to my surprise, that the social characters of the human mind are, one and all, traceable to the operation of instincts that are related to the functions of the female and not to those of the male. That the mind of women should have exercised so fundamental an influence upon human development in the conditions of historical patriarchal societies is inconceivable. I was thus led to reconsider the early development of human society, of its fundamental institutions and traditions, in the light of the matriarchal theory of social evolution... To the evolutionist who goes beyond anthropological speculation, it cannot but appear notable that *no trace of patriarchal organization is to be found in the animal world*...(my italics)"[271] This view constitutes an important update of Lafitau, Bachofen, Morgan and Veblen a Darwinian view more factual and less speculative. It responds to scientific advances in biology and in comparative psychology contributed at the time.

In 1930 cultural critic H.L. Mencken wrote about Briffault: "Primitive society, like many savage societies of our own time, was probably strictly matriarchal. The mother was the head of the family...What masculine authority there was resided in the mother's brother. He was the man of the family, and to him the children yielded respect and obedience. Their father, at best, was simply a pleasant friend who fed them and played with them; at worst, he was an indecent loafer who sponged on the mother. They belonged, not to his family, but to their mother's. As they grew up they joined their uncle's group of hunters, not their father's. This matriarchal organization of the primitive tribe, though it finds obvious evidential support in the habits of higher animals, has been questioned by many anthropologists, but of late one of them, Briffault, demonstrated its high probability in three immense volumes. [*The Mothers: A Study of the Origins of Sentiments and Institutions*]. It is hard to escape the cogency of his arguments, for they are based upon an almost overwhelming accumulation of facts. They not only show that, in what we may plausibly assume about the institutions of early man and in what we know positively about the institutions of savages today, the concepts inseparable from a matriarchate color every custom and every idea. They show also that those primeval concepts still condition our own ways of thinking and doing things, so that 'the societal characters of the human mind' all seem to go back 'to the functions

---

271 Briffault, R. (1927). Ibid. Vol 1. Preface. P.v.

of the female and not to those of the male." Thus, it appears that man, in his remote infancy, was by no means the lord of creation that he has since become."[272] Although Lewis Morgan and Thorstein Veblen had also written in the Darwinian spirit of evolutionary adaptation, the theoretical advance of Briffault consists in further rooting the issue of matriarchy through a comparative approach to other species and, through almost redundant buttressing, from every possibly imaginable field of investigation.

What is popularly known as the Briffault Law, the core of this magnificent opus reads as follows: "The female, not the male, determines all the conditions of the animal family. Where the female can derive no benefit from association with the male, no such association takes place."[273] Briffault continues, in the same paragraph: "Where male cooperation is useful, the male seeks out or follows the female, and it is the latter who determines the segregation of the group and selects its abode."[274] He provides overwhelming evidence from diverse species using an evolutionary benefit-cost analysis, as well from all possible anthropological, historical, and even literary and folk resources.

Unfortunately, the female influence in contemporary and past patriarchal societies has been largely circumscribed to a family immanence, deprived of the accruing transcendence of civil society. Ten thousand years of patriarchy have been unable to erase from memory the previous two hundred thousand, to count only the full humanoid form. The earliest maternal influence in every specimen of the species remains the cornerstone of human identity, as we are finding out through incontrovertible psychoanalytic neurobiology.[275]

---

272 Quoted in Wikipedia, entry on Robert Briffault. H. L. Mencken, Treatise on the Gods, Blue Ribbon Books, 1930, p. 84.
273 Briffault, R. (1927). *The Mothers: a study of the origins of the sentiments.* Vol. 1. Female Home Makers. P. 191. New York. The Macmillan Company. Online in Hathi Trust Digital Library. Accessed from <http://babel.hathitrust.org/cgi/pt?id=mdp.3901 5009106751;view=1up;seq=10> on 2013-06-17
274 Briffault, R. (1927). *The Mothers*. Ibid.
275 Schore, A. (1994). Affect Regulation and the Origins of the Self. The Neurobiology of Emotional Development. Hillsdale, N.J. Lawrence Erlbaum Associates. Online in

1.4.4 The Briffaultian Dialectic and Biological Economy

This is a sample of the scope of Briffault's reasoning: living matter is an energetic system that must constantly renew itself through partial destruction and reconfiguration; these are dialectical processes comparable to catabolism and anabolism. Rebuilding itself (self-maintenance) is matter for economic reasons because it selects reactions, and supports their repetition, which are favorable to present conditions. Matter seeks not simply to repeat, but in the process save energy through ways to manage it more efficiently. This is how adaptation works, the coherence of living matter. Unfavorable conditions produce restlessness in living organisms, a signal that necessities are unfulfilled. These unfavorable conditions thus promote search, foraging and ultimately compromise through variation. In all this, the basic necessity is for energy to operate and generate development. A corollary is that abundance of energetic resources tends to produce complacency while scarcity propels activity.

Instincts, rigid in lower species but in the more advanced progressively pliable, are the primary mechanisms of organismic mobilization. Instincts become dispositions, tendencies, drives, impulses, attitudes and habits. A selective process guided by a natural coherence, discriminating markers of value and usefulness, is necessary. These are our feelings. The function of emotion is to register the use-value of objects and events, and through their emotional correlates, instincts are modified by learning. Human instinctive tendencies are thus mediated by emotions, that in turn are subject to the determination of natural and social heredities, of genome and culture.

Relationally, when for physiological reasons two cells come into contact or fuse, the result is an equilibrium between their favorite reactions. Each one must react synchronically and reciprocally to the other. Merger, as in the fusion of gametes or fertilization, is an evolutionary strategy of survival economically superior to the prior

---

Questia. Accessed from <http://www.questia.com/read/57185676/affect-regulation-and-the-origin-of-the-self-the> on 2013-03-07.

one of cellular fission or self-fragmentation.[276]

The conjugation of protozoa is also the beginning of the process of sexual reproduction. "The most favorable effects of conjugation will naturally result when an organism which has acquired varied activities and adaptations in its struggle against unfavorable conditions conjugates with one which has retained a greater power of nutrition. The latter is typically a female organism and the former a male."[277] This is a collaborative economy of organismic relations toward a better adaptational outcome. It is the female who provides the built-in power of nutrition, the economic substrate for adaptation.

Humankind is part of this dialectic of the biological constitution, but it also developed an economic signal par excellence, the word or meaningful signal, that also stems two-pronged from evolution and tradition, where human history bifurcated from evolution. Briffault subordinates thought to language.

Important also is longevity, which provides enhanced experience and chances of learning by exposure to unfavorable conditions. In the process of learning, adaptation increases at the expense of plasticity, which is precisely the capacity to adapt to varied circumstances. The more brain reactions are hardwired in one direction, the less they can go in another one. Specialization ultimately inhibits the plastic capacity for growth and enhances fixity, or lack of adaptability to diverse circumstances; this has been verified in neurobiology.

Growth and reproductive capacity are inversely proportional to specialization and differentiation. "An unspecialized organism that has had no occasion to adapt itself and become modified and differentiated feeds well, grows quickly, and reproduces freely; a highly

---

276 Investigation at the time Briffault was writing had recently shown that isolated unicellular organisms frequently deteriorate unless they can conjugate with others, and that this is how cells came to be in the first place, by incorporating other cells to make them their organelles. This is also how capitalist mergers and acquisitions are themselves the germ of socialism within the capitalist system.

277 Briffault cites the studies of Maupas and Peptone. Briffault, R. (1927). he Mothers. Ibid. P. 88

modified organism, specially adapted to particular conditions and functions, assimilates poorly, grows slowly, and has little or no power of reproduction."[278] The same way it diminishes the capacity to reproduce, longevity lessens the ability to cope with unfavorable conditions, even if the repertoire of experience is much richer. This is the basic paradox of the life cycle.

Briffault dialectically applies the new, evolutionary epistemology to human origins, with many consequent, theoretical implications for our theory of origins.

1.4.5 About Sexuation

Almost prophetically, if one considers the late cloning developments, and recursiveness, Briffault told us that: "In simple multicellular organisms any detached group of cells will reproduce the whole organism, since each cell inherits the same dispositions which, by their reactions, gave rise to the organic structure. The greater the degree of specialized adaptation or differentiation of the cell or tissue, the less, as in protozoa, will be the power of reproduction."[279] This is plasticity versus specialization.

Briffault points out that some species reproduce through virgin females even tough males exist alongside, exclusively female reproduction's being the rule in families of sawflies and caddis flies, for example. Parthenogenesis is a common phenomenon that does not require a conjugal male. This type of reproduction without sexual involvement is exclusively female. "So far as regards the process of reproduction, no profit results to the female type from conjugation; the race as a whole gains, however, by preserving and acquiring the adaptability of the male type… In sexual reproduction each of the two opposite tendencies is corrected and supplemented by the other. The resulting organism partakes of the male and of the female dispositions. Whether it develops into a male or into a female depends

---

278 Briffault, R. (1927). Ibid. P. 87.
279 Briffault, R. (1927). Ibid. P. 88-89.

essentially upon conditions of nutrition; abundant food giving rise to an excess of females, scarcity to an excess of males. But each organism, whether male or female, inherits the benefits of maternal nutritive tendencies, and of the active, adaptive paternal qualities."[280] This may have deep unexplored implications, for example in the male-female ratio of the human species as a marker of the historical dialectic of abundance and scarcity, and the effect of war in maintaining an artificial scarcity through the sacrifice of males.

The fundamental dynamic relation between the sexes is most clearly expressed as a design of nature to achieve species survival benefit through the timely expression of opposite instinctual proclivities. This principle also seems to apply in self-psychology in the correlative polarity of *me*, the rich reservoir of the historical ensemble of the social relations, and *I*, the operational agent that takes from it.

One of the main problems with most anthropological narratives of origins is their "adultomorphic" nature, their lack of a developmental approach. They start from gendered adults' contending to create culture in one way or another. This is most typically exemplified in Hegel's metaphor of the master and slave, where two immature adults meet and demand a human recognition that neither is capable of giving. Recognition has to be given, and it is the mother who inaugurates it.

The lack of a developmental perspective has marred origins theories. It is here that developmental psychology logically fills the gap. Here it is possible to build on the evolutionary perspective illustrated by Briffault in his work *The Mothers*. Matriarchal narratives are guided by a developmental perspective, because mothers give development to all others. The paradigm opposite to Hegel's is in Vygotzky's "zone of proximal development,"[281] a collaborative

---

280 Briffault, R. (1927). Ibid. P. 91.
281 Vygotsky, L. S. (1978). *Mind in society: The development of higher psychological processes.* Chapter 6 Interaction between learning and development (79-91). Cambridge, MA: Harvard University Press. Accessed from <http://www.cles.mlc.edu.tw/~cerntcu/099-curriculum/Edu_Psy/EP_03_New.pdf> on 2014-09-28.

model.

1.4.6 Developmental Factors in Briffault's Theory

The relation of mother and offspring is, like all life-processes, a mutual adjustment and coordination of actions and reactions. Lengthy gestation in humans results in larger and better-quality offspring at birth, at the cost of smaller numbers. Relative to weight, human gestation is twice as long as that of elephants, which lasts nearly two years. The cortex of the brain so crucial in humans is generally also larger, bulkier, and more complex than that of other animals.

As happens with all organisms, speed in cell reproduction decreases with specialization in humans; bodily growth, therefore, is for the most part in inverse proportion to age; the higher we proceed in mammalian evolution, the longer we find the period of development. The protraction of immature infancy is the most far-reaching and momentous factor in the evolution of the higher animals, including humans.

The period of immaturity in humans does not have the primary purpose of bodily growth, except for the brain, which is stimulated to grow by functional development in interaction with its particular environment. The incomplete development of the brain at birth is much more pronounced in the human baby than in any other species; and this ultimately becomes an advantage as the brain has the opportunity to grow in context. Sensorially, of the distant relational senses, olfactory tracts develop first, visual tracts drag on later, and lastly the auditory paths achieve their unique discriminatory human power. Brain immaturity is also what allows for the crucial social mediation of learning and education.

Economically, the prolongation of gestation and the relative parasitism of the offspring due to the prolongation of its immaturity are serious handicaps for the survival of the female and require high energy expenditures on her part. It is to this necessity that the maternal instinct to provide for the successful growth of the offspring responds.

Through physiological adaptations, one of the manifestations of the maternal instinct is emotion, affective value, which expands, grows, and develops into uniquely human morality. In lower animals the maternal instinct remains physiological, but with evolution, particularly in the quadrumana, it becomes a psychological phenomenon. The maternal instincts are the product of the adaptive evolution of organisms, not a primary tendency of life. They require appreciable time to develop and their evolutionary development is marred by many instances of abandonment, neglect, infanticide, and even maternal cannibalism of the newborn, which can be observed in many species and perhaps even in archaic humans.

1.4.7 Instincts, Tendencies, and Myths

For Briffault, it is a general misconception that affection is part of the attraction between the sexes. Nothing is further from the truth. Sexual hunger is accompanied by cruelty, not love. Cruelty is a natural tendency in predatory animals, and its sexual expression usually takes place as violence, bodily injury, and rape.

The alternative instinct, distinct in origin, function and character, arises only when cooperation is needed in the care of the offspring. This is the *mating instinct*, opposite to the sexual one. The default mode among animal species is separation of the sexes. Sexual association is usually rare and transient, and devoid of cooperation or male protection. Sexual and mating instincts are antagonistic in nature and lust is originally opposed to love.

The repertoire we humans usually experience historically, our range of emotions, is a social modification of the natural instincts. The instinctual characteristics of both genders are inherited by the offspring; those of the opposite sex usually remaining more latent. Through interaction, there is a mutual adjustment of instincts in both sexes. A universal filial instinct is independent of sex, and it has been significantly limited and constrained by civilization. It is a manifestation of affection and respect for the mother today, more clear in the lower cultures. Maternal instincts produce a strong attachment in the offspring that includes dependency. In less developed cultures this phenomenon is lifelong.

All young animals attach themselves to the first creature, animal or human, that will look after them. This is usually the mother. The reliance upon the mother extends to others, even members of different species, provided they are not hostile or dangerous. Taming in animals and "chumship," cliquishness and clannishness in youngsters, are extensions of the maternal bond. The so-called social instincts are developed within the confines of the family; they are a result of the prolonged period of maternal care in infancy.

The social instincts have been typically mystified in literature, but the reality pointed out by Briffault is that originally organisms are attracted towards others by *hunger,* the attraction's being purely selfish and destructive. The need for food leads to group dispersion. "The truth is that there is neither any intrinsic social instinct or any instinct of solitude for its own sake. Such abstract predilections may operate in the realms of culture and conceptual thought, but they have no bearing on the behavior of unsophisticated life. Other impulses, such as the sexual impulse, or the infantile dependence of offspring, may keep or bring animals together; or they may, as does the competition for food, drive them apart; but whether they come together or seek segregation their behavior is not the effect of any 'gregarious or 'antigregarious' disposition, but of a need for the satisfaction of which either aggregation or solitude is favorable...All familial feeling, all group sympathy, the essential foundation, therefore, of a social organization, is the direct product of prolonged maternal care, and does not exist apart from it...In regard to individuals that are not members of the family group, the original instincts of the cautious, competitive animal, retain their full force; the stranger is regarded with spontaneous hostility and hatred."[282] The "social in-

---

282 Briffault, R. (1927). Ibid. P. 157.

stinct" is merely the extension of the maternal instinct for Briffault, and in these lines there is a sketch of how females of the species, mothers, not only reproduce but originally invented culture.

Groups of associated animals originate from reproductive, not cooperative or social functions and all quadrumana are also polygamous, according to Briffault. Packs of canines that seem to forage cooperatively are only adventitious and temporary; they are the exception to the rule. Sexual association is determined by the reproductive needs of the female. The competition of males is truly not for the possession of a particular female but for access to the largest possible number of females, Herds are usually led by females as are migrations, rudiments of a social feeling's being more developed among the carnivores. Animal families are originally constituted by mother and offspring and males, often absent, are not an essential part of them.

1.4.8 From Family to Herd

Here Briffault sketches for us the opposite evolutionary foundations of family and civil society. Herds are not simply associations of families; herd and family are opposites. Herd association means the dissolution of the maternal group or family. In the family, the male's activities are conditioned and dictated by the instincts of the female; not so in the herd, where there is a shift and male instincts predominate.

To impregnate as many females as possible, the masculine instinct manifests itself in the herd. The herd is the exclusive product of the sexual impulse, and mating or maternal instincts have no place in it. "When the mother, in obedience to the sexual impulse, joins the herd, she renounces the exercise of those maternal instincts which directly conflict with the sexual instincts, and abandons her male offspring. The family group is abolished. The circumstance of polygamy or of monogamy has no bearing on the essential constitution of the groups. The maternal instinct is not atrophied as a result of polygamous intercourse, but the polygamous group results from the atrophied condition of the maternal instinct; polygamy is an effect, not a cause...What does matter is whether the operation of the maternal instincts is prolonged or shortened, and whether the group formed by those instincts is or not broken up by a different association in which the maternal are supplanted by the sexual impulses."[283] Here, maternal and sexual impulses are opposites, and relate in an inverse way, one growing at the expense of the other.

The herd is therefore the masculine expression, the same way the family is the female's. The conditions required by a family are obtained by the segregation of the female, who retires and secludes herself from the herd. While herbivorous females tend to separate from their offspring to join the male herd, carnivorous females are joined by the male, whose sexual instinct is inhibited by the maternal function. Whenever association of large numbers of animals takes place, there is a tendency for the matrilocal family group to lapse into a patrilocal herd. The male herd, product of ephemeral sexual impulses, is not a stable association, as is the family.

The earliest human societies were primarily reproductive units. The human group did not develop out of the animal herd, its distinctive characteristic being the unparalleled development of a social instinct that only prevails in families through dependence and prolonged association. Physiologically, the human species is characterized by prolonged gestation and prolonged immaturity of the offspring, both linked to maternal functions that make herd life incompatible with it.

By the same token, it is not possible to imagine that an isolated family could have alone survived predatory natural conditions to develop language and mind. The beginning of humanity, like that of life itself, demands propitious conditions. Still, extant family-based scattered groups are the exception, unsuccessful families' being pushed out to unfavorable conditions by more advanced groups. "That the social human group should be much larger than the ani-

---

283 Briffault, R. (1927). Ibid. P. 192.

mal family is a condition of human progress no less indispensable than the permanency of its character. All that is involved in human evolution postulates a much larger group than the family, and we, in fact, find all human communities above the most miserable and degenerate, in much larger groups, and the larger those groups, the greater, as a rule, is their cultural and social development."[284]

1.4.9 Exogamy

After analyzing several possibilities, Briffault concludes that there is only one way the female constitution of the family could have been maintained and expanded. Sons would leave the group and daughters remain to pair with males from other groups. Exogamy became the rule and the identity of the original family group was conserved. "The germ of human development lay in the feminine family group nursed to more powerful maturity by the maternal instinct; the fruits of that development were possible only by the formation of larger associations."[285] Any other arrangement would have resulted in the destruction of the original family group, based on the maternal instinct, and such experiments would have been eliminated by natural selection.

The exogamic system became the most important and inviolable rule. Sibling marriage and male sexual predation in families were thus avoided. A milder form of inbreeding is still extant: cousin marriage. The rule of exogamy derives from the constitution of the maternal group. If females were to leave the group, it would be destroyed by the loss of its maternal constitution. Additionally, women clearly have a tendency to a more sedentary character compared to drifting men, and mothers needed to drive their male offspring away to encourage exogamous sexual unions. Males moved into the bride's household or visited, and were bound by the rules and obligations of the mother-in-law's household.

---

284 Briffault, R. (1927). Ibid. P. 199.
285 Briffault, R. (1927). Ibid. P. 202.

There is plenty of proof — in Briffault's words — that, contrary to the tirades of earlier historians, women in primitive societies were not in abject conditions but on the contrary held the uppermost authority. Men in many extant groups that he mentions are still clearly subordinate to the maternal rule.

1.5 HOW WOMEN INVENTED CULTURE: MY READING OF CHRIS KNIGHT

"For language to work, in short, there has to be a deeper, sub-linguistic level of mutual understanding already built up in relation to the most important things and underpinning any agreement on the more superficial level of purely linguistic usage."

Chris Knight.[286]

1.5.1 Method and Building Blocks

For language to work, there must be a ground that Marx called the ensemble of the social relations, and that G.H. Mead called attitude. Humans all carry that ground in the *"me"* part of our-selves.

Totemism, myth, religion, philosophy, and science are successive historical explanatory forms that emerge from that collective ground. Their succession reflects changes in how we relate to each other in the production and reproduction of our lives. The succession of forms is dialectical, not linear, with variation according to conditions. It does not discard past forms but builds upon them, in part conserving them. A totem is replaced by a banner, insignia or designation. A myth may be today an ideological rendition or a temporary patch for an unfinished theory, and religion is alive, as is philosophy here trying to coexist, there jostling with science.

The issue with myth, religion or philosophy is not to discard them as merely obsolete, unintelligible, or meaningless, but how to understand them in the context of the different conditions of their respective historical moments. It is the meeting of diverse horizons,

---

286 Knight, C. (1991). *Blood Relations. Menstruation and the Origins of Culture*. Introduction. P. 18. New Haven and London. Yale University Press.

sender and receiver, that brings our understanding. As a manifesta-tion of a social form of relation, every myth fits its nook in the large puzzle of history. As it happens, with dreams myth interpretation endeavors to find the historical context that lends it coherence, the compromise of different horizons. Therapeutic dreams fit interper-sonal puzzle gaps caused by dissimilar perspectives, just as actions fulfill needs.

What stamps legitimacy on the understanding of a myth is its fit into the context, the larger story. Marx said: "Darwin has interested us in the history of Nature's Technology, *i.e.*, in the formation of the organs of plants and animals, which organs serve as instruments of production for sustaining life. Does not the history of the productive organs of man, of organs that are the material basis of all social or-ganization, deserve equal attention? And would not such a history be easier to compile, since, as Vico says, human history differs from natural history in this, that we have made the former, but not the latter? Technology discloses man's mode of dealing with Nature, the process of production by which he sustains his life, and thereby also lays bare the mode of formation of his social relations, and of the mental conceptions that flow from them. Every history of religion, even, that fails to take account of this material basis, is uncritical. It is, in reality, much easier to discover by analysis the earthly core of the misty creations of religion, than, conversely, it is, to devel-op from the actual relations of life the corresponding celestialized forms of those relations. The latter method is the only materialistic, and therefore the only scientific one. The weak points in the abstract materialism of natural science, a materialism that excludes history and its process, are at once evident from the abstract and ideological conceptions of its spokesmen, whenever they venture beyond the bounds of their own speciality."[287] Sociobiological constructs today,

---

287 Marx, K. (1887). "Machinery and Modern Industry." In: *Capital.* Volume One. Chap-ter Fifteen. Footnote 4. First English Edition. Trans: Samuel Moore and Edward Aveling, edited by Frederick Engels. Moscow, USSR. Progress Publishers; (Orig. Pub. 1867). Online in MIA. Accessed from <https://www.marxists.org/archive/marx/works/1867-c1/ch15.htm> on 2015-01-24.

such as "memes,"[288], mechanically applied from a natural to a social field of science, are examples of natural science's abstract materialism. Abstract materialism is a remnant of idealism, a fractured science that portrays the fracture of its ground, class-directed society.

In his early analysis of myth leading to the theory of historical matriarchy, Bachofen, as did Frazer and, most recently, Max Weber, for the most part took the easy way: they looked at the determining effect of religion on social organization. Their theories reflect their historical period. Marx took the opposite, much harder, path. It is much more difficult, as he said, to properly make the correlations starting from the relations of production. But we can safely say, using the developmental approach of scientific psychology, that early mythical explanations show the necessity of alienation of human infancy. Like very young children, the species could not stand on its own yet, not to talk about produce either materially or spiritually, as compared to today's norms. Young children, and correspondingly young humanity, had to lean on an external object, the mothers as they do today. Mothers, then phylogenetic infants, also had to spiritually lean, because philosophical or scientific explanations were not possible then. They had only nature in the form of totems to reflect their identity, plus the imaginary representation of nature and group-belonging as a sacred unity, as God. God, the projection of goodness, righteousness and perfection, in other words morality, became the imaginary companion of mothers. This was the first human display of creative collective imagination made possible by language. Regarding historical matriarchy, in the wake of Bachofen, Morgan and Frazer, the critical work of Robert Graves, Merlin Stone, and Marija Gimbutas, among other feminists, has accomplished a better scientific approximation. Additionally, the work of Jean Piaget, Lev Vygotsky, and other developmentalists allows for an inference as to how the phylogenetic infancy of humanity may have looked regarding intelligence and mythical knowledge.

---

288 Dawkins, R. (2006.). *The Selfish Gene*. Oxford and New York. Oxford University Press. (Orig. Pub. 1976). Accessed from <http://www.arvindguptatoys.com/arvindgupta/selfishgene-dowkins.pdf> on 2015-01-28.

Developmentally, the phylogenetic mythical stage of explanation would grossly correspond to the ontogenetic pre-operational stage of Piaget.[289]

Chris Knight also chooses to take the difficult road. Basing his argument on the work of Levi-Strauss on myth, he interprets it critically, and buildd upon it based on the sociology of Marx and the current empirical facts of anthropology and sociobiology. Marx provides the fundaments of his method; Levi-Strauss the value of the pervasive universality and structural unity of myth; and sociobiology provides the counterpoint, the ideological challenge. This is a contest about an historical period that, by natur,e remains mythical, and has to be reconstructed archeologically.

1.5.2 The Old Patriarchal Hypothesis Inverted

Darwin, for the first time, made the questions of human origins and the invention of culture a pressing one for science; before him, the puzzle had been resolved largely through faith-based religious creationism. Darwin's patriarchal bias, as is Hegel's, and Freud's, is revealed in his lopsided emphasis on competition and the Malthusian survival of the fittest, generally understood as the survival by raw material force that generally applies to the food chain. Saying that males fight to have access, instead of saying that females choose fit partners, is a typical patriarchal inversion.

Freud, among others, borrowing from the anthropology and biology of his day, postulated along the same lines his theory of origins in *Totem and Taboo*.[290] Brothers collaborate to kill the alpha father and culture is then created on the foundation of guilt. Freud's purpose was to find the parallelisms between primitivism and neuro-

---

289 Piaget, J. (1952). Origins of intelligence in children. Trans. Margaret Cook. New. York. International Universities Press. Online in University of Pittsburgh. Accessed from <http://www.pitt.edu/~strauss/origins_r.pdf> on 2017-02-12.

290 Freud, S. (2012). Totem and Taboo Resemblances Between the Psychic Lives of Savages and Neurotics. Trans: A. A. Brill. Online in Project Gutenberg. EBook #41214. Accessed from <http://www.gutenberg.org/files/41214/41214-h/41214-h.htm> on 2014-10-04

sis, regression in development. The social organization of the alpha male is not historical but still natural, and thus legitimate.

Murderous destructive solidarity is thus the ground of the patriarchal social contract for Freud. Solidarity replaces the natural precedent of the food chain. It is the resulting fear of loss of protection and Oedipal guilt that result in counterphobic rules, such as the incest taboo, religion and exogamy, that in themselves perpetuate the memory of the idealized tyrant. The mark of the bloody event is left in the human mind as the structuring universal human signature of the Oedipus Complex. To his credit, Freud resorts to mythology to close the circle, if wrongly. Freud's inverted myth replaces the one of the historical carnage of mothers.

From a matriarchal standpoint, it is Bachofen's Orestes, not Freud's Oedipus, that bespeaks the true tragedy that structured the gender split in the human mind. Maternal dependence is so crucial that the antagonistic inversion had to be catastrophic in nature. Margaret Mahler[291] documented the psychology of human separation and John Bowlby[292] and Mary Ainsworth,[293] among others, deepened the understanding of traumatic separation and loss that must also apply phylogenetically to the species. The obvious disorders in our forms of attachment respond to an original separation trauma.

The selfish pyramidal organization of chimps, considered the paradigm of transition to humanity, particularly because of the high genomic share with the human species, has been recently challenged by contemporary primatology. Bonobos, with the same genetic sharing, if not higher, display a completely different social organization: peaceful, sedentary, and with features closer to what has been de-

---

291 Mahler, S. and Pine, M.M. and F., Bergman, A. (1973). *The Psychological Birth of the Human Infant,* New York: Basic Books.

292 Ainsworth, M. D. S., & Bowlby, J. (1991), "An ethological approach to personality development." American Psychologist, 46, 331-341. Accessed from <http://www.psychology.sunysb.edu/attachment/online/ainsworth_bowlby_1991.pdf> on 2015-08-10.

293 Ainsworth, M. D. S., & Bell, S. M. (1970). "Attachment, exploration, and separation: Illustrated by the behavior of one-year-olds in a strange situation." Child Development, 41, 49-67.

scribed as a possibly matriarchal human society. In self-feeding, for example, bonobo males defer to females. More importantly, bonobos use sex as contingency in social regulation, including conflict resolution. Bonobos perversely foreplay in all sorts of imaginable sexual combinations, usually prior to eating, and, in the presence of male conflicts, females use sexual maneuvering to mediate, appease, distract and resolve.[294] These facts are in support of Knight's theory.

From an anthropology perspective, Chris Knight offers an alternative theory to Freud's, that also starts from solidarity, more persuasive female solidarity. His theory is supported by data from several sources and foremost by the good fit of its facts into a logic of nature. It had been pointed out by Paul Turke[295] that males, having access to many mates reduces confidence of paternity and therefore paternal care, and that ovulatory concealment, synchrony, and extended sexual receptivity pressured protohominids to share their reproductive interest, and for males to behave paternally. Male tendency to sexually monopolize multiple females had to be countered. Data from the literature on several species, including modern humans, was presented to support Turke's argument. The synchronization of ovulatory rhythms to the cycles of nature, such as the moon's, had been found in some species, marine in particular,[296] and a tendency to menstrual synchronization in females sharing living quarters had also been described.[297] Also, in the anthropological literature Sahlins had argued that although primate societies were ridden with violent conflict about food, hierarchy and sex, hunter-gatherer humans were egalitarian and organized, through rules

294 De Waal, F. (1995). "Bonobo Sex and Society The behavior of a close relative challenges assumptions about male supremacy in human evolution", Scientific American, vol 272, no 3, p 82-88.
295 Turke, P.W. (1984). "Effects of ovulatory concealment and synchrony on protohominid mating systems and parental roles." Ethology and Sociobiology. 5:33-44.
296 Knight, C. (1991). *Blood Relations.* Ibid. Chapter 7, The Shores of Eden. P. 223 ff.
297 McClintock, M.K. (1971). "Menstrual Synchrony and Suppression." Nature 229, Pp. 244 - 245. McClintock, M.K (1978). "Estrous Synchrony and its Mediation by Airborne Chemical Communication (Rattus Norvegicus). Hormones and Behavior 10: 264-276.

and taboos that subordinated distribution and sex.[298]

Additionally, science historian Donna Haraway[299] had unmasked the political nature of modern theories about human origins, and motivated a new generation of young, feminist, female primatologists to conduct their research critically. The active alpha-male and passive-female theories were questioned; and the agency and unique evolutionary interests of females were brought to the table. Knight uses these threads.

1.5.3 The Primacy of Solidarity and Blood

Solidarity, not competition, is the basic ingredient of culture in Knight's view, and females have the natural endowments and proclivity. Solidarity originates practically, in the process of fulfilling natural needs. It is instinctually grounded. Solidarity in primates on the basis of their genetic benefit, for example, is by no means a groundless construct.[300]

To the primitive mind, females have the enviable capacity to cyclically control the flow of the most awesome and revered life element, blood. Blood is life, and it is therefore the equivalent of spirit and soul. Flowing menstrual blood in women is a signal that regulates sexual access, and an alert that the fertile phase of a cycle is predictable. Blood entails separation but also anticipates conjunction, moving away and moving towards, the most basic, elementary, opposite relational structures of a natural society. Moving against, this is the next relational possibility, the extra-domestic domain of males.

Female solidarity was originally achieved through a synchronized sexual strike, particularly directed to the alpha male. Females

298 Sahlins, M.D. (1960). "The origin of society." Scientific American. 203(3). 76-87. Online in Radical Anthropology Group. Accessed from <http://radicalanthropologygroup.org/sites/default/files/pdf/class_text_036.pdf> on 2015-02-27.
299 Haraway, D. 1989. *Primate Visions. Gender, race and nature in the world of modern science.* New York & London. Routledge.
300 Knight, C. (1991). *Blood Relations.* Ibid. P. 18.

used the synchronization of ovulation along the lunar cycle, and, foremost, menstruation as the visible signal to enforce solidarity. Females' menstruating simultaneously blocked the access for the alpha male without violence. The economic advantage was the inclusion of all males, not only the alpha. This has obvious gene-pool benefits and advantages to the increase in population. Besides, sexual access could be made contingent on productivity. During the strike period, males could focus on the hunt. Males will come home bringing with them meat, the outcome of their effort. Social value shifted from the prowess of the alpha to productivity; sexual access became the reward. This was a way to motivate uninterested males to contribute their effort to the remarkably difficult and costly task of raising children. The biological cost of child-raising had been left for the females to incur previously.

Using the sociobiology metaphor, Knight says: "…memes which specified something about how society should be organized…could never have percolated through a population riven by boundary disputes, inequalities, or power conflicts, for the simple reason that the dominant and subordinate, those in one coalition and those in the next, would have had such very different interests or perspectives. Wherever a political or sexual-political meme traveled from brain to brain, replicating itself in identical copies, it could only have been because the individuals so connected already possessed much in common. They must have shared the same social and political interests, providing them with a common vantage point from which to view their world. In this context, the fact that so many widely dispersed contemporary populations of hunter-gatherers (among other peoples) share mythologically and ritually codified memes of the kind says much about the scope of coalition-forming which the human revolution must have entailed."[301] Shared necessities, common problems, and interests breed solidarity.

The human female loss of estrus and her continuous sexual receptivity, of which anthropologists have usually made so much,

---

301 Knight, C. (1991). *Blood Relations*. Ibid. P. 19.

does not impress Knight; more important is menstruation. Even before "no-access" menstruation made females partners in the rhythms of nature, and there they found the possibility for forms of social regulation, first solidarity and next no access; if nature is cyclic, why not society? Although the research on the synchronization of female ovulation and menstruation is inconclusive, the following quotation by a scientific skeptic is relevant: "Whether or not menstrual synchrony occurs in humans is still an open question. Ovarian cycles in vertebrates have adapted to a wide range of environmental stimuli (McClintock, 1981, 1983a, 1983b), McClintock (1983a, pp. 136-140, Table I) listed 36 species of mammals in which reproductive synchrony, suppression, and enhancement occur in female groups in natural environments. Eighteen of these species, not including humans, are shown as having synchronous ovarian cycles as the result of interactions between females; eight of the species are primates. There is no *a priori* reason why humans should be an exception."[302]

To make it universal and to avoid the possibility of cheating, menstruation can be faked through the use of natural colorants such as hematite, red ochre, and fruit juices that resemble and that can last longer than blood. Bodily painting can easily mimic menstruation to bring all females on line.

Menstruation could then become institutionalized along the cycles of the moon. This was reinforced by rituals of segregation and those of return with the products of hunting. Social rules and habits converge and make sense, spread through matrilineal blood moieties, and eventually result in forms of exchange, and exogamy. The latter are associated with not eating your own kill and not having sex within your own family. Here we can fit totemism, myth and ritual, and the art of body-painting, the language of signals as symbolic first-order mediations. Matriarchal social solidarity enforces the first

---

302 Clyde Wilson, H. (1992). "A Critical Review Of Menstrual Synchrony Research." Neuroendocrinology. Vo. 17. No. 6. pp. 565-591. Online in University of California in Santa Barbara Psychological and Brain Sciences. Accessed from <https://labs.psych.ucsb.edu/roney/james/other%20pdf%20readings/reserve%20readings/wilson.pdf> on 2017-02-12.

negation-based social rules: "No access," and "no meat, no sex." Women condition men to cooperate in the collective survival under the *quid pro quo* of sexual gratification. This is not prostitution, as some would think because it does not go against the social rules, but, on the contrary produces them.

The blunt factual "no" is as much a subversion of the natural order of things as killing the tyrant was for Freud, only not as destructive, but because of the constructive nature of the protagonism of the female instinct. Synchronized menstruation does not intend to destroy alpha males, but only to help them postpone gratification along with everyone else. Solidarity in refusal also means universal access at the behest of the females. Access is restored, it is universal, all inclusive, provided all males successfully bring meat from the hunt for females and their families. In social interaction, this is equivalent to reciprocal action with mutual gain. In the meantime, males of moieties can only eat at their mothers', and they can only have sex outside, at their consorts' abode, not their mothers'. The central organizing rule is "not of or with your own," that means both "no incest," and "no eating of your own kill."

Solid evidence is presented by Knight from the anthropological record for solidarity, for cultural cyclicality, and for the power of blood and menstruation in the aboriginal mind. The same is true for what is available about female synchronization, sexual economic transactions, and the findings of crayons for body painting and early mining for red pigments. In other words, every step of the theory is well grounded on facts, to the extent the state of anthropology permits. This is a well-grounded theory that totally inverts the mainstream valuation of the phenomenon of female menstruation.

Most important, however, is the coherence of the narrative that for the first time seems to solve many problems that could not be solved before within the scope of the traditional patriarchal theories.

1.5.4 The "Meme" Compromise

There are two opposite familiar dreams interspersed in the human sciences: one is to find, as in natural science, "the unit" of social phenomena; the other, similarly, seeks "the elementary structures." Two ideological tendencies are here in conflict with each other. The unit is an extension of the Robinson Crusoe paradigm, usually embodied in the adult patriarchal white male. The elementary structures paradigm operates differently; it represent the focus on relations. Exclusive focus on the first one tends to be ideological, the second's being more realistic, as in nature everything is related to everything else.

The unit approach is analytic and it included intrapsychism in psychoanalysis. This has substantially shifted to the relational paradigm as psychoanalysis has evolved.[303]

Since Leucippus and Democritus, the atom was considered to be the indivisible unit of matter, but today the atom is considered a set of yet smaller interrelating particles. Similar conceptualizations in the new discipline of linguistics led to the phoneme,[304] that also consists of sets of anatomical and physiological relational structures. In biology, Mendel discovered the gene, the unit of heredity, that also consists in a structure of relations between smaller nucleotides and molecules. The quests continues along these two paradigms. The search for the unit prevailed during the last period of idealism. There has been a shift in modernity that started with the grand narratives. This shift tends to synthesize and integrate seemingly disparate sciences, and here sociobiology has taken the lead.[305]

303 Mitchell, S.A. (1988). *Relational Concepts in Psychoanalysis. An Integration.* Cambridge, MA. Harvard University Press.

304 Trubetzkoy, N.S. (1969). *Principles of Phonology.* Trans. Christian A. M. Baltaxe. Berkeley and Los Angeles. University of California Press. (Orig. Pub. 1958). Accessed from <http://www.ucpress.edu/op.php?isbn=9780520015357> on 2015-01-27.

305 Tooby, J., and Cosmides, L. (1992). "The Psychological Foundations of Culture." In Barkow, J. Cosmides, L., Tooby, J., Edi-tors. *The Adapted Mind: Evolutionary Psychology and the Generation of Culture.* New York: Oxford University press. Accessed from: <http://www.cep.ucsb.edu/papers/pfc92.pdf> on 2014-10-27.

Political economy is most telling in this regard, with commodity as unit of exchange for the satisfaction of human needs in capitalism. Marx saw the commodity as the cell of bourgeois economy, but within it was an whole history of human relationships, human needs, and the history of the form of their fulfillment. This is how Marx strenuously analyzed the unit commodity as a first step, but only then synthesized the outcome of his analysis in a practical social theory based on historical laws with predictive capacity. In such theory, there is a prediction to a return to matriarchal equality and communism, to a true human universality.

In the historical moment of evolutionary science, the meme is an attempt to spiritually replicate the gene, rather mechanically, applying the unit construct to consciousness: not a bad metaphor if it were not for the ideological dangers. The gene is the unit of organic replication. The organism is the vehicle of genes, a larger unity.[306] The danger is alienating human agency largely determined by freedom, modeling it exclusively biologically and therefore regressively. In other words, the danger is legitimizing alienation on powerful biological grounds. The signature of humanity is to have in part exited biological determinism through its own mediations. The replication of consciousness includes creative imagination.

Knight accepts the challenge of sociobiology and compromises to a point, accepting the meme as a metaphor of the unit of conceptual transmission, while placing it in the larger context of Marxist sociology and historical materialism. Anthropology, if anything, often uses small historical fragments to reconstruct full objects from the past through synthesis, logical connections, and imagination. In psychoanalysis the unit symptom serves a similar purpose. But, like commodities, phonemes, genes, and memes, symptoms are reducible to relational moments. They are, besides symbolizations, condensations and displacements within processes, narratives and

306 Dawkins, R. (2006.). "Introduction to the 30th Anniversary Edition." In: *The Selfish Gene*. Oxford and New York. Oxford University Press. (Orig. Pub. 1976). Accessed from <http://www.arvindguptatoys.com/arvindgupta/selfishgene-dowkins.pdf> on 2015-01-28.

theories that lost them. Like psychoanalysis, anthropology largely conducts its work by renewed attempts to complete the big puzzle, often based on hypotheses that change with historical changing conditions. Hypotheses are subordinated to the larger determinations, and only confirmable by their perfect fit.

Genes and memes are good examples of the fetishism of the analytic, unit-guided method. In the dialectical method one necessarily leads to two, and two to three, and we do not always know from which we are starting. They each give the first impression, as the atom did, that they are indivisible units, until their substratum, the more elementary set of relationships, is discovered. There is motion in nature, and motion is a relationship; but activity and agency are qualitatively different from motion like one, two, and three. Today's subjectivity is the rich accomplishment of the whole human history of human relations, and still in formation everyday. Like Freud's entelechies, the alienating-meme theory regresses us back to nature and the object, and unwittingly or not attempts to redact history and subjectivity with a strike of the pen.

Knight takes up the challenge of sociobiology for two reasons. First, as an anthropologist he cannot simply ignore it; he has to refute it with science. Second, the kernel of truth in it, the formal expression of ideology in the interpretation of the facts, must be exposed. Sociobiology is to today's Marxism what political economy was to Marx, Knight tells us. Here are represented two historical moments, industrial capitalism and its financial corporatist bubble desperate for legitimization, to appear natural, from biology.

The meme's gene-extension theory of agency can thus be best understood within the larger philosophical context of Hegel and Marx's theory of alienation, and Lukacs' reification. The fetishism of the meme is a historical reflection of the fetishism of commodity.[307]

---

307 Marx, K. (1887). "The Fetishism of Commodity and the Secret Thereof." In: Capital. Vol. 1. Ch. 1. Section 4. First English edition Trans: Samuel Moore and Edward Aveling, edited by Frederick Engels. Moscow, USSR; (Orig. pub: 1867). Progress Pub-lishers. Online in MIA. Accessed from <https://www.marxists.org/archive/marx/

The same way Marx built upon the theories of Smith and Ricardo, Knight does upon Paul Turke's sociobiology. Instead of looking for a line of development from hunter-gatherers to bankers, he moves from ovulatory synchrony to capitalism transcended. In Turke's theory there was gender egalitarianism amounting to a kind of coalition-building and communism. As Meszaros would say, sociobiology is now in its historical "moment" the way political economy was then.[308] But all historical ripples do not have the same effect; the pebble falling in the water makes waves differently from the meteorite. I say this to compare the mechanical poverty of the meme that jumps from brain to brain to the dialectical richness of Marx's alternative, his "ensemble of the social relations."[309] Although these paradigms are not incompatible, it is a matter of taking sides. Their synthesis, if they were thesis and antithesis, would be the ensemble of all possible "memes" produced by all generations, going back to Mitochondrial Eve that is present in the *me* part of each self, except that each meme has a material human act beneath it. Memes would have been exclusively jumpstarted by mothers, then inverted by men, the equivalence of a communal relational history forced into an individualistic one. Then we have to ask: was this a necessary break in natural continuity? And if so, has the break overstayed its welcome?

Quoting Lucien Seve: "In this way, one conceals behind the individual's lack of biological equipment at birth the fabulous wealth of his eccentric social equipment, one transforms the crying fact of the individual's total pre-established insertion in a determinate world of social relations into an 'almost complete lack of pre-established integration', and thereby the necessity, of individual life-processes disappears behind the antiquated myth of the freedom of an 'Ego'

works/1867-c1/ch01.htm#S4> on 2015-08-11.

308 Meszaros, I. (2005). *The Power of Ideology.* London and New York. Zed Books.

309 Marx, K. (1969). *Theses on Feuerbach. Sixth.* Trans: W. Lough. Marx/Engels Selected Works, Volume One, p. 13 – 15. Mos-cow, USSR. Progress Publishers, (Written: by Marx in the Spring of 1845, but slightly edited by Engels; Orig. Pub: As an appendix to Ludwig Feuerbach and the End of Classical German Philosophy in 1888). Online in MIA. Accessed from <> on 2014-10-29.

which so-called scientific psychology borrows uncritically from traditional philosophy. Is it not time to consider the lesson there is to be drawn from this sort of failure? No genuinely relational theory of personality, no effective surpassing of the impasses of psychological substantialism and naturalism and therefore no really scientific theory of personality are possible, so long as one does not take Marx's crucial discovery absolutely seriously, that in reality the human essence is the ensemble of social relations within which men not only produce their subsistence but are themselves produced."[310]

1.5.5 The Creation of Consciousness

In animals need creates coherent drive for search and foraging through the mediation of prewired instincts that, compared to their human equivalents, instinctual dispositions, are rather rigid and stereotyped. Nature places pleasurable contingencies as part of the process of reinforcement in the satisfaction of necessities, one of the most compelling being orgasm or satiety.

What makes possible the transition from animal to human in instinctual evolution is that humans can introduce endless material and cultural mediations, in consciousness ultimately leading to abstract operations. In the gap between stimulus and response, animals have a very limited capacity to choose. Humans learn to voluntarily delay their response to a much greater extent in order to introduce mediations. In studying intelligence in animals, Kohler found that chimps introduce instrumental mediations: for example, to reach a banana. They use a stick to reach it, a box to climb on top and get closer, or even the combination of both.[311] Today we know that many species instrumentally mediate. The limitation of animals is that their operations remain bound to their perceptual environment,

---

310 Seve, L. (1974). "The Articulation of the Psychology of Personality with Marxism." In: *Man in Marxist Theory.* Online in MIA. Accessed from <https://www.marxists. org/archive/seve/works/1974/ch2/2_0.htm> on 2015-01-29.
311 Köhler, W. (1956). The mentality of apes. London: Routledge and K. Paul. (translated from the 2nd revised edition by Ella Winter).

having little capacity to generalize. Humans, on the other hand, developmentally reach these capacities and go beyond, through learning. Not only can we delay our response, but we introduce abstract mediations from memory, from prior experience. Here language and consciousness are a great advantage. The culmination of this process in humans is the anticipatory proposition "if... then," that Piaget makes a cornerstone of his formal operational stage. This capacity allows humans to, in our minds, change perspectives by experimenting with notions such as independent and dependent variables.[312] As Marx put it: "A spider conducts operations that resemble those of a weaver, and a bee puts to shame many an architect in the construction of her cells. But what distinguishes the worst architect from the best of bees is this, that the architect raises his structure in imagination before he erects it in reality. At the end of every labor-process, we get a result that already existed in the imagination of the laborer at its commencement."[313]

Knight's human revolution altered the instinctual process by delay or inhibition, and by the introduction into it of self-produced abstract mediations. The end result is the unique capacity to anticipate and regulate of the human brain that already has recorded past events in its very shape, situations, positions, operations, *etc.* Knight tells us that, instead of females displaying their estrous hind, and offering access for a share of food to the meat-holding alpha male, women revert the process completely through the sex strike. Those earliest women reached the stage where they were able to reason: if we were to coordinate the signal "menstruation," then all males would have to wait and we could introduce mediation. Solidarily postponing copulation through the manipulation of the symbol men-

312 Inhelder, B. and Piaget J. (1958). The growth of logical thinking from childhood to adolescence: An essay on the construction of formal operational structures. (A. Parson and S. Milgram, Trans.). New York: Basic Books.

313 Marx, K. (1887). "The Labour-Process Or The Production Of Use-Values." Trans. Samuel Moore and Edward Aveling, Ed. Frederick Engels. First English Edition. Section 1, Chapter 7. *Capital.* Vol. 1. Part 3. Moscow, USSR; Progress Publishers. Online in MIA. Accessed from <https://www.marxists.org/archive/marx/works/1867-c1/ch07.htm> on 2015-08-11.

struation (that means no access), females collectively coerced the males to bring food to them first. Males were consequently rewarded in a new, regulated, universal sexual access. Theirs is now a society with rules, and, therefore with a collective form of consciousness and morality, a contract. The ritualistic exchanges were integrated with the cycles of nature and with totemism and mythology for success.

The sexual exchange is based on selfishness, particularly for males from the point of view of aggression, pleasure and hierarchy.[314] The sexual instinct tamed, however, becomes the ground of planning, universal welfare, and altruism in that it takes now into consideration the universal condition of the group. The arrangement is adaptively beneficial to the species and blossoming culture makes it a mutually beneficial economic arrangement that includes all individuals in archaic clannish economic units; the economy of nature changes its form into the historical economy. The social organization that inevitably results includes a structure of new social roles, social events and regularities. Males hunt, females subsequently cook and distribute in a division of labor. The corollary is a reflexive reciprocal internalization of forms of relationship in consciousness. In this process what was originally purely instinctual behavior has been transformed through socially complex complementarity, through rituals, and routines, habits and customs into collective culture, the seed of an individual self. At the end of this process, somehow the original natural sequence was inverted, anticipatory imagination's displacing the immediate goal of satisfaction, and placing it in the context of a consensual and mutual strategic planning. These are the first sparks of the unique characteristics of *Homo sapiens*, the ape that mediates.

Consciousness emerges from transforming the simple life reflex, or instinctual sequence, into a mediated, reciprocally intentional, and therefore socialized, complementary relationship. This relation-

---

314 Dunn, Kate M; Cherkas, Lynn F; Spector, Tim D (22 September 2005). "Genetic influences on variation in female orgasmic function: a twin study". *Biology Letters* (Abstract) 1 (3): 260–263.

ship is at once productive and reproductive, including sexual and economic exchanges and cyclic signaling at the root of language. It was jumpstarted and its foundation continues to be laid in each individual human by the females of the species, first through their invention, solidarity, and from there on through their altruism, the foundation of morality.

A consensual contractual and reciprocal equality in the sexual use of the body as exchange, leading to a social contract, takes the place of what before was the equivalent of rape in Briffault's view. Emerging subjects become involved in strategic planning of life cycles with gradually fewer and fewer obvious economic rewards. The phenomenon of the lunar cycle, a quality different in the sun, introduces in the mind the notion of sameness in change, the basic dialectic of reason. Behind it, goddesses are first projected by the mothers' mind to explain the intelligence of nature, as well as the agency of humans. These projections recognize the fact that all human logic comes from the good sense of nature.

The human individual, independent of gender, is foremost indebted to the reproductive mother. The individual emerges from that original universality that is mother: that is, immediate, linked to nature, and designed to satisfy natural necessity. It is the mother's task not only to materially reproduce herself to perpetuate the species, but to also reproduce the spirituality of each one of her progeny by putting in place the first-order mediations. Mother births each individual and psychologically has to endow him or her with enough capacity to survive within a reasonable degree of autonomy and independence, even in the jungle of civil society created by men. Within the early natural division of labor, males are in charge of distant and defensive functions, and are even ejected by mothers from the maternal group when sexually mature. Psychologically, closest to a father figure is the mother's brother, and then perhaps the older brother. While adult males forage, hunt, go to war, and deal with the outside world and civil society, females typically take care of the immediate needs of gens or family. They prepare the food for the family and tend to those who need care.

Reproduction is for the species the first most useful and valuable form of activity besides subsistence. For human society to emerge, women have achieved the feat of engaging the unlikely cooperation of men towards economic goals. Male primates typically do not instinctually provide for their progeny, leaving that to the mothers; human females had to change that and did. This was possible at the point when our species could overcome nomadic life, and settle in stable, agricultural homes and communities. Agriculture, and domestication in particular, made women independently productive. Their response was increased activity, adding their responsibility to tend to fields and animals while continuing to take care of the family. This eventually led to better skills, surplus accumulation, and eventually their spoiled sons' overriding them and installing patriarchy at their cost.

By the time the *sapiens* phenomenon came along, consciousness had evolved, through trial and error, in other species. Knight tells us that: "It is now recognized that chimpanzees, gorillas, gelada baboons, and other primates are rational beings able to set themselves goals, work out long-term strategies, memorize the essentials of complex social relationships over periods of time, display distinctive personalities, cooperate, argue among themselves, engage in deception, exploit subordinates, organize political alliances, overthrow their "rulers" — and indeed, on a certain level and in a limited way, do most of the things that we humans do in our localized, small-scale interactions with one another."[315] This is the confirmation and supporting evidence for what Darwin had already said in The Descent of Man.[316] The end of the myth of human conscious exclusivity was brought about by Darwin, based on evidence that consciousness had been slowly evolving.

---

315 Knight, C. (1991). Blood Relations. P. 127.
316 Darwin, CR (1882). *The Descent of man, and selection in relation to sex.* London: John Murray. 2nd edition. p.83. Online in Darwin Online. (Orig. Pub. 1871). The Complete Work of Charles Darwin Online. Accessed from <http://darwin-online.org. uk/content/frameset?itemID=F955&viewtype=text&pageseq=1> on 2012-10-09.

Compared to primates, humans have the advantage of a more complex nervous system that has partially developed in synchrony with the environment, and use of the hands almost exclusively in productive labor,[317] along with more complex forms of memory, and better capacity to classify, reason, and practically generalize from one situation to another. All these capacities are built, through mediations introduced by labor. They replace the simple sensory-motor reflex as Piaget has shown, enlarging it to the complexity of consciousness.

The icon *Homo Sapiens*, in accordance with the present evidence of science, ought to be updated, since it neither originates in Homo, nor has, in its patriarchal detour, acted with wisdom.

1.5.6 Solidarity and Social Regulation

This is how Darwin spoke about the social instinct. "The development of the moral qualities is a more interesting problem. The foundation lies in the social instincts, including under this term the family ties. These instincts are highly complex, and in the case of the lower animals give special tendencies towards certain definite actions; but the more important elements are love, and the distinct emotion of sympathy. Animals endowed with the social instincts take pleasure in one another's company, warn one another of danger, defend and aid one another in many ways. These instincts do not extend to all the individuals of the species, but only to those of the same community. As they are highly beneficial to the species, they have in all probability been acquired through natural selection."[318] Briffault recommended we change the highly mystified word *love* and replace it with the clearer one *mating;* it is from maternal birthing that tendering and motherly altruism derive, birthing is giving,

---

317 Engels, F. (1934) *The Part played by Labour in the Transition from Ape to Man.* Trans. Clemens Dutt. Moscow, USSR. Progress Publishers. (Orig. Pub. 1895, written 1876). Online in MIA. Accessed from <https://www.marxists.org/archive/marx/works/1876/part-played-labour/> on 2015-01-28.

318 Darwin, CR (1882). *The Descent of man, and selection in relation to sex.* Ibid. p.610.

birth, and here is where the maternal instinct resides, in that costly giving. The new instinct is simply to place the other, the child, before the self, altruism present already in other species. Mothers entice fathers to help against their instinctual priorities. Today we have changed the word *sympathy* that Darwin used for *empathy,* which means putting oneself in the place of the other. Sympathy was a form of identification; empathy includes the more dynamic projective identification. The natural bases for these processes has recently been confirmed by the presence of mirroring neurons in the frontal cortex of primates and humans that constantly makes vicarious the activity of the other. Empathy simultaneously leads to, and derives from, altruism.

Social regularities such as customs, modeled along the cycles of nature of which female fertility is one, became the foundation for expectations, therefore for social regulation, and for its corollary, organized social productivity. From mere randomness, regulated social activities such as rituals became regular and obligatory. Regulation is the essence and necessary ingredient of social life, and it includes the balancing of instinctual tendencies that are opposites, primarily mating to reproduce, flying from danger, and fighting for survival.

Sexual abstention during the hunting season is a well-documented fact in ethnology, as are the regulations about contact with menstruating women. What is not well known, is that cultures have been reported (Knight tells us) that copy menstruation from women by inflicting wounds on themselves. This must be seen as an identification, and residue, of a larger process of substitution of female social institutions for male ones after the patriarchal coup. "The myths allege that ritual power originally belonged to women. 'We took these things from women', as a learned Aboriginal put it during a performance of the great Kunapipi ceremony, referring to the cult's jealously guarded secrets."[319] Merlin Stone in her book *When God*

---

319 Berndt, C. H. and R. M. Berndt (1951). *Sexual Behaviour in Western Arnhem Land.* Viking Fund Publications in Anthropology 16. New York: Wenner-Gren. P. 55. Quoted by Knight, C. (1991). *Blood Relations.* P. 46.

was a Woman has amply documented the relation between sex and ritual in early matriarchal societies, where high priestesses were the leaders, including queens, in settled Mediterranean societies that were invaded by Indo-European nomads.[320]

Males replicated menstruation, copied it from females as genital laceration of warriors and male initiates, facts already known to the classical anthropologists. These facts were, however, always presented by mainstream patriarchal anthropology in an inverted form. Menstruation, the pride of women and envy of men, became a curse of females to be avoided at any cost by males. Instead of rendering the pride of its social power, it was made into a social handicap and a source of shame. Intentional menstruated body painting besides male menstruation contradicts the male theories about menstruation. Knight tells us that "...virtually throughout the world women have believed in their sexually controlled influence on the hunt even when distant from the scene,"[321] This is women's belief in their own idiosyncratic power which has been largely quelled.

Solidarity, as well as social regulation, was torn from women's hands and turned into patriarchal power, and Knight points out cultural differences between groups that ritualize female menstruation and those that choose the male version. "Where hunter-gatherers focused mainly on female initiation rites (as was generally the case among the San and some other African groups), then the mythico-ritual structures were not necessarily oppressive of women... her blood was taken to be potentially beneficial, immensely powerful — and mythically connected with male hunting success... But when hunter-gatherers — as in much of Australia — put the major emphasis on male initiation ritualism... The major structural feature remained gender segregation. Every ritual began with the women and children, as a group, repulsed in some symbolic sense from the space occupied by ritually active men."[322] Overall, Knight's story is a correction of the Freudian notion of penis envy. Envy was also

---

320 Stone, M. (1976). *When God was a Woman.* New York. Barnes and Noble.
321 Knight, C. (1991). *Blood Relations.* P. 391.
322 Knight, C. (1991). *Blood Relations.* P. 41.

inverted.

The relational structures of culture start, then, with their bases in blood and its language, regulated productive activity, and female solidarity. This is what Freud called sublimation, the social transformation of raw instinct.[323]

1.5.7 Double Jeopardy, The Black Mother

Culture, according to Knight, emerged revolutionarily, a Darwinian adaptational transition in the Hominin group, although not through the man-the-hunter myth as has been traditionally represented. Australopithecines lived very much like apes. While the evidence for organized hunting in Europe is fifty thousand years old, that for *Homo sapiens* goes back to Africa 150.000 years ago, extending globally halfway from then to the present. This process has been gradually revealed through interdisciplinary consolidation of data in the human sciences in the last four decades, and includes findings from disciplines as varied as sociobiology and paleoanthropology. It rests on the biological fact Briffault had pointed out that, in sexuated species, it is the females who develop the strategies for evolutionary change.

The first "classes" in human history, the mental representation of humanity as two contrasting particularities within the universality of the species, cognitively same and different, were sex and generation, male-female and child-adult; all other human classes are man-originated. The only "race" was the negroid, black-African. From there on, populations evolved into various races according to natural conditions. Populations migrating usually north of the equator and getting less exposure to sun lost their melanin pigment and changed other morphological characteristics. Skin protection from UV rays is necessary for high amounts of sun exposure. According

---

323 Freud, S. (1929). *'Civilisation and Its Discontents.* Electronic Edition. Online in Chrysoma Associates Limited. Bucking-hamshire. England. Accessed from <http://www2.winchester.ac.uk/edstudies/courses/level%20two%20sem%20two/Freud-Civ-il-Disc.pdf> on 2015-08-11.

to this principle, the only color prevailing initially, at the emergence of *Homo sapiens* was black. Skin color changed with genetic mutations due to migrations. "The first Black who went out to populate the rest of the world exited Africa through the Strait of Gibraltar, the Isthmus of Suez, and maybe through Sicily and Southern Italy."[324]

Europe and the first world have had trouble with this notion that compounds the fear of matriarchy. It has been proposed, for example, that only *Homo erectus* originated in Africa, *Homo sapiens* allegedly being European in origin. As Diop shows, the current evidence favors the concept that the initial populations of Europe that must have come from Africa were black. He places the arrival of the Grimaldian Negroid in Europe at about 40,000 years ago, and only twenty thousand years later did the Cro-Magnon appear in Southern France, the prototype of the Caucasoid or white race.[325]

The resistance to accept such facts is of course plainly owing to racism. A negroid original Eve is unimaginable and even revolting to some white supremacists.

1.5.8 The Snake Symbol

The rainbow snake legend is one of the most universal and compelling symbols of origins in human cultures. The same way males took menstruation and tried to appropriate it from females and upon failing turned it into a deprecatory handicap, they did with the female symbol of the snake turned into phallus. The snake is the symbol of self-sufficient conjunction and disjunction because, in its extreme postures, straight and recoiled, it can symbolize both sexes. This morphological ambiguity regarding primitive sex and reproductive relations makes it the most basic symbol of universality. It not only unites in itself both natural classes, but, by opening and closing, it signifies one and all, zero to infinite, zero and one bit.

---

324 Diop, C.A. (1991). *Civilization or Barbarism. An Authentic* Anthropology. Trans. Yaa-Lengi Meema Ngemi. Chicago, Illinois. Lawrence Hill Books. (Orig. Pub. 1981). P. 11.
325 Diop. C.A. (1991). *Civilization or Barbarism.* Ibid. P. 23.

It is this fabulous morphological ambiguity that has made the Rainbow Snake a universal mythical image in many variations, as Knight points out, and for both cultures and anthropologists a projective test. It says something very profound and yet very simple about our early origins as attested by the many ethnological representations of early goddesses holding or being surrounded by snakes.[326]

The legends Knight refers to usually depict a snake that is also a rainbow that connects waterholes. The serpent going into the waterhole, and dealing with water, is already a symbol of copulation. But it also ingests women, in the reverse way women eject newborns. This is why the rainbow snake may be the mother of all myths.

In the Old Testament the serpent in paradise represents wisdom, and Eve and Adam are punished for Eve's making the wise choice. The many old legends of men slaying dragons, monsters and the like, are a reflexion of the matriarchal coup that attempted to slay women's subjectivity.

Ouroboros circling itself to bite its own tail, an old metaphor used to signify totalization or closing the circle of understanding, also creates the space for the germinal egg of the cosmos, the Orphic Egg, the cosmic egg wherefrom good-sense deities arose.

---

326 Stone, M. (1976). *When God was a Woman.* New York. Barnes and Noble.

1.6 THE PSYCHOANALYTICAL EVIDENCE

"The relationship that stands at the origin of all culture, of every virtue, of every nobler aspect of existence, is that between mother and child; it operates in a world of violence as the divine principle of love, or union, or peace."

Bachofen[327]

"Far from producing a culture, as Levi-Strauss' mythological narrative would have it, male power enters tardily on to the scene, transforming and politically colonizing a cultural landscape long since formed by others."

Chris Knight[328]

1.6.1 Myths in Psychoanalysis

Anthropology is akin to psychoanalysis because it is the biography of history, of human agency; it goes back all the way to the origins of the history-makers that started as mythologists and had no way except oral tradition to make their narratives durable. Because the mind is the product of that history, some sort of developmental isomorphism must be possible between the growth process we observe in psychoanalysis and the same in anthropology, for the species at large; the two must have a common denominator.

327 Bachofen, J.J. (1967). "Introduction to Mother Right." In: Myth, Religion, and Mother Right. Selected Writings of J.J. Bachofen. Trans. Ralph Manheim. With a Preface by George Boas and an Introduction by Joseph Campbell. P. 79. Princeton, N.J. Princeton University Press.
328 Knight, C. (1991). *Blood Relations*. P. 512.

While anthropology tries to trace our cultural stages and the language we use back into our earliest forms, evolutionary before being historical, psychoanalysis endeavors to accomplish the same with each individual, going back to the pre-Oedipal mother to start the whole individual narrative. In this sense segments of the history of civilization become like large inkblots upon which historians and anthropologists project their inescapable subjectivity and cultural biases. One of the explanatory attractors in that task is trauma, the catastrophic disruption of a normative process. Hypotheses generated in this fashion always have to pass the test of scientific common sense, the fit of theory within an operating historical paradigm.

The subjective paradox applies to all sciences, because subjectivity is the only producer of a consciousness that then has to be validated by other subjectivities coming from various perspectives. This is how reality is culturally defined, always moving from alienated myth to truth. What Meszaros calls the active side,[329] which I equate with good sense, is the collective guarantor for our imaginary alienation's not leading us astray. Good sense is the natural ground and brilliant speculation its superstructure. Good sense is more universally shared and its safeguard in turn is limited perspective, which must be complemented by other perspectives. We must keep in mind, however, that reasoned consensus in a class society is by nature multiple, not necessarily good sense but commonsense.

Freud did make use of the anthropological evidence available at his time, particularly in his later works, starting with *Totem and Taboo*, and then *The Future of an Illusion, Civilization and its Discontents, Moses and Monotheism,* and other minor works. The fact that Freud's Oedipal metaphor assumed a central place in his theory of origins is an ideological anomaly. Freud had to frame his theory within the boundaries of his family, class, civil society, and the prevailing individualistic paradigm of the, Victorian Age. It is with Victoria that women started to find their voice, whether clear

---

329 Meszaros, I. (2011). *Social Structures and Forms of Consciousness.* Vol. 2. Ch. 1. The Nature of Historical Determination. Ch. 1. P. 34 ff. New York. Monthly Review Press.

or symptomatic, so this is paradoxical.

The most recent analysis of the structure of myth by Levi-Strauss and others, along with the work on human development of Hegel, Marx and Darwin, leading to Freud, Piaget, and Vygotsky, and linguists leading to Lacan as well as anthropologists such as Chris Knight-not to mention the multi-pronged feminist contribution-constitute challenges to old scientific paradigms in the human sciences. The purpose of the present work is to start a conversation about consciousness and ideology topics neglected by psychology as political and subjective.

The common ground of Bachofen and Freud has been proposed by Ellenberger to be *repression*. In this light, Ellenberger pairs hetaerism with polymorphous perversion, gynecocracy with the pre-Oedipal period, the Dionysian with the phallic stage, Orestes' myth with Oedipus, and patriarchy with the phallic stage. Repression would be the infantile amnesia of Freud, and Bachofen's myths would be screen memories and symptoms.[330] This comparison of two mythical structures is a good point to start our search for psychoanalytic evidence of matriarchy.

1.6.2 The Counterpoint to Freud

Henri Wallon (1879-1962) was a neuropsychiatrist, also a well-known socialist contemporary of Freud's, who developed an alternative theory of development that inspired the intelligence theory of his better-known disciple Jean Piaget.[331] Contrastingly, Wallon worked with cognitively challenged children and developed a theory of developmental stages determined by the dialectical interaction of emotion and cognition and the observable cyclical periodicity

---

330 Ellenberger, H.F. (2008). *The Discovery of the Unconscious: The History and Evolution of Dynamic Psychiatry.* P. 223. New York. Basic Books. (Orig. Pub. 1970)

331 Wallon, H. (1984) The Psychological Development of the Child. Trans. Michael Vale. (Written: 1965) Jason Aaronson. Online Version: Wallon Internet Archive (marxists.org) 2001. Accessed from <http://www.marxists.org/archive/wallon/works/1965/ch10.htm> on 2012-06-02.

of child development. Emotion is first, the newborn's cry followed by wordless affectivity and impulsivity. The impact of the external world, through maternal regulatory influence on sensorimotor activity and mirroring, makes possible the entrance into language and cognition. Henceforth being able to say NO! (an oppositional affective overflow) reiterates emotion, but external reality prevails again. The child accepts the primacy of cognition through the mediations introduced by the mother. The latency of emotion is made manifest again by the transformations of adolescence. There is room in the theory for the affective and cognitive entrance of the father, the proxy of the real external world and the carrier of devastating cognitive and affective triangulation.

Cognitively, for Wallon, the child starts from an initial self-other indifferentiation. Through mirroring and imitation it moves to self-perception. Children assimilate others, identify with them, but simultaneously influence and transform them in reality and imagination. Imitation is part of a child's play and mastery of reality. Not randomly, but adaptively, the child selects positive, affectionate feelings that work in the family environment. In play and imagination, the child assumes the roles of close persons, wishes to be them, and to have their size and magical qualities; the mother is the prototype. A latent awareness of inequality eventually brings feelings of envy and hostility against those same models that represent self-alienation in others. Resentment of their frustrating superiority engenders a feeling of inferiority in the child.

Identificatory ambivalence is not Oedipally parsed along gender lines, but is all-inclusive and leads to gender identity, sexual preference, and developmental deviations contingent on the reverberational emotional characteristics of self and reciprocal players, besides factors such as degree of exposure and intensity during development. In the universal process of development, hate eventually supersedes love, Oedipally. Hate is an ingredient in the subjective process of separation and individuation necessary for life in civil society.

Less ambitious and imaginative than Freud, but more in tandem with observation and proof, Wallon has been quite influential in developmental psychology and also in French psychoanalysis particularly that of Lacan.

1.6.3 Psychoanalysis, Marxism, and Feminism

Psychoanalysis was born of the muted voice of oppressed women who could only speak in code. It was a discipline contemporary with Marxism that could clearly see the class oppression of workers, but not so clearly that of women. Feminism shares with Marxism the goal of equality and with psychoanalysis the repudiation of repression. The three started as critical theories of bourgeois capitalism; compartmentalized, they have had separate and unequal destinies.

Well-known psychoanalysts influenced by Bachofen's matriarchal theory are Ian Suttie, who was also significantly influenced by Briffault, Otto Rank, also influenced by Karl Marx and Georg Groddeck, Groddeck himself, who usually does not get enough credit for his influence in early psychoanalysis, Sandor Ferenczi, Karl Jung, Erik Fromm, Wilhelm Reich, and John Bowlby among others. They are all in one way or another dissidents from the psychoanalytic mainstream and I will briefly summarize what is most important in their work for the purpose of this book.[332]

Ian Suttie (1898-1935) was a Scottish psychiatrist credited with being a precursor of the object relations school in England. In his main publication, *The Origins of Love and Hate*, he brings forth the issue of the social taboo on tenderness. I quote: "While in the physical sciences this justifies itself on methodological grounds, in psychology it has been carried to such an absurd length (*e.g.* Behaviorism) as to betray an underlying bias of anti-emotionalism. Yet it may seem incredible that so harmless and amiable emotion as tenderness, the very stuff of sociability, should itself come under a taboo... The

---

332 Burston, D. (1986). "Myth, Religion and Mother Right. Bachofen's Influence on Psychoanalytic Theory." Contemporary Psychoanalysis. Volume 22, Issue 4.

idea that tenderness is a primal independent reality and that it undergoes repression will seem untrue and even absurd unless supported by much evidence...What we call tender feelings and affection is based not on sexual desire, but upon the pre-oedipal emotional and fondling relationship with the mother and upon the instinctual need for companionship which is characteristic of all animals which pass through a phase of nurtured infancy. In our culture in particular the brusqueness of the cleanliness-training, the frequent and prolonged separation of mother and infant and the mother's own intolerance of tenderness (the result of her 'puritan' upbringing) bring about a precipitate 'psychic parturition,' attended by an anxiety, acquisitiveness, and aggressiveness which is reflected in our culture and economic customs and attitudes. This process of parturition or psychic weaning must be intensely painful even where not aggravated by jealousy of a supplanter...The distress of this process must after all be far greater than that attending sexual repression; for, in the case of psychic weaning, the child is being deprived of something it has enjoyed 'from time immemorial'; while in sexual repression it is merely being forbidden something that is reserved for 'grown-ups'. To the anger attending the thwarting of tenderness-feelings must be added the grief for the loss of the mother and above all the anxiety caused by her changing attitude."[333]

This is an enunciation of precisely the phenomenon that concerns the present work. I designate it as the unilateral imposition of the patriarchal instinctual disposition, characterized by Suttie as anxiety, acquisitiveness and aggressiveness, superimposed upon the severing of the child from the maternal disposition that must be repressed in civil society.

Suttie believes the *repression of affection* to be a cumulative phenomenon. Increasing as it becomes habitual with generations. Love becomes anxious, aggressive, and possessive, mothers themselves reinforcing this trend through habitual acculturation. Our societies,

---

333 Suttie, I. (1935). *The Origins of Love and* Hate. Chapter VI. The "Taboo" on Tenderness. P. 80 ff. London Kegan Paul, Trench, Trubner & Co. Ltd. Reprinted by Routledge in 2005.

compared with those with matriarchal influence, produce different social prototypes or characters: "Under matriarchal cultures, such as that of ancient Teutondom, no distinction was made between the virtues proper to a man and those of a woman…It is quite conceivable then that features of our mode of upbringing , which I have vaguely generalized as *tenderness taboo,* create an artificial mental differentiation and consequent emotional barrier between adult males on the one hand and women and children on the other."[334] I could have not said it better. Suttie provides an important landmark in the argument of this book, namely that social practices unilaterally undergirded by the male instinctual disposition have left an indelible mark in the psychic structure of both genders.

Otto Rank (1884 –1939) was a psychoanalyst and a teacher. He postulated the *birth trauma*[335] as a critical event that leaves a scar in our patterns of thinking, motivation, and emotion. A uterine paradise lost led to separation anxiety and the drive to re-unite, to return. Rank explored human creativity and emphasized the existence of a psychoanalytically neglected rich psychological life before the father becomes significant in the Oedipal period. Neurobiology is proving him right. Rank foretells Melanie Klein and her school's pre-Oedipal focus. Like Suttie, Rank was critical of the emotionless attitude proclaimed by Freud for psychoanalysis, and also of the eradication of emotion as analytic goal. He stressed the importance of Exploring the Dark Continent of Maternal Power.[336] Rank inspired the present work to propose a second universal human trauma, the paternal intrusion in the mother-child bond that creates triangulation phenomena as a prolegomenon for civil society.

Georg Groddeck (1866-1934), German physician, novelist, and literary critic, pioneer in psychosomatic medicine. He influenced Freud, who accepted him in the psychoanalytic circle. He also in-

334 Suttie, I. (1935). Ibid. P. 95.
335 Rank, O. (1952). *The Trauma of Birth.* New York. R. Brunner.
336 Rank, O. (1996). *A Psychology of Difference:* The American Lectures. P.97 ff. Selected, edited, and introduced by Robert Kramer. With a foreword by Rollo May. Princeton. Princeton University Press.

fluenced Ferenczi and Fromm in particular. His main book is the well-known *The Book of the It.*[337] He is credited with ushering in psychosomatic medicine and particularly the symbolic aspect of symptoms. Symbolically, a penis erection makes a man such only for a few seconds, leaving him a child for most of his life, he said; also: "the highest form of human pleasure is maternity and for this men envy women. When a man has a large paunch, it is an expression of his desire to give birth; falling back represents a desire to crack the head open and give birth, as Zeus did to Athena. Groddeck's own goiter only disappeared when he became aware that it was caused by his fantasies of pregnancy."[338] From Groddeck we draw the grounding of psychology on it, on matter and the body wherefrom it emerges, in a cultural form that is linguistically symbolized.

Hungarian psychoanalyst Sandor Ferenczi (1873 – 1933) is best known for his disagreement with Freud about sexual abuse that Freud had considered pathogenic briefly but then discarded, deeming it for the most part female fantasy. Ferenczi treated difficult patients and promoted *active therapy* against mirror-like neutrality and silence. From side effects of pernicious anemia, at the end of his life Ferenczi was ostracized, mocked, and even labeled mentally ill. He was punished for starting to deconstruct Freud. His paper *The Confusion of the Tongues*, where he discusses the traumatic incoherence of a dialogue of adult lust with child tenderness, is amongst the most original and famous in psychoanalysis. In his book *Thalassa: A Theory of Genitality*, Ferenczi suggests that the womb's amniotic fluid remains a symbol of a universal wish to return to the anaerobic origins of life in the sea. From Ferenczi we borrow the courage to speak truth to power.

Carl Jung (1875–1961) contributed to the understanding of myth and religion. He is better known for his theory of individuation, the

---

337 Groddeck, G. (1961). *The Book of the It*. New York. Random House.
338 Biancoli, R. (1995). "Georg Groddeck's influence on Erich Fromm's Psychoanalysis." Online in George Groddeck. Accessed from <http://www.indepsi.cl/ferenczi/vinculaciones/groddeck/articulos/art-dest26-ing.htm#top> on 2014-10-01

collective unconscious, and the human archetypes that underlie universal social roles. Through him we find access to the psychological symbolism of myths and a bridge to the universality of the ensemble of the social relations.[339]

Erich Fromm (1900-1980) was a member of the Frankfurt School of sociology. As mentioned, he was influenced by Groddeck and also by Marx. Like Wilhelm Reich, Fromm endeavored to establish a direct link between Marxism and psychoanalysis, his theory being very influential in the neo-Freudian movement, where he collaborated closely with Karen Horney, whom he influenced politically. Relatedness and individuation were central concerns of Fromm's. Gender behavioral differences are for him a result of historical and cultural conditions, not anatomically or physiologically determined. He is critical of the extreme patriarchalism of Freud, who mistakenly transformed affective yearnings into sexual feelings. A patriarchal gender war has made men and women members either of a victorious or of a defeated group. Equality between men and women is not the equivalent of lack of differences. He proposed a humanistic and democratic socialism as a constructive alternative to present-day destructive and alienating society.[340] This book draws much of its critique of patriarchalism and the return to a society of substantial equality from Fromm.

Wilhelm Reich (1897–1957) is perhaps the most expressly matriarchal psychoanalyst as well as the most expressly Marxist. His most popular work in the psychoanalytic circles is the first part of *Character Analysis*.[341] His most important political and psycholog-

339 Jung, C.G. (1972). *The Structure and Dynamics of the Psyche* (Collected Works of C.G. Jung, Volume 8). Part lll. The Struc-ture of the Psyche. 2nd Edition. Trans. Gerhard Adler and F.C. Hull. Princeton, N.J. Princeton University Press.

340 Fromm, E. (1991). *The Sane Society,* London and New York. Routledge. Accessed from <http://historicalunderbelly.files.wordpress.com/2012/12/erich-fromm-the-sane-society.pdf> on 2014-10-01.

341 Reich, W. (1972). *Character Analysis.* Third, enlarged edition. Newly translated by Vincent R. Carfagno. Edited by Mary Hig-gins and Chester M. Raphael, M.D. New York. Farrar, Straus and Giroux. (Orig. Pub. 1933). Full text available from the Wilhelm Reich Infant Trust. Accessed from <http://www.wilhelmreichtrust.org/charac-ter_analysis.pdf> on 2015-08-15.

ical work is *The Psychology of Fascism,* where he analyzes the impact of patriarchy on character structure. I quote: "The patriarchal authoritarian sexual order developed from the fundamental changes taking place in late matriarchy, such as economic independence of the chief's family from the maternal tribe, increasing barter trade between the tribes, development of the means of production, etc. This patriarchal sexual order then became the basis of authoritarian ideology by depriving women, children and adolescents of sexual freedom, by making a commodity out of sexuality, and by putting sexuality in the service of economic suppression. Under these circumstances, sexuality, in fact, came to be distorted into something demoniacal which had to be restrained. 'Under the pressure of patriarchal demands, the chaste sensuality of matriarchy appeared as the raging of sinister elements. The Dionysian turned into 'sinful desire,' into something which patriarchal culture can experience only as chaotic and 'filthy.' With the development of distorted, lascivious, sexual structures, patriarchal man becomes enmeshed in an ideology in which 'sexual' becomes inextricably associated with 'filthy,' 'low' and 'demoniacal'."[342]

There are for Reich three layers in the psyche, that are "…autonomously functioning representations of social development. In the superficial layer, the average individual is restrained, polite, compassionate and conscientious. There would be no social tragedy of the animal, man, if this superficial layer were in immediate contact with his deep natural core. His tragedy is that such is not the case. The superficial layer of social cooperation is not in contact with the biological core of the person, but separated from it by a second, intermediary character layer consisting of cruel, sadistic, lascivious, predatory, and envious impulses. This is the Freudian 'unconscious' or 'repressed'; in sex-economic language…In [the biological core]

---

342 Reich, W. (1946). *The Mass Psychology of* Fascism. III. The Race Theory. 3. Racial Purity, Blood Poisoning, And Mysticism. P. 68. Trans. Theodore P. Wolfe. New York. Orgone Institute Press. (Orig. Pub. 1933). Accessed from <http://www.relatedness. org/Mass_Psychology_of_Fascism.pdf> on 2014-09-28.

deepest layer, man, under favorable social conditions, is an honest, industrious, cooperative animal capable of love and also of rational hatred. In character-analytic work, one cannot penetrate to this deep, promising layer without first eliminating the false, sham-social sur-face."[343] I do believe this the best metaphor to describe exactly what patriarchy has done to the natural structure of the mind by interposing its destructive layer of secondary-order mediations behind the original, first-order ones introduced by mothers. It amounts to saying, with Horney, that between the actual self and the real self there is interposed the idealized, patriarchal false self.

An important contribution of Reich is to have emphasized the span of history as matriarchy, patriarchy, and the society of the future, a matriarchal type of compromise. The belief in matriarchy, and its supersession by authoritarian slavery-engendering patriarchy in macro-history, are elements in the present work borrowed from Reich.

Finally John Bowlby (1907–1990) introduced the ecological perspective, with an emphasis on our natural roots, and inspired empirical work done by his disciples, particularly Mary Ainsworth (1913-1999), in the area of mother-child attachment, and human relatedness in general, an indispensable ingredient to our present understanding of how we relate, conflictually, in our class society.[344]

1.6.4 The Matriarchal Alternative to Freud's Patriarchalism

I will not go into an overview or detailed critique of Freud's own theory, something that has been done by others, including Karen Horney. The reason Freud was not able to reach to the level of deep political class issues[345] that he only superficially discussed in a cou-

---

343 Reich, W. (1946). The Mass Psychology of Fascism. Ibid. Preface to the third Edition
344 Ainsworth, M. D. S., & Bell, S. M. (1970). "Attachment, exploration, and separation: Illustrated by the behavior of one-year-olds in a strange situation." Child Development, 41, 49-67.
345 Lichtman, R. (1982). The Production of Desire: The Integration of Psychoanalysis into Marxist Theory. New York. Free Press.

ple of his passages referring to revolutions and particularly the Russian one,[346] is that he could not extricate himself from the patriarchal paradigm that automatically entails the endorsement of hierarchy and class rule. On the other hand, it is to Freud's credit that he based his psychological theory of repression and the unconscious on the model of political repression. Woman and mother Karen Horney, was able to challenge and deconstruct Freud based on her critical, "feminine psychology," often derided by the psychoanalytic mainstream. Horney must be read as a feminist deconstruction of Freud.

Where Freud most missed the boat as concerns the present work is precisely in his most brilliant work on group psychology. Along with the most compelling explanation about the psychology of the leader *vis à* vis the group, and the psychology of the narcissism of small differences, Freud joins the patriarchs of the time in their misrepresentation of the psychology of groups as impoverished and regressive. This is pure ideological pablum.

From all women analysts that surrounded Freud, Karen Horney was the only one to openly disagree with his feminine psychology and ultimately with most of his patriarchal theory. Although Freud

---

346 "There are also men of action, unshakeable in their convictions, impervious to doubt, and insensitive to the sufferings of anyone who stands between them and their goal. It is owing to such men that the tremendous attempt to institute a new order of society of this kind is actually being carried out in Russia now. At a time when great nations are declaring that they expect to find their salvation solely from a steadfast adherence to Christian piety, the upheaval in Russia – in spite of all its distressing features – seems to bring a promise of a better future. Unfortunately, neither our own misgivings nor the fanatical belief of the other side give us any hint of how the experiment will turn out. The future will teach us. Perhaps it will show that the attempt has been made prematurely and that a fundamental alteration of the social order will have little hope of success until new discoveries are made that will increase our control over the forces of Nature, and so make easier the satisfaction of our needs. It may be that only then will it be possible for a new order of society to emerge which will not only banish the material want of the masses, but at the same time meet the cultural requirements of individual men. But even so we shall still have to struggle for an indefinite length of time with the difficulties which the intractable nature of man puts in the way of every kind of social community." Freud, S. (1933). *New Introductory Lectures on Psychoanalysis.* Lecture XXXV. A Philosophy of Life. London. Hogarth Press. Online in MIA. Accessed from <https://www.marxists.org/reference/subject/philosophy/works/at/freud.htm> on 2014-10-04.

and Horney share the common ground of the unconscious that has been challenged only by the existentialists, and although Horney recognizes her debt to Freud, their divergences can be judged by the emblems of their theories: *ego* for Freud, a narrow individualistic and even " intrapsychic" perspective, and *self* for Horney, a totalizing and relational perspective. After Freud, mainstream ego psychology ended up endorsing a theory of uncritical adaptation to a cultural system that Freud questioned but was not able to challenge. Horney offered, on the other hand, an alternative, the inherent critique of an alienating neurotogenic society. In a most timely fashion, Horney uniquely proposed a return to a morality of evolution.[347] This means returning to good sense, to recognizing and respecting the boundaries of nature that mandate humans to be such. With the challenge of sociobiology today, this Horneyian thread is essential to pursue. Ego-psychology after Freud took on a capital model of ego-accumulation and ego-growth; self-theory on the other hand, has sought the restoration of coherence lost to neurotic idealization, the imaginary flight unconstrained by good sense. Horney's theory of a falsified self is shared by that of several other psychoanalytic pioneers such as Alfred Adler, Donald Winnicott, and Heinz Kohut. They all propose the rescue and return to a real self. The real self, I propose here, cannot be grounded upon other than "the total ensemble of the social relations" of Marx,[348] particularly the good sense of respect of natural boundaries that matriarchal rule practiced for two hundred thousand years.

With Wilhelm Reich, we could redefine an unconscious that takes into consideration the bad faith of Sartre, precisely by the influence of class in the determination of consciousness. This secondary type of mediation is what results in ideology, the corruption of

---

347 Horney, K. (1950), *Neurosis and Human Growth*. Introduction. p. 13. Online in Internet Archive. Accessed from <https://archive.org/details/NeurosisAndHumanGrowth> on 2014-07-18.

348 Marx, K. (1969)." Theses on Feuerbach." Marx/Engels Selected Works, Volume One, p. 13 – 15. Trans: W. Lough. (Written: Spring of 1845, edited by Engels). Moscow, USSR. Progress Publishers, Online in MIA. Accessed from <https://www.marxists.org/archive/marx/works/1845/theses/theses.htm> on 2015-01-30.

the real self by the introduction of an intermediate layer between the actual and the real self, of idealization based on sophistry and false reasoning. Here is introduced the spurious need for patriarchal repression as the original form of values has to be hidden, introducing a continuous internal struggle between truth and convenience. I quote from where Freud most clearly defined repression: "Suppose that here in this hall and in this audience, whose exemplary stillness and attention I cannot sufficiently commend, there is an individual who is creating a disturbance, and, by his ill-bred laughing, talking, by scraping his feet, distracts my attention from my task. I explain that I cannot go on with my lecture under these conditions, and thereupon several strong men among you get up, and, after a short struggle, eject the disturber of the peace from the hall. He is now 'repressed,' and I can continue my lecture. But in order that the disturbance may not be repeated, in case the man who has just been thrown out attempts to force his way back into the room, the gentlemen who have executed my suggestion take their chairs to the door and establish themselves there as a 'resistance,' to keep up the repression. Now, if you transfer both locations to the psyche, calling this 'consciousness,' and the outside the 'unconscious,' you have a tolerably good illustration of the process of repression."[349] This metaphor illustrates how gradually, starting with the voice of women, and then extending to children, slaves, bondsmen, wage-workers, unions, and the ninety-nine percent today, an overwhelming majority of humanity has been kept "outside" of mainstream patriarchal discourse and reasoning. Patriarchal bad faith creates the unconscious, but the repressed will forever attempt to return to its critical, politically incorrect place. The way Freud sees the disturber is the same as he sees group psychology vis a *vis à* the patriarchal ego.

---

349 Freud, S. (1910). "The Origin and Development of Psychoanalysis." Second of the Lectures delivered at the Celebration of the Twentieth Anniversary of the opening of Clark University, Sept., 1909; translated from the German by Harry W. Chase. First pub-lished in American Journal of Psychology, 21, 181-218. Online version in Classics in the History of Psychology. An internet educa-tional resource developed by Christopher D. Green, York University, Toronto, Ontario. Accessed from <http://psychclassics.yorku.ca/Freud/Origin/origin2.htm> on 2012-09-09.

Compare this Freudian statement to Horney's: "As I have elaborated in an earlier publication,[350] repression of hostility helps to render a person defenseless, because it makes him lose sight of the danger which he should fight. If he represses his hostility, it means that he is no longer aware that some individual represents a menace to him; hence he is likely to be submissive, compliant, friendly in situations in which he should be on his guard. This defenselessness, in combination with the fear of retaliation, which remains in spite of its repression, is one of the powerful factors accounting for the neurotic's basic feeling of helplessness in a potentially hostile world."[351] Horney's warning expresses our alienation, our transformation into idealized aliens that have lost the capacity to identify the aggressor, a threat to our survival. No one can deny that this capacity is a cornerstone of successful animal evolution. The capacity to identify the aggressor is corrupted through the mystification incurred in ideological education, in corrupt mass media, in deceiving public relations and diplomacy, in the creation of false needs through advertising, and in the rewarded production of forged spirituality by paid ideologues. This is most clearly seen politically when people vote and elect into office their worst oppressors, which happens again and again.

From these two quotations it is possible to infer very clearly the different vantage points on the same phenomenon of the unconscious. Freud acknowledges the political aspect of repression but Horney expands on the very dangerous consequences of disrupting a dialogue.

The incongruent philosophical phenomenon of alienation was first spotted by Spinoza who asked himself why men fight for their servitude as stubbornly as if it were their salvation.[352] The same ques-

---

350 Horney refers here to: Horney, K. (1937). *The Neurotic Personality of Our Times.* Ch. 4. New York. Norton.

351 Horney, K. (1947). "Anxiety." In: *New Ways in Psychoanalysis.* P. 203. London. Kegan Paul, Trench, Trubner & Co.

352 "But if, in despotic statecraft, the supreme and essential mystery be to hoodwink the subjects, and to mask the fear, which keeps them down, with the specious garb of religion, so that men may fight as bravely for slavery as for safety, and count it not shame

tion is echoed by Hegel and Marx, and most recently by Fromm,[353] Horney,[354] and Meszaros,[355] all champions of addressing the same social phenomenon, alienation, that Horney and other psychoanalysts talk about in clinical practice, and that amounts to introducing immorality in evolution. Patriarchal ideology hides the phenomenon of alienation by pretending, with its own social scaffold, that it is the natural order.

1.6.5 Confirmation from Developmental Neurobiology

Developmental psychology has not usually been taken into consideration in the debate about matriarchy. Part of the reason is the rejection of the principle of recapitulation, that phylogeny summarizes ontogeny.[356] This principle, which does not apply mechanically to the details of evolution, does so to its larger trends, from simplicity to complexity, from homogeneity to heterogeneity, and from objectivity to subjectivity. In between the lines, this principle is also the landmark of the structuralist movement, in its belief that simple and complex operations of the mind are recursive. Every infant is the result of a biological program that starts as two cells conjoining, one and two, thesis and antithesis, in turn becoming sublated into multicellularity, organized specialization of parts, and anaerobic, self-sufficient autonomy. After birth, the organism, particularly through its brain evolves relationally, fitted to an average expectable environment, to reproduce consciousness in the process. Each sexuated or-

but highest honour to risk their blood and their lives for the vainglory of a tyrant; yet in a free state no more mischievous expedient could be planned or attempted." Spinoza, B. (1997). A Theologico-Political Treatise. Preface. The Project Gutenberg Etext #989. This is Part I Chapters I-V. (Originally published posthumously in 1677). Trans. R. H. M. Lewes. Accessed from <http://www.gutenberg.org/cache/epub/989/pg989.html> on 2012-09-14.

353 Fromm, E. (1961). 5. "Alienation." *Marx's Concept of Man.* New York. Frederick Ungar Publishing. Online in MIA. Accessed from <https://www.marxists.org/archive/fromm/works/1961/man/ch05.htm> on 2014-10-04.

354 Horney, K. (1950). *Neurosis and Human Growth.* New York. Norton. Online in the Internet Archive. Accessed from <hor-ney_human_growth_djvue> on 2015-08-15.

355 Mészáros, I. (1970). *Marx's Theory of Alienation.* London. Merlin Press.

356 Gould, S.J. (1977). Ontogeny and Phylogeny. Harvard. Harvard University Press.

ganism goes from parasite to symbiote to reciprocal, from object to subject very much along the same broad strokes of evolution. It is based on this premise that Herbert Spencer defines evolution as the process from incoherent simplicity to coherent complexity.

Fecundity, fertility, and capacity to give life and care for others are largely, if not exclusively, feminine prerogatives. It has been found empirically that human females tend to be better than males as regards empathy, verbal skills, social skills and security-seeking, among other things, all protective devices of a kind, while men tend to have an advantage in attributes such as independence, dominance, spatial and mathematical skills, rank-related aggression, and other psychological characteristics, different adaptational devices.[357] This implies a differently wired brain that we do not understand well as yet. These measurable differences are universally imprinted dispositions that external influences and conditions have the power to shift from their sexual determination. Conditions may make women man-like Amazons and vice versa. They reflect a basic difference in the newborn brain that we are starting to discern: the superior male efficiency in spatial ability, and the greater female skill in speech, for example, are adaptively necessary if we put them in the context of the most basic divisions of labor between the sexes for survival of the species.[358] Again, we must keep in mind that brain morphology is not written in stone, and that, on the contrary, the brain after birth continues to develop, largely determined by its particular environment, most importantly the social one.[359]

From the significant advances in the study of the nervous system during the last decades, we have growing evidence that the human brain differs between the sexes both structurally and functionally, in ways that are becoming clearer as research methodologies ad-

---

357 Wilson, E.O. (1992). Sociobiology. Harvard University Press.
358 Moir A. and Jessel D. (1993). "Brain Sex". New York. Dell Publishing.
359 Schore, A. (1994). Affect Regulation and the Origins of the Self. The Neurobiology of Emotional Development. Hillsdale, N.J. Lawrence Erlbaum Associates. Online in Questia. Accessed from <http://www.questia.com/read/57185676/affect-regulation-and-the-origin-of-the-self-the> on 2013-03-07.

vance.[360] This is the manifestation of the sex-determined instinctual dispositions that results in some differential forms of behavior. That gender differences are reflected in the brain is clear today; what is not, is that culture, through the principle of reciprocal action, not only modifies but is modified by the brain. The relation between culture and genome is reciprocal. If women in ancient Germany, for example, are described as equal to men in body size, while today they are on the average twenty-five percent smaller, that historical variation is bound to be cultural.

The peculiar advantage of psychoanalysis as compared to other evolutionary sciences, including philosophy, is that it studies the human relation from inside, not introspectively or "objectively," but intersubjectively. Although this is not easy to grasp, this is the same advantage Spinoza and Hegel introduced with their philosophical Monism, which linked myth, religion, philosophy, and science, as a necessary, developmental continuum. Psychoanalysis studies individuals *in vivo,* so to speak, through reciprocal intersubjective mechanisms that include biographical fragments, gaps, memories, utterances, idiosyncrasies, and the history of mirroring, introjection and normative correction, all within a total narrative. Classical humanism tended to look at the origin of consciousness in the relations between adults (witness Plato and his Republic), or even Hegel and his Master-Slave parable. The acknowledgment of the most basic relation, mother and developing child, was so transparent that it was not visible.

Freud, however, was forced precisely by the intersubjectivity inherent in medical practice to change this perspective and adopt a developmental stand that is necessarily historical and developmental hence, his bodily based stages that are so because they are social stages. Freud could understandably only perceive the glare of the most explicit relational features between mother and child such the oral introjection, the anal projection, the phallic submission and its

360 Society for Women's Health Research. "Sex Differences Extend Into The Brain." ScienceDaily. ScienceDaily, 3 March 2008. <www.sciencedaily.com/releases/2008/02/080229171609.htm>.

consequence, both historical and ontogenetic, repressed latency, be-fore a scarred genitality. In spite of himself, his ideological perspec-tive was intrapsychic, not relational. This is how the phallic stage and the Oedipus Complex became for him the displaced center of human development. Melanie Klein, who focused on the pre-Oedi-pal phenomena although still plagued by an Oedipal bias, was the first female to protest, if unconsciously. The Oedipus Complex is the manifestation of our universal biographical triangulation that forces women, unfortunately, to shift their original love object.

Neurobiology points out that the first organ involved in a re-lationship, following the philogenetic order, is still phemomon-ic olfaction, present at birth. Newborns can recognize the odor of their mothers' garments within minutes after birth.[361] What is most observable, however, by the untrained eye, is the oral relation that Freud chose as his beginning point. Neurobiology has thrown light on how the sensorial development applies to the bond between hu-mans, each sense having its own moment and span. We will know in detail how the mother-child relationship unravels sensorially to ul-timately produce balanced consciousness, the interplay of instincts. Even the food chain has its balance, with the ultimate dialectic's probably being the constant battle between regulation and balance.

All human senses are developed "to make sense" in their very particular way, but together they surrender to reason and conscious-ness. There are, according to Marx, many more than five human senses.[362] All the natural senses are socially transformed and they must, along with the historical ones, play into the total symphony of consciousness, our constant relationship with nature. This hap-pens within the pentagram of culture that starts with duets of mother

---

361 Vaglio, S. (2009). "Chemical communication and mother-infant recognition." Com-municative and Integrative Biology 2(3): 279–281. Online in PubMed Central. Ac-cessed from <http://www.ncbi.nlm.nih.gov/pmc/articles/PMC2717541/> on 2015-02-02.

362 Marx, K. (1959). "Private Property and Communism." In: Economic and Philosophic Manuscripts of 1844. Trans: Martin Mulligan. Moscow. Progress Publishers. Online in MIA. Accessed from <https://www.marxists.org/archive/marx/works/1844/manu-scripts/comm.htm> on 2014-11-05.

and newborn and extends to larger and larger melodies based on the foundation of that mother-child relationship.

The work of Allan Schore[363] represents the most comprehensive blend of psychoanalysis and neurobiology relevant to the necessary focus of mother-and-child interaction in the formation of the human subject and the self. The Oedipal focus of psychoanalysis for a long time stood in the way of this kind of understanding. Schore points, out for example, the obvious but neglected fact that in the first year or human infancy communication "is not verbal but non-verbal communication, a specialization of the right hemisphere."[364] We must point out that it is precisely the right hemisphere that is then usually overridden by the left in hierarchical society. Schore shows the implication for mental disorders as disorders of self-regulation. It is the fashion to present these disorders as "genetic," to conceal the social damage. The great advantage of Schore's method is that his neurobiology is interpersonal. He proposes that a critical period of growth in the right hemisphere, from the last trimester of pregnancy to the middle or end of the second year, precedes the spurt of growth of the left hemisphere in human infancy. The neurobiological bond during the first three or four years of life is maternal.

Psychology methodologically applies the epigenetic model. It does not start with mature relations. It starts with genesis as far back as possible. In humans, as in other mammals, every newborn is forced to leave the anaerobic uterine existence, a parasitic and rather paradisiacal experience where all needs are met by the host. In humans every fetus is then evicted, not kindly but by crude mechanical ejection through the narrow vaginal canal of the mother. This may be the most traumatic experience in the life span. Every single part of the fetal body — skin, muscles, bones, sense receptors, and organs

---

363 His many writings but particularly: Schore, A. (1994). *Affect Regulation and the Origin of the Self. The Neurobiology of Emo-tional Development.* Ibid.

364 Schore A.N. (2014). "Early interpersonal neurobiological assessment of attachment and autistic spectrum disorders." Frontiers in Psychology. 5:1049. Online in Allan Schore's Website. Accessed from < http://www.ncbi.nlm.nih.gov/pmc/articles/PMC4184129/ > on 2015-02-02.

— is subjected to a huge external pressure that, through the stimulation of proprioceptors, must awaken all the kinesthetic sensations. This is how sensibility is primed, including pressure, pain, position, direction, displacement and rhythm, simultaneously. Subsequently, the opposite force of expansion is triggered oxygen's forcing itself into the virtual space of the lungs through oral and nasopharyngeal spaces. This is accompanied by a sudden temperature change, from uterus to room temperature. There follows the manipulations of the body of the newborn by others against threatening gravity.

The mother is obviously the first organizer and the first regulator; she offers also the first cognitive template, her image to be internalized sense by sense, fragment by fragment, and gradually bundled together to arrive at the uniquely human total puzzle of a self-image. Our first "self" is vicarious ontogenetically, as the image of a goddess was phylogenetically, our projection of the fused maternal-self into one.

Piaget's theory of intelligence starts with functional integration of reflexes, but it neglects the role of the organizing mother as scaffold. Mother provides aliment from her body and with it goes the grammar for all coming relations. This is how *internalization of form* starts, the grammar of existence, the how-to. The mother piggybacks forms, symbols, emotional values, and ultimately meanings upon the infant's reflex infrastructure while it is being connected and integrated by the nervous system. Consciousness starts with behavioral conditioning that, made more complex, becomes learning. Mother does start from the intuitive belief that her newborn has a "theory of mind," to develop that theory in the child. She talks "motherese" to the baby much before the baby can understand.[365] The mother is repeating what happened phylogenetically; she invented culture and reinvents it again and again with every single child.

Most crucial for the development of subjectivity, Schore tells us, is *foveal eye contact*, a form of visual synchronization that gradu-

---

365 Alaugnier, P. (2001). *The Violence of Interpretation. From Pictogram to Statement.* Philadelphia. Taylor and Francis.

ally takes place during the first year of life, optimally intense at the time of breastfeeding and continuing to operate through the separation individuation process. Nature designed the optimal fovea-to-fovea synchronization distance by considering the breast-to-face distance. The part-object mouth-breast relationship Freud emphasized is invisibly accompanied by an intense gaze-dialogue of imaginary and reverberating objectification and subjectification, through synchronizations taking place in the fovea of the retina.[366] This has the effect of priming the visual sense as the primary relational sense in humans, superseding the pheromonal olfactory sense that prevails in other species.

The foveal synchronizations that start to occur during breastfeeding remain as the basic scaffold of interpersonal relationships. The iris of the eye regulates welcome and caution by relaxing and tightening up respectively. In the mother-and-child relationship, this is part of the first axis of language, bound to the protolanguage of emotion and mutual affect regulation.

With foveal eye contact arises human pride, the first and most fundamental of social emotions, and Schore tells us that the first year of life is about our mothers, celebrating our gestures and attitude unconditionally. This is how mothers intuitively convey to their children, with emotion and enthusiasm, the full recognition of their being human that Hegel talked about. This is also the origin of self-esteem based on positive reflected appraisals[367] for a whole crucial year, recorded in dopaminergic brain tracts that will continue to mediate pleasure through life.

1.6.6 The Premises of Human Intersubjectivity

Hearing one's own screech at birth is the first premise for intersubjectivity, because the cry creates a reflection of one's own sound,

366 Schore, A. (1994). "Visual Experiences and Socioemotional Development. In: *Affect Regulation and the Origins of the Self.* Ibid. Ch. 6. P. 71ff.
367 Sullivan, H.S. (1953). The Interpersonal Theory of Psychiatry. Ed. Helen Swick Perry and Mary Ladd Gawel. New York. Norton.

what will become speech when coming from others. Others, particularly the mother, intrusively interrupt one's cycle of sound and silence. Similarly the image of the addressing other, the mother, will be internalized visually to form a body image.

Reflected appraisals is the second premise, the internalization of other's evaluations of one's self. This occurs through social activity that is intersubjective, meaning a reciprocal chain of mutually determining events. This is the source of human pride, shame, and self-esteem. It occurs through the process that Hegel called recognition, being accepted as fulfilling the requirements for a member of the species with its benefits and obligations.

The third, and most important, premise is the frustration of one's demand when mother for the first time says "No"! after months of saying yes to every whim during the first year of life. As they did phylogenetically, mothers with the word and gesture "No"! open the gates both of culture and of the self. Here is where the activity gap between stimulus and response begins to be widened and occupied by first-order maternal mediations. This is what Freud called postponement of gratification that first comes from without. Frustration by a mother who has been fulfilling all necessities is equivalent to the eviction from the psychological paradise of early narcissism, and an analogue of the trauma of birth. Allan Schore provides us with details about the corresponding structural brain changes to these premises in the nervous system, neurotransmitter changes, and the concomitant muscular changes reflected in postural demeanor.[368]

Schore tells us that we grow, during our whole first year of life, to expect a celebratory and totally predictable mother image initially experienced as undifferentiated from ourselves, one that we were exposed to thousands of times through each and all of our senses, which she switched on by leaving her signature all over the brain along with our first identity. Paradoxically, we also become motor-

---

368 Schore, A. (1994). *Affect Regulation and the Origins of the Self. The Neurobiology of Emotional Development.* Part III. Late Infancy. P. 199 ss. Hillsdale, N.J. Lawrence Erlbaum Associates. Online in Questia. Accessed from <http://www.questia.com/read/57185676/affect-regulation-and-the-origin-of-the-self-the> on 2013-03-07.

ically autonomous through her ministrations, able and eager to explore the rest of the world with our own senses and skills.

As we start to independently explore our environment, we do so attached to an invisible leash that manifests itself in periodic millisecond foveal synchronizations with our mother. These keep us as if within the earlier safe container, our psychological first bubble extended. We must constantly return to the mother, for tactile feedback first, and then gradually for the more distant sound of her voice or even her flexible arm-length's presence as we map the contours of our environment with our proximate senses.[369] Mother remotely controls the child with her demeanor, particularly her facial expression, upper mostly, through her eyes and retinal fovea. The child reads the score and moves accordingly, counting on her usual approval. But, knowing areas of danger, the mother sets limits through her concern for safety. There comes a time when we want to insert the clip into the electric outlet because it logically fits, and that is when all hell breaks loose. Not only does our mother scream, she says "No"! with her whole being. Her posture and demeanor are drastically transformed: her face takes on a totally new countenance, until now totally unknown to us. Her new witch-image does not fit the thousands of imprints we have in our memory album; this new woman is a diabolical person. We for the first time have seen the face of catastrophe, and nothing could be worse. This is probably the phylogenetic image that, historically, triggered patriarchy.

Programmed for this event by evolution, for the traumatic cognitive dissonance of an unprecedented bundle of sensory data impossible to fit into any previous category of "mother," not only do we get consequently startled and upset, but in mirroring fashion, respond to this cognitive and emotional assault with our own peculiar change of demeanor. We Assume a fearful face and typically bent head laterally, averting our gaze, and suspending all motor initiative.

369 Pine, F., Bergman, A., Mahler, M.S. (2000). *The Psychological Birth of the Human Infant: Symbiosis and Individuation.* New York. Basic Books. Online in Questia. Accessed from <http://www.questia.com/read/98427085/the-psychological-birth-of-the-human-infant-symbiosis > on 2012-10-11.

We are magically paralyzed for the first time.

Most important, this highly dramatic event has also a crucial cascading effect in the biochemistry of the brain that hardwires entirely new brain tracks, routes of dysphoria embedded to balance those previous ones of pleasure from thalamus to cortex, involving also the parasympathetic branch of the autonomic nervous system.[370] The dopaminergic tracks that up to now have held hegemony in the brain now come to face opposite ones chemically connected to interact through completely new and different neurotransmitter tracks that lead to shame. This is reflected in the common expression "I wanted to disappear." In the motorically limited child the earliest defense mechanisms of freezing and camouflage result from hyper excitation concurrent with hyper-inhibition. They make themselves manifest for the first time in this mother-child interaction. These are also the earliest motoric and sensory dissociative defenses, frequent in children who are subject to abuse very early in their lives, traumatic stress' producing a parasympathetic form of freeze in creatures that are not physiologically ready to motorically fly away from danger.[371]

1.6.7 The Alternative to Master-Slave: Developmental-Historical-Cultural Paradigm

This "No"! event must, unconsciously, have been the basis for the Hegelian paradigm of self-consciousness origination, his theory of human recognition. It was mistakenly presented as the parable of two adult males' confronting each other, both demanding recognition. Typically, they got into a struggle to death, as is expected of male warring. Hegel leaves untouched interpersonal development, how the two adults got there, how they obtained their consciousness

---

370 Schore, A. Affect Regulation and the Origins of the Self. Ibid.
371 Perry, B. D. (1994a). Neurobiological sequelae of childhood trauma: post-traumatic stress disorders in children. In M. Murberg (Ed.), Catecholamines in Post-traumatic Stress Disorder: Emerging Concepts. (pp. 253-276). Washington, D.C. American Psychiatric Press.

and thirst for recognition. The Hegelian paradigm does, however, explain the introduction of slavery, the main "accomplishment" of patriarchy. The conflagration cannot result in death, because death would make recognition impossible; thus, slavery.

The slavish alternative to death entails a social contract that inaugurates exploitation of the vanquished by the victor, the establishment of slavery and dominant social hierarchy. This is how Hegel's first psychology is put forward in his *Phenomenology*,[372] the first modern sketch of a psychoanalytic theory. The master-slave paradigm in the origins of self-consciousness supersedes Plato's previous more mechanical, social-class model, in *The Republic*: guardian-king philosopher, civil servant, and worker, isomorphic with the psyche's virtues of wisdom, courage and desire. Hegel's theory starts with the master-slave or thesis/antithesis binary, and the synthesis comes later in the *Philosophy of Right*.[373] Interestingly, Hegel's first sketch eliminates the mediating middle class and leaves only the two poles, king and worker. While Freud took the Platonic model in his tripartite theory[374,375], Marx follows Hegel in

372 Hegel, G.W.F. (1967). *Hegel's Phenomenology of Mind.* From Harper & Row's Torchbooks' edition (1967) of the Phenome-nology (1807), translated by J B Baillie (1910), from University of Idaho, Department of Philosophy, thanks to Jean McIntire. § numbers from the Baillie translation have been inserted into the text of the Baillie translation and linked to explanations by J N Findlay. Φ links to original German text: Phänemenologie des Geistes. Online in MIA. Accessed from <https://www.marxists.org/reference/archive/hegel/phindex.htm> on 2014-10-05.
373 Hegel, G,W,F. (1820). *Hegel's Philosophy of Right.* Translated: by S W Dyde, 1896. First Published: by G Bell, London, 1896. Preface and Introduction with certain changes in terminology: from "Philosophy of Right", by G W F Hegel 1820. Prometheus Books; Remainder: from "Hegel's Philosophy of Right", 1820, translated, Oxford University Press; First Published: by Clarendon Press 1952, Translated: with Notes by T M Knox 1942. Online in MIA. Accessed from <https://www.marxists.org/reference/archive/hegel/works/pr/philosophy-of-right.pdf> on 2017-02-26.
374 Plato. (2008). The Republic. Trans. B. Jowett. Online in The Project Gutenberg EBook of The Republic, Ebook # 1497. (Written around 380 BCE). Accessed from <http://www.gutenberg.org/files/1497/1497-h/1497-h.htm> on 2012-11-03.
375 Plato. Phaedrus. (sections 246a–254e). Plato in Twelve Volumes, Vol. 9 translated by Harold N. Fowler. Cambridge, MA, Harvard University Press; London, William Heinemann Ltd. 1925. Online in Tufts' Perseus. Accessed from <http://www.perseus.tufts.edu/hopper/text?doc=Plat.+Phaedrus+246a&fromdoc=Perseus%3Atext%3A1999.01.0174> on 2014-10-05.

his capital-wage worker antagonism. In Freud's syllogistic schema of the mind the mediating ego the "go between,"[376] is Plato's middle class: auxiliaries, civil servants, and the military. The take-home message in all this is that form of government is universally internalized in the form of the self.

Politicians in general, as we well know, love the middle class to which they generally belong. They speak for the middle class caught in the dream to ascend and the nightmare of sinking. Middle-class ideology has the danger of fascism, and Freud's own theory has been used by the inventor of public relations and master spinner, Edward Louis James Bernays, Freud's nephew-in-law.[377] The real ideological split of class society is depicted in Hegel and Marx's binary theories, but the third element, middle class, is, since Plato, the compromising component.

Hegel's and Marx's models are entirely adultomorphic; here is what Sartre says about it: "Today's Marxists are concerned only with adults; reading them, one would believe that we are born at the age when we earn our first wages. They have forgotten their own childhoods. As we read them, everything seems to happen as if men experienced their alienation and their reification first in their own work, whereas in actuality each one lives it first, as a child, in his parents' work."[378] Sartre should have added particularly in her mother's work, which creates the core of subjectivity. Freud, on

376 Freud, S. (1932). "The Anatomy of the Mental Personality." From Lecture XXXI (1932). New Introductory Lectures on Psy-choanalysis. London. Hogarth Press. On-line in MIA. Accessed from <https://www.marxists.org/reference/subject/philosophy/works/at/freud2.htm> on 2014-10-05.

377 Bernays, E.L. (1955) The engineering of consent. University of Oklahoma Press. (Orig. Pub. 1947). Quote from Wikipedia. See also Adam Curtis' award-winning British television series "The Century of the Self" that focuses on how Sigmund Freud, Anna Freud, and Edward Bernays influenced the way corporations and governments have used herd consciousness to manipulate democ-racy.

378 Sartre, J.P. (1960). "The Problem of Mediations & Auxiliary Disciplines" Part II of Search for Method. In: An Introduction to Critique of Dialectical Reason. Trans: Hazel Barnes. Source: Existentialism from Dostoyevsky to Sartre (2nd part). New York. Vintage Books. Online in MIA. Accessed from <https://www.marxists.org/reference/archive/sartre/works/critic/sartre3.htm> on 2016-05-02.

the other hand, clearly influenced by Darwin, included in his theory a developmental line of bodily zones, connected to an intrapsychic machine-deploying libido, and only incidentally connected to an object with little power of determination. Starting with Melanie Klein however, some of Freud's disciples turned the Freudian model around first to consider concomitant internalized object relations, leading eventually to such a fully relational intersubjective theory as psychoanalysis has evolved into. Freud's main theoretical limitation is his displacement of interpersonal relations (that some considered the concern of sociology), into intrapsychic entelechies. That is in part reflected in Freud's need for a peculiar form of internal energy, libido. But, as in religion, the Freudian intrapsychic drama is a replica of the real, reciprocal, hierarchical, and oppressive one.

The obvious crucial role of the mother, highlighted by Schore and the neurobiologists, is not acknowledged in psychoanalytic theory, with the exceptions of females, interestingly: Melanie Klein, Margaret Mahler, Mary Ainsworth, and Karen Horney besides feminist writers such as Naomi Schor, Julia Kristeva, and Luce Irigaray. Freud does not tell us that all part-objects are initially undifferentiated in terms of self and mother, and that our body image is the copy of the mother's image. He does not recognize that, independent of gender, we all introject first our mother's image, and that our individuation comes from a previous maternal imaginary merger. These are by no means trivial matters, because early relational processes are the groundwork for all later identifications that will conserve them. The mother first contributes her instinct as the universal human moral ground. The father is a latecomer into these identificatory events, and is clearly the more incidental figure, his function's having been previously fulfilled by the maternal uncle. Against all this, Freud universally places the father at the center of child development and of the family.

This is not to deny that Freud does have the incontestable merit of (like Spinoza) rooting human psychology in our bodies, and developing a whole theory from that perspective. The correction of the

relational deficit in Freud's theory started not by chance with Melanie Klein, and continued with Mahler, Fairbairn, Sullivan, Horney,
and others.

The alternative to the Hegelian paradigm, the maternal one, has
been offered by the historical-cultural-instrumental school of Lev
Vygotsky, and is condensed in his concept of *Zone of proximal development*.[379] This is an alternative model of human development,
eminently relational and educational, based on the collaborative
couching of the less developed child by the more advanced mother.
This is not a psychoanalytic, but a psychological-educational, model. To take place, transformative education needs a fertile zone of
readiness that mothers and educators rather intuitively build upon.
Instead of focusing on the individualistic outcome that is tested as
skill in the current mainstream, the Vygotskian educational model
shifts the focus to the relationship between educator and learner.
Intelligence is here interpersonal, as a common ground of fertility
and possibility makes actuality of skill possible. A related theory
is that of Brazilian educator Pablo Freire, that links education with
practical needs instead of accumulation of useless knowledge, as
in the capitalist model.[380] Both Vygotsky and Freire are inspired by
Marx's psychology.

In this alternative paradigm, consciousness and intelligence are
measured relationally, on the premise that what the learner can accomplish alone is less than what he can accomplish in collaboration
with the educator. "When it was first shown that the capability of
children with equal levels of mental development to learn under a

379 Vygotsky, L. (1978). "Interaction between learning and development." From: Mind
and Society. (pp. 79-91). Cambridge, MA. Harvard University. In: Gauvain, M. and
Cole, M. (1977), Editors. Readings on the Development of Children. Second Edi-
tion. Press. New York. W.H. Freeman and Company. P. 33. Online in Carnegie Melon
Psychology. Accessed from <http://www.psy.cmu.edu/~siegler/vygotsky78.pdf> on
2014-09-14.
380 Freire, P. (2005). *Pedagogy Of The Oppressed*. 30th. Anniversary Edition. Trans.
Myra Bergman Ramos. With an Introduction by Donaldo Macedo. New York and
London. Continuum. Accessed from <https://libcom.org/files/Freire/Pedagogyofthe-
Oppresed.pdf> on 2014-10-05.

teacher's guidance varied to a high degree, it became apparent that those children were not mentally the same age and that the subsequent course of their learning would obviously be different. This difference...is what we call the zone of proximal development. It is the distance between the actual developmental level as determined by independent problem-solving and the level of potential development as determined through problem-solving under adult guidance or in collaboration with more capable peers."[381] Vygotsky goes on to add that the zone of proximal development defines areas in the process of maturation, "buds" or "flowers". Independent problem-solving, on the other hand defines only "fruits." This alternative model is the matriarchal, family model of education.

The same principle has been operational in psychoanalysis with the concept of "timing," in which an interpretation by the analyst is totally barren unless the patient has arrived, faced with a puzzle, at the point whether s/he can see that unique opening. This means that both minds are properly synchronized upon a common ground, even though their scopes differ.

Along with the psychoanalytical evidence and the evidence from neurobiology, the developmental-historical-cultural paradigm not only reinforces the theory of early matriarchal dependency and development but offers an alternative framework for psychology that is integrative, holistic, and based on cooperation and regard for the individual child as equal.

---

381 Vygotsky, L. (1978). "Interaction between learning and development. Ibid. P. 33.

1.7 NO! NEGATION AND HUMAN ACTIVITY

"The universal is a people, a group of individuals in general, an existent whole, the universal force. It is of insurmountable strength against the individual, and is his necessity and the power oppressing him. And the strength that each one has in his being-recognized is that of a people. This strength, however, is effective only insofar as it is united into a unity, only as will. The universal will is the will as that of all and each, but as will it is simply this Self alone. The activity of the universal is a unity. The universal will has to gather itself into this unity. It has first to constitute itself as a universal will, out of the will of individuals, so that this appears as the principle and element. Yet on the other hand the universal will is primary and the essence – and individuals have to make themselves into the universal will through the negation of their own will, [in] externalization and cultivation. The universal will is prior to them, it is absolutely there for them – they are in no way immediately the same.

Hegel[382]

We are rather forced to conclude that consciousness is an emergent from such behavior; that so far from being a precondition of the social act, the social act is the precondition of it. The mechanism of the social act can be traced out without introducing into it the conception of consciousness as a separable element

---

382 Hegel, G.W.F. (1805-6). The Philosophy of Spirit (Jena Lectures). (Also known as "Realphilosophie" II). Part III. Constitu-tion. Online in MIA, Accessed from <https://www.marxists.org/reference/archive/hegel/works/jl/ch03.htm> on 2016-02-27.

within that act; hence the social act, in its more elementary stages or forms, is possible without, or apart from, some form of consciousness.

Mead[383]

1.7.1 The Place of Negation in Evolution

Motion occurs through negation, and so does universality. Movement of an object in space negates one point to occupy the next, and a line is a succession of points negated. Equally in time, each instant is negated by the next, and when I finish saying *present* it has been already negated as *past*. This was the reasoning of Hegel in the *Phenomenology*, the work through which he found himself rediscovering the dialectical method, the logic of motion. Since everything in the universe is in constant motion, the real logic of the universe is not Aristotelian formal logic but Hegelian dialectical logic. In psychology, sensation is negated by perception, perception negated by thought; and in terms of development, each stage is negated by the subsequent one. Democritus already had said what scientists generally accept today, that the universe is in constant motion, that we do not cross the same river twice. This is equivalent to saying that the universe is a constant act of negation. This is antithetical to "there is no alternative."

Motion could not be understood using the formal logic of Aristotle, because in it negation means annihilation, disposal, disappearance, or suppression. Science has taught us that in the universe energy may not disappear; and that when it seems to disappear it has been only transformed. Hegel built his dialectic along the same tenor: negation is sublation, the thesis and the antithesis, in the

---

383 Mead, G.H. (1967). Mind, Self, and Society. Section 2 The Behavioristic Significance of Attitudes. Chicago. University of Chicago Press. P. 18. (Orig. Pub. 1934). Accessed from <http://www.brocku.ca/MeadProject/Mead/pubs2/mindself/Mead_1934_07. html> on 2012-10-10.

Hegelian syllogism, are really assimilated into a synthesis through a struggle and a final compromise of sorts. The universe, being an ensemble of matter and energy forms, moves by transformation from form to form, matter and energy themselves being transitory forms. In the last instance, nothing is disposable except for form. We can see that this is the opposite of what Plato had to say about the matter. What we humans dispose of, particularly in wasteful capitalism, nature has to recycle, no matter how long it takes; that is how we are posing a problem to ourselves, to our nature, in terms of unsustainable waste. This was expressed as the first law of thermodynamics of Carnot and Clausius, that states energy cannot be created or destroyed, only transformed. Logically, if the universe is expanding as we are told, it is because it did and will again contract. It may be that the expansion is only the diastole of a universal pulse.

One of the main differences between the logic of Aristotle and that of Hegel is that in the latter negation is transformative conservation, supersession, or sublation. Hegel uses the term sublation[384] to indicate that in his system what is negated is conserved, not destroyed. His concept is here congruent with the first law of thermodynamics. In this view, the universe is a struggle between embodied forms of material energy, some highly organized, some the opposite. An example of the former is life, and of the latter entropy, the progressive and regressive tendencies always at work in matter. Freud did see this correctly, at least from the point of view of physics, in his Eros and Thanatos drives. I postulate that, although both sexes have both drives, Eros is the default as the maternal drive, while Thanatos has proven itself historically to be the patriarchal option. Constant instinctual polarization, rather than titration, is probably due to both historical factors' scarcity being uppermost, if now not natural, but artificially created through war.

Evolution is the history of forms of energy's becoming complex. Before consciousness (the paradigm of conserving dialectical

---

384 Wikipedia. "Aufheben." Accessed from <https://en.wikipedia.org/wiki/Aufheben#cite_note-Walter_Kaufmann_1966.2C_p._144-3> on 2015-08-17.

negation) appeared in the scene, negation was mechanical, as Hegel describes it at the beginning of the *Phenomenology*.[385] Consciousness introduces a more complex form of negation, formal-only negation possible through reflection or representation. Representation reproduces only the form. This becomes most visible in *language*: the negation of the image in turn becomes the negation of its material object. Linguistic representation makes possible to shift negation from an analogue (perceptual) to a digital brain-form. It should be clear from all the above that Hegel saw negation as a form of alienation in its most general sense, change of form.

It is legitimate to say that culture is part of the process of negation, and so is its analogue, the self. They are both the result of adaptive, evolutionary processes. That the same processes that took place in natural history occur ontogenetically in the development of individuals is a truism, even if rejected by mainstream science in its mechanical version. Although the gestural "No"! is expressed prior to humans in concrete, non-linguistic ways, through destruction, the constructive "No"! that conserves and sublates is the human *no*. In this light repression, foreclosure, both political and psychological, is both a physical and a logical impossibility. This is the reason the symptom returns.

1.7.2 The Dialectic of Desire

The highest evolutionary form of negation, linguistic negation most characteristic of humans, is what creates human desire as an analogue of natural need. We have seen in the two previous chapters the important function of female and mother's saying "No"! in the origination of culture, both in the history of the genus as well as in the biography of the individual. In phylogeny, women solidarily

---

385 Hegel, G.W.F. (1807). "I: Certainty at the Level of Sense Experience – the "This", and "Meaning." In: *The Phenomenology of Mind.* From Harper Torchbooks' edition of the Phenomenology, from Uni-versity of Idaho, Department of Philosophy by Jean McIntire. Online in MIA, Hegel by Hypertext. Accessed from <https://www.marxists.org/reference/archive/hegel/works/ph/phprefac.htm> on 2015-07-11

created a symbolic pause in sexual access, a non-natural mediation postponing the satisfaction of the instinctual sexual necessity; this not only created desire, but allowed mothers to universally place contingencies on its satisfaction. Ontogenetically, the satisfaction of a child's want is postponed by the care-taking mother, who introduces a gestural and linguistic symbol, "No"!, a new mediation in the behavioral continuity of the developing child. In both cases, the purpose is regulation, and particularly, as Schore points out, regulation of affect, the primary language. Mothers were able to use intuition because they were evolutionarily programmed to strategize for the species. They were able to act within the constructively possible, based on their life-instinct. In other words, they had the intuitive capacity to act within a safe and ready zone of learning, as proposed by Vygotsky. The signals of natural need and want in this fashion began to be transformed, rerouted, to create signals of regulated human desire. The cultural grammar of desire is based on the maternal intuition of what is necessary and constructive. We can observe this taking place intuitively, without maternal training.

Anthropologically, the sex strike could accomplish the first group sublimation through negation. This transition was so important that it was reinforced with myth and ritual. Culture is the result of the regulation of instinctual behavior through successful regulation of affect. The physiological and chemical ground of these processes is being studied by neurobiology. This amounts to the contingency-based constructive transformation of instinctual activity by human mediation that ultimately results in choice, alternatives, and free self-determined human activity. Motherly "No"! is what initiates the process of postponement and the production of desire. Before desire was created by a sublated form of negation, satisfaction was immediate and based on demand and force. After "No"! becomes an institutionalized linguistic signal, a less coercive form of learning accelerates, as it makes physical restraint unnecessary. Satisfaction is then postponed through internal mechanisms that trigger the signal from the self. This is internalized self-control or self-regulation, what we call the self. This whole process, institutionalized through education, becomes part of the social reality of culture.

What produces human desire is the combination of instinctual need and its frustration. That is why human desire is most effectively produced by a titration of exposure and concealment. Desire is a characteristic of humans because only humans can postpone, through learning, the satisfaction of natural necessities. It is the postponement of satisfaction, Freud pointed out, that opens the space for sublimating mediations and, therefore, for culture. The delay in satisfaction still leaves the image of the object in mind and kindles the imagination and consciousness. For desire to appear, the satisfying object and event must become negated to paradoxically enhance the drive. Desire results from the imaginary representation of the partially concealed object. Ultimately it is language that becomes the mediating instrument, concealer, and displayer. The highest desire in humans is the desire to be recognized as such through language.

Intrinsically, by teaching the child self-regulation, to delay satisfaction, the mother is teaching the central function of social regulation.[386] This is the ultimate key to human success, and it consists in the capacity to titrate proximity and distance, activity and self-constraint, disclosure and concealment, in a social space determined by historical circumstances.

Psychologically, the child's inborn temperament and the mother's socially tempered personality are not necessarily well-fitted at the outset of their intersubjective journey; they require a mutual process of assimilation and accommodation to arrive at *goodness of fit*.[387] There is an evolutionary individual sequence from a) *temperament*, the inborn nature of the child's form of reactivity, to b) *character*, the deep remainder of the early learned configuration of interpersonal drives, to c) *personality*, the appearance form, in attitude and gesture, of the adult fitted into circumstantial social roles. Dialectically, temperament is overriden by character, which is in

---

386 Schore, A. (1994). *Affect Regulation and the Origins of the Self.* Ibid. P. 31
387 Chess, S. and Thomas, A. (1996). *Temperament in Clinical Practice.* London and New York. The Guilford Press

turn overriden by personality.

It has been proposed, *i.e.* by Cloninger,[388] that temperament entails innate differences in learning habits as well as skills proclivities in the brain. These come to be manifest in procedural, long term memory that involves the amygdala and limbic system of the brain. Character, on the other hand, represents differences in concept-based goals, and values related to propositional, semantic memory, manifest in the brain areas of hyppocampus, and neocortex. The two contribute to forming the personality.

The first object that the child needs is necessarily partial, for example the skin or the breast, as mother and self are initially not integrated into a total image. To integrate and differentiate mother and self is a first necessity, the mother becoming the object of desire. This is in part because the mother has the power to regulate, to satisfy needs, and also to postpone their satisfaction by externally controlling the activity of the infant. Desire for the object is based on the object's properties that satisfy a hierarchy of needs, both material and psychological. The first material need of the child is aliment, along with safety. The feeling of safety is conveyed by the mother's willingness to respond. Needs evolve into a complex, culturally determined hierarchy.

1.7.3 Being and Nothingness

Being is the most abstract category of all, becoming other from nothingness. Jean Paul Sartre follows Spinoza, Hegel and Marx in assuming the unity of reality and its successive appearances. As it is for Hegel the objective logic of being and essence, for Sartre the essence of reality is the history of its appearances,[389] not starting

---

388 Cloninger, R.C. (1998). "Temperament and Personality." Ch. 20. In: Squire, L.R., Kosslyn, S.M. (1998). *Findings and Cur-rent Opinion in Cognitive Neuroscience.* Cambridge, Massachusetts. MIT Press..

389 Sartre, J.P. (1956). *Being and Nothingness. A phenomenological essay on ontology.* Trans. Hazel E. Barnes. New York. Philosophical Library. Online in Dominican House of Studies, Priory of the Immaculate Conception. Accessed from <http://www.dhspriory.org/kenny/PhilTexts/Sartre/BeingAndNothingness.pdf> On 2014-11-06.

with God but with Matter, that has changed appearances until it has been able to produce its self-consciousness in humans. Self-consciousness appears to come from nothingness, but it is in fact nothing but the aggregate of all the social relations in history preceded by the good sense of nature. Sartre says that man produces being from nothingness, but he is incorrect. For Marx, each individual is produced by a collective consciousness that has had a number of historical appearances, the last being current ideology and science. This duality is not in the dialectical nature of consciousness; it is a split caused by the division of the human species into social classes. Ideology is a vestigial overgrowth, a mixture of religion, philosophy and spinning sophistry. The puzzling question is why a species, *Homo sapiens,* came to produce not consciousness but alienation, an ideology against its own interests. How could the good sense of nature have allowed for this contradiction? The first philosopher to be puzzled by this question was Spinoza.

The Hegelian type of motion as appearances that included evolution and history is, in fact, a condensed form of epigenetic developmentalism. When Sartre proposed that man makes himself out of nothingness, through choices, he ignores the determinism of both culture and nature. We are not, and never will be, free of either. We must breathe, eat, have shelter, before we do anything else. Sartre cannot see that what philosophically appears today as nothingness is the huge ensemble of all the history of the social relations repressed. As Sartre himself said, to construct my so-called free identity, I have to produce myself by building upon what my parents produced through their particular choices for me.[390] But my parents had to produce themselves from whatever their own parents chose for them and so on back to mitochondrial Eve. We are the product of the most comprehensive and inclusive collective work. This is why Marx said in his *Thesis on Feuerbach* that the essence of man is the

390 Sartre, J.P. (1989). "Existentialism Is a Humanism." Trans: Philip Mairet. In: *Existentialism from Dostoyevsky to Sartre,* ed. Walter Kaufman. Oklahoma, OK. Meridian Publishing Company; (Orig. Pub. 1956). Online in MIA. Accessed from <https://www.marxists.org/reference/archive/sartre/works/exist/sartre.htm> on 2016-05-03.

ensemble of the social relations.[391]

In Hegelian logic, an object's successive appearances are syllo-gistic, each step's being a thesis to be confronted by its antithesis and resolved in a synthesis. All objects in the universe are in the same type of motion through negation that conserves. Appearance is thus synonymous with developmental stage, and its succession applies not only to objects but, after the inception of consciousness, as an adaptation in evolution also to object representation in conscious-ness. The essence of an object, as well as of the consciousness of it, is the history of their appearances. The consciousness of totemism is still vestigially present in religion and in politics. Totemism was su-perseded, some of its features conserved, in mythology, and it is still present in the emblems of ideology. Religion, organized mythology is still vestigially alive, and so is philosophy that partially super-seded it and in turn is still present in science. These are successive historical presentations of consciousness. Matriarchy was the thesis superseded by the antithesis (patriarchy) that could only build itself epigenetically, upon the achievements of matriarchy. The synthesis is still in the future as potentiality, but its germs lie in present ide-ologies.

What occurred phylogenetically repeats itself, although not me-chanically, in every newcomer to the species. Being becomes con-scious through the relation of the newborn to its mother, but such consciousness is not enough for civil society. This is the human id-iosyncrasy and the paradox of evolution. Self comes from mirroring alienation in (m)other.[392] Universally and independent of sex, our original being is alienated mother-being.

The particular way the mother vicariously managed our satisfac-

391 Marx, K. (1938). *Theses on Feuerbach. 6. In: The German Ideology.* London. Law-rence and Wishart. (Written in 1845). Online version Marxists Internet Archive. Ac-cessed from <http://www.marxists.org/archive/marx/works/1845/theses/index.htm> on 2012-09-09.

392 Lacan, J. (2002). "The Mirror Stage as Formative of the I Function, as Revealed in Psychoanalytic Experience." Trans. Alan Sheridan. In: Ecrits. 1. Pp. 3-9. New York. Norton. Online in Western Illinois University. Accessed from <http://faculty.wiu.edu/D-Banash/eng299/LacanMirrorPhase.pdf> on 2014-11-06.

tion and frustration, our fulfillment and disappointment, outside of ourselves, when internalized becomes the psychological grammar of our social self-regulation. It is the very first ground of our personality, and it is alien. It does not come from nothingness, but from mother.

Our personality is the objectification, the last appearance in a succession after character and temperament. It contains assimilated identifications built upon that of our mother. Mothers precede father, teachers, heroes, love objects, authority figures, *etc.* Personality is what we display as the result of the activity of our initially ex-centric self. Our personality is the way we make ourselves objective, the way we represent to others the type of subject we are or want to be. Self is the manager of that representation that originally was managed by our mother.

This process of identification and transformation is ongoing throughout life. We are always in reciprocal and reverberating social intercourse with others. We thus build being not from nothingness, but from others.

1.7.4 The Chess Game of Intersubjectivity: A Battle of Negations

Intersubjectivity, as described by George Herbert Mead, is like a constant chess game played by subjects, except that each subject is always playing with many others. The game entails the synchronization of attitudes that start from instinctual dispositions, followed by the symbolic, meaningful conversation of gestures that reverberate. Each act reciprocally triggers a reaction, another act, and so on, starting a chain of reciprocal behavioral modifications that involve both attitudes and gestures. In humans, this game is mainly mediated through language. "There is an organization of the various parts of the nervous system that are going to be responsible for acts, an organization which represents not only that which is immediately taking place, but also the later stages that are to take place."[393] Here

---

393 Mead, G.H. (1967). *Mind, Self, and Society.* Section 2 The Behavioristic Significance

Mead refers to attitudes, what Briffault called instinctual dispositions. In clinical situations; a similar process was described by Melanie Klein as projective identifications, intersubjectively.[394] Two
subjects collude to bring about a reenactment of old, unresolved
conflict, bringing us back to the concept of transference in Freud[395]
that operates in the same fashion, except that the analyst becomes
aware of the projective attempt and resists entering the collusion in
order to therapeutically work with it. Family theorists such as Ivan
Boszormenyi-Nagy have also illustrated these archaic mechanisms
in clinical practice.[396] The key element in a chain of reverberating
reciprocal social acts is that attitudes are constantly being negated
by gestures changed by words that eventually result in social events
and outcomes. But already the Greek philosophers had said the same
thing more succinctly: that the virtue of the subject is in its fitness
for its object. For Mead the *me* part of the self is a condensation of
the history of social acts. Marx expressed this as the ensemble of all
the social relations.

The main characteristic of this game of intersubjectivity is that it
mediates all behavior, its ultimately coercive force being not physical, but moral: the history of culture has modified gestures, particularly through language. What appears as freedom conceals the fact
that culture is largely the government of the dead, as Comte said;
our ancestors built it. Language is ultimately an alien script, and
spontaneous attitudes are changed by anticipation, by political correctness. Social role as a powerful part of language that already determines the infrastructure of power and hierarchy in any particular

of Attitudes. Chicago. University of Chicago Press. P. 11. (Orig. Pub. 1934). Accessed
from   <http://www.brocku.ca/MeadProject/Mead/pubs2/mindself/Mead_1934_07.
html> on 2012-10-10.

394 Klein, M. (1946). "Notes on Some Schizoid Mechanisms." In: Klein, M. (1975). Envy
and Gratitude and Other Works. 1946-1963. (The Writings of Melanie Klein, Volume
3). London. The Hogarth Press.

395 Freud, S. (1920). "Transference." Chapter XXVII, Section Three in: *A General Introduction to Psychoanalysis.* Online in Bertelby. Accessed from < http://www.bartleby.
com/283/27.html> on 2015-05-07.

396 Boszormenyi-Nagy, I. and Spark. G.M. (1984). *Invisible Loyalties. Reciprocity in In-
tergeneratioonal Family Therapy.* New York. Brunner and Mazel.

relation. Sartre illustrated the sacrifice of the self to the social role.[397]

In the Hegelian parable of master and slave, the social game starts to take place between symmetrical adults who vie for recognition. Since without recognition they are not human yet, they engage as animals in the manner Mead illustrates, through emotional expression. Warriors as they were, they express their attitude and engage in battle to death. Fear of death subordinates the slave, who then proceeds to develop gesture into language. From symmetry, contending males created subordination.

The case is different in the Vygotskian, matriarchal paradigm, because the players are not symmetrical but complementary to start with, mother and child. Mother's function is to give recognition. The relationship cannot be symmetrical since the mother is sapient and the infant is not. The mother instinctually gives of herself to the child until the child is able to start building up her or his own consciousness.

To teach the game of sociality the mother intuitively gives to the child according to the child's readiness to receive. The mother is constantly anticipating an outcome from the child's potentiality that the child will realize and eventually appropriate for his/herself by internalization.

These are the two contrasting paradigms in the game of intersubjectivity, Hegelian and Vygotskian. They express opposite instinctual dispositions or attitudes.,

1.7.5 Playing and Being Played: The Dialectic of Agency

In psychoanalytic practice, we frequently find players whose life-game is clearly being played by someone else. We focus only on the tip of the iceberg, the unconscious of the patient, often leaving alone the bad faith of the alien agent. In a psychoanalysis fo-

---

397 Sartre, J.P. (1992). *Being and Nothingness.* New York. Washington Square Press. (Orig. Pub. 1943). Online in Scribd. Ac-cessed from <http://www.scribd.com/doc/10268925/Sartre-Being-and-Nothingness#scribd> on 2015-11-02.

cused on consciousness, on ideology, the same phenomenon would be observable in everyone. We all constantly struggle with relatively minimal success to re-appropriate our real self from mystifying patriarchal rules. The purpose of psychoanalysis is to place the subject in command of his or her own life, but to what extent this is possible without an analysis of culture is a moot point. Paradoxically, since we all were initially played by our mothers, we all have the vulnerability, and perhaps even the desire to go back to that type of safety. The premise of psychoanalysis, as Karen Horney saw it, is that it is never too late to rescue one's true agency and real self, of course in a social, constraining context.

After the mother has finished endowing the child with the awesome quality of self-regulation, if biased by her own background, the titration of interpersonal distance and intimacy is the key to social success. The father usually enters the picture representing the shift from the narrow network of mother and family to the ever-expanding one of civil society. Opposite to the family relational emphasis on giving and cooperation guided by needs, civil society is more about contributing and taking. Needs are to a large extent determined by others. The relative safety experienced in the average family is replaced by a paranoid outlook. In civil society, everyone has to negotiate self and social role. The existential freedom that Sartre points out is limited by a cultural window, often narrow. Success in civil society is largely compliance.

Negation produces desire and this applies materially to scarcity. Hegel pointed out in the *Phenomenology* that need or desire after deprivation overcomes the animal state of complacency associated with satiation. Capitalism uses this premise to produce artificial scarcity through the production of spurious needs. The universal equivalent of the object of desire has been transformed into money, not only desire for the object but identification with it. The object money is a material representation of human objectification. Money is social human labor, objectified while transforming the riches of nature that satisfy necessities. Mystification, confusion, and reification or subjection to the object are all components of alienation, becoming other than human, object-like.

Our agency has as its boundary that of others unless it becomes solidarity. The social role is the demarcation of the limits of individual agency in a social field. Freedom has its limit in that of others. In competitive class or civil society the game consists not only in finding our strengths but also the vulnerability of others. This logic of negation in families is usually constructive, while that of civil society tends to be destructive, as in present-day universally imposed austerity towards capital growth. Here the different instinctual dispositions of male and female are manifest.

The mother phase in psychoanalysis is named pre-Oedipal, and it sets in place all the first-order mediations for the child to be able to enter the triadic structure of civil society, where alliances around interests and exclusion of opposites result in opposite social classes. The mother has first taught the basic intersubjective strategies in family life, which are preponderantly based on necessity, but in civil society are often replaced by artificial needs.

We are always actively playing but also being played by the larger forces of nature, society and history. This dialectic is represented in our consciousness as consciousness and self-consciousness, and in our self as *I* and *me*.

1.7.6 Negation and Totality

Judging by the cultural consequences of females of the species' solidarity in saying "No Access"! to their counterparts, and subsequently mothers' universally saying "No!" to children for the same purpose, Knight and Shore have outlined negation, in anthropology and psychoanalytic neurobiology respectively, as the generative principle of analogic culture and self.

In terms of recursiveness, mythology had already understood

this. In the Pantheon,[398] at the beginning there were goddesses. Chaos, deep and empty darkness, was the first and Gaia, munificent Mother Earth, the second. Various male and female gods came then, Tartaros, a thunderous pit under the world that becomes the prison of undesirable gods, and Eros, the God of desire.[399] These are the original protagonists. We still tend to think of earth and origin as feminine.

While goddess Chaos produces mostly darkness and negativity, particularly through her daughter Night that births her whole family through parthenogenesis, including her children Sleep and Death, it is not so with Gaia, who has the most genealogical importance for humans. Broad-breasted to represent abundance, she portrays the origin of earth, then the center of the universe, and the earliest forms of evolution. Made of a concoction of fire, soil, air and water, Gaia not only impregnates herself, but is able to achieve virgin birth. She delivered two sons, Ouranus and Pontos, Heaven and Sea, both of whom she then proceeds to consort with in sexual intercourse. She has two families and a crop of second generation Titans that populate the first, divine world. With Pontos she only engenders sea-beings and monsters; with her favorite Ouranus, she procreates a brood of three couples, born siblings-in-marriage to the first families of Titans, besides Monsters and Cyclops. The latter are the strongest and most ferocious forces of nature imprisoned by Ouranus, unfortunately in the very entrails of Gaia, who feels usurped and irremediably offended.

Natural consorts of their sisters the brother-Titans contribute the third generation of gods. One of them, the youngest male Cronus the horned one, is also the rebellious one. Jealous of his lusty father, Cronus promptly aligns with Gaia's hurtful resentment of Ou-

398 Hesiod. The Homeric Hymns and Homerica with an English Translation by Hugh G. Evelyn-White. Theogony. Cambridge, MA.,Harvard University Press; London, William Heinemann Ltd. 1914. (Written circa 700 BCE). Online in Perseus Digital Library, Tufts University. Online in Hesiod. Theogony. Accessed from <http://www.perseus.tufts.edu/hopper/text?doc=Perseus:text:1999.01.0130> on 2013-08-29.

399 Hard, R. (2004). The Routledge Handbook of Greek Mythology. Based on H.J. Rose's Handbook of Greek Mythology. P. 22. New York and London. Routledge.

ranus. Mother and child plot against the inventor of tyranny, and Cronus eventually manages to castrate his father with a sickle as he is about to cover Gaia. Then, in the second *coup d'état* — Ouranus had already dethroned Gaia — Cronus both supplants the ruler and consolidates patriarchal succession once and for all. This is the first patriarchal version of Oedipus.

His father emasculated, Cronus throws away the bleeding remains, but the spilling blood still manages to impregnate Gaia for the last time. The result of the first unplanned pregnancy is three Erinyes, avengers of wrong, and thirteen giants, their unwelcome size condemning them to loom under the mountains as volcanoes. From the froth of the testicles that land in the sea arises well-known Aphrodite.

Male Titans, now unquestioned rulers of the universe, proceed to express their instinct by inventing war, Titanomachy, deployed against the third, aspiring generation of gods. From his sister Rhea, Cronus has given birth to a new cohort of gods, now called Olympians because of their residence. This is an age of prosperity, but Cronus himself is obsessed with the return of the repressed, the murder of his father. He consequently devours his first five newborn children, swaddling clothes and all, afraid that they will grow up to maim and supplant him as he did with his father. It takes Rhea until her sixth pregnancy to figure out a trick to save her child. Conspiring with her parents upon the birth of the one shining God, Zeus, she hides him and places a stone instead within his swaddle, for Cronus to gulp down.

Zeus grows up to fulfill the feared prophecy and commits patricide. Becoming the new ruler, he forces his father to regurgitate his brothers, and enlisted for his coup Monsters, Giants and Cyclops in a ten-year war. Politically astute by nature, he exiles his former allies, along with the Titans, back to the underworld.

Only two Titans escaped who had aligned with Zeus and were of use: Prometheus named for his forethought, and Epimetheus for his afterthought. The two brothers-in-thought were assigned the task of populating the world with a new species of mortals. Epimetheus became busy devising horns, wings, beaks, hoofs, tails, and all sorts of complicated bodily parts, hides and colors seemingly intended for trans-humans. Prometheus, with feminine intuition, focused on making all humans simply dramatic agents in the image of the gods.

Prometheus had to fuel and empower his puny invention, and for that purpose stole the secret of fire from Mount Olympus to bestow it to his humans. With fire comes brainpower and the arts of civilization. Irate, Zeus makes Prometheus pay dearly. He is bound to a rock at the mercy of a vulture that everyday feeds on his hardly recouped liver.

Humans made in the image of gods are also punished by Zeus through the bequest of Pandora, "full of gifts." The first mortal woman came with her proverbial box. She has the power to startle and lead men astray at first sight, her descendant women destined to torment the patriarchal race. The only silver lining here is that there is hope at the bottom of Pandora's box.

This is how, according to Greek mythology, we transitioned from female origin through female negation, and from the realm of the material to that of consciousness.

1.7.7 Negation is Sublation

The negation of nature does not destroy; it conserves and transforms. This is what Hegel in his *Logic* called sublation. "Thus, for instance, the temperature of water is first of all indifferent in relation to its state as a liquid; but by increasing or decreasing the temperature of liquid water a point is reached at which this state of cohesion alters and the water becomes transformed on the one side into steam and on the other into ice."[400] Along the same line Clausius says that in a closed system, energy cannot be created or destroyed;

---

400 Hegel, G.W.F. (1830). *Encyclopedia,*.Collected Works, VI, p. 217. Moscow. Progress Press. Quoted by Engels. Engels, F. (1925). *Dialectics of Nature.* First Published: in Russian and German in the USSR in 1925, except for Part Played by Labour, 1896 and

only transformed. The issue remains whether the whole universe is an open system in the way that the observable universe is.[401]

Slavery, conserving the vanquished instead of killing them, could be legitimized in history as a form of sublation as Hegel did in his recognition passage. The Jesuits, however, documented the fact that American indigenous peoples adopted their vanquished into their tribes rather than making them slaves; that may have been the matriarchal model.[402] Sublation is also the epistemological model for Freud's notion of the return of the repressed: the memory of a trauma does not simply fade into nothingness but remains active and reiteratively attempts to return in the disguised form of symptoms. "The main differences between the various neuroses are shown in the way in which the repressed ideas return..."[403]

One of the negative consequences of the hypostatization of logic into formal logic by the Greek Sophists is the introduction of negation as annihilation. "Aristotle's logic is concerned with separate, discrete (self-)identities in a deductive pattern. Hegel dissolves this classical static view in a dynamic movement towards the whole. The whole is an overcoming which preserves what it overcomes. Nothing is lost or destroyed but raised up and preserved as in a spiral.

Natural Science and the Spirit World, 1898; Transcribed: by Sally Ryan and jjazz@ hwcn.org 1998/2001; Notes and Fragments transcribed by Andy Blunden 2006. Online in MIA. Accessed from <https://www.marxists.org/archive/marx/works/1883/ don/index.htm> on 2017-03-02. Source: Hegel for Beginners, by and Andrzej Krauze, Published by Icon Books, 14 of 175 pages reproduced here, minus the abundant illustrations.

401 Bertalanffy, L. von (1968)."The Meaning of General System Theory." Chapter 2 of *General System Theory. Foundations, Devel-opment, Applications.* New York. George Braziller. Pp. 30-53. Online in Monoskop. Accessed from <http://monoskop. org/images/7/77/Von_Bertalanffy_Ludwig_General_System_Theory_1968.pdf> on 2015-08-20.

402 Thwaites R. G. (Ed.)(1896). "Iroquois, Lower Canada; 1653." Preface to Volume 40. *The Jesuit Relations and Allied Documents Travels and Explorations of the Jesuit Missionaries in New France 1610—1791.* Cleveland: The Burrows Brothers Company, Pub-lishers. Accessed from <http://puffin.creighton.edu/jesuit/relations/relations_40.html> on 2015-08-20.

403 Freud, S. (1957). "The Unconscious." In: Strachey, J. Ed. The Standard Edition of the Complete Psychological Works of Sigmund Freud, Volume XIV (1914-1916): Pp. 159-190. London. The Hogarth Press and the Institute of Psycho-analysis.

Think of the opening of a fern or a shell. This is an organic rather than mechanical logic. Hegel's special term for this 'contradiction' of overcoming and at the same time preserving is *Aufhebung*, sometimes translated as 'sublation'. For anything to happen, everything has to be in place. Quantum theory, postmodern cosmology, chaos theory, computer interfacing and ecology all essentially subscribe to this view of 'totality' in question, without being 'hegelian'."[404] I would say being unconsciously Hegelian.

1.7.8 Negation and Contradiction

The most problematical contradiction in Hegel is that although for him knowing is an act -"He grasps labour as the essence of man"-[405] the only labor he recognizes is abstract mental labor. Hegel practices the alienated philosophy called idealism. And yet Hegel has the merit of being able to make of all philosophy a synthesis, a continuous historical dialogue up to his time. Philosophy is for the first time one historical narrative with a logic, rather than a bundle of theories as had been thought before. In this dialogue, different philosophers come into the narrative, contributing from their various historical perspectives separate aspects of nature, consciousness, and self. Hence Hegel's dialectical monism.

Contradiction for Hegel is precisely the mechanism of motion and of human activity. Knowing is a contradictory act because it recognizes its object while negating it, and in its stead constructs its imaginary replica. The secret of the success of Hegel's logic in science is that it does not simply discard contradiction as formal logic did; it makes it the core of its system. There is no waste to dispose of, and instead totality is the whole of a sublated reality that

---

404 Spencer, L., and Krauze, A. (2012). *Hegel for Beginners*. London. Icon Books. Excerpts online in MIA. Accessed from <https://www.marxists.org/reference/archive/hegel/help/easy.htm> on 2014-10-08.

405 Marx, K. (1959). "Critique of Hegel's Philosophy in General." *Economic and Philosophic Manuscripts of 1844*. Trans: Martin Mulligan. Moscow. Progress Publishers. (Orig. Pub. 1932). Online in MIA. Accessed from <https://www.marxists.org/archive/marx/works/1844/manuscripts/hegel.htm> on 2014-10-08.

conserves all.

Hegel paraphrased: Each of the parts of philosophy is a whole, a circle rounded and complete in itself. In each of these parts, however, the philosophical Idea is found only in a particular specificity or medium. The larger circle, because it is a real totality, bursts through the limits imposed by the specific mediums, giving rise to itself. The whole of philosophy in this way resembles a circle of circles. The Idea appears in each sub-circle, but at the same time aggregates into itself all the peculiar phases, and each is a necessary member of the organization.[406] Here I represent the circle as Ouroboros, the serpent that, by joining its beginning and end, recoils to represent all in a circle.

Knowing is full presence of mind attached to its object by a formal image and mediated by its linguistic symbol as historical culture. Alienated himself by his idealism, Hegel rather honestly portrays his alienation in his *Phenomenology*, which besides the philosophical moment in history contains the projection of his own self-analysis. He said himself that his phenomenology was his psychology. He is looking for the lost coherence that he calls the *absolute idea*, that has been lost in ideological particularities, unable to reach the monolithic universality of a human species. He cannot grasp the fact that his absolute, abstract idea of God at the beginning of evolution is simply coherent matter, something Spinoza had already grasped. Hegel did not fully understand the meaning of Spinoza's monism.

---

406 The complete quote is: "Each of the parts of philosophy is a philosophical whole, a circle rounded and complete in itself. In each of these parts, however, the philosophical Idea is found in a particular specificality or medium. The single circle, because it is a real totality, bursts through the limits imposed by its special medium, and gives rise to a wider circle. The whole of philosophy in this way resembles a circle of circles. The Idea appears in each single circle, but, at the same time, the whole Idea is constituted by the system of these peculiar phases, and each is a necessary member of the organisation." Hegel, G.W.F. (1830). Encyclopaedia of the Philosophical Sciences. Part One. I. Introduction to the Shorter Logic. § 15. Trans:y William Wallace, with Foreword by J N Findlay. Oxford. Clarendon Press. Online in MIA. Accessed from <https://www.marxists.org/reference/archive/hegel/works/sl/slintro.htm#SL15> on 2014-10-08.

1.7.9 Negation and Praxis

Marx did close the gap in the Hegelian circle with his concept of praxis, which is the application of Spinoza's monism. "Frederick Engels, with whom I maintained a constant exchange of ideas by correspondence since the publication of his brilliant essay on the critique of economic categories… arrived by another road… at the same result as I, and when in the spring of 1845 he too came to live in Brussels, we decided to set forth together our conception as opposed to the ideological one of German philosophy, in fact to settle accounts with our former philosophical conscience. The intention was carried out in the form of a critique of post-Hegelian philosophy. The manuscript [*The German Ideology*], two large octavo volumes, had long ago reached the publishers in Westphalia when we were informed that owing to changed circumstances it could not be printed. We abandoned the manuscript to the gnawing criticism of the mice all the more willingly since we had achieved our main purpose – self-clarification."[407]

This paragraph illustrates Marx and Engels' accomplishment in their concept of praxis. What Marx is saying is that what really matters is not the publication but the fact that collective consciousness, in them as individuals, has arrived at a landmark point in its developmental insight. Their theory is their comprehensive self-understanding, which corrects Hegel by inverting him from idealistic ground to a materialist, scientific one. Matter (or energy), starts the total process of evolution and then of history, which becomes Marx and Engels' full historical past, found through their self-analysis. Their body of theoretical work is the projective test that takes place not at the academic desk but intersubjectively, one with the other in reciprocity and mutual validation, besides being a test in activism. In the exploited workers (today, the ninety-nine percent) they see the most universality, the class with the potential of becoming con-

---

407 Marx, K. (1977). A Contribution to the Critique of Political Economy. Moscow. Progress Publishers, with some notes by R. Rojas. (Orig. Pub. 1859). Online in MIA. Accessed from <https://www.marxists.org/archive/marx/works/1859/critique-pol-economy/preface.htm> on 2014-1008.

sciously for itself.

The backbone of Marx and Engels' undertaking, and self-understanding, is political economy, the most unconscious and yet palpable part of humanity that at the time was gradually coming to light with the classical economists, particularly Smith and Ricardo, mystified by class ideology. The keystone of Marx and Engels' theory is their lifetime praxis and the practical exercise of their intersubjectivity as critical friendship and collaboration.

Praxis is thus not just another word for practice. Practice takes place in the context of the ideology that subverted consciousness. Scientific theory and practice are melded in praxis and neither one can be intelligibly separated from the other. In other words, praxis is coherent practice rooted in natural activity, natural good-sense practice. Historically, theory was ideologically separated and fragmented into specializations by the division of labor during patriarchy, particularly with the class division of manual and mental labor. It represents the interests of the ruling class, a minority. Marx had used the term praxis once in his 3rd Manuscript of 1844 (not published until 1932) and Lukacs used it again in 1923; since then it has been commonly used by Western Marxists.

Lukacs: "The premise of dialectical materialism is, we recall: 'It is not men's consciousness that determines their existence, but on the contrary, their social existence that determines their consciousness.' Only in the context sketched above can this premise point beyond mere theory and become a question of praxis. Only when the core of existence stands revealed as a social process can existence be seen as the product, albeit the hitherto unconscious product, of human activity. This activity will be seen in its turn as the element crucial for the transformation of existence. Man finds himself confronted by purely natural relations or social forms mystified into natural relations. They appear to be fixed, complete and immutable entities, which can be manipulated and even comprehended, but never overthrown. But also this situation creates the possibility of praxis in the individual consciousness. Praxis becomes the form of action appropriate to the isolated individual; it becomes his ethics. Feuerbach's attempt to supersede Hegel foundered on this reef: like the German idealists, and to a much greater extent than Hegel, he stopped short at the isolated individual of 'civil society'."[408]

Praxis is what psychoanalysis endeavors to achieve through clinical work. Unfortunately, psychoanalysts are also victims of the same class-determined ideological repression as their patients, their own unconscious constraining their work within an ideological, particularistic context that limits the boundaries of their theory out of the reach of ideology. Only when we close the circle of history for ourselves, bringing back together our practice and our theoretical consciousness, full universal social consciousness may be achieved, inherently political. Only becoming one wholehearted presence and presentation, as Karen Horney proposed,[409] will we be able to eliminate the gap of unconscious and ideology and achieve being through a real, coherent self.

408 Lukács, G. (1967). *History & Class Consciousness.* What is Orthodox Marxism? 5. Trans: Rodney Livingstone. London. Merlin Press. (Written: 1919-1923). Online in MIA. Accessed from <https://www.marxists.org/archive/lukacs/works/history/orthodox.htm> on 2014-10-08.
409 Horney, K. (1987). *Final Lectures.* Ed. Douglas Ingram. New York. Norton. P. 33.

1.8 ONE AND TWO IN THE DIALECTIC OF NATURE AND SOCIETY

1.8.1 One Prototype, Two Sexes

Spinoza's Monism is the response to Descartes' dualism, but it all started with pluralism in mythology, religion and early philosophy. This is the advance of cognition that looks for universality, the common denominator of all that exists. In dualism, mind could not be explained from the point of view of matter until Spinoza, for whom God, the analogue of mind, was inherent in matter, its evolutionary good sense. Their separation and antagonism were the product of formal logic reasoning that, through analysis, fragmented and hypostatized motion. This method, among other things, artificially separates the object from its necessarily sequential presentations, its evolution, development, and history. In reality, as in dialectical logic that is suited to its motion, number one is already the negation of zero, and together with it makes number two. This is the beginning of the infinite numerical sequence. Each number negates its opposite and brings a new dimension to the particular totality. This is the math that was applied by Hegel's theory of the origins of consciousness in master and slave. Each requires the other, is dependent on the other for its identity. Similarly, in biology, one cell originally became two through its own fission, creating its own contradiction. Or a cell internalizes another to make it its organelle and enhance its complexity. This is how prokaryotes became eukaryotes. The same process continues to produce complexity, the heterogeneity of Herbert Spencer, through parallel processes of conservation and differentiation, similar to those of assimilation and accommodation that Piaget found in intelligence. In this light, the process of differentiation that in an organism has been taking place internally, through the differentiation and specialization of organs, becomes morphologically externalized as sexuation requiring a complementary external organ. Here we go back to the germ of plurality; two produce one, the individual, and simultaneously three, the family. This new form of complexity from sexuation also leads to better adaptive capacity through reshuffling of chromosomes in meiosis checks and balances for more efficient use of energy and minimization of waste, the paradigm of which is consciousness, formal production without waste.

The all-encompassing dialectical process inherent in our nature that forces us to inevitable social activity is arbitrarily negated today by the ideologues of the *status quo* who, sadly, believe they benefit from denial. They formulate their mystifying motto "there is no alternative." Like evolution, history moves through alternative forms.

On the other side, human sexuated reproduction, for example, allows meiosis: halving the number of chromosomes to then complement them with those of the partner from the opposite sex. The subsequent fusion of two halves, spermatozoid and ovum, as gametes equal but structurally opposites, reconstruct the unit again, the blueprint for the whole human individual. Here plurality starts individuality.

Here is where Plato made the mistake of hypostatizing a myth attributed to Socrates: "A gift of gods to men, as I believe, was tossed down from some divine source through the agency of a Prometheus together with a gleaming fire; and the ancients, who were better than we and lived nearer the gods, handed down the tradition that all the things which are ever said to exist are sprung from one and many and have inherent in them the finite and the infinite." From this horizontal dialectic of opposites Plato created the binary hierarchy of idea over matter. This is how idealism was engendered. Plato continues: "This being the way in which these things are arranged, we must always assume that there is in every case one idea of everything and must look for it—for we shall find that it is there—and if we get a grasp of this, we must look next for two, if there be two, and if not, for three or some other number; and again we must treat each of those units in the same way, until we can see not only that the original unit is one and many and infinite, but just how many it is.

And we must not apply the idea of infinite to plurality until we have a view of its whole number between infinity and one; then, and not before, we may let each unit of everything pass on unhindered into infinity. The gods, then, as I said, handed down to us this mode of investigating, learning, and teaching one another; but the wise men of the present day make the one and the many too quickly or too slowly, in haphazard fashion, and they put infinity immediately after unity; they disregard all that lies between them, and this it is which distinguishes between the dialectic and the disputatious methods of discussion."[410] One, many and infinite is the Hegelian syllogism of individuality, particularity and universality that Plato complains the Sophists are mishandling. The idea is the Trojan Horse that Plato introduced to replace matter, the cosmic object, of which the idea is only its evolutionary sense.

In this context, sexual dimorphism is the original plurality of one species that brought about the complementarity of sexual behavior and of sexual characteristics of sexuated organisms, from algae to *Homo sapiens*. Had Linnaeus had available the evidence we have today, he may have named the species *Almae Matres* or *Femina Mediatrix* on the ground that our evolutionary default form is not *Homo* but *Femina*, and we are not *sapiens* having lost our good sense. The original morphological sex determination is for the most part genetic, which means allele or gene grounded. However, gender and sexual behavior are also determined by environmental and social conditions, such as the size of an organism relative to others of its population, temperature, seasonality, or other conditions more numerous and complex in humans. The genomic revolution has greatly increased our knowledge of sex-determination systems. [411]Sexual identity is even more complex and overdetermined: witness today's sexual fluidity.

---

410 Plato. *Philebus.*16c-e, 17a. Online in Perseus, University of Chicago. Accessed from <http://perseus.uchicago.edu/perseus-cgi/citequery3.pl?dbname=GreekFeb2011&getid=1&query=Pl.%20Phlb.%2016c> on 2016-05-14.
411 Beukeboom, L. and Perri, N. (2014). *The Evolution of Sex Determination.* Oxford University Press.

In evolution, sexuation entails dimorphism, two morphs of the phenotype, to produce more complex and efficient fitness based on paired conjugation of genes. Dimorphism is the dual appearance or formal difference between males and females of the same species, in color, shape, size, and bodily structures,which is caused by the inheritance of one or the other sexual pattern in the genome. The presence of a particular gene (SRY), on the Y chromosome in humans, causes the male development of the testes, and the subsequent release of hormones which cause the overall morphological changes from the female default.[412] This determines differences in bodily organs of particular significance, brain dimorphism, and it may determine any number of behavioral differences.

In humans, the sex ratio at birth is remarkably consistent across human populations, with 105–107 male births for every 100 female births, a fact already documented for three centuries. More than 30 demographic and environmental factors have been studied regarding their possible effects on the sex ratio at birth, among them family size, parental age, parental occupation, birth order, race, coital rate, hormonal treatments, exposure to environmental toxins, stress, several diseases, and war.[413]

War is a significant social factor in the determination of sex. A small but significant increase in male births during and after war has been documented in Europe and the U.S. in both the First and Second World Wars, and in the U.S. for the Korean and Vietnam Wars. Biological explanations for the observed increase in sex ratio during war include the stress suffered by adult males, affecting the viability of XY-bearing vs. XX-bearing sperm, changes in the age structure of the population, and higher frequency of intercourse, leading to conception earlier in the menstrual cycle, all of which have been

---

412 Berta P, Hawkins JR, Sinclair AH, Taylor A, Griffiths BL, Goodfellow PN, Fellous M (November 1990). "Genetic evidence equating SRY and the testis-determining factor". Nature 348 (6300): 448–50.

413 Hesketh, T. and Xing, Z,W. (2006). "Abnormal sex ratios in human populations: Causes and consequences." Proceedings of the National Academy of Science of the United States of America. vol. 103 no. 36. Online in CrossMark. Accessed from <http://www.pnas.org/content/103/36/13271.full> on 2015-04-24.

independently associated with increased sex ratios. On the other hand, evolutionary explanations argue that the increase represents an adaptive equilibrium to compensate for the unbalanced loss of males in war.[414]

Son preference is another significant factor that takes place pre-natally through sex determination and sex-selective abortion, and after birth through neglect and abandonment of females and higher female mortality. Studies have shown that unequal access to health care is the most important factor, especially in societies without health insurance. In 1990, Sen estimated that differential female mortality had resulted in approximately 100 million "missing fe-males" across the developing world,[415] and at least two other au-thors have arrived at similar estimates.[416] The highest percentages of missing females occurs in the Indian subcontinent.[417]

The consequences of war, son preference, and missing females are not only social but have biological repercussions. They lead to significant alteration of the male/female ratio, with excess of males that in some rural areas of China have been reported as high as 130:100. According to Hesketh and Xing it is not in dispute that over the next 20 years in parts of China and India, there will be a 12–15% excess of single young men, unable to have families in societies where marriage is universal and social status and accep-tance depend on it. They believe one social consequence of excess of males is increased violence and crime; others are antisocial be-havior, migration, sex trafficking and increase in sex workers and homosexuality.[418]

The social equivalent of sexual dimorphism is gender assignment,

---

414 Hesketh, T. and Xing, Z,W. (2006). "Abnormal sex ratios in human populations: Causes and consequences." Ibid.
415 Sen A. K. (1992) British Medical Journal. 304:586–587.
416 Klasen, S. (1994) World Development. 22:944–948. Coale, A. (1991) Population and Development Review. 3:518.
417 Hesketh, T. and Xing, Z,W. (2006). "Abnormal sex ratios in human populations: Causes and consequences." Ibid.
418 Hesketh, T. and Xing, Z,W. (2006). "Abnormal sex ratios in human populations: Causes and consequences." Ibid.

a social factor that reciprocally influences the sexual dimorphism by culturally enhancing or inhibiting behavioral manifestations of sex determination. These are phenomena such as conditioning, modeling and learning, and social tolerance of deviations from the norm. Fashion, for example, symbolically enhances some sexual characteristics while reducing others.

One example of a body dimorphism with behavioral association is the so called D2:D4 ratio or finger length ratio, the ratio of the length of the index finger to that of the ring finger that has been shown to be consistently a sexually dimorphic trait and a marker of sex. According to several studies, both men and women have relatively shorter index than ring digits, and this is what is expressed as D2:D4 ratio, by dividing the length of D2 by that of D4. However, the ratio is consistently lower in males. Smaller, more masculine, digit ratios are thought to be associated with either higher prenatal testosterone levels, or greater sensitivity to androgens, or both. Studies show that men with more masculine finger ratios are perceived by females as being more masculine and dominant, and also tend to perform better in a number of physical sports. It has been also hypothesized that digit ratio correlates with propensity to engage in aggressive behavior. In a study, the relationship between trait aggression, assessed using a questionnaire, and finger-length ratio, was researched in both men and women. It was found that in fact, men with lower, more masculine, finger-length ratios had higher-trait physical aggression scores. But the authors found no correlation between finger length ratio and any form of aggression in females. The authors concluded that these results are consistent with the hypothesis that testosterone has an organizational effect on adult physical aggression in men.[419]

---

419 Baileya, A.A., Hurd, P.L. (2005). "Finger length ratio (2D:4D) correlates with physical aggression in men but not in women." Biological Psychology. Volume 68, Issue 3, March 2005, Pages 215–22.

1.8.2 The Natural Design "Makes" Sense

The natural "design" literally "makes" sense. The constant interplay of singularity, plurality and universality in various sequences of evolution produces a particular direction in the variations of nature, most clearly when we consider organism and environment as a dialectical pair, as Darwin did. Opposite phenomena, such as bifurcation in speciation, and nesting, are paradigmatic of process.

As an example, the female body is, materially and spiritually, the human ground; it is the original universality of "we are all born equally." The female body is designed to, from its own protein, build progeny along with its consciousness infrastructure. But it is the mother who also jumpstarts consciousness, making complete the individual of the species, individuality independent of the duality of sex. The male body contributes an average of 280 million spermatozoa per ejaculation, each containing half of the initial genetic program for each new individual to be produced. The female body contributes one ovum only but, as opposed to the spermatozoid that ends its mission with fertilization, she conserves her structure in the fertilized ovum, and from it through progressive fission, replication, differentiation and organization produces the fetus. The mother is the constructive ground, the Petri dish, the culture, wherein each human individual grows. After birth, each newborn builds itself ingesting from, and therefore destroying maternal tissue to build its own. This form of relationship in biology is called parasitism, generally meaning that there is no reciprocity, although this is not completely true; the mother is proud of her accomplishment and derives some benefit.

It seems a great paradox, from the point of view of biological economy, that we fuss over the issue of abortion, the termination of a life that is still parasitic and only rudimentarily invested with potential. At the same time, we uncritically engage in killing by the troves the most biologically costly and potentially enhanced youth of the population in its prime of life, in war. Malthusianism has provides a pseudoscientific, and mostly unconscious, biological premise, the survival of the fittest, for the unrestrained expression of the male instinct to destroy while its female opposite is repressed with the females themselves.

Two hundred thousand years of female leadership based on gentile group ideology and harmony with nature, if acknowledged, creates a contrast with ten thousand years of male rule and civil society. The original gens was based upon the female instinctual disposition of giving, tending and growing, and was historically replaced by its opposites in patriarchy. Civil society is the expression of instinctually male-determined hierarchical and dominant group formations, few taking from the production of all, the opposite of the gentile or clannish form of consciousness. Civil society, through the institution of the hierarchical state legitimizes the use of violence for the benefit of its ruling class.

The individual's entrance into civil society entails a qualitative jump from matriarchal to patriarchal dispositional orientation and it unbalances the individuals' natural instinctive dual disposition, repressing altruism in the service of paranoia. Almost universally, the political characteristic of modern societies is male dominance. This situation, through habit, has become ideology and therefore "natural," affecting all individuals, independent of sex, conditioning their brain. In practice the characteristics of family group life are repudiated, while those of civil society are enhanced. The end result is dominant patriarchy and therefore the total subversion of the natural design of a balanced, altruistic and moral coherence. This is, along with its ultimate expression the economic condition of capitalism imposed by patriarchy, which has led humanity to its present crossroads.[420]

Being is the all-inclusive, one, experience of all subjects, through their naturally endowed consciousness and their historical form of self in constant metabolic relationship with nature and society. The phenomenon of reification, resulting from spurious patriarchy, turns

---

420 Meszaros, I. (2001). *Socialism or Barbarism. From the American Century to the Crossroads.* New York. Monthly Review Press.

being into a type of object-having which is by nature not universal but particular, exclusive, and alienating. The effect of the alienating phenomenon, as observed in psychoanalysis, is nowhere better reflected that in the ideological fetishism of penis envy and castration anxiety as they were constructed by Freud.[421]

1.8.3 One Brain, Two Hemispheres

Autopsies, brain sampling and microscopic examination, although useful for centuries in understanding the brain, could not be conducted in living subjects, and in any case do not allow us to draw clear behavioral conclusions. Pathology-based learning always came too late and had the same limitation. This has been largely resolved recently with neuro-imaging that allows us to see the brain in motion. We are learning to map the connective functionality of the brain in relation to our behavior, and to make observable, previously inaccessible subjective experiences such as memory, pain, cognition, emotions, *etc.*

One way imaging is done is by measuring the activity of brain areas by measuring their consumption of oxygen supplies through the speed of blood flows correlated with behaviors or experiences. Functional magnetic resonance imaging (fMRI) employs a powerful electrical magnet to detect those changes in blood oxygenation and flow that occur in response to the neural activity that underlies observable behavior.[422]

There are by now a significant number of studies that document sexual dimorphisms by measuring volumes and functions of parts of the brain in animals as well as in humans.

Dimorphic behavioral prototypes are maternal behavior in fe-

---

421 Fromm, E. (1997). *To Have or to Be?* London and New York. Continuum. (Orig. Pub. 1976). Accessed from <https://keimena11.files.wordpress.com/2011/11/erich-fromm-to-have-or-to-be-1976.pdf> on 2015-08-21.
422 Devlin, H. (2008). "University of Oxford: FMRIB Centre: Introduction to fMRI. Online in Nuffield Department of Clinical Neurosciences. " Accessed from < http://www.fmrib.ox.ac.uk/education/fmri/introduction-to-fmri/ > on 2014-08-09.

males, and aggression or rough-and-tumble play in males. So-called maternal behavior, such as displaying sensitivity to the infant cues, being sociable with the child independent of context, fulfilling the child's needs such as grooming and nursing has been correlated to a number of brain areas such as the amygdala, hypothalamus, nucleus accumbens, and specific areas of the cortex.[423] Amygdala and hypothalamus are a complex of subcortical nuclei of the brain involved in perceiving, discriminating, and consequently releasing feelings and behaviors in context. Networks of specific subcortical and cortical circuits act in concert to support aspects of parental response to infants for example, including in those responses ensembles of emotion, attention, motivation, and empathy, that determine appropriate decision-making, including feeling, thinking, and acting. This is how infant-released stimuli activate basal forebrain regions, which in turn regulate brain circuits handling specific nurturing and caregiving responses. The integrated understanding of the brain basis of parenting has profound implications for mental health and psychopathology.[424] Overall sex determination has been highly correlated to the hypothalamus, which is connected to the pituitary gland that in turn control hormones. Research has shown that several hormones such as oxytocin, prolactin, estradiol and progesterone are essential for the onset and maintenance of maternal behavior.

The sexual dimorphism seems to be greater among brain areas that, in previous animal studies, had been identified as showing greater levels of sex steroid receptors for sex hormones during critical periods of brain development. Sex steroid hormones have a determining role in the sexual dimorphisms of humans, including

423 Leckman, J. F. and A. E. Herman (2002). "Maternal behavior and developmental psychopathology." Biological Psychiatry 51(1): 27-43.
424 Swain, J.E., Lorberbaum, J. P. et al. (2007). "Brain basis of early parent–infant interactions: psychology, physiology, and in vivo functional neuroimaging studies." Journal of Child Psychology and Psychiatry. Volume 48, Issue 3-4, pages 262–287, March/April 2007.

behavioral dimorphisms.[425],[426]

Contrasting behavioral tendencies can be mapped in the brain, and then traced to developmental variations in hormonal systems. The universal default morphology after reproduction is female, but the Y chromosome carries the gene that determines hormonal exposure at a critical period in embryonic development and in turn determines masculine behavior. In experiments with rodents, hormonal manipulation can criss-cross behavior. For example, mounting male sexual behavior can be transformed into female arching of the back for coitus and vice versa. The lifelong effects of early exposure to sex hormones is "organizational," meaning that they alter brain function permanently. The same manipulation at later stages or in the adult cannot reproduce the effect.

The issue of hemispheric lateralization as correlated to sex is a provocative one in terms of gender determination in the proclivity toward war, or peace, for example.[427] However, the only documented fact in this regard so far, studying brain connectivity, is that while male brains are optimized for intra-hemispheric communication, female brains connect more inter-hemispherically. "The developmental trajectories of males and females separate at a young age, demonstrating wide differences during adolescence and adulthood. The observations suggest that male brains are structured to facilitate connectivity between perception and coordinated action, whereas female brains are designed to facilitate communication between analytical and intuitive processing modes."[428] These very early find-

425 Goldstein, J.M., Larry J. Seidman, L.J., Horton, N.J., et al. (2001). "Normal Sexual Dimorphism of the Adult Human Brain Assessed by In Vivo Magnetic Resonance Imaging." Cerebral Cortex 11 (6): Pp. 490-497. Accessed from <http://cercor.oxford-journals.org/content/11/6/490.full> on 2014-08-08.

426 Allen, L.S., Hines, M., Shryne, J.E., and Gorski, R.A. (1989). "Two sexually dimorphic cell groups in the human brain." The Journal of Neuroscience, 9 (2): Ppl 497-506. Accessed from <http://www.jneurosci.org/content/9/2/497.full.pdf+html> on 2014-08-08.

427 Olson, J. (2011). *The Whole-Brain Path to Peace.* San Rafael, CA, Origin Press.

428 Ingalhalikara, M., et al. (2014). "Sex differences in the structural connectome of the human brain." Proc. Natl. Acad. Sci. PNAS (USA). 111:823–828. Online in PNAS. Accessed from <http://www.mit.edu/~6.s085/papers/sex-differences.pdf> on 2015-

ings are still to be understood hypothetically. Similarly, "left-hemisphere regions are biased to interact more strongly within the same hemisphere, whereas right-hemisphere regions interact more strongly with both hemispheres. These two different patterns of interaction are associated with left-lateralized functions, such as language and motor abilities, and right-lateralized functions, such as visuo-spatial attention."[429]

The gender bias to hemispheric lateralization may manifest itself in analytic vs. intuitive and piercing vs. relational forms of subjectivity, according to sexual disposition, as proposed in the present work.

1.8.4 The Cultural Effect

In terms of gender, reports of the relation between brain and behavior have been highly biased in the past, generally attributing intellectual advantages to white males; this is how science can be self-serving. Only relatively recently has it been considered that the brain has been demystified and considered just another adaptive organ, its morphologies therefore determined by environmental conditions, including social-historical ones. Intelligence and personality in particular among the most studied brain properties, had their differences once attributed to race or cranial configuration. Neurobiology, in particular, is giving us a truer picture, particularly about how significantly social contingencies may interact with critical and sensitive periods of development.

Cultural research has shown that intelligence, problem-solving capacity, is adaptively shaped by cultural particularities of human groups.[430] This follows the general trend of animal life that makes

03-25.
429 Gotts, S. J. et al. (2013). "Two distinct forms of functional lateralization in the human brain." Proc. Natl. Acad. Sci. PNAS (USA). 110(36): E3435–E3444. Online in PNAS. Accessed from <http://www.ncbi.nlm.nih.gov/pmc/articles/PMC3767540/> on 2015-03-25.
430 Gottfredson, L. S. (2004), "Intelligence: Is It the Epidemiologists' Elusive "Fundamental Cause" of Social Class Inequalities in Health?" Journal of Personality and

both morphology and intelligence adaptive functions, meaning reciprocally determined by organism and environment. Animals display the best adaptive intelligence they need to survive in the particular environments they inhabit, their particular forms of intelligence emphasizing and highly developing the senses, and organs, that are most useful for thriving.[431] Humans are no exception to this general rule.

In humans in particular, the social division of labor is a most important determining factor. It makes complex the natural division of labor based on sex, artificially determining variations in intelligence according to skills, and according to the demands of cultural conditions. One of those usually neglected conditions is social class, that automatically provides diverse access to resources and education. Social selection starts with child-rearing. The natural sexual division of labor has endowed females with skills for tasks having to do with reproduction, tending, growing and caring for the young and needy within an immediate family environment. Males, on the other hand, without the reproductive function are better equipped for problem-solving in predatory conditions outside of the immediate confines of the family. Family activities and reproduction have, from the standpoint of civil society, not been considered as significant as labor and production outside the family. This has led to the exploitative situation imposed on "working women" with industrialization, that feminists call "double burden,"[432] or unpaid "second shift."[433] The reason is that political economy has been developed, like most of modern science, by the patriarchal mainstream. Early matriarchs practiced an economy of the gift, still present but for the most part invisible according to Vaughan that, from the profit point

Social Psychology, Vol 86(1), Jan, 174-199.

431 Shettleworth, S.J. (2010). *Cognition, Evolution and Behavior* (2 ed.). Oxford Press, New York. Draft of Chapter 1 accessed from <http://psych.utoronto.ca/users/psy460/files/Shettleworth_ch_1.pdf> on 2015-08-24.

432 Moen, P. (1989). *Working Parents. Transformations in Gender Roles and Public Policies in Sweden.* University of Wisconsin Press.

433 Hochschild, A. and Machung. A. (1990). *The Second Shift. Working Families and the Revolution at Home.* New York. Avon Books.

of view, makes no sense.[434]

The fact that maternal labor is probably the costliest investment of human energy for the species has been generally ignored. The same has happened with maternal expression, particularly of affect, language, and cognition as landmarks of development. That human expression, besides explicit speech is implicitly emotional, bodily based, substantially facial and reverberational,[435] its foundation being set by the mother. Social referencing —the tendency of a person to look to a significant other in an ambiguous situation for clarifying information— observable at about the age of eight months, is the reciprocal transactional phenomenon by means of which children, based on the face of the mother, test reality.[436] The impairment in the neural systems that respond to the emotional expressions of others that is learned this way can have devastating effects in both maternal care and in child development.[437] This capacity is preceded by a facial, eye-based non-verbal dialogue that takes place as early as two months, when foveal synchronization can be best observed between mother and child. By this time, infants are already responding to the specifics of timing and emotion of their mothers' expressions, and show signs of confusion and distress when the mother is instructed to keep a still face and ignore their intuition of their infant's emotional cues.[438] The study of the effect of stress and alienation on this type of delicate and momentous human imprinting is still in its infancy.

That familiar faces evoke a stronger response in parts of the

434 Vaughan, G. (1997). *For-Giving: A Feminist Criticism of Exchange.* Austin, Texas. Plainview Press in collaboration with the Foundation for a Compassionate Society. Ch. 1., P. 15. Free download from < http://www.gift-economy.com/forgiving.html> on 2016-03-21.
435 Markova, I. (1982). *Paradigms, thought and language.* London: Wiley.
436 Walden T.A., and Ogan T.A. (1988). The development of social referencing. Child Development. 59(5):1230-40.
437 Blair, R. J. R. (2003). "Facial expressions, their communicatory functions and neuro-cognitive substrates." Philosophical Transactions of the Royal Society of London Series Biological Sciences. 358(1431): 561-572.
438 Trevarthen, C. and K. J. Aitken (2001). "Infant intersubjectivity: research, theory, and clinical applications." Journal of Child Psychology and Psychiatry 42(1): 3-48.

brain associated with *theory of mind*: the ability to attribute mental states such as intents, desires, pretense, *etc.*, to others indicates the particular importance of the mother's face in development. There is a weaker response in the amygdala that is more involved with instinctual meaning and less influenced by social learning. "These response modulations appear to go beyond developing a visual memory for the appearance of a face. The perception of a familiar face activates a distributed network of brain structures related not only to visual familiarity but also to knowledge about a person's personality, attitudes, and intentions; to episodic memories associated with that person; and to the emotional response to that person... The knowledge about the other person is retrieved spontaneously and appears to play an integral role in the recognition of familiar individuals."[439] Specific networks in the brain involved with theory of mind the anterior paracingulate cortex, the superior temporal sulci and the temporal poles bilaterally have been already identified.[440]

Experiments have also shown that looking at pictures of one's own child, as compared to others, evokes stronger responses in areas associated with emotional responses and theory of mind in the brain. This kind of reciprocal intense exposure in the maternal relationship makes it unique. Activations in areas such as the amygdala, insula, and bilateral orbitofrontal cortex "may reflect the mixture of intense attachment and vigilant protectiveness that characterizes the maternal relationship but not other close relationships"[441]

A long trajectory of research in animals has identified a very specific area, the cingulate cortex of the temporal lobe, and its connected, medially located, thalamic nuclei as important in mammalian mother-infant attachment. Infants emit characteristic distress noises and mothers respond protectively. Specifically, the cingulate,

439 Gobbini, M.I., Leibenluft E, et al. (2004). "Social and emotional attachment in the neural representation of faces." NeuroImage 22(4): 1628-35.

440 Gallagher, H.L., Frith, C.D. (2003). "Functional imaging of 'theory of mind'" Trends in Cognitive Science. 7(2):77-83.

441 Leibenluft, E., Gobbini, M. I., et al. (2004). "Mothers' neural activation in response to pictures of their children and other children." Biological Psychiatry 56(4): 225-32.

subcortical medial thalamus, and medial prefrontal and right orbitofrontal parts of the cortex display more activity with infant cries than with other noise. There is a highly developed discriminatory capacity in the brain for type of infant noise, particularly in the right side of the brain, that is equivalent to linguistic discrimination. This work is advancing, identifying more areas of the brain selectively involved, and substantiating the fact that elaborate neural mechanisms mediate maternal love and unique, diverse, and complex maternal behaviors. These are at the neurological bases of the altruistic behaviors that so much puzzled Darwin.

Evidence of brain dimorphism has come from research on ADHD through functional imaging studies. They have found that, exposed to the same environments, boys" and girls' brains respond differently in terms of ADHD phenomenology.[442] In general, and already telling, is the fact that the attention deficit is more prevalent as a form of manifestation in females, while the hyperactivity is more perceptible in males. Interestingly, most child psychiatry diagnoses that are not clearly organic have a higher prevalence in males during childhood particularly externalizing disorders. This general rule shifts during adolescence, when females become more vulnerable, particularly to depression and internalizing disorders, to a great extent owing to socially determined factors.[443] It must be kept in mind, as Carol Gilligan and others points out, that the patriarchal culture tends to devalue and pathologize female behaviors that differ from the male cultural paradigm.

The brain is dimorphic according to sex, and particularly the language of mothering, which is highly emotional. Removing emotion from cognition in human expression, for the sake of "objectivity," is a cultural phenomenon.

---

442 Dirlikova, B., Roscha, K.S., Crocettia, D., et al. (2015). "Distinct frontal lobe morphology in girls and boys with ADHD." NeuroImage: Clinical. Vol. 7,, Pages 222–229.

443 Gilligan, C. (1982). *In a Different Voice Psychological Theory and Women's Development.* Harvard University Press, Cam-bridge, Massachusetts.

1.8.5 Behavioral Dimorphism

In an experiment, rats that had been housed together harmoniously in a laboratory became aggressive when exposed to strange rats. Their aggressiveness was selective to the same-sex rats. Male rats mainly attacked male intruders, and so did females for their kind. Experimenters then manipulated the hypothetical hormonal requirements behind such behaviors, and confirmed another sex-bias phenomenon. Castration decreased aggressive behavior in males, but removal of ovaries did not in females. Male hormonal replacement then brought castrated males back to their old aggressive routines; not the case for females. Females treated with replacement female hormones did reduce or block their attacks of intruder females, but did not alter their low level of attack toward males. Male hormones in females also slightly reduced attacks toward female intruders, but increased the probability of attack toward male intruders.[444]

The authors of this study concluded that the sex-discriminatory specificity of aggression and the differential influence of hormones suggest different mechanisms responsible for aggression in males and in females. They are sexually dimorphic in their response to stimuli eliciting aggression. It is not that males are aggressive and females nonaggressive by nature; they both have the trait and expressive capacity, but these are differently mediated by conditions along the sexual divide.

Studies that review human sex differences in aggressive behavior in the social psychology literature agree that men are more aggressive than women particularly when it comes to physical aggression and producing pain, and that women, are more likely than men to be responsive to the contingencies of aggression, such as harm done, guilt and anxiety, as well as danger to self.[445] Aggression is a

---

444 Debold, J.F. Miczek, F.K. (1981). "Sexual Dimorphism in the Hormonal Control of Aggressive Behavior of Rats." Pharmacol-ogy Biochemistry and Behavior. Volume 14, Supplement 1, Pages 89–93.
445 Eagly, A.H., and Steffen, V.J. (1986). "Gender and Aggressive Behavior: A Meta-Analytic Review of the Social Psychological Literature." Psychological Bulletin. Vo. 100, No. 3, Pp 309-330. Accessed from <www.saylor.org/site/wp-content/up-

shared behavioral predisposition, but its deployment differs according to gender and circumstances. Social stereotypes are probably a compounding mediating factor.

The application of animal findings to the human species is of limited use because of the different instinctual wiring. In humans, cultural norms reshape instinctual impulsivity. It is a well-known phenomenon that dehumanizing the enemy blocks human empathy and facilitates aggression.[446] In that regard, mass destruction terms such as "ethnic cleansing"[447] and "mowing the lawn,"[448] displace the emotional reaction to their equivalents "genocide" and "holocaust."

In mammals, close contact with other members of the species during early life provides the sense of security necessary to assertively explore the world and eventually forage independently. In most species, the mother is the secure base, although in some it may be the father or the group at large. Where maternal attachment is evident, security and novelty-stress management capacity can be measured selectively both in recorded behavioral responses to events, and in hormonal levels, and compared to other situations. Capacity for handling exploratory stress response is related to forms of attachment, in humans to the mothering one.[449] Human forms of attachment have been particularly studied since Bowlby,[450] and particularly through the work of his disciple Mary Ainsworth[451] and her

loads/2011/07/psych406-7.2.pdf> on 2014-08-08.

446 Bandura, A., Underwood, B., Fromson, M.E. (1975). "Disinhibition of aggression through diffusion of responsibility and de-humanization of victims." Journal of Research in Personality Volume 9, Issue 4, Pp 253–269.

447 Naimark, N. (2007). "Ethnic Cleansing, Online Encyclopedia of Mass Violence. Accessed from <http://www.massviolence.org/Ethnic-Cleansing> on 2015-08-24.

448 Feffer, J. (2014). "Mowing the Lawn in Gaza." Foreign Policy in Focus. Accessed from <http://fpif.org/mowing-lawn-gaza/> on 2014-08-09.

449 Sachser, N. and Kaiser, S. (2010). "The Social Modulation of Behavioral Development." Ch. 17. In: Kappeler, P. (Ed.). *Animal Behaviour: Evolution and Mechanisms.* London and New York. Springer.

450 Bowlby, J. (1982). Attachment and Loss. 2 vols. Second Edition. New York. Basic Books. (Orig. Pub. 1969). Accessed from <http://www.abebe.org.br/wp-content/uploads/John-Bowlby-Attachment-Second-Edition-Attachment-and-Loss-Series-Vol-1-1983.pdf> on 2014-08-09.

451 Ainsworth, M. and Bowlby, J. (1965). *Child Care and the Growth of Love.* London:

school. Their empirical findings are well fitted to Karen Horney's basic relational categories of moving toward, against and away,[452] that are rooted in instinctual mating, fighting and flying, and to theories of conflict. They include the notions of choice and conflict according to circumstances or conditions. The basic relational reciprocity postulated in the concept of *goodness of fit* of Stella Chess and Alexander Thomas[453] illustrates the highly reciprocal nature of the relational choice embedded in the character of humans.

End-game aggressive behavior varies according to environmental stimulation more than it does to predisposition. Darwin linked male aggression to sexual selection, that in turn would determine difference of size and strength between males and females.[454] But we cannot ignore the effect on body size of physically challenging occupations selected by males, and also the cultural bias that favors child-like qualities in the female.[455]

Darwin credits Wallace with pointing out the important fact that, in humans, evolution made a turn from the simplicity of physical morphology to intelligence in the response to the demands of the environment.[456] Making tools and building shelters for protection from inclement weather came along with the development of the human intellect. Humans have sheltered themselves from the effects of mere natural selection by the use of instruments, first our hands, then useful parts of raw nature, and finally consciousness and language. Unfortunately, despite our having proven high intelligence capacity, it seems obvious today that we have lost the most basic

Penguin Books.

452 Horney, K. (1945). *Our Inner Conflicts. A Constructive Theory of Neurosis.* New York. Norton. Online in Internet Archive. Accessed from <https://archive.org/details/OurInnerConflicts> on 2024-08-09.

453 Chess, S. and Thomas, A. (1999). *Goodness of Fit: Clinical Applications from Infancy through Adult Life.* Philadelphia. Brun-ner/Mazel.

454 Darwin, C. (1874). *The Descent of Man, and Selection in Relation to Sex.* Second Edition. London. John Murray. Darwin Online. Accessed from <http://darwin-online.org.uk/converted/pdf/1874_Descent_F944.pdf> on 2014-08-07.

455 Morris, D. (2004). *The Naked Woman. A Study of the Female Body.* New York. St. Martin's Press. P. 3.

456 Darwin, C. (1874). Ibid. Ch. 5. p. 127.

elements of good sense of our adaptive relations with each other and with nature. That is the reason *Homo sapiens* does not really define us well any longer.

1.8.6 A Human Dimorphism that is Not: Natural -Social Class

If we follow the logic of Wallace and Darwin, evolutionary determination changed from mere morphological adaptation and survival force to a radically new form in the human species: self-consciousness. Complex labor and its concomitant intelligence are the foremost adaptive qualities of the new species, both being trans-formations of instinct, of mere material activity and its sense. Two instinctual dispositions combined, male and female, could naturally and logically lead to various forms of consciousness, of self and of intelligence, according to their titration. I will call the two main divergences first, analytical subjective consciousness that pierces reality and separates to understand analytically; and second other a synthetic form of subjectivity or consciousness that, in opposite form infinitely conserves and ensembles in a totality. This is similar to what Freud called Thanatos and Eros respectively, without attrib-uting them gender selectivity.[457] This would be the dimorphic struc-ture of consciousness that operates reciprocally and dialectically to exercise its own constraints, and balance. I illustrate this graphically at the end of this book. I believe the two brain hemispheres to have been originally biased to one or the other type of consciousness, polarized according to sex, mutual constraint's being the purpose of their pairing and achieving balance, according to environmental conditions, particularly scarcity and abundance.

Patriarchal history, however, that introduced inequality and the exploitation of mothers, and with them those considered weak by the

---

457 Freud, S. (1922). Beyond the Pleasure Principle. The International Psychoanalyti-cal Library. No. 4. Trans. C.J.M. Hubback. London and Vienna. The International Psycho-Analytical Press. Online in the Internet Archive. Accessed from < https://ia800501.us.archive.org/2/items/BeyondThePleasurePrinciple_633/freud_sig-mund_1856_1939_beyond_the_pleasure_principle.pdf> on 2015-08-26.

new standard of their sons' being better skilled for the demands of civil society, brought with it a huge antagonistic dichotomy, a split or dehiscence in what was originally only self-resolving dialectical opposition. This is the original trauma of human consciousness. An artificial, force-based hierarchy subverted the natural horizontality of the sexual division of labor and in its place put the class-based, vertical division that still prevails in capitalism today. Initially enslaving more than half of the species, women, children, the elderly and the handicapped, today ninety-nine percent in the public perception, took place at the cost of repressing female subjectivity, converting it into silence and lack of transcendence. Although silence does not abolish consciousness, it blockades its expression and usefulness. The initial silence of the female human half, imprisoned in her *famula*[458] role as handmaid, or female servant, has evolved to become ideology, halved truth. Regardless of culture, humanity, first by force, then by habit, has had to internalize the artificial situation as "human nature." This has been accomplished by power élites, conquerors and missionaries, and presently, in the more civilized world, by ideologues who speak in the name of formal democracy. Language, like consciousness, is unbalanced, all binaries being hierarchical. The purpose is to impose the values of the hegemonic world class, first exclusively patriarchal and constructed upon the inverted ruins of the matriarchal foundation. Today, the white male is still fighting to resurrect his hegemony in various quarters.

What is natural is moral, not so what is historical. Human morality was constructed upon the blueprint of natural good sense and coherence, the ways of nature. From this point of view Karen Horney uniquely speaks about a *morality of evolution*, a morality that can be tested by going back to its natural roots and direction.[459] Today more than ever, we are faced with the compelling and terrifying fact that nature has started to reassert her morality against our false one

---

458 Wikipedia. Noun (genitive famulae). 1 female slave; maid, handmaiden, maid-servant. 2 temple attendant.
459 Horney, K. (1950). "A Morality of Evolution." In: *Neurosis and Human Growth*. New York. Norton.

of imbalance.

The artificial human monomorphism that inhumanly ties one of the wings of the human lark results in the transformation of consciousness into ideology, clearly class-generated after the patriarch.

1.9 THE ASCENDANCE OF PATRIARCHY AS NEGATION THAT MUST BE NEGATED

"We see paternity falling back from Apollonian purity to Dionysian materiality, so preparing the way for a new victory of the feminine principle, for a new flowering of the mother cults."

Bachofen[460]

1.9.1 From Biology

Also says Bachofen: "Despite appearances to the contrary (fostered by anthropocentric nursery stories), a distinct role for male parents does not exist in nature. Fatherhood says Sebastian Kramer was invented by humans during the agricultural revolution about six thousand years ago. Symbolized by the new God-king, it incorporated the mother's originally superior role in primate families, the control or ownership of children. The male deity could even make his own offspring without female help. This inflated political figure was designed to compensate for the male's modest role in procreation, once the facts of life were known. Patriarchy was born out of an envious attack on mothers."[461] Here Bachofen agrees with Briffault. The attack is still going on in the form of the male legislation of the female body, particularly seen in the laws about her decisions to abort.

"A Chimpanzee family consists of only a mother and her chil-

---

460 Bachofen, J. (1992). *Myth, Religion and Mother Right.* Preface by George Boas, introduction by Joseph Campbell, translated by Ralph Manheim. Princeton NJ: Princeton University Press. P. 116. (Orig. Pub.1967)

461 Kramer, S. (1991). The Origins of Fatherhood: An Ancient Family Process. Family Process. 30:377-392. Accessed from <http://sebastiankraemer.com/docs/Kraemer%20origins%20of%20fatherhood.pdf> on 2015-03-28.

dren. After the mating, the father has no further part in the child's development. Indeed, neither we [the observers] nor the chimpanzees normally have any idea who the father is. This is one of the major differences between human and chimpanzee societies,"[462] adds Jane Goodall. Paternity developed from the envy of maternity, and from the illusion that paternal heredity, the transfer of an object, accumulated wealth, would eternalize the patriarch.

Gorilla and chimpanzee males are primarily interested in competing for the defense of their group and alpha status; even coitus with females in heat is not as important. Male gorillas carry infants on their shoulders primarily to protect themselves from attack by other males. Even in gibbons that remain sexually paired and that parent together, the bulk of tending for the young is performed by the female, as is the case for bonobos. Marmosets, like birds, share parental tasks but their social roles are not antagonistic. Only in humans do mother and father become hierarchical, male parents' having difficulty behaving as females. This is an historical rather than biological determination of human behavior.

Research has suggested that patriarchy is somehow correlated to the domestication of cattle and to pastoralism. Matrilineal descent seems to be infrequent in societies that raise livestock. Matrilineal cultures become patrilineal when they acquire cattle. Testing for co-evolution of cattle and descent, researchers concluded: "The results support the hypothesis that acquiring cattle led formerly matrilineal Bantu-speaking cultures to change to patrilineal or mixed descent."[463] Domestication of animals was probably an offshoot of male-implemented agriculture; and it obviously made accumulation more feasible than storing perishables.

Domestication was also a way to finally fathom the mechanism of reproduction through sexual intercourse and therefore the nec-

---

462 Goodall, J. (1978). *In the shadow of man.* London: Collins English Library. P. 76.
463 Holden, C. J. and Mace, R. (2003). "Spread of cattle led to the loss of matrilineal descent in Africa: a coevolutionary analysis." Proceedings of the Royal Society of London. 270, 2425–2433. Accessed from <http://rspb.royalsocietypublishing.org> on March 31, 2015

essary role of males. Before that, pregnancy had been attributed to other causes. As late as the mid-twentieth-century, the Na of China believed the function of the male in reproduction was to "water" the independent germinative ground of the female.[464] The mechanisms of female fertilization and the gestation of children being unknown, all children were only identifiable, placed in a narrow consanguine class, by the obvious precedence of their particular mother. Knowledge of paternity came late in history, as did Oedipus.

Barbara Smuts, reviewing primatological evidence, gives an excellent review of hypothesis about the origins and future of patriarchy. There are various forms of social life among the apes, she concludes, and with them various forms of sex relations have also been described. She explores the evolutionary and adaptive hypothesis for the establishment of patriarchy in humans by drawing from primatology research, and states that "patriarchy is a product of reproductive strategies typically shown by male (and, to a lesser extent, female) primates, which in humans have undergone unusually effective elaboration," and that "natural selection has favored in humans the potential to develop and express any one of a wide range of reproductive strategies, depending on environmental conditions." In her review *gender solidarity* emerges as an outstanding factor, and *violence* has an ultimate determining role. She concludes with lessons that can be learned from evolution and history to correct the protracted patriarchal imbalance.[465]

1.9.2 Identity Change

Neolithic learning of domestication made humans aware that it took a male to impregnate a female and produce offspring, Le-

464 Cai, H. (2001). *Society Without Fathers or Husbands. The Na of China.* Trans. Asti Hustvedt. New York. Zone Books.
465 Smuts, B (1995). "The Evolutionary Origins of Patriarchy." Human Nature, Vol. 6, No., 1, pp. 1-32. Accessed from <https://isites.harvard.edu/fs/docs/icb.topic1001965. files/Course%20Materials_Week%205/Evolution%20of%20Patriarchy%20 Smuts%201995.pdf> on 2017-04-07.

rner argues.[466] However, several other factors such as the development of the division of labor, the technical possibility of surplus accumulation, enhanced social status based on ownership, growth of commerce through bartering, and the discovery of value through exchange contributed to male ascendance. The original matriarchal economy, based on non-profit giving alone, was obviously unsustainable in the context of civil society. A shift of the center of gravity of society from communal gentile values to those of civil society was required.

Along with their new consciousness of paternity, men were able not only to roughly identify their sons, but also to invest their pride and material goods in them as their own externalization and objectification. This contributed to the realization of a fantasy of immortality. Their command of commerce and barter outside the gens gave patriarchs the ability to accumulate, while their subsistence was always assured by women, children, and slaves working agriculturally. The amount of labor invested on objects for exchange eventually came to be the measure of value. This was a totally new, radically different form of economy, opposite to that of the matriarchy, from societies that had a tenuous division of labor based on need and instinctual disposition in a naturally cohesive gentile group. There was a gradual shift to a different type of social metabolism where competition in civil society supplanted domestic collaboration and a necessity-based economy. Yet the domestic form survived as a vestige of matriarchy and perhaps the seed for a future society.

The word *family* originally meant the group of slaves at home. The meaning grew to include all property of the *paterfamilias,* including relatives, adoptees, captives of war, and domesticated animals. Owning slaves that implicitly agreed to recognize the patriarch as their owner and ruler, as well as their protector and vicarious source of subjectivity and consciousness, made it possible for patriarchs to create the state, with its exclusive right to the monopoly of violence and terror. Patriarchs were owners of lives and bodies

---

466 Lerner, G. (1986). *The Creation of Patriarchy.* Oxford. Oxford University Press.

of their slaves who literally had no say. Slavery was a major detour from the morality of evolution in a species designed for the universality of consciousness, equality, and freedom. This was the primal trauma that started with the war on women for hegemony. It entailed the silence of all who were subordinated in the social hierarchy, the forceful suppression of their instinct to speak up. The role of repression in neurosis was elucidated but simultaneously concealed by Freud, who attributed all instinctual disposition and agency to the male of the species..

Slavery remains extant to this day in the form of wage labor. In return, enhanced productivity feeds the universal dream of class ascendance. The symbolic change of human identity manifested in a patronymic name, along with patrilineality, patrilocality, and inheritance all inversions of previous matriarchal institutions is a footnote in the light of eons of evolution and two hundred thousand years of successful matriarchal history. As Freud indicated, also in reverse, a most difficult transmogrification of consciousness is necessary to shift from mother to father love. Many succumb to "mental illness"in the process.

A substantial part of our human identity is the internalization of our whole history as culture.

1.9.3 The Fate of Mothers

In terms of consciousness and subjectivity, the domination by the patriarch over his family placed extraordinary conditions on women. Corollary notions of womanhood became objectification, virginity, sexual exclusivity, wife-possession, adultery, negative menstrual taboos, patriarchally dictated birth control, estranged body management; and, central to all, the exclusivity of patriarchal heredity and his dream of immortality, largely represented in the masculinized objectifications of culture and cultural institutions. Children, particularly the first-born son, the son of *primae noctis* and its *droit du seigneur,*[467] or, counterphobically, the youngest son, became able to challenge the authority of the mother at home, and to exclusively inherit a reinforcement of hierarchy. Worst of all was the damage done to the subordinate's subjectivity by his deprivation of expression and transcendence.

Sexual taboos initially imposed by mothers on sons that weaned late became first generational, and then extended slowly to heterosexually include a progressively ample circle of consanguine relatives on both sides of the family, to end in present monogamy. This is historically reflected in orderly arranged kinship nomenclatures documenting all the stages of family organization and containing their consequent sexual taboos. These were logically recorded by Morgan in his *Systems of Consanguinity and Affinity of the Human Family*[468] and *Ancient Society*. From these, Morgan was able to reconstruct the stadial history of the evolution of the family from its initial animal promiscuity. Generational incest, when it occurs within the nuclear family, is for the most part a father-daughter phenomenon today.[469]

Some of the notions of womanhood, mother status, and family etiquette were still absent in the mind of the indigenous tribes of North America in the seventeenth century, when Jesuit missionaries such as Lafitau and Paul Le Jeune described their customs. The Montagnais-Nascapi in the Labrador Peninsula, for example, lived in extended family groups that practiced parity in labor and sexual equality. Their sexual relations were temporary non-exclusive monogamy, and for that they were considered "very lewd" by the Jesuit in his letters to his superiors in France. They practiced solidarity in family interests, but both men and women were sexually free. Le

467 In Feudalism the right of the Lord to sleep with all brides for the first three or four nights. See: Gage, J.M. (2002). Woman, Church and State. Ch. 4. "Marquette." Amherst, N.Y. Humanity Books. Unabridged Edition.
468 Morgan, H.L. (1871). *Systems of Consanguinity and Affinity of the Human Family.* Washington, D.C. Smithsonian Institution.
469 Herman, J., and Hirschman, L. (1977). "Father-Daughter Incest." In: Signs: Journal of Women in Culture and Society. 2 (4): 735-756. Accessed from <http://link.springer.com/chapter/10.1007/978-1-4684-4754-5_16#page-2> on 2015-08-27.

Jeune documents that males preferred to take the children of their sisters as heirs, a remnant of matriarchal organization. In the Jesuit's mind this represented the infidelity of wives. This rendition runs against that of the native himself, who responds to the priest's judgment as follows: all children, the Nascapi man tells the Jesuit, not only one's own, are loved equally. And he adds: it is the French that are weird for loving only their own children.[470] The Nascapi had no patriarch, no chief, and, as explicitly described by Le Jeune, abhorred social hierarchy. They still managed their lives and affairs consensually and in a communal form. Le Jeune even explicitly says to his superiors that were they to agree to have a chief, they could then be blessed with the gift of French civilization. The Montagnais-Nascapi ethnology is in many other ways a mirror image of that of their dire enemies the Iroquois. These aborigines were revisited after a century-and-a-half of anthropological research by Eleanor Leacock,[471] who is to them what Lewis Morgan is to the Iroquois. It is an irony of history that it was two North American anthropologists who would reveal the still live and equal female transcendent subjectivity in the recently discovered New World.

The female hostile devaluation was crafted by patriarchs to override natural balances and produce social hierarchies, all condensed in the notion of gender. This was achieved through slavery, reification, exclusion, exploitation, and gagging, all variations of political and psychological *repression*. Initially imposed by force, through habit they became custom and etiquette and were made to look natural with the complicity of science. The main strategy was the inversion of the female status.

Women today are painstakingly undoing this historical detour, unlearning what is so deep that it appears as natural, and starting

470 Le Jeune, P. (1633). In: The Jesuit Relations and Allied Documents. Travels and Explorations of the Jesuit Missionaries in New France.1610—1791. Vol. VI. Québec. 1633–1634. Chapter VI. On Their Vices And Their Imperfections. P. 251 ff. Cleveland: The Burrows Brothers Company, Publishers, M DCCC XCVIII. Accessed from <http://puffin.creighton.edu/jesuit/relations/relations_06.html> on 2015-03-31.
471 See for example her collection of essays: Leacock, E. (2008). *Myths of Male Dominance*. Chicago. Haymarket Books.

to offer a constructive alternative, a contrast to the hopelessness of *there is no alternative*.

1.9.4 Active Correlation and Mediation

Vladimir Mikhailovich Bekhterev was the first psychologist to develop the very useful notion of first- and second-order mediations in the nervous system.[472] Unlike other behaviorists, he advocated for a science of behavioral, reflexive subjectivity, to include the study of consciousness as behavior. With Hegel, Bekhterev deserves the first place in pioneering the study of consciousness. Like Freud a neurologist, he started from the brain's central property that he called *correlative activity*, rejecting a psychology without consciousness proposed by other behaviorists. His first premise was thus that the brain is the organ that actively correlates reality and consciousness. It accomplishes this through mediatory conditioning, animal reflexes, and instincts, transformed into reality-oriented human behavior. Active correlation takes place through a complex, heterogeneous mediatory organ, the brain, and this is the signature of the human species.

Today we understand the design of the human brain for its active correlation as mediated by an other, a first mediator, the mothering one, everyone else bringing influence secondarily through second-order mediations. Internalized, the mother-mediator becomes the self, mediation being the uppermost characteristic of the human species. Paradoxically *neoteny* the retention, by adults in a species, of traits previously seen only in juveniles or developmental retardation, turns into the advantage of being able to learn through mediations. Maternal first-order mediations for the first time switch on all

---

472 Bekhterev, V. M. (1923). *General foundations of human reflexology.* Chapter 3. Quoted by: Vygotsky, L.S. (1999). "Con-sciousness as a problem in the psychology of behavior." Trans: Nikolai Veresov. In: Undiscovered Vygotsky: Etudes on the pre-history of cultural-historical psychology. European Studies in the History of Science and Ideas. Vol. 8. pp. 251-281. Frankfurt. Peter Lang Publishing (Orig. Pub. 1925). Online in MIA. Accessed from <https://www.marxists.org/archive/vygotsky/works/1925/consciousness.htm#n6> on 2015-04-08.

the senses and brain reflexes in a very particular form of symbiotic relationship. Not only the brain, the central station, but the whole human organism, would be unable to survive if left to fend on its own and without relational human mediations.[473] The human infant has to be not only protected and looked after; its innermost drives have to be regulated from outside. What the brain does is to avidly internalize, and conserve, to later retrieve and reproduce, not so much the material relationship itself, but its form or grammar. This is how the infant brain materially seems to construct *forms* Plato believed to exist independently. Every psychological first-order mediation is interpersonal, a dependent protoself connected to an executive other.

Ontogenetically, the mother is thus the first-order mediator, an external executive organ, and there is no good reason to believe that she was not so also phylogenetically. Even today, the relationship with the mother is legally recognized as primary. The most important psychological function of the father in child-raising is to represent the second-order mediations necessary for civil society.[474] As Freud illustrated, the emotional and cognitive impact of the father on the growing child is a relative late and incidental event, as proven by single-parent families. In the present family form, the Oedipal-period triangulation takes place after the age of about three, bringing with it the possibility of alliance and exclusion. By this time all the basic structures of the mind, first-order mediations, are in place.

Marx discussed alienation as the substitution of primary- by secondary- order mediations, a notion endorsed by Meszaros.[475] The

---

473 Somel, M., Franz, H., et al. (2009). "Transcriptional neoteny in the human brain." Proceedings of the National Academy of Sciences of the United States of America. Accessed from <http://www.pnas.org/content/early/2009/03/20/0900544106.full.pdf> on 2015-08-28.

474 For the difference between first and second order mediations see among others of the same author: Meszaros, I. (2011). *Social Structure and Forms of Consciousness.* Vol. 2. New York. Monthly Review Press.

475 Meszaros, I. (1970). *Marx's Theory of Alienation.* Ch. 2. Genesis of Marx's Theory of Alienation. Online in MIA, István Mészáros Internet Archive. Accessed from <https://www.marxists.org/archive/meszaros/works/alien/meszaro1.htm> on 2015-04-08.

latter are the result of the patriarchal upset. First-order mediations are the essential incorruptible elements in the relation of man to nature and man to man, the original bridging. Male second-order mediations, superimposed and repressive, became alienating when made to appear as if they were natural and first-order.

Mediations are Bekhterev's correlations and through them psychologically we move from the original disorganized state of our minds at birth, incoherent homogeneity of the object brain, to our mature status, the "coherent" heterogeneity of a subject. Retracing evolution collaboratively, mothers build good-sense through first-order mediations.

1.9.5 The Patriarchal Second-Order Mediations

The mother had put in place all the social conditionings necessary for the child to survive, and thrive, in a protected but limited social environment that was collaborative in nature, and essentially based on an ethics of giving. But this is a subversive ethics in the larger expanse of nature and although not exclusive to the human species, highly sublimated into altruism and morality. So-called civil society, transformed by males through second-order mediations, remains still the prior ethic of the food chain. The fragile human family has had to survive in a hostile environment transformed by male dominance to its bourgeois form. In the bourgeois family, the father is the emissary of civil society and his function is to prepare the young for the Hobbesian struggle that is to come.

Can the large human family, the species, the achievement of evolution that enshrines altruism and collaboration — giving-to-produce rather than taking or destroying-to-produce— survive the onslaught of prior survival of the fittest, compounded by its historical reappearance in civil society? The large solidarity-based human family has been brought back to the competitive survival of civil society at a time when universal solidarity is not only morally, but materially, possible in the form of substantial equality.

The original intent of the social contract between social classes represented in the state, was to legally mediate, which means starting from the antagonism of conflicting sides, a lawful compromise according to law and precedent. Law is the second-order mediatory process after morality.

From first-order learning, a form of family social conditioning, civil society moved to introduce second-order education by civil society. Family-learned skill in civil society became authority. Similarly, learned self-control became policing. Sharing is institutionalized as taxation, and survival loses its peremptoriness to wasteful profit. The peaceful shelter of the family is invaded by media-produced spurious needs including constant war in the name of safety. Paradoxically, civil society can only survive by creating an organ of control, the state, "government" built after the first-order model of matriarchal family governance based on fulfilling the needs of all.

The original family, the gens, was transformed into subsequent forms to facilitate the reproduction, not of truly free individuals, associated producers, that the gens originally was, but of an spurious external order imposed by patriarchal civil society and based on accumulation, waste, and profit. The only way this could be accomplished was by the destruction of the full subjectivity that produced families to replace it with the one that reproduces civil society. This took place in the open-slavery stage of patriarchy.

Patriarchs started slavery within the family by shifting its center of gravity from maternal competency to force-based division of labor. The patriarchs failed in their attempt to fully objectivize women. This failure has assured the survival of humanity to this day, in the fact that mothers still put in place the first-order mediations for all. Patriarchs have talked about democracy since the inception of slavery, while mothers have continued to practice it in the narrow context of the family. The productivity-oriented model of slavery grew to include, besides women children, the colored, the weak, the propertyless, the immigrant, the religiously infidel in the eyes of the master, all categories that street wisdom in today's jargon calls the ninety-nine percent dominated, by the remainder one.

What probably started as a balanced mediation through a social contract between, opposite gentes (only symbolically), became one-sided domination and social class hierarchy buttressed by the force of the state. This detour in the morality of evolution, based on the balance of equal but opposite instinctual dispositions, led us to where we are now.

1.9.6 "You Are Not the Only Victim"

These words are the culmination of the comedic tragedy portrayed in the Swedish film *Force Majeure*,[476] A vacationing Swedish working family in the French Alps is suddenly frightened, while having lunch in an outdoor restaurant at their resort, by the growing prospect of a catastrophe, an explosion-triggered avalanche that makes everyone in the place abandon everything and scurry for cover. The exception is Ebba, the young mother who clutches her boy and girl, unable to lift and carry them to safety while she, to no avail, calls on her husband Thomas for help. Thomas has, in fact, already fled, snow boots on and all. It turns out to be a false alarm.

Ebba suffers an acute stress reaction not to the avalanche that turned out to be only a cloud of snow dust, but to what the crisis revealed about her family structure, the unwritten family contract of patriarchal protection broken. A victim of acute stress, she cannot go back to business as usual and is obsessed. She tries to clarify what happened with her husband, but he remembers things very differently, he insists. She talks it over with acquaintances and visiting friends and finds it impossible to confirm her memory because Thomas insists that his memory of the event is not the same.

But when his own smartphone reveals the recorded fact that Thomas indeed ran for his life abandoning his wife and children, he finally breaks down as his idealized image is destroyed. This is

---

476 Ostlund, R. (2014). Force Majeure (Turist). Referenced in the Internet Movie Database. Accessed at <http://www.imdb.com/title/tt3630276/> on 3015-08-29.

when he falls apart, sobbing uncontrollably, and at the end finally utters the sad truth: "Look at me, you are not the only victim." A few maneuvers are necessary for Ebba to restore the family to baseline, to go back home after vacation.

One central take-home message is that catastrophe brings us back to our natural instinct, and that such instinct turns out to be opposite in male and female. True protective altruism is the disposition of the mother, not the father.

1.9.7 The Negation of the Negation

Motion is the negation of previous negations. The personifications of patriarchy, including, famously Margaret Thatcher, tell us that "there is no alternative" to the social structure we are living. This does not mean hopelessness, but either ignorance or denial of the cosmic facts of motion and evolution. The motto is so popular as to have been abbreviated in the acronym TINA. Were we to accept this injunction, there would indeed be no hope. We are living in a constant state of war, not only bloody but pervasive and abstract. A constant war on human consciousness is deployed by ruling-class ideology. Wikipedia lists one hundred and ten bloody wars in the twentieth century alone.

In his famous finches, Darwin observed how the beak, the instrument for their nourishment, varied to accommodate to type of food they survived on. The same is true for the human instrument of consciousness deployed through language; our consciousness is shaped by the pablum we are fed by media and education. This is an illustration of how fitness is a dialectical relationship with the environment, and if our ecology has been perverted, so has our consciousness. Object and subject reciprocally transform each other as they fulfill their evolutionary function. Today, humans are raised to be fit for war and children are desensitized to the emotional effects of violence through television and games. The problem is that being fit for war reciprocally creates the need for war. This is the reason most of the functions of society have been militarized. In the United States, the National Rifle Association calls for universal gun ownership as a deterrent: good guns neutralize bad guns, we are told. The gun has become in America the most sacred symbol of patriarchal fitness. After all, we are all without exception, men and women, equipped for a gun.

Our hands and brains produce technology that today is geared for war. These are the same brains and hands that in the original society were not used to destroy but to produce humanity. There is only one alternative and one way out of the present predicament we are in, and that is the negation, the supersession of both, patriarchy and capitalism. Whether patriarchy and capitalism will eventually see the need for a transition, or else continue the now nuclear race to barbarism, we do not know. In any event, in case we do not destroy ourselves it is predictable that the next historical stage is likely to be a synthesis constructed over the templates of matriarchy, with synthesis constructed over the template of matriarchy.

This will be a society of give-and-take, a society that will balance both human instinctual dispositions to constraining each other. The precedent is there in matriarchy for a new society based on a return of the primacy of first-order mediations: collective self-control against police control, acceptance and parity for all forms of human heterogeneity, production for use, not exchange or accumulation and profit, abolition of the division of labor particularly mental and manual, the abolition of social hierarchy, and a return to a natural morality of evolution based on the fulfillment of true human needs.

Only this would make possible a classless society based on consciousness instead of ideology, one in which the individual self can be truly realized, as there would be no state to be internalized for the management of a class split.

1.9.8 A Society Without Fathers or Husbands

As if waiting for the last minute, evidence has come from anthropology about a society without the holy family. This is what the mainstream has always asked about: full evidence. The recent publication of impeccable ethnographic work by Chinese anthropologist Hua Cai has finally shown the remnants of a society without the roles, functions, or even words for father and husband.[477] I will in what follows draw briefly from Cai's book.

The Na is part of four minority groups in the Yunnan and Sichuan districts of China, about 250,000 people called by the majority of Chinese Mo-So. Some of these groups have not reached the stage of the written word. Na means black, and the life of this group centers around raising buffalo, cows, horses and mules. Each household keeps dozens of chicken and several pigs, pork being their preferred food. Until 1956, they were ruled by chiefs but then came communist rule and their functionaries. Their social stratification is visible in their housing and attire. The upper class are descendants of chiefs, and the only strata to be patrilineal and patrilocal. There is a middle class composed of commoners and estranged previous upper class members that lives matriarchally and following the custom of *the visit* that I will describe below. There is a third class of estranged middle class and lumpen. The total number of Na is about 30,000.

There is a swat of public land administered by a male chief. Land can be sold only by the aristocrats, but others can pawn and rent. Each commoner has a plot of land for cultivation and serfs are also given land plots. There are two religions, Na religion and Buddhism, and priests are of both genders.

The Na believe the newborn comes exclusively from the female, the function of the male in intercourse being to water the female seed for reproduction. This is seen as a favor the male does for the female. Instead of consanguinity, the Na refer to being of the same bone, the mother's. Every child is born in a maternal household of people of the same bone. Each generation traditionally consists of brothers and sisters living together for life and working within the

---

477 Cai, H. (2001). *Society Without Fathers or Husbands. The Na of China.* Trans. Asti Hustvedt. New York. Zone Books.

same household. Brothers and sisters participate in raising the sisters' children. The incest taboo is expressed in the law that "those who eat from the same bowl and the same plate must not mate."[478] Almost all active mothers are in their teenage years, and there is a taboo on sexual evocation that includes the prohibition of telling the child who the *genitor* is, if known. The form of these families goes against all previously found family structures and contradicts Murdock's axiomatic kin structures,[479] and Westermarck's universal marriage.

There are two chiefs in every group, and generally the female chief is concerned with all that refers to domestic life, while the male is in charge of external affairs. Succession is generally determined by age, oldest daughters, and nephews of the chiefs. Within the group, the chiefs have no particular privilege and, if anything, work harder. To the extent it exists, social hierarchy has been imposed by a succession of Chinese governments.

All sexual relationships are open, even though there is some degree of contractual unions in the different strata. Some couples agree to grant each other mutual sexual privilege and some even agree to cohabitate. All, however, continue to on occasion practice the *furtive visit,* the oldest custom of the group.

During the communist regime in China, four reforms have been implemented in the past century trying to impose marriage, patriarchal rule and descent, and different forms of private property, with minimal success. The reasons provided by the government to convince people to shift have been health/epidemiological reasons and economic ones, besides that of joining the lifestyle of the Chinese majority. Incentives have been rather unsuccessfully provided for marriage and monogamy. In response, people have married, but the rate of divorce has been sky-high. Penalties have been applied for noncompliance with the government rules, and visiting has been

---

478 Cai, H. (2001). *Society Without Fathers or Husbands.* Ibid. P.125.
479 Murdock, G.P. (1949). Social Structure. P. 42. New York. Free Press. Online in Accessed from <https://archive.org/stream/socialstructurem00murd#page/42/mode/2up> on2016-05-26.

forbidden. People still continue with their old practice for the most part, practicing the visit and open sexual relations. While in 1963, after the first reform, the marriage rate in the population was 8.5 percent, in 1989, well after the more punitive fourth reform the marriage rate was 2.5 percent, and all persons still practiced the furtive visit.

The prevalent modality of sexual life, the furtive visit, requires mutual heterosexual consent between adults and excludes consanguine relatives. The usual custom is the man visiting the woman at night, usually after the woman has previously consented to the visit. This is entirely a private affair and must be furtive, including a ban on talk about sex. The man must avoid being perceived by the male relatives of the woman he is visiting. There are usually a multiplicity of partners for both participants and they are designated as acquaintances, not friends, because the rule of furtiveness keeps them from openly visiting at their respective homes. In 1989, the furtive visit was practiced exclusively by 57% of the population.

There is another form of the visit which is the *conspicuous visit*. In this variation, there is family acknowledgment of the relation through a meal ritual. This form signifies the couple's sexual privilege in sexual access decided by both partners; it does not exclude furtive visits, but is a form of temporary priority dissolvable by either party at will. The sexual evocation taboo restricts the issue to a private matter and is not the concern of any other member of the family. Here the couple are designated as friends. In 1989, the conspicuous form of the visit was practiced by 28.5% of the population.

Besides the furtive and conspicuous forms of visit there is also cohabitation practiced by 12% of the population in 1989, either uxorilocal or virilocal. Cohabitation is mostly considered a last resort to preserve a household, usually after adoption attempts have failed, and usually with no sisters in this type of family. This is a social solution to a biological problem. Here again, the desire of either partner can break the relationship at any time, although both of their families have been involved in approving the contract. This is the form with the most continuity; and the children take the name of the family that provides the locality.

Finally, there is also the usual form of marriage which is only virilocal, also related to lack of female members in the particular family, and agreed upon by both families. If the couple separates, they are prohibited from returning to their families of origin, and the separation must be negotiated and approved by the chiefs. This is the uppermost expression of a social, not natural form of liaison. Here, contrary to all other forms, the name of the members of the family is that of the father's family of origin. The children have become relatives by marriage, not by blood.

Cai points out talking about the visit: "Its complete opposition to the mode of marriage makes us confront, for the first time in the course of human history, a society based on an institution other than marriage. The existence of this institution provides a new type of institutionalized sexual life that makes it possible to consider marriage as only one modality of institutionalized sexual life. We can therefore posit the visit and marriage as different types of institutionalized sexual life and treat them as separate categories."[480] This posits a gambit to the mainstream theory of marriage and the holy family. Of course mainstream anthropology may predictably retort that the Na are the exception that confirms the rule, and this is predicted by Cai. [481] The fact that marriage is almost exclusive to the high social-class strata confirms the economic nature of the bourgeois family.

The Na society is matriarchal, because the maternal lineage provides the identity and name of individuals, property is communal and matrilineal in transmission, there is a sexual division of labor, and seniority is the only natural hierarchy.[482] Kinship is purely matrilineal, there is no exchange of women, fidelity is considered shameful rather than something to be proud of, cohabitation or marriage are traditionally illicit if not dictated by biological needs, and sex has a completely different meaning than that of the mainstream.

Cai concludes that the furtive visit, the conspicuous visit, and cohabitation were the only modalities of sexual existence prior to the Qing dynasty in China.[483] He argues against mainstream anthro-

---

480 Cai, H. (2001). *Society Without Fathers or Husbands.* Ibid. P. 426.
481 Cai, H. (2001). *Society Without Fathers or Husbands.* Ibid. P. 442.
482 Cai, H. (2001). *Society Without Fathers or Husbands.* Ibid. P. 461.
483 Cai, H. (2001). *Society Without Fathers or Husbands.* Ibid. P. 413.

pology, particularly Radcliffe-Brown,[484] who fiercely defends marriage and patriarchy as universal and transhistorical.

This is where the exception could become the rule.

---

484 Radcliffe-Brown, A.R. (1952). *Structure and Function in Primitive Societies.* Glencoe Ill. Free Press. Accessed from <http://monoskop.org/images/b/b6/Brown_Radcliffe_ Alfred_Structure_and_Function_in_Primitive_Society_1952.pdf> on 2015-08-27.

1.10 HOW MATRIARCHS MANAGED WAR

"The dancers performed first a series of complicated and wild movements in which clubs, spears, boomerangs, and shields were brandished. Then 'all at once the mass divided into groups, and with deafening shrieks and passionate cries they sprang into one another in a hand-to-hand fight. One side was speedily driven out of the field and pursued into the darkness, whence howls, groans, and the stroke of clubs could be heard, producing the perfect illusion of a terrible massacre.'[485]

1.10.1 The Need for War

War is an historical phenomenon, not a natural one. What species do in the food chain is not war; it is a form of destruction designed to maintain constructive equilibrium and fitness variation. In this chapter I rely fundamentally on the most comprehensive historical work of Evelyn Reed, in her seminal book *Woman's Evolution, from Matriarchal Clan to Patriarchal Family.*[486]

Reed points out the existence of two views on the matter of how tribes emerged from herds. One is through segmentation of fission of blood-related groups, and the other from affiliation or fusion, of disperse groups that may or may not have been blood-related before. Reed brings both viewpoints together. It is possible that first off-shoots of consanguine groups split apart and wandered afar. At the same time when cannibalism was still operative in human society and strangers were edible animals, sticking together and magnitude were safeguards for the group. It was also desirable to make alli-

---

485 Grosse, E. (1897). *The Beginning of Art.* New York. Appleton. Quoted by Reed, E (1975). *Woman's Evolution from matriar-chal clan to patriarchal family.* New York and Toronto. Pathfinder Press. P. 235.

486 Reed, E. (1975). *Woman's Evolution from matriarchal clan to patriarchal family.* Ibid.

ances with neighboring groups for the same reason. "Progressive combinations" led group units to develop into tribes. Moieties on the one hand, and maternal clans, phratries and tribes on the other, could have originated through the two opposite processes mentioned, from maternal primal hordes.[487]

The immediate social danger originally was cannibalism, the same danger that prompted the earliest social covenants. This is a remnant of the food chain to be socially eradicated. According to Reed, the danger is gradually eliminated through social institutions that simultaneously overcome but conserve the instinctual drive. Reed quotes the Arapesh in the pages of Margaret Mead: "Your own mother, Your own sister, Your own pigs, Your own yams that you have piled up, You may not eat. Other people's mothers, Other people's sisters, Other people's pigs, Other people's yams that have piled up, You may eat."[488] Eating was originally equivalent to mating and similar taboos applied to both cannibalism and incest. The safety of the family was guaranteed in this fashion, but it was otherwise outside of the gentes or clans, the domain of males.

Dialectical social processes, both centripetal and centrifugal, created divisions such as moieties as well as division of labor, and at the same time produced, through aggregation, larger social units such as nations and federations that went well beyond the realm and manageability of families. In the same fashion, exchange created bonds that reinforced the need for larger social units. This had inevitable effects on personal identity and its consequent expansion to include even non-consanguine others and enemies. It became a matriarchal practice to adopt prisoners of war before slavery came into place.

Psychologically, what originally was a need to mirror matures into a need for reciprocity. This is reflected in the exchange systems, first the economic system of gifts, and also that system of war.

487 Reed., E (1975). *Woman's Evolution.* Ibid. P. 195 ss.
488 Mead, M. (1963). *Sex and Temperament in Three Primitive Societies.* New York. P. 83. (Orig. Pub. 1935).

Gift-giving was fundamental in early societies and the backbone of their economy. Giving was not originally barter; it was the logic of use: what I cannot use must be used by others, not wasted. Giving became part of social ceremonies and institutions in a society that was communal that did not have the notion of "private." A refusal to give or to accept gifts was against the etiquette of those societies, and even the great, and at times destructive potlatches, were reciprocated.

1.10.2 Death Exchanges and Blood Revenge

Death also fell within the category of exchange, and people's death, not having a scientific explanation yet, was usually attributed to magic from neighboring groups. Turf-related exterminations can be understood on the grounds of the food chain; more interesting is the concept of death reciprocity that falls within the logic of exchange. Reed points out that although this system has been called warfare by anthropologists, it does really have a very different logic behind it, not at all comparable with what we understand as modern warfare. Territorial conquest by armed force was not a concept in the primitive mind yet. Death reciprocity was. As it was during confrontation, death was caused also outside of it, magically.

Applying vengeance directly by killing a neighbor in return had the negative possibility of misunderstanding, the alternative group's not knowing exactly the explanation of the occurrence and therefore possibly snowballing into more killing. This is why the institutionalization of war was necessary, to make sure that actions were explained and clarified before action was taken. Neighboring groups that operated equally, with an equal level of psychological development, would meet periodically to discuss their grievances and arrive, in a more sophisticated fashion, to combat arrangements and settling accounts. It was possible, for example to regulate fighting, to fight until the right number of victims was arrived at on one or both sides. There was as much reciprocity in the blood revenge as there was in the gift. After accounts were settled without territorial or any other gain and reciprocity achieved, life would then go back to business as usual. This was in fact a form of regulated justice. Everything's being communal, the whole group, not individuals, was held responsible and accountable. The whole kin is answerable for the death of each member, and blood revenge was originally matrilineal, the mother's brother being the center.[489]

This is how killing of people who may not even be enemies was morally justified; it was part of reciprocity, of a natural process of exchange. It was based on the *principle of equivalence*, a notion absolutely necessary as a condition for exchange, as groups were moving from a use economy to an exchange one. With the institutionalization of exchange and property came war proper, a fact that takes us to the patriarchal shift.

1.10.3 The Sublimation of Aggression: Sports and Art

To expiate death or malfeasance, morality demanded economic substitutes more than the continuation of the cycle of death. Mock fights or sham fights were an alternative, a first mediation. Fighting was further regulated to avoid death, although exceptions were granted. Sham fights were prearranged along the same procedures that had been implemented for blood revenge. They were often in fact reconciliation fights, which would seem paradoxical, perhaps a form of face-saving duels. Scalping was taking a small piece of skin from the head of the vanquished, in terms of economy a great improvement from killing.[490]

It eventually came to be that injuring the contender was not so honorable as forgiving him even in fight, avoiding the last blow or the scalping, while having had the opportunity to do the injury. It is not difficult from this point to see sports like Japanese jujitsu, karate, or gladiators as sublimated forms of settling accounts. It is a logical

489 Reed, E. (1975). *Woman's Evolution.* Ibid. P. 219.
490 Reed, E. (1975). *Woman's Evolution.* Ibid. P. 231.

step from this to group or team sports representing communities. According to some, soccer would have started with decapitated heads as the ball, before they evolved to the inflated leather ball. It makes sense that sports, including the Olympics, may have originated from funeral games. "In our concepts a dance performed by mock skeletons may be called a "dance of death." But in savage society, where it represented a victory over death through a mock representation in dance-and-drama form, it was really a "dance of life"[491] The dance is a wonderful social organizer, because it integrates all participants into one motion.

Other forms of art have similar origins and similar effects as pointed out by Reed: they include oratory, songs, poetry, satire and jokes that at times were represented in the form of artistic combats. Competitive satirical poetry, such as in South American *trovas*, is still a frequent cultural form of expression in some societies.

1.10.4 The Role of Women

Matriarchal communities were free from internal strife. Although reports of peace ceremonies center on the activities of men, it was women who made the preparations, including gifts. Not being warriors or hunters, women were less suspicious and more prone to establish communication, particularly with stranger women. Opposite to men, whose reaction to aliens was knee-jerk preemptive defense, as it is still today, women did tend rather to explore the possibility of conserving and growing.

The following is of another Reed's quotations[492] of Margaret Mead: "And whereas the lives of the men are one mass of petty bickering, misunderstanding, reconciliation, avowals, disclaimers, and protestations accompanied by gifts, the lives of the women are singularly unclouded with personalities or with quarreling. For fifty quarrels among the men, there is hardly one among the women.

---

491 Reed, E. (1975). *Woman's Evolution.* Ibid. P. 235.
492 Reed, E. (1975). *Woman's Evolution.* Ibid. P. 263.

Solid, preoccupied, powerful, with shaven unadorned heads, they sit in groups and laugh together, or occasionally stage a night dance, at which, without a man present, each woman dances vigorously all by herself the dance step that she has found to be most exciting. Here again the solidarity of women, the inessentiality of men, is demonstrated."[493] Women do the work that lies behind what men exchange. And Reed adds: "Women played the key role in making men into brothers and teaching them how to make brothers and brothers-in-law out of other men."[494] Not only did women take care of all the details of ceremonies and gifts, but they also made early arrangements for future mating of children from exchanging groups. Additionally, love dances and free sexual parties often followed ceremonial exchanges between groups, and these are usually moralistically ignored or depicted as debauchery by current standards. Love dances often followed war ones, but they are not paid attention to, because such female freedom is an insult to the patriarchal ethos.

According to Reed, some early anthropologists describe women as ambassadors who conducted peace negotiations' being highly respected, even if they included sexual favors. Sexual intercourse was a most natural form of relationship and it did not have the present connotation and implications. Women were good ambassadors because they were less likely to be killed; women as companions were often protective for strangers.

1.10.5 Sublimation and the Aggressive Instinct

We have seen the evolution of male's instinctual disposition from crude forms of blood revenge to ritualistic ceremonies that gradually abolish hostility, and the important role of women in this process. This represents the mechanics of what Freud called sublimation. It results from balancing two equivalent domains of life, inside and outside, we and they, and love and death. It is very important to keep in mind that sublimation first consists in balancing, and second in

---

493 Mead, M. (1963). *Sex and Temperament in Three Primitive Societies.* Ibid.P.257.
494 Reed, E. (1975). *Woman's Evolution.* Ibid. P. 264"

displacing; it is a balanced displacement.

This is what Freud left unfinished when he responded to Einstein's question "Why War?"[495] Freud invoked the death instinct as an irrevocably natural instinctual disposition, but did not take into consideration that instinctual dispositions evolve through sublimation, through balanced displacement. War is not an exception, and therefore there is hope. With the political repression of women in patriarchy, their contribution to the whole of society, coming from the inside of the prison-family, could only have little perceptible effect in civil society. In the latter, the male instinct then proceeded to expression without its appropriate natural constraining force. Thanatos at the expense of Eros has brought humanity to the situation we are in.

---

495 Einstein, A, and Freud, S. (1931-2)."The Einstein-Freud Correspondence." Online in Arizona State University. Accessed from <www.public.asu.edu/~jmlynch/273/documents/FreudEinstein.pdf> on 2016-11-07

PART TWO (A): TOWARDS A PSYCHOANALYSIS OF CONSCIOUSNESS

"My general consciousness is only the theoretical shape of that of which the living shape is the real community, the social fabric, although at the present day general consciousness is an abstraction from real life and as such confronts it with hostility. The activity of my general consciousness, as an activity, is therefore also my theoretical existence as a social being.

Above all we must avoid postulating "society" again as an abstraction *vis-à-vis* the individual. The individual is the social being. His manifestations of life – even if they may not appear in the direct form of communal manifestations of life carried out in association with others – are therefore an expression and confirmation of social life. Man's individual and species-life are not different, however much – and this is inevitable – the mode of existence of the individual is a more particular or more general mode of the life of the species, or the life of the species is a more particular or more general individual life.

In his consciousness of species man confirms his real social life and simply repeats his real existence in thought, just as conversely the being of the species confirms itself in species consciousness and exists for itself in its generality as a thinking being.

Man, much as he may therefore be a particular individual (and it is precisely his particularity which makes him an individual, and a real individual social being), is just as much the totality – the ideal totality – the subjective existence of imagined and experienced society for itself; just as he exists also in the real world both as awareness and real enjoyment of social existence, and as a totality of human manifestation of life.

Thinking and being are thus certainly distinct, but at the same time they are in unity with each other."

Karl Marx, *Manuscripts*[496]

---

496 Marx, K. (1959). *Economic and Philosophic Manuscripts of 1844.* Private Property and Communism (3). VI. Trans: Martin Mulligan. Moscow, USSR. Progress Publishers. (Orig. Pub. 1932. Written 1844). Online in MIA. Accessed from <https://www.marxists.org/archive/marx/works/1844/manuscripts/comm.htm> On 2016-02-01.

2.1 THE EVOLUTION OF CONSCIOUSNESS: FROM NATURAL SENSE TO NATURAL SELECTION AND FITNESS

"The physician can only shrug his shoulders when he is assured that 'consciousness is an indispensable characteristic of what is psychical', and perhaps, if he still feels enough respect for the utterances of philosophers, he may presume that they have not been dealing with the same thing or working at the same science. For even a single understanding observation of a neurotic's mental life or a single analysis of a dream must leave him with an unshakable conviction that the most complicated and most rational thought-processes, which can surely not be denied the name of psychical processes, can occur without exciting the subject's consciousness."

Freud, *The Interpretation of Dreams*.[497]

"But also when I am active scientifically, etc. – an activity which I can seldom perform in direct community with others – then my activity is social, because I perform it as a man. Not only is the material of my activity given to me as a social product (as is even the language in which the thinker is active): my own existence is social activity, and therefore that which I make of myself, I make of myself for society and with the consciousness of myself as a social being."

Marx, *Private Property and Communism*.[498]

497 Freud, S. (1955). *The Interpretation of Dreams*. Trans. James Strachey. New York. Basic Books. P. 612. (Orig. Pub. 1900). Online in Questia. Accessed from <http://www.questia.com/read/99555894/the-interpretation-of-dreams> on 2012-11-20.
498 Marx, K. (1959). *Economic & Philosophic Manuscripts of 1844*. Private Property and Communism. Trans. Martin Mulligan. Moscow. Progress Publishers. (Written 1844.

2.1.1 From the Big Bang to Consciousness

Freud became aware of the fact that since most psychic processes are unconscious, it would be impossible to bring to consciousness all the stimulation that is coming through the senses, including internal stimuli. As a matter of fact, filtering huge amounts of stimuli through mechanisms such as focusing, attention and concentration, and brain structures such as the thalamus and reticular activating system, is one of the main tasks of the central nervous system. Functionally, Freud's work is based on a small portion of the unconscious, the actively repressed. The bulk of the unconscious is reality that we discard or are unable to reach, besides what we inherit from the ensemble of the social relations. The latter was better illustrated by Carl Jung, who included the notion of a *collective unconscious*, consisting of latent memories from both historical and evolutionary past, and archetypes.[499] a layer of the unconscious shared with all members of the human species. This layer contains the bias that makes us biased towards an already modified context, the average expectable environment of Hartman.[500] At birth, ancestral memories are already present in our brain as is the predisposition for language. The same is illustrated in Marx's quotation above and in his sixth thesis on Feuerbach.[501]

It is a task of science to trace evolution starting from the big bang, our current scientific myth, as well as the specific pathways to human self-consciousness. Consciousness as antithesis to reality

Orig. Pub. 1932). Online in Marxists Internet Archive. Accessed from <http://www.marxists.org/archive/marx/works/1844/manuscripts/comm.htm> on 2012-11-20.

499 Jung, C.G. (1972). *The Structure and Dynamics of the Psyche* (Collected Works of C.G. Jung, Volume 8). Part lll. The Structure of the Psyche. 2nd Edition. Trans. Gerhard Adler and F.C. Hull. Princeton, N.J. Princeton University Press.

500 Hartman, H. (1958). *Ego Psychology and the Problem of Adaptation.* Trans. David Rapaport. New York: International Universities Press. (Orig pub. 1939)

501 Marx, K. (1969). "Theses on Feuerbach." Trans: W. Lough, Marx/Engels Selected Works, Volume One, p. 13 – 15. Moscow: Progress Publishers. (Written: by Marx in the Spring of 1845, but slightly edited by Engels; First Published: As an appendix to Ludwig Feuerbach and the End of Classical German Philosophy in 1888). Online in MIA. Accessed from <https://www.marxists.org/archive/marx/works/1845/theses/theses.htm> on 2015-06-08.

is only the form of reality internalized, virtually and digitally reconstructed as a hologram embedded in the brain.[502] The particular form of the holographic representation of reality is given by a concrete set of social relations that, advancing historically, have transformed evolutionarily-based sense into socially-based consciousness. This process goes from animism, magic thinking and mythology, through organized religion and philosophy, to today's science and ideologies. Ideologies, alternative non-scientific explanations, are based on the fact that consciousness is split by the opposite interests of class society. Consciousness was pristine in animals and in humans probably up to the initiation of slavery after the patriarchal coup. Consciousness had been synchronic with its objective reality as long as it remained aligned to morality, the sense of evolution. Spurious social hierarchy and socioeconomic, class with its ideology of idealism, came into human history at the beginning of written history. Philosophical idealism, the Sophists and Plato in particular being their main authors, came to be when science was already possible; it delayed the birth of the sciences for centuries. With the surplus of second-order mediations introduced by patriarchy, consciousness became corrupted. Forced to serve a class, it lost its universality and became class ideology. We started to see the world differently through the lens of social class, and religion openly started to repress science. The negation of patriarchy that will necessarily come along with the negation of capitalism will make it possible for consciousness, not without strong class resistance, to eventually return to the original unity of a universal human praxis.

In 1929 American astronomer Edwin Hubble found evidence that galaxies are moving away at velocities that are proportional to their distance from the earth.[503] This was much-needed evidence that the universe is expanding. Confirmation soon came from New

---

502 Pribram, K.H. (1971). *Languages of the Brain: Experimental Paradoxes and Principles in Neuropsychology.* New York. Prentice Hall/Brandon House.

503 Hubble, Edwin (1929). "A relation between distance and radial velocity among extra-galactic nebulae". Proceedings of the National Academy of Sciences of the United States of America. 15 (3): 168–173. Accessed from <http://www.pnas.org/content/15/3/168.full.pdf+html> on 2015-08-27.

Jersey Nobel Prize winners Arno Penzias and Robert Woodrow Wilson, who serendipitously discovered cosmic microwave background radiation, a type of electromagnetic energy that most cosmologists agree is the best evidence for the expanding model of the universe, in 1964.[504] Before these developments, there had been no inkling as to whether the universe was expanding or contracting, and Einstein initially believed it was shrinking.

The data only confirms that the universe, today, expands. It does not, however, deny, but implicitly affirms the opposite phenomenon: the universe can only expand from a prior state of contraction. That is the problem that remains unsolved; it is the universe in a pulse of eons.

The concept of expansion is what Belgian Monsignor, astronomer and physicist Georges Lemaitre, used for his proposal of what has been called, and is generally accepted, the Big Bang as the theory of the origins of the universe. Based on the general relativity theory of Einstein, Lemaitre postulated that the universe originated in a huge explosion, the rapid expansion of matter from a state of extremely high density and temperature.[505] Einstein is said to have diplomatically called this the most beautiful theory of creation. The alternative pulsating theory of the universe, of phasic systole and diastole, is more logical and has been proposed by some.[506]

The attractiveness of the expanding only model is ideological. It still leaves room for creationism. Additionally, the expansion of capital is the hidden cornerstone of capitalist epistemology and political

---

504 Penzias, A.A.; R. W. Wilson (July 1965). "A Measurement Of Excess Antenna Temperature At 4080 Mc/s". Astrophysical Journal Letters 142: 419–421.

505 Lemaître, G. (1931). "Expansion of the universe, A homogeneous universe of constant mass and increasing radius accounting for the radial velocity of extra-galactic nebulæ". Monthly Notices of the Royal Astronomical Society 91: 483–490. (Orig. Pub. 1927). Online in The Smithsonian/NASA Astrophysics Data System. Accessed from <http://adsabs.harvard.edu/abs/1931MNRAS..91..483L> on 2013-08-13.

506 Woods, A., and Grant, T. (2005). *Reason in Revolt. Marxist Philosophy and Modern Science.* Second Edition. Part 2. Time, Space and Motion. London. Wellred Publications. Online in: In Defense of Marxism. Accessed from <http://www.marxist.com/science-old/revolutioninphysics.html> on 2013-08-14.

economy, corrosively spilling into other sciences such as evolutionary theory (survival of the fittest) and psychology (good narcissism).

Unconstrained expansion as ego only leads to reciprocal impoverishment along the same logic as capital. It is mediated by force, not by reason. This was a matter of concern for Albert Einstein, who raised the question to Freud in the context of war. Freud answered with the instinctual disposition of Thanatos, the death instinct.[507] But expansionary war and Thanatos are food-chain laws, contrary to the conscious capacity to sublimate through mediations that Freud himself proposed. Why war is an exception to the sublimatory march of civilization, Freud left unanswered. Paradoxically, not only does war prevail; it has become so entrenched that a substantial part of the capitalist economy is dedicated to its production. This creates artificial scarcity, the signature of the capitalist patriarch.

In English and the Romance Languages, the concept and word war are opposites to those of nature. As opposites, nature is goodness and war the perversion of historical phenomena. Nature destroys only to produce higher forms; war produces to wastefully destroy and retrogress. The word nature comes from the paradigmatic phenomenon of birth, natus in Latin, but it also more generally means the course of things,[508] implying that nature is really a constant birth. The alternative to war is the re-birth of humanity, literally the true renaissance that has not taken place yet. This is what Hegel arduously tried to illustrate with his new dialectic in the *Phenomenology:* a psychology of the constant syllogism of birth's conserving negation without destruction.[509] Marx was inspired to pick up the torch, but both Hegel and Marx's theories have been made powerful symbols,

---

507 The Einstein-Freud Correspondence (1931-1932). Accessed from <http://www.public.asu.edu/~jmlynch/273/documents/FreudEinstein.pdf> on 2015-04-10.

508 Online Etymology Dictionary. Nature. Accessed from <http://www.etymonline.com/index.php?allowed_in_frame=0&search=nature&searchmode=none> on 2014-03-28.

509 Hegel, G.W.F. (1807). *Phenomenology of Mind.* From Harper Torchbooks' edition of the Phenomenology, from University of Idaho, Department of Philosophy by Jean McIntire. Online in MIA, Hegel by hypertext. Accessed from <https://www.marxists.org/reference/archive/hegel/works/ph/phconten.htm> on 2015-04-11.

the converse of what they are by ruling class ideology.

The challenge of science is to explain this birth-based course of nature and history, in better terms than did previous religious and philosophical forms of explanation. Unfortunately, science, like its predecessors, is not free of cooption by ideology. When science loses its universality to serve narrow class interests, it gives in to ideology.[510]

Before the Big Bang, dense matter was probably in a state of entropy, static incoherent homogeneity. We could say that natural sense started with motion, with the Big Bang, the explosion of a small egg of dense chaotic matter (linguistically related to mother),[511] suddenly taking the form of energy, matter at work. Here the beginning of evolution is also the beginning of natural sense, of the evolutionary direction of matter to end up in consciousness: seeing itself through a selected *sapiens* species. That is as far as we know and as far as we can explain logically. In between good sense and consciousness are myriads of negating mediations, first natural and then historical.

Sense is direction in evolution. I use coherence as a relationally more complex notion that advances sense. Fitness is an example of advancing coherence in relation to context. Consciousness, subsequently, is a particular form of fitness, of adaptation, that includes the capacity to represent, anticipate, and respond in action while introducing mediations. The awesomeness of conscience emerging from good sense compelled in the human mind the image of a God.

2.1.2 The Nature of Science

The purpose of science is to practically sort out, organize, legitimate, and institutionalize the historical process of knowledge, its

---

510 Meszaros, I. (2005). *The Power of Ideology.* London. Zed Books. Revised Edition. (Orig. Pub. 1991).

511 Online Etymology Dictionary. "Matter." Accessed from <http://www.etymonline.com/index.php?allowed_in_frame=0&search=matter> on 2016-05-28.

foundations and practices, and to systematically disseminate its theory and method towards an enhanced universal quality of the human life of the species. Science is historically the best form of explanation and the way to give social activity its most adaptive form. Integral to scientific practice is the parallel development of accessible theory, its transmission to all humans. Accessible theory is transmissible through a translation of technical jargon into common-sense language while advancing the education of communities. Science possesses characteristic instruments for obtaining and presenting evidence such as observation, verification, experiment, proof, and reasoning. These have been developed from previous forms such as fantasy faith, speculation, and authority.[512] The stages to knowledge have superseded each other conserving and discarding, with science emerging from the previous forms.

The signature of science is its legitimacy attained through its practicality, logical coherence, replicability, and consensuality. The universality of the scientific syllogism gives a consensual stamp to individual and particular practices. A tripod sustains the scientific syllogism: 1) Historical and evolutionary relativity, the *universal* quality. Science is subject to the limitations and biases of the time, in terms determined by the social modes of production that constantly change. Keeping this in mind, including the determination of class in hierarchical societies and its child ideology, makes it possible to critically penetrate deeper into the structure of natural and historical phenomena. This principle was first formulated by Heraclitus, who said that everything is in motion.[513] 2) the particular quality is characterized by a limited, partial perspective within an historical paradigm[514] usually offered by a segment of science that

---

512 Encyclopedia of Marxism. Science. Online in MIA. Accessed from <https://www.marxists.org/glossary/terms/s/c.htm> on 2015-04-12.

513 Engels, F. (1970). Socialism: Utopian and Scientific. II [Dialectics]. Trans: Edward Aveling. In: Marx/Engels Selected Works, Volume 3, p. 95-151. (Written: Between January and March of 1880. Orig. Pub. 1880. Moscow. Progress Publishers. Online in MIA. Accessed from <https://www.marxists.org/archive/marx/works/1880/soc-utop/ch02.htm> on 2916-05-29.

514 Kuhn, T. S. (1966). *The Structure of Scientific Revolutions,.,* 3rd edition. Chicago:

has achieved its historical moment,[515] and that spreads to influence other sciences. This helps the scientist go beyond the observable phenomena and discover the structure, the set of relations and forces that constitute the particular object of study. 3) Lastly, all scientific events have individual protagonists, usually in teams today, and the fact that often discovery takes place individually and often simultaneously indicates the readiness of the scientific field for the new step. No scientific problem arises unless its solution is within reach. Every discovery fits into a whole puzzle like a dream. The practical end of all science is the organized application of knowledge towards the enhancement of the quality of life of the species. True science fulfills these three conditions, the core of which is universality.[516] In psychoanalysis the same principles apply, the object of study being the relationship of an individual's consciousness to her reality and its historical and biographical alterations.

Unfortunately, the practice of science is not immune to the damage done by class ideology. It is the latter, for example, that distributes resources, ranks needs, and dictates the form taken by the scientific practice. The dominant class has the political power and the material means to hire ideologues whose function is to legitimate detoured scientific practice. It subordinates it, for example, to the prevalent needs of profit and capital expansion.

The failure of previous modes of cultural explanation preceding science is due precisely to their lack of universality. Globalization has somewhat changed this perspectival isolation by facilitating communication particularly with the growth of social media. Religion, a particularly narrow form of explanation based on superstition and unchallengeable belief, still holds a grip on a very substantial segment of communities, including scientific ones that subordinate

University of Chicago Press.

515 Mészáros, I. (1970). Marx's Theory of Alienation. London. Merlin Press.

516 See excellent article on this subject by: Ollman, B. (1978). "Marxism and Political Science: Prolegomenon to a Debate on Marx's Method." Chapter IV In: *Social and Sexual Revolution: Essays on Marx and Reich.* New York. South End Press. Online in Dialectical Marxism, The Writings of Bertell Ollman. Accessed from <https://www.nyu.edu/projects/ollman/docs/ssr_ch04.php#2> on 2016-05-29.

fact to dogma. Religious exclusion inherently deprives a science of its universality, and therefore legitimacy.

August Comte was the first modern philosopher and sociologist trying to classify the sciences within a unitary system that subordinated science to sociology.[517] In his attempt to capture the religious fervor, in the end Comte tried to make of sociology a religion. Comte's model was subjected to critical review by Spencer[518] in turn critiqued by Wundt.[519] A reasonable review and synthesis of the issue of the unity of science, up to his time, was offered by Cogswell,[520] who used two parameters to classify sciences, method and object. Pierce made an attempt at a logical classification but started from the wrong foot, separating theoretical and practical sciences.[521] All sciences are subject to the dialectic of theory and practice in their particular field. A purely theoretical aspiration to the status of science was metaphysics; Freud similarly attempted his metapsychology.

The problem behind these recurrent classificatory attempts was pointed out by Marx. Because of the antagonistic division of labor and competitiveness in a class society, Marx saw the fact that every science speaks its own language and disregards that of the others.

---

517 Comte, A. (1980). *System of Positive Philosophy.* London. Translated and condensed by Harriet Martineau. Two volumes. Online in Internet Archive. (Orig. Pub. 1893). Accessed from <https://archive.org/stream/positivephilosop01comtuoft/positivephilosop01comtuoft_djvu.txt> on 2017-03-09.

518 Spencer, H. (1854). "Reasons For Dissenting From The Philosophy Of M. Comte." In: Essays: Scientific, Political and Specu-lative, 3 volumes. Vol. 2. London. Williams and Norgate. 1891. Online Library of Liberty. Accessed from <http://oll.libertyfund.org/titles/336> on 2015-04-16.

519 Danziger K, (1980). "Wundt's Psychological Experiment in the Light of His Philosophy of Science." Psychological Research. 42, 109-122. (Wundt Centennial Issue). Online in Springer-Verlag. Accessed from <http://www.kurtdanziger.com/wundt%20experiments.pdf> on 2015-04-16;

520 Cogswell, G.A. (1899). "The Classification of the Sciences." The Philosophical Review. Vol. 8, No. 5 (Sep.,), pp. 494-512. Online in Jstor. Accessed from <> on 2015-04-13.

521 Peirce, C.S. (1931). The Classification of the Sciences. Vol. 1. The Collected Papers. Principles of Philosophy. 2. A Detailed Classification of the Sciences: §4. The Divisions of Science. Accessed from <http://www.textlog.de/4261.html> on 2015-04-13.

This makes it impossible for various sciences to find a common ground: "We know only a single science [said Marx] — the science of history. One can look at history from two sides and divide it into the history of nature and the history of men. The two sides are, however, inseparable; the history of nature and the history of men are dependent on each other so long as men exist. The history of nature, called natural science, does not concern us here; but we will have to examine the history of men, since almost the whole ideology amounts either to a distorted conception of this history or to a complete abstraction from it. Ideology is itself only one of the aspects of this history."[522] I would add that matriarchy was in that history the transitional hybrid of the two, including primitive communism as economy and the early forms of myth and religion. The long history of matriarchy went along with the morality of evolution, avoiding the confrontation with nature we face today.

On these premises, it is appropriate to look for the presence and types of coherence and consciousness from their historical origins, their evolution, and their various forms of presentation up to their final form of consciousness and ideology. Stages of evolution of their objects are the concern of different sciences from their particular vantage points. Unified, they all will lead to a history of the universe and of its ultimately natural property, consciousness. We must keep in mind, however, that this project is impeded by ideology.

2.1.3 Natural Sense in the First, Inorganic World, Physics and Chemistry

The explosion of the Big Bang, a moment in the pulse of the universe in the present work's view, is a chemical reaction but also a physical and cosmological phenomenon. Fire requires specific con-

---

522 Marx, K., and Engels, F. (1932). *The German Ideology.* Critique of Modern German Philosophy According to Its Representa-tives Feuerbach, B. Bauer and Stirner, and of German Socialism According to Its Various Prophets. Part I: Feuerbach. Opposition of the Materialist and Idealist Outlook. A. Idealism and Materialism. (Written 1845 to mid-1846). Online in MIA. Accessed from <https://www.marxists.org/archive/marx/works/1845/german-ideology/ch01a.htm> on 2015-04-13.

ditions for its realization, such as fuel, oxygen, and heat, in certain proportions. This event is a form of natural transformation that in its details has a particular sense or direction. It requires conditions that have to be selected. The previous state of entropy —a quantity of matter in a state of disorder or randomness without enough thermal energy to convert itself into mechanical work— as we have seen, seems an apt conceptualization of the status matter reached before the Big Bang expansion.

With the thermal expansion of the original quantity of matter, cosmology, chemistry and physics from different vantage points offer the first level of scientific understanding of our universe and world. Analogically, these sciences were originally undifferentiated from each other and from other disciplines such as natural history, philosophy and religion, and they were largely mythical and religious in character. Their theories probably started in Sub-Saharan Africa some 20,000 years ago, perhaps also independently in the Orient. They spread as humans migrated. Egyptians and Sumerians had early cosmological theories, as well as the Babylonians who postulated a flat earth floating in infinite "waters of chaos."[523] Indian cosmology proposed a cycling trillions of years existence of one universe preceded by an infinite number of previous universes. From there we have evolved to the most recently accepted, and rather universal, theory of a universe somehow born 13.772 billion years ago[524] in a Big Bang. Most cultures have postulated an anthropomorphic God as the creator and beginning of all, the trend's continuing presently in its Intelligent Design form.

Humans have scientifically recorded chemical events most verifiable since the alchemists' observation of chemical regularities, and the subsequent postulate of chemical laws after Irish natural philosopher, chemist, physicist and inventor Robert Boyle (1627-1691) separated chemistry from the rest of natural science. Chemical law-

---

523 Wikipedia. "Ancient Egyptian creation myths." Accessed from <https://en.wikipedia.org/wiki/Ancient_Egyptian_creation_myths> on 2017-03-09.

524 space.com. "How Old is the Universe?" Accessed from <http://www.space.com/24054-how-old-is-the-universe.html> on 2017-03-09.

fulness points to a first form of selectivity in nature that we have substantially altered with industrial chemical practices. Although natural selection is a notion mostly applied to organisms, we already can see its roots in chemistry. If an organism's selective goal is fit adaptation towards enhanced reproduction, the same parameter applies to mineral matter in its selective, naturally useful combinations that are at the core of organisms and their metabolism. Usefulness in nature drives direction, and direction is teleological, moving toward higher means of conservation in the constructive and complex use of energy. Simple matter tends to become complex, and from random coherent, at least from the point of view of our understanding.

Inorganic matter, the elements and minerals of the universe, after the Big Bang, evolved to produce organic molecules leading to life through photochemistry. This advancing process required more complex forms of relations to save energy for regulated use. As use-save options increased, higher forms of storage and complexity must have evolved in parallel. Evolutionary plausibility, as seen by our scientific consciousness, has to first match the boundaries of chemical feasibility, as the respective sciences advance.

Coherence is to chemistry what Darwin's fitness is to biology. They are forms of economic advance in the deployment of forms of matter and energy. Fitness is reflected, for example, in the capacity of a variant type to invade and displace the resident population in competition for available resources.[525] But this has to be understood in the larger context of the general direction of nature as a totality. This is what ideology neglects, the cooperative side, highlighting only competitiveness for lack of a dialectical method. Capitalism is the application of the biological model of the food chain that does not logically fit the overriding cooperative design of the human species. A more nuanced definition of fitness in human terms is the collective achievement of a better, more energetically economic form

---

525 Demetriusa, L. Ziehec, M. (2007). *Darwinian fitness.* Theoretical Population Biology. 72: 323–345. Online at www.sciencedirect.com. Accessed from <http://www.mcz.harvard.edu/Departments/PopGenetics/pdf/2007_07_-_Darwinian_fitness.pdf> on 2015-02-05.

of social organization in tandem with nature. This better fulfills the syllogistic requirement of human universality.

We can thus say that evolution is the movement from randomness to the lawfulness of economic coherence, or, as Herbert Spencer put it, from incoherent homogeneity to coherent heterogeneity in the dialectical processes of energetic dissipation of motion and its obverse integration as structured matter.[526]

The destructive peculiarity of the chemical reaction as a form of relation was pointed out by A.N. Leontiev.[527] Participating substances in a chemical reaction must reciprocally destroy themselves to produce new forms. Chemistry's being one original form of energetic relation in the mineral universe was thus a highly intrusive and destructive relationship, as we can see in the Big Bang.

Besides chemistry, the other prevailing form of energetic relation in the mineral universe is not intrusive, but distant and out of reach. It operates through rather invisible reciprocal forces. The branch of science properly concerned with the nature and properties of matter and energy from this perspective, is physics. Astrophysics offers a relational perspective quite opposite to that of chemistry. From this perspective objects relate negotiating their distance through forces, obstacles and boundaries. Opposite natural forces, centripetal such as gravity and centrifugal such as expansion of matter, regulate and are regulated by variables such as mass and energy, in order to balance each other in a game of constant motion. Objects must negotiate their optimal distance though force.

All this reciprocity is what produces harmony and equilibrium, at the level of the atom: a small nucleus surrounded by a cloud of electrons operating within the parameters of attraction and repul-

526 Spencer, H. (1867). *First Principles.* 2nd ed. Chapter XVI.: The Law Of Evolution Continued. § 128. London: Williams and Norgate,). Accessed from <http://oll.liberty-fund.org/titles/1390> on 2015-04-12.
527 Leontiev, A.N. (1981). "The problem of the origin of sensation.". In: *Problems of the Development of the Mind.* Trans. M. Kopylova. Pp. 7-53). Moscow: Progress Publishers. Source: Paul Ballantyne's site at York University. Accessed from: <https://www.marxists.org/archive/leontev/works/1981/sensation.htm> on 2015-04-12.

sion. Scientists today believe that strings in atoms vibrate, and that those vibrations contain the information that makes objects take their particular form. At the level of human society, it is similarly the activity of individuals with degrees of consciousness that collectively accrue to revolutions and new stages. This is how far we have advanced in demystifying the nature of matter and energy.

The fundamental rule of nature as a system with boundaries, objects in relations, is that energy and matter are not produced or destroyed, only constantly transformed. Everything has an energetic price that quantitatively will eventually lead to a qualitative jump. The huge surplus of transformation represented in evolution is an economic process advancing complexity and coherence. This process seems to be guided by an inherent advancing force similar to the unidirectional cosmic arrow of time. Humanity, designed by evolution with the capability to supersede this process through conscious collaborative mediation, not through competition, has not learned this lesson yet, although it is unconsciously subject to it through the power of good sense.

Survival, conservation, and progress irrevocably involve the constant transformation of energy, and energy moves back and forth into its more structured and stable form of matter. Energy is matter at work and matter is energy at rest.

These two, chemical and physical, levels of object relations are the most basic and fundamental in science. They are superseded by more advanced and complex developments, but always remain operative as the constant ground of all other forms of evolution.

2.1.4 Organic Matter

Organic matter, the concern of organic chemistry and biology, is the ground of life. In 1924 Soviet biochemist Alexander Oparin[528] and, independently, Indian-British scientist J.B.S. Haldane[529] in 1929 almost simultaneously came up with the same hypothesis. If the primeval atmosphere reduced to lower oxidation states, and there were a supply of energy such as lightning or ultraviolet light, a variety of organic compounds, the building blocks of life, could have been generated from prior inorganic cosmic matter. In a fine moment for science, graduate student Stanley L. Miller and his teacher Harold C. Urey at the University of Chicago confirmed this hypothesis in the laboratory.[530] They simulated a primitive environment by using simple substances methane, ammonia, hydrogen, and water, the theorized necessary elements for the appearance of life, placed them in a closed system, and provided extrinsic energy through an electric current simulating lightning. In this fashion, they were able to produce proteinogenic amino acids and other organic compounds.

Organic matter may have also been deposited on the surface of the earth by meteorites that have been found to have carbon and amino acids. Large amounts of carbon were necessary and a process of polymerization (the formation of large molecules) was necessary. Enzymatically, ribozymes such as RNA could have facilitated the process.

Highly destructive chemical relations were tamed, buffered by liquid water at a time when the temperature of the surface of the earth made it possible for water not to be hot and gaseous but temperate and liquid. Buffering is an act of compromising to reduce the extreme corrosiveness of excess acidity or alkalinity. Water is the buffer *par excellence:* its dissolving capacity bringing with it the

528 Oparin, A. I. (1952). *The Origin of Life.* Online in Universitat de Valencia. Accessed from <http://www.valencia.edu/~orilife/textos/The%20Origin%20of%20Life.pdf> on 2012-11-10.

529 Haldane, J. B. S. (1954). *The Origin of Life.* New Biology, 16, 12. Online in Universitat de Valencia. Accessed from <http://www.uv.es/~orilife/textos/Haldane.pdf> on 2012-07-21.

530 Miller, S. L. (May 1953). "Production of Amino Acids Under Possible Primitive Earth Conditions" (PDF). Science 117 (3046): 528–9. Online version in Jester. Accessed from <http://www.abenteuer-universum.de/pdf/miller_1953.pdf> on 2012-08-20.

pH compromise. Motion from oceanic waves concentrated organic substances prior to their becoming organisms.

It is well known that carbon is common to more that half of organic substances. A rich source of energy, in excess, like oxygen, it produces adverse ecological effects when over-combusted, as everyone knows today. Oxygen is second in volume to carbon in the composition of organic matter and in high concentrations is also very toxic to life. Many early forms of life-extinction were caused by excess oxygen in the atmosphere. In smaller concentrations, however, oxygen is indispensable to life as we also know. The first form of activity nature exacts from our bodies immediately after birth is breathing to draw oxygen from the air. Our life depends on the constant act of respiration. Oxygen is one of the most abundant elements in the universe and metabolically it is reduced to waste as carbon oxides that are recycled by plants back to oxygen.

Organic matter is the source of proteins, lipids and carbohydrates, among other nutritious substances. Proteins are the backbone of life, and some specialize as enzymes that facilitate or inhibit life-sustaining metabolic processes. Lipids are abundantly used as membranes that, like bubbles, surround cells and organs providing them with boundaries and a first degree of separation and safety, while remaining porous enough for nutrition; they also serve as an important repository of stored energy. Carbohydrates are the first fuel in metabolic processes providing the easiest most immediate access to energy.

Organic matter typically breaks down after the life cycle of its compounds is completed. It recycles itself through microorganisms and soil biota surrounding it, animal and plant life. In this process, complex molecules are again broken down and made simple to be used again. Water and a third component of organic matter, nitrogen, are highly useful as the main protagonists in recycling. Hydrogen, the final element of organic matter, with oxygen forms water, the *sine qua non* of life. Although not so abundant as carbon or oxygen in organic matter, hydrogen is the most abundant element in the universe, about 90% by weight.[531] It is awesome to see the coherence of selection in operation, as science gradually unveils it to us in metabolic processes. It is even more breathtaking when one considers that parallel and reciprocal social and conscious metabolisms follow highly similar selective processes.

The compounded, buffered, and enzymatically mediated nature of organic matter makes life possible. Through polymerization, buffering, enzymatic mediation, and the creation of permeable boundaries for the importation and use of energy, and through energy storage and conservation inside of organisms, nature introduced the necessary mediating elements for the huge evolutionary qualitative jump of life. The next similar step was consciousness.

2.1.5 Life

Life is built upon the ground of organic matter, but its beginning is far from clearly demarcated as yet. Intermediate forms of life, difficult to fit into present classifications, such as viruses, have led some to question the old definition and classification of the three kingdoms. The main characteristic of life is that, by creating regulatory mechanisms and boundaries, it internalizes chemistry from previous forms, and other organisms that have partially transformed chemistry, to sustain itself metabolically and to store surplus energy. Not having to depend on immediate external sources of energy gives life a first degree of freedom.

Compared to the previous stages where the destructiveness of inorganic relations prevailed, life is the first attempt of nature in evolution to introduce conservation and place it above destruction. Life does this by internalizing and regulating destructive chemical processes, setting membranes and boundaries within boundaries, and dividing the work of organisms in selected ways for efficiency, assigning different functions to different organs. These are all evo-

---

531 See Web Elements. Online. Accessed from <http://www.webelements.com/hydrogen/> on 2015-04-10.

lutionary adaptive mechanisms, archaic forms of organization that initially respond predominantly to external pressures. This is how life introduces the first two basic natural mediations, regulation and division of labor, whereupon their historical equivalents have originated.

Life is insurgent from the point of view of entropy. Natural history is the fascinating epic of these two giants, life and entropy, constantly battling for hegemony in nature, with episodes where life has been almost destroyed. It would seem that, given the comparative fragility of life, David vs. Goliath, at the end entropy may after all reign. The main weapon of life is its good sense, evolved into coherence and consciousness. The human active role in this process is the question raised by the Anthropocene period of evolution, the epoch when humans exercised hegemony to substantially transform nature.[532] Artificial unconstrained war on nature has called for a response, a return from her latency that we are witnessing.

Conscious life is the most recent reenactment of the old battle between destruction and production, now partially influenced by consciousness that can alter its path. Life internalizes these opposites for her benefit as organic metabolism, subject to regulation to achieve delicate homeostasis or balance. Homeostasis is in reality constant reciprocal homeodynamics, because the stasis in nature is illusory, a temporary structure at best. Sensitive regulatory mechanisms provided with feedback and feed-forward loops evolutionarily started the processes of self-communication and information, the paradigm of which is a nervous system. They are the prolegomena of consciousness. Encrypting, reading, and conserving signals gave life the capacity to encode in memory, to store images or forms, including the direction and grammar of events. This may have started with nucleic acid in living cells, ribonucleic acid or RNA, whose function is mainly to act as a messenger carrying instructions. These

---

532 Steffen, W., Richardson, K., et al. (2015). Planetary Boundaries: Guiding Human Development in a Changing Planet. Sci-encexpress. January. Accessed from <Planetary Boundaries- Guiding human development on a changing planet- Steffen.pdf> on 2015-05-20.

regulate the synthesis of proteins that in some viruses carry the genetic information itself.

Natural compulsion, lawful and binding necessity, yields to the freedom of communication, that allows the possibility for self-regulation. Need and freedom become the polarities of life, freedom's being the capacity to introduce mediations. Life is a zero-sum game whose strategy consists in transformational displacements of matter and energy, mediations; these result in coherent complexity. War destroys achievements of evolution, and handicaps humanity. War goes against all evolutionary economy. In the context of evolution war is the opposite of planning to avert unnecessary destruction. *Homo sapiens,* like any other animal must spend part of its life on maintenance and reproduction. Humans, unlike other species, have through mediations developed the most economic means to deal with material imperatives such as food, shelter, temperature regulation, reproduction, safety, and escaping from predation. Those economies are what allow for freedom and leisure, that in turn result in alternatives, speculation and spirituality. These capacities historically produce civilization.

Life sustains itself through ascending sublation, conservation internalized, always in the context of satisfaction first of natural necessities. Life evolves through creating complexity and, seemingly paradoxically, coherence.

2.1.6 Organisms

Irritability and excitability are terms used to define a property of living bodies that become activated by external influences. Biology is the science that deals with life and organisms. Organisms' complexity is what Herbert Spencer called heterogeneity, which has accrued through supersession of stages entailing a growing capacity for self-regulation. This results in capacities such as self-maintenance and selective reproduction. This growing capacities in turn allow for better energy utilization, and a relative autonomy or limited independence from the material imperatives in relation to the environment.

Organisms can be autonomous because they can store energy for immediate use, in view of the fact that the environment does not always provide it on demand.

Layered bio-chemical accretions in shallow waters formed by trapping and binding sedimentary grains by microbial films, especially cyanobacteria, are considered the oldest fossils related to the origins of life more than 3.7 billion years ago.[533]

It is not easy to define organisms but they are essentially living objects made of DNA, and usually organized in genes, chromosomes, cells, and specialized organs with boundaries. They are open systems obtaining and using energy from their environment and producing waste, while establishing a self-regulated and adaptive reciprocity with their environment. They therefore have an internal metabolism that replicates and is subordinated to the external one of nature at large. In humans the life-cycle of organisms, consisting in birth, growth and development, reproduction, decline and death is compounded by society. Organisms are the highest form of material organization in evolution and they have a range of complexity going from simple proto-bacteria to humans. It is estimated that here are currently 8.7 million species of life on Earth, 6.5 million on land and 2.2 million in oceans.[534] More than 99 percent of all species that ever lived are estimated to be extinct and this gives an estimate of the obduracy of the battle.

Four characteristics of organisms are outstanding in what respects the evolution of consciousness. First is the capacity to store energy, a mediation that frees organisms and gives them pause for strategic mediation and variation. Second, the metabolic transfor-

---

533 Stromatolite. WikipediaAccessed from <http://en.wikipedia.org/wiki/Stromatolite> on 2015-04-10.

534 Science Today. (August 24, 2011) "How many species on Earth? About 8.7 million, new estimate says" Source: Census of Marine Life. Accessed from <https://www.sciencedaily.com/releases/2011/08/110823180459.htm> on 2017-03-10.

mation of energy is the result of the internalization of previously external environmental mechanisms from prior stages in evolution. Third, this comes with the consequent capacity to maintain an optimal, buffered internal balance between destruction and production in their processes of transformation of energy with higher chances of survival. Fourth, self-control is particularly applicable to the property of consciousness. Self-control starts metabolically and advances to autonomy, particularly with the development of a specialized nervous system, in some of the more advanced or higher organisms.

These characteristics define fitness, a measure of the skill of an organism to strategically deal with an environment in which hostility and predatoriness prevail.

2.2 FROM NATURAL SELECTION TO LEARNING

"Revélame algo conciencia,!

Háblame Dios poderoso!"

(Reveal me something conscience,!

Speak to me God almighty!)

Rafael Pombo - The Hour of Darkness[535]

"Ownership and property are doubtless quite foreign to the feminine. At least sexually. But not nearness. Nearness so pronounced that it makes all discrimination of identity, and thus all forms of property, impossible."

Luce Irigaray.[536]

"This Logos holds always but humans always prove unable to understand it, both before hearing it and when they have first heard it. For though all things come to be in accordance with this Logos, humans are like the inexperienced when they experience such words and deeds as I set out, distinguishing each in accordance with its nature and saying how it is. But other people fail to notice what they do when awake, just as they forget what they do while asleep."

535 Pombo, R. (1856). La Hora de Tinieblas. A poem. Online in Biblioteca Virtual. Banco de la Republica de Colombia. Accessed from <http://www.banrepcultural.org/blaavirtual/literatura/pombo/pombo2.htm> on 2014-03-17. (my translation).
536 Irigaray, L. (1977). "This Sex Which Is Not One." P. 31. Trans. Katherine Porter and Caroline Burke. Ithaca and New York. Cornell University Press. Accessed from < https://caringlabor.files.wordpress.com/2010/11/irigaray-this-sex-which-is-not-one.pdf> on 2015-05-07.

Heraclitus[537]

"The less you are and the less you express of your life—the more you have and the greater is your alienated life."

Marx[538]

Pombo protests the inability to understand his alienated existence that he finds absurd, and poetically demands to no avail an explanation from his consciousness, or else from God. Irigaray's answer clarifies the alienation we share with Pombo: ownership and private property are inimical to our universal feminine disposition. Heraclitus depicts alienation as our inability to understand the abiding Logos. As Erich Fromm asks critically quoting Tennyson's poem "Flower in the Crannied Wall": why do we have to pluck and kill the flower to learn, to understand; why not just enjoy it?[539] Marx closes the circle: having alienates our being. In history having as a compulsive way of social life was instituted by the instinctual disposition of men; back to Irigaray.

2.2.1 The Meaning of Evolution

The evolutionary process is about being, about developing means to soften the impact of destructive natural force, ultimately changing material force, into spiritual force. Morality, the drive of spiritual force derives from altruism, being able to place others before oneself. This phenomenon appears in evolution with mam-

---

537 Heraclitus. Pre Socratic Fragments (DK 22B1). Wikipedia. Accessed from <http://en.wikipedia.org/wiki/Heraclitus> on 2014-08-18.

538 Karl Marx quoted by: Fromm, E. (2008). *To Haver or to Be?* Ibid. P. xviii.

539 Fromm, E. (2008). *To Haver or to Be?* London and New York. Continuum. P. 14. (Orig. Pub. 1976). Accessed from <https://giuseppecapograssi.files.wordpress.com/2013/08/erich-fromm-to-have-or-to-be-1976.pdf> on 2017-03-10.

malian maternity. As long as they are dependent, mothers will fight and at times give their lives for their heirs. This is what mothers "have" and that is what captures their instinctual disposition. Unnecessary object-having, particularly at the expense of others, is an artificial ethos invented by men and leading to the alienation and reification of the species. Morality in humans is the highest expression of consciousness and precludes alienated forms that keep the species bound to the old food-chain morality of material force, opposite to its spiritual equivalent and not fit for humans. This is true particularly in epochs of abundance whereas in those of scarcity we may regress to material force. Morality is good sense at its best. The patriarchal split has altered the balance of evolution in that a few individuals are free of scarcity at the cost of the majority suffering it. The natural cycles of scarcity and abundance have been artificially altered by their subjection to the spurious phenomenon of class.

What Heracliteus called Logos is the coherence of nature, its good sense, in its greatest expression human consciousness that had before been expressed as God. Heraclitus tells us that things make sense when we stop to think and make sense of them. The sense that we make of things is only a reflection of the sense inherent in them. The sense of their motion is our logic, the coherence of their fitting relations and parts our totality. When our consciousness and sense synchronize in the apprehension of reality and our actions correspond to that synchronization, then we have praxis that is inherently moral and no need for a separate morality.

This is why the word evolution originally meant *unrolling what was rolled-up*.[540] In Hegel's terms, it is looking at the succession of presentations of the evolving object, appearances that together reveal the particular essence of that object as it unfolds in its motion, development or history. Seventeenth- and eighteenth-century natu-

---

540 Online Etymology Dictionary. "evolution" (n.) 1620s, "an opening of what was rolled up," from Latin evolutionem (nominative evolutio) "unrolling (of a book)," noun of action from evolvere (see evolve). Online Etymology Dictionary. "Evolution." Accessed from <http://www.etymonline.com/index.php?allowed_in_frame=0&-search=evolution&searchmode=none> on 2014-02-14.

ralism made the notion and word evolution popular.[541] A new attitude
of questioning suspicion, what is behind it, took over epistemology
at the same time capitalism was entering its hegemonic stage. This is
how capitalism came to benefit from a science it now politically rejects, particularly in its social form. The Renaissance had planted the
seeds of phenomenology and hermeneutics for the Enlightenment to
grow and develop. Middle-Ages dogmatic scholasticism was over
with the fall of Constantinople to the thriving Ottomans. This was a
time of accelerated social change. It was also the feared encounter
of East and West in Europe and Asian commerce. Capitalism took
advantage and modern globalization, the virtual connection of all
major parts of the world, advanced.

The philosophical underpinnings of evolution were laid not so
much by René Descartes, as the mainstream still claims, as they
were by Baruch Spinoza's revolutionary two-faced monism that ma-
terialistically revealed God as the good sense of nature, resolving the
old philosophical problem by explaining dying idealism. Descartes'
mind-body dualism only put God in parenthesis for now and left it
mystified for others to decipher.[542] For Spinoza, when one looks at
one side of being one sees nature, but looking at the other side there

---

541 "The idea of organic evolution was proposed by some ancient Greek thinkers but was
   long rejected in Europe as contrary to the literal interpretation of the Bible. Lamarck
   proposed a theory that organisms became transformed by their efforts to respond to
   the demands of their environment, but he was unable to explain a mechanism for this.
   Lyell demonstrated that geological deposits were the cumulative product of slow processes over vast ages. This helped Darwin toward a theory of gradual evolution over
   a long period by the natural selection of those varieties of an organism slightly better
   adapted to the environment and hence more likely to produce descendants. Combined
   with the later discoveries of the cellular and molecular basis of genetics, Darwin's theory of evolution has, with some modification, become the dominant unifying concept
   of modern biology." Oxford Online Dictionary. "Evolution." Accessed from <http://
   www.oxforddictionaries.com/us/definition/american_english/evolution> on 2014-02-
   14.
542 "Prop. VII. Proof: Substance cannot be produced by anything external (Corollary,
   Prop vi.), it must, therefore, be its own cause—that is, its essence necessarily involves existence, or existence belongs to its nature." de Spinoza, B. (2009). The Ethics. Trans. Part I. Definitions. Concerning God. R.H.M. Elwes. (Orig. Pub. 1677).
   Online in Project Gutenberg Ebook #3800. Accessed from <http://www.gutenberg.
   org/files/3800/3800-h/3800-h.htm> on 2014-01-29.

is its logos, God the good sense of motion.

Of course, Descartes' compromise was better received by the patriarchal mainstream. Spinoza's radical discovery was quickly rejected, silenced and ignored, or repressed. Spinoza was and remains excommunicated by the religious hierarchy of his time. His message, however, like fire in powder, spread unrestrainedly if quietly. Every philosopher after him was unable to escape his influence. The simple but elegant and huge statement that nature and God are the same had repercussions in all branches of philosophy, and ushered in the human sciences that had been so far kept at bay by a dogmatic dead-end theology.

The Platonic dualistic alternative that Descartes still clung to, measurable versus imponderable being, was, however, eagerly adopted by the natural sciences and obstinately survives to this day. Freud was one of its victims with his metapsychology. It took some time, but Hegel picked up Spinoza's thread and developed it into a full philosophy, a coherent narrative seeking to heal the rift. Unfortunately, idealist Hegel started from the wrong foot. At the beginning was the idea, God that subsequently embodied itself and alienated itself as nature instead of the other way around. Instead of sense's being a property of matter, it was the other way around. God evolved, incidentally losing itself in his creation, the natural process of evolution. Evolution allowed God to rescue himself through the human species in nineteenth-century Prussia, in the haystack of philosophy, and in the needle of no less than G.W.H Hegel himself; in his philosophy.[543] It is not difficult to see here an attempt to marry Christianity and Evolution, an opportunity the Vatican missed. The unintended result is a dialectical method to explain motion and activity. This method came to supersede the formal logic of Aristotle, a logic of statics.

---

543 Hegel, G.W.F. (1817) "The Absolute is Mind (Spirit) - this is the supreme definition of the Absolute." Philosophy of Mind § 384. Encyclopaedia of the Philosophical Sciences Part III. Online in Marxists Internet Archive (MIA), Hegel by Hypertext. Accessed from <http://www.marxists.org/reference/archive/hegel/works/sp/suintrod. htm> on 2014-03-17.

In spite of all efforts, the tectonic event of Spinozist philosophy could not be hidden. Hegel's was the main aftershock, but not the last one. After Hegel, his disciple Ludwig Feuerbach carefully dissected the structure and function of religion and God.[544] Then came Karl Marx, who moved Feuerbach's romanticism into a scientific anthropology. The essence of humanity that had been attributed to God was "In its reality it is the ensemble of the social relations."[545] These are the successive presentations, the Hegelian essence of humanity in its material and overdetermined history.

Using Hegel's own argument —that the creation is a part of the creator— Feuerbach had concluded that the creator is none other than humanity. "Religion is the disuniting of man from himself; he sets God before him as the antithesis of himself."[546] Religion is a necessary historical alienation. Feuerbach is the first humanist; his God is human consciousness that started with the good sense of nature.

Anthropologists have been puzzled about the fact that all human groups, without exception, practice some form of religion. Some have seen this fact as a proof of an anthropomorphic God, external to humanity. Religion is in fact proof of God, if we conceive God as the good sense of nature, including ours. Man first magically explained the coherent sense of natural phenomena through religion. Magical thinking become institutionalized as religion is the first form of consciousness. It is animistic, hybrid, nature-like, as in totemism, a projection from the primitive, stumbling human mind that still has to heavily lean on nature, an anaclitic form of explanation that we still see in the magic explanations of young children.

---

544 Feuerbach, L. (1854). *The Essence of Christianity.* Trans. George Eliot, (Orig. Pub. 1851). Online in MIA. Accessed from <https://www.marxists.org/reference/archive/feuerbach/works/essence/> on 2015-04-21.

545 Marx, K. (1938). Theses on Feuerbach. 6. In: The German Ideology. London. Lawrence and Wishart. (Written in 1845). Online version Marxists Internet Archive. Accessed from <http://www.marxists.org/archive/marx/works/1845/theses/index.htm> on 2012-09-09.

546 Feuerbach, L. (1854). *The Essence of Christianity.* Ibid. Part I, The True or Anthropological Essence of Religion.Chapter II. God as a Being of the Understanding.

Incidentally, Hegel refused to accept the challenge of Feuer-bach's materialist argument, and Feuerbach, in turn, disrespect-fully called his master a closet materialist unable to face up to the implications of his own theory. The skirmish spread to the Young Hegelians who split into politicized right and left factions, each bet-ting on hegemonizing their ideologies drawn from the chest war of Hegelian ambiguity. This was the beginning of the modern form of bipolar ideology.

The last Spinozist aftershock came with Darwin, and with Marx and Engels, with whom philosophy finally bowed to science. While Feuerbach was proclaiming that "God is the self-consciousness of man freed from all discordant elements,"[547] Darwin was unfolding the natural coherence of the live body of nature with his theory of natural selection.[548] Marx, on the other hand, at the peak of the mod-ern critical movement, was proposing a critique of critical criticism in his *Holy Family* critique of the Young Hegelians.[549] The critical movement had started with the timid Cartesian doubt and the implo-sive pantheism of Spinoza, transformed itself into critique by Kant and critique of critique by Hegel, and was relentlessly augmented with all sorts of implications both for science and politics.

Unifying God and nature, Spinoza had made possible a new and much-needed anthropology in the social sciences to replace the old theology. This made it possible for Marxist sociology to undertake the critique of capital as the unconsciously alienated core of reified human relations. The relational nature of the social practice of capi-tal is still highly mystified, and remains buried in the deepest recess-

547 Feuerbach, L. (1841). *The Essence of Christianity.* Ibid. Part I. Ch. IX. The Mystery of Mysticism, or of Nature in God.

548 "Man in the rudest state in which he now exists is the most dominant animal that has ever appeared on the earth." Darwin, C.C. (1871). *The descent of man, and selection in relation to sex.* Vol. 1. P. 136. London: John Murray. 1st ed. Darwin Online. Ac-cessed from <http://darwin-online.org.uk/converted/pdf/1871_Descent_F937.1.pdf> on 2014-02021.

549 Marx, K. (1956). *The Holy Family. or Critique of Critical Criticism. Against Bruno Bauer and Company.* Trans: Richard Dixon. Moscow. Foreign Languages Publishing House. (Orig. Pub.1845). Online in MIA. Accessed from <http://www.marxists.org/archive/marx/works/1845/holy-family/> on 2014-11-22.

es of the human unconscious.

Psychoanalysis, that claims to understand the unconscious, has neglected the study of the elephant in the room, the historical form of human relations as capital. The theories of the current epidemic of narcissism first proposed by Freud,[550] Federn,[551] Kernberg,[552] and Kohut[553] have focused not on the social relations but on the individual's "intra-psychic" phenomena. Karen Horne,[554] has uniquely portrayed narcissism as a reaction formation, through idealization, to the impoverishment capitalist culture imposes on the personality of human individuals.

God, like the proverbial chickens, has come home to roost as narcissism, the detoured power of the ensemble of the social relations, the essence of man, that sublates the compelling and awesome coherence of nature and history. Spinoza re-discovered it from its alienation after Heraclitus, Hegel exposed its method and ways, Darwin provided the proof in nature, and Marx applied it to human history and its future projection.

2.2.2 Rewind to Heraclitus

Heraclitus of Ephesus was the first philosopher to detect the coherence of nature as logos and also the fact that humans did not understand logos and called it God. Heraclitus' philosophical understanding was based on two dialectical principles: that everything is

550 Freud, S. (1925). "On Narcissism. An Introduction. Tr, James Strachey.(Orig. Pub. 1914). Accessed from <http://www.freud2lacan.com/docs/On_Narcissim_with_Introduction.pdf> on 2015-05-01.

551 Federn, P. (1928). "Narcissism in the Structure of the Ego." In: Federn, P. (1952). Ego Psychology and the Psychoses. New York. Basic Books. Chapter accessed from <http://www.sakkyndig.com/psykologi/artvit/federn1928.pdf> on 2014-11-22.

552 Kernberg, O. (1975). *Borderline conditions and pathological narcissism.* New York: Jason Aronson.

553 Kohut, H. (1971).*The Analysis of the Self: A Systematic Approach to the Psychological Treatment of Narcissistic Personality Disorders:* By Heinz Kohut. Monograph Series of the Psychoanalytic Study of the Child Monograph No. 4. London. Hogarth Press; New York: International Universities Press.

554 Horney, K. (1950). *Neurosis and Human Growth.* New York. Norton.

constantly in motion, and that such motion is caused by the struggle of opposites. This is an explanation without resorting to an alien God. "For this reason [he said] it is necessary to follow what is common. But although the Logos is common (sense), most people live as if they had their own private understanding,"[555] not the common one. This is what makes good sense common sense that is not necessarily good. Understanding is not private but social, and it builds up by accretion from the opposites of dialogue, in the same fashion capital builds privately from accrued social labor.

I believe this may have been the first time ideology was historically detected, by Heraclitus, as the illusory private appropriation of what by necessity must be social understanding, if only by the fact that every statement is a relation between speaker and listeners, subject to the process of challenge, discussion, and compromise, therefore change. If we all did not all share the same logos, the good sense that comes from the morality of evolution, we would be unable to communicate through language. But logos and language are corrupted when they serve narrow class interests not the universal. This is how we usually become narrowly brilliant but widely stupid through the division of labor; we can't see the forest for the tree. This results in the most alienated one percent leading ninety-nine to the precipice.

By artificially separating the Logos, the grammar of nature in motion, from its original material ground, the Sophists and particularly most philosophers from Plato to Bacon and Spinoza, enshrined idealism as the high ground binary in philosophy. Idealism spread like wildfire because of its explanatory usefulness for the dominant class in denying reality. Religion based on faith was relied upon for its legitimation. A handy tool in the hands of patriarchal thinking, idealism functioned by repressing the previous mode of thinking, the philosophy and logic of motion, epitomized by Heraclitus' dialectic, which had grown from the old matriarchal traditions of good sense. From its evolutionarily dialectic form, logos was transformed

---

555 Heraclitus. Ibid. (DK 22B2)

into stultified formal logic, the patriarchal logic of analysis without synthesis, of progression without regression, leading to the appearance of stasis where motion was. This is the same logic that today tells us there is no alternative to the horror of the way most humans live.

Paterfamilias, to fully assert his social dominance, had to appropriate, and reconstruct, mostly by logical inversion, every previous form of social institution assiduously constructed by mothers through dialectical first-order mediations along the parameters of moral consciousness and natural morality. The patriarchal version included a formal logic based on static, analytic, and imaginarily abstracted forms of objects rather than on the practical operation on objects themselves in their relationship with the senses. Formal logic flourished like weed, taking over the space of the previous logic, only to serve the interests of patriarchs that wanted to see themselves, and still do, as eternally in command. Formal logic hypostatizes the dialectical processes of things separating its syllogistic moments and changing its method to a fetishized form of analysis and objectivity that does not properly totalize, except religiously. It is like disassembling your car to fix it and not reassembling it. Analysis is congenial to the patriarch because it represents destruction; analysis *ad infinitum* without return to the original mainstream of common sense, its synthesis, ultimately destroys everything through alienation. We are thus, as a result, living an epoch of scientific incoherence, of fragmentation and absurdity, well described by artists but perpetuated by hired middle-class thinkers, ideologues, and politicians.

The questionable honor falls to Plato and most of his cohorts to have analytically disembodied coherence by enshrining form over matter, idea over object. The maneuver was happily endorsed by most philosophers who proceeded to analytically continue the attack on good-sense and synthesis. Aquinas and the holy fathers were accomplices. The independent idea of an ideal and separate God as governor of the universe still prevails in many minds.

The human mind thus became alienated from its purpose by its own products, religion and philosophy, which within the social class determined division of labor by assigning spiritual work to a middle class hired by the dominant class. Material workers were made to produce for, not the fulfillment of needs of the collective, but for those of the dominant class to hoard.

2.2.3 Fitness, Newtonian Reciprocity, and Darwinian Sexual Selection

Darwin usually takes the credit for solving the mystery of evolution although Alfred Russel Wallace did it simultaneously and independently. But it was in fact Hegel who had first outlined evolution in his cryptic philosophy that drew from Spinoza. How is it that nature and sense came to be and why is it that they are what they are today? was the question Hegel addressed, and what is their relation? Already long before Hegel the whole theory of evolution had been sketched in the practice of artificial selection, invented by farmers who chose and criss-crossed preferred specimens to reproduce better ones with desired characteristics both in animal and plant species; that was human selection. Besides, Lyell had found almost concurrently that geological time was much more protracted than its theological version, and Lamarck and many others had already followed threads leading to a full evolutionary theory. Typically, de Candolle is quoted as saying for example, not unlike Malthus, that: "All the plants of a given country... are at war one with another. The first which establish themselves by chance in a particular spot, tend, by the mere occupancy of space, to exclude other species the greater choke the smaller, the longest livers replace those which last for a shorter period, the more prolific gradually make themselves masters of the ground, which species multiplying more slowly would otherwise fill."[556] De Candolle and Malthus, endorsed by Darwin, could

---

556 The quote is from Lyell in : Darwin, C., and Wallace, A.R. (1858). "On the Tendency of Species to form Varieties; and on the Perpetuation of Varieties and Species by Natural Means of Selection." A presentation to the Linnaean Society on 1 July 1858.

not see however, the larger sense, the coherence leading to selection that was encoded in their belief in God.

Even Darwin's grandfather Erasmus had already sketched evolutionary theory for the most part. I quote a brief excerpt from his poem *The Temple of Nature*:

"ORGANIC LIFE beneath the shoreless waves

Was born and nurs'd in Ocean's pearly caves;

First forms minute, unseen by spheric glass,

Move on the mud, or pierce the watery mass;

These, as successive generations bloom

New powers acquire, and larger limbs assume;

Whence countless groups of vegetation spring,

And breathing realms of fin, and feet, and wing."[557]

With their concept of natural selection, Darwin and Wallace simultaneously unveiled the mechanism for the evolving relation between species and environment, reproduction, variation, all relations of reciprocity, of action and reaction in Newton's terms. But, most important, they discovered the logic and grammar of evolution, the *reciprocal determination* of life and environment the same reciprocity Newton had found in physics. In patriarchal hands however, this reciprocity is verticalized, as happens with all binaries that become hierarchical: the adjective *natural* is subordinated to the noun *selection,* as collaboration is subordinated to competition that fits well with the model of operation of the current ideology of capitalism. The larger all-encompassing cooperation, nature's turning objects

Zoo-logical Journal of the Linnean Society 3: 46–50. Darwin Online. Accessed from <http://darwin-online.org.uk/content/frameset?itemID=F350&viewtype=text&pageseq=1> on 2014-01016.

557 Darwin, E. (2008) *The Temple of Nature. Origin of Society. Canto I. Production of life. V. Organic Life.* The Project Gutenberg EBook (#26861) of The Temple of Nature; or, the Origin of Society. London. T. Bensley, Printer, Bolt Court, Fleet Street. (Orig. Pub. 1803). Accessed from <http://www.gutenberg.org/files/26861/26861-h/26861-h.htm> on 2012-05-12.

into subjects for energetic economy for example, is not seen yet.

Long before we knew it, since its inception, natural evolution had been taking place within its own lawfulness. Our knowledge of it is itself only a step within that whole process. This does not mean evolution was meaningless, devoid of sense or purely random; it means only that our species became ready for that knowledge of the dialectic of randomness and lawfulness. Guiding itself by its own natural laws, evolution had taken its specific direction and sense, going through the huge punctuations of minerality, organicity, life, and consciousness, the big jumps. Darwin only decoded the mechanisms for our minds, now ready for the knowledge after centuries of alienated dogma. Astronomers, physicists, chemists, geologists and anatomists, to mention only a few, had already deciphered within their narrow fields some of the lawfulness of their objects of study. Evolution-in-itself long preceded its knowledge by us, our species' understanding of it. Darwin, introducing the concept of natural selection, fathomed a more complex form of coherence. His concept was more visible and applicable in his field of biology, and took historic precedence because it serves as a new paradigm for other sciences. Before him Newton had found the law of reciprocity, expressed in his third law of motion, the law of action and reaction.[558]

Our understanding itself is then framed in its own evolutionary history. It is assembled from partial representations of properties of objects. Both phylogenetically and ontogenetically, our knowledge was first sensorial and partial in the way Piaget, and Freud, described for the young child. It was magical and concrete before growth made learning possible. The use of our hands and senses transforming reality then turned magic into logical reason within a framework that had been placed there by ancestors with the name of culture. Darwin saw "selection" as the coherence and "fitness" as the outcomes of natural relations. Similarly, Hegel had already

---

558 Newton, I. (1846). *The Mathematical Principles of Natural Philosophy.* Book One. Axioms or Laws of Motion. Law III. p. 83. New York. Daniel Adee. Online in Internet Archive. Accessed from <https://archive.org/stream/newtonspmathema00newtrich#page/n87/mode/2up> on 2014-01-17.

seen thesis and its antithesis not to be random, but fit to each other for a synthesis. Epistemologically, a pivotal shift of focus was taking place from (patriarchal) separate analytic object back to relational (matriarchal) bound synthetic objects. Things had been seen that way before the Sophists. Sense, coherence, fitting, selection, consciousness are all relational concepts connected in an evolution that is natural, mineral, organic, live, animal, conscious, but also epistemology, irritability, sensation, perception, language, thought and knowledge. Raw forms of material coherence are reproduced in consciousness according to the same grammar.[559]

Newton had already formulated the law of reciprocity long before Hegel and Darwin. This is the law of relations, not of objects. "To every action there is always opposed an equal reaction: or the mutual actions of two bodies upon each other are always equal, and directed to contrary parts."[560] Human object relations are no exception, and historically the return to dialectics, motion and relations is already the return of a matriarchal way of seeing nature as an ensemble of relations.

The reciprocity Darwin sees between species and environment is first an external form of reciprocity, fitness akin to Newton' plan-

---

559 "What are the consequences of coherence? It results in properties that are characteristic of biological systems. These include the high efficiency of energy transfer and transformation which often approaches 100%; the ability of communication at all levels within cells, between cells and between organisms capable of resonating to the same frequencies; the possibility for sensitive, multiple recognition systems utilizing coherent electromagnetic signals of different specific frequencies, such as for example, the organization of metabolic activities within the cell, the operation of the immune network and a host of other biological functions involving specific recognition between hormones or ligands and their receptors; and finally, the stable persistence of the working system arising from the inherent stability of coherent states." Ho, M.W. and Popp, F.A. (1989). "Gaia and the Evolution of Coherence." Presented at the 3rd Camelford Conference on The Implications of The Gaia Thesis: Symbiosis, Cooperativity and Coherence, November 7-10, 1989. Online in I-SIS. Accessed from <http://www.i-sis.org.uk/gaia.php> on 2014-03-06.

560 Newton, I. (1846). *The Mathematical Principles of Natural Philosophy.* Book One. Axioms or Laws of Motion. Law III. p. 83. New York. Daniel Adee. Online in Internet Archive. Accessed from <https://archive.org/stream/newtonspmathema00newtrich#page/n87/mode/2up> on 2014-01-17.

etary relations. In his formulation of sexual selection, Darwin goes one step further however, and sees the reciprocity internalized within the species. Sexual selection, is the internalization of reciprocity within species: predominantly competing males are paired with predominantly selective females, although they both have the full range of options between the extremes of competition and selection. The understanding of this process, and its implications, has been refined but it remains somewhat elusive and mystified. "What governs sexual selection is the relative parental investment of the sexes in the offspring. Competition for mates usually characterizes males because males usually invest almost nothing in their offspring."[561] This line of thinking had been started by Bateman's experiments pairing opposite-sex drosophila;[562] it highlights the fact that in sexuated reproduction it is females of species who materially mediate, meaning they not only select, but invest and produce lending their body as the cultural medium.

The human mode of reproduction is an exquisite form of live reciprocity endowed with the most compelling contingencies, and it is also an absolutely necessary prelude to subjectivity.

2.2.4 Sexual Selection, Instinct, and Emotion

Mate preferences are based on the detection of properties in the selected object through visual, vocal and chemical cues that appraise health, development, and fitness, including aesthetic fitness, the latter being largely culturally determined in humans. These preferences and properties have evolved in plants and animals through sexual selection. Although selection pressures always shape the standards, there are other determining elements such as level of development, habits, and cultural upbringing.[563]

561 Trivers, R.L. (1972). "Parental investment and sexual selection.: In: Campbell, B. ed. *Sexual Selection and the Descent of Man,* 1871-1971, Chicago. Aldine-Atherton, pp. 136-179. Accessed from <http://www1.appstate.edu/~kms/classes/psy2664/Documents/trivers.pdf> on 2015-05-
562 Bateman, A.J. (1948). "Intrasexual Selection in Drosophila. Heredity, 2, pp. 349-368
563 Grammer K., et al. (2003). "Darwinian aesthetics: sexual selection and the biology of

Sexual selection thus takes place through some form of agency, a self found through sensual perception but based on a new, more complex dialectic of sameness and difference that implies a higher cognitive capacity, compared to previous levels of natural selection. Mates are selected that belong to the same species and therefore have the same morphological characteristics, except for sexual morphology that is different and opposite in primary, genital, and secondary sexual characteristics. Freud very narrowly coined the term "penis envy," leaving out reciprocity, the male envy of female characteristics he had to search for. Psychologically in humans, envy is the fitting emotion also underlined by Melanie Klein more evenly.[564] Cognitively, it is the perception of desired properties and skills in the sexual object that compellingly bind to it because of its fitting, complementary design.

Sexual selection operates driven by the binary opposition of the sexual instinct but, as we know after Freud, it can be overriden by cultural mediations toward sublimations and other forms.[565] In Chapter VII of *On the Origin of Species*, Darwin explained instincts as *behavioral adaptations* that have evolved both by natural and sexual selection. Darwin provided many examples of instinctive behaviors in animals, and suggested how such behaviors could have evolved. In particular, he proposed that animal *social behavior* was the result of natural selection's acting at the level of groups such as families, rather than through individuals.[566] Darwin contrasted instincts and intelligence, not without suggesting the necessary continuity between them. He pointed out the analogy between animal instinctive behavior and human intelligence. Instincts are not acquired or learned, they are stereotyped behavioral programs inherent univer-

beauty." Biological reviews of the Cam-bridge Philosophical Society. 78(3:)385-407.

564 Klein, M. (2002). *Envy and Gratitude*. New York. Free Press.

565 Lasch, C. (1991). *The Culture of Narcissism. American Life in an Age of Diminishing Expectations*. New York. W. W. Norton & Company

566 Darwin.C. (1859). "Instinct". Chapter 7 in The Origin of Species by Means of Natural Selection or The Preservation of Favoured Races in the Struggle for Life. London: John Murray: Pp. 234-263. Online in A Mead Project source page. Accessed from <https://www.brocku.ca/MeadProject/Darwin/1859_7.htmL> on 2-16-09-26.

sally to a particular species. They do not involve the human complex mediations of judgment, reason or choice. Instincts are opposite to habits that are learned in their stead.

In his later book, *On the Expression of Emotions in Men and Animals*,[567] Darwin explained the role that emotions play in the biology of animals, and extended those explanations to humans. Emotion is our animal intelligence and the internal language between the two opposite forms of consciousness within ourselves, consciousness and self-consciousness. He argued that emotions are essentially biological processes analogous to other physiological adaptations, and that the methods by which they can be studied are similar to those by which any other inherited trait can be scientifically analyzed. I propose that emotion is a legitimate and legitimizing internal, language placed within the gap that goes from perception to action.

Instinct is the beginning of intelligence and consciousness in animals, and emotion is a form of signaling, a protolanguage closer to nature and internal but powerfully communicational and reverberational with others. Emotion is more legitimate than speech.

2.2.5 Mirroring and Imprinting, from Affiliation to Recognition

Mirroring and imprinting are mechanisms that allow animals to affiliate, to "know" what species they belong to, and partake of its species' specific benefits and liabilities. Imprinting is the acquisition of the species' affiliation capacity, a sort of animal external identity. This occurs usually when the young is exposed to a species-specific analogue during a critical period of development. Mirroring allows an animal to, for the first time, recognize itself in the other, its particularity within the universality of its species in practical terms.

The discovery of specialized mirror neurons in the frontal cortex of primates and humans is a recent landmark in developmental and

---

567 Darwin, C. R. 1872. The expression of the emotions in man and animals. London: John Murray. 1st edition. Darwin Online. Accessed from <http://darwin-online.org.uk/content/frameset?pageseq=1&itemID=F1142&viewtype=text> on 2015-08-29.

comparative neurobiology. In Italy neurobiologists serendipitously found that monkeys in the laboratory, through specialized motor neurons in the frontal, so-called executive, cortex of the brain, constantly mirrored each other's actions. One day, while a monkey was sitting idly, one of the researchers came in and picked up a peanut. The observing monkey's frontal cells fired as if the monkey was picking up the peanut, even though the animal had not moved at all; his brain was merely expressing envy and sameness. It was the same group of neurons that fired when the monkey was not merely watching but doing it. Here the monkey-subject's neurons were mirroring the related researcher-object's motion, the monkey anticipating the motion himself; learning by imitation.[568]

Here we have neurobiological evidence for what Freud called identification. Others before him had simply called it imitation. The implications of this brain phenomenon had been already behaviorally described by Henry Wallon, who had proposed that the young's play is a creative form of imitation in the development of subjectivity, through mirroring other subjects.[569] Jacques Lacan popularized mirroring as a specific stage of development he called the mirror phase.[570] It is important here to remember, however, that the first mirror of the infant, and therefore the first concrete human identification, is universally the mothering one.

Hegel had previously proposed mirroring *recognition* as the source of human desire, not for the other as object, but for being reciprocally recognized and confirmed as a subject by the other. For Hegel the desire for recognition differentiates humans from animals.

---

568 Gallese, V., Fadiga, L., Fogassi, L. & Rizzolatti, G. (1996). "Action recognition in the premotor cortex. Brain, 119, 593-609.
569 Wallon, H. (1984) The Psychological Development of the Child. Trans. Michael Vale. (Written: 1965) Jason Aaronson. Online Version: Wallon Internet Archive (marxists.org) 2001. Accessed from <http://www.marxists.org/archive/wallon/works/1965/ch10.htm> on 2012-06-02.
570 Lacan, J. (2002). "The Mirror Stage as Formative of the I Function, as Revealed in Psychoanalytic Experience." Trans. Alan Sheridan. In: Ecrits. 1. Pp. 3-9. New York. Norton. Online in Western Illinois University. Accessed from <http://faculty.wiu.edu/D-Banash/eng299/LacanMirrorPhase.pdf> on 2014-11-06.

Animal, or sexual, desire is desire for the object or its property. Human subjects build their species-specific identity through a mirroring relationship with other subjects that for Lacan extend to include, the symbolic order of culture, that produces subjectivity.[571] The first and foremost other subject is the mother, who puts in place all the necessary first-order cultural mediations for all.

2.2.6 Reciprocal Envy and Imitation

Typically Freud thought (penis) envy to be unilateral as far as women are concerned. Hegel portrayed the envy-based desire for recognition through the struggle to death of contending males. We owe to Melanie Klein the acknowledgment of the universal phenomenon of envy in the earliest phases of development, envy's being the introjecting force that jumpstarts subjectivity in children, independent of sex. Klein defined envy as the angry feeling aroused by seeing that another person possesses and enjoys something desirable to the subject, followed by the demand to have it. The feeling is often accompanied by an impulse to take it away for the self, or spoil it for the other.[572] Contrary to the male view, this is a universal view of envy as a constructive phenomenon.

What Freud called superego Klein empirically described as the object formally internalized by the developing subject, analogous to the oral incorporation of milk from the breast. The internalization of the mother includes that of her culture; the mother is the first carrier of cultural symbols and prerogatives, such as language. The first part-object internalized is the mother's breast that becomes the landmark for the superego, a giver and taker. The breast is internalized on the basis of envy of its plentifulness and giving goodness, although it also has the alternating qualities of absence and hostile

571 Evans, D. (1966). *An Introductory Dictionary of Lacanian Psychoanalysis.* London: Routledge. P. 133.

572 Klein, M. (1928). "Early Stages of Oedipus Conflict." International Journal of Psychoanalysis, Vol. 9, Pp. 169-80. Online in Scribd. Accessed from <https://www.scribd.com/doc/215382037/Klein-Melanie-Early-Stages-of-Oedipus-Conflict-International-Journal-of-Psychoanalysis-Vol-9-1928-169-80> on 2015-05-07.

frustration. The latter is what later, sublimated, is to become constraining fear of a bad object. Here Klein was a better naïve dialectician than Freud.

The original phenomenon regarding subjectivity proper in humans is thus animal envy that takes the sublimated cultural forms of desire and fear, the universal schizoid binary of Ronald Fairbairn.[573] This has an epistemological resonance with Briffault's description of the original sexual act as a brutal form of rape, the brutal takeover and penetration of the other's body, having nothing to do with love, which for Briffault is instead a sublimation of the mating instinct, not of sex.[574] Food-chain envy culturally evolves to become a dysphoria, a painful affliction based on the unrequited desire for the possession of the advantage of the other. Klein postulates that envious impulses, oral and anal-sadistic in nature, operate from the beginning of life, initially directed at the feeding breast and then at parental coitus. Envy for Klein moves from object to relation, and to alliance. She sees envy as a manifestation of primary destructiveness, constitutionally based, and worsened by adversity, the natural ethics of the food chain.

What is later experienced as the destructive attack on the good object, based on the initial lack of discriminatory capacity between good and bad, causes the necessary depressive position in development. Depression here means emotional integration based on cognitive advance; it is a sort of logical guilt. Original envy logically leads to persecution and persecution boomerangs into the self as paranoia, the first form of anxiety. Guilt is logically the integrative second stage. Klein came to see more mature gratitude, a further stage, as an expression of love, the life-instinct, and the antithesis of

---

573 Fairbairn, R. (2001). *Psychoanalytic Studies of the Personality* London and New York. Routledge. (Orig. Pub. 1952).

574 Briffault, R. (1927). *The mothers: a study of the origins of sentiments and institutions.* New York. The Macmillan Company. Printed in the U.S. By J.J. Little & Ives Co New York. Online in Hathi Trust Digital Library <http://catalog.hathitrust.org/Record/001109898>. Accessed from <http://babel.hathitrust.org/cgi/pt?id=mdp.3901 5009106751;view=1up;seq=10> on 2013-06-17.

destructive envy.[575] This completes the Kleinian dialectic.

Karen Horney expresses the same dynamic, but now in the envious simultaneous dread and attraction between the sexes, in essence the same phenomenon but reciprocal. "Men have never tired of fashioning expressions for the violent force by which man feels himself drawn to the woman, and side by side with his longing, the dread that through her he might die and be undone." [576]And she continues: " 'It is not,' he says, 'that I dread her; it is that she herself is malignant, capable of any crime, a beast of prey, a vampire, a witch, insatiable in her desires. She is the very personification of what is sinister.' "[577] Horney presents her evidence from art and literature, including psychoanalysis. The droit du seigneur, or *jus primae noctis,* comes not so much from the sexual greed of the patriarch as from the recognition of his courage to penetrate a woman for the first time and maybe judge that it is safe. Man objectifies his fear, says Horney, and his counterphobic glorification of women conceals his dread. Here the castrating one is the woman and the envy turns around.

The female is designed to internalize, to place within boundaries and add up, a crucial evolutionary mechanism that, as listening, is not to be equated with passivity, but seen as another form of activity. The male, on the other hand, is designed to externalize, perform, and destroy. How these natural roles were totally subverted leads to the notion of "morality of evolution." For Horney, men fear not castration but its symbolization of ridicule, rejection, and loss of self-respect. This fear led to the institution of patriarchy. In childhood, these feelings are the result of anatomical disproportion related to size and power more than to any other cognitively perceived property of adulthood or of the opposite sex.[578] Women and men's

---

575 Klein, M. (1957). "Envy and Gratitude." In: *The Writings of Melanie Klein.* Vo. III. Pp. 176-235. London. Hogarth Press.

576 Horney, K. (1932). "The Dread of Women. Observations on a Specific Difference in the Dread Felt by Men and by Women Respectively for the Opposite Sex." In: Horney, K. (1967). *Feminine Psychology.* Norton. New York. P. 134.

577 Horney, K. (1932). "The Dread of Women. Ibid P. 135.

578 Horney, K. (1932). "The Dread of Women. Ibid. P. 142.

dread and desire are reciprocal, but historically compartmentalized as antagonistic. Beauty ideals and power ideals are transformed historically. Reciprocal envy is at the heart of imitation.

2.2.7 Imitation and Learning

Envious mirroring reciprocity of subjects within a common infrastructure of feelings and cognitions are the necessary foundation of imitation and learning. Canadian psychologist Albert Bandura was a behaviorist who had to go beyond the narrow mechanical premise of behavior-environment interaction that he found insufficient to explain human behavior. Bandura developed a Social Cognitive Theory, a form of reciprocal determinism. Our behavior, he said, is socially determined by that of others whom we reciprocally determine. Imitation is based on the useful appraisal of better competency, skill or advantage in the other. Upon close contact, the better-skilled becomes the role model. One important characteristic of this process is its functional value: vicarious learning and vicarious reinforcement. Children learn to behave by observing.[579] Needless to say the most crucial other in this early process is the mother.

Bandura's theory is akin to that of Russian psychologist, founder of the historical-cultural school, and developmentalist Lev Vygotsky. What Vygotsky called *Zone of Proximal Development* consists precisely in that relational segment where change is possible through collaboration. This is like a scaffold where the learner can develop, where he/she is ready to collaborate with the knower or teacher, as a ground of soil is ready for the seed. This is how Vygotzky from the viewpoint of education sees intelligence as a relationship rather than as a privately owned property. "The zone of proximal development (ZPD) has been defined as "the distance between the actual developmental level as determined by independent problem solving and the level of potential development as determined through problem solving under adult guidance, or in collaboration with more capable

---

579 Bandura, A. (1986). Social foundations of thought and action: A social cognitive theory. Englewood Cliffs, NJ: Prentice-Hall.

peers."[580]

The history of the understanding of learning properly starts with Pavlov and his laboratory experiments in conditioning dogs. Pavlov piggybacked sound upon the image of food; he conditioned a new reflex upon an unconditioned, instinctual one. Learning is conditioning in the Pavlovian fashion. The theory had been already proposed by Sechenov, Pavlov's teacher, and after Pavlov came the waves of behaviorist line of psychology that initially rejected thought and introspection as part of behavior. This problem was corrected by the school of Vygotsky, particularly by A.N. Leontiev. Unfortunately the works of this school remain for the most part inaccessible for the English reader. The study of learning, the juxtaposition of conditioning on instinct, starts a whole new era in psychology and the understanding of consciousness.

The first proxy, alter-ego is the mother, and her method is intuitive.

---

580 Vygotsky, L. S. (1978). Mind in society: The development of higher psychological processes. P. 86Cambridge, MA: Harvard University Press.

2.3 FROM LEARNING TO CONSCIOUSNESS -ACTIVITY TO REFLEXION

"In physiology, it is not hard to be a materialist - but just try to be one in psychology."

L. Vygotsky[581]

"Just as Darwin discovered the law of development of organic nature, so Marx discovered the law of development of human history: the simple fact, hitherto concealed by an overgrowth of ideology, that mankind must first of all eat, drink, have shelter and clothing, before he can pursue politics, science, art, religion, etc..."

Engels -Speech at the Gravesite of Karl Marx.[582]

"Human beings are ultimately actuated by impulses, such as those towards nutrition and reproduction, which are common to all animals. They are also actuated, like animals, by more specialized instinctive dispositions."

Briffault. The Mothers.[583]

581 Quoted in: Leontiev, A.A. (2005). *The Life and Creative Path of A.N. Leontiev.* Journal of Russian and East European Psy-chology, vol. 43, no. 3, May–June, pp. 8–69. P. 16. Accessed from <http://xa.yimg.com/kq/groups/25194687/320109047/name/A.+A.+Leontiev+-+43+n°3+A+vida+e+o+trabalho+criativo+de+A.+N.+Leontiev+(em+ingles).pdf> on 2012-07-26.

582 Engels, F. (1951). "Speech at the Graveside of Karl Marx." *In Karl Marx and Frederick Engels Selected Works.* Moscow. Foreign Languages Publishing House. (Orig. read 1883). Online in MIA. Accessed from <http://www.marxists.org/archive/marx/works/1883/death/burial.htm> on 2013-01-13.

583 Briffault, R. (1927). *The mothers: a study of the origins of sentiments and institutions.* 3 volumes. Vol. 1. Ch. II. Traditional Heredity. P. 45. New York. The Macmillan Com-

2.3.1 The First Ingredient of Learning: Activity

Subjective activity meets objects in the environment that pose all sorts of problems from obstruction to destruction, but these are the same that produce self-enhancement and self-reproduction in the process of problem-solving. To discriminate, subjects have evolutionarily been provided with a nervous system that allows them not only to discriminate but, most important, to anticipate. All novelty is considered suspicious until an exploratory relationship with the new object has determined its properties.

Freud's various paragraphs about women reveal his patriarchal unconscious motivation in its often dumbfounding bluntness. He disposes of female activity in his libido theory, assigning to women only passivity and masochism. Activity in psychology is the equivalent to motion in physics; we cannot either exist or think without being active. That is the degree of Freud's hostility towards women, not unusual in the patriarchal literature. There can be no psychology without activity and if Freud were to be true, there would be no female psychology for Horney to write about.[584] The first presupposition of psychology, spiritual activity, has been almost totally neglected in Western psychology. We owe the reintegration of activity to psychology largely to Russian psychologist A. N. Leontiev.[585] Although the binaries of Freud, such as id and superego, or sadism and masochism, have a dynamic and reciprocal nature, there is a lag when it comes to gender; in a form of patriarchal enactment, all privilege goes to men.

The first case Freud saw not neurologically but psychodynam-

pany. Printed in the U.S. By J.J. Little & Ives Co New York. Online in Hathi Trust Digital Library <http://catalog.hathitrust.org/Record/001109898>. Accessed from <http://babel.hathitrust.org/cgi/pt?id=mdp.39015009106751;view=1up;seq=10> on 2013-06-17.

584 Horney, K. (1967). Feminine Psychology. Norton. New York. (Orig. Pub.1932).

585 Leontiev, A.N. (1977). "Activity And Consciousness." Published in Russian in the journal Voprosyfilosofii, n. 12, p. 129-140 (1972) and English in the book Philosophy in the USSR, Problems of Dialectical Materialism. (Moscow, 1977, p. 180-202). Online at MIA. Accessed from <http://www.revistadialectus.ufc.br/index.php/RevistaDialectus/article/viewFile/156/95> on 2015-05-13.

ically, in terms of conflict, is that of a healthy young mother who upon trying to feed her newborns would get terribly ill. Freud was called and successfully hypnotized the patient, who was then able to breastfeed her second child. But the problem recurred after her next delivery that, again, responded positively to Freud's hypnotic intervention. Writing about this case, Freud for the first time talks about *psychological conflict*, and, inspired by Schopenhauer,[586] explains it as a clash of will and what he calls counterwill.[587] This prompted Freud to review his practice and focus on free association in order to overcome the repressive censorship of the mind, incidentally modeled on social repression. But he could not see that the repressive censorship of the mind is an internalization of that of hierarchical social relations.

Had Freud read his contemporary, anthropologist Robert Briffault, he would have been able to find the evidence for the female instinct in female anthropology and evolutionary science, not in the mystified overstatement of Eros, but in the material phenomenon of human reciprocity: in the mother's capacity to give, altruism, the foundation of benevolence, empathy, and moral sense. This is the opposite of the capacity to take of the males of the species. Altruism is the peculiar instinct of social animals that Darwin so much puzzled about and that Freud totally missed. This artistic instinct, the ground of empathy and humanization, is biased to females of species, not only human, paradigmatically through their mothering and tending activity.

Females are biologically programmed to, from their body and mind, invest in their progeny. This is precisely the root of their instinctual activity and disposition. Females give in for fertilization, give life from the ground of their body, give proteic aliment from

---

586 Schopenhauer, A. (2011-2). The World as Will and Idea. (1909 Sixth Edition). Online in Project Gutenberg. 3 Vols.

587 Freud, S. (1950). A Case of Successful Treatment by Hypnotism: With Some Remarks on the Origin of Hysterical Symptoms through 'Counter-Will.' Editor and Translator: James Strachey. The Standard Edition of the Psychological Works of Sigmund Freud. Vol. 1. P. 115. (Orig. Pub.1892-3).

their breast, and, most important, through gestures and words, give mediating consciousness while caring for their young. They serve as the vicarious or proxy blueprint of subjectivity. They go through harboring a costly uterine parasitism, collaborating in a costlier infant symbiosis, negotiating contradictory childhood dependence, and finally colluding in the long struggle for separation each human has to negotiate. These are various relational manifestations of the feminine instinctual disposition, and they place every single human being at the threshold of consciousness and morality, planting the seeds of a self, and self-regulation, in every individual and in every culture. Women are the carriers of universality.

The first characteristic form of human activity, and of human evolutionary adaptation, is labor. Labor introduced the unique form of human mediation in evolution, and maternal labor-and-delivery is the prototype of labor. The mother concretely introduces the first mediation by placing herself as the instrument of production of each newborn, *Almae Matres,* and by putting in place all the first-order elements of social regulation that lead to culture. The estranged, alienated form of labor we have had since slavery, along with the fetish of commercial exchange instead of use, is second-order mediation introduced by insurgent sons. Culture is the creation of mothers and so is the self, both internalizations of self-regulation, one collective, one individual, both derived from the way mothers regulate, from the outside first, each individual. Maternal pedigree was historically known long before the paternal one.

The most valuable maternal mediation in humans is the endowment of her offspring, through learning, with a self that starts vicariously from her caring and regulating activity. This is the template for the child's later self-regulatory capacity or self. The original self, the mother's, is highly altruistic, wholeheartedly giving, and built cooperatively through instinctual maternal intuition of delicate critical and sensitive stages in development recently described by neurobiologists.[588] Maternal altruism actually started long before hu-

---

588 Knudsen,E.I. (2004) "Sensitive Periods in the Development of the Brain and Behav-

mans in other mammalian species. If consciousness stems from the internalization, the mirroring of the activity of the mothering one, morality arises from its very particular altruistic form. Even when the mother says *no* to her child, it is not for selfish self-assertion but a form of protective altruism.

Historically, between human groups the first form of social exchange was the gift, that was correctly designated by Mauss as "the total social fact"[589]: social structure's transcending the individual and capable of exercising social control. The gift expresses social pleasure, and it is, even today, reciprocal and universal even though today its magnitude is almost made invisible,[590] through market equivalence, exchange, and profit. Everyone naturally strives to be able to give and enjoys giving, not for return but for moral self-satisfaction; even hungry billionaires set up their charities. Albert Camus, in his novel *The Fall*, illustrates the selfish perversion of altruism in patriarchal society.[591] It is quite difficult, in a capitalist society based on the extraction of profit from the transactions with others, to conceptualize the transcendental importance of the gift, derived from the female instinct, in the formation of human identity. In anthropology, gift-giving has been illustrated for example in the

---

ior." Journal of Cognitive Neuroscience 16:8, pp. 1412–1425. Accessed from <http://synapse.princeton.edu/~sam/knudsen_critical_periods_jcn_2004.pdf> on 2016-06-20.

589 "These phenomena are at once legal, economic, religious, aesthetic, morphological and so on. They are legal in that they concern individual and collective rights, organized and diffuse morality; they may be entirely obligatory, or subject simply to praise or disapproval. They are at once political and domestic, being of interest both to classes and to clans and families. They are religious; they concern true religion, animism, magic and diffuse religious mentality. They are economic, for the notions of value, utility, interest, luxury, wealth, acquisition, accumulation, consumption and liberal and sumptuous expenditure are all present..." Mauss, M. (1966). *The Gift.* Trans. Ian Cunnison. London. Cohen and West Ltd. Pp. 76-77. Online in Internet Archive. Accessed from <https://archive.org/details/giftformsfunctio00maus> on 2014-02-06.

590 Vaughan, G. (1997). For-Giving: A Feminist Criticism of Exchange. Austin, Texas. Plainview Press in collaboration with the Foundation for a Compassionate Society. Ch. 1., P. 15. Free download from < http://www.gift-economy.com/forgiving.html> on 2016-03-21.

591 Camus, A. (1991). *The Fall.* Trans. Justin O'Brien. New York. Random House.

social custom of the potlatch,[592] an ancient and fundamental social institution.[593] Forbidden by occupying patriarchal cultures where it still existed, the potlatch loudly expresses the matriarchal imprint.

The female instinctual sexual determination is the manifestation of the life-instinct, the insurgent original manifestation of the natural drive to produce and grow, to give and fight for life against the morality of the food chain that in humans is subordinated to it. Freud's death instinct highlights the other side, the necrophilic nature of the male instinct unrestrained by patriarchal subjection and leading to war.

The natural active proclivity of females is instinctually different to that of males.

2.3.2 Freud's Flight from Activity

By resorting to natural science, thermodynamics, as a model for his theory, instead of sticking with philosophy, the mother of psychology, Freud left the dramatic realm of human psychology for what would, paradoxically, become an idealist metaphor in the guise of science, thermodynamics, the play of physical forces. Freud became entangled in the metaphor and in the process of translating from one realm, behavior, to the other, he had to resort to metapsychology inspired by metaphysics. Karen Horney's theory endeavors

---

592 "The second reason for the discontent among the Indians is a law that was passed, some time ago, forbidding the celebrations of festivals. The so-called potlatch of all these tribes hinders the single families from accumulating wealth. It is the great desire of every chief and even of every man to collect a large amount of property, and then to give a great potlatch, a feast in which all is distributed among his friends, and, if possible, among the neighboring tribes." Boas, F. (1888). "The Indians of British Columbia," The Popular Science Monthly, March 1888 (vol. 32), p. 635-636. Google Free Ebook. Accessed from <https://play.google.com/books/reader?id=pc4WAQAA-IAAJ&printsec=frontcover&output=reader&authuser=1&hl=en&pg=GBS.PA628> on 2014-02-06.

593 The boats of the young woman were loaded with her dower: boxes filled with blankets, valuable copper plates, and the *gyiserstal* — the latter being a heavy board, cut so as to represent a human jaw-bone. The front is set with sea-otter teeth. This object is given' to the bridegroom, who thus obtains the right to command his wife to talk or to be silent." Boas, F. (1888) "The Indians of British Columbia," Ibid.

to deconstruct and reverse that. Freud's metapsychology is a regression, in that its premise is belief in controlling entelechies. The ego is something one "has," and something one is encouraged to grow in the image of capital. Freud was not successful in extracting the method, dialectic, from the metaphor, thermal motion. This is how concrete human activity became reduced to abstract cathecting libidinal energy, imponderable and attributed to men. Freud's theory then had to be subject not to transactional, but to physical, laws of a simple mechanical reciprocity unable to handle the complexity of human behavior. Energy in the human organism belongs to different domains, physiology and biochemistry, in psychology being a metaphor at best. Fairbairn began to correct this problem with his definition of libido as *object-seeking tendency.*[594] In the domain of psychology, social activity is the analogue of energy. The prototype of object-seeking is consciousness that cannot exist if it is not attached to an object.

In his effort to gain scientific recognition in an epoch in which thermodynamics was considered cutting-edge, Freud and his teachers tried to mold their theories accordingly. Helmholtz had applied the revolutionary principle of the conservation of energy to the nervous system, based on the law that the amount of energy contained in a closed physical system always remains constant.[595] Freud's teacher Ernst Brucke, in his *Lectures on Physiology* of 1874, included humans as energy systems subject to the law of the conservation of energy: "psychodynamic." Bowlby writes: "During the 1840s, Brücke had been one of a group of dedicated young scientists, of whom Helmholtz was the leader, who were determined to show that all real causes are symbolized in science by the word 'force.' Since the achievements of the Helmholtz school soon became famous, it

---

594 Fairbairn, W.R.D., (1981). Psychoanalytic Studies of the Personality. London: Routledge and Kegan Paul, (Orig. Pub. 1952).

595 Helmholtz, H.L.F. (2001). *On the Conservation of Force.* Introduction to a Series of Lectures Delivered at Carlsruhe in the Winter of 1862–1863. New York: P.F. Collier & Son, 1909–14. Tr. Edmund Atkinson. Online in Bartleby.com. Scientific Papers. The Harvard Classics. Scientific Papers. Vol. XXX. Accessed from <http://www.bartleby.com/30/125.html> on 2012-07-27.

was natural that Freud, working under one of their number, should have adopted their assumptions."[596] This became Freud's theoretical cornerstone. However, what applies in physics, as I said in the case of entropy, does not necessarily apply the same way at the level of psychology.

Human activity, the most complex form, is necessarily intersubjective. In psychodynamics it became reduced to abstract forces. Karen Horney and others corrected this by applying the concept of interpersonal forces, in Horney simply moving towards, against and away, the equivalent of the most basic mating, fighting and flying.[597]

2.3.3 Activity in the Cultural-Historical (Instrumental) School Perspective

Human activity, as opposed to its animal analogue is much more complex, mediated by human relations that include labor, meaning, language and consciousness. It is determined culturally because culture has the purpose of defining reality, how everything relates to everything else. Practically, how to go about approaching reality culturally takes into consideration the experience of all previous generations. Culture is the synchronic manifestation of the diachronicity of history, the history of human mediations. Mediation is instrumentality, the definition of a thing by revealing its relation to another thing,.[598]

Activity's equivalent in physics is reciprocal action, and in physiology, sensory-motricity. In psychology it is the action of a subject

---

596 Bowlby, John. (1973). *Separation: Anxiety and Anger.* Volume: II. p. 401.New York. Basic Books. Online in Questia. Accessed from <http://www.questia.com/read/6986636/separation-anxiety-and-anger> on 2012-10-10.

597 Horney, K. (1950). *Neurosis and Human Growth.* New York. Norton.

598 Mediation is the "Existence or definition of a thing by revealing its relation to another thing. The properties of things are revealed in their interconnection with other things. A mirror mediates the thing it is reflecting and its image. Mediated knowledge is knowledge, for example, related through past experience and reflection which enables us to recognise things in the stream of impressions." Encyclopedia of the Marxists Internet Achive. Mediation. Accessed from <http://www.marxists.org/glossary/terms/m/e.htm> on 2012-07-27.

reciprocally determined by its subjectified object. In fact, the subject is always irremediably related to the object that defines it, even when that object is itself. This is how the material process of evolutionary human social practice comes about: subjective relation to an objective reality that has been previously subjectified, mediated by properties unique to the subject, such as reflection and mediation. In practical activity, the subject consciously realizes itself, becomes objectified, through labor and meaningful words. It subjectivizes whatever its object happens to be at any time, and thus makes everything it touches cultural and historical.[599] This is the true meaning of the Midas myth. The object, however, in turn seeks to objectify its subject the most tragic example's being reification, the "fetishism of commodities."[600] Here humans see all their potential, activity and power not in themselves but in the object money. Money, they believe, can get everything for them. They don't know money can get them only what they deposited into it, starting with slavery.

Activity, the real power, is an essential psychological notion neglected in Western psychology globally, more than just by Freud. This is partly due to the still prevalent analytic focus on objects at rest, and the consequent formal form of logic that goes with it this in spite of the compelling scientific evidence of the constant universal and internally determined motion of the cosmos. Materialist psychologists, particularly in the Soviet Union, have filled the gap in psychology; they have defined activity as the fundamental man-world interaction. A. N. Leontiev (1903-1979) among them became the carrier of the banner of activity theory in psychology. It was however his teacher Vygotsky[601] who, after Marx,[602] brought the

599 Leontiev. A.N. Quoted in : Leontiev, A.A. (2005). "The Life and Creative Path of A.N. Leontiev." Ibid. Pp. 55-6.
600 Marx, K. (1887). "The Fetishism of Commodities and the Secret thereof." In: *Capital*. Part 1. Chapter 1. Section 4 - First english edition., Moscow, USSR; Progress Publishers. (Orig. Pub: 1887). Trans: Samuel Moore and Edward Aveling, edited by Frederick Engels. Online in MIA. Accessed from <https://www.marxists.org/archive/marx/works/1867-c1/ch01.htm#S4> on 2015-09
601 Quoted by Leontiev, A.A. (2005). The Life and Creative Path of A.N. Leontiev.Ibid. p. 34.
602 Marx talks for example about "forms of intercourse" in the German Ideology. See

core notion to the forefront of psychology.

The approach to psychology proposed by Vygotsky and Leontiev in the tradition of Marx, Darwin, and Romanes[603] is particularly concerned with providing an evolutionary account of the origin of consciousness in animal psychology.

For Leontiev activity is the main unit of vital processes in an organism. It is similar to the social act of Mead,[604] who replaces activity by tendency. Leontiev does not want to put activity to rest as tendency implies; tendency is subordinated to activity. Activity implies that the subject's vital relation to reality is constantly determined by its object. Maslow expresses this in his popular saying that if the only tool you have is a hammer, everything looks like a nail,[605] which the Greeks had in their ethics said differently: virtue is goodness of fit. *Eudaimonia* for Aristotle, "good living," is to human virtue what sharpness is to a knife. This is what Horney translated as "morality of evolution," living in peace with nature. Types of subjective activity are determined by the form of their objects. Darwin saw it in the finches' beaks shaped to their type of food.

To the unbiased observer we humans, today, must look like

Marx, K. (1932) *The German Ideology.* Part I: Feuerbach. Opposition of the Materialist and Idealist Outlook. D. Proletarians and Communism. "Forms of Intercourse." Marx-Engels Collected Works, Volume 5. Moscow. Progress Publishers. (Written: Fall 1845 to mid-1846). Accessed from <http://www.marxists.org/archive/marx/works/1845/german-ideology/ch01b.htm> on 2012-08-19.

603 George Romanes (1848 –1894) was a Canadian-British evolutionist and Darwin's mentee, who pioneered comparative psychol-ogy. See for example: Romanes, G.J. (2012). *Animal Intelligence.* The International Scientific Series, Vol. XLIV. Project Gutenberg EBook #40459. Accessed from <http://www.gutenberg.org/files/40459/40459-h/40459-h.htm> on 2015-09-04.

604 Mead defines the social act as follows: "An act is an impulse that maintains the life-process by the selection of certain sorts of stimuli it needs. Thus, the organism creates its environment. The stimulus is the occasion for the expression of the impulse. Stimuli are means, tendency is the real thing. Intelligence is the selection of stimuli that will set free and maintain life and aid in rebuilding it." Mead, G.H. (1967). *Mind, Self, and Society.* Chicago. University of Chicago Press. (Orig. Pub. 1934). Accessed from <http://www.brocku.ca/MeadProject/Mead/pubs2/mindself/Mead_1934_07.html> on 2012-10-10.

605 Maslow, A., (1966). *The Psychology of Science: A Reconnaissance.* New York. Harper.

money.

2.3.4 The Genesis and Evolution of Activity According to Leontiev

Leaving aside motion that in the realm of physics was already found to be reciprocal by Newton, Leontiev traces activity from its simplest evolutionary biological form, *irritability*. The amoeba "knows," and "selects" what to engulf, as does the insect-eating plant. Activity is reciprocally determined action, a sort of concrete mutual recognition and reciprocal operation that in this case takes place between a more advanced subject, amoeba, or insect eating plant, and an object, they pray on. They metaphorically shake hands, select each other, before the destruction of the object one as aliment by the surviving one takes place. This goes on from bottom to top of the food chain. The ones that remain throughout the chain will evolve through the complexity they owe to their objects. Human consciousness is uniquely the last, indestructible, object only because it objectifies itself as civilization. Civilization destroyed human consciousness will be with it.

What determines the human species in its bifurcation from the food chain for Leontiev is self-consciousness. Consciousness is the totalizing process that can understand itself by looking behind phenomena. Although animals continuously close circles of stimulus-response in their complex interactions with their environment, they do not *totalize* their experience in a cultural form, as we humans constantly must do. Like them, we destroy to produce, but through cultural mediations maintain and enhance. We all contribute through our constant process of objectifying ourselves in our practices. The totality of culture, as in a puzzle, takes each human self-objectification, and places it in its fitting place, its niche in the whole, the totality. That is uniquely human totalization.

Leontiev attributes the failure of stimulus-response behaviorism to its premise of immediacy, the lack of acknowledgement of mediation. The mediating processes build consciousness and that is why labor is privileged, because labor is the mediating activity *par excellence*. Leontiev says that mediating processes realize a person's actual life in the objective world by which he is surrounded as a social being; mediatory processes are human activity.[606] Here it is not meant that physiological or neurological processes determine psychology, but rather dramatic, social, relational processes. Sociality is inherently mediation. The operations and the language of mental activity are different from biological processes; consciousness is constantly mediated by social being, by the actual social life that determines its form: hence ideology.

It is important to reiterate that all material existence is characterized by reciprocal action, two-way connectivity or exchange. Human activity is a highly developed form of reciprocal action. Brain reflection is a higher manifestation of the physical phenomenon of reciprocal action.

If we go back to the seemingly mindless interactions of inorganic chemistry, we already see in them the embryo of what is much later to become psychological reflection. Given the appropriate conditions, each substance through its properties responds to the precise properties of the other. The two chemical substances in question do not engage by pure chance; they recognize and select each other as they do with optimal circumstances for their embrace. What we could call proto-reflection or proto-mind here is the essential component of reciprocal action that goes back to inorganic, mineral matter. Similarly, the selective interactions of planets and stars with their orderly orbits and simultaneous forces of attraction and repulsion, and perhaps even the galaxies being somehow alike in their behavior, interact with each other on the basis of the engagement of opposite forces of reciprocal selection and action.

As regards the blossoming animal psyche, its first stage is traditionally agreed to be sensory since Hobbes. Romanes credits

---

606 Leontiev, A.N. (1977). *Activity and Consciousness.* In: Philosophy in the USSR, Problems of Dialectical Materialism. Pp. 180-202. Trans. Robert Daglish. Moscow. Progress Publishers. (Orig. Pub. 1972). Accessed from <http://www.marxists.org/archive/leontev/works/1977/leon1977.htm> on 2012-07-28.

Hobbes with being the first psychologist and quotes from *Leviathan*: "All the qualities called sensible are, in the object which causeth them, but so many motions of the matter by which it presseth on our organs diversely. Neither in us that are pressed are they anything else but divers motions; for motion produceth nothing but motion.... The cause of sense is the external body or object, which presseth the organ proper to each sense, either immediately, as in taste and touch, or mediately, as in hearing, seeing, and smelling; which pressure, by the mediation of the nerves, and other strings and membranes of the body, continued inwards to the brain and heart, causeth there a resistance, or counter-pressure, or endeavour.... And because going, speaking, and the like voluntary motions, depend always upon a precedent thought of whither, which way, and what; it is evident that the imagination [or idea] is the first internal beginning of all voluntary motion. And although unstudied men do not conceive any motion at all to be there, where the thing moved is invisible; or the space it is moved in is, for the shortness of it, insensible; yet that doth not hinder, but that such motions are. These small beginnings of motion, within the body of man, before they appear in walking, speaking, striking, and other visible actions, are commonly called endeavour."[607] Endeavor is activity.

This quality or property, the sensitivity of sensory organs, has evolved one notch up from the previous more undifferentiated protoplasmic irritability. The difference is that while irritability is governed by properties of objects that are directly related to survival, the sensory psyche responds to already mediated, therefore less immediate and more distant, properties of the objects. At this stage, activity becomes a response, not to direct and selfish first-order survival needs, but rather to their second-order mediations. The plant, for example, responds to light not because of its direct impact in itself, but because light is what mediates the production of nutri-

---

607 Romanes, J. (2007). *Mind and Motion and Monism.* London Longmans, Green, and Co. Oxford and New York. Horance Hart, Printer to the University. (Orig. Pub. 1895). Online in Project Gutenberg. Ebook #22283. Accessed from <http://www.gutenberg. org/files/22283/22283-h/22283-h.htm> on 2012-10-10.

ents. Pavlov in his laboratory introduced mediations experimentally paired to unmediated reflexes. Already present in vegetal organisms, the sensory psyche has expanded beyond immediacy.

Activity theory starts from the premise that previous natural object-orienting processes based on reciprocal action evolve to become *meaning* as we reach the highest processes of human activity. Activity theory has been considered somewhat akin to American Pragmatism, Ecological Psychology, and some aspects of Systems Theory. [608]As we can see, activity theory is an offshoot of the theory of evolution.

2.3.5 Learning Activity

The behaviorist model wrongly assumes that all animals, including man, learn the same way. The stimulus-response sequence (S-R) in the model of irritability, is only the starting point. This model is based on external, observable phenomena that cannot explain subjectivity. Ignoring the issue, as behaviorism did originally, leaves it unsolved. Yet, the core principle, a relationship between two objects, is the same, except that now one of the objects is consciousnesses. The S-R phenomenon is the dialectical basis, the model and foundation, of all learning. In learning the hyphen is replaced by mediations.

Internal processes that traditionally had been the focus of introspection are not reducible to the S-R formula. This is where Freud started. In his *Interpretation of Dreams,* Chapter 7, he focuses on the gap between perception and motor response, more complex versions of S-R. In the gap are a series of memory containers in which the mediations of activity have been conserved. Triggered by either exogenous or endogenous stimuli, the dream essentially reversed their process and instead of motor response moves back to imagi-

---

608 See: A Glossary of Terms in Activity Theory. Compiled by Dr. S. R. Harris, 2007. Accessed from <http://www.coedglas.org.uk/PDFs/AT_Glossary2007.pdf> on 2012-05-24.

nary perception.[609] The pearl in all this is that mediations, human activities recorded in memory, can be accessed from the gap between perception and motor response.

This was an insolvable problem for behaviorists until Vygotsky included mediation, culture, and history in the equation. Through mediations, learning, culture and history totally transform the very nature of both the stimulus and the response. The original limited view of learning, ignored the fact that learning produces transformation by deinstinctualizing instincts through the introduction of growingly complex and abstract mediations that in humans replace instinct with habit. It is as if at birth all learning organisms were, yes, blank slates, but biased, phylogenetically predisposed, by the mediations of previous generations. It is on the already existing bias that cultural-historical conditioning works, transforming and enhancing it, and constantly conserving its modified form to endow it, from those who leave, to those who come anew.

There are basically two traditional types of learning: classical conditioning and operant conditioning. The first addresses learning of involuntary responses, as for example when the sound of a bell stimulates saliva flow in the Pavlovian dogs. Operant conditioning, on the other hand, is concerned with learning of voluntary responses, as when a desired behavior is reinforced by a reward or an undesired one is punished. In the classical version learning takes place through the mediatory pairing of unconditioned and conditioned stimuli, a regularly goes with b. In operant conditioning mediation occurs when a response is either preceded or followed by reinforcement: a or c are paired to occur with b.

Behavior (B) can then itself be considered to be in the midst of its reinforceable or inhibitable antecedent stimulus (A), and its reinforceable or inhibitable consequences (C). Here mediation may occur before, during, or after. This is easily remembered as ABC,

---

609 Freud, S (1913). *The Interpretation of Dreams.* Chapter VII The Psychology Of The Dream Activities. (b) Regression. Trans. A.A. Brill. Pp 422ss. New York. Macmillan. Source: Wikisource. Index:Freud - The interpretation of dreams.djvu. Accessed from <https://en.wikisource.org/wiki/Index:Freud_-_The_interpretation_of_dreams.djvu>

and is the basis for understanding how behavior can be reinforced or inhibited, for example by fear of punishment, which is what prompts Freud's repression. Positive reinforcement rewards behavior and thus encourages its reoccurrence. Negative reinforcement produces the need to repress, escape, or cause to vanish the punishable or painful behavior. Punishment can occur by aversive stimulation or by removal of rewards. Behavioral psychology is the most simple but fundamental psychology, very useful in training animals and the young human.

The difference between reflex and instinct is in the degree of complexity. Instincts usually consist of sequences or cascades of bundled reflexes, the characteristics of which are stereotypye and immediacy. A reflex action is typically involuntary, which means governed outside of consciousness. Although reflex and instinct are similarly triggered by stimuli, instinct is more complex and more susceptible of influence, and of learning, than a reflex because it already involves a degree of intelligence, natural mediation. Freud correctly pointed out instincts have a source, charge, aim and object, and the same applies to reflexes. Rangel stated that "...some reflex acts are essentially unconscious, whereas instincts, in the higher animals at all events, appear always to involve consciousness. Instincts accordingly depend more largely than reflexes upon the operations of the higher brain centers. If the activity involves a number of acts, each one of which, considered singly and alone, is relatively useless, but all of which taken together lead up to some adaptive consequence, such as the building of a nest, the feeding of young, etc., it will be safe to call the action instinctive."[610]

Conditioning is a form of mediation conducive to learning. It starts with pairing the stimulus of unconditioned reflexes, part of instinctual behavior, with associated stimuli. In other words, it is a

---

610 Angell, J.R.(1906) "Reflex Action and Instinct", Chapter 15 in *Psychology: An Introductory Study of the Structure and Function of Human Conscious.* Third edition, revised. New York: Henry Holt and Company: 283-293. P. 288. Online in A Mead Project Source Page. Accessed from <https://www.brocku.ca/MeadProject/Angell/Angell_1906/Angell_1906_o.html> on 2015-09-09.

transformation of the external form of governance of the response at its source. The most elementary forms of conditioning were first demonstrated in animals by Pavlov.[611] In humans there are infinitely more complex processes particularly brought about by the mediation of language, instruments, meaning, consciousness, in other words culture. Some of the reflexes that are typical of human infants disappear as they become unnecessary, or are transformed with time and maturation, although they may return with neurological damage. Conserved reflexes in adults, which are usually tested during neurological examinations, such as the knee jerk, remind us or our basic natural condition, our old philogenetic ground.

Conditioning occurs upon prior reflex behavior through time linkage, as we saw, and can be both established and extinguished experimentally. It constantly occurs, however, in real life and forms the ground for the earliest forms of learning, and also for subliminal manipulation, as in advertising, mass media and public relations. Marketing in particular resorts to regressive instinctual and emotional behavior to create artificial consumerist needs.[612]

Classical or Pavlovian conditioning is plain associative learning. After pairing the two types of stimuli the organism will respond to the conditioned stimulus with the unconditioned response. In other words, the animal's nervous system has the capacity to associate the two through a unitary response.

The capacity of, through material activity, introducing mediations between stimulus and response, is the root of all consciousness in the view of Leontiev.

---

611 Pavlov, I.P. (1927). *Conditioned Reflexes: An Investigation Of The Physiological Activity Of The Cerebral Cortex.* Trans. G. V. Anrep. Online in: Classics in the History of Psychology. An internet resource developed by Christopher D. Green. York University, Toronto, Ontario. Accessed from <http://psychclassics.yorku.ca/Pavlov/> on 2015-09-06.

612 Baddeley, A. (2002). "Conditioning and Advertising." P. 158 ff. in: *Human Memory. Theory and Practice.* Revised Edition. Hove. East Sussex. UK. Psychology Press. Taylor and Francis.

2.3.6 From Need to Sense, and Repetition: Instinct and Habit

The adaptive form of psychic reflection grows concurrently with the complexification of the animal organism, particularly the brain, in its three functional areas: sensation, motricity, and mediatory mentation. These three areas develop not in parallel but in reciprocity; each affects the others. Any development in one area affects development globally, although each maintains its own degree of autonomy and has its hegemonic moments in development. Their progression is triggered by biological need. Sensorially, a stimulus fits a specific receptor, motorically the outcome of an action is satisfaction, and mentally it all starts to "make sense" in a larger context natural and cultural.

All the necessary conditions for this process' having being fulfilled, the practical yield is a positive adaption; repetition hardwires the particular sequence of mediations in the nervous system to replace instinct with habit. Saying that the sequence started from natural necessity is equivalent to saying that it started from instinctual adaptation, because instincts are the first pre-wired adaptive modules towards the fulfillment of natural necessities. This is why instinct is an adaptive bias in the organism that nature programmed following its evolutionary strategy in order to, through growing complexification, originate higher orders in its economy. Consciousness is the most economic of operations, because it works as an abstract guide to practice with minimal morphological requirements. As regards sense, the important contribution of Leontiev is to have pointed out that, as mentation, it is not exclusive of man or higher animals, but can be traced back all the way to organic interactions based on irritability and beyond, chemical complementarity, recognition, selection, and reaction. Leontiev's sense is the first step in natural coherence, dialectical consciousness being the final stop.

The role of repetition in learning was well illustrated by Piaget, not as a mechanical phenomenon but as a form of reciprocal action that may begin randomly with reflexes, but that ultimately leads to useful adaptive temporary forms of equilibrium, eventually disrupted by new needs but epigenetically conserved. Piaget's *circular reactions* start as reflexes, sensorimotor cycles that combine with each other by chance and produce complexity through a mutual, reciprocal process of assimilation and accommodation; primary circular reactions are the first habits. Complexified reflexes here become behavioral units that continue to expand and, conserving themselves epigenetically, further psychologically complexify. This is the foundation of intelligence for Piaget based on the operation of opposites.

For these processes to occur in the higher order of the mind, the earlier ones were necessary; properties of objects had to have developed their own physical, chemical or biological senses for detecting properties of other objects in their interaction. This is most clear in animals. Spiders respond to the vibrations caused a tuning fork because, biologically, they make the same sense as those of an insect. This is a fitting response from a biased sensorial level. Vibration acquired the sense of food for the spider during its species' evolution. "The biological sense of any influence is not constant for an animal, but on the contrary varies and develops during its activity in accordance with the objective associations of the corresponding properties of the environment. The sense connections that arise in the activity of animals, it must be noted, are conditioned reflexes with a specific, and (one can even say) extraordinary character. They differ markedly from the conditioned associations that form the mechanism of behaviour itself, i.e., connection by which behaviour is realized."[613] Sense of food links arises first, and behavioral conditioned associations appear and disappear slowly and gradually with time and changing conditions. Additionally, as the particular habit for food-seeking is acquired, the subjectivized animal recognizes itself, as it were, in the object-stimulus, actively seeking it.

Operations differentiate as sensoryimotor modules, their degree of complexity characterizing the stage of development of the psy-

---

613 Leontiev A.N. (1981). "An outline of the evolution of the psyche" (pp. 156-326). *Problems of the Development of the Mind.* Trans. M. Kopylova Moscow: Progress Publishers. There is an Online Edited version by Paul F. Ballantyne, Ph. D. Accessed from <http://www.igs.net/~pballan/Leontiev1981chapt2.htm> on 2012-05-24.

che. They lay the basis for the evolution of new forms of automatization of animal experience, wired as motor habits with economic gain. Habits, through associative conditioning, are formed in animals from learning to overcome obstacles, the form of the habit's being determined by the character of the obstacle. Learned and hardwired through repetition, sensorimotor modules can then be generalized to new situations, where the reciprocal processes of assimilation and accommodation integrates them and makes them part of motor memory, automaticity.

The motor elements forming part of the habits of animals may be both innate and acquired. They become fixed in sequence or structure in the course of chance motor trial-and-errors during the formation of the given habit. Their success resides in the fulfillment of particular needs, adaptation.

More complex habits automated into habitual *operations* are observed only in animals that have a cerebral cortex. The formation and arrangement of systems of cortical conditioning is the physiological base of habits. In the brain the subcortical basal ganglia, caudate nucleus, putamen and *globus pallidus* are particularly involved with habitual behavior and automaticity.

Motor habits require a new form of representation in memory, and it is well established that animals have such representational capacity.

2.3.7 The Problem of the Origin of Sensation[614]

In Russian, language activity is defined as a coherent system of both internal mental processes linked to motivation, and concurrent external behaviors directed to achieve conscious goals.[615] This is akin to what Marx called praxis, except that the latter has the

---

614 This section is based on Leontiev's article with the same title. See below.
615 Robbins D. (2012) Unity of Vygotsky-Leontiev-Luria within Diversity: Understanding the Past to Shape the Future of Russian Activity Theory and Cultural-Historical Theory. (Unpublished Paper). Accessed from <http://faculty.ucmo.edu/drobbins/pdf/unity.pdf> on 2012-05-23.

connotation of being guided by a free consciousness, not by corrupt ideology. Praxis starts with sensation, which Hegel properly defined as what moves animals out of their complacency, meaning that sensation disturbed a previous equilibrium or stillness. Freud and the neurologists shared this view.

Leontiev surveys previous efforts to explain the beginning of sensation, from a scientific standpoint. He classified these efforts into the anthropsychism of Descartes, that sees mind as exclusive of man, the panpsychism of Robinet[616] and Fechner[617] that considers the psyche as a universal property of nature, the biopsychism of Hobbes, Haeckel[618] and Wundt that circumscribes mind to life, and Darwin and Spencer's neuropsychism that considers the psyche an exclusive property of the central nervous system.[619] This gives us an idea of the magnitude of the issue to which we can add pantheism of Spinoza, a historical form of panpsychism, the good sense of nature expressed as God.

Life is a particular complex form of reciprocal interaction between organism and environment that is nested and recursive, meaning it operates in both realms. From this external form of relationship, a process of internalization creates a next level of internal representations of its forms in consciousness. These come to determine the

---

616 Jean-Baptiste-Rene Robinet (1735-1820) was a French materialist and deist member of the Encyclopedists. He wrote *On Nature* as well as five supplementary volumes of the *Encyclopedia* of Diderot.

617 Gustav Theodor Fechner (1801-1887) was a German experimental psychologist who founded psychophysics and formulated Fechner's law, — that subjective sensation is proportional to the logarithm of the stimulus intensity.— a landmark in the emergence of psychology as an experimental science.

618 Ernst Heinrich Philipp August Haeckel (1834 – 1919) was a German biologist, naturalist, philosopher, physician, professor, and artist who discovered, described and named thousands of new species, mapped a genealogical tree relating all life forms, and coined many terms in biology. Haeckel promoted and popularized Charles Darwin's work in Germany and developed the influential but no longer widely held recapitulation theory ("ontogeny recapitulates phylogeny").

619 Leontiev, A.N. (1981). "The problem of the origin of sensation" (pp. 7-53). In Problems of the Development of the Mind. (Trans. M. Kopylova) Moscow: Progress Publishers. Online Extracts from: Paul F. Ballantyne, Ph.D. March, 4, 2005. Accessed from <http://www.igs.net/%7Epballan/Leontiev1981chapt1.htm> on 2015-09-09.

possibility of internal adaptive anticipatory states within the living organism, which constitute the essence of learning. These are outgrowths of an original protoplasmic irritability, and the subsequent levels, reflex and instinct, the result of mediations. What we immediately see as internal capacity for externally triggered sensitivity is, at a deeper glance, already functionally linked with the environment by specific receptors to that type of sensitivity. This fitting pair constitutes the primary source of mentation and consciousness.

Mind is a property of living, highly complex and organized material bodies, expressing their ability to reflect a reality that appears external but is also internal because they are part of it, not exception. This ambiguity of reflection has been made possible by evolutionary and biographic, reflexive and instinctual, mediations, specific in form to particular species. The resulting interactive processes are ingrained in internal organs and they are afferent and efferent, sensory and motor, fitted to reflect the specific necessary margin of the reality around the organisms, according to their needs and the history of their mediations. Reality exists independently but it is also a part of them, always interconnected and reciprocal, requiring a common ground for their operational opposition: only discerned stimuli trigger specific response. Any *knowledge* of the objective world through psychic phenomena is a function of a material, embodied subject, itself part of the same world. The psyche thus lies within the one and only world, particular forms of object relations, not outside it, in the second world of God, as idealist philosophers once thought.

Upon these premises, comparative psychology looks for the genesis of psychic phenomena in the material world, in previous, less developed forms of life, to trace its evolutionary development toward the peak of human consciousness. This process has no end, and it goes beyond life and even beyond the Big Bang. Starting with the most basic phenomenon, we already find an obstacle: while ascertainment of sensation is simple in a human subject that has the capacity to corroborate, it is much more difficult in previous organisms that have to be judged by their morphological changes or external behavior, not to talk about mineral chemical reactions and planets' motional orbits that are equally reciprocal and fitted to sense each other.

That is how the reciprocal action of the subjective and the objective aspects of the psyche, far from being mechanical or static, is eminently dialectical, reciprocally relational. The structure of an evolutionary relationship changes throughout the process of growth and development both phylogenetically and ontogenetically, by simultaneously enhancing their codependent opposition and relative autonomy. In this process there are transitions as well as relatively autonomous moments for each side. Subjectivity emerges from an directionally organized original protoplasm that has a particular structural organization already biased toward consciousness. The fact that the relationship subject-object is reciprocal, mutually determinative, eliminates the one-sidedness of materialist and idealist perspectives. A purely external comparison of subject and object is artificial; it neglects the profound concrete evolutionary process that naturally transforms the object into the subject. It is helpful, to throw light onto the issue of the origin of subjectivity, to start the inquiry from the conditions that engender life, keeping in mind that, as Marx pointed out, consciousness arises out of natural necessity, not by chance: language, the expression of consciousness, only arises from the dire necessity of intercourse with others.[620]

---

620 The larger quote is: "Only now, after having considered four moments, four aspects of the primary historical relationships, do we find that man also possesses "consciousness," but, even so, not inherent, not "pure" consciousness. From the start the "spirit" is afflicted with the curse of being "burdened" with matter, which here makes its appearance in the form of agitated layers of air, sounds, in short, of language. Language is as old as consciousness, language is practical consciousness that exists also for other men, and for that reason alone it really exists for me personally as well; language, like consciousness, only arises from the need, the necessity, of intercourse with other men. Where there exists a relationship, it exists for me: the animal does not enter into "relations" with anything, it does not enter into any relation at all. For the animal, its relation to others does not exist as a relation. Consciousness is, therefore, from the very beginning a social product, and remains so as long as men exist at all. Consciousness is at first, of course, merely consciousness concerning the immediate sensuous environment and consciousness of the limited connection with other persons and things outside the individual who is growing self-conscious. At the same

Subjects are organisms that operate not through energy directly derived from external sources of stimulation, such as the sun, oxygen, or aliment, but through metabolic breakdown of their own stored energy upgraded for their particular purposes. A machine in comparison, a car, an airplane, a robot, is a passive conduit of external energy, its particular form given by man; the machine only transforms energy into external motion and wear of its parts. Leontiev calls this process dissimilation of energy, to contrast with organic energy that had already been assimilated, metabolized, and stored with a purpose. Metabolic assimilation and dissimilation are the opposites of mechanical work and they give an advantage to the organism: it does not have to rely on immediate sources of external energy for its operations. Unlike a machine, through assimilation and dissimilation, internal and external work, organisms are always in constant self-renewal. Unlike the machine, if the input of energy ceases, the organism has buffering alternatives through the sacrifice of its own less crucial tissues for the sake of the most important ones, to maintain essential functions. Starved, animals may consume half of their own tissues before they die. The mediation provided by a two-way, anabolic and catabolic, process of exchange of substances in metabolism, is the most significant feature of the

time it is consciousness of nature, which first appears to men as a completely alien, all-powerful and unassailable force, with which men's relations are purely animal and by which they are overawed like beasts; it is thus a purely animal consciousness of nature (natural religion) just because nature is as yet hardly modified historically. (We see here immediately: this natural religion or this particular relation of men to nature is determined by the form of society and vice versa. Here, as everywhere, the identity of nature and man appears in such a way that the restricted relation of men to nature determines their restricted relation to one another, and their restricted relation to one another determines men's restricted relation to nature.) On the other hand, man's consciousness of the necessity of associating with the individuals around him is the beginning of the consciousness that he is living in society at all. This beginning is as animal as social life itself at this stage." Marx, K. (1968) The German Ideology. Part I: Feuerbach. Opposition of the Materialist and Idealist Outlook. Part I: Feuerbach. A. Idealism and Materialism [4. The Essence of the Materialist Conception of History. Social Being and Social Consciousness]. History: Fundamental Conditions. Marx-Engels Collected Works, Volume 5. Moscow. Progress Publishers. (Written: Fall 1845 to mid-1846). Online in Marxists Internet Archive. Accessed from <http://www.marxists.org/archive/marx/works/1845/german-ideology/ch01b.htm> on 2012-08-23.

reciprocal interaction between living, proteic bodies and the objects that provide their nutritional support. The latter are destroyed, but conserved within the subject, becoming part of its structure besides being a reserve.

Clearly the organism is an advance in evolution, a new form of dealing with destructive interaction and preservation. Inorganic bodies ceased to exist as a result of their interaction, as we saw in chemical reactions, or even in the mechanical weathering of rock by water, for example. A living organism's self-preservation is a necessary condition for its continued interacting existence. But this new form of relation, characteristic of life, does not simply discard the old one; it internalizes it. It makes it the foundation of its own metabolism that makes prior external destruction internal, and part of its self-renewal. The organism remains alive precisely because its own particles are continuously decomposing and regenerating anew; therefore the organism constantly becomes other than itself, renewed. Subjectivity is the consciousness, the parallel virtual con-servation of the object that persists. In these advanced and complex organic interactions, paradigmatically dialectic, it is a requirement of evolutionary coherence that to find usefulness in the use of its object, the subject must be appropriately designed to fit with it; in this sense, the subject is guided by the object it selects. The sub-ject must be equipped and prone to recognize or properly reflect its object, that is, to anticipatorily replicate its form. A form of pro-to-consciousness is already present in these material facts since the beginning, the Big Bang. Consciousness does not emerge finished, it is a series of presentations.

Subjectivity arises from a long evolutionary coherent process that we discover *a posteriori*. It includes simultaneous self-renewal, self-destruction, and conservation. In the coherent chain of interac-tions of objects with their changing environment, the subject is the one that conserves and remains. If the default before subjectivity was destruction, after it, it is conservation. Internalization is the pro-cess that determines subjectivity. The metabolism of other objects is reproduced internally. Eventually it requires a specialized nervous system for these blind functions to become mentation. The subject assimilatorily destroys objects by reducing them to more primitive levels of useful internal chemical interactions that it needs for its adaptation. Evolution is naturally coherent, constructive destruction, and its coherence is dialectical random teleology, based for the most part on trial and error, but having an energetic aim of best utilization toward enhancement of heterogeneity, complexity, and ultimately self-consciousness.

The self, the organ that metabolizes consciousness and self-consciousness, is the signature of the human species. It is unique in that it is the only organism-like, metabolic phenomenon in nature that has the capacity to operate with abstracted forms, images and digits only, with representations. For that purpose, it requires the infrastructure of the brain. The subject has the advantage of an evolutionary trajectory that has assimilated and conserved, epigenetically and morphologically, previous forms of historical relations. It has the consequent capacity to be able to fit into its totality new types of phenomena by assigning them to a class of similar ones. This creates conceptual syllogistic particularity, a great evolutionary advantage. Unlike animals, humans do not find their conditions of existence in raw nature but in humanly transformed nature. This essential feature is what Marx called the ensemble of the social relations, that internalized is the essence of man.[621] This is how history is objectified in the large morphological process of civilization, superimposed on evolution that is not denied but conserved in latency.

Humans transmit their reciprocally transformed subjectivity to their progeny upon a foundation exclusively laid by mothers during the earliest years. Subjectivity is spiritual activity embodied in destructible yet necessary social objects, agencies and institutions: culture. This is how each generation is involuntarily inducted, at its

---

621 Marx, K. (1938). *Theses on Feuerbach*. 6. In: The German Ideology. London. Lawrence and Wishart. (Written in 1845). Online version Marxists Internet Archive. Accessed from <http://www.marxists.org/archive/marx/works/1845/theses/index.htm> on 2012-09-09.

arrival, into the ongoing material and spiritual activity of the previous ones. The incoming generation in turn transforms both sectors, material and spiritual, for the next generation in line. Again, this recursive historical phenomenon, in its totality, is the invisible snowball called by Marx the ensemble of the social relations.

2.4 ANIMAL INTELLECT TO CONSCIOUSNESS

"But an animal only produces what it immediately needs for itself or its young. It produces one-sidedly, whilst man produces universally. It produces only under the dominion of immediate physical need, whilst man produces even when he is free from physical need and only truly produces in freedom therefrom. An animal produces only itself, whilst man reproduces the whole of nature. An animal's product belongs immediately to its physical body, whilst man freely confronts his product. An animal forms only in accordance with the standard and the need of the species to which it belongs, whilst man knows how to produce in accordance with the standard of every species, and knows how to apply everywhere the inherent standard to the object. Man therefore also forms objects in accordance with the laws of beauty."

Marx[622]

2.4.1 A New Evolutionary Necessity: Desire for Recognition

Marx is overtly optimistic about the conditions of production of man because he is speaking here about human potential, not about the conditions of production at the time he was writing that could not have been called free. The important contribution of Marx in this regard in not to try to differentiate humans from animals on the bases of consciousness, but on the bases of how they materially

---

622 Marx, K. (1959). *Economic and Philosophical Manuscripts of 1844.* Estranged Labour, XXIV. (Written: Between April and August 1844; First Published: 1932. Trans: by Martin Mulligan. Moscow. Progress Publishers.Online in MIA. Accessed from <https://www.marxists.org/archive/marx/works/1844/manuscripts/preface.htm> on 2017-03-16.

reproduce their lives and make themselves what they become. We know we cannot differentiate humans from animals even on the bases of morality.

Hegel was the first one to capture in his writings the essential need of mirroring in the achievement of subjectivity, even if he did it in a particularly patriarchal way, through competing war on each other rather than on the basic cooperative mother-child developmental relationship. In nature necessity is what jumpstarts animal activity, says Hegel in the *Phenomenology*. In its human version, necessity is evolutionarily sublimated to include an abstract form of need: desire for recognition. Animally we fight for objects; humanly we struggle for abstract recognition that we call identity. A national flag is an example of an abstract symbol the recognition of which humans collectively demand, even giving their lives for it. The recognition-seeking ego of self-consciousness is for Hegel the manifestation of the genus in the individual, of our universality.[623] This is the opposite of Freud and his mainstream followers, who saw the ego as individuality. The core difference between the psychology of Freud and that of Hegel, Marx, and Vygotsky, is that the self is not an efflorescence that emerges from the inside through effort, but rather a reciprocally constructed type of human agency, a relational operational structure. Individuality evolutionarily emerges from universality.[624] The desire for recognition drives humans to grow through constructive mother-child projective identifications that start from the original identity merger with the mother.

Natural necessities are satisfied by activity upon well-fitted, spe-

623 Hegel, G.W.F. (1807). "The Ego and Desire." In: The Phenomenology of Mind. B. Self-Consciousness (1). IV: The Truth which Conscious Certainty of Self Realises. 3. The Ego and Desire. From Harper Torchbooks' edition of the Phenomenology (1807), from University of Idaho, Department of Philosophy by Jean McIntire. Online in MIA. Accessed from <https://www.marxists.org/reference/archive/hegel/works/ph/phb.htm#3> on 2014-11-25.

624 Baldwin, J.M. (1911). *The Individual and Society or Psychology and Sociology.* CHAPTER III. Social Competition and Indi-vidualism. Boston: Richard G. Badger. Pp. 77-117. Online in the Mead Project. Brock University. Accessed from <https://brocku.ca/MeadProject/Baldwin/Baldwin_1911/Baldwin_1911_03.html> on 2017-03-10.

cific objects. In humans these at first-natural necessities evolve to become humanly produced social needs. I quote from Marx: "Man is a natural being endowed with vital powers, an active natural being. Vital forces exist in him as tendencies and abilities as instincts. A suffering, conditioned and limited creature, like animals and plants, the objects of his instincts exist outside him, independently. Yet these are objects that he needs essential objects, indispensable to the manifestation and confirmation of his essential powers. To say that man is a real and vigorous sensuous being, is to say that he needs real, sensual objects to fulfill himself, his life; he can only express his life through those objects. To be real, to have real objects, and to be a real object for a third party, is one and the same thing."[625] Marx never ceases to emphasize the compelling nature of human dependence on the fulfillment of natural necessities, the foundation of his theory of alienation. We forget that we have to first breathe and eat before we can do anything else. It is the consequent leisure provided by the fulfillment of those needs that opens the space for other material and spiritual practices.

The connection between how we humans behave and think, our psyche, and our particular form of life and culture has been the concern of philosophers before Marx. Plato, for example, in various works, brings up the important analogy between form of government and the soul. A triad of soul's virtues is analogous to three social classes.[626] King-philosophers, civil servants, and workers are

---

625 Marx, K. (1959). *Economic and Philosophic Manuscripts of 1844* Critique of Hegel's Philosophy in general. D. Absolute Knowledge *(In The Phenomenology).* Trans. Martin Mulligan. Moscow. Progress Publishers. Online in MIA. Accessed from <https://www.marxists.org/archive/marx/works/1844/manuscripts/hegel.htm> on 2015-05-23.

626 "Again, let us put it in this way. The proper functioning of the money-making class, the helpers and the guardians, each doing its own work in the state... would be justice and would render the city just." ... "Then, my friend, we shall thus expect the individual also to have these same forms in his soul, and by reason of identical affections of these with those in the city to receive properly the same appellations." The three class virtues are wisdom, courage, and temperance titrated differently according to class. Plato (1969). Republic. Plato in Twelve Volumes. Vols. 5 and 6. (434c and 435b and c). Trans. Paul Shorey. Cambridge, MA, Harvard University Press; London, William Heinemann Ltd. (Written 380 BCE). Online in Perseus. Accessed from <http://

respectively represented in the soul as wisdom, courage, and temperance. In Phaedrus' metaphor the psyche is like a chariot pulled by two winged horses, one noble and white and one ignoble and black. The charioteer's function is to manage and compromise the pulling opposites.[627] Here Plato is talking about government and self-government but also about class, upper, middle and lower.

Freud's structural theory is similar, except that Freud transforms the drama of class into the entelechies, id, superego and ego. The id is instinctual disposition, the working class, and the superego the capitalist. The ego is the go-between, the class politicians love because it provides their ideology and, if that fails, the necessary force. Elsewhere, Freud defined the ego as a man on horseback, who has to hold in check the superior strength of the animal,[628] and also as id modified by the influence of the external world.[629]

Dialectically, Freud could have seen a dual instinctual disposition, female and male, and psychic energy oppositely distributed, not all masculine. Here we can see the exclusively human psychological necessity to be achieved through mutual recognition, according to Hegel, as well as through Horney's self-realization: the needs of each individual to produce herself or himself truthfully, according to the goal of nature for the species, reciprocally balanced self-consciousness. Looking at the issue this way, we can easily see the effect of the Hegelian lack of recognition in women that occurred with the establishment of civil society. "The real self... is the alive, unique, personal center of ourselves; the only part that can, and wants to grow. We saw that unfortunate conditions prevent its unimpeded growth from the very beginning. ...our interest has been centered

www.perseus.tufts.edu/hopper/text?doc=Perseus%3Atext%3A1999.01.0168%3A-book%3D4%3Asection%3D434c> on 2015-09-14.

627 Plato. (360 B.C.E). *Phaedrus.* Trans. Benjamin Jowett. Online in The Internet Classics Archive. Accessed from <http://classics.mit.edu/Plato/phaedrus.html> on 2015-09-10.

628 Freud, S. (1923). *The ego and the id.* Standard Edition. The Psychological Works of Sigmund Freud, Ed. Trans. J. Strachey. London. Hogarth Press. 19: 1-66. P. 15

629 Freud, S. (1920). *Beyond the pleasure principle.* Standard Edition of the Psychological Works of Sigmnd Freud. Ed. Trans. J. Strachey. London. Hogarth Press. 18: 1-64.

on those forces in the individual which usurp its energies and lead to the formation of a pride system which becomes autonomous and exerts a tyrannical and destructive power."[630] Who could say this better than a woman who experienced growing in hierarchical capitalism, and what could illustrate it better than the present political structure?

2.4.2 The Opposite of Necessity is Accident

If we take into consideration the dialectic of necessity and accident, we may realize that things that happened historically may not have been necessary in the original design of the species to achieve full humanity. Opposite to necessity is accident, "Chance, or Accident is a transient, non-essential property of a thing or process, as opposed to what is essential, necessary and substantial. Denial of the objectivity of chance is called Determinism, which leads to the fatalistic view that everything is necessarily as it is and predetermined. Knowledge of the Necessity of things is the basis of all rational, conceptual thought and action. Denial of the objectivity of Necessity, the idea that historical events are the outcome of the chance occurrences and individual actions, etc., is associated with Voluntarism. For dialectics, Chance and Necessity are inextricably linked. Necessity asserts itself through the interaction of millions of accidents, while each such 'accident' is the outcome of a necessary sequence of causes."[631] This can be graphically illustrated as a curve, let's say seasonal temperature or trade graphs, that has a necessary trend behind a composite of constant accidental corrections, peaks and valleys. The graph of human history would be the same, if we look, for example, at the history from slavery to equality. To find the direction of the morality of evolution as a trend, it is necessary to go first through the accidents of human history.

Necessity creates the basic coherent bond between reciprocal

---

630 Horney, K. (1950). *Neurosis and Human Growth*. New York. Norton.Ch. 6. "Alienation from Self. P. 155-175.

631 Marxist Internet Archive. Glossary of Terms. "Chance and Necessity." Accessed from <https://www.marxists.org/glossary/terms/c/h.htm> on 2015-05-14.

objects; accident is its temporary detour from encountered obstacles. Initially in evolution, at the chemical level, necessity as we have seen, was highly destructive. At the two ends of evolution, chemical substances lose their nature to produce the new while we in contrast change our bodies constantly to keep it the same, replacing slow morphological change with intelligent operation. The subjective strategy of evolution is conservative, the subject dependently prevailing. Organisms with strong boundaries and complex organs can internalize more fragile external objects along with their chemical properties, and control them for their own survival. Subjective identification works similarly.

Internalization places objects under subjective control through internal metabolic processes. Not only are objects metabolized, but with them their form and structure that become part of the metabolizing subject. Sense and coherence grow in parallel with material complexity and heterogeneity of organisms, ultimately to become consciousness proper. As complex systems, organisms have inner subsystems of clearly boundaried organs that advance their increasingly complex adaptational capacities through division of labor and specialization. Those systems require the development of boundaries between their organs and functions, boundaries within boundaries. This is well illustrated by cells and their organelles, for example. Through complex internalization, objects produced subjects and subjectivity was born from objectivity. This process implies the growth of relational needs an their accidents.

It is inevitable that internal necessities become as compelling and rigid as external conditions, and, paradoxically, evolutionary obstacles. Ideology dependent on spurious needs, supplants consciousness, and appears equally compelling.

Consciousness subordinates sense and coherence, fitness and selection in the model of sublation. It is in fact sense that dictates the ultimate direction of consciousness behind its flows and ebbs. Ideology is ultimately confronted by critical thinking, the return to good sense. The universal process of civilization must confront its repressions, unfortunate cultural conditions. The ultimate boundaries of human consciousness are delineated by natural sense, and by natural necessity, not by accident. Bad faith and repression use the syllogism to make sense latent and produce ideology, but sense comes back to the peak in a correction. At times consciousness becomes symptomatic, encoded; this is when psychoanalytic interpretation can be useful.

It is on this ground that Karen Horney poised the concept of a morality of evolution, the fact that we humans cannot escape good sense. As long as consciousness and good sense are at odds we are outside of the boundaries of our necessary natural course: hence ecological conundrums.

The adaptational advantage of consciousness, properly synchronized with good common sense, is that it allows humans to economically achieve adaptive feats that other species of animals can only accomplish through very slow and costly morphological change. Consciousness produces economic efficiency by changing the environment through its forms, first in its imagination. Old necessities may be made latent but they will always return. Humans produce their own needs through conscious mediation that for the most part are accidental.

The notion of the anthropocene denotes the huge, accidental human effect on nature. During this period of approximately two hundred thousand years, which is incidentally when matriarchy started, we humans have gravely trespassed the coherence of nature.[632] Geologists do not take into consideration that more than ninety-five percent of that time was matriarchal, when humanity lived largely in harmony with nature. It is only during the last ten millennia at most, and particularly during accelerated capitalism, that destructive technology and wasteful accumulation have prevailed.

---

632 Steffen, W., Richardson, K., et al. (2015). *Planetary Boundaries: Guiding Human Development in a Changing Planet.* Sci-encexpress. January. Accessed from <Planetary Boundaries- Guiding human development on a changing planet- Steffen.pdf> on 2015-05-20.

We can consider learning as the incorporation of accident or chance into the sequence of reflex need-fulfillment, a contingency in which only first-order mediations may have been historically necessary. From this vantage point the corruption of the morality of evolution is the artificial creation of accidental needs for capital gain. This phenomenon is so familiar that we do not usually see it, a function of "the media." It results in the creation of artificial scarcity. Accidental capitalist second-order mediations, in turn, make ideology necessary to rationalize the false needs. Ideology reshuffles the natural syllogism inherent in the human relation by translocating individual, particular, and universal. Insecure and threatened by our own species, we are compelled to accumulate out of fear.

Life replicates itself at the molecular level following the scripts of genomic memory that have stored in them previous forms of adaptation, including their necessities and accidents. Consciousness is the equivalent of the genome with the difference that it stores, in brain morphology, the virtual forms of previous adaptations, first-order maternal and second-order paternal. The latter are not universal but class-determined and therefore particular. The human resilience, our survival in spite of ourselves, is due to the degree of good sense upon which we must capitalize to combat ideology.

In the patriarchal tradition, human science has until recently disregarded the study of growth and development that were traditionally the business of mothers. Developmental psychology, necessarily with a relational and matriarchal perspective, is thus a relative latecomer in the human sciences with Hegel, Darwin, Freud, Piaget, Marx and Vygotsky, among others.

2.4.3 Activity Become Labor

Animal activity that started with sensation and the reflex arc, a constant circle reiteratively opened by natural necessities and social needs, and closed by actions, is where A.N. Leontiev's activity psychology finds its origin. The theory is inspired by Hegel, Marx, and

Leontiev's mentor Lev Vygotsky. When the open circle of activity is mediated by a part of nature using another to modify a third, closing with a useful purpose, the satisfaction of a necessity, activity has become labor.

Through active, productive labor that requires a social agent, tools and raw materials, humans can express, extend, and transcend themselves creatively through selfobjects[633] they produce to depend on, at the same time leaving their signature in nature. Laborers see themselves objectified in their labor activity of self-expression. This is the reason unemployment is not only a material but also a spiritual problem: it denies humans the natural right to realize themselves in creative expression, in the survival project of the species. Language is already a relational tool, an instrument used to express consciousness, to plan, and to congenially penetrate nature to transform it into culture as Vygotsky sees it.[634]

Through certain activities, some of which nature coherently endowed with pleasurable contingencies, such as the satisfaction of hunger and reproductive necessities, individuals periodically re-enter the state of equilibrium disrupted by necessity. The result for the Greek philosophers varied from happiness to ataraxia. Naturally rewarded activities are instinctual and, through sensate individuals, serve the preeminent purpose of survival of the species. Upon these activities as a ground, through mediations upon them, human consciousness constructed morality.

Consciousness is a type of activity adaptively geared to satisfaction of human necessity, not in the abstract but materially. It can lead to freedom when the criteria of universality have been met. Conscious self-realization is seeing oneself realized in the realization of others, and the contingency is a moral one. It is undeniable at first hand that mothers paradigmatically have this experience with their

633 Selfobject is a term coind by Heinz Kohut to designate the dependence on the self on objects that complement it. Kohut, H.(1971), *The Analysis of the Self.* New York: International Universities Press. p. 3.
634 Vygotsky, L. (2012). *Thought and Language.* Ed., Trans. Eugenia Hanfmann, Gertrude Vakar, and Alex Kozulin. Cambridge MA. MIT Press.

children. This is the opposite of Freud's satirical penis envy. Philosophers have said that this makes subject-object identity possible, meaning the point where human representation is accurate and practical, not distorted by ideology.[635] Consciousness and good common sense synchronize again in history, returning to the morality of evolution, when the better adjusted unselfishly labor for the less advantaged, as mothers do. There we are back to the gift economy.

This is how human labor is a generalization of the first form of labor, mother's labor-and-delivery. Mother unselfishly lent her first instruments, body and mind, to the reproduction and maintenance of the species with only moral reward; but her son by enshrining individuality, detoured the species from its natural, moral path. For Hegel and Marx it would then be the personifications of labor that would be able to redeem the species. If mother objectifies herself in the selfobject child, we all become without exception mother-objects even if sons have historically, that is, accidentally, recoiled. Most of us wage-laborers, we are all producers in the raw, natural image, of mothers.

Labor modifies nature through mediation that make nature human, human's being no exception but the most privileged segment of nature. Mother's labor is the template for all subsequent labor. Through labor humanity's powers and capacities are made manifest. Through labor humanity advances itself materially and spiritually, humanizing a nature that wants to be morally humanized. Nature wants to see itself, its altruism, in humans, just as the mother sees herself in her child. Marx endorses and develops the Hegelian principle of human objectification not as alienation, but as the enhancement of nature. This vision Marx considered the deepest part of our unconscious in the sense that it is the most repressed. This is the reason he dedicated his life to the study of the most unconscious, alienated part of our culture, our human bond not objectified but reified, turned capital.

Vygotsky wrote that a tool is to man what adaptation is to other

635 Meszaros, I. (1995). Beyond Capital. New York. Monthly Review Press. P. 347 ff.

species. He considered language and consciousness, to be tools the same as sensations leading to motions that were preliminary adaptations.[636] Necessity remains the compelling lawfulness of nature that requires adaptation and tool, and sets limits to freedom.

In this light, we can say that productive labor preceded humans in sexuated, particularly mammalian, species, but animal labor is limited to the production and reproduction of individuals of their species. Human labor is the reproduction of reproduction.

2.4.4 Leontiev's Developmental Anatomy of Activity

Shifting in full to a historical, developmental, and epigenetic perspective is a major epistemological contribution of the historic-cultural-instrumental school of psychology. In this basic new approach to human science Freud and Piaget, among others, had already made attempts similar to Vygotsky's: Freud's use of the body as the ground of psychology, and Piaget's beginning with the reflex.

Human activity, originally focused on external objects, becomes internalized, as a driven complex system with its own structure, internal relationships. [637]With the brain development, it necessarily grows engaged with an environment that is growingly hybrid, always natural but more and more historical. Kant had already introduced the notion of a mind active in constructing its representation of reality as the marker of humanity. Fichte had located this activity in the *I*. The seminal materialist contribution of Marx here is to point out that Kant and Fichte's abstract activity could not have emerged from nowhere; it had to concretely have started from material labor. As we have seen, that labor is originally the mother's.

In psychology, Vygotsky picked up and followed the thread of Marx. He deciphered culture and symbolism as working tools and

---

636 Lloyd, P. and Fernyhough, Ch. (1999). *Lev Vygotsky: Critical Assessments,* Volume 1. Ibid. P. 59.
637 Leontiev, A.N. (1979). "The problem of activity in psychology." In J.V. Wertsch (Ed.). The concept of activity in Soviet psychology. (pp. 37-71). Armonk, NY: Sharpe. (p. 46)

objectifications of man, language (that is first external but becomes internalized) becomes the cardinal instrument binding the species. Vygotsky also emphasized the distinction between universal meaning and individual sense: in the use of language, the same distinction Freud made in *The Interpretation of Dreams* when he parsed idiosyncratic from conventional meaning in dreams. The gap between consciousness and sense is in this duality that has to constantly be negotiated dialectically. The person internalizes culture as consciousness, but her or his drive must be constantly measured and checked in the context of ideology in class society. This process is somewhat similar to Piaget's assimilation and accommodation processes in intelligence, because the individual not only yields to culture but s/he can also transform it. His disciples Leontiev and Luria picked up and further developed Vygotsky's developmental ideas.[638]

Protoplasmic *irritability,* being the first form of internally driven activity needs a trigger, an event external to it. It also requires the possibility of a distinctive gap before a motor or secretory response. In its most archaic form, an irritable protoplasm selectively responds to properties of objects upon which it directly depends. The amoeba for example engulfs bacterial food and the Venus Flytrap encloses its insect. Irritability is the first manifestation of the S-R, and its gap, expressed by the hyphen, is the space where mediations will be evolutionarily introduced to gradually arrive at consciousness from sense.

In more complex *sensation*, the next notch up, activity depends not directly upon properties or qualities of objects, but upon an already mediated relationship. A plant responds to sunlight not directly but with the additional purpose of using it in metabolic reactions. The environmental influence unchains in the plant internal reactions: the stimulus becomes a signal or trigger. A signal is a conditioned stimulus that triggers the fulfillment of a necessity.

---

638 Shames, C. (1989). "Activity Theory: A Marxist Approach to Psychology." Science and Nature, Nos. 9/10, 1989, pp. 54-64. Accessed from <http://www.autodidactproject.org/other/sn-9-10-activity.html> on 2013-08-29.

Ivan Sechenov, the founder of physiology, had already proposed that sensation in humans becomes cause, then purpose, while motion becomes effect. Purpose is a qualitative transformation that transcends physiology and already places us in the field of psychology.[639] Freud had to reluctantly partake of the same journey. He had to shift from neurophysiology to psychoanalysis under the influence of his friend Breuer.[640]

After sensation comes *perception*, sensation mediated, at a distance. The nervous system has developed the capacity to form images, as well as the dimensions of learning and memory. Correspondingly *motor responses* or *actions* have also developed into more complex *operations*. There is more room for flexible variation according to conditions as well as for generalization and better discrimination of objects. Habitual, learned behavior, is now possible.

In the next stage, *animal intelligence*, problems can be solved in two steps that now may involve instruments. Complex actions mediate or are preliminary to other complex actions, all with the same purpose. *Understanding* now involves complex relations of properties of *whole objects*. A monkey 1) climbs on a box and 2) simultaneously uses a stick to reach the banana.[641] Coherent actions are organized by a single purpose. They are also discriminatingly generalizable to other situations.

Motive or purpose arises from the fit of need and object. *Human consciousness*, unlike that of the chimp, does not remain bound to

639 Lloyd, P. and Fernyhough, Ch. (1999). *Lev Vygotsky: Critical Assessments,* Volume 1. P. 58. London and New York. Routledge.

640 Breuer, J., and Freud, S. (2006). *Studies On Hysteria.* Translated from the German and edited by James Strachey In collaboration with Anna Freud Assisted by Alix Strachey and Alan Tyson. New York. Basic Books, Inc. Publishers. Online in Internet Archive. Accessed from <https://ia801406.us.archive.org/2/items/studiesonhysteri037649mbp/studiesonhysteri037649mbp.pdf> on 2017-03-20

641 Wolfgang Kohler (1887 – 1967) made chimps face a variety of problems regarding obtaining food that was not directly acces-sible. Food was put on the other side of a barrier that dogs and cats in previous experiments had been unable to circumvent. The chimps, however, presented with the same situation, immediately started to explore circuitous routes to the food. See Köhler, W. (1956). The mentality of apes. London: Routledge and K. Paul. (translated from the 2nd revised edition by Ella Winter).

the perceptual environment. It can abstract, detach, and operate formally.

2.4.5 Historical Precedents

Instinct consists of conserved packages of previous forms of activity adaptationally developed by repetition, then slowly transcribed in the genomic memory. Behavioral sequences are preprogrammed to be adaptively triggered by specific environmental cues. If the triggering environment changes, instincts must reciprocally change and vice versa. This largely happens through mediation, the incorporation of readiness for accidents into what was previously considered readiness for expected sequences of necessity. Learning modifies instinct.[642] Instincts are considered exclusively the property of animals, but plants often exhibit the same patterns. Darwin postulated the ascending hierarchy reflex-instinct-intelligence but did not emphasize their evolutionary continuity and rather recused himself on the matter.[643] It was his disciple George Romanes who emphasized the epigenetic continuity.

Romanes' goal was to do for psychology what Darwin had done for biology, to map evolution and continuity. Before Leontiev, Romanes had started his evolutionary schema from the protoplasmic quality of *excitability*, Leontiev's irritability. He saw psychic evolution as ascending along three developmental lines: emotion, will, and intelligence.

These three parallel developments for Romanes took place through the natural substratum organized in the following sequence:

---

642 Tolman, C.W. (1987). "The Comparative Psychology of A.N. Leontiev, U.S.S.R." In E. Tobach (Ed.). Historical Perspectives and the International Status of Comparative Psychology (pp. 203-209). Hillsdale: LEA. Online in MIA. Accessed from <http://www.marxists.org/archive/leontev/comment/tolman.htm> on 2013-10-04.

643 Tolman, C.W. (1987). "Theories of mental evolution in comparative psychology: Darwin to Watson." In E. Tobach (Ed.). Historical Perspectives and the International Status of Comparative Psychology (pp. 15-23). Hillsdale: LEA. Online in York Uni-versity (pballan@comnet.ca). Accessed from <http://www.igs.net/~pballan/Mentevol.htm> on 2013-08-30.

1) protoplasm, 2) nervous system, 3) discrimination of pleasure-pain, 4) capacity of conservation as memory, 5) organization of primary instincts, 6) association by physical contiguity, 7) recognition of off-spring as self-same and development of secondary instincts, 8) association by formal similarity, 9) capacity to operate through reason, 10) human recognition of persons with rights, 11) communication of ideas, 12) recognition of pictures (imagination), 13) understanding symbols and words, 14) reporting dreams, 15) understanding operational mechanisms, 16) using tools, and, 17) morality. This sequence, for Romanes, applies both phylogenetically and ontogenetically, to species going through the ascending steps in the same fashion the developing child does.[644] Whatever shortcomings in the detail, the general evolutionary trend is well-delineated in terms of growing complexity. It traces back consciousness to a proteic property, and morality ultimately stemming from what Darwin called altruism, the maternal instinct.

The more difficult question to be worked out is how those transitions take place, and how they are all conserved, sublated, in evolution. Darwin, like Romanes, would argue that they originate in necessary adaptations to the environment. Subsequently, Mendel independently discovered the mechanics of their transcription, conservation, transmission and mutation.[645] On the other hand Engels proposed that dialectical jumps, sudden changes, in quality, accrue from accumulated quantitative change as in boiling water or ice.[646]

Darwin argues that there is no qualitative difference between man and animals as far as particular mental faculties is concerned,

644 Romanes, J.H. (1888). *Mental Evolution in Animals.* London. Kegan-Paul, Trench & Co. Online in Internet Archive. Accessed from <http://archive.org/stream/cihm_16907#page/n11/mode/2up> on 2013-08-30.

645 Mendel, G. (1865). Experiments in Plant Hybridization. Read at the February 8th, and March 8th, meetings of the Brünn Natural History Society. Trans. W. Bateson. Online in Electronic Scholarly Publishing Project. Accessed from <http://www.esp.org/foundations/genetics/classical/gm-65.pdf> on 2013-08-31.

646 Engels, F. (1998). Dialectics of Nature. II. Dialectics. Online in the Marxists Internet Archive. (Orig. Publ. 1925). Accessed from <http://www.marxists.org/archive/marx/works/1883/don/ch02.htm> on 2012-09-29.

the difference being only quantitative. He starts from the simple premise that since man and animals operate through the same senses, their intuitions must also be the same. This is true for instincts such as self-preservation, sexual love, the love of the mother for her new offspring, the predisposition of the infant to suck, and so on. Darwin then challenges the prevailing view of the inverse relationship between instinct and intelligence. He ponders the effect of will on instinct, and the possible Lamarckian transformation of intelligent actions into inheritable instinctual behavior. Most important, he disputes the general assumptions that go with previous creationism.

Darwin endorsed Herbert Spencer's notion that intelligence probably originated in simple reflex actions delayed,[647] a view that Pavlov, Piaget and Freud would also later endorse. Spencer contributed significantly, not only to the divulgation of evolutionary theory, but with his own philosophical foundations for it and its extension to phenomena other than biological, particularly his principle of the journey of all evolution from incoherent homogeneity to coherent heterogeneity, at first glance a paradox. This is for him the most fundamental principle of evolution.[648]

Darwin sees some degree of overlapping and reversion between instinct and intelligence combined with a certain degree of mutual interference. For him this implies that there must be parallel inherited modifications in the human brain. Through the development of complex interconnections, the brain inhibits some areas from responding instinctively to stimulations, creating intelligent pathways as mediations in their place. In this regard not far from Freud's *Psychology for Neurologists,* Darwin observes that persons of limited intelligence tend to react in more impulsive and stereotyped manners. On the other hand, habit for Darwin, through its reiteration and

---

647 Spencer, H. (1855). *The Principles of Psychology.* London. Longman, Brown, Green and Longmans. Online in The Online Library of Liberty. Accessed from <http://oll.libertyfund.org/?option=com_staticxt&staticfile=show.php%3Ftitle=1394> on 2013-08-30.

648 Spencer, H. (1867). First Principles. 2nd ed. Chapter XVI.: The Law Of Evolution Continued. § 128. London: Williams and Norgate. Accessed from <http://oll.libertyfund.org/titles/1390> on 2015-04-12.

summation, does modify and strengthen natural instincts.

Spencer, Darwin, Romanes and Marx are the precursors of Leontiev's psychology of activity. Around the theory of instinct also converged Freud, who defined drive as "a measure of the demand made upon the mind for work,"[649] activity that he saw as requiring energy. Marx similarly placed the herd instinct at the foundation of social consciousness,[650] a notion still in need of development. Instinct is definitely inserted as an important step in the natural history of consciousness.

2.4.6 About Contingency

Contingency is chance or accident that as we have seen, can become integrated as a new type of necessity in the learning process. This is what happens with the historical creation of needs, and the classical example is the experiments of Pavlov with his dogs in the laboratory. Upon a natural reflex, salivation in response to the perception of food, an incidental, simultaneous sound is contingently connected and then made equally operational. When the dog salivates in response to the sound, we then say that the dog has learned; it *anticipates* the image of food. This is how animals are trained, and also how our human education begins, the mother's being the first educator.

From a necessary mediation that was natural, we derived an artificial contingent mediation, a contingency learned by time simultaneity. This elementary process of connection between the necessary and the contingent is the foundation of all learning.

---

649 Freud, S. (2000). *Three Essays on the Theory of Sexuality.* P. 34. Trans. James Strachey. New York. Basic Books. Place of publication: New York. (Orig. Pub. 1905). Online in Questia. Accessed from <http://www.questia.com/read/8909177/three-essays-on-the-theory-of-sexuality> on 2013-08-31.

650 Marx, K, and Engels, F (1968) The German Ideology. I. Feuerbach: Opposition of the Materialist and Idealist Outlooks. A. Ide-alism and Materialism. History: Fundamental Conditions. Marx-Engels Collected Works, Volume 5. Moscow. Progress Publishers. (Written: Fall 1845 to mid-1846). Accessed from <http://www.marxists.org/archive/marx/works/1845/german-ideology/ch01b.htm> on 2012-05-20.

In evolution, life produced consciousness through mediation of instinct, a fact Freud,[651] as much as Pavlov, Darwin, and Marx, deserves full credit for independently discerning in his theory. Nietzsche pointing out our humiliating subordination to nature,[652] Groddeck saying that "we are lived,"[653] and Comte proposing that we are "governed by the dead,"[654] offer different perspectives that, connected, lead to a theory of consciousness. Their common denominator is in the fact that they agree our past forged our present. That huge evolutionary past consists ultimately in natural coherence leading to animal instinct then mediated by innumerable historical contingencies.

In his materialism Feuerbach went only halfway toward recognizing anthropology in the mediations of theology,[655] but Marx added that human conscious life remains always biologically rooted.[656] We have seen that life became consciousness long before it produced humans. But human consciousness cannot produce life.

We are paradoxically victims of our natural endowment, the ability to place accidental mediations upon our good sense. Human alienation is the ability to ideologically manipulate conscious facts

651 Freud, S. (1927). *The Ego and the ID.* Trans. Joan Riviere. London. Hogarth Press; Institute of Psycho-Analysis. Online in Questia. Accessed from <https://www.questia.com/read/72395649/the-ego-and-the-id> on 2014-11-24.

652 Nietzsche. F. *On the Genealogy of Morals. A Polemical Tract.* Trans. Ian Johnston. Accessed from <http://home.sandiego.edu/~janderso/360/genealogytofc.htm> on 2015-05-24.

653 Laplanche, J., and Pontalis, J.B. (1973). *The Language of Psychoanalysis.* New York. Norton. Online in the Internet Archive. Accessed from <https://archive.org/details/TheLanguageOfPsychoanalysis> on 2014-11-24.

654 Comte, A. (1875). *System of Positive Polity.* Ch. 7, "Limits of Social Variation. London. Longsmans, Gree, and Co. P. 381. Google Free eBook. Accessed from <https://books.google.com/books?id=SQ3TAAAAMAAJ&pg=PA381&lpg=PA381&dq=where+did+comte+say+that+the+dead+govern&source=bl&ots=heu8PsPdpv&sig=ljIE7YF9hL3W8KaXOcb_SXYqwpA&hl=en&sa=X&ei=jAVjVfjlKovXsAWWzILABQ&ved=0CFMQ6AEwCQ#v=onepage&q=where%20did%20comte%20say%20that%20the%20dead%20govern&f=false> on 2015-05-24.

655 Fine, R. (2001). *Political Investigations: Hegel, Marx and Arendt.* P. 78. London. Routledge.

656 Warminski, A. (1995). "Hegel/Marx: Consciousness and Life." Pp. 118-141. Yale French Studies. No. 88.

and truths corrupting consciousness. Ideology is the result, the tendentious interpretation of facts in the interest of a social class.[657] Universal consciousness is the only antidote.

2.4.7 The Construction of Object, Subject and Relation: Reflection and Habit[658]

We have seen that sensations better equip organisms for a wider adaptive range as compared to mere sensibility. Better discriminatory capacity results particularly when sensations of different organs are bundled together to represent full objects. Evolutionarily sensitivity enhances the object, on its way to becoming a subject. The subject is characterized by discriminatory capacity and choice. This is possible thanks to the evolution of the reflecting capacity of the nervous system.

The emerging subject continues to be in part governed by the properties of its sensed object. Its form reciprocally depends on it, indicating that there was anticipation in their having been made to fit each other. Reflection of whole objects through more complex perception, the assembly of their properties through integrated sensations. This requires further development of the nervous system. Along with discriminating power, motor power must also increase in complexity.

The discriminatory capacity of consciousness resides in its appropriation of forms, internalized images of whole objects. It includes their context, boundaries, properties, and conditions. This degree of complexity is what allows for *operations*, the non-conscious, automatic aspect of actions that are at the root of *habits*. Through habitual repetition, conscious actions become automatic operations.

---

657 Meszaros. I. (1995). *Beyond Capital. Towards a Theory of Transition.* New York. Edition Published by Monthly Review Press. Ch. 5.

658 Tolman, C.W. (1987). The comparative psychology of A.N. Leontiev -U.S.S.R. In E. Tobach (Ed.). Historical Perspectives and the International Status of Comparative Psychology (pp. 203-209). Hillsdale: LEA. Accessed from <http://www.igs.net/%7Epballan/Leontiev.htm> on 2012-05-23.

At the sensorial stage activity is stereotypical, unable to solve new problems or old problems under different conditions; the corresponding behavior is instinctual. At the perceptual stage, the animal has developed a wider repertoire of simple operations called habits. Habits are more complex and plastic than instincts, making it possible for an activity to be transferred from its original context and tested in a new situation, generalized. Consciousness conserves the previous capacities and in humans can perceive itself.

2.4.8 Memory and the Unconscious

A parallel development is necessarily that of memory, the capacity to store images of objects and events to operate with in practice. Memory helps generalization, classification, as well as recollection and comparison of prior experience. The subject-object relationship of reflection becomes more dynamic. The subject becomes more complex as activity growingly organizes around more detailed and differentiated information about object, properties and context. But subject and object change, reciprocally transformed by their interactions. The resulting direction in the evolutionary process is not only toward subjectivity but also improved objectivity. Objectivity becomes the degree of perceptual and cognitive congruity, a closer identity of image and object, a more accurate representation. Subjective truthfulness includes the synchronicity of consciousness and intuitive sense that form morality. In this process memory contributes, consciously or unconsciously, the background of unique prior experience.

Memory becomes the hallmark of learning and anticipation. Our understanding of memory has significantly advanced recently. There are two broad categories of memory according to neuroscientists, *declarative* and *nondeclarative*.[659] The first is the most familiar, because of its specific conscious component. Nondeclarative memory

---

659 Squire, L.D, (1994). "Declarative and Non-declarative Memory." In: Schachter, D.L. and Tulving, E. (1994). Memory Systems 1994, Cambridge, MA. MIT Press. Pp. 233-268.

includes the types of memory systems that do not have a conscious component but do have an unconscious impact on behavior. These include memory of skills and habits, of associative or conditioned learning, of sensitization, *etc.* Nondeclarative memory is more involved with automatic know-how. Contrary to what we used to think, memory is not localized just in one part of the brain, the hippocampus, but is distributed to a number of different areas.

Artificial intelligence and computer science have contributed to the lexicon of memory besides psychology. There is in terms of time short-term, and long term memory, in terms of consciousness implicit and explicit, in terms of form of operation procedural, episodic, or semantic,[660] besides the well-known random access RAM and read-only ROM. This gives an idea of how complex the field of memory has become.

The unconscious of Freud[661] seems to fit into the category of implicit memory, although the notion of such an unconscious structure within consciousness has been challenged by J.P. Sartre on philosophical grounds.[662] Unconscious memories of pathological significance, according to Freud were dynamically repressed and they were strongly linked to instincts. Learned repression, initially parental and subsequently self-imposed, causes the observable phenomenon of silence from which Freud inferred *the unconscious*. The unconscious was first a noun, a topography; but in the structural theory it became an adjective, a property. Silence is the loss of transcendence, according to Simone the Beauvoir[663] for whom silence does

660 See for example <http://www.human-memory.net/types.html> accessed on 2015-05-22.

661 Freud, S. (1900). *The Interpretation of Dreams.* F. The Unconscious and Consciousness -Reality. Pp. 1036ss. Online in: Freud Complete Works. Ivan Smith. 2000, 2007, 2010. Accessed from <https://www.valas.fr/IMG/pdf/Freud_Complete_Works.pdf> on 2017-03-21.

662 Sartre, J.P. (1956). *Being and Nothingness. A phenomenological essay on ontology.* Trans. Hazel E. Barnes. New York. Philo-sophical Library. Online in Dominican House of Studies, Priory of the Immaculate Conception. Accessed from <http://www.dhspriory.org/kenny/PhilTexts/Sartre/BeingAndNothingness.pdf> 0n 2014-11-06.

663 De Beauvoir, S. (1972). *The Second Sex. Ch. 2.* Psychology. Trans. by H M Parshley, London. Penguin. (Orig. Pub. 1949). Online in MIA. Accessed from <https://www.

not abolish immanence, the heart of consciousness. The notions of immanence and implicit memory allow for a better understanding of the operation of ideology, the result of the repression of consciousness. Perhaps it is better to say that the unconscious is what is not perceived in the subject's act of *selective perception,*[664] the signals of which are however perceived by an interlocutor.[665] Freud's classification of conscious preconscious, and unconscious is still a useful tool in dealing with memory in clinical practice, although it must be seen from a different perspective, relational.

2.4.9 Animal intellect

The next stage of the evolution of the psyche arises again from the accruing development of complex characteristics. Here the problem-solving behavior of Kohler's[666] experimental apes provides the paradigm. Apes have the ability to solve *two-phase tasks.* This is a more complex form of what we saw in chlorophyll as mediation of sunlight for plant nutrition. The ape, first, picks up a stick or climbs a box, to, second, obtain food. Activity is organized around food, but it now incorporates an action with a goal not directly related to the food, instrumentation. The animal's activity is governed not only by the properties or by the objects, as it was before, but also by the instrumental relations among objects.

With this step, the middle level of the structure of activity emerges. It is now a complex of distinct actions organized around a motive

marxists.org/reference/subject/ethics/de-beauvoir/2nd-sex/> on 2015-07-23

664 Fuchs, T. (2012). "Body Memory and the Unconscious." Phaenomenologica, Vol. 199, 2012, pp. 69-82. Accessed from <http://www.klinikum.uni-heidelberg.de/fileadmin/zpm/psychatrie/fuchs/Body_memory_Unconsious.pdf> on 2015-05-22.

665 Lacan, J. (1968). *The Language of the Self. The Function of Language in Psychoanalysis.* Trans. Anthony Wilden. Baltimore, MD. The John Hopkins University Press.

666 Wolfgang Kohler (1887 – 1967) made chimps face a variety of problems regarding obtaining food that was not directly acces-sible. Food was put on the other side of a barrier that dogs and cats in previous experiments had been unable to circumvent. The chimps, however, presented with the same situation, immediately started to explore circuitous routes to the food. See Köhler, W. (1956). *The mentality of apes.* London: Routledge and K. Paul. (translated from the 2nd revised edition by Ella Winter).

and subject to variations of operations depending on conditions but firmly directed at specific goals. Actions attain a degree of autonomy from their objects and their context allow them to detach from one situation, object or activity, and apply to another as generalization. This can be seen by placing these animals in new problematic situations; instead of randomly moving about to express motor readiness, as a chicken does when exposed to inaccessible grains of corn, apes experiment with different approaches formally geared to the solution of the specific problem. These approaches have been gathered and conserved from prior experience, and are detachable from them.

It is obvious that, with the evolution of the capacity to reflect relations, including instrumental ones, among objects, the subject is not only increasing its scope of reality and context understanding; it is also increasing its power to deal with it. This is happening abstractly, with a degree of detachment from the immediacy of perceptual environment and conditions. Here we find the foundation for human thought. Comparatively the apes remained substantially bound to the immediacy of their perceptions while humans problem-solve thinking.

The most highly organized mammals rise to the higher level of mental evolution, animal intellect. Reflecting objects and their relations makes possible discriminatory social relations. The animal stage has also been called *manual thinking* because it is still hybrid.[667]

A first feature of this form of intellectual activity is that solutions to problems are not found randomly, through trial and error, but through selected anticipatory operations. A second feature is that, having solved a problem once, animals are able to solve similar problems without preliminary trials, indicating the use of memory. When the circumstances are similar a solution once applied is easily

---

667 Based on Leontiev A.N. (1981). "An outline of the evolution of the psyche" (pp. 156-326). Problems of the Development of the Mind. Trans. M. Kopylova Moscow: Progress Publishers. There is an Online Edited version by Paul F. Ballantyne, Ph. D. Accessed from <http://www.igs.net/~pballan/Leontiev1981chapt2.htm> on 2012-05-24.

retrievable from memory. Solutions are transferred selectively only to similar situations, indicating a capacity to classify. At least two different operations are linked in the solution of a problem, such as fetching a short stick to bring a larger one closer to solve a problem, a two-phase task.

Köhler and his followers consider the solving of two-phase problems to be a composite of two steps: first the animal's "insight," and second the transfer of a solution from an earlier repertoire. Köhler explained insight as the faculty to correlate different objects through perceiving them as part of a single integral situation that he called *gestalt*, a new ontological boundary of perception. This is the operational scope of anticipation. Leontiev rejects the gestalt principle and sees insight not as wider perception but as a preparation, an anticipatory phase itself, preliminary and not directly related to the biological goal, but governed by the second phase, the motor realization phase. This new preliminary phase, anticipatory insight, is for him what characterizes the *origin of intelligence*. The animal now can solve a problem in various ways, independent of problem form.

The generalization involved in these two-task operations now includes, besides the principle of similarity of things, that of obstacles, and of situational relations. The animal is now generalizing not only the perceptual relations but also the situational connections between things and its motor capacity. These generalizations come up during the activity itself, not separately. The preparatory activity elicited by the object of biological interest leads the psychic understanding of the animal. Animal activity always leads understanding, and is for Leontiev a material explanation without need of gestaltist presuppositions.

The new infrastructure that distinguishes the brain of higher mammals is the cortex of the frontal lobe of the brain, developed through further differentiation of its prefrontal fields, and intellectual behavior proper to higher mammals is the upper limit of the evolution of the animal psyche before man.

The psyche is always the shadow of activity. It lags behind, although with its paradoxical capacity to anticipate. Activity and conscious reflection have a reciprocal effect. If new forms of activity create disparities, the result is a new form of reflection and so on. This is a dialectical process of spiral movement.

2.5 HUMAN CONSCIOUSNESS

"The spider makes operations resembling the operations of the weaver, and the bee creating its waxen cells disgraces some architects. But from the very beginning, the worst architect differs from the best bee in that before building the cell of wax, he already has built it in his head. The result, which is received at the end of the process of work, already exists in the beginning of this process in an ideal form in a representation of a person. The person does not only change the form given by nature, but in what is given by nature he, at the same time, realizes his conscious purpose, which as a law determines the way and character of his actions and to which he must subordinate his will."

Marx[668]

2.5.1 Humans' New Consciousness

The last stage of the evolution of psyche for Leontiev is the stage of human consciousness, based on the capacity to abstract, and to operate with mediated abstractions rather than with immediate objects. In the progressive order of the contributory governance of activity by objects, we have started from properties, moved to objects, then to relations, but now we have all combined in meanings; how it is that things make sense, or better yet, how it is that we make

---

668 Marx, K (1887). *Capital.* Volume One. Part III: The Production of Absolute Surplus-Value. Chapter Seven: The Labour-Process and the Process of Producing Surplus-Value. Section 1. The labour-process or the production of use-values. First english edition. Trans: Samuel Moore and Edward Aveling, edited by Frederick Engels. Moscow. Progress Publishers. (Orig. Pub. 1867). Online in MIA. Accessed from <http://www.marxists.org/archive/marx/works/1867-c1/ch07.htm> on 2014-08-18.

sense of things. Making sense is applying value judgments to relations. Besides memory and habit, other well-differentiated cognitive functions enter into play in full, along with an extreme complexification, through redundant connectivity, of the cerebral cortex and the different parts of the central nervous system.

Alexander Luria, another member of the cultural-historical-instrumental school, in parallel shifted the attention of neurology from the search for localization of functions to that of the connections between systemic ensembles. "The idea of the nervous system as a most complicated system, of a series of separate apparatuses, acting, thanks to very delicate and changeable connections, in a manner comparable to the telephone system, was considered the basic theory of nervous activity almost from the very first. But in the second half of the nineteenth century it appeared that we had already reached the limit of understanding the secret of this complicated machine."[669] Luria moved from Pavlovian conceptions of excitation and inhibition to the necessarily more complex ones of organization and disorganization of connected systems, with the cortex, and particularly language, having the main regulating function in the process as a whole.[670]

The evolutionary advance in humans is best illustrated for Leontiev in collective labor -the ability of large groups of subjects to coordinate and exquisitely fine-tune their modes of producing their lives collectively, individually apportioning their divided social labor with an ultimate and distant common goal in mind. Here human actions are socially articulated in such a way that the actions of each individual complement the entire series of actions of the others. This happens historically, leading toward a final grand symphony we call culture and, all cultures interconnected, building the process of civilization. This entails the conservation of all previous forms of activi-

---

669 Luria, A.R. (1932). *The Nature of Human Conflict or Emotion, Conflict and Will.* An Objective Study of Disorganization and Control. Trans. Horsley Gantt. New York. Grove Press, Inc. P. 4. Online in MIA. Accessed from <https://www.marxists.org/archive/luria/works/1932/nature-conflicts/luria-conflicts.pdf> on 2015-05-31.
670 Luria, A.R. (1932). *The Nature of Human Conflict or Emotion.* Ibid. P. 7.

ty renovated by each generation in many diverse cultures, as a single process called *history*.

Component micro-actions are the contribution of individuals through the division of labor, and give a particular historical form to the unity that we call *mode of production*, capitalism. In its present form, the integration of social actions allows for the constant improvement of not only material but also enhanced spiritual tools and technological advancements.

With the development of this complex type of human production that is simultaneously self-production, operating reciprocally as cause and effect, comes *subjective consciousness*. This means moving from the realm of nature into the new one of human society, and being able to partially overstep the compellingness of natural selection and natural necessity, transform them into latency, and substitute them in part by human choice through the creation of mediatory needs as immediate alternative to natural necessities. The intersubjective introduction of a new level of reciprocal action, meaningful and implemented through speech activity that creates human consciousness, brings the ability to collectively and consensually "make" sense.

It is here that the metaphorical snake, Ouroboros, bites its tail, where the end can apprehend its beginning and the beginning its end. Evolution can make sense of its beginning in the chemical reaction, its shift from destructive chemistry to constructive life, and its trajectory from sense to consciousness, from natural coercion to human freedom, from randomness to morality.

The analytic division of activity into individual parts, followed by its social reintegration into a mediated, universal synthesis, presupposes that each subject can, in reciprocity with all the others, apprehend the nature of the relationship between divisive abstraction, particularity, and synthetic concreteness toward totality. This in turn requires a universal anticipatory understanding of the sources, motives, aims, and objectives of mediation. Meaningful relationships are no longer exclusively natural; they have reached a new qualitative stage: sociality.

For every human to meaningfully participate in a partial but co-ordinated function within the huge collective activity of the species, humanity requires that all individual actions be understood in the context of distant multilayered mediations of all others. This complex of relations must be reflectively apprehended and conserved by each subject. Each individual must realize the full *sense* of his actions. "Personal sense is a pre-logical function referring to the individual's reflection of those general meanings of the objective world, which are principally acquired during social learning/acculturation. In the process of social learning, individuals acquire not only the meanings of different artifacts, situations *etc.*, but also emotional evaluations of situations. Personal sense is the realization of meaning in a subject's life activity, in relation to their needs and motives. Personal sense determines the significance of any situation for the individual, and as such is closely connected with both their general and situation-specific motivation."[671] Consciousness of the sense of an action comes from the reflection of its object as a conscious goal, of its motive and intention, in its larger context. Sense is the individual cog of meaning that produces collective consciousness. And in this sense consciousness can only rest upon the ensemble of the social relations.

The dialectical syllogistic grammar of sense and consciousness is individuality, and universality mediated by their cultural particularity. In class society that has historically become universal individuality and universality have become antagonistic, the syllogism adapted to class' becoming ideology. The split has made ideologies as irreconcilable as classes are. The result is forms of consciousness that are not universal, but perspectival, corrupted forms of antagonistic consciousness. To the degree that consciousness is not universal it is ideology. Ideology will reign supreme as long as there are social groups with interests other than those of the species. Con-

671 Harris, S.R. (2007). A Glossary of Terms in Activity Theory. Accessed from <http://www.coedglas.org.uk/PDFs/AT_Glossary2007.pdf> on 2012-05-24.

sciousness, being by nature universal and dialectically consensual, is reduced to ideological particularities by social class. This is best observed in the political narrative.

The end of ideology and the consequent re-integration of consciousness to make sense of reality will not mean the end of the dialectic of society. It would be the return to the natural struggle of man with nature made conscious. The history the species has been making so far has been unconscious since the time when one instinctual disposition, feminine, was repressed leaving the other, masculine, un-dialectically unconstrained, like a vehicle with accelerator but no brakes.

2.5.2 Conditions for the Emergence of Human Consciousness

Human consciousness has conserved all the properties of animal consciousness and has built upon them. It can arrive at conscious judgments of value based on precedents forged by past generations of human experience. It can plan, anticipate and operate accordingly, based on relations as abstract as the relations between mathematics and logic. Those relations are sociohistorical and can be very far apart both in time and space from the immediacy of natural relations, thus acquiring an appearance of autonomy.

As we have seen, human consciousness is grounded in the unique form of very complex activity of humans that is divided labor, that connects all the ingredients of perception, conserved memory of prior generational experience, the consequent capacity to anticipate, and reason. The corollary of these complex connections in the social individual is the production of culture, of history, and of the self, all produced collectively. The instrument hand could only attain its instrumental perfection, and its privileged turf in the sensory and motor cortex of the brain, through its use in productive social labor, the same's being true for the instrument language. Labor shapes the brain and its emergent quality, consciousness.[672] Unemployment,

---

672 Engels, F. (1934). *The Part played by Labour in the Transition from Ape to Man.*

forced idleness, besides the obvious effects has deleterious ecological consequences for the brain and human self-expression.

Man's consciousness overrides its sensorial roots and becomes completely abstract and autonomous; but it still depends not only on sensory feedback and brain energy to reflect reality objectively and opportunistically as animals do, but also and most importantly on the form of its particular society, of its particular historical mode of production. Consciousness must always operate within the larger man-made contexts of theory and ideology, explanations of reality's having been successively mythological, religious, philosophical and scientific. Our reality testing, is normal if our consciousness subscribes to the mainstream grammar of our particular historical mode of production; otherwise we become incidental and at risk. Human generations continue to transmit their thinking to their successors, objectively, even after their death, through durable cultural devices and memory objectifications.

The perception of reality reflected in man's consciousness constructs an imponderable world of inner experience and self-observation. Evolutionary variation in the size and structure of the brain relative to total body weight seems to be the marker of the ascent of man from its apish predecessors. New areas of the cortex, not fully differentiated in the brain of apes, which later achieved full development in the brain of man, are already distinguishable in the Neanderthal human, as casts of the inner surface of their skull indicate. Such areas are located in the frontal lobe, as well as in the parietal and temporal lobes.[673] The form of the homunculus of Penfield proportionally attests to the importance of manual labor and of communication in the new morphology of the brain.[674]

Trans: Clemens Dutt. Moscow. Progress Publishers. (Written 1876, Orig. Pub. 1895-6. Online in MIA. Accessed from <https://www.marxists.org/archive/marx/works/1876/part-played-labour/> on 2015-06-01.

673 Leontiev, A.N. (1981). "An outline of the evolution of the psyche" (pp. 156-326). Problems of the Development of the Mind. (Trans. M. Kopylova). Chapter 2. Moscow: Progress Publishers. Section online in MIA. Accessed from <https://www.marxists.org/archive/leontev/works/1981/evolution.htm> on 2015-05-28.

674 Penfield, W., and Jasper H. (1954) Epilepsy and the functional anatomy of the human

Qualitatively, through mediation, the human senses improved, as did the motor capacities as compared to their contemporary primates. The rise of labor and cultural human sociality were rather slowly pursued by evolution, if we look at all preliminary random attempts at excellent sensory and motor skill in so many other species. It is evolutionary trial-and-error toward *Homo sapiens* by combination, titration, and readjustment of the five senses. Pre-adaptations, including two-phase problem-solving actions, constituted conditions by which, during evolution, cooperative labor and human society based on labor, could arise.

Labor is the mediating bridge between man and nature, the process of man's applied activity to nature. It is ultimately nature through one of its agents, humans, compounding itself in order to modify the rest of itself, nature. All human labor literally starts with maternal labor, not exclusive to humans, in which the female lends herself as the first mediatory instrument in reproduction. As a first-order mediation, labor comes from the natural phenomenon. Upon this dramatic fact that involves great evolutionary investment and cost, the production of the new human is achieved that will utterly depend on otherness for success. Humanity develops industrial labor capacity from the ingredients of maternal labor: instrumental reproductive objectification. All human labor is reproductive objectification.

Labor so derived has two typical features. The first is the extension of the body through instruments: foremost the hands that, in psychoanalytic terms are self objects, instrumental extensions that augment the self.[675] The second is that production is as social as the initial maternal reproduction was. If the newborn is the outcome of a natural relation, labor extends the feature to a collective collaboration to produce culture internalized as self in each individual. The success of the species depends on individuals' functioning integratively with nature and with each other, as members of a given so-

---

brain. Little, Brown, Boston.
675 Kohut, H. (1971). The analysis of the self. New York: International Universities Press.

ciety. Only through relations with others does each human relate to nature. Labor as an emergent societal construct is a process socially mediated by tools.

Humans' characteristic sociohistorical use of tools has a natural history that reveals its own evolution. We see the rudiments of tool use among animals using a piece of nature to operate on another. These differ qualitatively, however, from man's tools, which are implements of collective labor. Unfortunately humans were instrumentalized, made means instead of ends, in patriarchal slavery.

In collective labor, from an individual's standpoint every member of the group performs his or her labor to satisfy his or her needs; but the result of individual actions does not in itself lead to the immediate satisfaction of needs. Individual labor is only a mediation within collective labor, originally for survival. The goals of the social individual's actions, only a part of the total ensemble, do not directly coincide with what motivates him or her. The immediate reason of her activity is individual survival needs, while the mediated reason is social production, the complementary survival of the species. In class society the species-survival mode is designed by a ruling minority. The mediated activity appears divorced from what previously was immediate action.

The outcome of the collective process that satisfies the group's survival necessities simultaneously meets the needs of each participating individual, even though his or her role in the group process may appear incidental. The preparation and the realization of operations characteristic of the two-phase actions of higher animals, mediations introduced within gaps of time and space, have been stretched out to socially fit humans. Two-phase intelligent actions that in animals are linked by perceptual links in humans become abstract connections between motives and goals collectively synchronized and alienated in social institutions, such as the market. Collective activity is the necessary basis of individual activity. The connection between the distant goal of an activity and its immediate objectives has been, in human activity, transformed from its natural form to a sociohistorical one. Human relations have become primordially social rather than merely natural.

It is the social context of mutual dependency that makes consciousness necessary, as a specifically human form of adaptation, reflection of humanized reality. Separate individual actions synchronized as collective activities require a synthesizing human science that covers a span from the political economy of the base to psychology and ethics of the superstructure. Conscious individual actions can then make sense.

2.5.3 The Metamorphosis of Human Consciousness

In human consciousness operational coherence reaches a new qualitative stage. Spider, weaver and bee can successfully operate on reality to transform it and fulfill their needs. They instinctually do know what they are doing but, unlike humans, they don't know that they know. They also do not have an experience or a notion of self, and much of their behavior, if they are social animals, mirrors group behavior.

Human consciousness is the highest stage in the evolution of natural sense and coherence. This more complex consciousness is an adaptation to new evolutionary conditions and complexity. Prior to full-fledged human meta-consciousness there were previous forms of biological coherence in sensory-motor information, in perceptual-motor forms of instinctual signaling, in genetic coding, and in instinctive relations. The new form of fitness achieved in symbolic communication required all those previous steps. Signaling and meaning systems evolved to become highly independent of the immediate environment resulting in language and abstract consciousness.

Storage of life experience and learning in the form of memory became objectified in culture making it possible for every individual in the species not to have to reinvent the wheel from instinctual drives. Consciousness is a form of ecological economy, every new individual's benefiting from the lived experiences of all those in preceding generations. What foods to eat and what operations to safely and economically perform on the environment were for the most part delineated by ancestors. This capacity required among other things, human speech, the most developed form of communication that required a very slow and lengthy evolutionary process of bodily transformation, including cranial, facial, laryngeal, oral and nasopharyngeal structures in particular, besides the corresponding change in brain structures.

Our type of consciousness required a highly recursive central nervous system with an excessively redundant wired and interconnected central station, the brain, a network of hubs of specialized anatomical, physiological, structural, functional chemical and electrical distributed networks or connections.[676] Neurons not only hook up with each other but create their own complex excitatory and inhibitory feedback and feed-forward loops, both memorial and anticipatory, and connect all parts of the whole with each other in successive evolutionary layers of ascending complexity, where their evolutionary history is inscribed. The various sensory receptors, simultaneously responding to selected parts and properties of the encircling environment, register the physical reality of the natural and social milieu. All this has its developmental precursors in the neurological and cognitive structure of previous species.

Due to their speedy abstract and combinatorial nature, language and consciousness, using new sets of signaling and coding relations, economically facilitate communication and collaboration. They require the epigenetic conservation of all their previous steps even though they may look separate and autonomous. They also lead to new cognitive domains such as eminently practical aesthetic sense, scientific drive, and morality.

To achieve their new qualitative status, language and conscious-

---

676 van den Heuvell, M.P. ,Sporns, O. (2013). "Network hubs in the human brain." Trends in Cognitive Sciences December 2013, Vol. 17, No. 12. Pp.683-696. Online in Elsevier Cell. Accessed from <www.cell.com/trends/cognitive-sciences/pdf/S1364-6613(13)00216-7.pdf> on 2017-03-23.

ness evolutionarily required the new genetic condition of two mirroring sexuated subjectivities, cognitively same and different, hori-
zontally symmetrical and complementary. On a developmental level
of verticality, each subjectivity must travel successive stages from
total anaclysis to relative autonomy, from mother-regulation to optimal self-regulated dependency on others. The phonemic coding
system of language that expresses consciousness and largely internalized becomes self-regulation has been relationally built and
consensually tested and maintained for generations. It was originally close to one shared universal consciousness in mythology that
Levy-Strauss could not decipher for lack of method.[677] The universality sought for by consciousness was destroyed by the split created
by patriarchy in the enslavement of the female half of the species.
The coding system of language has the evolutionary advantage that
it can be economically objectified, diffused, materially stored, and
generationally transmitted as collective civilization.

This was implicitly Darwin's point of view, and more explicitly
that of his disciple George Romanes.[678] It appears logical that animals have only as much intelligence as they need for survival while
man, fortunately or unfortunately, has the surplus that allows among
other things imagination and distortion.[679] If we look at the whole
process in terms of growing coherence, to achieve the human level

---

677 Levi-Strauss, C. (1964-1971). *Mythologiques.* Four-volume. Originally written in
   French, the works were translated into Eng-lish by John Weightman and Doreen
   Weightman. The four volumes of Mythologiques are: 1. The Raw and the Cooked
   (Le Cru et le cuit) - First published 1964. Translated in 1969. 2. From Honey to Ashes
   (Du miel aux cendres) - First published in 1966. Translated in 1973. 3. The Origin of
   Table Manners (L'Origine des manières de table) - First published in 1968. Translated
   in 1978. 4. The Naked Man (L'Homme nu) - First published in 1971. Translated in
   1981. Reprinted in English by University of Chicago Press.
678 Romanes, G.J. (1895). *Mind, and Motion and Monism.* London. Longmans, Green,
   and Co. Online in Project Gutenberg. Accessed from <http://www.gutenberg.org/
   files/22283/22283-h/22283-h.htm> on 2014-08-20.
679 Couchman, Justin J.; Coutinho, M. V. C.; Beran, M. J.; Smith, J. D. (2010). "Beyond
   Stimulus Cues and Reinforcement Sig-nals: A New Approach to Animal Metacog-
   nition". Journal of Comparative Psychology 124 (4): , 356 –368. Online in National Center for Biotechnology Information. Accessed from <http://www.ncbi.nlm.nih.
   gov/pmc/articles/PMC2991470/> on 2014-08-20.

of self-consciousness nature had to first go through many random trial and error attempts in other species.

Although consciousness can be said to be the exclusive property of some species, its roots go back to the universal coherence of nature, even at its mineral and physical levels. "The Earth is a highly structured natural spaceship. Its biosphere is a perfect information-and energy-processing thermodynamic mill that has been operating on this planet without excess or waste for the last four billion years. The biospheric mill runs on the flow of energy from the Sun, exploiting the free-energy differential between the incoming solar radiation and surrounding space, its 'source' and 'sink.' It structures and builds molecular matter on the planet's surface into systems of increasing size and complexity, from crystals and macromolecules to organic species and planetary ecologies."[680] This resilient natural form of coherence is what many still believe to be a God.

No other object or species in the universe, so far as we know, has the qualitative type of consciousness of humans, even though some animals such as great apes, dolphins, and rhesus monkeys seem to get quite close, and some we know excel humans in narrow forms of sensory-motor intelligence.[681] The various fields related to comparative psychology and sociobiology as of late have made great strides in understanding these similarities and differences.

The evolutionary advantage of language, and consciousness, is that they allow members of a species to socially mediate their relations with nature. Mediation by definition is to introduce change in the relation between the parties involved. This allows humans to determine their own behavior through self-created codes.

Even though gene codes mix and realign through meiosis at fertilization, more complex cultural codes have the advantage of being

680 Laszlo, E. (2014). "Information and Coherence in Nature;–and the Cancer of Human-World Incoherence." P. 5. Systema: con-necting matter, life, culture and technology. Volume 2 Issue 1: 04–10. Accessed from <www.systema-journal.org/article/view/258/210> on 2014-08-20.
681 Boysen, S. (2009). *The Smartest Animals on the Planet. Extraordinary Tales of the Natural World's Cleverest Creatures.* Buffalo, N.Y. Firefly Books.

universal, consensual and reciprocal, collaborative and thus highly plastic and relatively reversible. They require shared transmitter and receptor mechanisms specifically designed to deal with information not physical but symbolic. This is not to deny that behind them are chemical and electrical mechanisms. They however operate in a qualitatively different way that makes human consciousness an emergent property of the human nervous system that cannot be mapped or traced back to any single set of physical structures.

The self, the internalized human regulator, requires mirroring and reciprocal reverberation. It regulates individuals through constant reciprocal feedback from other selves external and previously internalized through identification. Human conscious coding for regulation is relational and it starts to be build upon the ground of the mother-child relationship.

The human condition precludes mere governance by the raw, unmediated laws of nature. Determining the proper adaptive direction in humans is the role of morality. Laszlo warns us: "However, there is a potential disadvantage in the rapidity of the spread of cultural codes in that they can go off in non-evolutionary directions. Non-evolutionary directions such as technology that serves one's own values and aims at the expense of others', can be maintained for a while, but are not sustainable."[682] Morality is the compass of the self.

We acutely know today that nature is starting to speak about the effects of the ecological damage caused by ideology, the idiosyncratic perversion of human consciousness. It is very possible that natural catastrophe may make us regress to earlier instinctual behavior before we can mend our consciousness fragmented by social class. We have pushed nature too far into latency.[683,684] Over ninety-five percent of scientists, the possible carriers of our most

---

682 Laszlo, E. (2014). Ibid. P. 6.
683 Laszlo, E. (2014). Ibid. P. 6.
684 Meszaros, I. (2010-1). Social Structure and Forms of Consciousness. 2 vol. New York. Monthly Review Press.

advanced consciousness, agree that we are in a danger zone.[685]

What seems clear is that we have lost our natural coherence, detoured from the morality of evolution, in order to accommodate class ideology that goes against species universality.

685 Doran, Peter T.; Maggie Kendall Zimmerman (January 20, 2009). "Examining the Scientific Consensus on Climate Change". EOS 90 (3): 22–23. Online in Accessed from <tigger.uic.edu/~pdoran/012009_Doran_final.pdf> on 2014-08-20.

2.6 THE MAIN HISTORICAL BIFURCATIONS OF CONSCIOUSNESS

2.6.1 Hybrid Consciousness: Totemism and Blood

I chose the term historical bifurcations to emphasize the likeness of the development of consciousness and natural evolution. Since Darwin's *Origins* evolutionists propose bifurcation as the mechanism of speciation in the tree of life. Although bifurcation appears directionally opposite of the syllogism, it is not if we realize that all conscious bifurcation start from a previous synthesis become thesis. As descent with modification, bifurcation is a form of supersession that conserves its past structure. Every new form is an antithesis that overrides the previous one while conserving it. Opposite to previous more destructive forms of adaptation, consciousness operates economically, meaning with minimal costly morphological transformation of nature. Totemism, for example, is today the national flag or group insignia.

In natural evolution the bifurcation leading to *Homo sapiens* was of the same kind. The morphological modification was neoteny. This is a selective form of growth with heterochronic retardation, changes in the timing of certain anatomical areas as they grow. This led to pedomorphosis, in human adults anatomical closeness to the orangutan infant rather than to the adult great ape. This resulted in favored brain size over mandibular size along with positive allometry. This occurs through operational genes' being de-repressed that had been previously repressed.[686] The phenomenon of repression and derepression has been seen in biology, particularly in genetics and biochemistry.[687] As a result of all this the brain, underdeveloped

---

686 Gould, S.J. (1977). *Ontogeny and Phylogeny.* Cambridge Massachusetts, London England. The Belnap Press of Harvard University Press.
687 See Wikipedia. Derepression. Accessed from <https://en.wikipedia.org/wiki/Derepression> on 2016-07-13.

at birth, acquires the advantage of growing in an extrauterine, social environment that shapes it.

One main characteristic of the *sapiens* type of consciousness is its tendency to *totalize*, meaning to classify and fit every new piece of information into a single existing explanatory puzzle or paradigm. To totalize, consciousness has historically used paradigms of growing complexity starting from totemism and mythology, followed by organized religion, philosophy and science, successively. All these have remained operative in spite of science's having attained hegemony as best explanatory model.

In history there have been many forms of consciousness, as Hegel documents for philosophy in his *Phenomenology*,[688] summarized by Trejo.[689] Forms of consciousness where for Hegel failed historical attempts at truthful totalization, and at times even defense mechanisms. Linked to each other, they illustrate how human certainty has developmentally appeared starting from sensation, theories of mind.

In this chapter I will select only the larger, most encompassing forms of historical bifurcation of consciousness keeping in mind that the individual consciousness is first and foremost a manifestation of its collective form. The individual however has the faculty of altering it in the same fashion s/he has the capacity to leave his or her imprint in the natural world. This does not mean that individuals make history; history is made collectively. Many of the previous forms of consciousness continue to operate, the main one's being religion. I start with totemic consciousness, which I consider qualitatively unique because of its hybrid form meaning that humans were, at their infancy, still in a strong anaclytical relationship with nature, with their animal form. In totemism humans saw themselves

---

688 Hegel, G.W.F. (1807). *Phenomenology of Mind.* Harper Torchbooks' edition of the Phenomenology, from University of Idaho, Department of Philosophy by Jean McIntire. Online in MIA, Hegel by hypertext. Accessed from <https://www.marxists.org/reference/archive/hegel/works/ph/phconten.htm> on 2015-04-11.

689 Trejo, P. (1993). "Summary of Hegel's Philosophy of Mind. Online in philosophy eserver.org. Accessed from <http://philosophy.eserver.org/hegel-summary.html> on 2014-08-22.

pertaining to the same class as their selected totem. This means they thought that with their totem they even shared descendancy and their blood.[690] The totem is a symbol of collective identity of a group of blood-bound individuals, and this is the beginning of the syllogism, individual versus universal, that started not with individuals but with a rather over-inclusive universality. This universality, lost in slavery, is what humanity yearns to recover in the political concept of true substantial equality.

Istvan Meszaros, following the historical method of Marx, proposes that forms of consciousness reflect the developing material relations of society.[691] The autonomy of consciousness finds its limit in its material dependence on life, without which it is not possible. Human life on the other hand must be maintained through the activity of labor. In the age of totemism humans leaned substantially on Mother Nature in the same way an infant clings to her mother. Here the given universality of nature starts to be parsed into the particularity of opposite, self-differentiating groups, various forms of blood linkage in societies based on blood affinity. Totemism that appears as the first form of symbolic human consciousness goes beyond the immediacy of animal intelligence, introducing the symbolic mediation of their hybrid totem, part themselves, part external nature, part supernatural and sacred.

Developing consciousness, as reflected in children's stages of *intelligence* (practically deployed consciousness in problem solving and learning, observable consciousness in language) had already evolutionarily blossomed in partial forms in plants and animals. Totemism is more properly the beginning of self-consciousness, the exclusively human second layer of metaconsciousness. This is the characteristic that defines our species as so-called *Homo sapiens*.

Totemic consciousness uses analogy to classify objects by sim-

---

690 Lang, A. (1911) *Method In The Study Of Totemism*. Glasgow. Printed at the University Press by Robert Maclehose & Co. Ltd. Online in Project Gutenberg. Accessed from <http://www.gutenberg.org/files/46546/46546-h/46546-h.htm> on 2017-03023.

691 Meszaros, I. (2010-2011). *Social Structure and Forms of Consciousness*. 2 Vols. New York. Monthly Review Press.

ilarity or contiguity. The totemic self, like Konrad Lorenz's geese, was the natural object that was accidentally there at the critical time of imprinting. From the experience of self-as-nature it condensed in the totemic symbol object and subject for the first time. Similarity stems from accidental proximity and a selected property like life, the analogue of blood. My identity then is my group mediated by the totem, its arbitrary symbol.[692] All members of my *species* share the same categories of life, blood, group, and symbol, therefore being all the same but simultaneously each different on geographical and symbolic ground: the dialectic of sameness and difference. The life of the totem is my life and the form of the totem my spirit. My group identity thus leans on the natural object I was socially imprinted upon, and it is anaclytic and inseparable, supported by coercive rituals, laws and taboos consensually imposed and maintained by my gens.

Consensual reality-testing, magically totalized in this explanatory model where the sacred can explain what the profane cannot, is thus achieved on the bases of *belief.* Costly ritualistic coercion props up the sacred domain upon which moral authority becomes based. With authority comes the profane hierarchy within the group that before may have been based on physical force, but is now instead on symbolic coercion. Humans live in a consanguine group upon which is projected the hierarchical morphology of their bodies, with a head, members, and organs that become institutions in the group. The group is a body, a *corporation.* This would become a society with its head in the state, its executive organ. This is a practical social division of labor modeled after bodily metabolism. As this group evolves, religion, philosophy and science are attempts at totalizing explanation. Shamans or priests provide leaders and groups with information, if still magical, nevertheless crucial for their survival of a cohesive group.

---

692 Durkheim, E. (1915). The Elementary forms of Religious life. Ch. 7. Trans. Joseph Ward Swain. London. George Allen and Unwin, Ltd. Online in Internet Archive. Accessed from <https://archive.org/stream/elementaryformso00durkrich#page/n15/mode/2up> on 2014-08-20.

It is to Scottish ethnologist and lawyer John Ferguson McLennan that we owe the notion that all of humanity must have gone through a period of totemic life,[693] although he did not fully understand the social and psychological implications in terms of individual identity and group and self-organization. English founder of cultural anthropology Edward Burnett Tylor did advance the notion that totemism also represents the need to classify[694] that is closely related to the needs to belong and to totalize. Totalization is a temporary closing of the circle with an explanation that is, here, mythological. It was Feuerbach, however, who discovered in God the condensation of all the virtues of the group, and in religion the earliest form of anthropology.[695] Emile Durkheim arrived at the same conclusion studying totemism: if the totem animal is at once the symbol of God and of society, he reasoned, it must be because god and society are the same.[696] Diverse human groups in this fashion became particularities geographically self-determined progressing from gentes to clans, tribes, nations, confederacies, city-states, and modern nations. Same humans, different identities. If I have the blood of the totem and so do all my totemic affiliates, I am in a conceptual class where I belong; this is my identity. Other groups are the same but vary in their symbolic identity.

French sociologist Emile Durkheim later pointed out the functional notions of profane and sacred, the latter's being the unconscious and its correlates symbolism, law, and morality. Freud, within

693 Mc.Lennan, J.F. (1870) . *The worship of animals and plants.* Part I.—Totems and Totemism. Extracted from Fortnightly Review, vol. 6 (1869) and vol. 7 (1870). On-line in masseiana.org. Accessed from <http://www.masseiana.org/mclennan.htm> on 2014-08-20.

694 Tylor, E. B. (1870). *Researches into the early history of mankind and the development of civilization.* Second Edition. P. 286. London. John Murray. Free EBook. Google. Accessed from <https://play.google.com/books/reader?id=AIMIAAAAQAAJ&printsec=frontcover&output=reader&authuser=0&hl=en&pg=GBS.PP1> on 2014-08-20.

695 Feuerbach, L. (1854). The *Essence of Christianity.* Trans. George Eliot, (Orig. Pub. 1851). Online in MIA. Accessed from <https://www.marxists.org/reference/archive/feuerbach/works/essence/> on 2015-04-21.

696 Durkheim, E. (1912) The Elementary Forms of the religious life. Trans: Joseph Swain. London: George Allen & Unwin Ltd. P. 206.

his own Oedipal theory, adopted some of the anthropologist's views, integrating them into his evolutionary group psychology.[697] Finally, Chris Knight highlights the important blood connections, the strongest possible natural connection susceptible of symbolization in the primitive mind, used by our female ancestors to invent culture.[698]

In totemism the dialectical foundations are set for a collectively derived personal identity that simultaneously includes the immediate group and its ritualistic and coercive hierarchical practices. Totemism survives in gentes (Latin: begotten) that become families (Latin: servants) in patriarchy, It is the purest form of consciousness if in its infancy.

In his form of a totemic soul, consciousness was linked originally with life, blood and group.

2.6.2 The Imaginary and the Infatuation of Consciousness with Itself: Mythology and Art

It has been said that art is the result of the capacity to constructively regress. We regress because we have been there, and this is the epoch when we lived the magic of art. Originally it was a developmental stage of consciousness. Mythology and art starts to separate consciousness from its strong symbiosis with sensual life and become creative through a shift to imagination, anticipation and prediction. Here consciousness moves from its yield to the external totem to the infatuation with its own power to project. It projects reverse perception and displays in full its own power of representation. A new imponderable world emerges, an expressionist virtual image that, if poorly understood, is empowered with the animistic drive of magic. This is how the real world is explained by the vir-

697 Freud, S. (1919). Totem And Taboo Resemblances Between The Psychic Lives Of Savages And Neurotics. Authorized English Translation, with Introduction By A. A. Brill. London. George Routledge & Sons, Limited. (1912-3). Online in Project Gutenberg. Accessed from <http://www.gutenberg.org/files/41214/41214-h/41214-h.htm> on 2015-08-03.
698 Knight, C. (1991). *Blood Relations. Menstruation and the Origins of Culture.* New Haven and London. Yale University Press.

448

tual one. Mythology becomes a form of explanation emerging from imagination and its power to totalize through a loose, emerging logic. The prolegomena of ideology, myth is still used by hierarchical culture, largely through the art of political spinning. Life is an animistic anthropomorphic self-projection that spreads through inanimate objects. We can see here the beginning of *alienation*. Not only does consciousness spiritualize and animate the world but, through belief, it surrenders itself to its own creation. We have been struggling to understand this since Spinoza. The various gods of polytheism are idealized projections of forms of natural motion and human agency. Ideal gods replace the single totem, and establish their own moral hierarchy reflecting the developing material hierarchies of society stemming from social status and enhanced skill in material production. Gentes grow and divide, enlarging into more complex social structures.

Hierarchy is a set of vertically stratified particularities, *i.e.*, roles within the group, endowed with different characteristics and values. Values emerge from usefulness, skills and attributes. As Freud illustrated, the value of the leader is the resultant of idealized group projections. Freud, however, did not see in this mechanism the replica of the mother child relation when the child perceives difference in magnitude. Other natural roles such as lieutenants of the leader or deputies, priests, ideologues, followers, antagonists, and scapegoats are inserted in the hierarchy. Hierarchies political, religious and military, in particular, emerge eventually to form full social institutions. This social organization is reflected, if inverted and idealized, in the narratives of mythology. Following Durkheim, who found the elementary structures of religious life in emotion, society, the sacred, and belief, Levi-Strauss tried without success to achieve the same for myth.[699] To arrive at a satisfactory explanation, myth must be

---

699 Wikipedia. Mythologiques is a four-volume work of cultural anthropology by Claude Lévi-Strauss and the culmination of his structural work. Originally written in French, the works were translated into English by John Weightman and Doreen Weightman. The four volumes of Mythologiques are: 1. *The Raw and the Cooked* (Le Cru et le cuit) - First published 1964. Translated in 1969. 2. *From Honey to Ashes* (Du miel aux cendres) - First published 1966. Translated in 1973. 3. *The Origin of Table Manners*

understood in its historical context and logic, with its predecessing and its succeeding forms, as well as to the modes of production that also produced it.

The great paradox of consciousness is that, although in the last instance it can only express itself individually, the individual is for the most part the vehicle of the expression of others, largely prior generations that preceded him or her. The individual mind utterly depends upon a syllogistic, triangular set of concentric relationships: individuality, the particularity of group, and the universality of the species that must be ultimately reckoned as the foremost natural determining factor. This triad is one from which Aristotle, and Hegel logically derived their respective methods, formal and dialectical, and similarly Freud intuited his triangular Oedipus Complex, with the mother representing the particularity of the family and the father the universality of a civil society for the individual.

Mythology replaces totemism to become a richer form of consciousness in a culture that is still emerging. It comes with the growth and encounter of groups and thus incorporates a larger collective consciousness. Totemism was exclusionary as religion continues to be, reinforcing its group differences. While totemism was dealing with group identity, mythology extends its concern to reflect wider social issues. Opposite classes of gods contend for power for example, personifications of good and evil. In the Greek pantheon the continuity of Titans, Olympians, and humans is an example, as is also the transition from Gaia's preeminence to that of her son-husband Ouranus, who starts the male line of power. Growing inclusion and classification are characteristic of mythology's logic, reflecting new capacities in the human mind and brain.

Solidarity also expands to include others through marriage relations and group exchanges that agglutinate rather than separate neighboring groups. The boundaries of the group are enhanced and

---

(L'Origine des manières de table) - First published in 1968. Translated in 1978. 4.*The Naked Man* (L'Homme nu) - First published in 1971. Translated in 1981. Reprinted in English by University of Chicago Press.

so are the political possibilities eventually leading to the imperialism of the earlier cultures, Sumerian, Babylonian, Persian, and Egyptian and their wars for hegemony. In a moment of dialectical clarity, Freud made the connection between monotheism and Egyptian imperialism.[700]

Gentes that were external to each other and unconnected, excluded as "others," begin to be seen as same through exchange. This process is reflected in the growing complexity of incest laws, marriages and kinship systems. Groups of sisters from one gens or tribe can collectively consort with groups of brothers from another instead of just their moieties.

Mythology is thus about plurality of intermingling agents' being recognized as mirrors of the self. It must explain the emerging lawfulness and contradictions with a logic that is similar to that of a child. The boundaries of the sensorimotor world are expanding to recognize other groups as equal. Mythology tries to totalize an expanding world; it remains the totalizer par excellence.

In its mythological form cognition is not divorced from emotion. A form of transition between totemism and religion, it shows characteristics of both. Myth differs from religion in its lack of dogma and institutionalization. Transmitted through oral tradition, it is susceptible of individual distortions. What Andrew Lang[701] and early anthropologists saw as capricious has its own form of developmental logic similar to the one Piaget found in the evolution of intelligence in children.

Myths thus become accrued narratives of successive generations reflecting changing types of human relations, developing cultures and subjectivities, therefore many contending and changing val-

---

700 Freud, S. (1939). Moses and Monotheism. Trans. Katherine Jones. London. The Hogarth Press and the Institute of Psychoanaly-sis. P. 36. Online in the Internet Archive. Accessed from <https://archive.org/details/mosesandmonothei032233mbp> on 2014-10-18.

701 Lang, A. (2015). *Myth, Ritual and Religion.* (Orig. Pub.1887). Online in eBooks@ adelaide. University of Adelaide. Australia. Accessed from <https://ebooks.adelaide. edu.au/l/lang/andrew/myth-ritual-and-religion/> on 2016-07-17.

ues. Here consciousness is confronted with its paradox that, being collective, it can only speak through individuals. There is evidence that mythology was originally matriarchal in nature, and that such hegemony ended with the patriarchal political coup that largely inverted it. This is the view of Bachofen,[702] of Graves.[703] and most recently of Stone[704] and others.

Because of their artistic quality, myths appeal to the emotional and the subjective, and this makes them politically expedient at times. The virtual world of myth is populated by ideals that replace the ghosts of a comparatively pitiful reality and this is its their therapeutic value as narcotizers.

Old literary achievements such as Homer's and Hesiod's focus on the Trojan War and its aftermath. For the genesis of the world and the intersection between oral tradition and durable written language, myth and religion, we have the Bible. The Hellenistic and Roman cultures preserved mythology in their religious forms. Myths survive and still today we need to create myths to close the circle and totalize our understanding. They often compete with scientific theories and at times hybridize with them. During the scientific revolution of the Renaissance Hermeticism was a contending force, a popular alternative explanation. The same was the case as recently as with the *Lebensraum* of Hitler,[705] an alternative to "Jewish" science, and Manifest Destiny in the United States. Today's equivalents are American exceptionalism,[706,707] creationism, or intelligent design, or

---

702 Bachofen, J. (1992). Myth, Religion and Mother Right. Preface by George Boas, introduction by Joseph Campbell, translated by Ralph Manheim. Princeton NJ: Princeton University Press. P. 116. (Orig. Pub.1861).

703 Graves, R. (1948). *The White Goddess.* A Historical Grammar of Poetic Myth. London. Faber and Faber Limited. Accessed from <http://72.52.202.216/~fenderse/The-White-Goddess.pdf> on 2015-07-24.

704 Stone, M. (1976). *When God was a Woman.* New York. Barnes and Noble.

705 Shelley Baranowski. (2011). *Nazi Empire: German Colonialism and Imperialism from Bismarck to Hitler.* Cambridge UK. Cambridge University Press.

706 Koh, H. H. (2003). "On American Exceptionalism." Faculty Scholarship Series. Paper 1778. Online in Yale Law School Legal Scholarship Repository. Accessed from <http://digitalcommons.law.yale.edu/fss_papers/1778> on 2015-09-23.

707 Democracy Now! Broadcast of 09-23-2015. Noam Chomsky on George Orwell,

for that matter even astrology, since for most people who lack access to science, myths appear more practical an alternative.

The psychological study of myth and its similarity to dreams and delusions led Swiss psychoanalyst Carl Jung (1875-1961) to postulate a hybrid, bridging principle between nature and society similar to Freud's instinct. This is the inherited *archetype* (Gr. original model), a set of unlearned universal organizing social principles concerned mainly with primal social roles and their function in the psychology of the person. Jung saw archetypes as wired biologically and triggered socially, according to a collective unconscious, ancestral memory, an even deeper form of the unconscious than Freud's, historically represented in mythology.[708]

It has been said that scientific theories are our current myths and religions. Some scientists still admit to the mythic nature of their theories, particularly in the midst of competing ideologies.[709] In class society the attainment of objectivity in science is impossible. Science is always contaminated by ideological myth.

2.6.3 Hierarchy, Discipline and Morality: Religion

Religion is the historical synthesis of totemism and mythology. Popular, folk mythology with its capricious emotionality gives place to more cognitively systematized and hierarchical religion that, in its transition, still keeps the polytheistic form of myth. In fact, myth tended to be almost omnitheistic, comprehensively animistic. Mature religions are monotheistic and reflect more integrated and hierarchical societies. As society advances in its organization, it needs to firm up the syllogistic relation between itself as a whole and the individual as her partial agent. It inverts the natural order

the Suppression of Ideas and the Myth of American Exceptionalism. Accessed from <http://www.democracynow.org/2015/9/22/noam_chomsky_on_the_myth_of> on 2015-09-23.

708 Jung, C.G. (1980) The Archetypes and the Collective Unconscious. Trans RFC Hull. Princeton NJ. Princeton University Press. [Orig. Pub. 1959?].

709 For example: Knight, C. (1991). *Blood Relations. Menstruation and the Origins of Culture*. New York and London. Yale Uni-versity Press.

into a purely virtual domain based not on perception but belief. To do this legitimately and give preeminence to individual leaders that are somehow connected with God, it needs coercive rituals that reinforce an imposed view that is contrary to perceived reality. In reality the leader is not different from other individuals except in attributes of skills; power rests in the projection of the group.

Ritual is a costly natural adaptation we already see in biology, but in humans it takes on its own characteristics, including the element of explanatory power of spurious mediation. Religion therefore has to be ideological and political in nature. Its function is to legitimize the specific form of social organization of the group. While rituals were initially attached to unexplained natural events such as birth, puberty, death, hunt, lunar cycle, seasons, etc., [710]in religion the periodic exercise of ritual separates the sacred from nature and assumes a regulatory capacity, its own nature dealing with the sacred and using it to explain the world and its events. Religion evolves ideologically to mystify, hand in hand with coercive politics.

In monotheism religion achieves its most organized form, but unfortunately it confronts other monotheisms that question its universality. Feuerbach's important theological finding is that the powerful individuality of an ideal anthropomorphic God represents the accrual of all possible individual virtues and powers of a group that no individual can possibly have. God consists of all powers, assets and virtues, imaginarily put together resulting in an ideal anthropomorph. In a similar form, Freud saw the same projection, now involving all groups, in imperialism. At its peak religion became the culture of its time, scientifically an inverted anthropology representing the growing hierarchy implemented by patriarchs.[711]

---

710   van Gennep, A. (1961). *The Rites of Passage.* Trans. Monika B. Vizedom and Gabrielle L. Coffee. Chicago. University of Chi-cago Press. London. Routledge and Kegan Paul Ltd. (Orig. Pub. 1909).

711   Feuerbach, L. (1841). *The Essence of Christianity.* Source: Introduction from The Fiery Brook, remainder from The Essence of Christianity. Trans: Introduction translated by Zawar Hanfi, 1972, remainder translated by George Eliot, 1854. Online in MIA. Ac-cessed from <http://www.marxists.org/reference/archive/feuerbach/works/essence/index.htm> on 2014-08-21.

Particularly in collective rituals, religion is still largely practice in an emotional language. The psychology of religion is powerful group psychology. Religion, however, in the practice of its leaders strives to shift more and more toward the cognitive, ideological domain to be useful. This is how it becomes concerned with an alienated theology based on dogma, drawn from a nascent philosophy. Religious experience in ecstasy or trance can lead to alternative forms of consciousness, hallucinatory, the remnants of an old collective animistic form. Emotional religious practice did ultimately become more and more compartmentalized into periodic ritualistic episodes, while priests and monks worked on its explanatory structure competing with, and subordinating, philosophy and science. This is how the famous Inquisition came to be a political phenomenon of censure and repression.

French founder of sociology Auguste Comte (1798–1857) represents the historical conundrum of religion, philosophy and science. After his brilliant encyclopedic career the first positivist philosopher of science surrendered to religion and advocated the religious practice of sociology guided by the political motto of *order and progress*. What Comte wanted was his science to have the emotional passion and practical fervor of religion. Instead, science has become alien to the masses and largely ideological, its objectivity's being measured by its lack of critical power. The science of climate change is the paradigm of class division.

According to Comte's Law every branch of knowledge goes through the same three syllogistic stages: fictitiousness, abstractness and concrete evidence. These correspond to religion, metaphysics, and science. Although here is captured in brief the evolution of consciousness, it lacks a base in material life and remains a religious explanation.

Comte writes: "The whole economy of the human mind is subject to that general law prevailing throughout the Real Order, according to which the nobler phenomena are everywhere subordinate to those which are grosser but also simpler and more regular, sensation. Thus it is that Man is entirely subordinate to the World, as each living being is to its own environment. Now by a legitimate extension of this Biological dependence to the Mental functions, we at once get the essential principle of the Intellectual Economy. For it consists in the necessary and continual subordination of our Subjective Conceptions to the Objective Materials from which they are constructed; a truth substantially established by Aristotle in the aphorism: There is nothing in the Understanding that did not originally spring from Sensation; elucidated by the addition of Leibniz: except the Understanding itself; and completed by Kant's distinction between Objective and Subjective Reality. But from the Biological point of view, this dependence of Intellect on Sensation is perfectly analogous to that of the bodily Functions upon the Environment which controls the whole vital Existence."[712] We can see some of Marx here, as we can in many other passages of Comte's encyclopedic work. Consciousness is subordinated to matter however, as Marx sees it.

French sociologist Emile Durkheim (1858-1917) contributed to the elucidation of religion and its meaning in society, particularly as the form of communion and solidarity of collective practice and the defense of that sacred realm, a virtual image of nature.[713] Passion does not originate from religion but from the solidarity of communion. Feuerbach reduced God to idealized man, [714]and Engels says that: "this God is, however, himself the product of a tedious process of abstraction, the concentrated quintessence of the numerous earlier tribal and national gods. And man, whose image this God is, is therefore also not a real man, but likewise the quintessence of the

---

712 Comte, A. (1876). *System of Positive Polity: Social Dynamics; or, The General Theory of Human Progress*. Vol. 3. Ch. 1. P. 15. London. Longmans, Green and Co. (Orig. Pub. 1853) Online in Internet Archive. Accessed from <https://play.google.com/books/reader?id=y8MYAAAAIAAJ&printsec=frontcover&output=reader&authuser=0&hl=en&pg=GBS.PR16> on 2013-04-02 .

713 Durkheim, E. (2012). *The Elementary Forms of the Religious Life*. Trans: Joseph Ward Swain. EBook #41360. Online in Project Gutenberg. Accessed from <http://www.gutenberg.org/files/41360/41360-h/41360-h.htm> on 2014-08-21.

714 Feuerbach, L. (1841). *Ibid.*

numerous real men, man in the abstract, therefore himself again a mental image."[715] Feuerbach's decoding of God and theology is well known; what is less known is his appeal for a continued religion of sensuality and love, including sexual love, an idea that goes back to old matriarchy.[716] Not love, so much as its general solidary form is the glue of human universality.

Religion was culture for many centuries and its current revival as fundamentalism is proof of the fact that new thinking cannot simply discard the old. Solidarity is experienced as religion because religion was the first form of organized solidarity after women invented culture through solidarity, as we saw in the chapter on Knight. As we endorse new ways of thinking that we deem progressive, based on solidarity, we must be mindful of the fact that we are just picking up a thread, and building on an old foundation.

Based on emotion, belief and authority, religion could not satisfy the demands of consciousness, thus the shift to philosophy.

2.6.4 The Infatuation with Form, Reason and Speculation: Philosophy

Philosophy challenges but cannot separate from religion until it understands it. God and the leader are at the top of the hierarchy and mutually reinforced. In some cultures leader and God are the same. The anthropological understanding of religion and God starts with Spinoza, and continues with Hegel, Feuerbach, Marx and Engels. With Freud and Durkheim Marx and Engels contribute, all from their disciplinary vantage points, to move the issue from philosophy to science. God is an alienating analgesic defense for Marx, [717]a nec-

---

715 Engels, F. (1946). *Ludwig Feuerbach and the End of Classical German Philosophy.* Part 3. Feuerbach. Trans: Progress Pub-lishers. (Orig. Pub. 1886). Moscow. Progress Publishers. Online in MIA. Accessed from <ww.marxists.org/archive/marx/works/1886/ludwig-feuerbach/ch03.htm> on 2014-08-25.

716 Stone, M. (1976). *When God was a Woman.* New York. Barnes and Noble.

717 Marx, K. (1844). A Contribution to the Critique of Hegel's Philosophy of Right. Introduction. Online in MIA. Accessed from <https://www.marxists.org/archive/marx/works/1843/critique-hpr/intro.htm> on 2015-11-04.

essary sociological structure of representation for Durkheim,[718] and, more concretely, a psychological condensations of projected ego ideals of the group for Freud.[719] These explanations overlap and are not exclusive, reinforcing each other, products of scientific perspective. Religious belief advanced reasoning and philosophical idealism but dogmatism had limited its philosophical power. Abstract notions, although all originally stemming from real-life phenomena as Comte and Marx pointed out, had subordinated matter to the ideal world, thanks to Plato's ideas, his true realities.[720]

Engels: "The great basic question of all philosophy, especially of more recent philosophy, is that concerning the relation of thinking and being. From the very early times when men, still completely ignorant of the structure of their own bodies, under the stimulus of dream apparitions (1)[721] came to believe that their thinking and sensation were not activities of their bodies, but of a distinct soul which inhabits the body and leaves it at death — from this time men have been driven to reflect about the relation between this soul and the outside world. If, upon death, it took leave of the body and lived on, there was no occasion to invent yet another distinct death for it. Thus arose the idea of immortality, which at that stage of development appeared not at all as a consolation but as a fate against which it was no use fighting, and often enough, as among the Greeks, as

---

718 Durkheim, E. (1915). The Elementary forms of Religious life. Ch. 7. Trans. Joseph Ward Swain. London. George Allen and Unwin, Ltd. Online in Internet Archive. Accessed from <https://archive.org/stream/elementaryformso00durkrich#page/n15/mode/2up> on 2014-08-20.

719 Freud, S. (1922). Group Psychology and the Analysis of the Ego. Trans. James Strachey. London. The International Psychoan-alytic Press. Online in the Internet Archive. Accessed from <http://www.gutenberg.org/files/35877/35877-h/35877-h.htm> on 2015-01-14.

720 Plato. *The Republic.* Trans: B. Jowett. Online in Project Gutenberg. Release Date: August 27, 2008 [EBook #1497]. Last Up-dated: November 5, 2012. Accessed from <http://www.gutenberg.org/files/1497/1497-h/1497-h.htm> on 2015-06-05.

721 Original footnote in the quotation: "Among savages and lower barbarians the idea is still universal that the human forms which appear in dreams are souls which have temporarily left their bodies; the real man is, therefore, held responsible for acts committed by his dream apparition against the dreamer. Thus Imthurn found this belief current, for example, among the Indians of Guiana in 1884."

a positive misfortune. The quandary arising from the common universal ignorance of what to do with this soul, once its existence had been accepted, after the death of the body, and not religious desire for consolation, led in a general way to the tedious notion of personal immortality. In an exactly similar manner, the first gods arose through the personification of natural forces. And these gods in the further development of religions assumed more and more extramundane form, until finally by a process of abstraction, I might almost say of distillation, occurring naturally in the course of man's intellectual development, out of the many more or less limited and mutually limiting gods there arose in the minds of men the idea of the one exclusive God of the monotheistic religions."[722] Like its predecessors, mythology and religion, philosophy was concerned with representing the truth in theory, but the correspondence function of thinking and being continued to be gradually eroded, and with philosophy the gap became more blatant, particularly since the Greek Sophists endeavored to show that any individual viewpoint could be rationally proven for a fee. This idealism, until Spinoza, was the means for closing the circle of understanding. Philosophers after Spinoza starting with the Bacons in England, Roger and Francis, called for science to take the matter in its hands utilizing proof and experiment. Unfortunately science is not immune to being kidnapped by ideology.

Explanatory deficits result from the fact that the material forces of production and reproduction of our lives advance faster than their representation in the mind as theory. Material forces and relations change before their progress can be reflected in their knowledge superstructure. Explanations become obsolete. Additionally organized social thinking, corrupted by ideology in class society, may benefit from the slowness of change.

The emotional component of thinking came to be seen as accept-

---

722 Engels, F. (1946). *Ludwig Feuerbach and the End of Classical German Philosophy.* Part 2: Materialism. Trans. Progress Pub-lishers. Moscow. Progress Publishers. (Written and Orig. Pub. 1886). Online in MIA. Accessed from <http://www.marxists.org/archive/marx/works/1886/ludwig-feuerbach/index.htm> on2014-08-23.

able in religion but not so in science. It was apportioned with all that is feminine, weak, and illogical, in science contrary to objectivity. Subjectivity, the metabolic source of consciousness, was devalued by ideology because of its split nature. This happened along with other logical binaries that were verticalized and made hierarchical, one ascending at the cost of the other. Mathematics and formal logic ascended in value because of their highly abstract nature.

In the West, philosophy came at the zenith of Greek patriarchal domination, wealth accumulation, and leisure to think, linked to slavery and the division of manual and spiritual labor. During feudalism religion appropriated philosophy and became the ideological bulwark of monarchic domination. Because patriarchal consciousness endeavored to overthrow all matriarchal forms of life, largely closer to nature, it used strong repressive maneuvers to forget the past. Religion has been a most useful instrument of repression. Philosophy more subtly can distribute into diverse fields of knowledge different areas of inquiry, and originally all branches of knowledge were philosophies.

In philosophy consciousness suffers its most blatant transformation into class ideology because it is closer or even hybridized with a science that eventually will make its reasoning untenable, besides the fact that philosophy is secular. The utopia of consciousness would have the compelling identity of totemism, the beauty of mythology, the passion of religion, and the truthfulness of science. We are at the scientific stage of consciousness historically, but science has been unable to avoid the effects of ideology. The result is that we can be brilliant while lacking good sense.

2.6.5 Proof and Experiment: Science

Sooner or later scientific materialism, the instinct of the earliest philosophers, had to be re-sparked to fight the corrupt idealism of Plato and the Scholastics. This was initiated by English philosopher Francis Bacon (1561-1626), who endeavored to eliminate the idealist bias pervasive in medieval philosophical thinking. Francis Bacon had been preceded in this challenge by his unrelated homonym (1214-1292?) Roger Bacon, an English philosopher and Franciscan friar who had already called for an empirical study of nature. Francis proposed inductive reasoning, starting from the individual perception of real facts. Facts are perceived through the senses before they are properly processed by reason to arrive at working axioms and at scientific laws after the mind has been cleansed from distorting notions. The latter are constraints that Bacon calls idols, false gods.

If friar Roger Bacon strangely precedes Francis in the new chain of science, the next link is even more strange. This is excommunicated Portuguese-Dutch Sephardic Jew Baruch Spinoza (1632-1677), who makes it possible to understand and reconcile idealism from a materialist, scientific perspective. God or nature, he says, meaning they are identical, God being the good sense of nature. This means that what scientifically may have appeared as natural randomness turns out to be lawful and axiomatic good sense. We can however, only understand it *a posteriori,* looking back historically, when our consciousness has evolved to be able to reach such capacity in its stage of science. Hegel (1770-1831) picks up and develops the Spinozist thread albeit still idealistically inverted.

Hegel reversed would indicate that good sense was already there in the Big Bang, it survived, and that it embodied each particle of it. Infantile animistic "distortions" that started with totemism, grew more abstractly and spread to become culture. What good sense is to matter culture is to humanity, the first form of culture's being necessarily religion. Culture is thus the good sense of a new species, because good sense has been evolving along with nature to become consciousness. God finally apprehended itself as consciousness in philosophy, particularly with Spinoza and Hegel.

The new method proposed by Francis Bacon is intended to keep us from reverting into idealism. Its inductive method transforms the Aristotelian syllogism in preparation for the dialectic of Hegel that shuffles the three cards: individual, particular, and universal. Proof and experiment legitimize the method by constraining reason and imagination. Knowledge is power attached to the senses and their good sense. All this is reflected in the title of Bacon's main work: *The New Instrument*,[723] aimed at Aristotle's first principles: self-evident propositions. We have seen that instrument is what in human nature mediates and ultimately leads to consciousness.

Natural science is, of course, for Bacon the paradigm, with physics at its heart and matter as its object. That man can know nature only by obeying its laws is an admonition. That movement is not only mechanical and external, but inherent in matter itself, and impelling is a notice to the scholastics. Only the senses are infallible and the truest source of knowledge. Science is experimental and consists largely in the application of reason to the data provided by the senses.

Bacon jumpstarts the modern scientific method and is critical of what, in light of the new discoveries, is superstition. He, however, must leave the theological realm, including psychology, alone.

---

723 Bacon, F. (1863). *The New Organon or True Directions Concerning the Interpretation of Nature*. This rendition is based on the standard translation of James Spedding, Robert Leslie Ellis, and Douglas Denon Heath in The Works (Vol. VIII), published in Boston by Taggard and Thompson in 1863. All bracketed statements are the additions of the editor. In addition to some minor stylistic changes, spelling, punctuation, and capitalization have been revised to conform to current American usage. (Orig. Pub. 1620). Accessed from <http://www.constitution.org/bacon/nov_org.htm> on 2012-09-21.

2.7 THE SCIENTIFIC EXPLANATIONS OF CONSCIOUSNESS AND THE SELF

2.7.1 Mechanical Explanations

Mechanicism first tries to explain all natural phenomena on the basis of mechanical laws, meaning that the only factors operating in the organization of natural systems are physical factors. It excludes any non-material vital organizing notions. This was early scientific materialism, the first vanguard of the young scientific insurgency. Motion is still conceived as external displacement, such as astronomers observe it in stars and planets. Mechanicism is the first developmental stage of modern materialism, of science, and it was not fully superseded in physics until relativity and quantum theories.

English philosopher Thomas Hobbes (1588-1679) further systematizes Bacon's materialistic conception of the world. Hobbes sees humans as sophisticated machines, and time and space as mental constructs. Thought for the first time is conceived as part of the physical operation of the human body and all ideas start with sensations. Representations and notions are reflections of reality in our brain. Animal activity is the result of discomfort and its aim is wellbeing, volition's being the movement of the will springing from strong desire. Humans are driven by animal nature and by utilitarian self-interest. These are still familiar revolutionary concepts of the seventeenth century.

Political philosophy is a main interest of Hobbes. Only through the social contract and commonwealth, *Leviathan*,[724] can a corporate state develop agreements and avoid constant war of man against man. Here is the foundation of European liberal thought, including

---

724 Hobbes T. (1996). *Leviathan*. Ed. Richard Tuck. Cambridge and New York. Cambridge University Press. (Orig. pub.1651). Online in Project Gutenberg. Accessed from <http://www.gutenberg.org/ebooks/3207> on 2012-09-21.

rights of the individual, natural equality, and harmony of civil society through a representative state.

A different take is that of French philosopher René Descartes (1596-1650), who rejects the scholastic tradition and endorses science. Like Bacon, Descartes believes education has fed us judgments before we had full use of reason; having been brainwashed, we cannot arrive at any certainty or truth. We must at a point doubt and question everything we have assumed to know.

That I am presently engaged in the activity of thinking is the only given I can take for granted. Along with Locke, Hume, and the English Sensualists, in the matter of method Descartes relies on hypothesis and experiments rather than on prior Aristotelian syllogistic demonstrations. In that fashion he can arrive, if not necessarily, to certainty to speculative hypothesis and theory, mechanics being the paradigm. In this light, animals are machines made of earth by God, man additionally having language, and a soul. His new method is highly mathematical and Descartes introduces methodical doubt[725] for the first time to challenge dogmatism, placing the seeds of later critical theory. To be true, any statement must survive the test of the most severe skeptical scrutiny by reason.

Most human behavior, like that of animals, can be explained mechanically, but there is a big difference. His "I think, therefore I am" clearly reflects a shift of philosophy from God to a humanity, a humanism that makes possible inductive first-person psychology. What characterizes humans is not the depth of any animal capacity, as many animals put us to shame as far as particulars is concerned; it is the sensorial repertoire leading to the flexibility and combinatorial capacity of reason, especially manifest in thought and language.

Fearful of the Inquisition, in a conciliatory fashion Descartes divides man into two substances and leaves the issue of God to theologians. His concern is the human body, to be explained me-

---

725 Descartes, R. (2008). *Discourse on Method*. Online in the The Project Gutenberg EBook of A Discourse on Method, by René Descartes. Ebook #59. (Orig pub 1637). Accessed from http://www.gutenberg.org/ebooks/59 on 2012-09-26.

chanically. Although we always start from ourselves, our thinking, false perceptions, dreams, illusions and imaginations can lead us to false forms of knowledge we must be aware of. Error can also be owing to emotion and to the subjective diversity of opinions.

The main property of the material substance is spatial extension and its mechanical nature cannot fully explain the mind that is different and unique. The relationship between mind and body is not reciprocal but parallel.

There are four methodological prescriptions in Cartesian reasoning: to prevent hasty conclusions and only accept as true, axiomatic, observable evidence; to, analytically, divide any given problem into the greatest possible number of parts for a simpler analysis of each; to, progressively, start from the simplest and move on to the most complex; and to, methodically, constantly reevaluate results. For himself, Descartes also sets four rules: uphold law and custom even if in doubt; be firm and decisive even if in doubt; master self and desire rather than fortune and the external; and do not deviate from your project and self-prescribed method. This is his advice to scientists.

Sensations and passions of the soul are the result of mechanical motions dependent on nerves that connect to the brain in parallel. Nerve fibers float in a fine substance called animal spirits that penetrate the brain. Pores in the brain expand or contract to produce muscular activity. Sensations lead to passions and emotions according to their magnitude and beneficial or harmful nature. Passions marshal the soul to select and adopt or reject. Animal spirits mediate the passions to produce results. Wonder, love, hatred, desire, joy, and sadness are the primary passions; all others are composites of them. Descartes does not discard emotions.

The practical psychology of Descartes is best illustrated in his letters to Elizabeth[726] and in his last book *The Passions of the Soul.*[727] In the letters he answers queries and gives advice to princess-philosopher Elizabeth of Bohemia, with whom he corresponded for several years. In *The Passions* he discusses his theory of feelings connected through the animal spirits to the pineal gland, as designed by God with a natural logic of affective states. Fleeing in fright or fighting in anger are predispositions of the body. It is inevitable that passions can become our enemies and harm us. His therapeutic advice is a positive attitude that can keep passions away from the senses and imagination, turning our attention to objects that provide gratification. Only through the intellect can passions be dealt with. Descartes through his own positive attitude was able to overcome his sickly nature (he tells us): a cough and paleness he inherited from his mother and that had been poorly prognosticated by doctors.

Good and happiness are for Descartes the ultimate goals of morality. The supreme good is virtue, the use of the free will to attain the best possible outcome. Happiness is inner satisfaction acquired by the wise man, even in the absence of fortune's favor. We aim at virtue to attain happiness. Descartes still endorses the view that supreme happiness, consisting solely in the contemplation of the divine majesty, is reserved for the next life. Through the cultivation of reason and sound judgment, philosophy is a form of therapy for the universal illnesses of the mind, vices and passions such as sadness or fear, that stand in the way of happiness.

The proverbial Cartesian dualism continues to be entrenched in human science, in spite of the advances in the monistic and dialectical line of thinking of Spinoza and Hegel. Neurobiology in particular has advanced the understanding of the complexity of con-

---

726 Descartes, R. (2007) *The Correspondence between Elisabeth, Princess of Bohemia and Descartes*. Trans. Lisa Shapiro. Chicago: University of Chicago Press. (Orig. Pub. 1684).

727 Descartes, R. (1989). *The Passions of the Soul*. Trans. Stephen Voss. Indianapolis, Cambridge. Hackett Publishing Co. (Orig. Pub. 1649). Also online in Claremont Graduate University: The Descartes Web Project. The Passions of the Soul. Accessed from <http://net.cgu.edu/philosophy/descartes/Passions_Letters.html> on 2012-09-26.

sciousness. On the other hand, the identification with the machine, a human product, reflects the alienation of human power.

2.7.2 Spinoza and the New Science

Cartesian dualism is a split form of consciousness that started with Plato and the absurd preeminence of ideas over things. It does not make sense to Dutch-Portuguese philosopher and lens grinder Baruch Spinoza (1632-1677) who dissents from the religious and philosophical mainstream. He was excommunicated from the Jewish community at age 23, and still is. He was placed in the Catholic Index of banned books, and his books burned. Yet his peer philosophers endorsed him: "It is therefore worthy of note that thought must begin by placing itself at the standpoint of Spinozism; to be a follower of Spinoza is the essential commencement of all Philosophy," said Hegel. [728]Not only ethics and cosmology, but even fields as diverse as political science, linguistics, and neurobiology pay tribute to him today during a well deserved recognition and revival of his influence.[729] With Spinoza and Hegel, philosophy transfers its banner of understanding to science.

To say that material extension and imponderable thought are two properties of the same object, as Spinoza said, is saying that nature and idea or God are two sides of the same coin, thus bridging the gap between philosophical idealism and materialism. This is how his critique of Descartes offers a scientific alternative to dualism. This places the philosophical foundation for one encompassing science during the Enlightenment by Spinoza, and makes possible Biblical criticism for example, developed into modern hermeneutics. Spi-

---

728 Hegel, G.W.F. (1892-6). *Hegel's Lectures on the History of Philosophy*. Section Two: Period of the Thinking Understanding. Chapter 1. The Metaphysics of Understanding. A2. Spinoza. Trans. E.S Haldane. The lectures were first published between 1833-36 in volumes 13-15 in the first edition of Hegel's Werke. Online in MIA. Accessed from <https://www.marxists.org/reference/archive/hegel/works/hp/hpspinoz.htm> on 2016-07-23.

729 See for example: Damasio, A. (2003). *Looking for Spinoza. Joy, Sorrow and the Feeling Brain*. Orlando, FL. Harcourt Inc.

noza's pivotal importance as the bridge between classic philosophy and modern science cannot be overestimated.

For the first time since Plato Spinoza made it possible to think of one coherent whole, one totality to be understood by one unified discipline, instead of antagonistic philosophical viewpoints, one monolithic science. Religion is anthropology and theology is psychology. One universe, being guided by its own lawfulness and need, its own sense, can begin to be deciphered by science. Being the coherence of nature, God is also my innate consciousness located within myself; in *me*. I embody the property of nature that has evolved, subjectively, to best decipher and understand itself, myself, naturally. Saying that God rules the universe is saying that natural good sense is to be understood from inside, humanely. From inside I can understand God in the totality of my species, in society. The lawful coherence of nature, God, is particularly accessible in human nature because here it can look at itself, internally. This is the Spinozist thread picked up later by Hegel, Feuerbach, Marx, and Durkheim within a holistic, totalizing philosophy that makes it possible to understand evolution as one single process from Big Bang to Self.

Everything happens through the operation of necessity, whether natural or man- made. "By God, I mean a being absolutely infinite that is, a substance consisting in infinite attributes, of which each expresses eternal and infinite essentiality."[730] There is continuity, everything necessarily connected; natural sense is the seed of human consciousness. Absolute infinity is totality, achievable by thought, the infinite attribute of matter.

Necessity is the first ruler, the driver of nature that humans endeavors to make latent through freedom to mediate; but freedom is only possible upon the knowledge of necessity. Freedom is the human capacity to know how we are determined by necessity, and, through our own mediations, the additional capacity to introduce

---

730 Spinoza, B. (2010) *Ethics*. Part 1. Concerning God. Definitions. VI. Online in Wikisource. The Free Library. Accessed from <http://en.wikisource.org/w/index.php?title=Ethics_(Spinoza)/Part_1&oldid=2171549> on 2012-09-27.

our own historical needs. Through adequate ideas about the meaning of what we are and do, legitimized by our emotions and moral feelings we, humans, can gradually become relatively free while still depending on nature, that we are in the first place. Unfortunately, it is misunderstood freedom that has placed us at odds with nature.

We can augment or diminish nature both inside and outside of ourselves. We can also distort our knowledge of nature, and misguidedly abuse ourselves by abusing nature which we have done. Our natural activity become agency, driven from inside, is not just subordinated to the coerciveness of evolution and of natural selection that are determined externally. Abandoning the good sense of nature is violating the morality of evolution. The advantage to introduce mediations, becoming freer and more God-like or self-determined cannot divorce itself from the necessity of natural morality. This notion is central to Karen Horney's theory of narcissism. Idealized distortion falsifies our good sense self-image the same way Plato's idealism historically split our self-understanding.

Logically, Spinoza paved the way for Hegel and Marx, in the human sciences, as Descartes and Newton had done for natural science. "The order and connection of ideas is the same as the order and connection of things."[731] The logic we use reflects how natural phenomena operate in the first place. This is a huge statement that unifies epistemology and phenomenology: it tells us that the secret to logic is to follow the logic of the thing itself and from it draw the form of our understanding. This notion inverts Plato by properly placing the idea in its proper position, part of the thing.

A corollary is the relation between reason and emotion. Reason, opposite to what scientific ideology proclaims in the name of objectivity, cannot override and suppress its compass emotion. Emotion can however be overridden by a more fitting, more sublimated, or appropriate emotion. Discarding or subordinating emotion undermines reason. Emotion made a hierarchically determined binary of

---

731 Spinoza, B. (2010) *Ethics*. Part 1. Ibid. On the Origin and Nature of the Mind. Part 2. Proposition VII.

cognition, was, historically, subordinated as female was to male, or object to idea. But the natural phenomenon and its function can only be repressed to come back home to roost. Cognition without its other constraining side, emotion, leads the species to its *idiot savant* form of brilliant foolishness.

Along the same lines, in ethics good and evil are derivatives of pleasure and pain. For Spinoza the highest virtue is the intellectual love or understanding of the universe. "The knowledge of good and evil is nothing else but the emotions of pleasure or pain, in so far as we are conscious thereof,"[732] and: "By good I mean that which we certainly know to be useful to us."[733]

The method of Spinoza, advancing definitions, axioms, propositions and proofs, is the application of the scientific method. Any science that does not aim at ultimately fitting in a synthesis of all science retains only a narrow perspective. To Spinoza we owe a philosophical preparation for the project of a monistic science without the Cartesian split.

2.7.3 John Locke and the "Self"

Empiricism is the new perspective highlighted by English thinker John Locke (1632-1704) the representative of the new science in England, spreading its influence from the developments of Newton in physics, Boyle in the study of gases, and Sydenham in medicine, all following in the footsteps of Bacon and Hobbes. Locke ushered in modern liberalism in political life and we can find his signature in most of the parliamentary constitutions of modern states. Political liberalism is possible when every citizen has the psychological infrastructure to internalize within consciousness the structure of the modern governing state.

Knowledge has been tracked to its root, sensation, the agree-

---

732 Spinoza, B. (2010) *Ethics*. Part 1. Ibid. Part 4. Proposition VIII.
733 Spinoza, B. (2010) *Ethics*. Part 1. Ibid. On Human Bondage, or the Strength of the Emotions. Part 4. Definitions. I.

ment or disagreement of ideas with perceptions. The old certainty of identity is being replaced by motion, variation, coexistence, and opposition. Cartesian certainty is opinion, common sense. The same way in nature every animal has enough intelligence to survive, every human person in society has enough knowledge to address fundamental concerns. Excess knowledge is not necessarily good. The concept of substantial equality is making political headway as kingship is questioned.

Along with this democratic leveling comes the responsibility of each person to be a moral agent autonomously responsible for her/his actions and opinions, besides being contractually free. The new common sense is accountable to that of the majority.

Personal knowledge is universal and there are no innate ideas or practical principles, as Descartes believed. Our mind at birth is a blank slate upon which social experience will write what is deemed useful. Based on sensations, the vehicles for our ideas, conscious reflection provides us with a map of our own mental operations. Operations with ideas allow us not only to reflect reality but to also create illusions. We re-cognize things through organizing their material parts, and our words signify our ideas. Here Locke is getting quite close to a construct of *self*, the common sense organizer universal to all humans. Democracy simultaneously starts to make sense because we can now internalize repression on the model of political repression making the latter unnecessary.

Perceptual and reflective capacity, Descartes notwithstanding, extend to the animal kingdom. Animals also have knowing perceptions. Only abstraction, operating with operations, makes morality possible. This is also how ideas such as mode, substance, and relation, are simply derived from abstractions.

Locke's theory of the mind originates modern conceptions of identity and Self -"that thinking thing that is in us"-[734] provoking

---

734 Locke, J. (1690). *An Essay Concerning Human Understanding*. Chapter 27. §27. Suppositions that look strange are pardonable in our ignorance. Online in Enlightenment. Accessed from <http://enlightenment.supersaturated.com/johnlocke/BOOKIIChap-

a new current of philosophical work and psychology. By placing thinking, feeling, and reflexivity together to arrive at the central notions of individual autonomy and self-control, Locke sets the foundations for liberal democracy, human rights, and accountability. To adjust and survive in culture, an internal map of culture is necessary, self-consciousness, and that map is actively organized by what we call the self.

Locke for the first time defined the self as the continuity of consciousness originating in experience through sense perception. A *person* is a "thinking intelligent being, that has reason and reflection, and can consider itself as itself, the same thinking thing in different times and places"[735]

The science of the self proper in psychology started later with Hegel and his *Phenomenology* but here, in Locke, are its roots. Like Plato before him, and Hegel afterwards, Locke presents us with isomorphs: culture and self.

2.7.4 The Skepticism of Hume

Scottish philosopher David Hume (1711-1776) whose moral philosophy is a psychology,[736] was very skeptical about an entity called self. Hume's psychology is explained mostly in *A Treatise on Human Nature*, books Two ("On the Passions") and Three ("On Morals"),[737] where we can already see a sketch of the id and superego of Freud. However, there is no such a thing as a standing self for Hume; there is only a continuous sequence of experiences that leave impressions in the mind. Hume is of the opinion that, bombarded

---

terXXVII.html> on 2015-09-24.

735 Locke, J. (1690). *An Essay Concerning Human Understanding*. Chapter XXVII. §11. Consciousness makes personal Identity. Ibid.

736 Cohon, R. (2010). *Hume's Moral Philosophy*. Online in Stanford Encyclopedia of Philosophy. Accessed from <http://plato.stanford.edu/entries/hume-moral/> on 2012-09-21.

737 Hume, D. (2010). *A Treatise on Human Nature*. Online in Project Gutenberg EBook #4705. (Orig. Pub. 1789). Accessed from <http://www.gutenberg.org/files/4705/4705-h/4705-h.htm> on 2012-09-21.

by a constant input of external and internal "impressions," the mind cannot have constancy or identity. A self, as a discrete entity, cannot be simply construed from a series of mercurial impressions. Hume sees the constant activity of the self but cannot see it as a phenomenon. Different forms of memory found by neuroscience and the phenomenon of identity in change help us to understand the conundrum of Hume. Besides explicit memory that has its own localization in the medial temporal lobe of the brain and in the diencephalon, there are various forms of unconscious implicit or non-declarative memory. Those involve skills and habits, priming, simple classical conditioning of emotional responses and skeletal musculature, and the non-associative learning of habituation and sensitization. In the brain these have been mapped to different areas such as striatum, neocortex, amygdala, cerebellum, and reflex pathways.[738] The permanence of the self is in agency besides all these forms of memory, partially accessible through what Freud called preconscious and part-unconscious or inaccessible.

Morality for Hume is an interpersonal phenomenon originating in emotions coming from approval or disapproval while interacting with others. This is Hume's crucial contribution and the foundation of Karen Horney's theory of idealization, false self-presentation for political correctness. Consequent social emotions are pride and shame; other emotions arise from impressions of good or evil, pleasure or pain, usefulness and uselessness. Emotions shape the will, and reason alone is never enough motivation for human actions. The strength of the will must come from passion, and "is" and "ought to be" are at the core of human morality.

Hume also elaborates about empathy that for him involves moral appraisals of character traits, demeanor, and actions that stem from reverberating interpersonal feelings. Observation of others produces approval or disapproval that respectively go with pleasure and dis-

---

738 Squire, L.R. (2004). "Memory systems of the brain: A brief history and current perspective." Minireview. Neurobiology of Learning and Memory 82: 171–177. Online in Elsevier, www.sciencedirect.com. Accessed from <http://amyalexander.wiki.westga.edu/file/view/memory+systems.pdf> on 2016-07-27.

pleasure. Hume foretells the phenomenon of mirroring.

2.7.5 Kant's Dual Self

Hume's theory of a non-self has been called "Bundle theory"[739] and it contrasts with that of German philosopher Immanuel Kant's (1724-1804), who takes the opposite stand: there are two discrete selves, one empirical and one transcendental. We start to see here the twofold nature of subjectivity,[740] experience and behavior. This duality is expanded by American philosopher G. H. Mead (1863-1931) who proposes it as *I* and *me*,[741] and by French philosopher Simone de Beauvoir as "immanence" and "transcendence."[742] William James went farther proposing a larger number of selves.[743]

The mind for Kant *organizes* the manifold of raw sensations and intuitions along a spatial-temporal grid through a set of functions, among them knowledge generated by the application of concepts. The way our mind is put together for Kant does in fact reflect the way physics tells us nature is put together. Cognition requires not only perceptions but also *a priori* transcendental concepts or cate-

---

739 Azeri, S. (2008). The Riddle of Subjectivity: The Humean Notion of the Self. University of Otawa. Ontario. Canada. Library and Archives = Bibliothèque et Archives Canada, 2008. Canada. Accessed from <http://www.collectionscanada.gc.ca/obj/thesescanada/vol2/002/NR41626.PDF.> on 2012-09-09.

740 Azeri, S. (2008). The Riddle of Subjectivity: The Humean Notion of the Self. University of Otawa. Ontario. Canada. Library and Archives = Bibliothèque et Archives Canada, 2008. Canada. Accessed from <http://www.collectionscanada.gc.ca/obj/thesescanada/vol2/002/NR41626.PDF.> on 2012-09-09.

741 Mead, G.H. (1934). "The 'I' and the "me"", Section 22 in Mind Self and Society from the Standpoint of a Social Behaviorist (Edited by Charles W. Morris). Chicago: University of Chicago. Pp. 173-178. Online in https://brocku.ca/MeadProject/. Accessed from <https://brocku.ca/MeadProject/Mead/pubs2/mindself/Mead_1934_22.html> on 2016-07-25.

742 de Beauvoir, S. (1972). The Second Sex. Ch. 2. Psychology. Trans. by H M Parshley, London. Penguin. (Orig. Pub. 1949). Online in MIA. Accessed from <https://www.marxists.org/reference/subject/ethics/de-beauvoir/2nd-sex/> on 2015-07-23.

743 James, W. (1890). The Principles of Psychology. Chapter X. The Consciousness of Self. Online in Classics in the History of Psychology. An internet resource developed by Christopher D. Green. York University, Toronto, Ontario. Accessed from <http://psychclassics.yorku.ca/James/Principles/prin10.htm> on 2015-06017.

gories to organize the representation of reality. This is where nature and history meet. Our understanding translates phenomena into notions, and here again we have the roots of the duality *I* and *me*.

Categorical preconditions of experience such as time and space reflect real phenomena, but have no existence outside experience; they have to be imported from the mind. This is the case for mathematics and natural science. They are historical derivatives from our sensations and intuitions, applying themselves to our perceptions but having nothing to do with reality itself. They are transcendental, in the sense of non-natural. Here is the Platonic and Cartesian split in operation.

On the other hand, the outcome of the operations of the mind, the transcendental unity of apperception, constantly synthesizes toward totality. Apperception includes the use of past experience to recognize the present, and is the mechanism that organizes our multiple simultaneous sensations from their original chaos. "The first pure cognition of understanding, then, upon which is founded all its other exercise, and which is at the same time perfectly independent of all conditions of mere sensuous intuition, is the principle of the original synthetical unity of apperception."[744] This is the transcendental self of Kant, in which Marx includes besides "I" "the ensemble of the total of human relations," the *I* and *me* of Mead.[745]

The idealist views of Kant have become mainstream pillars of modern cognitive science that, separate cognition from emotion. The core of this method is postulating unobservable mental mecha-

---

744 Kant, I. (2003). *The Critique of Pure reason.* Chapter II. Of the Deduction of the Pure Conceptions of the Understanding. SS 13. The Principle of the Synthetical Unity of Apperception is the highest Principle of all exercise of the Understanding. Online in The Project Gutenberg EBook of The Critique of Pure Reason, by Immanuel Kant. (EBook #4280). (Orig. Pub. 1781). Accessed from <http://www.gutenberg.org/files/4280/4280-h/4280-h.htm> on 2012-09-28.

745 Mead, G.H. (1934). "The 'I' and the "me"", Section 22 in Mind Self and Society from the Standpoint of a Social Behaviorist (Edited by Charles W. Morris). Chicago: University of Chicago. Pp. 173-178. Online in https://brocku.ca/MeadProject/. Accessed from <https://brocku.ca/MeadProject/Mead/pubs2/mindself/Mead_1934_22.html> on 2016-07-25.

nisms in order to explain observed behavior,[746] the same error Freud fell into postulating psychic agencies to explain behavior. The "transcendental" mind is Freud's metapsychology,[747] not theological but still idealist.

Kant correctly argues that our consciousness, always linked to particular objects, has to reconstruct from synthetic intuition, inclusion of context, classification, and totalization. Imagination depends on memory that conserves, retrieves and reproduces object, context and meaning. This is the process of conceptual recognition. Sensual experience needs reproductive imagination that, in turn, needs conceptual recognition.[748] This is close to Lacan's three orders, real, imaginary and symbolic.[749]

In the last instance the real, for Kant, cannot be known; all we can count on is our perception of it. Our logic is already there prior to our experience, and our experience catches phenomena, appearances behind which logic discovers an inaccessible reality. Logical judgments apply only to the phenomenal appearances. We may believe but can't really know. Against Spinoza, Kant still separates reality from consciousness.

Kant's moral theory[750] is most familiar. Actions are morally right as measured by their dutiful motives, not by any other selfish interests. A duty is the need to submit to a law that applies to the universe

---

746 Brook, A. (2008). "Kant's View of the Mind and Consciousness of Self", The Stanford Encyclopedia of Philosophy (Winter 2011 Edition), Edward N. Zalta (ed.). Accessed from <http://plato.stanford.edu/archives/win2011/entries/kant-mind/> on 2012-09-27.

747 Freud, S. (1963). *General Psychological Theory: Papers on Metapsychology.* (Orig. Pub. 1923). New York. Touchstone, Simon and Schuster, Inc.

748 Kant, I. (2003) Ibid. SS 6. SECTION III. Of the Pure Conceptions of the Understanding, or Categories.

749 Felluga, D. (2011). "Modules on Lacan: On the Structure of the Psyche." Introductory Guide to Critical Theory. Online in Purdue U. Accessed from <http://www.purdue.edu/guidetotheory/psychoanalysis/lacanstructure.html> on 2016-07-27..

750 Kant, I (2002) *Fundamental Principles of the Metaphysic of Morals.* Online in The Project Gutenberg EBook of Fundamental Principles of the Metaphysic of Morals by Immanuel Kant. (Ebook #5682). (Orig. Pub. 1785). Accessed from <http://www.gutenberg.org/cache/epub/5682/pg5682.html> on 2012-09-28.

of human actions. According to this *Categorical Imperative* each one of us must always act as if we are setting a lawful precedent for everyone else. We must treat ourselves and humanity, always as an end, not as a means. This is the old Golden Rule that capitalism egregiously ignores. It is altruism or empathy in practice.

Like Hume, Kant is faced with the problem of culture. History bestows upon us the knowledge produced by all previous generations, a knowledge that reciprocally shapes us starting with our brains. All knowledge, including knowing skills, is inherited as culture. That is the real transcendence, the real *a priori*, not abstract but as material as nature. Social knowledge gives form to our essence, *sapiens*, the ensemble of the social relations that constitutes my essence. Freud did get close with his notion of superego, and Mead and Baldwin[751] with their socializing *Me*.

2.7.6 The Hegelian Dialectic Monism

After Kant came the absolute idealism of German philosopher Johann Gottlieb Fichte (1762-1814) and the more moderate objective idealism of German philosopher Friedrich Wilhelm Schelling (1775-1854) contemporaneous of Hegel. Fichte criticized any concessions his predecessor may have made to materialism. He continues with the idea of a transcendental ego constituted by reason, will, knowledge and activity. The individual is a natural moral agent bound by living in a society of like individuals. There is also a supra-individual pure ego that encompasses all empirical egos. Knowledge is activity and nature can be known only by acting upon it. It is interesting that ego, the most accessible part of the self in observable behavior, is the focus of philosophical, attention before the self. In psychoanalysis, also, ego theory also preceded self theory.

G. W. F. Hegel (1770-1831) is an objective idealist who rep-

---

751 Baldwin, J.M. (1901). Dictionary of Philosophy and Psychology. New York. The Macmillan Company. Online in Classics in the History of Psychology. An internet resource developed by Christopher D. Green. York University, Toronto, Ontario. Accessed from <http://psychclassics.yorku.ca/Baldwin/Dictionary/> on 2016-07-28.

resents the peak and the end of the tradition of German idealism that contains the seeds of human science in particular. Hegel is the bridge to scientific materialism, and in fact his disciple Feuerbach accused him of being a closet materialist. Hegel makes his main concession to materialism by rescuing the dialectical method that was used by the Pre-Socratics. This "new" method is a logic critical of Aristotelian formal logic, a logic of motion and development. He focuses on self that is more than ego and supersedes it. Ultimately not concomitant with his own historical method, Hegel decrees his society to be the end of history, of a theodicy. Having already in his *Phenomenology* discovered the key to humans' liberation from patriarchal capitalism, he fought for the rest of his life to avoid facing the implications of his theory that were then uncovered by his disciples. At the end he was another apologist of the *status quo* in Prussia. He is a Spinozist in that for him God and nature are one, a Heraclitean in that he proposes a logic of motion and activity, the constant negation of stasis, but also a Platonist in that his origin of everything is still in the idea, in God. In fact Hegel was the first philosopher to see in philosophy a continuous historical dialogue, a chain of failed attempts at reaching truth.

Hegel sees rationality as analogic with reality, not separate or *a priori* but embedded. With reality, rationality evolves developmentally. As idealist, he still starts from God that embodied and alienated himself in nature, recovering himself in Prussian culture and particular in Hegel's philosophy. Logic is not transcendental but natural, and it is not difficult to infer from his theory that God is the logic of evolution, the Verb.

The study of logic thus investigates the fundamental structure of reality itself, the human mind's always moving syllogistically from perception to challenge to compromise that restarts the process all over again. This logic of motion is illustrated in the narrative of the history of philosophy itself. Each time a theory seems to have settled it is challenged on the basis of its inherent contradictions. What Hegel aspired to accomplish, and Kant failed to achieve, was to heal the old philosophical gap between idealism and science reigning from Plato to Descartes, through the development of a systematic monist philosophy that conserved the place of God. Having been educated in formal logic is a major challenge to understand the novelty of Hegel's narrative, his philosophy of motion and development that tries to explain nature and history, matter and consciousness, society and self, and natural and social science within the parameters of history. I will review some of his main categories relevant to the present work.

Hegel starts his major work with the *Phenomenology of Spirit,*[752] a logical beginning for an idealist. Already this first work is a scientific blueprint of psychoanalysis, and the spirit in question is the mind, subjective spirit, but also culture. *Culture* is objective spirit arising from the collective interaction of all individuals in society, abstract universality that makes the concrete individuality of the ego possible. This is what Lacan means when he says that we don't make language but on the contrary language makes us. This syllogistic premise: all men (universal), are made through culture (particular), individuals (individual). Reality and consciousness are married in history and, most important, it is impossible to understand one without the other; the understanding of their marriage is the truth. Understanding is in motion and has to be approached in motion. Motion is oppositional negation, and the negation of that negation. Time for example, is the constant negation of successive moments.

Understanding must be ethical, not misunderstanding. *Ethics* is the interaction of opposites individual freedom challenged by social duty. An ethical life must be based on the recognition of one's stake in the general good of human society. The important inference is

---

752 Hegel, G.W.F. (1967). *Hegel's Phenomenology of Mind*. Harper & Row's Torchbooks' edition (1967) of the Phenomenology (1807), translated by J B Baillie (1910), from University of Idaho, Department of Philosophy, thanks to Jean McIntire. § numbers from the Baillie translation have been inserted into the text of the Baillie translation and linked to explanations by J N Findlay. Φ links to original German text: Phänemenologie des Geistes. Online in MIA. Accessed from <https://www.marxists.org/reference/archive/hegel/phindex.htm> on 2014-10-05.

that there can be no peace of mind, no quality of life, as long as one single human suffers. Social order starts in family life with its spontaneity, emotional reciprocity, and common identity. The challenge to family life, its moving opposite, is civil society, where regulation of difference occurs through exchange, consent and compromise. The result of global social compromise is the State, a sort of larger family that actualizes the larger collective will of civil society. The State to sociology is the Self of psychology.

Among cultural phenomena, *Art* is the compromising transcendence of the subject-object dichotomy that reveals their underlying unity; the regression of the subject with the ascension of the object. Starting as plain symbolic representation, it is constantly challenged by a cultural style that at the time of Hegel was Romanticism. *Religion* challenges art and their compromise is *Philosophy*. Here is the compromise between rationalism and empiricism, versions of the old split in philosophy. *History* is challenged only by "the Absolute," the *Spirit* of dialectical idealism, God. Their ultimate compromise is the Prussian Monarchy, the model of a human society, Hegel's inconsequence with himself, with his whole theory. In today's lingo: "there is no alternative."

The major contribution of Hegel is to have revived the new logic of the Ionians, applicable to processes and motion and making a paradigm of evolution possible; the ancient logic had been inherited from matriarchy, where progress was achieved not through destruction but through conserving compromise, sublation. Hegel reconnects us to the mainstream of logic after the long detour of patriarchy, dialectics representing the true logic of nature.[753] Hegel is the first modern evolutionist; his logic operates according to its main principle, the inclusion of contradiction as a necessity in motion that

---

753 Engels, F. (1925). *Dialectics of Nature*. First Published: in Russian and German in the USSR in 1925, except for Part Played by Labour, 1896 and Natural Science and the Spirit World, 1898; Transcribed: by Sally Ryan and jjazz@hwcn.org 1998/2001; Notes and Fragments transcribed by Andy Blunden 2006. Online in MIA. Accessed from <https://www.marxists.org/archive/marx/works/1883/don/index.htm> on 2017-03-02.

we call dynamics.

Constant motion is reflected in the fact that time and space operate through a constant self-negation; they are and immediately cease to be. Time and space through motion deny their here-and-nowness since when I finish experiencing it is already there-and-then. In space every point denies and is denied by its next. The motion inherent in everything is prompted by the fact that all physical and social objects harbor within themselves a binomial contradiction that seeks a compromise of self-renovation. Although opposites are in conflict, they finally embrace and compromise.

One example in physics is matter and energy; it is only through their different forms of embrace and dance that the infinite variations of reality can be produced. An analogue, from computer science, is the way one and zero bits combine to result in their universe of imagery and meaning and their artificial intelligence. It is the same in Horney's psychology, moving toward, against and away, the titration of the three trends' producing character and psychopathology.

A tenet of dialectical thinking is that change can occur quantitatively, *i.e.*, cold to hot water, by small variation or qualitatively, as a jump (water, ice, steam), and that quantity and quality are in a dialectical relation in opposition to each other. Niles Eldredge and Stephen Jay Gould have illustrated this in science with their theory of punctuated equilibrium in evolution.[754]

Operation by contradiction, qualitative and quantitative change, and the negation of the negation, the reiteration of constant motion, are the central features of dialectics. If we see the dialectical method as simply a reflection of the processes of nature, then it is logical that these are lawful processes based on necessity. Darwin's context and relationship in variation, Sartre's analysis and synthesis, progression and regression in methodology, and Marx's base and su-

---

754 Gould, Stephen Jay, & Eldredge, Niles (1977). "Punctuated equilibria: the tempo and mode of evolution reconsidered." Paleobiology 3 (2): 115-151. (p.145). Online in a Reprint from Paleobiology. Accessed from <http://www.nileseldredge.com/pdf_files/Punctuated_Equilibria_Gould_Eldredge_1977.pdf> on 2012-09-29.

perstructure in society are examples of the application of dialectical thinking. Freud was at times a naïve dialectician.[755]

We have already seen that the psychological equivalent of physical motion or energy is activity. The reality of the psyche, according to materialist monist principles, is the result of the active evolution of one substance only, matter, bifurcating at some point, most visibly in the animal stage of evolution to produce reflection through irritability and sensation. Although matter at this all-comprehensive point is almost as much of a fictional generalization as it is God, the difference is that science accepts the hypothesis of matter as a gradually testable and provable one that has already been materially supported through the discovery of molecules and atoms and their manipulable components and properties.

2.7.7 Hegel's Psychology

After his early writings in theology, Hegel's psychology started as the philosophy of the *Subjective Spirit* in the *Phenomenology*.[756] Spirit or mind is moral freedom that manifests itself historically and hence its various terms reflect developmental stages. Moral freedom is the only pathognomonic human phenomenon but it has its roots in the good sense of nature. This perennial and teleological good sense evolved successively through organismic sensitivity, to sensation, perception, thought, knowledge, language, consciousness, intelligence, self, and morality subjectively, in each individual human. The objective transformation of nature by subjects, through their labor, reciprocally determined this growth, and this is the *objective*

---

755 Rendon, M. „Philosophical Paradigms in Psychoanalysis". J. Amer. Acad. Psychoan. 14, (4), 1986. pp 495-506.

756 Hegel, G.W.F. (1967). Hegel's Phenomenology of Mind. B. Self Consciousness. 3. Lord and Bondsman. From Harper & Row's Torchbooks' edition (1967) of the Phenomenology (1807), translated by J B Baillie (1910), from University of Idaho, Department of Philosophy, thanks to Jean McIntire. § numbers from the Baillie translation have been inserted into the text of the Baillie translation and linked to explanations by J N Findlay. Φ links to original German text: Phänemenologie des Geistes. Online in MIA. Accessed from <https://www.marxists.org/reference/archive/hegel/phindex.htm> on 2014-10-05.

spirit of the *Philosophy of Right,* [757] subjective spirit objectified. This dialectical process of reciprocity is necessary because the concept of God, alienated itself in nature, must through freedom re-appropriate itself. We must remember that, since Spinoza, God is good sense, the purpose, of both evolution and history. God's alienation means that good sense has been lost and it is no longer good sense. All this is simply to say that alienation is the loss of good sense, that good sense was lost in the randomness of nature, and that the task of the human species is to recover its good sense.

Freedom is the sense of autonomy, rationality, and self deter-mination produced by the unique human capacity to mediate, and, most importantly, self-mediate. Hegel insists on the distinctness of human self-consciousness from the needs-based good sense, coher-ence, and previous consciousness of the natural world. The human spiritual reality has transcended, freed itself from nature's coercion and laws, and is something separate and different. As an idealist He-gel goes too far in terms of the idea of God's being at the beginning and at the end. This is not so problematic however, if we consider God to be the good sense of nature.

To understand Hegel's psychology that is not separate but irre-mediably attached to its object, the universe, it is necessary to look at it historically: as events conserved and conceptualized. We must look at it epigenetically: each event generates the next. And finally, we must look at it teleologically: as having a sense and a meaning. That is how psychology itself comes from anthropology that in turn comes from philosophy, religion, mythology, totemism, etc.

The other crucial characteristic of Hegel's psychology is that philosophically it is the history of failures. The history of explana-tion from totemism to science is the history of failures to explain the cosmos and all that it includes in its evolution up to consciousness. However, each failure is an advance, and it is buttressed by all pre-vious failures that are conserved in history. This negative view leads

---

757 HeHegel, G,W,F. (1820). Hegel's Philosophy of Right. Translated: by S W Dyde, 1896. (First Published: by G Bell, London, 1896).

us to the notion of negation itself, the ground of dialectical logic, as we have seen, a logic of motion.

Psychology has been concerned with phenomena, manifold and sundry: perception, attention, memory, will, *etc*. Hegel's goal is to get behind phenomena and logically link their successive epigeneses that constitute their essence. If Hegel starts with God, we place in His stead nature's good sense or direction as the ground upon which the whole structure is built. Psychology starts with the concept of *soul* that is not yet psychological, but religious and therefore anthropological. The soul is conserved as the oldest psychological phenomenon upon which the rest of psychology is going to be built. The soul is unconscious. Upon the soul comes consciousness that is able to phenomenologically classify; we can see that this property is not exclusively human, because animals practically classify good and harmful. Upon that animal consciousness is built self-consciousness, psyche, and self. This is consciousness of consciousness, alien to any other species but the human. This is how psychology is integrated into the wider scientific realm of evolution and history. Operational self-consciousness, after ascending, reached its plateau with the Greek philosophers and has continued from philosophy to science. Whether it will continue to ascend in science or else descend to death is up to us, whether or not we recover our lost good sense.

We can thus say that our mediations are accidental, because we know the cosmos will go on without us, and the true meaning of this accident that is humanity is that we are closer but still unable to explain. I believe the answer is not in consciousness, the mind, or science, its last stage. I believe it is in morality, what Horney most properly called *the morality of evolution*. This morality is going back to our evolutionary good sense, the fact that we were designed to be fully human, universally so, and we, alienated in the object money, are putting obstacles to that goal. We have misunderstood the meaning of wealth inherent in *being* because we have historically displaced it to *having,* through the second-order mediations of patriarchy and capitalism. Hegel tried to say this with his notion of *recognition,* but because of his ideology ended up trying to square the circle.

The alternative to Hegel, the matriarchal metaphor within the Marxist tradition, is represented by Vygotsky as a horizontal form of reciprocal development in which a more developed self, mothering, freely contributes to the development of the less developed one, depending child. What allows for growth and development for Vygotsky is the *zone of proximal development,* the overlapping intersubjective area where learning is possible. This is similar to agriculture, placing the seed where the land is ready, and also to what psychoanalysts called *timing,* not interpreting before the patient is ready. Both paradigms, Hegelian and Vygotskyan, can be conducive to human substantial equality, because the first belongs in civil society and the second in the by-nature ethical family. It is in civil society that we needed "ethics," and the State is the failed attempt to bring civil society to a family morality.

The subjective spirit of Hegel is *individual* consciousness, also *universal* because it is partaken of by all members of the species, culture internalized with a regulatory self-analogue of the State. Objectified through labor, subjective spirit becomes culture that in turn is internalized as consciousness. Culture is thus produced through the objectification of historical subjects, through labor that transforms nature and creates technology, and regulatory institutions that includes "ethics," because in split-class society there is not one morality as there was in the original gens, but two or more.

Hegel was part of the Romantic movement[758] that had its roots in Spinoza, aiming to rescue the unity of nature and mind from a dry rationalistic philosophy failing to explain them. Nature, governed by lawful and compelling necessity, entails the endless evolutionary dependency of objects upon each other even though they may appear separate and autonomous at first sight. The movement of evolution becomes part of the shared essence of all connected material and

---

758 Taylor, C. (1989). *Sources of the Self. Te Making of the Modern Identity.* Cambridge. Cambridge University Press

spiritual objects, because subjectivity emerges from objectivity. The issue for an evolutionary science then becomes to find the universal logical connections. The huge epistemological shift is from *objects* to their *relations* and from phenomena to what matters, essence. Consciousness appears as self-reliant as nature because it mirrors the self-reliance of nature. Consciousness is nature.

Hegel saw the empiricists before him as wrongly separating subject and object, and emphasizing their difference rather than their co-dependence and truthful isomorphism. His novelty is to have made the two realms continuous. Nature is objective because it appears external and so autonomous that it required a God to explain its good sense. Thought on the other hand is subjective because it is internal, it exists only inside of itself, and it does not need anything else to exist (in Hegel's view). Thought challenges natural necessity with its freedom, its lack of dependency on objects, except that today we know it relies on glucose, oxygen and blood circulation to operate. That the world is self-unfolding, externalization, or self differentiating activity, is the Darwinian kernel in Hegel's thought, a huge compromise with materialism.

Hegel thus presaged Darwin's theory of evolution by stating that nature is to be viewed as a system of stages, emerging of necessity one from another in succession. However, he qualified this further by stating that such evolution occurs within the terms of the idea or logos. Logos is only the inherent coherence of nature as we see it after our brain has evolved to be able to do so. Nature comes to exist *for itself*, reflexively, in the human brain. Spirit/Mind for Hegel is mistakenly the absolute that in fact is only the other side of matter.

In summary Hegel's psychology is still subordinated to theology, but its scientific translation and method render it useful. In spite of being the kernel of psychology, Hegel's theory cannot extricate itself from idealism, split ideology. In spite of all the evidence he produces, Hegel cannot see the fact that, developmentally, we evolved from nature to, quite late, being able to conceptualize a God, particularly in a monotheistic form.

From reflections, sensations and perceptions come, first, partial representations of properties and then total representations of objects and the world. Reflections become ideas in memory, then narratives, theories, and ambitious grand narratives such as Hegel's own. Changes in nature transform the psyche in diverse ways that we learn to arrange into classes or particulars. A myth such as God served the purpose of closing the circle of understanding, the historical *panchreston* that also failed. Based on syllogistic oppositions, Hegel's logic operates within the continuity of evolution and history, reflecting the motion of nature in that one event succeeds another. The three syllogistic elements, individual, particular and universal, take turns in mediating each other; each synthesis is a new thesis, singled out, then paired by its opposite, and finally triangulated in a continuous recursive chain.

This is the model for intellectual and moral development. Subjectivity is the expression of human individuality, which in turn derives from the universality of culture to which it must, morally, return. An individual biography starts with temperament and moves to character or attitude, personality and self first being shaped in the context of family and culture, then of civil society and government. Freedom cannot exist without the knowledge of necessity.

Individuality manifests itself in will and judgment. Judgment is individual sense or coherence, morally applied consciousness. We each started with perceptions of colors, smells, sounds, *etc*, becoming meaningful from their attractive or repulsive qualities, their usefulness. Meaning becomes consensual but conserves its idiosyncracy because: "It is important to include here the line of connection by which anger and courage are felt in the breast, the blood, desire in the reproductive system, irritation, and contemplation, intellectual activity in the head, which is also considered the centre of the sensible system."[759]

---

759 Hegel GWF. (1830). "The Soul." The Encyclopedia of the Philosophical Sciences in Outline. C. The Philosophy of Spirit. Section one: Subjective spirit. A. The Soul. § 318. Online in Marxists Internet Archive. Accessed from <http://www.marxists.org/reference/archive/hegel/works/sp/sssoul.htm> on 2012-09-29.

Most important to keep in mind is Hegel's culture-consciousness and state-self isomorphisms that had been sketched since Plato. The full secret of self is revealed as of government, as self-governance.

2.8 THE METABOLISM OF CONSCIOUSNESS:[760] CRITIQUE OF MARX'S PSYCHOLOGY

"Historical materialism is that view of the course of history which seeks the ultimate cause and the great moving power of all historic events in the dialectic of sex: the division of society into two distinct biological classes for procreative re-production, and the struggles of these classes with one another; in the changes in the modes of marriage, reproduction and childcare created by these struggles; in the connected development of other physically-differentiated classes [castes]; and in the first division of labor based on sex which developed into the [economic-cultural] class system."

"All past history [note that we can now eliminate 'with the exception of primitive stages'] was the history of class struggle. These warring classes of society are always the product of the modes of organization of the biological family unit for reproduction of the species, as well as of the strictly economic modes of production and exchange of goods and services. The sexual-reproductive organization of society always furnishes the real basis, starting from which we can alone Work out the ultimate explanation of the whole superstructure of economic, juridical and political institutions as well as of the religious, philosophical and other ideas of a given historical period."

Shulamith Firestone,[761] *The Dialectic of Sex*

---

760 Here I apply Meszaros' theory mostly based on: Meszaros, I. (2010-2011). Social Structure and Forms of Consciousness. 2 Vols. New York. Monthly Review Press.

761 Firestone, S. (1970). *The Dialectic of Sex: The Case for Feminist Revolution.* New York. Bantam Books. Online in The Internet Archive. Accessed from <https://teori-

2.8.1 The Basics

In the above quote Firestone paraphrases Engels in *Socialism, Utopian and Scientific*,[762] to shift the emphasis from the economic determination of history so visible in patriarchy, and particularly in capitalism, to its older biological imperatives, instinctual and sexual, from which psychology starts. That there are two sexual classes before the socioeconomic ones, and that those two struggle in different ways, countering force with solidarity, has been demonstrated in observation of apes, evolutionarily close to humans.[763]

Marx rooted his theory of society upon Freud's mercurial "other" instinct, self-preservation that initially Freud called ego instinct.[764] I argue that the self-preservation instinct's first manifestation is *maternal altruism*. This instinct is manifest in other species before the human, as the maternal investment in her progeny and the maternal determination to protect, defend, and develop her offspring at her own risk. I believe in this regard Marx and Freud complement each other. Marxist political economy is the science of the other, even more deeply repressed and mystified unconscious: our survival economy. Marx put it very simply: before we do anything else, we have to breathe, eat, and take care of our biological imperatives. Here we must remember that survival implies destruction.

In the reproduction of the species the instrument is the body and in sexuated species two bodies are required, making reproduction an externally dependent phenomenon. Instead of two's coming from one, as happens in parthenogenesis, in sexual reproduction for the

aevolutiva.files.wordpress.com/2013/10/firestone-shulamith-dialectic-sex-case-feminist-revolution.pdf> on 2015-09-25.

762 Engels, F. (1970). *Socialism: Utopian and Scientific*. Marx/Engels Selected Works, Volume 3, p. 95-151. Moscow. USSR. Progress Publishers. (Orig. Pub. 1880).

763 Smuts, B (1995). "The Evolutionary Origins of Patriarchy." Human Nature, Vol. 6, No., 1, pp. 1-32. Accessed from <https://isites.harvard.edu/fs/docs/icb.topic1001965.files/Course%20Materials_Week%205/Evolution%20of%20Patriarchy%20Smuts%201995.pdf> on 2017-04-07.

764 Freud, S. (1913). *The Claims Of Psychoanalysis To Scientific Interest*. P. 2818. Online in Ivan Smith: Freud - Complete Woks. Accessed from <https://www.valas.fr/IMG/pdf/Freud_Complete_Works.pdf> on 2017-04-08.

purpose of better quality the equation is inverted: one comes from two. I have pointed out that, with the exception of the 50/50 meiotic combination the contribution of each sex is significantly different, that of the father being limited to copulation and single-spermatozoid fertilization. All the producing, growing and development, tasks during the initial period of life, are the burden of the mother. She imprints the psychological first order mediations (let's say attitudes, gestures, and their translation into meaningful symbols) necessary for natural and social survival in a hostile world, particularly considering that her infant is always premature. The first psychological imprint and blueprint are maternal, as are the first form of proxy-consciousness and self: that most archaic, outer, matriarchal self, becomes the ground of *me* before ego can say *I*.

2.8.2 Why Metabolism

In medicine the concept of metabolism, the internalization of chemical processes for self-regulation, illustrates the mechanisms that keep organisms alive through constructive anabolic processes and destructive catabolic ones. Although this is usually applied to physiological processes, it also applies to psychological ones. Metabolism is the living dialectic of an organism, and through it survival energy is provided to an open system along with the mechanisms for its use and the disposition of toxic waste, the beginning and end of metabolism. Metabolism transforms; it destroys forms of energy to create new ones useful and to its advantage. It also allows for energy storage in regulated amounts that will serve predictable needs. Metabolism makes it possible to accelerate responses to environmental changes without necessarily involving slow and costly changes in bodily morphology. In this regard, consciousness is the paradigm of metabolism.

Through ingestion and disposal of waste, internal metabolism is ecologically connected to the larger natural one contributing to the larger homeostasis. It also connects, uniquely, through consciousness, to the social metabolism. In this regard, through our senses we internalize social universality to transform it into cultural particularity through individual activity. The formal waste of redundancy and uselessness of myriads of sensations that are discarded is compounded by the imbalance of ideology that precludes true consciousness aimed at skirting the necessary return to human universality. Conscious metabolism is a byproduct of its material analogue and is always irremediably connected to it. Humans are mediators with additional moral responsibility in the chain of larger processes of nature. Metabolism is a dynamic process that sustains life. The metabolism of an infant is different from that of an adult and it is partially external, mother-managed.

Marx contributed to the early science of ecology when he pointed out the negative impact of urbanization. Capitalism, industrialization, and their consequences, particularly in the handling of waste, have created what he called a *metabolic rift*.[765] After him, Istvan Meszaros has championed the understanding of the concept of metabolic processes in society and consciousness.[766] Central to the understanding of metabolism are the concepts of *system, boundaries, self-regulation*, and *homeostasis*; also the concept of *recursion*, that reflects the fact that, in a complex system, subsystems operate in similar, analogic metabolic ways. This is the case for culture and consciousness, and political government and self.

Leontiev tells us that first-order sensual food links with nature clearly manifest in infancy as instincts mediated by the mother. Development moves humans to second order (conscious) operations through associations that appear and disappear slowly with environmental conditions.[767] New habits for food-seeking are acquired, be-

765 Bellamy Foster, J. (1999). "Marx's Theory of Metabolic Rift: Classical Foundations for Environmental Sociology." American Journal of Sociology. Volume 105 Number 2 (September): Pp. 366–405. Online in UNC.edu. Accessed from <http://www.unc.edu/courses/2008spring/geog/804/001/210315.pdf> on 2016-08-06.
766 Meszaros. I. (1995). Beyond Capital. Towards a Theory of Transition. New York. Edition Published by Monthly Review Press.
767 Leontiev A.N. (1981). "An outline of the evolution of the psyche" (pp. 156-326). Problems of the Development of the Mind. Trans. M. Kopylova Moscow: Progress

cause the surrounding conditions, starting with the body itself, have changed. This happens phylogenetically and ontogenetically, and the subject-animal is equipped to recognize itself differently, as the receptor of those changed conditions. This is possible through the plasticity of its senses and consciousness. Before it eats, the subject must recognize itself as properly fitted for the object that stimulates its hunger.

This is the beginning of a metabolic consciousness that builds upon instinct, and that sparks as the fitting picture and grammar of the relationship with its environment are internalized as part of consciousness. The active mirror-like emerging structure in the brain develops during the life process to be able to mirror it, including itself. Conscious metabolic internalization is purely formal although still based on brain chemistry. Food chain and conscious mediation part ways as forms of metabolism, but remain connected.

Through the new seemingly endless capacity of learning based on new needs fulfillment, a gradual differentiation of adaptive operations also appears, sensory-motor modules that characterize the evolutionary stage of the perceptive psyche we share with animals. More advanced conditioned learning lays the foundations for the evolution of automatized experience. This is how bundled automated sensory-motor operations susceptible of accommodation appear as sensorimotor *habits*. Metabolically, we have then replaced instincts with cultural habits.

Perceptual-motor habits appear in animals through the same associative conditioning where consciousness starts. Habits arise from actions developed to overcome obstacles, and are determined by the character of the obstacles they face. After they have been learned, they are hardwired through repetitive use, but, unlike instincts, they can be unlearned. Learned new strategies are tried in similar situations and, through reciprocal processes of assimilation and accommodation, fitting generalizations take place that are integrated into

---

Publishers. There is an Online Edited version by Paul F. Ballantyne, Ph. D. Accessed from <http://www.igs.net/~pballan/Leontiev1981chapt2.htm> on 2012-05-24.

an automatized memory that releases them according to perceived conditions.

The sensorimotor elements forming part of the repertoire of habits of an animal may thus be both species-specific innate movements, or movements acquired through experience and learned into habit. These are movements neurologically ensembled in reflex sequences, structures, or modules bundled in the course of chance trial-and-error attempts to solve problems. Their success resides in the final fulfillment of needs, in their repetition and generalization, and in their economic automation.

Psychology studies the most complex operations of a subject that grow from total dependence and vicarious selfhood to self-consciousness and relative autonomy. Psychoanalysis, in particular, focuses on those always-developing relationships from a direct intersubjective stand mediated by theory. Developmental psychologists have successfully filled many theoretical gaps particularly in family life. Similarly, Marx, Engels and others in sociology have explored the domain of civil society.

The brain is split in two halves that represent a natural duality. This duality may parallel sexuation and therefore dual instinctual consciousness in ways we don't understand yet. It is possible that brain dominance reflects the imbalance historically created by patriarchal domination. In its vertical dimension, the brain tells a phylogenetic history from its reptilian to its human form. Areas that we know are involved with habit are the basal ganglia, caudate nucleus, putamen and globus pallidus. Specialized areas of the cortex, particularly prefrontal, have more to do with discrimination, choice, anticipation, imagination, problem-solving, and values. That new motor habits require new forms of representation in memory has been well established in animals.[768]

---

768 See for example: Carruthers, P. (1998). "Animal Subjectivity." PSYCHE, 4(3), April. Accessed from <http://www.theassc.org/files/assc/2377.pdf> on on 2015-06-12. Also: Rolls, E.T. (2001). *"Representations in the Brain."* Synthese 129: 153–171. Kluwer Academic Publishers. Accessed from <http://redwood.psych.cornell.edu/discussion/papers/rolls_representation.pdf> on 2015-06-11.

From mechanisms that fulfill basic natural needs to complex high-order mental functions, humans arrive at self-consciousness. This is a metabolic process of growth that operates phylogenetically and ontogenetically. It includes reciprocal adaptive processes such as assimilation and accommodation to changing external and internal conditions. The highest form of self-consciousness is morality, a sublimation of selective maternal altruism.

2.8.3 The Origins of Metabolic Consciousness

Consciousness is a phenomenon to be understood as a form of evolutionary unfolding that has taken different successive forms. This is the way Hegel approached it in the phenomenology. Most recently, the developmental psychologists from the cultural school, following Darwin and Romanes, track the phenomenon back to protoplasmic irritability that eventually evolved to become neuron and muscle. From irritability came sensation, and from the latter perception, thought, institutionalized knowledge, theory, culture, mythology, religion, philosophy, and science. Finally, praxis will come from the true unity of consciousness and human practice. This is an ontological sequence of forms of consciousness.

The specifically human form of consciousness occurred when animal consciousness became self-consciousness, consciousness of consciousness. For consciousness to recognize itself it has to become subjective. This qualitative change was probably the outcome of a long quantitative one in the animal kingdom that culminated in verbal and artistic communication. Chris Knight has suggested that the first form of art may have been body painting unfortunately perishable, used by women for solidarity purposes, to introduce the mediation of labor as a conditioned contingency of sexual access.[769] This is a well-documented and very plausible hypothesis.

Metabolism is a typical dialectical process, a play of opposites.

---

769 Knight, C. (1991). Blood Relations. Menstruation and the Origins of Culture. New Haven and London. Yale University Press.

Derived from the Greek word for change,[770] the structure of the word indicates that they understood the concept. *Metabolism* today is the ensemble of internalized physical, chemical, and psychological processes that allow an organism to regulate its life through operations, internal and external processes of destruction and production (negation, and negation of the negation). Already in his science-fiction novel *Autodidact Theologian* Syrian physician Ibn al-Nafis (1213-1288) is said to have explicitly stated that the body and its parts are in a continuous state of dissolution and reconstitution.[771] This has been scientifically proven to be correct. Reciprocal metabolic processes, have been well documented in physiology and are for the most part well understood today, including the important role of specialized proteins as enzymes and catalysts that facilitate and inhibit metabolic processes. Italian physiologist Santorio Sanctorius (1561-1636) experimented for years with his own metabolic balance. In 1614, in his book *Ars de statica medecina,* he was probably the first to publish results of a controlled study of metabolism. He weighed himself before and after different activities, eating, sleep, working, sex, fasting, drinking, and excreting, and concluded that most of the food he ingested was spent in "insensible perspiration."[772] This study, a first step in the understanding of metabolism, became the model for future physiological experiments.[773]

Selection is an intelligent natural process and more so sexual selection, which improves population health and protects against extinction.[774] Also, by its external dependency sexual selection con-

---

770 Etymonline. "Metabolism." Accessed from <http://www.etymonline.com/index.php?allowed_in_frame=0&search=metabolism> on 2016-08-07.

771 See Wikipedia: Ibn al-Nafis. Accessed from <http://en.wikipedia.org/wiki/Ibn_al-Nafis> on 2015-06-09.

772 See University of Exeter. Center for Medical History. Accessed from <http://humanities.exeter.ac.uk/history/research/centres/medicalhistory/projects/santoriosantorio/> on 2015-06-09.

773 See for example: The American Physiological Society *Timeline of Physiology. Endocrinology and Metabolism.* Accessed from <http://www.the-aps.org/mm/hp/Audiences/Sections/E-M/E-M-Timeline> on 2015-09-28.

774 Lumley, A, J. Michalczyk, Ł, et al. (). "Sexual selection protects against extinction." Nature 522, 470–473 (25 June 2015).

nects itself to the rest of nature. Historically, social institutions such as family, civil society, and the state have their own independent but interrelated, formally recursive metabolic processes. The family must prepare the individual for civil society and the latter must produce the individuals to run the state. These are metabolic substructures within larger metabolic structures all interconnected. The notion of psychological metabolism applies the physiologic model to the mind, and it is concerned with the processes of elaboration of internalized perceptions to meaningfully arrive at thoughts, knowledge, theories, and consequent social practice. The function of judgement requires the critical distinction between ideology and consciousness, *good sense* and *science*, as well as between commonsense and good sense. Common sense is the ideological perversion of good sense.[775]

Although mediated by chemical processes, psychological processes have their own, different level of explanation, at a higher level of abstraction and with different notions. The central issue here is then to what extent and how metabolism deviates from reflecting the morality of evolution, based on two instinctual dispositions reciprocally determined. This concern was one of philosophy before psychology. It immediately conjures the issue of mind autonomy, and particularly the function of a critical mind and self-government. Karen Horney saw the main distorting process as idealization in psychology, and this is corroborated by the historical detour of idealism in philosophy.

Even before humans it is mothers in other species that assure the proper operation of the basic survival skills for their expectable environment. These skills must be operative in each individual as a part of its consciousness. This means metabolically patriarchy is a historical antithesis of matriarchy, exclusive to few species in the most developed apes, and particularly to humans. If we consider it

---

775 Gramsci, A. (1999). *Selection from the Prison Notebooks.* III. The Philosophy of Praxis. 630 ff. Edited and translated by Quentin Hoare and Geoffrey Nowell Smith. London. Elecbooks. Accessed from <http://abahlali.org/files/gramsci.pdf> on 2017-04-10.

a necessary human adaptation to civil society, how is it that it has become an obstacle to the unfolding of history, manifested in war? How is it that its ideology is expressed in a lack of alternative?

Historical consciousness transformation takes place through a syllogistic logic that reflects the grammar of a reality that is itself metabolic. Hegel conveyed this when he compared language in consciousness to water in reality. Both are neutral universal solvents in their respective domains.[776] That so many individuals besides Charles Darwin and Alfred Russell Wallace for (example, Darwin's grandfather naturalist and poet Erasmus Darwin, French naturalist Jean-Baptiste Lamarck, British lawyer and geologist Charles Lyell, and philosopher Herbert Spencer, not to mention Hegel himself) almost simultaneously arrived at the same conclusion, from so many different syllogistic perspectives and particular points of view, is proof that the water of consciousness rather collectively had re-solved a riddle of nature. Consciousness is not an individual prerogative. This is why Marx believed that when a problem appears it is because the material conditions for its solution are within reach.[777] This means the subject is metabolically connected not only to the object of his study but also to the collective pulse of consciousness.

This coincides with naturalists' starting to shift their attention from things to relations, an epistemological and heuristic jump. Consciousness internalizes not only the image of its object, but also its properties, functions and relations, arriving at "Being-for-itself." The autonomy of the subject resides in that inner relation with its opposite that includes itself and the relation. Humans become con-

---

776 Hegel, G.F.W. (1969) *Hegel's Science of Logic.* The Doctrine of the Notion. Section Two: Objectivity. Chemism. The Chemical Process. §1583. Trans. by A. V. Miller. Sydney, Australia. Allen & Unwin. (Orig. Pub. 1812). Online in Marxists Internet Archive. Hegel by Hypertext. Accessed from <http://www.marxists.org/reference/archive/hegel/works/hl/hlobject.htm#HL3_729> on 2012-10-28.

777 Marx, K. (1977). *A Contribution to the Critique of Political Economy.* Preface. Moscow. Progress Publishers. (Orig. Pub. 1859). Online in MIA. Accessed from <https://www.marxists.org/archive/marx/works/1859/critique-pol-economy/preface.htm> on 2017-04-12.

scious of their selves when they realize their *being* is collective.[778] This is where we started and where we must return after the detour of patriarchy. This is the lesson Hegel synthesized in the metaphor of the master-slave dialectic. My self-image is contingent on that of all others. I am master and slave.

Metabolic consciousness is no exception to evolution, as we used to think; it is a more complex adaptive function in epigenetic continuity with animal habit and instinct, and beyond.[779]

2.8.4 First- and Second-Order Social Metabolism

Society's metabolism is constituted by individual units, the equivalent of cells that, as in previous organisms, are both separate and connected by the material processes of reproduction and production. Additionally and idiosyncratically, they are also separate and connected by constant psychological mirroring and recognition. Consciousness is formal reproduction that requires reflection and reciprocal mirroring between nature and subject and society and subject. Formal reproduction and production in humans lead to history, civilization, culture, and their corollary internal selves. Paradoxically, individuals psychologically emerge from the universality of culture to become its authors, not individually but particularly. That phenomenon is always present in a culture and social class, the latter initially gender-based and subsequently becoming socioeconomic. The historical transitions from evolution are characterized by a change in form of mediations, determined by two opposite instinctual dispositions.

---

778 Hegel, G,W,F, (1817 & revised up till his death in 1831). *Encyclopedia of the Philosophical Sciences.* Part One. First Subdivision. VII. Being. A. Quality. (b) Being Determinate. Reality, Being-for-another & Being-for-self. § 95. Online in MIA. Accessed from <https://www.marxists.org/reference/archive/hegel/works/sl/slbeing.htm> on 2015-06-08.

779 Vygotsky, L.S. (1931). "Genesis of Higher Mental Functions." In: *The History of the Development of the Higher Mental Functions.* Vol. 4. Pp. 97-120. The Collected Works of L. S. Vygotsky. Online in MIA. Accesed from <https://www.marxists.org/archive/vygotsky/works/1931/higher-mental-functions.htm> on 2015-06-12.

[780]The first human society was the gens, similar to what today we call an extended family, socially tied by blood or consanguinity, and self-understood animistically, through totemism, the first form of explanation. First-order mediations, material and psychological, that applied to this first form of social organization are as follows: Society was *matriarchal* (matrifocal, matrilineal), and matrilocal-continuing the natural strategies of female selection and female hegemony. Gender-wise it was substantially equal. Following a family model, it was oriented to the universal fulfillment of natural necessities. We can call it a *horizontal* society in very primitive conditions of subsistence. The first economy was based on transformative extraction from nature through the use of primitive *tools,* and the immediate, social *use* of goods produced. The value of objects was therefore exclusively *use value*, and any surplus was immediately given to others in need of it or as a gift. There was no institutionalized exchange or exchange value, but instead an economy based on *gift*. Land was not owned but shared communally, although gentes, being nomadic, had temporary boundaries. This is probably what Marx called "primitive communism." Engels says of it: "In the old communistic household, which comprised many couples and their children, the task entrusted to the women of managing the household was as much a public and socially necessary industry as the procuring of food by the men. With the patriarchal family, and still more with the single monogamous family, a change came. Household management lost its public character. It no longer concerned society. It became a private service; the wife became the head servant, excluded from all participation in social production."[781] This took place with the emergence of the patriarchal civil society. The form of consciousness was *totemic* because later mythology and re-

---

780 Meszaros, I. (2010-2011). Social Structure and Forms of Consciousness. 2 Vols. New York. Monthly Review Press.

781 Engels, F. (2000). The Origin of the Family, Private Property and the State. 4. The Monogamous Family.Trans. Alick West. Marx/Engels Selected Works, Volume Three. Online Version: Marx/Engels Internet Archive (marxists.org). Accessed from <http://www.marxists.org/archive/marx/works/1884/origin-family/index.htm> on 2012-09-14.

ligion emerged from it. There was no notion of private property, of civil society, or of a repressive state.

Second-order mediations were introduced by the patriarchal shift to hegemony, only ten thousand years ago at the most. We do not know exactly how and why this U-turn took place but it may have been by conditions of natural scarcity that required accumulation, when a more sedentary life was possible with home-like abodes, and perhaps by a narcissistic collusion of mothers with their sons. A required condition was the development of an opposite to the family, a qualitatively different *civil society* outside of it formed by males. Extra-familiar affairs including chiefdoms, had always been delegated to males, and warriors. It is logical that males being in charge of this external domain, would become the hegemons of civil society.

Second-order mediations, in many instances merely the inversion of their first order analogues, started with hierarchical and repressive *governance*, patriarchal *religion*, the development of institutions in civil society culminating in the state, an economy based on exchange and accumulation and commodification of goods. Most remarkably, the gens became totally subordinated to civil society and, as Engels points out, became private with the ensuing of the status of women, children, slaves and animals as mere property of the paterfamilias. The family was thus totally transformed.

The *Homo sapiens* species is inherently vulnerable in that it needs surplus of production by those capable because they have to, morally, take care of the needs of children, the elderly, and the handicapped. Only the middle layers of young and adults, initially mothers and their brothers and sisters, are the ones that must assure the survival of the whole gens, consisting of three or four generations of affiliated gentes. The productive challenge to the species as a whole is its vulnerability and privilege that is solved through productive instrumental collaboration. Social altruism, morality, emerges from the central characteristic of the human species.

Different from mammalian families that may be in a similar

biological predicament of vulnerability, the human species has the adaptive advantage of a double layer of consciousness, consciousness and self-consciousness, along with a larger brain relative to body size. The cost of this benefit is twofold: expensive anatomical changes related to erectile posture and language, and to the female pelvic capacity to deliver a large brain volume at birth, yet prematurely. Relative to most other mammalian species in the same social predicament, human newborns are more helpless their brains not even being developmentally midway at birth. That single brain-disadvantage however, ultimately results in the idiosyncrasy of humans: their brain grows to maturity not in the meager and solitary confines of the uterus, but precociously subject to the shaping stimulation of a rich social environment that includes language and culture.

With erectile posture, evolution made the forelegs available for manipulative transformation of nature, the beginnings of which we can see in other species such as rodents. In erect humans, forelegs became highly sophisticated attached instruments, laboring hands, the first mediatory tools. Hands acquired skills that left their history imprinted in the brain.[782] After the necessary internal processes of development, morphological and psychological, came the capacity of consciousness to externalize itself, to store the surplus memory of its human activity in cultural artifacts.

Social metabolism became more complex according not only to specialized skills and functions and division of labor, but also to social roles. Hand labor became manufacture and continued to extend itself to industry, commerce, and technology. Spiritual labor that started with religion transformed itself into philosophy and ideology as well as science. Language and its corollary consciousness heeded the regulatory functions of humans.

First-order versus second-order, matriarchal and patriarchal, human forms of social and psychological metabolism derive from

782 Engels, F. (1934). The Part played by Labour in the Transition from Ape to Man. Trans: Clemens Dutt. Moscow. Progress Publishers. (Written 1876, Orig. Pub. 1895-6. Online in MIA. Accessed from <https://www.marxists.org/archive/marx/works/1876/part-played-labour/> on 2015-06-01.

two different instinctual dispositions and are designed to reciprocally constrain each other's expression achieving a necessary balance. Matriarchal metabolic processes were based on the preeminence of altruism, relationships, equality, and universal need fulfillment. Their patriarchal opposites are based on egocentricity, individual wealth accumulation, exchange, hierarchy and subordination to the object capital. With the oppression of women, the unconstrained expression of the masculine instinctual disposition has led the species to the present crossroads.

2.8.5 The Metabolisms of Consciousness as Ideology

If consciousness is a reflection of reality, ideology is a disorder of psychological metabolism, of consciousness. The difference is that consciousness reflects the universal interests of the species while ideology distorts, offering as universal what is only in the interests of a particular group. It is therefore a syllogistic disorder.

Animals come into the world with a form that is reciprocally shaped to fit the form of their particular environments. That animal form is determined by a genetic map, a natural transcription that determines their form. Animal metabolism is circumscribed by this particular form of coherence, which responds to specific geographical and environmental determinants, by idiosyncratic instincts and by their dispositions, including the limited capacity to learn. Animal consciousness is relatively simple compared to that of *Homo sapiens*. Metabolic ingestion of matter selectively, metabolic transformation to grow, mature, and reproduce within the constraints of the food chain, and a limited capacity to transform their environment characterized them along with morphological change to adjust to changes in the environment. For these processes, animals have just enough intelligence, enough capacity to learn to solve problems that permits the survival of their species within the balance of the metabolic food chain.

Each generation of humans, on the contrary, not only finds a new world transformed by all previous generations, a transformation that contributes to a global historical growth called civilization. Humans create their own needs to mediate their natural ones, and in the process transform the world for the next generation. Historically, humans have thus entered into a metabolic relationship not with a limited environment, but with the whole world.

Human transformation of the world occurs through a process of objectification, the transformation of their individual subjectivity into objective forms of nature. This process started with mothers' strategically transforming the environment through natural and sexual selection. Initial consciousness, necessarily matriarchal, was universal in that there was little individual differentiation besides that dictated by material imperatives such as gender, age, and health status. It can be surmised logically that during matriarchy consciousness was rather uniform in human groups, undivided. The world was then seen, so to say, through matriarchal eyes and a highly natural perspective, close to the morality of evolution based on the new trait of a highly cooperative altruism.

With the radical shift that caused the advent of patriarchy, as we have seen there was a qualitative change that affected most of the types of mediations applied to nature by mothers in the style of objectification dictated by their instinctual disposition. This counterintuitive event, as it turned out, resulted from the point of view of the morality of evolution in an unbalanced patriarchal ideology, particularly in its present capitalistic form corrupted by wealth accumulation, unsustainable waste, exploitative hierarchy, and the continuous creation of spurious needs through education and manipulative advertising. In this alienating enterprise, a small segment of patriarchs who along with the material conditions of production have attained control of the spiritual ones, using myth, art, religious belief, and even science as means to mystify humans into believing that their narrow interests are the natural order. This is manifested in the ecological damage to consciousness that is alienation.

In this fashion human spiritual metabolism becomes compartmentalized, politics in civil society's becoming the paradigm. Every issue that comes up has at least two political explanations. Most characteristically, the opposition between these explanations is often unbridgeable and a logical compromise is not possible. We cannot operate dialectically. Resolution of antagonistic issues then can only take place by force. The logical solution is thus war, for which we are always prepared in magnitudes incompatible with our own and most other species' survival. We have lost the meaning of the notion *we*, the essential notion of universal human solidarity for the sake of *I*. This syllogistic damage is manifested in pathological mental conditions, the most typical being *narcissism*. We have also lost the notion that, like the object, the subject is part of the same universe: that we live in a cosmic moving vehicle with limited capacity that was designed to recycle its reasonable level of waste; and we have made it toxic. Patriarchal capitalism is premised on the creation of metabolic needs that are spurious, their persistence irreversibly damaging nature for generations to come, trespassing our boundaries.

The concept that our historical species process is collective, and that no single individual or particular group of individuals can solve our universal problem has become alien. That we elect and reelect individuals and groups that only represent their own interests has been a puzzle since Spinoza. This is our individualistic ideology at its peak and its rationalization is paradoxically not even produced by the bearers of the particular interests, but by hired ideologues, typically of the middle class, sophisticated slaves.

Mediated by alienating words, by ideologies, our instruments such as judgment and reality testing cannot work because they have been transformed into an invisible prison we all inhabit internally. We see the world not the way it is but the way the mediating lens of ideology makes it look. Since through education, at all levels, and through the dominant class-owned media we have all been "refurbished," it is as if we are vehicles trying to operate with oil that were designed for gas. "Feuerbach resolves the religious essence (ideology) into the human essence (consciousness). But the human essence is no abstraction inherent in each single individual. In its reality it is the ensemble of the social relations."[783] The human essence is concrete, constantly accruing human universality at its most inclusive level. This is the essence that has been kidnapped and alienated by the particularity of ideology, detouring the species from the morality of evolution. The ideal human essence to be emulated is male, white, moneyed, competitive, and ruthlessly exploitative. Reality, in fact, has it differently; in its inclusiveness and universality it is independent of all particular determinations. This means that as long as there is even if only one individual in the world that is being exploited, and suffers unnecessarily, freedom is impossible for me, and for each one of us.

The ensemble of the social relations Marx talks about goes back to Mytochondrial Eve and it is what constitutes the second layer of consciousness and is more critically reflected in the second level of self. It is not linearly stored as in a library, but contained in the form of our bodies and brains. Our morphology tells the story of our long history of adaptations, culminating with a consciousness that remains latent because of ideology. It is also stored in language and culture, including cultural institutions that model the structure of our selves. It is the function of our mothers to produce humans ready for the cultural environment we constantly create.

Stemming from the evolutionary capacity for metabolic internalization of forms that so much captivated Plato's imagination, the structure of consciousness is designed to reduce evolutionary cost that before was slow and morphological, through conscious operations that can now be conducted abstractly. This is possible thanks to the second layer of consciousness that represents our human es-

---

783 Marx, K. (1969). *Theses on* Feuerbach. Trans: W. Lough, Marx/Engels Selected Works, Volume One, p. 13 – 15. Moscow: Progress Publishers. (Written: by Marx in the Spring of 1845, but slightly edited by Engels; First Published: As an appendix to Ludwig Feuerbach and the End of Classical German Philosophy in 1888). Online in MIA. Accessed from <https://www.marxists.org/archive/marx/works/1845/theses/theses.htm> on 2015-06-08.

sence and unique quality, the ensemble of the social relations and its moral universality. Its formal, iconic and semantic representations contain the history of our relation with nature and the relations within our own species, culturally. These are parsed as syllogistic classes that serve as the template for our consciousness, to be applied as the paradigm of human practical operational adaptation. This is how, economically, we can avoid material destruction by making it formal and dialectical by the inclusion of planning, dialogue and compromise. Dominant ideologies have tinkered with this natural process, distorting it wherever it can serve their hegemonic purposes.

The function of language in this process, originally possibly coming from affective grunts and progressively complex sounds carrying meaning, is hard to overemphasize. It is through language that we connect, plan, diverge, dialogue, and compromise. As Hegel said, language is the solvent, the water of consciousness. Already the cry at birth has characteristics that prompt adults morally to respond. We can see consciousness only through its objectivization in language, but ideologically language often serves not consciousness but its censored product, ideology.

Ideology is a form of regression in evolution because it must be not dialectical but antagonistic, representing the irreconcilable interests of different particularities such as capitalism and the wage worker. Instead of compromise, this form of opposition only triggers cascades of competitive gambits that in history have been the successive social paradigms of slavery, feudalism, and capitalism. The regressive nature of ideology has its foundations in forms of adaptation evolutionarily prior to consciousness, the food chain in particular, as best formulated by Reverend Thomas Malthus.[784] The fallacy in this theory, unfortunately endorsed by Darwin, is precisely to have its premise in a pre-conscious natural morality. It is

---

784 Malthus, R.T. (1798) *An Essay on the Principle of Population As It Affects the Future Improvement of Society, with Remarks on the Speculations of Mr. Goodwin, M. Condorcet and Other Writers* (1 ed.). London: J. Johnson in St Paul's Church-yard. Online in Internet Archive. Accessed from <https://archive.org/details/essayonprincipl00malt> on 2017-04-12.

precisely in order to skirt such destructiveness that consciousness was designed. The proof is the fact that social planning, including proper education, has not been furthered as a consequence of its predictions. On the opposite, a "pro-life" label hides its opposite, that most apocalyptic of destructive ideologies particularly thriving through the production of all sorts of wars on nature and society, and on consciousness and good sense. When so many things don't make sense, as is the case today, then we must question sense itself, (that is, common sense, good sense corrupted by ideology). Ideology has reached its spun limit.

Our consciousness is alienated through reification. This means that the highest values and prerogatives of our species, condensed in the word *Being,* have been through ideology slipped to *Having.* This is the process of surrendering our subjectivity, our power, our wealth and transcendence, to one object, money, and its main satellite constructs of commodity, profit and market. Instead of our species' qualitatively growing we have to make sure that capital, quantitatively, is. This requires repression by governments and constant ideological spinning, because our good sense remains alive in spite of the onslaught. Any sign of good sense must be repressed, most often unfortunately by ourselves, because we have internalized the governmental model of repression. We do it for political correctness, meaning pleasing our oppressors.

In Engels' words: "And when such an ideologist constructs morality and law from the concept, or the so-called simplest elements of 'society,' instead of from the real social relations of the people round him, what material is then available for this construction? Material clearly of two kinds: first, the meager residue of real content which may possibly survive in the abstractions from which he starts and, secondly, the content which our ideologist once more introduces from his own consciousness. And what does he find in his consciousness? For the most part, moral and juridical notions which are a more or less accurate expression (positive or negative, corroborative or antagonistic) of the social and political relations amidst which he lives; perhaps also ideas drawn from the literature on the subject; and, as a final possibility, some personal idiosyncrasies. Our ideologist may turn and twist as he likes, but the historical reality which he cast out at the door comes in again at the window, and while he thinks he is framing a doctrine of morals and law for all times and for all worlds, he is in fact only fashioning an image of the conservative or revolutionary tendencies of his day - an image which is distorted because it has been torn from its real basis and, like a reflection in a concave mirror, is standing on its head."[785] The ideologist produces commonsense to combat good sense.

Since the only weapon we have to fight ideology is ideology itself, we must differentiate ideologies good and bad; this test is in the true universality, the concrete inclusiveness of the ideology as it regards the species.

2.8.6 Two Instinctual Dispositions, One Morality of Evolution

I have insisted on the notion of two opposite instincts present in Freud's writings (but male and female, not Freud's view) to underline the depth of our human dialectical structure in nature, which goes into our natural roots to include pre-historic instinctual determinations. In the food chain a subject can make another its object. This is what capitalist reification tries to do, reflected in the need "to have." The historical, unnatural need to hoard-if-useful-for-a-rainy-day is institutionalized, a regression from being the rich subject of nature Marx talked about,[786] to a state of slavery. Our need to have transfers our power to the alien object.

---

785 Engels, F. (1947). *Anti-During. Anti-Dühring. Herr Eugen Dühring's Revolution in Science Part I: Philosophy. X. Morality and Law. Equality.* Trans, Emile Burns from 1894 edition. Moscow.Progress Publishers. (Orig. Pub. 1878). Online in MIA. Accessed from <https://www.marxists.org/archive/marx/works/1877/anti-duhring/ch08.htm> on 2016-05-31.

786 Marx, K. (1973). *Grundrisse.* Notebook III. The Chapter on Capital (Continuation). Surplus value... etc. Trans: Martin Nicolaus. London, UK. Penguin Books in association with New Left Review; <https://www.marxists.org/archive/marx/works/1857/grundrisse/ch06.htm#iiic> on 2017-04-12.

Species sexuation operates as reciprocal sexual selection that Darwin parsed in two categories, males fighting for access and females selecting the fittest. Here is already a division of labor, material and spiritual. However, both sexes have both skills even though there is a sexual bias that can be overcome through cultural mediations. This kind of instinctual structure conjures up a delicate balance that depends upon simultaneous external and internal reciprocal regulation.

Freud could not figure out the instinct of women and therefore decided to adjudicate to women the virtue of passivity. He wrote: "Man is an animal organism with (like others) an unmistakably bisexual disposition. The individual corresponds to a fusion of two symmetrical halves, of which, according to some investigators, one is purely male and the other female. It is equally possible that each half was originally hermaphrodite. Sex is a biological fact that, although it is of extraordinary importance in mental life, is hard to grasp psychologically. We are accustomed to say that every human being displays both male and female instinctual impulses, needs and attributes; but though anatomy, it is true, can point out the characteristics of maleness and femaleness, psychology cannot. For psychology the contrast between the sexes fades away into one between activity and passivity, in which we far too readily identify activity with maleness and passivity with femaleness, a view is by no means universally confirmed in the animal kingdom. The theory of bisexuality is still surrounded by many obscurities and we cannot but feel it as a serious impediment in psychoanalysis that it has not yet found any link with the theory of the instincts. However this may be, if we assume it as a fact that each individual seeks to satisfy both male and female wishes in his sexual life, we are prepared for the possibility that those [two acts of] demand are not fulfilled by the same object, and that they interfere with each other unless they can be kept apart and each impulse guided into a particular channel that is suited to it. Another difficulty arises from the circumstance that there is so often associated with the erotic relationship, over and above its own sadistic components, a quota of plain inclination to aggression. The love-object will not always view these complications with the degree of understanding and tolerance shown by the peasant woman who complained that her husband did not love her any more, since he had not beaten her for a week.

The conjecture that goes deepest, however, is the one which takes its start from what I have said… It is to the effect that, with the assumption of an erect posture by man and with the depreciation of his sense of smell, it was not only his anal eroticism which threatened to fall a victim to organic repression, but the whole of his sexuality; so that since this, the sexual function has been accompanied by a repugnance which cannot further be accounted for, and which prevents its complete satisfaction and forces it away from the sexual aim into sublimations and libidinal displacements."[787]

Because of his ideological perspective, Freud could not see the instinct of women and the glaring differences between the human sexes. For lack of a dialectical perspective, he could not see them as oppositely designed for reciprocal constraint. He could not see repression behind women's passivity or unconstrained aggression in men's success. An alternative society in which both women and men equally shared governance leading to substantial equality was for Freud impossible to imagine.

2.8.7 All Psychology is Group Psychology

The universality of humans, the foundation of what we usually call equality, resides in the fact that we are all members of the same species, designed with the same determinations and possibilities, all to benefit from the gifts of nature and from the productive activity of all. On these grounds, we ought to all be able to perceive reality uniformly and correctly, according to the same instrument, consciousness, to reach the best approximation to collective truth.

787 Freud, S. (1929). 'Civilisation and Its Discontents. Electronic Edition. Online in Chrysoma Associates Limited. Buckinghamshire. England. Accessed from <http://www2.winchester.ac.uk/edstudies/courses/level%20two%20sem%20two/Freud-Civ-il-Disc.pdf> on 2015-08-11.

At first sight, we also ought to be able to send and receive correct information to and from each other along those identical parameters through a language we have developed communally. We know this is not the case, however, in part because some of the most outstanding initial variations are sex and age determinations, for example, which entail different needs and interests. Besides, being located at different points in space and time, under different ecological conditions, nations, races and cultures also dictate different needs and interests. Different needs and interests lead us to perceive and experience the world differently. Additionally, the second-order mediations of patriarchy, particularly capital, create spurious needs such as excess private property that ego comes to depend upon. This is how rather universally money, the universal equivalent of property and wealth, comes to replace the earliest fetish God, now reified. God was the sublimation, collective imaginary precursor, of what now can be materially achieved: an easier life, freer from compelling natural needs. In imagination, the more money, the more freedom.

The reification inherent in money psychologically limits and diminishes our unique consciousness. There are more wealthy individuals and more wealthy nations today than ever before. Our advance as a species cannot be said to have grown apace. If anything, looking at our society today what jumps at our senses is its high level of incoherence. Successful corruption has replaced morality. Human values universally corrupted by capital turn morality inside out. Our consciousness turned ideology precludes proper perception and protest through desensitization that gradually blunts the moral response. Ideological mystification, logical spinning that making universal the interests of dominant groups, makes class reality appear as if it were universal reality. The capacity to mystify, acquired religiously and developed philosophically, has contaminated scientific thinking. The assault on our senses and reason leaves us perplexed and often sick. As we mirror each other, we wage war in the name of peace and humanitarianism that remain abstract. We fiercely oppose therapeutic abortion while approving wasteful and costly genocidal war. Again, and again we vote for our oppressors to decide our destiny. We impoverish ourselves by giving power to corporations whose speech is money. And we let the market decide our political and economic destiny. When we open the newspaper, we see more absurdity, nonsense and corruption everyday. We read about events that make no sense. This is ultimately because, instead of destroying to produce we produce to destroy, the logic of capital. When so many things don't make sense, we must examine sense itself, and yet when we do that we find pockets of brilliance. Our mental illnesses reflect our modes of alienation, but we choose not to look at them socially because that would mean critical thinking, not political correctness. Our psychological textbooks show our misguided search for genetic causation.

The war on terror is conducted with compounded state-terror that only breeds more terror. Good sense and critical mind are innocent bystanders. The species operates like a bird trying to fly with one wing. We look at "the economy," as rulers define it, as an indicator of wellbeing, without realizing it is largely a war economy. In the meanwhile, the ground we stand on is caving and our stoicism is not wisdom but the folly of alienation. Ideology has saturated our natural sense to the point that we are collectively unable to identify our aggressor; we instead identify with him. This shows the depth of our tragic alienation, our detour from natural being.

Like political economy, the science of scarcity has paradoxically transformed itself into *capitalist economy,* the "science" of the creation of artificial scarcity, psychology opted for intrapsychism, individualist psychology. Its role is to promote ego and executive functions, mirroring society. The science of capital-like ego excludes the unheard-of, science of *me* that is human history. Presented as a series of individualistic and random events, history loses its coherence, its dialogical nature. What Freud defined as his unconscious is in fact only the tip of the iceberg. It leaves untouched the whole realm of bad faith[788] and of falsified consciousness[789] through which we have been programmed to operate as we do with the results we see as natural. Political repression, necessary after the historical patriarchal coup, has been quite well captured in psychoanalysis as neurotic repression. The phenomenon of self-repression is so culturally pervasive that it became universal and the cornerstone of psychoanalysis.[790] Its analogue, political repression, behind which is economic repression, has been the motive for the long struggle for freedom since patriarchy was put in place.

Repression is very central to our present condition and it started with women's depriving themselves not only of their natural leadership role but of their transcendence, voice, and expressive capacity. The same model has then been applied to children, the elderly, and to anyone not male, white, and wealthy. It has also been applied to nature by overuse and exploitation. We have come to thrive in production of waste, mortgaging faster and faster the natural resources of our children.[791]

Groups are the natural units of the human species. They reproduce themselves naturally in concentric cycles, starting with the nuclear family in which the first group structures are integrated in the developing mind. Family experience and thinking are based on

788 Sartre, J.P. (1992). Being and Nothingness. New York. Washington Square Press. (Orig. Pub. 1943). Online in Scribd. Accessed from <http://www.scribd.com/doc/10268925/Sartre-Being-and-Nothingness#scribd> on 2015-11-02.

789 Engels, F. (1968). "Engels to Franz Mehring." Marx-Engels Correspondence. Abstract. Trans: Donna Torr. New York. International Publisher. (Written 1893). Online in MIA. Accessed from <https://www.marxists.org/archive/marx/works/1893/letters/93_07_14.htm> on 2017-04-14.

790 Freud, S. (1917). The History of the Psychoanalytic Movement. Trans: A.A. Brill. New York. The Nervous and Mental Disease Publishing Company. Online in Internet Archive. Accessed from <https://archive.org/details/historypsychoan00freugoog> on 2017-04-14.

791 "Humans have gone into "ecological debt" earlier and earlier in the year since the 1970s, according to data from the California-based think tank, which hosts Earth Overshoot Day every year. In 1971, Overshoot Day fell on December 24. Ten years later, it had moved ahead by a month to mid-November. It's arrived in August since 2005." Mosbergen, D. (2016). "We've Already Used Up Earth's Resources For 2016 — And It's Only August." The Huffington Post. August 9, 2016.

group identity and identification, and the family remains a protective device for life. The next group experience is in civil society, the opposite of the family. While families operate ethically, civil society operates legally. The premises of family's coming from the gens are solidarity, mutual protection and collaboration, and equality in the fulfillment of needs. Civil society as developed by patriarchs external to the family operates competitively and individualistically. The power of religious thinking in civil society has some of the characteristics of the family, idealized, and with an emphasis on morality. Religion and family get together in important family events such as birth, initiation into civil society, marriage, and death. Religion is also a source of morality in dealing with the contradictions of civil society. Military thinking is the secular application of family and religious thinking based on the abdication of the self to a leader representing a higher social symbol, such as a nation. Skill, trade or profession bring individuals into other social groups that are more present in their lives and where there is opportunity to titrate the two opposites of solidarity and competition. This also happens in sports groups.

Group psychology became a topic of scientific interest in the nineteenth century. Freud, who emphasized solidarity and brotherhood in the origins of culture,[792] saw regression in group psychology. This is how individualism penetrated psychology. Freud endorsed the current type of thinking crucial to patriarchal dominance that pejoratively saw the activity of groups as regressive. French social psychologist Gustave Le Bon (1841–1931), best known for his 1895 work *The Crowd: A Study of the Popular Mind*,[793] inspired racism and the political philosophy of Hitler and Mussolini. Le Bon

792 Freud, S. (1919). Totem And Taboo. Resemblances Between The Psychic Lives Of Savages And Neurotics. Authorized English Translation, with Introduction By A. A. Brill. London. George Routledge & Sons, Limited. (1912-3). Online in Project Gutenberg. Accessed from <http://www.gutenberg.org/files/41214/41214-h/41214-h.htm> on 2015-08-03.

793 Le Bon, G. (1996). *The Crowd: A Study of the Popular* Mind. Online in Project Gutenberg. Etext #445. Accessed from <http://www.gutenberg.org/cache/epub/445/pg445.html> on 2015-06-08. (Orig. Pub. 1895).

created the concepts of group mind, racial unconscious, Darwinian regression, contagion and suggestibility, all attributes of the herd-like group in action. This is quite opposite to Emile Durkheim's (1858-1917) view of the religious group experience, for example, as solidarity based on sacred social values. Others writing about group behavior at the time for the most part agreed with Le Bon, and so did Freud.

Freud furthered psychoanalytic support for Le Bon's theory. Freud roots suggestion in libido instead of mirroring, surrender to the love object, the leading patriarch. Although Freud does clarify some of the dynamics of group behavior, particularly in what concerns the social roles of leader and follower, his interpretation of the herd instinct and primal horde along the lines of Le Bon are precisely what patriarchal authority needs to rationalize the repression of revolutionary fervor, and the implementation of massive repression and fascism. We must remember that religion was one of the first forms of organized consciousness in organized society. Religion was the first form of culture.

In his *Group Psychology and the Analysis of the Ego*,[794] Freud, using the writings of Gustave Le Bon,[795] and Wilfred Trotter,[796] utilized the notion of herd consciousness that Marx had also talked about decades earlier with a developmental, not politically regressive, connotation. "On the other hand, man's consciousness of the necessity of associating with the individuals around him is the beginning of the consciousness that he is living in society at all. This beginning is as animal as social life itself at this stage. It is mere herd-consciousness, and at this point man is only distinguished from

---

794 Freud, S. (2011) *Group Psychology and the Analysis of the Ego*. Trans. James Strachey. Project Gutenberg [EBook #35877]. Accessed from <http://www.gutenberg. org/catalog/world/readfile?fk_files=2083370> on 2012-05-21. (Orig. Pub. 1921).

795 Le Bon, G. (1996) *The Crowd; study of the popular mind.* Ibid.

796 Trotter, W. (1908). "Herd instinct and its bearing on the psychology of civilized man - part 1." Sociological Review, July. Trotter, W. (1909). "Herd instinct and its bearing on the psychology of civilized man - part 2." Sociological Review, January. Trotter, W. (1919). *Instincts of the Herd in Peace and War* - 4th impression, with postscript. New York, MacMillan.

sheep by the fact that with him consciousness takes the place of instinct or that his instinct is a conscious one."[797] But like Le Bon, Freud believed that within a group individuals regress to an instinctual status of high suggestibility and "contagion" easily becoming more impulsive, changeable and irritable; in other words, more emotional and less self-repressed, we could say instead. In group experiences humans get in touch with the invincible power of solidarity. Le Bon's type of group psychology is used to see terrorism in the restlessness of hurting groups trying to speak up, today throughout the planet. Alienated from their consciousness, they may see their exploitation as stemming from race, religion or nationality, when in fact they are victims of economic forces that have been made invisible.

What is described as emotional thinking is the fervor or groups in action that have shed their political correctness to display their power. This is where we started in the original, matriarchal form of group expression that has been repressed since repression was politically installed: since slavery. It is useful to review briefly Freud's ideas in *Totem and Taboo*[798], to see how ideology inverts the logic of history. According to Freud, the original society, being of course patriarchal, was ruled by a powerful male that among other things in a Darwinian fashion precluded other males from sexual self-expression, access to the females. The excluded males invented solidarity in order to kill the patriarch. The murderous event naturally produced fear and guilt that, sublimated, became taboo, ritual, religion ,and social organization with its patriarchal morality. Here it is acknowledged that the transition from apehood to humanity is based

797 Marx, K. (1932). *The German Ideology. History,* Part I: Feuerbach. Opposition of the Materialist and Idealist Outlook. A. Idealism and Materialism. 4. The Essence of the Materialist Conception of History. Social Being and Social ConsciousnessFundamental Conditions. (Written in 1845-6). Online in MIA, Accessed from <https://www.marxists.org/archive/marx/works/1845/german-ideology/ch01a.htm> on 3015-0608.
798 Freud, S. (1919). *Totem And Taboo. Resemblances Between The Psychic Lives Of Savages And Neurotics.* Authorized English Translation, with Introduction By A. A. Brill. London. George Routledge & Sons, Limited. (1912-3). Online in Project Gutenberg. Accessed from <http://www.gutenberg.org/files/41214/41214-h/41214-h.htm> on 2015-08-03.

on solidarity. It is also recognized that emotion is a crucial factor in social organization. It remains so today, but we have been trained not to consider that a militarized state is a state based on fear.

Freud's scholarly construction of origins noticeably leaves females out, as the Catholic Church does in its Holy Trinity that puts the Holy Spirit in the place of the mother. It patriarchally reifies male self-expression as the agency of all humanity. If we assume, along with developmental theorists, that adulthood is only a late stage in development, we can't do it without women and generous collaboration. Labor starts with women's labor and productivity starts with delivery.

The human bond thus goes from parasitism through symbiosis and the trials of separation to a largely illusive individuation. From this perspective all psychology is group psychology, as we are finding out because human development stems from collaboration that includes transmission of culture. What we come to call identity started from otherness, and it has to constantly be maintained through other-mirroring and its constraining feedback.[799] This fact has not been given the attention it deserves. Our constant dependence on the other, materially and psychologically ideologically disappears with individualism.

The most important argument for the hegemony of the group in psychology is the fact that the individual mind, the only one that really exists, is made of what all previous other individuals, part of groups themselves, produced with their hands and minds. Mind is the collective outcome of individual activity. The essence of the mind is the ensemble of the social relations.[800]

Individualistic ideology led Freud's nephew Edward Bernays, with the acquiescence of Anna Freud, to use Freud's theory to po-

---

799 Goffman, I. (1959). *The Presentation of Self in Everyday Life*. New York. Anchor Books. Online as The presentation of self in everyday life. Published 1956 by University of Edinburgh, Social Sciences Research Centre in Edinburgh . Accessed from <http://monoskop.org/images/1/19/Goffman_Erving_The_Presentation_of_Self_in_Everyday_Life.pdf> on 2015-06-08.
800 Marx, K. (1969). *Theses on Feuerbach*. Ibid.

litically and commercially manipulate social groups. Bernays was in the business of "engineering mass consent" by altering social perception and subliminally or openly appealing to instinctual, emotional, and archaic impulses. Bernays believed that freedom to persuade and suggest, no matter what, is in the essence of democracy.[801] He was of course euphorically welcomed and pampered by the establishment, and became extremely successful in the field of "public relations" of which he is considered the founder. He provided corporations and the media with the proper psychological strategies, "scientifically" backed up, to create spurious needs in large audiences and subsequently to impel individuals to action: action predominantly against their own interests in the patriarchal model. Herd consciousness produced in such a fashion was the royal way to consumerism and to constant war. The promotion of political causes, typically oppressive in the interest of corporations, was the menu he had to offer in his public relations campaigns. This has been the most unfortunate episode in the misuse of psychoanalysis.

The Freudian theory of group psychology, if reinterpreted, can be useful in that it shows the mechanics of group leadership and group behavior. Today it is not love of the leader but the leader's promises, the articulation of constituent's needs in bad faith that operates the best. Of course the closer the interests, and the more common the purpose, the more powerful the reverberating feelings in groups of individuals in action. This is precisely what Durkheim pointed out in his studies of religion.[802] The power and resilience of religion are based largely on this phenomenon of affective communion. This is the fervor that Comte desperately wanted to bring into

---

801 Bernays, E.L. (1955) *The engineering of consent.* University of Oklahoma Press. (Orig. Pub. 1947). Quote from Wikipedia. See also Adam Curtis' award-winning British television series "The Century of the Self" that focuses on how Sigmund Freud, Anna Freud, and Edward Bernays influenced the way corporations and governments have used herd consciousness to manipulate democracy.

802 Durkheim, E. (1915). *The Elementary Forms of the Religious Life.* Trans: Joseph Ward Swain. London: George Allen & Unwin Ltd. Online in Project Gutenberg. Accessed from <http://www.gutenberg.org/files/41360/41360-h/41360-h.htm> on 2015-06-08.

his political sociology, a religious passion.[803] Religious and political fervor are easily observed in discussions of those matters, the defensive posture's revealing the ideological insecurity. Like religion, politics when real and alive is emotionally arousing. The eruption of emotion is a side effect of spontaneous group behavior.

As in anxiety, alienation makes groups express restlessness without true knowledge of its cause. Groups resort to close and expedient explanations that often conceal the real, universal cause. Artificial scarcity is often behind.

2.8.8 The Ensemble of the Social Relations

"No genuinely relational theory of personality, no effective surpassing the impasses of psychological substantialism and naturalism and therefore no really scientific theory of personality are possible so long as one does not take Marx's crucial discovery absolutely seriously: in reality the human essence is the ensemble of the social relations within which men not only produce their means of subsistence but are themselves produced"[804] The term ensemble of the social relations explains the complexity of human consciousness by basing it not in philosophical constructs but in social reality. It begins from human collaboration and teamwork as the ground of consciousness and it is opposite to the ideology of competitiveness and the survival of the fittest. It is psychology based on the other, universal ideology.

Let's start with Hegel, to whom we owe the distinction between consciousness and self-consciousness. This is how he defined consciousness: "The simple sensuous consciousness is the immediate

---

803 Martineau, H. (1893). *The Positive Philosophy of Auguste Comte*. London: Kegan Paul, Trench, Trubner and Co. Ltd. 2 vol. Online in Internet Archive. Accessed from <https://ia800309.us.archive.org/14/items/positivephiloso01martgoog/positivephiloso01martgoog.pdf> on 2015-06-08.

804 Seve, L. (1974). *Man in Marxist Theory*. The Articulation of the Psychology of Personality with Marxism. (2) The articulation from the side of psychology. Online in MIA. Accessed from <https://www.marxists.org/archive/seve/works/1974/ch2/2_0.htm> on 2017-04-18.

certitude of an external object. The expression for the immediateness of such an object is that "it is," and moreover a "This," a "Now" according to time, and a "Here" according to space, and different from all other objects and perfectly, determined (definite) in itself."[805] This consciousness is (this, here, and now) always bound to its object, pure experience without the mediation of language. It lacks abstract notions and the ability to communicate through language.

About Self-consciousness on the other hand Hegel said: "As Self-Consciousness the Ego intuits itself, and the expression of the same in its purity is Ego = Ego, or: I am I."[806] This second layer of consciousness is absent in animals and in humans is the outcome of a different type of relating based on social labor and communication.

Hegel's disciple Feuerbach added: "Thus understood, the animal has a simple, but man a twofold, life. In the case of the animal the inner life is one with the outer, whereas in the case of man there is an inner and an outer life. The inner life of man is constituted by the fact that man relates himself to his species, to his mode of being. Man thinks, that is to say, he converses, enters into a dialogue with himself."[807] It is humans' unique form of relation with their species that constitutes the qualitative change. Relation with species is simultaneously relation with nature and self-relation, because human species is also nature, a notion absent before Spinoza: human meant exceptional.

---

805   Hegel, G.W.F. (1967). Hegel's Phenomenology of Mind. Second Phase. A. The Sensuous Consciousness. 11. From Harper & Row's Torchbooks' edition (1967) of the Phenomenology (1807), translated by J B Baillie (1910), from University of Idaho, Department of Philosophy, thanks to Jean McIntire. § numbers from the Baillie translation have been inserted into the text of the Baillie translation and linked to explanations by J N Findlay. Φ links to original German text: Phänemenologie des Geistes. Online in MIA. Accessed from <https://www.marxists.org/reference/archive/hegel/phindex.htm> on 2014-10-05.

806   Hegel, G.W.F. (1967). Hegel's Phenomenology of Mind. Second Phase. The Self-Consciousness. 22. Ibid.

807   Feuerbach, L. (1972). The Essence of Christianity. §1 The Being of Man in General. Trans: Introduction translated by Zawar Hanfi,, remainder translated by George Eliot, 1854. Introduction from The Fiery Brook, remainder from The Essence of Christianity (Written: 1841). Online in MIA. Accessed from <https://www.marxists.org/reference/archive/feuerbach/works/essence/index.htm> on 2015-02-26.

Another Hegel disciple, Marx, picked up from there: "Feuerbach resolves the religious essence into the human essence. But the human essence is no abstraction inherent in each single individual."[808] The religious essence used to be abstract, based on a God-connected soul. Feuerbach translated soul into consciousness and, most important, God into society. In the abstract relation soul-god, Feuerbach discovers the relation human-species. Marx is not satisfied because human-species is still abstract; to become fully understood it must become concrete. The essence of humans that was alienated as soul-god has to be ponderable, verifiable. This becomes possible through the notion of *the ensemble of the social relations.* As "Human nature," and still as "species-being" the essence of humans is defined by a "dumb generality." The "ensemble of the social relations" is society, history and culture. These start as relations of production of life and survival that, to a great extent, determine the form of other relations. The ensemble of the social relations gives its form to the second layer of consciousness, the one that is not constantly bound, as plain consciousness, to its object. The ensemble of the social relations I compare to the memory of the species, the analogue of the genome.

Let's take for example Durkheim's notion of collective representation, the first human form of explanatory consciousness, religion: "Religious representations are collective representation which express collective realities."[809] The realities of religious representations can be found in history depicting the sequence of the ensemble of human relations. And, continues Durkheim: "Collective representations are the result of an immense co-operation, which stretches out not only into space but into time as well; to make them,

---

808 Marx, K. (1938). Theses on Feuerbach. 6. In: The German Ideology. London. Lawrence and Wishart. (Written in 1845). Online version Marxists Internet Archive. Accessed from <http://www.marxists.org/archive/marx/works/1845/theses/index.htm> on 2012-09-09.

809 Durkheim, E. (1964). *The Elementary Forms of Religious Life.* Subject of our Study. P. 10. Trans: Joseph Ward Swain. London. George Allen & Unwin Ltd. Online in Internet Archive. Accessed from <https://archive.org/stream/elementaryformso00durkrich/elementaryformso00durkrich_djvu.txt> on 2017-04-16.

a multitude of minds have associated, united and combined their ideas and sentiments; for them, long generations have accumulated their experience and their knowledge. A special intellectual activity is therefore concentrated in them which is infinitely richer and more complex than that of the individual. From that one can understand how the reason has been able to go beyond the limits of empirical knowledge. It does not owe this to any vague mysterious virtue but simply to the fact that according to the well-known formula, man is double. There are two beings in him: an individual being which has its foundation in the organism and the circle of *I* whose activities is therefore strictly limited, and a social being which represents the highest reality in the intellectual and moral order that we can know by observation — I mean society." [810]Durkheim focuses on intellectual activity, an activity that for Marx is relatively autonomous but in the last instance determined by real material activity, how we relate to each other at work for the reproduction of our lives. Collective representations express collective realities, group ideas, beliefs, and values not reducible to individual representations. Durkheim saw collaboration and solidarity here, but he missed the class struggle that made such collaboration, slavish and exploitative, as it still is. The collective symbolic capacity is developed in each individual according to parameters determined by his or her culture as Horney pointed out, through historically determined family and institutional education. Durkheim was also able to see how originally this collective representations were originated in religious experience involving coercive rituals.[811] That was the first form of cultural metabolism that created the two realms of life, the profane individual life and the sacred collective, echoing Hegelian consciousness and self-consciousness. Collective representations close the circle of understanding: they totalize for all through common-sense explanations based on collectively prescribed reality testing and judg-

---

810 Durkheim, E. (1964). The Elementary Forms of Religious Life. Subject of our Study. P. 16. Ibid.
811 Durkheim, E. (2012). *The Elementary Forms of the Religious Life*. Trans: Joseph Ward Swain. EBook #41360. Online in Project Gutenberg. Accessed from <http://www.gutenberg.org/files/41360/41360-h/41360-h.htm> on 2014-08-21.

ment. Durkheim's notion concretely, scientifically, confirms Marx's concept of the ensemble of the social relations.

Freud also explores in his double registry of unconscious dreams the meaning of which is simultaneously idiosyncratic and conventional. The idiosyncratic meaning is based on the personal experience of the individual and the conventional the common-sense, dictionary type of interpretation. It is the relation between these two registers that makes interpretation possible.[812]

This double registry that Freud saw along the lines of id-superego is essential for social action because it contains the common denominator of cultural reality testing. Its practical relevance comes from its universality, the shared social meaning of symbols. The notion of ensemble of the social relations implies more than episodic religion or dreams: it includes social life, the collective production of human life that can be produced only socially.

The ensemble of the social relations in this light emerges as a result of the social nature of the production and reproduction of human life. The psychological mechanisms involved are material and observable and described in history, psychology and sociology. They include mirroring, diffusion, imitation, fashion, alienation, reification, and, most importantly, ideology, all forms of collective representation. Like social institutions, collective representations transmit historical human objectifications that survive until they are superseded by new ones more fit to their changing object.

Conscious individuality can only develop from those collective representations' mediation by particular cultures. The peculiarities of so-called primitive peoples, for example, cannot be deduced from individual psychology alone. The psychology of the individual can only be understood as subordinated to institutional collective representation, reflecting material and historical modes of production of

---

812 Freud, S. (1913). The Interpretation of Dreams. Trans. A. A. Brill (Orig. Pub. 1900). Originally publish in New York by Macmillan. Online in Classics in the History of Psychology. Accessed from <http://psychclassics.yorku.ca/Freud/Dreams/> on 2015-01-15

human life. Different societies produce different psychologies, the common denominator's being where individual psychologies draw from. The needs of an African peasant are not the same as those of an American urbanite. Their intelligence differs accordingly and not quantitatively but qualitatively. Both can be geniuses at what they do and neither has the skill of the other.

We map reality iconically and analogically as animals probably do. However, because we live socially, we have to convert our mapping into digital signals for the nervous system to transmit, and consequently symbolize to meaningfully communicate with others. Here George H. Mead helps us understand the process with his triangle of linguistic symbol, meaning and social act. Durkheim's representation is Mead's symbol; they are possible through the social act that requires a common denominator. Sending and receiving meaningful messages requires that both participants share what Mead, as does Lacan, calls *big other*. "The principle which I have suggested as basic to human social organization is that of communication involving participation in the other. This requires the appearance of the other in the self, the identification of the other with the self, the reaching of self-consciousness through the other."[813] Conscious individuals are the product of social intercourse, and their self as a reflective process is not *a priori* given but is born of that interaction; it develops socially. Personality has at its base the ensemble of all biographical interactions of the individual. Even our body we cannot see as an object because there are parts of it that we can never see. We put together a body image from looking at other bodies and our whole body was originally the blueprint of our mother's. Mead's big other, the same as Lacan's, is the ensemble of the social relations of Marx. The best description of the dynamics of the ensemble of the social relations is George Herbert Mead.

813 Mead, G.H. (1934). Mind, Self and Society. (Ed. Charles W. Morris). Section 33 The Social Foundations and Functions of Thought and Communication. Chicago: University of Chicago (1934). Online in A George H. Mead source page. Accessed from <https://brocku.ca/MeadProject/Mead/pubs2/mindself/Mead_1934_23.html> on 2016-04-11.

Lévy-Bruhl concluded that the higher psychological functions of primitives, pre-logical and mystical, are profoundly different from those of civilized individuals. Psychological nature changes with social nature and pre-logical does not mean illogical but constructed through a different, earlier form of coherence, a different way of making sense and logic. It is phylogenetically what Jean Piaget describes ontogenetically for the child. We must however remember that, historically, a substantial part of early logical thinking was dialectical thinking before it became Aristotelian formal logic. Early dialectical logic may appear illogical and capricious to the untrained eye.

Lévy-Bruhl raised the question of the historical development of collective thinking. He showed that thinking is not a constant, but rather an historical variable. Comparative psychologists and symbolic interactionists have developed a similar line of thinking; they give genetic priority to the activity of the social protoplasm from which all individuality and individual thinking and consciousness emerges.

The available psychological information at his time on the study of so-called primitive man was reviewed by Vygotsky,[814] who pointed out some of the singular characteristics of primitive psychology such as cranial configuration, possible brain structure, and naturally adaptive perceptual acuity.

2.8.9 The Contribution of Meszaros: Social Structure and Forms of Consciousness

Meszaros more than any modern philosopher has been able to respond to the successive ideological challenges posed by the

---

814 Vygotsky, L. (1930). Primitive Man and his Behavior. In: A.R. Luria and L.S. Vygotsky (1992). *Ape, Primitive Man, and Child: Essays in the History of Behaviour.* Trans.y Evelyn Rossiter. Orlando. Paul M. Deutsch Press. Online in MIA. Accessed from <https://www.marxists.org/archive/vygotsky/works/1930/man/index.htm> on 204-09-12.

apologists of a desperate, dying capitalism. Weberianism, Existentialism, Structuralism, Postmodernism and Economic Liberalism among others, are all attempts to revitalize the capitalist status quo, a pathological form of social metabolism. The work of Meszaros is concerned with maintaining alive the philosophical argument that follows the rich legacy of Hegel and Marx, the only coherent alternative to capitalist ideology, based on the scientific study of history, its laws and regularities.

In spite of his acumen, Hegel was a victim of ideology in the form of idealism, and ended up an apologist for the Prussian Crown. As a philosopher and scientist, Marx was not only able to see farther in both historical directions past and future, but he was able to synthesize scientific viewpoints practically relevant such as philosophy, anthropology, political economy, and even ecology.[815] Marx studied the regularities of history, which he considered the backbone of all science, always keeping in mind their determining material ground. Unfortunately, although the mainstream of science has largely rejected Marx, this is for the most part not on scientific or logical grounds but on hearsay and political ideology.

Following Marx, Meszaros has been able to develop the understanding of social and conscious metabolism of the declining phase of capitalism against the neoliberal motto that there is no alternative. He has opened views for the transition to socialism, inspiring for example Hugo Chavez in Venezuela. Meszaros starts from the fact that our consciousness is irremediably determined by our type of social structure that we must live, and consciously reflect. This means the mechanisms of our consciousness, if uncritically assumed, are biased: they have been corrupted.[816]

That the structure of consciousness reflects the structure of soci-

---

815 Bellamy Foster, J. (2000). *Marx's Ecology. Materialism and Nature.* New York. Monthly Review Press.
816 Mészáros, I. (2010-11) *Social Structure and Forms of Consciousness.* First Volume: The Social Determination of Method. Second Volume: The Dialectic of Structure and History. New York. Monthly Review Press.

ety is not a new idea; it goes back to Plato and his *Republic*.[817] Plato describes a three-tier form of morality in consciousness, wisdom, courage and desire, based on the structure of a three-class political structure, guardians, civil servants and property-less producers. Morality's being virtue, Plato tried to square the circle by coming up with a just republic in a slavist society.

Most recently, Hegel also used the notion of social structure as analogue of consciousness in his *Philosophy of Right*, an ambiguous title that also applies to morality and law.[818] Following Hegel, Marx critically contributed his famous but usually misunderstood metaphor of base and superstructure. Our mode of production determines, in the last instance, not mechanically but dialectically, our consciousness, that in turn determines our mode of production. How we produce and maintain our life determines how we think, and vice versa. Plainly put, unless we are able to develop a critical mind based on the ideology of universality, we are thinking capitalistically, meaning according to the parameters of the ruling class only.

Marx says it most explicitly in these three rich paragraphs that I quote at length: "In the social production of their existence, men inevitably enter into definite relations, which are independent of their will, namely relations of production appropriate to a given stage in the development of their material forces of production. The totality of these relations of production constitutes the economic structure of society, the real foundation, on which arises a legal and political superstructure and to which correspond definite forms of social consciousness. The mode of production of material life conditions the general process of social, political and intellectual life. It is not the consciousness of men that determines their existence, but their social existence that determines their consciousness. At a certain stage of development, the material productive forces of society come into

---

817 Plato *The Republic*. Trans: B. Jowett. Project Gutenberg. Accessed from http://www.gutenberg.org/files/1497/1497-h/1497-h.htm on 2012-04-24.

818 Hegel G.W.F. (2001) *Philosophy of Right*. Trans: S.W Dyed. Batoche Books. Kitchener. Ontario Canada. Accessed from http://socserv.mcmaster.ca/~econ/ugcm/3ll3/hegel/right.pdf on 2012-04-30.

conflict with the existing relations of production or – this merely expresses the same thing in legal terms – with the property relations within the framework of which they have operated hitherto. From forms of development of the productive forces these relations turn into their fetters. Then begins an era of social revolution. The changes in the economic foundation lead sooner or later to the transformation of the whole immense superstructure." The problem leading to social restlessness is the incongruity between what we are doing to survive and what we think we are doing according to the historical explanation of the time. The metabolic explanation of our time is scientific.

Marx continues in the next paragraph: "In studying such transformations it is always necessary to distinguish between the material transformation of the economic conditions of production, which can be determined with the precision of natural science, and the legal, political, religious, artistic or philosophic – in short, ideological forms in which men become conscious of this conflict and fight it out. Just as one does not judge an individual by what he thinks about himself, so one cannot judge such a period of transformation by its consciousness, but, on the contrary, this consciousness must be explained from the contradictions of material life, from the conflict existing between the social forces of production and the relations of production. No social order is ever destroyed before all the productive forces for which it is sufficient have been developed, and new superior relations of production never replace older ones before the material conditions for their existence have matured within the framework of the old society." This means we have the science to precisely determine that our economy is producing largely for those who do not need, those who hold the reins of capital. The conflict is easily observable, particularly when rates of unemployment, poverty and even hunger and death are high.

Furthermore: "Mankind thus inevitably sets itself only such tasks as it is able to solve, since closer examination will always show that the problem itself arises only when the material conditions for its solution are already present or at least in the course of formation. In broad outline, the Asiatic, ancient, feudal and modern bourgeois modes of production may be designated as epochs marking progress in the economic development of society. The bourgeois mode of production is the last antagonistic form of the social process of production – antagonistic not in the sense of individual antagonism but of an antagonism that emanates from the individuals' social conditions of existence – but the productive forces developing within bourgeois society create also the material conditions for a solution of this antagonism. The prehistory of human society accordingly closes with this social formation."[819] Marx means that we may be merely ending human pre-history, and that true history will begin with the next society engendered by capitalism. The solution is within our reach, the end of our alienation, the end of having our oppressors, or their proxies whose agenda is to produce artificial scarcity and create spurious needs, represent our universal interests.

The first principle I draw from Meszaros is that social metabolism is *materially grounded*. It starts from the biological fact that the species must survive and it does it through labor that is historically divided and organized towards production. As we have seen, production requires destruction but the human species is equipped to operate productively with the least destruction. This is possible first of all physiologically through organs such as sensual body, nervous system, and brain, and their emergent phenomena: consciousness, reason, meaningful communication, collaboration and language. These organs and phenomena, parts of both the natural and social organisms. are material facts and have all been scientifically verified. Psychologically this means that my default operational mode is capitalist ideology, which I, however, have the freedom to question through my critical thinking.

---

819 Marx, K. (1859). *A Contribution to the Critique of Political Economy. Preface.* Trans. S.W. Ryazanskaya. Moscow, USSR. Progress Publishers. Online in MIA. Accessed from <https://www.marxists.org/archive/marx/works/1859/critique-pol-economy/preface.htm> on 2015-10-04.

The second principle is that these material facts and phenomena did not arise capriciously but through an evolutionary logic of *reciprocal action*, starting from the universal principle of action and reaction between organism and environment. Reciprocal action is the backbone of all forms of metabolism, and it means that the same way social structure determines the form of consciousness, that latter determines the former not mechanically but dialectically. Cause and effect both operate both ways within parameters of change. As both reciprocally change, they regulate each other according to those changes. Psychologically this is what allows my thinking to be critical, to create but also to distort, corrupt and falsify.

The third principle is that consciousness is collective, *total representation*. My individual consciousness cannot be without its collective counterpart, which it came from in the first place and to which it remains constantly attached, even if it is critically. Totalization means we have a theory for everything, an explanation nested in a larger consciousness. This means if we falsify nature we do so simultaneously with consciousness and morality. We cannot be happy if we see nature hurt, particularly if that hurt is the result of our actions. Psychologically this means that my consciousness is always double, as we have seen, individually and collectively. I cannot possibly shade my collective nature.

The fourth principle is that, recursively, we organize our society as *base and superstructure*, the base's being how we relate to each other and to the rest of nature in the process of producing and reproducing our lives. The form of the foundation necessarily determines the form of the whole edifice in the last instance; there cannot be edifice without foundation. The difference between this principle and the first is that here I am talking not about the brain as base of consciousness but about the particular historical form in which my relations are shaped with others and nature. If I live in a capitalist world I cannot avoid being part of hierarchy and exploitation unless I protest and rebel.

I would call these the four premises of social and psychological metabolism; and they have a historical dimension that Meszaros simplifies by saying that all organisms are born, develop and grow, plateau, and finally decay and die. There are increasing signs that the social form of organization for production we call capitalism is in the last phase, dying out as did all preceding ones, feudalism, slavery, and primitive communism. Since the previous ones all engendered their next, we can, if we look, find in capitalism the seeds of the next stage. Metabolism changes with development.

Our material imperatives are first taken care of externally by others: usually the mother in this manner determines our social nature. We can never survive independently of others and this handicap becomes our advantage because it makes us a collaborative species. Together we create society and the culture that created us in the first place. First we related instinctually but then we turned that around consciously. First came hunger disposed of in a family mode of existence, and later sexual desire that called for a civil society with rules, taboos and laws. Evolution endowed us with the capacity to discriminate the useful from the dangerous and we turned that into morality. We all have the capacity to see the right side of things. We can postpone satisfaction and elaborate for better quality and economy, of course within limits; we are not free to starve and survive. Simpler mediations, such as cooking, are closer to nature than second-order ones such as salting, smoking, refrigerating or genetically modifying food. Our survival as a species is crucial for a nature that seems to want to see itself truthfully, according to her self-produced consciousness. Humanity, however, has in the past and continues to introduce historic mediations, often disregarding the limits posed by the morality of evolution. Nature has already started to speak, to return from the latency we placed her into through our mediations.

Totalizing, explaining, produces consciousness. When corrupted, this function produces ideology instead. Corruption can occur through bad faith but also through the use of previous forms of explanation that have been superseded by science such as mythology and religion. Needs are like receptors that demand particular forms of satisfaction. They started as natural necessities (that remain as basic but have been made largely invisible as such) but have been substituted by humanly produced needs through mediations. Accumulation of goods may have served for the purpose of a rainy day, healthy reserves, but that has become unstoppable obesity ideologically rationalized. The necessity to use has been superseded by the need to accumulate and to exchange to accumulate. Useful things have turned out to be commodities. Today we accumulate in response to the fear of a scarcity we produce in the act of accumulation.

Through our actions we humans are being made. Human activity transforms nature, but also and at the same time transforms itself in its relations to nature, that includes itself. Psychologically accumulation makes us greedy and hoarding; we metamorphose from being into having..[820] We seem to have lost the foremost capacity of the brain, to properly anticipate and plan.

Because we cannot escape ideology, all being naturally contaminated, we need a measure to differentiate ideology from consciousness. That measure is universality, where we came from as individuals and where we must return before we become ashes. The original universal classes, men and women, have been also historically transformed into spurious socioeconomic strata. To accomplish that it was necessary to turn the horizontal complementarity of woman-man into the verticality of master and slave, as Hegel portrayed. This radical turn I propose is the universal trauma of humanity, not birth.

Here is where the ecological fault began. Only true pristine consciousness with a universal interest, following the morality of evo-

---

820 Fromm, E. (1997). To Have or to Be? London and New York. Continuum. (Orig. Pub. 1976). Accessed from <https://keimena11.files.wordpress.com/2011/11/erich-fromm-to-have-or-to-be-1976.pdf> on 2015-08-21.

lution, can offer an alternative to our present course of self-destruction. This consciousness is not theoretical but eminently practical and foremost universal, urgent, and political. We need to realign our morality with a goal of equal fulfillment of needs for all.

PART TWO (B): THE SELF

"This process of relating one's own organism to the others in the interactions that are going on, in so far as it is imported into the conduct of the individual with the conversation of the "I" and the "me," constitutes the self."

G.H. Mead[821]

---

821 Mead, G.H/ (). *"Mind Self and Society.* Section 23 Social Attitudes and the Physical World. P. 179. (Ed. Charles W. Morris). Chicago: University of Chicago (1934): 178-186. Online in A George H. Mead source page. Accessed from <https://brocku.ca/MeadProject/Mead/pubs2/mindself/Mead_1934_23.html> on 2016-04-11.

2.9.1 PROLEGOMENA TO THE NOTION OF SELF

The self is the metabolic agent of self-consciousness the result of the struggle and compromise with consciousness or with ideology in order to deal with the external world. "The self is not so much a substance as a process in which the conversation of gestures has been internalized within an organic form. This process does not exist for itself, but is simply a phase of the whole social organization of which the individual is a part. The organization of the social act has been imported into the organism and becomes then the mind of the individual. It still includes the attitudes of others, but now highly organized, so that they become what we call social attitudes rather than roles of separate individuals. This process of relating one's own organism to the others in the interactions that are going on, in so far as it is imported into the conduct of the individual with the conversation of the '*I*' and the '*me*,' constitutes the self"[822] I here turn to Mead's psychology of the self, which I consider the most compatible with the Hegelian and Marxian idea of two forms of consciousness. Marx's theory of the self was succinctly summarized in a footnote of *Das Capital*.[823]

2.9.1.1 The Soul in Ancient Mythology, Religion and Philosophy

The notion of self is a recent one. Historically it has gradually differentiated from what used to originally be the notion of soul. Soul was an over-inclusive notion, the first explanation of life, and

---

822 Mead, G.H. (1934). *Mind, Self and Society. Section 23 Social Attitudes and the Physical World*. P. 179. (Ed. Charles W. Morris). Chicago: University of Chicago (1934): 178-186. Online in A George H. Mead source page. Accessed from <https://brocku.ca/MeadProject/Mead/pubs2/mindself/Mead_1934_23.html> on 2016-04-11.

823 Marx, K. (1887). Capital. Vol.1. Ch. 1. Section 3. 2. The Relative Form of value. Footnote 19. First English edition of 1887 (4th German edition). Moscow USSR; Progress Publishers. (Orig. Pub. 1887). Trans: Samuel Moore and Edward Aveling, ed. Frederick Engels. Online in MIA. Accessed from <https://www.marxists.org/archive/marx/works/1867-c1/index.htm> on 2015-09-29.

also of the natural virtue of objects. The etymology of the word soul indicates that it most likely came to derive metaphorically from water or air, from their visible external motion's being the analogue of life's own internally driven activity.

Like religion, philosophy was always concerned with the mind or spirit, and with its relation to collective societies and to individual persons. Deriving the concept of soul from religion, philosophy historically came up with various theories of the soul. It has been considered part of God or its analogue, and this is the reason it is useful to understand God as the collective form of consciousness after Feuerbach.

Being the nursemaid of science, philosophy has advanced itself through paradox: as material conditions and perspectives change historically, extant explanations become out of sync, unsustainable, creating the need to argue for better explanatory constructs. Arguments produce hypotheses that challenge present explanations and are challenged by other arguments and hypotheses. Compromise is consensual, constrained by the differing perspectives of protagonists that are embedded in class perspectives. The class issue is what derails the forward process, because its perspective is not universal and it serves particular and narrow interests. Perspectives have their historical moments that may take the form of paradigms' becoming generalized and persisting longer. The core of philosophy is reason, a significant improvement from belief in authority, but like religion not as efficient as science. Commonly seen as a mosaic of independent or individualistic capricious forms of philosophical argument, Hegel linked all philosophical schools into a dialectical totality, a coherent narrative, by finding the historical and epigenetic threads that often linked their arguments as forms of compromise.[824],[825] His-

---

824 Hegel, G.W.F. (1833-36). *Lectures on the History of Philosophy by G W F Hegel.* Trans: E.S. Haldane (Given 1805-6). Volumes 13-15 in the first edition of Hegel's Werke. Online in MIA, Hegel by Hypertext. Accessed from <https://www.marxists.org/reference/archive/hegel/works/hp/hpconten.htm> on 2015-11-04.

825 Hegel,, G.W.F. (1822-30). *Lectures on the Philosophy of History.* Online in MIA, Hegel by Hypertext. Accessed from <https://www.marxists.org/reference/archive/hegel/works/hi/hiconten.htm> on 2015-11-04.

tory was a theodicy for Hegel: the history of philosophy was the narrative of the epic of God alienated in nature and reclaiming Himself in philosophy. If this was a metaphor, and to the point it may be, it is a wonderful one. It would be a history of our collective representations, the big other, struggling for understanding.

Kuhn provided an understanding of the dynamics of the scientific historical punctuations, and so does Meszaros with his notion of paradigmatic moments in history. From various standpoints, perspectives are integrated into new coherent totalities, scientific theories.[826] This point of synthesis is most clear in the theories of Hegel, Darwin, Marx and Freud, all of whom put together threads that had been created by others before them.

Regarding the antecedents of self in philosophy, there are of course the major punctuations in the narrative of philosophy: Socrates, Plato and Aristotle after the Sophists, Descartes and Spinoza after the Renaissance, Locke and Hume during the Enlightenment and after the Glorious Revolution, and Hegel and Marx after the Romantic movement and during the Industrial Revolution.

Speculative thinking, as we have seen, emphasizes reason, and has at its heart critical thinking that always has to fight present dogma. Critical thinking is challenging the seemingly obvious, and it is the method science inherited from philosophy. Science, however, is not immune to being coopted by ideology. Critical thinking has its own historical punctuations, most clearly the Syllogism of Aristotle, the Methodical Doubt of Descartes, the Critiques of Kant, the pugnacious Critical Critique of Hegel and finally the relentless Critique of Critical Criticism of Marx, one that addresses the danger of ideological class corruption. Feminist, antiracist and ecological critiques, besides philosophical critiques such as Meszaros' and others, are the most powerful living critical movements, and the most promising in terms of a future if society survives the onslaught of capitalism.

---

826 Kuhn, T.S. (2012). The Structure of Scientific Revolutions. 50th anniversary. Ian Hacking (intro.) (4th ed.). University of Chicago Press.

The quotation at the head of this chapter clearly indicates that the self is the ensemble of the collective human relations impossible in individualist isolation. In this regard, Mead validates Marx independently. This helps us understand how the self starts by being alienated phylogenetically and ontogenetically, its organizing quality originally attributed to imaginary constructs such as soul, totem and God. These in fact are a metaphor for the greater encompassing social protoplasm that psychologically produces individuals. The so-called animistic[827] period of self-history saw consciousness, soul and self projected outside precisely because there was no individuality yet to talk about. Animism evolved to early mythology and organized religion.

Animism and mythology, including religion, are deficient explanatory models based on faith and that is the reason philosophy replaces religious faith with secular reason. The early philosophers of the school of Miletus rejected the prevailing notion that the world was a work of imponderable gods and proposed instead tangible matter as its source; they were materialists. Matter became the first form of a scientific call for universality.

Soul that was the equivalent of life, motion, wind, sea, and blood, explained life and was attributed not only to everything alive, but also to everything useful, useful objects' having virtue, the quality of their performance. The Ionian philosophers drew from earlier Oriental and Egyptian knowledge that had already advanced natural science, geometry, geography, astronomy, and mathematics, gradually shifting from ineffable soul to matter and its forms.

But the phenomena of life and soul were so compelling, though so difficult to fathom, that metaphysical and epistemological idealism, under the influence of religion, took over philosophy again, alienating it for a long historical period. Anaxagoras in the fifth century before our era had already proposed the mind as the ordering

827 Tylor, E.B. (1871) *Primitive Culture: Researches Into the Development of Mythology, Philosophy, Religion, Art, and Custom.* London. John Murray. Volume 1 Online as Google eBook. Accessed from <http://books.google.com/books/about/Primitive_culture.html?id=AucLAAAAIAAJ> on 2012-09-24.

force of a changing nature, its coherence, but it was Plato who en-shrined reified ideas as the real world giving idealism, in alliance with religion, its most durable form until the Renaissance. Idealism has been a problem ever since. For the idealists, consciousness is the only known and knowable, and the idea of God as the ultimate agent and creator of the universe. The silver lining of idealism is that, by working with the forms and grammar of nature, it greatly developed domains of philosophy such as ethics, logic and episte-mology. Idealism, particularly in its Cartesian form, persists as a distortion useful to the ruling classes. Only healthy critical scientific consciousness can eradicate it.

2.9.1.2 Plural Discovery

It then took until the advent of two European philosophers, Des-cartes and Spinoza,[828] for philosophy to begin to shed idealism, and slowly pass its gavel to science. Descartes' dualism ushered in nat-ural science along with Newton, Copernicus and Leibniz; Spinoza with his monism made it possible to bridge the materialist-idealist dichotomy, thus opening the space for the human sciences particu-larly with Hegel and Marx, who represent the fusion of philosophy and science. It is a well-known fact that paradigmatic shifts and their foundational discoveries often come from multiple individuals: In-finitesimal calculus (Newton and Leibniz), Oxygen (Priestley, La-voisier, and Scheele), Evolution (Darwin and Wallace), DNA (Wat-son, Crick, and several others), are classic examples; more recent examples are the simultaneously discovered retrovirus of AIDS, and the race for the human genome. Merton[829] believes that multiple discoveries are the rule rather than the exception and this is a good illustration of how collective representation works.

---

828 Spinoza, B. (2009). *The Ethics.* Online in Project Gutenberg. EBook #3800. Accessed from <http://www.gutenberg.org/files/3800/3800-h/3800-h.htm> on 2012-09-19.

829 Merton, R.K. (1961). "Singletons and Multiples in Scientific Discovery: a Chapter in the Sociology of Science," Proceedings of the American Philosophical Society, 105: 470–86. Reprinted in Robert K. Merton, The Sociology of Science: Theoretical and Empirical Investigations, Chicago, University of Chicago Press, 1973, pp. 343–70.

Regarding the beginning of philosophy, Jaspers gives us a good example also in what he calls the Axial Period of History, the years between 800 and 200 BCE, and I quote: "The most extraordinary events are concentrated in this period, Confucius and Lao-Tse were living in China, all the schools of Chinese philosophy came into being, including those of Mo-ti, Chuang-tse, Lieh-tse and a host of others; India produced the Upanishads and Buddha and, like China, ran the whole gamut of philosophical possibilities down to skepticism to materialism, sophism and nihilism; in Iran Zarathustra taught a challenging view of the world as a struggle between good and evil; in Palestine the prophets made their appearance, from Elijah by way of Isaiah and Jeremiah to Deutero-Isaiah; Greece witnessed the appearance of Homer, of the philosophers Parmenides, Heraclitus and Plato, of the tragedians, Thucydides and Archimedes. Everything implied by these names developed during these few centuries almost simultaneously in China, India, and the West, without any one of these regions knowing of the others. What is new about this age, in all three areas of the world, is that man becomes conscious of Being as a whole, or himself and his limitations. He experiences the terror of the world and his own powerlessness. He asks radical questions. Face to face with the void, he strives for liberation and redemption. By consciously recognizing his limits he sets the highest goals. He experiences absoluteness in the depths of selfhood and in the lucidity of transcendence."[830] This could be called the Cambrian period of consciousness.

This is a sobering lesson for the current trend to copyright ideas for individual usufruct. Ideas are all only the cusp of the contribution of many previous generations of material and spiritual work, and could not have arisen up without the accrued foundations painstakingly set by those previous generations. Ideas are like collective historical chains, some of which have their particular paradigmatic

---

830 Jaspers, K. (1965) *The Origin and Goal of History.* Chapter One. The Axial Period. A. Characterization of the Axial Period. P. 2. New Haven. Yale University Press. Third Printing. (Orig. Pub. 1949). Online in Scribd. Accessed from <http://www.scribd.com/doc/52666907/Jaspers-Karl-The-Origin-and-Goal-of-History> on 2012-09-22.

moments; but they are contributed and shared by many. It is tempt-
ing to think that there is some sort of spirit that imbues individuals
with particular ideas, but this is not necessary as it may have been
in the past. We have the material elements to explain discovery and
invention as the fulfillment of collective needs engendered by human activity.

2.9.1.3 Early Philosophical Landmarks

Philosophy came not pure at first, but was a sort of alloy with
religion upon which it built itself, shifting from coercive to reasoned
explanations. Humans needed a more practical knowledge but of the
early philosophical groups some continued to be quasi-religious. Regarding origins explanations everything came from water for Thales
(c. 624-546 BCE); from infinite opposite particles for Anaximander
(c. 610-546 BCE); or from divine air increasing or decreasing its
density for Anaximenes (585-528 BCE). These were materialist mo-
nists who had logical arguments to promote their views. Xenophanes
of Colophon (C. 570-475 BCE) already saw polytheism as the result
of anthropomorphic self-projections, saying that if animals could
describe their gods, their gods would also look like animals, a deeply reasoned insight at the time. The notion of God however, did not
then have the precise religious connotation it does today, but was
sort of an explanatory panacea, the last logical resource to close the
circle of totalization, of necessary understanding, the human need.

Speculative ideas spread from groups of live actors rather than
from isolated thinkers. The history of philosophy is thus not just a
collection or a series of individuals' proposing their particular ideas.
It is not a series of concepts coming out one after the other, as we
often think of it. It is rather a logically linked historical change of
arguments, of thesis, antithesis, and synthesis dialogues that mirror
the productive evolution of society based on natural necessity, need-
fulfillment, and new need. Need engenders material production that
in turn creates new needs. In the collective dialogue some individu-

als emerge as representatives, more skilled participants in critically applying their good sense.

In a class society when enough wealth is accumulated in private hands some individuals became free to think rather than having to directly produce their immediate survival. These became philosophers and for the most part their clients came also from the leisured class. This was taking place as the division of material and spiritual labor appeared. Here also was the origin of education as different from training. The new philosophers became collectors and dispensers of a knowledge somewhat detached from practical reality across classes. Practical problem-solvers, lawyers, and therapists, as the Sophists advertised themselves, appeared to mediate the life-conflicts of those who could afford their services.

The oldest and purest form of logic in reasoning is mathematics, born of the need to quantify particularly for exchange. From it came geometry, physics and astronomy, greatly advanced by the Pythagorean group, a secretive pseudo-religious brotherhood that literally idolized their number. Pythagoras (571-490 BCE), was a self-disciplined vegetarian. He, among other things, described the mathematical relationship between musical notes and the physical characteristics of objects emitting them, applying mathematical sense to make music out of random noise. Pythagoras also mathematically described the planets' regularities, revealing the order that lies behind apparent chance and chaos. Mathematics was for Pythagoras a cleanser of the soul. His main claim to fame however, comes from having described the nature of the Soul, one of our earliest glances at the psyche described by him as divine air, immortal through reincarnations. Air is a logical metaphor for abstraction and reincarnation. For Pythagoras, life and man were totally embedded in the harmony of nature, a harmony derived from the sacred number that can apply a measure to everything to make it practically relevant to human life.

The school of Heraclitus of Ephesus (c. 535–c. 475 BCE) was another early group, now in love with paradox. They were the first dialecticians, methodic builders with the bricks of argument. For them it is not the apparent harmony of things but a constant chaotic struggle lying behind it that characterizes everything in nature and consequently in thinking. These were the first phenomenologists and for them the world draws its origin and unity from a live fire not unlike the Big Bang. Contraries that struggle and exchange places perpetually determine each other and are behind all the phenomena of the perceptible world, in a process of development fueled by necessity and its resulting struggle to fulfill itself. Natural necessity is the foundation of all logic, and if we want to thrive we need to listen to, and act, in conformity with it. Nothing happens by chance and nature is self-regulated, everything's being determined by laws. It is up to us carriers of perception and logic to find the reason behind phenomena. Hegel would later endorse the Heracliteans by clarifying that change is always paradox because it is based on negation. You can also see a lot of Marx in Heraclitus.

Conversely, the group of Parmenides of Elea (515-450 BCE) was of the belief that change is impossible and only an illusion. Appearance is false and deceitful and in this regard the data provided by the senses is practically useless. This worrisome conclusion is arrived at by Parmenides way before Plato, with whom idealism took the upper hand in philosophy for fifteen centuries.

A sort of materialist synthesis then saw the world not as either/or, but as a composite of mixed elements, water, earth, air and fire, combined through opposite forces, Love and Discord, the theory first proposed by the school of Empedocles of Agrigento (490-430 BCE). He was also the first proponent of Natural Selection: in nature change takes place but it only endures when it is a true response to need; otherwise it perishes. Let's keep in mind the recurrent notion of Necessity as an ingredient in these discussions.

Soon after that synthesis, again came a new split. Anaxagoras of Clazomenae (c. 500-428 BCE), brought philosophy to Athens and was the first philosopher accused of atheism and condemned to a death sentence which, unlike Socrates, he escaped. For him mind, indeterminate and autonomous, is separate from nature. The difference is qualitative. Chaotic elementary particles combine and separate to make objects under the guidance of Logos, the mind, also made of the lightest of particles. The idealist typically separates sense from nature.

This was a preamble to the more elaborate theory of atoms, for the first time advanced by Leucippus of Elea or Miletus (first half of 5th C, BCE) and his brilliant disciple Democritus of Abdera (c. 460-370). Atoms are packed in empty space and are the origin of everything, colliding with each other to produce events and the properties of things, whether natural or imponderable, including the soul. Whole worlds emerge and perish under the action of atoms. Our perception of objects owes to their capacity to emanate light substances that impact our senses to be then properly processed by reason. The soul is no exception to the materialist design, and events are caused by necessity, lawfully. Plutarch, quoted by Marx,[831] says that necessity is —according to Democritus— fate and law, providence and the creator of the world. The substance of necessity is motion, the impulse of matter. This is what I have called the progression sense-coherence-consciousness. Democritus, whose name means "chosen" was also a theorist of democracy, a form of government invented by the Greeks.

Up to this point we can classify arguments as either idealistic or materialistic. Hegel took sides with the idealist and saw the philosophical process as the struggle of an embodied spirit; Marx took the other path, collective labor and superstructure.

The message to take home from the pre-Socratics is that object-nature has two faces, materiality and sense, that, although ap-

---

831 Marx, K. (1902). The Difference Between the Democritean and Epicurean Philosophy of Nature. With an Appendix. In: Marx-Engels Collected Works, Vol. 1. Moscow. Progress Publishers. Part One. Difficulties Concerning the Identity Of the Democritean and Epicurean Philosophy of Nature (Original publication in 1841 as Marx's Dissertation). Online in Internet Archive. Accessed from <https://archive.org/stream/ Marx_Karl_-_Doctoral_Thesis_-_The_Difference_Between_the_Democritean_and_ Epicure/Marx_Karl_-_Doctoral_Thesis_-_The_Difference_Between_the_Democritean_and_Epicurean_Philosophy_of_Nature_djvu.txt> on 2012-09-16.

pearing separate and autonomous, are only, like mass and energy, two faces of the same thing: matter-God. Necessity is the expression of sense, the practical intelligence of nature. Our human soul is our good moral sense, God inside, the collective representation.

With the school of the sophists that comes next, philosophy becomes institutionalized in various forms, as education, as therapy, and as legal defense. Infatuated by the limitless freedom of thinking, the Sophists applied it lavishly to the affairs of daily life, problem-solving and legal defense now that private property was accruing. The Sophists brought the power of argument to new practical heights. Masters of erudition and eloquence, they often attacked religion, the previous form of explanation. Some Sophists advertised themselves as being able to win any argument, prove any point of view, or totally reframe any problem in practical terms, of course for a reasonable fee. Masters of spinning as their pupils, politicians, remain to this day, they did help people manage their lives through sophistry. Gorgias went to the extreme of arguing that nothing exists, that if anything does we cannot know it and that if we were to know it it would be impossible to talk about it. This argument is waterproof.

Coming from sophism, Socrates constitutes a significant punctuation in philosophy because he fine-tunes the instrument of therapeutic dialogue to tackle interrelated issues of personality, truth, morality and justice, or at least rationalization. In his dialogues the strategies of intersubjective dialogues are exposed. The main moral conundrum of the Greeks was to morally rationalize slavery, now extended from mothers to women in general, to children and animals alike, all objects, all property of the ruling *paterfamilias*. This is the question that Plato would answer with his negation of reality and in its place the development of idealism. Now everything could be explained sophistically, closing the circle with the panchreston of God if necessary and the authority of the doctors of the church. The question still haunts us and we deal with it as Plato did, primarily by first compartmentalizing, then separating, and finally subordinating morality to self-interest, unconsciously: that is, conveniently. This has been made possible by the reification of the world of ideas turned into explanatory entelechies.

2.9.1.4 Socrates: Truth as Labor and Delivery

In the Sophist period, philosophy was infatuated with itself and its power. Socrates (470/469-399 BCE) illustrates the difficulty inherent in trying to find the needle of truth in the haystack of sophist spinning. This is only possible because the interlocutors share the same cultural strategies of mystification they deconstruct. It is the same in psychoanalysis that deals with mental illness caused by a necessarily alienating society of which patient and therapist are both victims: "it takes one to cure one." The therapeutic aspect of Socrates' famous dialogues, transcribed for the most part by his disciple Plato, is in showing a method to arrive at the fact that the truth is closer to good common sense than it is to corrupt sophistry. In his work Socrates shifts the goal of dialogue from victory to truthful self-cleansing.

Ultimately one's virtue consists in how one applies oneself, as one's own instrument, to one's task of living with others. This is reflected in dialogue and narrative that also portrays personality and how one "attaches" to others. At any time this is the practical issue most essential in the self-determination of a person. Virtue is human value, the practical self-appraisal that can be corrupted through necessary idealization, as Horney portrayed in neurosis. But of course the patriarchal premise of living an ethical good life starts with accepting one's position in class society. This seems to solve the ethical dilemma if it implies that one is consenting to slavery. This is the origin and root of the philosophical rationalization of immorality.

Socrates gives a new twist to the notion of virtue, the aim to be as fully human as one wishes others shall be; he is here applying the Golden Rule that coincides with Horney's notion of morality of evolution: be human. This ultimately means use your uniquely human consciousness to the benefit of all, not yourself. This implies honestly doing what one thinks is right, even if everyone else is going the other way, and defending one's consciousness even in the face of harm.

Socrates does not dictate; he helps his interlocutor deliver his own truth. In this he follows the method of his midwife mother, also the psychoanalytic method, and foretells Vygotsky's paradigm of collaboration rather than master-slave confrontation. Here the better-adapted person collaborates with the learner one and morally shares in the outcome.

Socrates was very influential in the political life of Athens, having mentored some of its leaders. This also placed him in the midst of the political clash taking place at the time between the oligarchy he belonged to and those in favor of democracy. This all took place in the midst of the devastating Athenian turmoil that followed its defeat by Sparta in the final Peloponnesian war. Socrates was condemned to death, and refused the opportunity to escape or compromise. He was charged with impiety and corrupting the youth. By remaining defiant toward his jurors during the trial, Socrates endorsed his death sentence. His final lesson was that in class society morality is an innocent bystander.

2.9.1.5 Plato in the Age of the Person

Socrates' best student was Aristocles, nicknamed Plato as we know him. Plato (about 423–348 BCE) continued his teacher's interest in the triangle of person, society and ethics. These are the roots of the Hegelian syllogism, society's being the old protoplasm or thesis, the emerging individual person its antithesis, and morality their struggle and compromise. Here are also the roots of Freudian superego, id, and ego. Keep in mind that the person is the outward manifestation, perceived first, of the self. This is due to the fact that the person is clearly perceived first through its objectification in property.

For Plato knowledge can only take place based on previous knowledge, cognition's being really re-cognition; this is the base of his argument. We learn by matching new perception to previous forms in our mind, fitting it into a class of similar perceptions. The *a priori* retrievable mind forms are the eternal realities that our immortal soul acquired in previous existences. If this were really a metaphor, not to be taken literally, where previous existences could be childhood and adolescence, it would be a simultaneous explanation of "the ensemble of the social relations" of Marx, the "superego" of Freud, the "Ought" of Kant, the "shoulds" of Horney, as well as of Gods and Totems. William James called the same thing "empirical self," and George Herbert Mead "me." We will see that "me" is the "immanence" of Simone de Beauvoir, the second-class self that lost transcendence. But Plato's disciples, idealists, took him literally.

The soul is thus beyond the physical reality for Plato, as it remains in Freud's metapsychology its cognitive capacity being a supreme eternal form that, although coming from previous generations becomes detached from any materiality, thus is God-like. It is hard to believe that this sort of idealism became the backbone of medieval scholasticism and that it dominated philosophy through the Middle Ages. Ideas became the primary data of the mind instead of sensations, and objects became only incidental to their form. Sensory knowledge became deceptive and truth based on the soul's reminiscence.

Plato's subverted theory fits like hand-in-glove the interests of the corrupt Greek aristocracy because it subverts the representational relation of mind and reality by subverting its natural hierarchy. Idealism endorses instead a hierarchical social order of power that starts and is legitimized by God. All the horizontal, dialectical binaries, natural and spiritual, are similarly vertically rearranged according to the new hierarchy of class.

In the meantime, an effective recipe for the downtrodden: the good life only exists as other life, independent of what we perceive. This fits well the religious imagination.

The *Republic*,[832] the culmination of Plato's philosophical system, outlines the structure of an ethical human life and of a just state.
The three-class political construct is at the same time a triune psychological metaphor. Virtue is the axis of both social and subjective
structures, the compromise. The model presents society as, through
the division of labor, an organizing system for the sake of efficiency
and justice. Social classes are necessary, first the philosophically
competent leisure class of guardians to resolve disputes and guide
society, second the middle class military and civil servants needed to guarantee the security of the guardians, and third the manual
skill-based lower class of workers that guarantees the survival of
all. Their importance is idealistically inverted in the vertical ranking, and the class division is legitimized through the natural, val-
ue-laden metaphor of gold, silver and bronze respectively. Virtue is
class-determined, wisdom for the guardians, courage for the militant
middle class, and moderation for workers. The middle class is there
to guarantee this moderation. To maintain the balance of this just
system, individual skill and competency must be enhanced through
well-censored and institutionalized education.

Corresponding to the structure of the state the independent soul
of each individual has three parts. The first is the rational mind or
intellect that through its wisdom discerns real from unreal, of course
following the idealist guidelines, truth from falsity and virtue from
vice. The second, the spirited soul, will or volition, courageously
carries out the dictates of "reason." The third, the appetitive soul of
emotion and desire, is the soul of workers, women and the weak,
that typically want immediate satisfaction until they learn austerity.
The soul's virtues are titrated according to class.

In *Phaedrus,* Plato uses a different, more abstract, three-part
metaphor. First is the charioteer, the ego of Freud that controls a
lowly and downwardly driven black horse, the desiring id of Freud.

---

832 Plato. (1969). *Republic.* Plato in Twelve Volumes. Cambridge, MA, Harvard University Press; London, William Heinemann Ltd. Book 3. Section 415a. Accessed
from   <http://www.perseus.tufts.edu/hopper/text?doc=Perseus:text:1999.01.0168:-
book%3D3:section%3D415a> on 2012-11-03.

The black horse pulls side by side with a noble and upwardly white horse, the wise Freudian superego. Only the gods at the top of the hierarchy of being have two white horses and are thus free of debased human contradiction. They are the ones who set the standard for what is "good." When the good shines, it reveals its legitimate forms, knowledge and truth that only the few wise at the top can see; the rest are left to their pedestrian opinion.

Very important for our purpose here, *personality type and form of government are also analogues* in the Platonic scheme: they replicate each other. The extremes of both are aristocrat and tyrant, with other forms of government and personality types in between. The aristocrat has the good fortune of his rational, spirited, and appetitive souls working in harmony, a role model for classes in the just aristocratic republic. The greedy oligarch will tend to irrationally hoard and to form cliques with others of his kind, and the timocrat would usurp what rightly belongs to others. The democrat suffers from incontinence of desire; he will thus never be satisfied and his drive will ruin governments, while the tyrant would focus only on the satisfaction of his personal needs at the expense of the whole of society. Timely.

The great merit of Plato as it concerns us in psychology is to have, for the first time, posited the social structure and the form of consciousness as analogues or isomorphs. After him only Hegel picked up the thread in his *Philosophy of Right*,[833] and most recently Meszaros in his *Social Structure and Forms of Consciousness*.[834]

Plato fully installs idealism by splitting reality into two levels:

---

833 Hegel G.W.F. (1942). *Hegel's Philosophy of Right*. First Published: by G. Bell, London, 1896. Translated: by S W Dyde, 1896. Preface and Introduction with certain changes in terminology: from "Philosophy of Right", by G.W.F. Hegel 1820, Translated. Prometheus Books; Remainder: from "Hegel's Philosophy of Right", 1820, translated, Oxford University Press; First Published: by Clarendon Press 1952, Translated: with Notes by T M Knox 1942. Online in MIA. Accessed from <https://www.marxists.org/reference/archive/hegel/works/pr/philosophy-of-right.pdf> on 2016-08-17

834 Meszaros, I. (2010-2011). Social Structure and Forms of Consciousness. 2 Vols. New York. Monthly Review Press..

Factual reality is the ideal, and available only through aristocrati-cally privatized reason. Phenomenal, sensorial, or manifest reality is only illusory appearance. The ideal ultimately derives from, and leads to, God.

2.9.1.6 Aristotle on How to Think

That Aristocles and Aristotle have the same linguistic root as aristocrat is no mere coincidence. To have the leisure to philoso-phize they had to have the leisure guaranteed by ruling class. Pla-to's most brilliant student in the Academy, a brotherhood not unlike the Pythagorean community, was Aristotle (384-322 BCE). Like his teacher, Aristotle was concerned with a systematic theory and with a method that could unify knowledge. He endeavored to accomplish this through his syllogistic formal logic, still with us. Representing the peak of Greek philosophy Aristotle critiqued some of Plato's idealistic premises. Essence is not an alien form for Aristotle; it is something contained within the object itself and not separate, it pro-vides the form of the thing. Aristotle could not completely extricate himself from idealism and therefore his concept of essence remains formal as we can see. I will briefly review some relevant Aristote-lian notions starting with his logic.

Logic:[835] Immersed in language, logic reflects the way in which nature operates. This is a seminal idea for science that is not gener-ally understood. It was later picked up by Hegel. It means that logic does not come from the unknown or from the brain; it is inherent in the phenomena of nature and we copy it in our consciousness. The fundamentals of Aristotelian logic are contained in his laws of Iden-tity, Non-contradiction, and the Excluded Middle, that until Hegel prevailed unchallenged. Hegel radically inverted them. Using these principles, Aristotle thought he could get to the essence of things.

---

835 Aristotle. Aristotle Organon and Other Works. Organon III. Prior Analytics. Book I. Trans W.D. Ross and A.J. Jenkinson. Online in Internet Archive. Accessed from <http://ia600300.us.archive.org/18/items/AristotleOrganon/AristotleOrganoncollect-edWorks.pdf> on 2012-09-18.

The relationship between substance and form produces object individuality. For Hegel essence is the series of appearances of the object. This is verifiable.

Motion:[836] Motion is abstractly defined as potentiality turned actuality, going all the way back to a First Mover, a self-caused mind to be studied by theology. The goodness of the universe resides in its teleology, the will of the designer. We see here as in other notions of Aristotle the zigzagging of materialism and idealism. Again, Hegel redefined motion as negation.

Soul:[837] The soul is the unique virtue of life. The notion that all living beings have a soul is the central tenet of Aristotle's psychology. Connecting life with its environment, the soul is both nutritional and sensitive, and in humans exclusively universal and rational. The three requirements for the existence of the soul are the general potentiality of matter, the energetic individuality of form, and activity that leads to observation and knowledge. The notion of activity is central to psychology today in the cultural instrumental school of Vygotsky.

Sensation, thinking and desire:[838] Sensation is the passive capacity of the soul to register the subject's contact with external objects, a contact that turns into potentiality in the soul that in the object is actuality. The soul assumes the object's form, formally enacting its material reality. Pleasure and pain determine desire, and activity. Thinking further abstracts and combines forms independently of their external objects. Knowledge is information provided by the senses and subsequently modified by reason. The intellect includes a storage of possibilities that the agent uses as thoughts.

---

836 Aristotle. (2005). *Physics*. Book II. Part 7. Pp. 81-220. Translated by R. P. Hardie and R. K. Gaye. In: The Internet Classics Archive. (350 BCE). Accessed from <http://classics.mit.edu//Aristotle/physics.html> on 2012-09-16.
837 Aristotle. *Organon and Other Works. On the Soul*. Ibid. Pp. 1159-1255.
838 Aristotle. *Organon and Other Works. On the Soul*. Ibid.

Emotion[839] and imagination:[840] Emotions are notions actualized in physiological changes. Anger is a desire for retaliation accompanied by an upward surge of warm blood. This raises the question of whether the mind is really separate from the body. Imagination makes something that was sensed before reappear.

Morality,[841] will,[842] and personality:[843] Voluntary human activity is always ethical and entails moral responsibility with the final goal of happiness. To achieve excellence and be a good person, virtue postpones the satisfaction of desire, a balancing act between excess and deficiency, between desire and reason, regulation. Virtue is its own reward, as it leads to happiness. Permanently embedded virtues forge the individual's character or personality, the predispositions to act influenced by habits and experience. Lack of self-control is moral incontinence and weakness of the will. Friendship[844] is a form of reciprocity that conforms a moral community of fairness and rectification of individual wrongs. It is based either in pleasure, utility or altruism, all essential for a good life. Within that community, division of labor and private property are essential.

The four possible explanations:[845] When we don't know a cause we look for an explanation. There are diverse and at times competing explanations we usually call theories based on perspectives. These can be material, formal, efficient, and final in character. The variety of such explanations is complementary and necessary. The material explanations of a table answer the question what is it made of: the answer is wood. The formal explanations answer the question of how did it take its form: through the activity of the carpenter. The

---

839 Aristotle. *Nicomachean Ethics*. Translated by W. D. Ross. Oxford, Clarendon Press. Online in The Internet Classics Archive. Accessed from <http://classics.mit.edu/Aristotle/nicomachaen.html> on 2012-09-18.
840 Aristotle. *Organon and Other Works. On the Soul*. Ibid.
841 Aristotle. *Nicomachean Ethics*. Ibid. And other related works such as *Eudemian Ethics* and *Magna Moralia*.
842 Aristotle. *Organon and Other Works. On the Soul*. Ibid
843 Aristotle. Nicomachean Ethics. Ibid.
844 Aristotle: *Nicomachean Ethics*. Ibid. Book VIII.
845 Aristotle. (2005). *Physics*. Book II. Part 3. Ibid.

efficient explanation responds to how did it possibly come to be: through specific mediating tools. And the final explanations respond to what does it do, or what is it for; the answer, to fulfill the need to eat, or write, *etc*. The four explanatory models are not separate but interconnected moments of a process of knowing.

In Aristotle we have the categories necessary for a psychological science.

2.9.1.7 After Aristotle

Socrates, Plato, and Aristotle represent the heyday of philosophy, spanning about a century, and shaping philosophy as a collective and unified grand narrative operational to this day. After the three masters, the process of questioning and advancing knowledge continues, as school after school continue to pass on the torch in various parts of the world, although here I am focused only on Western philosophy. Three later schools are important perspectives that Hegel considered a variety of what we would call defense mechanisms. Marx was also concerned with them in his dissertation and the beginning of his disagreement with Hegel.[846]

The Epicureans return in full to a pre-Socratic materialistic conception. There are no gods in worldly affairs for them, but only matter and its own inherent motion, and things are independent of the knowledge we have of them. Things are the result of mechanically colliding atoms, and knowledge of them has to be acquired through the senses. The universe is eternal and infinite and all explanations are acceptable if they don't contradict good sense but perishable. What ultimately matters is ataraxia, tranquility attained by the

---

846 Marx, K. (1902). The Difference Between the Democritean and Epicurean Philosophy of Nature. With an Appendix. In: Marx-Engels Collected Works, Vol. 1. Moscow. Progress Publishers. Part One. Difficulties Concerning the Identity Of the Democritean and Epicurean Philosophy of Nature (Original publication in 1841 as Marx's Dissertation). Online in Internet Archive. Accessed from <https://archive.org/stream/ Marx_Karl_-_Doctoral_Thesis_-_The_Difference_Between_the_Democritean_and_ Epicure/Marx_Karl_-_Doctoral_Thesis_-_The_Difference_Between_the_Democritean_and_Epicurean_Philosophy_of_Nature_djvu.txt> on 2012-09-16.

knowing subject without unnerving dogmatism. Explanations must be eminently practical and geared to the satisfaction of personal consciousness rather than to any final understanding. The practical goal of philosophy is sober happiness based on the moderate fulfillment of desire and the avoidance of the pain of excess or frustration. Pleasure and pain are the original measures of good and evil. The Epicureans were politically egalitarian, and believed humans exit nature and enter the human realm by facing other humans. Human maturity is achieved when man subdues his natural desire and creates contradiction within himself. Our sensations reflect the world as it appears; when I hear, nature hears itself, and when I see, nature sees itself; I am the mirror of nature.

The Stoics' central belief is that life must be lived according to nature. For Zeno and his disciples psychology is part of logic since sensation is the basis of all knowledge. Dysphoria is an unnatural disturbance and happiness results from behavior that is moral and therefore congruous with nature. Negative emotions arise from morally avoidable false judgments. Virtue is happiness and only the wise are truly free. Another Stoic, Epictetus, was born a slave and for him philosophy became the way of life and liberating self-knowledge. An important formula for success in living is that external events are produced by fate which is uncontrollable, while actions we choose to take are our responsibility. Consequently, suffering results from trying to control the uncontrollable or neglecting to regulate the controllable. Like Epicureanism and Skepticism, Stoicism is a practical rejection of Plato's denial of reality. The world may crumble under my feet but I choose how I react.

The Skeptics or doubters were grouped around the Greek philosopher Pyrrho of Elis (c.360-c.270 B.C.E.) who questioned the very possibility of objective truth, erected doubt, before Descartes, as a central principle. Since everything can either be affirmed or denied, this uncertainty must lead to the suspension of all judgment. A practical indifference toward objects is the road to peace. They do not deny that truth exists, but refrain from pretending they possess it. Skepticism is a logical outcome of Sophism that calls for a revision of all premises. The contribution of Skepticism is its critical thinking.

2.9.1.8 New Birth: The Renaissance

The battle against Plato and idealism was not won by the Greek Renaissance. After it there came a historical gap when philosophy, in its idealist version, was largely co-opted by religion, a regression to faith and orthodoxy perhaps best represented by the Roman-African church father Augustine of Hippo (354-430 CE), born in what is today Algeria, who argued the sinfulness of nature and God and religion as the only protection. Italian priest Thomas Aquinas (1225-1274 CE), the other pillar of Catholicism, promulgated divine revelation and salvation.

For centuries medieval philosophy using Plato and Aristotle, became busy trying to rationalize Christian theology through dogmatic scholastic interpretation and argument. This situation finally started to change with the first symptoms of the Renaissance as Polish polymath Copernicus (1473-1543), German mathematician Johannes Kepler (1571-1630), and Italian physicist Galileo Galilei (1564-1642), each from his own perspective (respectively, theory, mathematics, and empirical proof) as a team proved beyond doubt that it is the sun, not the earth, that constitutes the center of our immediate universe. This was a blow to scholasticism that had held the opposite view.

The center of gravity also started to shift from God to man with the new Humanism of Giovanni Pico della Mirandola (1463-1494) and Giordano Bruno (1548-1600) in Italy, Desiderius Erasmus (1466-1536) in Holland, and Francisco Suarez (1548-1617) in Spain, among others. Here again we have an example of collective representation's moving simultaneously in various fronts. The new message was that it is immoral to wait for God to make our decisions, and we have ourselves the obligation, the capability, and the freedom to address our human issues and solve our problems. Philosophy took its corresponding turn and skepticism was revived through Michel de Montaigne (1533-1592) in France, who wondered how knowledge can be possible and even arrogant when the self is always changing, even escaping judgment and contradicting itself which Montaigne did in his *Essays*.[847] This honesty is a veiled attack on dogmatism.

2.9.1.9 The Scientific Method

Francis Bacon (1561-1626) endeavored to eliminate the idealist bias pervasive in medieval thinking. He proposed inductive reasoning, which means starting from the real sensual fact rather than the abstract generality. Facts are properly processed by reason, and can lead to axioms and scientific laws after the mind has been cleansed from prejudices that Bacon calls *idols*. These are *false gods* based on fantastic distortions, and can either be idiosyncratic or else cultural, linguistic, imposed by bad faith and ideology. His new method, intended as a substitute to Scholastic thinking, is based on unbiased observation, empirical knowledge characterized by accepting its roots in the natural world, and on experimentation geared to increase human power over nature. Knowledge is power and his main work: *The New Instrument (Novum Organum Scientiarum)*,[848] intends to replace the ideal realm of first principles.

Natural science is the paradigm of all science with physics at its heart and matter as its object. Man can know nature only by observing its laws. Movement is inherent in matter and the senses are infal-

---

847 de Montaigne, M. (2006). *Essays Of Michel De Montaigne*. Trans: Charles Cotton, Ed: William Carew Hazlitt. (Orig. Pub. 1877) Project Gutenberg. [EBook #3600]. Online in Project Gutenberg. Accessed from <https://www.gutenberg.org/files/3600/3600-h/3600-h.htm> on 2017-04-21.

848 Bacon, F. (1863). *The New Organon or True Directions Concerning the Interpretation of Nature*. This rendition is based on the standard translation of James Spedding, Robert Leslie Ellis, and Douglas Denon Heath in The Works (Vol. VIII), published in Boston by Taggard and Thompson in 1863. (Orig. Pub. 1620). Accessed from <http://www.constitution.org/bacon/nov_org.htm> on 2012-09-21.

lible, the true source of knowledge. Science is not contemplative but experimental; it applies reason to the data provided by the senses. These are the new premises.

Bacon is critical of the new humanism that he characterizes as words more than matter, style over substance. Although he propels the modern scientific method and is critical of superstition, he must leave the theological edifice rather untouched. This results in his conceptualization of a dual human soul, one natural and one rational, the latter created by God. Again, if we understand God as the collective representation, this is a lead to our theory of dual consciousness and self.

2.9.1.10 Mechanical Explanations

Philosophical mechanicism now tries to explain all natural phenomena on the basis of mechanical laws, at this time the vanguard in young science. However, it mechanically reduces qualitatively different natural processes: biological, chemical and psychological. Motion for example is not conceived as change but goes back to external displacement. The seeds of mechanicism were already in Democritus and it is understandable in the early astronomers that observed only the external motion of stars and planets. An early stage of materialism, it shifts from mathematics to mechanics.

English philosopher Thomas Hobbes (1588-1679) further systematized Bacon's materialistic conception of the world. For him humans are no more than sophisticated machines. Typically movement is only a secondary mechanical property of matter and the product of external force. Time and space are mental constructs. Thought is an instance of the physical operation of the human body, ideas developing from sensations. Representations and notions are nothing but mechanical reflections of reality in the brain. Animal activity is the result of discomfort and its aim is well-being, volition's being the movement of the will sprung from strong desire. Human's ultimate driving force is our animal nature and our self-interest.

Political philosophy was a main interest of Hobbes. Only through a social contract and a commonwealth embodying it through the creation of a protective *Leviathan*,[849] a corporate state emerging from civil society, can we avoid constant war, the natural tendency of man against man. Hobbes establishes the foundations of European liberal thought, including human rights based on equality.

Hobbes, in opposition to metaphysics, stressed that knowledge is based on experience. Psychology is a branch of anthropology. Man's nature is the sum of his faculties and powers, animal and rational. The powers of the mind are cognitive and motive. Motions in the external world cause motions in the brain. Sensations become complex ideas, cognitions. Animal warring appetites are the beginning of a response series starting from deliberation, through will, to action. We can see here the mechanical steps in psychology. Here we have a sketch of mechanical psychology.

Some consider Hobbes the founder of psychology in England, although he is best known for his political philosophy.

2.9.1.11 The Cartesian Compromise

French philosopher René Descartes (1596-1650) also rejects the scholastic tradition and endorses science. He compromises, however, by dividing substance into two types, material and spiritual. Material substance is characterized by extension or the capacity to occupy space. Mind is an internal substance with different and unique characteristics. The mind and body act in parallel fashion.

Descartes believes that as children we are fed judgments before we can exercise critical reason and consequently it is impossible to arrive at certainty, thus his methodical doubt.[850] That I can think is

---

849 Hobbes T. (1996). *Leviathan*. Ed. Richard Tuck. Cambridge and New York. Cambridge University Press. (Orig. pub.1651). Online in Project Gutenberg. Accessed from <http://www.gutenberg.org/ebooks/3207> on 2012-09-21.

850 Descartes, R. (2008). *Discourse on Method*. Online in the The Project Gutenberg EBook of A Discourse on Method, by René Descartes. Ebook #59. (Orig pub 1637). Accessed from http://www.gutenberg.org/ebooks/59 on 2012-09-26.

my only certainty and point of beginning. Hypothesis and experiments lead, although not to certainty, to theories, mechanical theory's being the paradigm. To be true any statement must survive the test of severe skeptical scrutiny by reason.

Human behavior can be explained mechanically. What characterizes humans is not the depth of any animal capacity but thought and language. Starting with "I think" can be deceptive because of imagination and false perceptions such as hallucinations. Passion also falsifies perception, as does the uncritical acceptance of opinions. Mechanical motions in the body and nerve connections to the brain explain sensations and passion, a major focus of Descartes. Nerve fibers float in animal spirits, fine substances with access to the brain. Pores in the brain expand or contract to produce the muscular activity of the body. Sensations trigger the passions and emotions of the mind according to their importance and usefulness or harmfulness. Passions influence the soul to desire things. Primary emotions are wonder, love, hatred, desire, joy and sadness; others are composites of these.

Descartes' views on happiness are expressed in his letters to Elizabeth[851] and in his last book *Passions of the Soul*.[852] In the letters he answers queries from, and gives advice to, princess-philosopher Elizabeth of Bohemia, with whom he corresponded for several years. He believes that feelings originate in mechanical bodily changes communicated through the animal spirits to the pineal gland. Emotions dispose the soul to want the things for which they have prepared the body, such as fleeing in the case of fright or fighting in that of anger. Passions can harm us but we have no choice but to live with them. Through the intellect we can deal with them. A positive attitude keeps passions away from the senses and the imag-

---

851 Descartes, R. (2007) *The Correspondence between Elisabeth, Princess of Bohemia and Descartes*. Trans. Lisa Shapiro. Chicago: University of Chicago Press. (Orig. Pub. 1684).

852 Descartes, R. (1989). *The Passions of the Soul*. Tr, Stephen Voss. Indianapolis, Cambridge. Hackett Publishing Co. (Orig. Pub. 1649). Also online in Claremont Graduate University: The Descartes Web Project. The Passions of the Soul. Accessed from <http://net.cgu.edu/philosophy/descartes/Passions_Letters.html> on 2012-09-26.

ination, by directing us to objects that can provide contentment and joy. Through his own positive attitude Descartes was able to overcome his sickly nature, he states, a cough and paleness he inherited from his mother that had been poorly prognosticated by doctors. Reason is master of the emotions.

Good and happiness are ultimate goals of humans. The supreme good is virtue and virtue is the use of the free will to attain the best possible outcome. Happiness is inner satisfaction acquired by the wise man even in the absence of fortune's favor. We aim at virtue to attain happiness, its supreme form's being the contemplation of God reserved for the next life. Even in disasters and pain, we can be content if we use our reason. Reason and sound judgment, philosophy itself, is a form of therapy for the universal illnesses of the mind that stand in the way of happiness.

Descartes' is a practical philosophy and a therapeutic psychology within the parameters of his time and we can see that his main contribution resides in including the nervous system in his psychology and focusing on emotion. Descartes also contributed the fundamental notion that the reflex is the unit of involuntary action.

2.9.1.12 The New Monism

Cartesian dualism does not make sense to Portuguese-descended Dutch philosopher and lens grinder Baruch Spinoza (1632-1677) who, in contrast to Descartes presents a comprehensive vision of the universe as one coherent whole guided by a logic of necessity. The processes of the mind are no exception to natural law, and humans must be understood the same as the rest of nature. This is a huge step that originates materialist scientific Monism. One substance, God, is two-faced, its other side being Nature. The beginning of phenomenology, this sounds like matter and energy in physics or object and subject in psychology. This is provided that energy and subject have a sense, like the universe: a logic of necessity. God is the good sense of nature that makes it intelligible and that does not rule by proxy but is embedded. Everything that happens occurs through the operation not of a supernatural forces but of lawful necessity. "By God, I mean a being absolutely infinite that is, a substance consisting in infinite attributes, of which each expresses eternal and infinite essentiality."[853] This is the definition of Nature, the part of the absolute we know.

For Spinoza body and mind are two attributes of the same substance; and he endeavors to develop the ethics of knowing. Each object has an equivalent idea and the idea of the human body is the mind. But minds vary and the capacity of the mind is directly proportional to that of the body. Human behavior has its central motive in the avoidance of pain. Some behaviors are unconscious, such as those that responds to passion. Deliberate behavior, activity, exercises consciousness. Ethics is practical, good being what serves the long-term interests of life. Ethics must include full knowledge of repercussions. The greatest human good is to understand one's place in the structure of the universe as a natural expression of necessity. Freedom is self-determination in the context of knowledge.

Necessity is the first ruler, the wise ruler of nature. Through reason nature allows necessity to be partially overruled by freedom's in humans, freedom being based on the capacity to know how we are determined by need. Better-fit ideas and emotional feedback make us freer. This means we increasingly become the cause of our own effects. This entails agency, overcoming the passivity of our earlier natural state of natural determination. As we become freer we become more God-like.

On the issue of logic Spinoza paved the way for Hegel. "The order and connection of ideas is the same as the order and connection of things."[854] Reason cannot override emotion; emotion can only be overridden by a stronger and perhaps a more rational emotion. They

---

853 Spinoza, B. (2010) *Ethics*. Part 1. Concerning God. Definitions. VI. Online in Wikisource. The Free Library. Accessed from <http://en.wikisource.org/w/index.php?title=Ethics_(Spinoza)/Part_1&oldid=2171549> on 2012-09-27.

854 Spinoza, B. (2010). Ibid. On the Origin and Nature of the Mind. Part 2. Proposition VII.

can be deactivated however by detaching them from their external cause. Lack of mastery of the emotions causes bondage and suffering.

Good and evil are derivatives of pleasure and pain. "The knowledge of good and evil is nothing else but the emotions of pleasure or pain, in so far as we are conscious thereof...By good I mean that which we certainly know to be useful to us."[855] The highest virtue is the intellectual love or understanding of the universe.

The method Spinoza uses, advancing from definitions to axioms, to propositions and proofs is the application of the scientific method in philosophy. His monism is his major contribution that has scientific methodological consequences far greater than those of Descartes. If we define mind as the idea of the body, we can define consciousness as the idea of the brain.

2.9.1.13 The Dialogue Continues

Philosophers continue their dialogue. German mathematician and philosopher Gottfried Leibniz (1646-1716) rejects some of the premises of Descartes. For him mind and body are separate realms in a non-causal relationship, a pre-established parallel harmony. Consciousness, soul and feeling are continuous with animals and not exclusive of humans. Leibniz also introduced the notion of unconscious mental representations, and for the first time connected language and mind.

Idealism came back in full with English bishop George Berkeley (1685-1753) who claimed to rely on common sense and the obvious, to argue against Locke's materialism:[856] only ideas directly perceived are real, and the qualities of objects are only human sensations. In other words things exist only as perceptions. God perceives

---

855 Spinoza, B. (2010). Ibid. Part 4. Proposition VIII.
856 Berkeley, G. (2003) . A Treatise Concerning the Principles of Human Knowledge. Online in The Project Gutenberg EBook of A Treatise Concerning the Principles of Human Knowledge, by George Berkeley. Ebook #4723. Accessed from <http://www.gutenberg.org/files/4723/4723-h/4723-h.htm> on 2012-09-27.

them all the time. Perception is caused by God.

There are no material substances for Berkeley. The most essential feature of substance is activity and mind or spirit is activity experiencing itself. Mind is active perception, self-perception and judgment. The notion of activity is the positive kernel of Berkeley's otherwise extreme theory.

2.9.1.14 Locke Consolidates the Self

English thinker John Locke (1632-1704) was one of the first philosophers to give serious attention to the question of individual identity, the self, which he saw as the continuity of consciousness. Psychology is about experience and there is nothing innate in terms of ideas or categories as Descartes believed. Our knowledge is experience mediated by ideas, and everything we can possibly think of is reducible to simple ideas. There are also complex ideas such as substances, modes, and relations, combinations of simple ideas. Experience provides the best explanations, not belief or reason alone. Locke's psychology is described in his *Essay Concerning Human Understanding,*[857] in which Locke expends considerable effort on the explanation and classification of ideas, the primary units of consciousness. Words, often confusing if not properly selected, represent our ideas.

Knowledge is the perception of the connection and agreement or disagreement of ideas. There is intuitive knowledge that directly perceives the connection between ideas in the clearest and most certain way. There is also demonstrative knowledge, when the connection between ideas is not obvious. Finally sensitive knowledge has to do with the relationship between our ideas and the objects in the external world that produce them.

---

857 Locke, J. (1690). *An Essay Concerning Human Understanding.* Chapter 27. §27. Suppositions that look strange are pardonable in our ignorance. Online in Enlightenment. Accessed from <http://enlightenment.supersaturated.com/johnlocke/BOOKIIChapterXXVII.html> on 2015-09-24.

This new model of science, empirical, in England was also embraced by Newton, Boyle and Sydenham among others, and is another example of collective consciousness' simultaneously operating through individuals coming from quite different perspectives. It follow in the footsteps of Bacon and Hobbes. Locke also propelled Hobbes' liberalism in politics.[858]

Capitalism established a new form of human relations after the previous ones, master-slave and master-bondsman. This was reflected in the need for a new type of government that emerged in England with the great convulsions of the seventeen century in which Locke lived. The rising bourgeoisie was able to achieve the compromise of parliamentary democracy from the monarchy. With the end of feudalism all individuals in society became the owners of their lives and bodies that had been totally or partially alienated before, and therefore the new mode of production required a new type of productive relation. In the previous forms of social relations some individuals, masters, had either total or partial control of others. In the new capitalist relation although the hierarchy propertied and property-less remained, all individuals were free to enter into contract in the process of production for the reproduction of their lives. Freedom to contract was not so much an external issue of legal persons and property; individuals now independently of property could enter into contract to buy and sell commodities, including labor power. This new type of transaction required knowledge of individual rights and state regulations, and this required a full self with power of attorney even if the contract were implicit. The self is this completed identity that in its form reproduces the political compromise; but that will become clear later: that the self is the result of the struggle of two opposites.

Self is thus about regulation outsourced onto the individual himself and it therefore requires the introjection of the master-slave relation that Hegel so keenly saw. This new psychological structure

---

858 Locke, J. (1690). Second Treatise on Civil Government. Online in Constitution Society. Accessed from <http://www.constitution.org/jl/2ndtr05.htm> on 2015-03-06.

that Freud saw later as superego and id is nothing but the internalization of political hierarchy. That is the reason it must be used for political correctness. It produces the docile citizen with his or her capacity to participate in political representation. Social control or regulation becomes more of an internal matter, in fact the most important for the functioning of society. From a psychological standpoint, Locke speaks for his time or, perhaps better, his time speaks through him. Each individual now had the necessary structure to define the limits of her or his freedom in class society. The new form of hierarchy had to be endorsed in the hope of climbing, freely ascending within it. The vertical structure of mastery and bondage had been internalized.

Each person is a moral agent responsible first of all to her/himself. Our mind at birth is a blank slate, and the property of sensations provide us with our ideas about the external world, that of reflection giving us a map of our mental operations; we arrive at knowledge through these two processes. The capacity to combine ideas allows us to create illusions. We recognize change by the fact that it reorganizes material parts.

Locke's theory of the mind inaugurates the modern conceptions of identity and self, provoking a cascade in the work of later philosophers such as Hume, Rousseau and Kant, and in Hegel who finally sketches a psychoanalytic theory in his *Phenomenology*. Locke gave its modern nuance to *the self* when he famously said is "that conscious thinking thing whatever substance made up of, (whether spiritual or material, simple or compounded, it matters not) which is sensible or conscious of pleasure and pain, capable of happiness or misery, and so is concerned for itself, as far as that consciousness extends." [859]We can notice the emphasis on the practicality and the morality of the self.

In this fashion, Locke placed thinking, feeling, and reflexivity together to arrive at the notions of autonomy and self-control. This

---

859 Locke, J. (1690). *An Essay Concerning Human Understanding*. Ibid. Chapter XXVII, §17. Self depends on Consciousness, not on Substance.

is absolutely necessary to a capitalist democratic society. Locke for the first time defined *the* self, against Hume's skepticism, as the continuity of consciousness. All knowledge originates in experience and particularly in sense perception and is therefore material knowledge. The person is a "thinking intelligent being, that has reason and reflection, and can consider itself as itself, the same thinking thing in different times and places"[860]

---

860 Locke, J. (2004). Ibid. Chapter XXVII. §9. Personal Identity.

2.9.2 FORMS OF SELF: SELF AND PERSON. AND CONSTIT-
UENT OPPOSITES: I AND ME

"The world is this actualization of divine Reason; it is only on its surface that the play of contingency prevails.

Hegel[861]

"In a sort of way, it is with man as with commodities. Since he comes into the world neither with a looking glass in his hand, nor as a Fichtian philosopher, to whom "I am I" is sufficient, man first sees and recognizes himself in other men. Peter only establishes his own identity as a man by first comparing himself with Paul as being of like kind. And thereby Paul, just as he stands in his Pauline personality, becomes to Peter the type of the genus *homo*."

Marx[862]

"The earliest education is most important and it undoubtedly is woman's work. If the author of nature had meant to assign it to men he would have given them milk to feed the child. Address your treatises on education to the women, for not only are they able to watch over it more closely than men, not only is

---

861 Hegel, G.W.F. (1971). *Philosophy of Mind.* Oxford, Clarendon Press. P. 62. Quoted by: Meszaros, I. (1995). *Beyond Capital. Towards a Theory of Transition.* New York. NY. Monthly Review Press. P. 469.

862 Marx, K. (1887). *Capital.* Vol.1. Ch. 1. Section 3. 2. The Relative Form of value. Footnote 19. First English edition of 1887 (4th German edition). Moscow USSR; Progress Publishers. (Orig. Pub. 1887). Trans: Samuel Moore and Edward Aveling, ed. Frederick Engels. Online in MIA. Accessed from <https://www.marxists.org/archive/marx/works/1867-c1/index.htm> on 2015-09-29.

their influence always predominant in education, its success concerns them more nearly, for most widows are at the mercy of their children, who show them very plainly whether their education was good or bad. The laws, always more concerned about property than about people, since their object is not virtue but peace, the laws give too little authority to the mother."

Rousseau[863]

2.9.2.1 Good Sense and Consciousness

In the first Hegelian quotation above, if we take divine reason to mean natural good sense, we leave the realm of idealism and enter scientific speculation; we have no quarrel then. This is what Locke meant by not choosing confusing words. Hegel would then be telling us that, deeper than the shiny patina of contingent consciousness or ideology based on our second-order, lies the natural imperative of evolutionary good sense. Although evolutionarily humans have been endowed with the brain infrastructure for abstract consciousness, if humanity is to survive it must first follow the coherent determinations of natural sense, material imperatives. This means we must obey a morality of evolution that today must be determined scientifically.

The management of the relationship between good sense and consciousness is the function of the self in individuals and government in the collective: morality and ethical law. The opposites, good sense and human consciousness, are analogues of the ones Marx discovered in collective society as base and superstructure.[864] Both

863 Rousseau, J.J. (2004). *Emile*. Book 1. Trans. Barbara Foxley. (Orig. Pub. 1762). Online on Project Gutenberg. Accessed from <http://www.gutenberg.org/cache/epub/5427/pg5427.txt> on 2016-08-20.

864 Marx, K. (1859). A Contribution to the Critique of Political Economy. Preface. Trans. S.W. Ryazanskaya. Moscow, USSR. Progress Publishers. Online in MIA. Accessed

have a great degree of autonomy in determining each other but, if it comes to antagonistic discord, in the last instance good sense must prevail. This is what seems to have happened in successful social revolutions so far. Were this not to happen, we would be crossing the limits of our natural turf and imperiling our survival as a species. It comes to individual morality versus class ideology in our culture. The force of this cultural process however is not predominantly from individual to society, but the other way around.

Culture is to individual consciousness what government is to self. The final compromise of the opposites moves *civilization. Sapiens,* the signature of the species, is the expression of this dialectical struggle, of its constant transformative metabolism. Class society corrupts natural sense ideologically. This results in the perplexing lack of common sense in politics, and in war as an obviously wrong survival strategy where ideologies clash, unable to compromise in a synthesis. This is a phenomenon of civil society, not family. It would therefore require making the whole of humanity a huge family, as originally intended, for the war phenomenon to subside.

Our present paradox is to have achieved high, even astounding, levels of knowledge in particular areas, to have solved the most difficult problems, reached the most outstanding technological advances, to have altered the natural demeanor of space and time changing the face of nature, and yet to have lost our most basic good sense. We collectively live a life that if examined is so absurd from the viewpoint of good sense that we would be astonished. But we have been desensitized to preposterousness, to the emotional effects of catastrophe, to immorality, to crisis and crime. Cataclysms must be increasingly huge to start to arouse some response. Nothing triggers our outrage any longer because we have been ourselves transformed by our own transformation of nature; the damage done to nature is in us because we have internalized the damaging structure. Our emotional capacity has been totally blunted by alternating shocks

---

from   <https://www.marxists.org/archive/marx/works/1859/critique-pol-economy/preface.htm> on 2015-10-04.

and gradual exposure, compounded desensitization and mystification by the mass media, sophisticated forms of conditioning. Television starts to do this damage to children as soon as they are ready to understand. The trick evolution has played on us is not so much to have made us a sexuated species, dual, dialectical and reciprocal by nature, designed to achieve a balance of our opposite drives, but to have also given us, in the form of freedom, the capacity to override the mutually constraining instinctual dispositions of our balanced sexuation. We have crossed the line of the natural sexual divide and made of it a spurious gap reflected in our universally split self and split class-culture.

2.9.2.2 The Sexual Divide

To complicate matters, the dialectic good-sense-consciousness, that syllogistically guides the fitness of the species and its final direction, has a dual instinctual ground that was designed by evolution to be mutually constraining in its dual instinctual proclivities, female and male. Our approach to the natural environment must be mediated by the constraint resulting from the opposition and struggle of the two opposite sexual instinctual dispositions, resulting in their final adaptive compromise. This is the root of what we call judgment, applied morality. The way this happens is that *I* instinctually tends to pierce and analytically penetrate reality, but is constrained by *me* that has the toolbox where *I* selects from. *Me* is formal objectification of all the past experience of the species designed to produce survival strategy. *Me* is the protoplasmic species beginning, gens, guided by a sense of *us*, and a maternal proclivity to equality and equal fulfillment of needs based on a morality of giving and tending. This is posited in the *bon sauvage* of Rousseau.[865] The original maternal tendency must contend with its own making, filial opposition's becoming patriarchal rule, the expression of *I* in civil society

---

865 Rousseau, J.J. (2011). *Emile*. Trans. Barbara Foxley. (Orig. 1762). Pub. Online in Project Gutenberg. Accessed from <http://www.gutenberg.org/cache/epub/5427/pg5427-images.html> on 2015-11-14.

paradigmatically portrayed in the *homo homini lupus* of Hobbes.[866] Bachofen tells us that mothers colluded with sons in the patriarchal coup.

Under conditions of catastrophe or crisis that bring about scarcity and is therefore a threat to the survival of the species, we regress to the more aggressive, destructive, approach of previous instinctual behaviors typical of the pre-human food chain. This is the expression of the male instinct. Conversely, under conditions of abundance we apply our maternal instinctual disposition. Crises and catastrophes are situations that prompt us to act rather than to delay and conjecture.

If we think about our present situation, however, we find a paradox that illustrates our deviation from the morality of evolution. The conditions of abundance and the possibilities of peace and stability were never greater for humanity than they are today. But instead of responding to this situation morally, our collectivities support the ongoing production of artificial scarcity. Thus we live "as if". Full access to resources and means is limited only to a very small segment of society that perpetuates itself through our internalization of hierarchy to make it look "natural." The result is that in the midst of abundance the majority of the members of the species lives in artificially created conditions of misery.

To compound this problematic paradox, the middle class, which characteristically provides the bulk of collective policing and explaining, survives thanks to a wage disbursed by the ruling class that dictates the ideology to be spread and the laws to be applied. The result is a society that produces a corrupted image of nature as enemy of the species, and as something to be limitlessly exploited.

How far can individualistic patriarchal ideology push the dialectic good-sense-consciousness before nature unilaterally corrects course is not possible to ascertain. But we may be currently living

---

866 Hobbes T. (1996). *Leviathan*. Ed. Richard Tuck. Cambridge and New York. Cambridge University Press. (Orig. pub.1651). Online in Project Gutenberg. Accessed from <http://www.gutenberg.org/ebooks/3207> on 2012-09-21.

in one of the moments Marx observed: "At a certain stage of development, the material productive forces of society come into conflict with the existing relations of production or – this merely expresses the same thing in legal terms – with the property relations within the framework of which they have operated hitherto. From forms of development of the productive forces these relations turn into their fetters. Then begins an era of social revolution. The changes in the economic foundation lead sooner or later to the transformation of the whole immense superstructure."[867] Here I substitute material productive forces for good sense, and existing relations of production with ideology, and I expect the same psychological outcome, a revolution in consciousness. Revolutions do not happen spontaneously, but through the unsustainable mismatch of good sense and consciousness.

It is not the tip of the iceberg, neurosis, but the bulk of universal ideological alienation that is the problem to be studied by applied psychoanalysis.

2.9.2.3 Collective Psychology, a Regression?

That all psychology is group psychology was only hinted at by Freud but expounded by Melanie Klein. Human psychology is always relational because the subject cannot be without its object that turns out to be another subject. But the original students of group psychology, including Freud, could not truly understand the collective nature of the mind because of their individualistic ideology. As we saw, they arrived at the conclusion, under the spell of individualism, that group psychology, the mother of individual psychology, is a regressive and impoverished form. In fact what is regressive are individualism and intrapsychism. Cognition pushes emotion aside because emotion is the narrative of good sense. Cognition can manipulate and produce any form of theory and even make it look natural and moral when it is not. Emotion warns us when we are going

---

867 Marx, K. (1859). A Contribution to the Critique of Political Economy. Preface. Ibid.

too far, at least those of us who have not been forced to excise our affect.

What group psychologists saw as destructive aspects of group behavior is based on the collective removal of the many constraints ideologically applied by an individualistic hierarchy of values based on repression. During group action, ideological parameters are shattered precisely because of their obsolescence. It is group psychology that applies to revolutions, which occur when the super-structural parameters of society no longer apply in the understanding of the material base, and ideology goes too far. Individuals mirror and reverberate in their common cause, the need for new forms of relations that are precisely mirroring and thus equalizing. Their good sense comes back from being stained by ideology. This is also what happens in artistic creation, among other things because art was the original form of human expression, emotional and cognitive at once. It is a regression not in the service of the ego but in the service of the *me*. Left on its own as the group evolves it will organize itself anthropomorphically, as a body with a head and functional organs and extremities. This is a natural tendency because the creation of social structures by humans is a projection of themselves as a group.

Good sense seeks to go back to the basic adaptive design of the species in its natural syllogistic structure and sexual duality: negation and negation of the negation. Good sense that I have also called coherence, as Gramsci pointed out, is corrupted by ideology,[868] resulting in what we see as actual common sense. But good sense itself is the residue of the old natural sense that goes back to the Big Bang and before. Its naturally rooted morality remains, if not individually, collectively impermeable to ideology and even if transitorily lost it is recoverable. In its manifest form good sense is buried in the alloy of commonsense, the ideological philosophy of

---

868 Gramsci, A. (1999). "The Study of Philosophy." In: *Selections from the Prison Notebooks of Antonio Gramsci.* Trans. Quentin Hoare and Geoffrey Nowell Smith. P. 630. London. ElecBook. Accessed from <http://courses.justice.eku.edu/pls330_louis/docs/gramsci-prison-notebooks-vol1.pdf> on 2015-10-15.

life, the worldview that Freud referred to as *weltanschauung*,[869] a basic holistic, totalized conception of life that every human needs. Common sense survives because of its vestigial good sense.

The function of the self, and of culture, is to titrate good sense and consciousness according to conditions or circumstances; in class society common sense has to negotiate at least two opposite ideologies. This is possible because all psychology is group psychology individually internalized.

2.9.2.4 The Relativity and Equivalence of the Self

As philosopher, and particularly as generally unacknowledged psychologist, Marx prophetically foresaw what we call self today. This is particularly remarkable considering that during Marx's time the notion of self had hardly been developed yet in a psychology that was infatuated with the ego, a part of the self. Psychology was still largely in the hands of philosophers. As the second quotation at the beginning of this chapter illustrates, Marx foretells the mirroring self-theory of today in the plainest of dramatic (non-reified) language that the late Georges Politzer (1903-1942) deemed necessary in psychology.[870] I can say "I am," only because in front of me I have a person who said "I am and you too." That person was not Paul but Mother. She was the first consistent person in front of us from the moment of birth; she imprinted our selves. Without that crucial relationship I could at best be a feral child.

My mother transmitted to me her pride in being human, and her assurance that I, like her, will grow to be big and know. She was the first Hegelian to recognize me not as master-slave but solidarily. I internalized my mother's image as she gradually turned on all my

---

869 Freud, S. (1932). "A Philosophy of Life." Lecture XXXV. In: New Introductory Lectures on Psycho-analysis. (Orig. pub. 1933). London. Hogarth Press. Online in MIA. Accessed from <https://www.marxists.org/reference/subject/philosophy/works/at/freud.htm> on 2015-10-15.
870 Politzer, G. (1964). *Critica de los Fundamentos de la Psicologia y el Psicoanalisis.* Buenos Aires. Argentina. C. Davalos, D.C. Hernandez. Libreros, Editores.

sensory buttons, my senses. She was my first mirror and self-image, the *socius* of Wallon, my original interlocutor and my first "other" and "Other."[871] She is the root of *me*. That earliest bond developed the basic internal structure, and the scaffold, of my whole consciousness and self-consciousness that will become one but forever remain dual, specular, subjective and objective. The self not only comes from the other but remains attached for its existence. The other is so crucial for the self that it must take the various forms described by Freud, Wallon and Lacan, and de Beauvoir, the archetypes of Jung, and the *Imagoes* of Melanie Klein.

In the chapter where Marx's footnote is quoted in *Das Kapital*, "The Relative Form of Value," Marx sets out to explain how the exchange value of a commodity lies hidden within its relationship with another commodity that shares with it a common ground: value. Value in commodities presents itself universally as price in money, the expression of the magnitude of their value. The amount of value in commodities necessary for their exchange is nothing but the amount of socially necessary human labor invested in their production. Human productive activity is connected through labor that is socially divided. In patriarchal capitalism it appears as if it is the commodities that have value and that can relate to each other through their price. Of the several forms of value Marx describes, the relative form is the most elementary.[872]

Marx says it is the same with man as it is with commodities.

---

871 Wallon, H. (1984). "The Role of the Other in the Consciousness of the Ego." Trans: Donald Nicholson-Smith. In: «Le role de l'autre dans la consciousness de moi» in The World of Henri Wallon. New York. Jason Aronson. (Written: 1946). Online in MIA. Accessed from <https://www.marxists.org/archive/wallon/works/1946/ch7.htm> on 2015-11-26.

872 "2. The Relative Form of Value." in: Part I: Commodities and Money. Chapter One: Commodities. Section 3 - The Form of Value or Exchange-Value. A. Elementary or Accidental Form of Value 1. The Two Poles of the Expression of Value: Relative Form and Equivalent Form. Marx, K. (1887). *Capital. A Critique of Political Economy.* Volume I. Book One: The Process of Production of Capital. Trans: Samuel Moore and Edward Aveling, edited by Frederick Engels. (Orig. pub: 1867). Moscow, USSR; Progress Publishers. Online in MIA. Accessed from <https://www.marxists.org/archive/marx/works/1867-c1/ch01.htm#S3a2> on 2015-11-16.

Our value is being human, a so-called identity that paradoxically comes in fact from the other. Human identity, the value is the common ground of humans that paradoxically starts as alterity, as the introjection and imprinting of the maternal identity. But the value of commodities remains always externally determined while humans develop to set the standards for their own values.

In psychoanalysis the most elementary relationship is mirroring, after the French Marxist psychiatrist Henry Wallon,[873] from whom Lacan borrowed the term mirror stage. The phenomenon Lacan describes is the arrival at identity: "This is me, not my mother." Mirroring the mother is the original ground of our self-consciousness from which identity, a copy of the maternal identity, emerges. Rather mechanical, I am I, the identity of formal logic is only a transitory stage to the dialectics of self-realization, my self constructs itself as the Lockean "sameness in change" that Erikson mistakenly defined as ego. [874]The mother was the first other, the live mirror that actively triggered the whole process so that what I build as "self" I build on what she and others built to make me. There can be no *I* without *me* even if the latter has not reached the status of grammatical capitalization.

Empathic mirroring has been confirmed to be present already in primates,[875] whose identity is even more dependent on the collective, on group psychology, because they don't achieve subjectivity and individuality. This sort of proto-mirroring is expressed in various degrees in other animal species, manifested in the affiliative and gregarious behaviors whereby animals recognize each other as

873 Lacan, J. (2002). "The Mirror Stage as Formative of the I Function, as Revealed in Psychoanalytic Experience." Trans. Alan Sheridan. In: Ecrits. 1. Pp. 3-9. New York. Norton. Online in Western Illinois University. Accessed from <http://faculty.wiu.edu/D-Banash/eng299/LacanMirrorPhase.pdf> on 2014-11-06.

874 Erikson E.H. (1956). "The problem of ego identity." Journal of the American Psychoanalytic Association. Jan;4 (1): 56-121.

875 Rizzolatti, Giacomo; Craighero, Laila (2004). "The mirror-neuron system." Annual Review of Neuroscience 27 (1): 169–192. Accessed from <http://www.kuleuven.be/mirrorneuronsystem/readinglist/Rizzolatti%20&%20Craighero%202004%20-%20The%20MNS%20-%20ARN.pdf> on 2015-11-21

of the same morphological kind and gregariously seek each other. This is the root of the relative form of self that in humans is also the most elementary, but of course more complex because the mother altruistically invests in being the vicarious self of the infant, who must internalize her form and agency before being able to say *I*. The bodily-form mother becomes the self's body image, and the mother-ly agency, including her piggybacking words upon actions to bring about consciousness, becomes consciousness and regulatory self.

The active, relative self develops as *I*. It selects and therefore applies useful morality that it finds in its opposite, the equivalent form of self or *me* coming from the O/other.

2.9.2.5 The Ambivalence of the Self

We have seen that qualitatively or formally different commod-ities like sugar and silver can be reduced to have quantitatively the same exchange value in bartering or in money only because they both contain quantifiable amounts of human labor. It is the amount of human labor necessary to produce them that determines their val-ue. Similarly, from the point of view of political economy Peter and Paul are equivalent. It is otherwise psychologically, because unlike commodities in the market, human relativity has the characteristics of sexuation, development, and anaclysis. The first human relation, unlike Peter-Paul is mother-child; it could not be more dissimilar in both actual quality and quantity. Besides the morphological dif-ferences of sex that already imply value in a class society, there is the implication of different instinctual dispositions, largely socially sanctioned. There are also the quantitative differences in size and skills, besides the fact that the mother must assume the role of proxy agent of the child if the latter is to survive. Moral consciousness, the ultimate determining value of humans, has the element of freedom in the mother and only potentiality in the child. That the mother must construct that child physically and spiritually is an imposition on her freedom. This experience is transformed socially through values

that have been constructed by predecessors in the form of historically contingent child rearing. The deepest difference between commodity and human is that of subject and object, the infant's being in
the object status at birth and made a subject through relational life
experience that starts with the mother. That we are all created equal
is only an illusion. We are genetically unique and, besides instinctual disposition we are born into a family with a particular history
that places us into a role full of expectations, in addition to a social
class that already hierarchically determines much of what is going
to happen in our lives. The recorded history of humanity reflects
the constant struggle to return to a condition of substantial equality,
such as has been described in matriarchal societies, a condition created by mothers originally.

We see mother-child love but ignore the practicality of a parasitic infant's destructively eating of the body of the mother who
willingly gives of herself. We proceed to grow up through identifications that imply envy, taking from others and appropriating their
values. From the biologically point of view a mother is a very costly
evolutionary object for the child to try to destroy even if she colludes in the process by giving of herself both materially and spiritually at her own cost. This could be depicted as a sublimatory projective identification with the aggressor that requires a type of morality
that only nature can provide, and that has been expediently inverted
by the parasitic patriarch. This in itself is the mother of axiological
inversions in patriarchy.

The pervasive human ambivalence of emotion comes from the
way we socially and morally organize in our imagination all these
natural and historical events. Science then challenges our construc-
tions and inversions.

2.9.2.6 The Dialectical Ground of the Self: Human Personality

The elementary polarity of dependent and ambivalent self is a
necessary moving part of the developmental process of subjectivity.

In opposition to prior species, in which the survival of the fittest is the norm, the new human morality, as we have seen, is based on altruism, making substantial equality in the fulfillment of needs possible as an adaptive goal for the species. This is mediated by human freedom, the unique achievement of the species.

Using our mediating consciousness toward the anticipation and planning the future of the species as a family unit, within the constraints of nature, would seem the logical mission of the species. Instead we have chosen, by allowing civil society to hypertrophy and return to the path of pre-human ethics, the Malthusian survival of the fittest, to deviate from the morality of evolution. This has only been possible through the creation of artificial scarcity that privileges the one-sided expression of the male instinctual disposition. The historical repression of women and the consequent suppression of their balancing instinctual disposition makes impossible the moral imperative of universal fulfillment of first-order natural necessities and necessary second-order historical needs, in that order.

The two alternative moralities, pre- and post-civil society, can be called Rousseauian and Hobbesian types depending on how human nature is seen as premise. Prior to civil society, maternal uncles first served the structural role in consciousness that later would be provided by the father, proxy of the extra-familial world that in the gens was subordinated to the matriarch. This was compounded by the rule of exogamy.

Father and civil society have historically come to represent the opposite to mother and family, with a radical transvaluation that replicates the original trauma, what for Freud was the Oedipal conflict. The sexual divide of the family in civil society becomes socioeconomic class divide. This new patriarchal dialectic of second-order mediations overrides the original female hegemony that was biologically determined. While the scope of consciousness is enhanced by the inclusion of the extra-familial world, triangulation traumatically disrupts the original mother-child relation, the Oedipal complex. If equality in need-fulfillment necessarily applied to the matriarchal gens through its gift economy, the norm for the new realm of civil society could not be based on the notion of equal fulfillment of needs, but on that of profitable negotiation of difference, This is how exchange value came to supersede use value.

Internalized, these processes in consciousness formed the structure of the psyche with a person's appearance in the external world displayed to others as a mask, behind which was the real old structure of the matriarchal gens, an ineffable soul that later would come to be designated self.

2.9.2.7 The Enhanced Form of Self -Narcissism

Historically collective consciousness shifts from its external alienation in idealized gods and magic to a growingly accurate representation of society, of the ensemble of the human relations. As God is gradually understood, external turns into an internal phenomenon. This process could have been translated into real human enrichment and quality of social life. Instead the subject has shifted alienation from god to money, from projected idealization to fetishistic reification. This is a new replica of slavery that ends up in pathological narcissism.

The first statement in any human dialogue is the demeanor of the parties, what their postures and paraphernalia mean. This is based on reverberating self and other appraisals of their expressive objectification that takes place through conspicuous selfobjects and personality. A significant amount of dialogue takes place non-verbally through bodily posture and eye contact.[876] Those reciprocal self-appraisals come from internalized original appraisals from significant others, particularly from the mothering one.[877] Schore points

---

876 See particularly: Reich, W. (1972). *Character Analysis*. Third, enlarged edition. Newly translated by Vincent R. Carfagno. Edited by Mary Higgins and Chester M. Raphael, M.D. New York. Farrar, Straus and Giroux. (Orig. Pub. 1933). Full text available from the Wilhelm Reich Infant Trust. Accessed from <http://www.wilhelmreichtrust.org/character_analysis.pdf> on 2015-08-15.

877 Sullivan, H.S. (1953). The Interpersonal Theory of Psychiatry. Ed. Helen Swick Perry and Mary Ladd Gawel. New York. Norton.

out how during the first year of life the proud mother encourages the narcissism of the infant by positively celebrating each and all of his or her behaviors.[878] Of course this interpersonal phenomenon is highly cultural. The necessary kindling of early narcissism for the purpose of later self-esteem necessarily comes to a halt drastically, when the mother for the first time says "No!" to her toddler in a warning and alarming manner that includes a radical maternal shift in demeanor.

When the mother is out-of-tune with the culturally accepted level of titration of useful narcissism she impairs, through excess or lack, the self-regulatory mechanisms necessary for the future person's realistic self-appraisal or self-esteem. Those interactions are essential as a foundation for self-regulation in future social life, which also requires empathy and emotionally guided optimal distances.

Pathological narcissism[879,880] is a self-regulatory deficit based on self-idealization. The externalized person is made to appear larger than the internal self. This is an inflationary phenomenon, as Horney pointed out, the surplus consisting in self-idealization objectified in demeanor. Culturally, narcissism logically fits the economic model of surplus appropriation and hierarchy in capitalism.[881]

Traditionally, the social standing of a person resides in his or her ability to grow outwardly through objectification; this introduces a psychological imbalance between immanence and transcendence,[882]

---

878 Schore, A. (1994). *Affect Regulation and the Origins of the Self.* The Neurobiology of Emotional Development. Hillsdale, N.J. Lawrence Erlbaum Associates. Online in Questia. Accessed from <http://www.questia.com/read/57185676/affect-regulation-and-the-origin-of-the-self-the> on 2013-03-07.

879 Horney, K. (1950), Neurosis and Human Growth. Introduction. p. 13. Online in Internet Archive. Accessed from <https://archive.org/details/NeurosisAndHumanGrowth> on 2014-07-18.

880 Kohut, H. (1971). *The Analysis of the Self.* Chicago. The University of Chicago Press.

881 Lasch. C. (1979). *The Culture of Narcissism. American Life in an Age of Diminishing Expectations.* New York. Norton. Accessed from <http://thezeitgeistmovement.se/files/Lasch_Christopher_The_Culture_of_Narcissism.pdf> on 2015-12-11.

882 de Beauvoir, S. (1972). *The Second Sex.* Ch. 2. Psychology. Trans. by H M Parshley, London. Penguin. (Orig. Pub. 1949). Online in MIA. Accessed from <https://www.marxists.org/reference/subject/ethics/de-beauvoir/2nd-sex/> on 2015-07-23.

between being and having, that is manifested at many levels. Narcissism is a production of surplus of god-like idealization according to a particular human value as Horney pointed out, a culturally determined form of pathology that falsely appears adaptive.

In capitalism persons must reciprocally recognize each other, hierarchically. Such a form of recognition based on objectification is part of the phenomenon of alienation in its particular form of reification, identification with the object that robs one's being. Recognition is a fundamental phenomenon for the form and maintenance of the self.

2.9.2.8 The Hegelian and Vygotskian Models of Self-Expansion

In his master-slave chapter Hegel illustrates how the victorious master, instead of killing the contending captive, preserves him to benefit from his work capacity. Here Hegel portrayed the patriarchal *modus operandi* based on exploitation, taking from others, of civil society.[883] Lev Vygotsky offered the opposite, family developmental paradigm, through his educational notion of the zone of proximal development.[884] Here self-expansion is based on giving to the other instead of exploiting him. We have seen these models operate in education, but they also do in life. Clearly these two models operate as complementary opposites and are necessary at different levels and conditions. The first is based on competitive taking, the second on cooperative giving. They are paradigms of personhood and self-

---

883 Hegel, G.W.F. (1967). Hegel's Phenomenology of Mind. From Harper & Row's Torchbooks' edition (1967) of the Phenomenology (1807), translated by J B Baillie (1910), from University of Idaho, Department of Philosophy, thanks to Jean McIntire. § numbers from the Baillie translation have been inserted into the text of the Baillie translation and linked to explanations by J N Findlay. Φ links to original German text: Phänemenologie des Geistes. Online in MIA. Accessed from <https://www.marxists. org/reference/archive/hegel/phindex.htm> on 2014-10-05.

884 Vygotsky, L. S. (1978). "Zone of Proximal Development: A New Approach." In: Mind in society: The development of higher psychological processes. Chapter 6. Interaction between learning and development. Cambridge, MA: Harvard University Press. Accessed from <http://www.cles.mlc.edu.tw/~cerntcu/099-curriculum/Edu_Psy/ EP_03_New.pdf> on 2014-09-28.

hood.

The Etruscans were the first to become aware of the monist duality self-person when they discovered that through a mask the self becomes able to represent a person other than what it is. Etruscan masks, part of religious rites, were found in the covers of funerary urns, made of bronze and representing the wish for immortalization while enhancing the social status of descendants. The Etruscan mask was also an attempt at durable objectification of the person.

Masks became an important expanded artistic form in Greek and Roman theatre, a way for the author and actor to express themselves as if they were someone fictitious, not morally responsible. Carl Jung emphasized the *persona* as the mask we choose to wear for the world, a central concern of psychoanalysis.[885] Legally, persons were historically created to represent property as their right. The prototype has since been the *paterfamilias* property owner of land and accoutrements, including family and animals alike. This took place after women had been legally objectified, that is, deprived of their political capacity.

Part of the phenomenon of alienation is the fragmentary separation and desynchronization of the exquisite connections of *I* and *me*, and of "self" and "person," all serving different functions in psychological life necessary for the aspiration to a real self. The human being paradoxically becomes impoverished as wealth is socially produced.[886] Human identification with property and the transvaluation of human power into money are the roots of modern and historical alienation. In a state of alienation each sphere of life, *i.e.*, economic, aesthetic, moral, etc., is independent of the others, each is focused on a specific area of compartmentalized activity alienated from the rest. Fromm quotes from Marx: "Alienation leads to the perversion

---

885 Jung, C. G. (1971). "Psychological Types." Collected Works of C.G. Jung 6. Princeton University Press. Online in Classics in the History of Psychology. An internet resource developed by Christopher D. Green. York University, Toronto, Ontario. Accessed from <http://psychclassics.yorku.ca/Jung/types.htm> on 2015-11-21.

886 Fromm, E (2012). To Have or to Be. London and New York. Bloomsbury Academic. Orig. Pub.1976]

of all values. By making economy and its values 'gain, work, thrift, and sobriety' the supreme aim of life, man fails to develop the truly moral values, 'the riches of a good conscience, of virtue, etc., but how can I be virtuous if I am not alive, and how can I have a good conscience if I am not aware of anything?' In a state of alienation each sphere of life, the economic and the moral, is independent from the other, 'each is concentrated on a specific area of alienated activity and is itself alienated from the other.' "[887] This social perspective of mental illness is not favored by academic human science that instead, in a false form of materialism, focuses on what it considers more legitimate but is in fact more alienating, genetics, biology and biochemistry, *etc.*

The same alienated type of thinking believes, for example, that artificial intelligence would rescue our lost good sense. What we have seen instead so far is the increase in unemployment as a paradoxical result of robotic production. Alienated, artificial intelligence would, like its natural analogue, work for capital, not for its creator.

A radical change in social paradigm, from Hegel to Vygotsky, is necessary.

2.9.2.9 The Structure of the Self: I and Me

We owe to American philosopher, sociologist and psychologist George Herbert Mead[888,889] the full outline of self consisting in the dialectical interaction of *I* and *me* that was in his own way endorsed

---

887 Fromm, E. (1961). "Alienation." Ch. 5 in: *Marx's Concept of Man.* New York. Frederick Ungar Publishing. Online in MIA. Accessed from <https://www.marxists.org/archive/fromm/works/1961/man/index.htm> on 2015-11-22. The numbers in parentheses are references to Marx's *Economic and Philosophic Manuscripts of 1848.*

888 Mead, G.H. (1934). "The I and the Me." Part 3, number 5 In: *Mind, Self and Society from the Standpoint of a Social Behaviorist.* (Edited by Charles W. Morris). Chicago: University of Chicago. Online in A George H. Mead Source Page. Accessed from <https://www.brocku.ca/MeadProject/Mead/pubs2/mindself/Mead_1934_22.htm> on 2016-03-12.

889 Mead, G.H. (1913.). "The Social Self", Journal of Philosophy, Psychology and Scientific Methods 10, 1913: 374-380. Online in MIA. Accessed from <https://www.marxists.org/reference/subject/philosophy/works/us/mead3.htm> on 2016-08-25.

by French psychoanalyst Jacques Lacan.[890]

Historically much before there was even a hint of self, the notion of person had been recognized because the person is what can be observed. Equally, much before the spotlight was turned on *me*, first by Karl Marx,[891] William James[892] and George Herbert Mead[893] there was *I*, or ego, because that is the visible part, the transcendent agent, of the self. The history of the notion of self proper starts with Locke in *An Essay in Human Understanding*; I quote: "...to find wherein personal identity consists, we must consider what person stands for;—which, I think, is a thinking intelligent being, that has reason and reflection, and can consider itself as itself, the same thinking thing, in different times and places; which it does only by that consciousness which is inseparable from thinking, and, as it seems to me, essential to it: it being impossible for any one to perceive without perceiving that he does perceive. When we see, hear, smell, taste, feel, meditate, or will anything, we know that we do so. Thus it is always as to our present sensations and perceptions: and by this every one is to himself that which he calls SELF..."[894]

Regarding the *me* component, which makes sense, Locke begins

---

890 Sharpe, M. (2017). "Jacques Lacan (1901-1981)." Internet Encyclopedia of Philosophy." Accessed from <http://www.iep.utm.edu/lacweb/> on 2017-04-25.

891 "The ensemble of the social relations." In: Marx, K. (1969). Theses on Feuerbach. Trans: W. Lough, *Marx/Engels Selected Works*, Volume One, p. 13 – 15. Moscow: Progress Publishers. (Written: by Marx in the Spring of 1845, but slightly edited by Engels; First Published: As an appendix to Ludwig Feuerbach and the End of Classical German Philosophy in 1888). Online in MIA. Accessed from <https://www.marxists.org/archive/marx/works/1845/theses/theses.htm> on 2015-06-08.

892 James, W.(1890). The Principles of Psychology. Chapter X. The Consciousness of Self. Online in Classics in the History of Psychology. An internet resource developed by Christopher D. Green. York University, Toronto, Ontario. Accessed on <> on 2015-06017.

893 Mead, G.H. (1913). "The Social Self." Journal of Philosophy, Psychology and Scientific Methods 10: 374-380. Online in MIA. Accessed from <https://www.marxists.org/reference/subject/philosophy/works/us/mead3.htm> on 2015-05-17.

894 Locke, J. (2004). *An Essay Concerning Humane Understanding*. An Essay Concerning Humane Understanding. Based on the 2nd Edition, Books I. and II. (of 4). Book 2. Chapter XXVII. On Identity and Diversity. §7-11. (Orig. Pub. 1690). Online in Project Gutenberg Ebook #10615. Accessed from <http://www.gutenberg.org/cache/epub/10615/pg10615.html> on 2012-09-22.

to adumbrate its material origins in relations, and interestingly he selects women as an example of the carriers of good sense. "This, however strange it may seem, is that which every day's experience confirms; and will not, perhaps, appear so wonderful, if we consider the ways and steps by which it is brought about; and how really it may come to pass, that doctrines that have been derived from no better original than the superstition of a nurse, or the authority of an old woman, may, by length of time and consent of neighbors, grow up to the dignity of PRINCIPLES in religion or morality. For such, who are careful (as they call it) to principle children well, (and few there be who have not a set of those principles for them, which they believe in,) instill into the unwary, and as yet unprejudiced, understanding, (for white paper receives any characters,) those doctrines they would have them retain and profess. These being taught them as soon as they have any apprehension; and still as they grow up confirmed to them, either by the open profession or tacit consent of all they have to do with; or at least by those of whose wisdom, knowledge, and piety they have an opinion, who never suffer those propositions to be otherwise mentioned but as the basis and foundation on which they build their religion and manners, come, by these means, to have the reputation of unquestionable, self-evident, and innate truths."[895] The *I* at the time, and much further, was propelled by its transcendent "will." This was the classical treatment of the ethical importance of human life that dates historically to the old Golden Rule, to the *Nicomachean Ethics* of Aristotle,[896] to the categorical imperatives of Kant,[897] and finally to the critique of superstructure and ideology of Marx.[898]

---

895 Locke, J. (2004). *An Essay Concerning Humane Understanding*. Ibid. Chapter II. No Innate Practical Principles. 22. How men commonly come by their Principles.

896 Aristotle. (350 B.C.E). *Nicomachean Ethics*. Trans: W. D. Ross Books III (chapters 1-5), and Book VII (chapters 1-10). Online in Classics MIT. Accessed from <http://classics.mit.edu/Aristotle/nicomachaen.html> on 2015-06-18.

897 Kant, I. (2004). *Fundamental Principles of the Metaphysic of Morals*. Trans. Thomas Kingsmill Abbott. Online in Project Gutenberg EBook #5682. (Orig. Pub. 1785). Accessed from <http://www.gutenberg.org/cache/epub/5682/pg5682-images.html> on 2016-08-28.

898 Marx, K. (1932). *The German Ideology*. to Marx-Engels Collected Works, Volume

Evolutionarily, the self, the active mirroring agent, stands upon the two legs of *I* and *me* as opposites; it is their compromise. I and me are instinct and history in a dialectical relation of representation that, in evolution, started from the duality of sexuation. The simplest form to represent the architecture of the self is the dialectical relation of *I* and *me*, I being the agency originally called instinct, subsequently will, and *me* the universal ensemble of the necessary and constraining social relations.

Imagine one leg amputated or chained; that is how humanity has moved since the invention of patriarchal slavery that initially targeted women and gradually extended to others but that psychologically affected all without exception.

We have seen how the dialectic one-and- two operates in consciousness after Spinoza. Similarly the self comes to be through a compromise between the instinctual *I* and the social *me*, outcomes of the two types of consciousness, for Freud roughly id and superego. *I* and *me* are subject and its objectification in history and culture. They are inalienable from each other and one cannot be without the other. They come from Hegel's monistic duality of consciousness and self-consciousness.

The subject is not only necessarily conscious but also necessarily expressive, communicative. Let's now look at what underlies these opposites. An internal template must be constructed after the mother for the child to be able to act and say "I." In fact "I am I," Aristotelian formal identity is a tautology. The Hegelian version is "I am me," the acknowledgment of "I am other," This means I come from alienation not only phylogenetically in religion, but also ontogenetically in the internalized image of my mother. From there stems the big other, the total ensemble of the social relations of Marx.[899] I am not possible, genomically and historically, without all

5. Moscow. Progress Publishers. (Written: Fall 1845 to mid-1846). Accessed from <http://www.marxists.org/archive/marx/works/1845/german-ideology/ch01b.htm> on 2012-08-19.

899 Marx, K. (1938). Theses on Feuerbach. 6. In: The German Ideology. London. Lawrence and Wishart. (Written in 1845). Online version Marxists Internet Archive. Ac-

others have made before me.

The collective me is what *I* builds upon, making self of what others made as culture. It is culture objectified in me, the first bricks put in place by the mother. It consists in maternal first-order mediations going back to Mytochondrial Eve, upon which patriarchal second-order mediations have been placed for ten thousand years. Human activity cannot take place without the fundamentals put in place by all previous human activity. Internalized, this social phenomenon is *me*, the "how to" prescribed by the corrective experience of all past generations objectified in form language and culture.

The invisible guidelines for human activity are largely provided by a grammar of ethics and etiquette that involves morality and judgment. *I* carries the material imperative of my natural instinct, agency, and transcendence, *me*, my historical genome, is a condensed representation of my social and historical evolution, what is other in me in all the iterations of otherness.[900] *me* can be psychologically compared to mitochondria, maternally traceable historically. In actuality however, today we are the result of the hegemony of *I* introduced through the patriarchal coup.

The perceptual-motor or executive organ of consciousness is then the self that consists of those two opposites, morally compelling *me*, how to, and instinctually driven *I*, agency. Wherever consciousness and self-consciousness intersect or overlap in their mutually self-constraining operations, there is the regulatory self. First and second layers of consciousness dialectically feed into organizers *I* and *me*.

Neurosis and ideology are both corruptions of consciousness that is not real consciousness but actual ideological manifestation. As Horney pointed out, surplus idealization is the product of polit-

---

cessed from <http://www.marxists.org/archive/marx/works/1845/theses/index.htm> on 2012-09-09.

900 See for example: Lacan, J. (1993). *The* Psychoses. The Seminar of Jacques Lacan. Book III 1955-1956. Trans. Russell Grigg, Ed. Jacques-Alain Miller. New York. Norton.

ical correctness in class society that has at least two forms of ideology. If idealization necessarily started from natural alienation, it subsequently takes an adaptive form. Individual idealization is a response to coercion that starts ideologically in the patriarchal family, but becomes the default mode in a civil society that must survive through surplus value. Part of this idealization paradoxically takes the form of reification, the identification with the thing that expands, selfobjects, money and wealth's being its paradigm.

The reason a masculinized *I* continues to be individually, and collectively, overvalued at the expense of the moral, feminine me, is ideology. The hypertrophy of *I* can only be maintained by creating the conditions of artificial scarcity through accumulation and subsequent reification which underlie capitalist life. Concomitantly, the fact that there is an alternative for which the precedent historically exists must be fiercely repressed.[901] Paradoxically, the manifest problem of capitalism is scarcity in the midst of abundance.[902] Under these circumstances the other is not *me* and *I,* unnaturally, loses its universality.

2.9.2.10 Balance and Polymorphism

Balance implies the self's dual polymorphism of opposites that facilitates the natural design of very flexible human adaptation besting the best way for changing environments and social-historical conditions. According to those conditions, changing with the individual's biography, the self can be Aristotelically located somewhere in between a number of extremes such as male-female, impulse-morality, immanence-transcendence, activity-passivity, *etc,* individual virtues achieved through balance between extremes. This type of complexity is what characterized variation in the human spe-

---

901 Vaughan, G. (2007). *Women And The Gift Economy. A Radically Different Worldview Is Possible. Toronto, Canada.* Inanna Publications And Education Inc. Accessed from <http://gift-economy.com/wordpress/wp-content/uploads/2013/08/womenandthegifteconomy.pdf> on 2015-11-27.
902 Meszaros, I. (1995). Beyond Capital. New York. Monthly Review Press.

cies manifested as unique personality.[903] Extremes in any of those dimensions mean imbalance, which translates into dysfunction or pathology.

We could simplify by saying that, relationally, self-regulation being the key issue in intersubjective relations, the final post is optimal distance or, what is the same, optimal dependence. The dynamics of this set of balanced extremes is necessary to adapt to constantly changing conditions. This is how Karen Horney proposed her interpersonal markers, moving towards, against, or away as sublimated derivatives of mating, fighting and fleeing, the most fundamental animal tendencies.[904] Bowlby's attachment theory[905] and Ainsworth's research on it[906] fit theoretically with Horney's typology. These relational theories are all about what Aristotle saw as virtue, regulation of opposite extremes. This means that optimal individuation is optimal dependency based on the acknowledgment of the needs and rights of others. Each individual must negotiate her or his relations within the complex social protoplasm, to find a niche that must be flexible to accommodate changing conditions. It is ultimately the Darwinian variation, polymorphism, which in humans accounts for unique individuality, that gives us the illusion of separateness. In fact we are primarily one social protoplasm, the species.

Although this has not been confirmed scientifically, it is highly likely that the animal brain was designed along the parameters of balanced instinctual duality, not mechanically but dialectically:

---

903 Aristotle (1997). *Nichomachean Ethics.* Trans. W. D. Ross. (Written 350 BCE). Online in Constitution Society. Accessed from <http://www.constitution.org/ari/ethic_00.htm> on 2015-11-14.

904 Horney, K. (1950). Neurosis and Human Growth. New York. Norton.

905 Bowlby J (1999) [1969]. Attachment. Attachment and Loss (vol. 1) (2nd ed.). New York: Basic Books. Bowlby J (1973). Separation: Anxiety & Anger. Attachment and Loss (vol. 2); (International psycho-analytical library no.95). London: Hogarth Press. Bowlby J (1980). Loss: Sadness & Depression. Attachment and Loss (vol. 3); (International psycho-analytical library no.109). London: Hogarth Press. Bowlby J (1988). A Secure Base: Parent-Child Attachment and Healthy Human Development. Tavistock professional book. London: Routledge.

906 Ainsworth, M., Blehar, M., Waters, E., & Wall, S. (1978). Patterns of Attachment. Hillsdale, NJ: Erlbaum.

two hemispheres that are opposites and yet can compensate and even stand for each other, and that, although overlapping in most respects, still have sex-determined unilateral biases we still do not understand well.[907]

2.9.2.11 First- and Second-Order Mediations

From instinct, consciousness grows through mediations starting with classical conditioning. Phylogenetically, first-order mediations in the constitution of consciousness were provided by the mothering one in the context of a familiar environment primarily concerned with nutrition, growth, and self-maintenance. Ontogenetically and rather metaphorically, Freud saw this as the oral period.[908] Besides orality, all the other senses such as olfaction, vision, audition, proprioception etc., are turned on by the mother mostly during the first year of life to altogether spark the dawn of consciousness. Maternal first-order mediations respond first and for the most part to natural needs, guided by a for-the-most-part intuitive morality of evolution. Their form of implementation, however, becomes more and more, through further mediations, culturally determined. Second-order mediations come to be in response to needs not necessarily natural but predominantly new social need, created by the human mediations. Humans develop many senses initially through conditioning and learning, arriving at social senses of propriety, justice, economy, aesthetics and morality, a practical sense and an abstract sense, *etc.*, to mention only a few. The maternal first-order mediations are originally geared to operate predominantly within the immediate context of the family, and the predominantly paternal ones are geared for life

---

907 Allen, L.S., Hines, M., Shryne, J.E., and Gorski, R.A. (1989). "Two sexually dimorphic cell groups in the human brain." The Journal of Neuroscience, 9 (2): Pp. 497-506. Accessed from <http://www.jneurosci.org/content/9/2/497.full.pdf+html> on 2014-08-08.

908 Freud, S. (2000). *Three Essays on the Theory of Sexuality.* Trans. James Strachey. New York. Basic Books. (Orig. Pub. 1905). Online in Questia, a part of Gale, Cengage. Accessed from <https://www.questia.com/read/8909177/three-essays-on-the-theory-of-sexuality> on 2015-11-24.

in civil society.

Since moral self-consciousness is the defining condition of being human, it is always deployed when we are awake and active, and have our senses tuned to reality.[909] Consciousness changes in form in altered states, the most typical being sleep or self-induced chemical imbalances of the brain. During sleep dreams, through the hallucinatory inversion of the operation of the sensory organs in the nervous system, appear to have a structure closer to our original form of mythological or magic thinking than to our mature cognition. The developmental transformations of consciousness in individuals, that may grossly repeat those of the species, are illustrated in the studies of intelligence and morality of child developmentalists such as Henry Wallon, Jean Piaget, Lawrence Kohlberg, and Lev Vygotzky among others. Our intelligence is how we deploy our consciousness practically, as the instrument of problem-solving.

The capability each one of us has to fully develop a unique self through rather uniform epigenetic stadial processes from childhood is something we owe to the process of mediatory learning. It requires the parallel maturation of the nervous system in tandem with the cultural environment in an interplay of needs and skills. The process of learning includes our induction into the wealth of what all previous generations of humans have contributed to the fund of culture. Each generation moves collective consciousness a bit forward through technological, scientific, and spiritual means, including ideological developments in class society. Each generation builds on top of the existing accrual of the contributions of all previous gen-

---

909 'Man appropriates his comprehensive essence in a comprehensive manner, that is to say, as a whole man. Each of his human relations to the world – seeing, hearing, smelling, tasting, feeling, thinking, observing, experiencing, wanting, acting, loving – in short, all the organs of his individual being, like those organs which are directly social in their form, are in their objective orientation, or in their orientation to the object, the appropriation of the object, the appropriation of human reality." Marx, K. (1959). "Private Property and Communism." In: *Economic and Philosophic Manuscripts of 1844.* Moscow, USSR. Progress Publishers. Online in MIA. Accessed from <https://www.marxists.org/archive/marx/works/1844/manuscripts/comm.htm> on 2015-11-28.

erations. This cultural bulk is then passed on to the next generation to continue to be expanded. All this wealth becomes part of culture and is reflected in the self of each individual, in the *me*.

Self as agent thus started from first-order mediations, largely implemented by the mothering one and internalized as actions and their learned forms. The *Me* part of the self is a sort of grammatical transcript of how-to's for action, compiled through the trial-and-error activity of all our predecessors. Like the genome, it consists of the mapped memory of all the productive mediations that humans have introduced in their dealings with nature and each other historically. Animals are externally guided through their genomic program and their instinctual intelligence; humans by the me part of the self.

2.9.2.12 Mediations and the Direction of the Species

The first material mediation necessary for the species to bifurcate as *Sapiens* was the use of tools,[910,911] parts of nature used by us, who are parts of nature with agency, to productively operate upon other parts of nature. This became possible after evolutionary bipedalism and hand instrumentalization for labor, with concurrent changes in posture and brain morphology. These morphological changes required bodily changes, particularly in the female, for gestation and premature birth. The ambiguous use of the word labor suggests that hand labor was modeled after mother's labor; re-producing. If this is true, the first instrument was the mother's body. Hand labor, contrary to maternal labor, had to first destruct in order to produce, but in signaling and writing, hand labor achieved the capacity to produce without destruction.

Since the inception of manual labor each generation has intro-

---

910 Engels, F. (1934) The Part played by Labour in the Transition from Ape to Man. Trans. Clemens Dutt. Moscow, USSR. Progress Publishers. (Orig. Pub. 1895, written 1876). Online in MIA. Accessed from <https://www.marxists.org/archive/marx/works/1876/part-played-labour/> on 2015-01-28.

911 Fedigan, L.M. (1986). The Changing Role of Women in Models of Human Evolution. Annual Review of Anthropology. 15:25-66.

duced its own material and spiritual mediations that in parallel have changed the form of the brain. All human history is recorded in the form of the brain that tells us of natural history going back to the origin of sensation. The horizontal and vertical components of the brain are records of adaptations grown complex through human mediation. Macroscopically, we start with a reptilian brain concerned only with dire survival of the organism, and end up with a cortical brain that can be concerned with the most trivial minutiae. The form of the human brain, which holds the secrets of the forms of consciousness, is determined by our collective history. This makes highly questionable the copyright of ideas that are necessarily built upon others' ideas.

Mothers introduced first-order mediations only for better adaptation: self-regulation, social organization, allocation of resources and forms of self-government.[912] These maternal mediations started hundreds of thousands of years ago. Much later came the patriarchal coup with its second order mediations built upon the first ones, at times their simple inversion. These are for the most part not mediations toward the fulfillment of natural necessities but mediations in response to historical needs that can be adventitious. Patriarchally created needs are characterized by their lack of constraints since they are built upon the foundation of silenced mothers who ran social affairs quite differently. Individualistic self-interest-oriented patriarchal needs lack the universality of their matriarchal predecessors. This is how we go to war in the name of a peace that is never realized; the manifest "peace" end is again and again overriden by the latent selfish end. Economically, the most basic perspective of humans, capital accumulation, overrides the most basic collective survival needs. This type of inversion is the patriarchal signature of secondary-order mediation and it is inevitably imprinted in all cultures today.

As it concerns us in psychology, the problem is that these material processes are all replicated in the self, and they become the

---

912 Meszaros, I. (1995). Beyond Capital. New York. Monthly Review Press. Pp. 138-9.

default consciousness unless subjected to critical review, a capacity that has been precisely atrophied since the patriarchal coup, replaced by all sorts of pseudo-critical sophistry. We are raised and educated in the patriarchal model, our own maternal constraints repressed with emotion and altruism. Our default mind becomes isomorphic with the prevailing ideology and our self with present government. This is what makes a true critique of the system so difficult in practical terms.

Wilhelm Reich said that: "In the superficial layer, the average individual is restrained, polite, compassionate and conscientious. There would be no social tragedy of the animal, man, if this superficial layer were in immediate contact with his deep natural core. His tragedy is that such is not the case. The superficial layer of social cooperation is not in contact with the biological core of the person, but separated from it by a second, intermediary character layer consisting of cruel, sadistic, lascivious, predatory and envious impulses. This is the Freudian 'unconscious' or 'repressed'; in sex economic language... ...In [the biological core] deepest layer, man, under favorable social conditions, is an honest, industrious, cooperative animal capable of love and also of rational hatred. In character-analytic work, one cannot penetrate to this deep, promising layer without first eliminating the false, sham-social surface."[913] Roosevelt similarly said "speak softly and carry a big stick."[914] The superficial layer of Reich is the tailpiece of matriarchy, ripped off from its natural core. It is necessary to remove the intermediate second-order mediations of patriarchy and free the back-tied left hand of humanity by letting women and those oppressed who have not been corrupted by patriarchy resume their due critical position in the governance of society.

In present times the aggressive layer is hardly disguised. Individualism hypertrophies *I,* here and now at the expense of historical *me.* The disregard of history in the form of social amnesia[915] is noto-

---

913 Reich, W. (1946). The Mass Psychology of Fascism. Ibid. Preface to the third Edition.
914 Roosevelt, T. (1901). Address at Minnesota State Fair. Accessed from <http://www.theodore-roosevelt.com/images/research/txtspeeches/678.pdf> on 2015-1-29.
915 Jacobi, R. (1997). *Social Amnesia.* Hassocks, Eng. Harvester Press,

rious and pandemic. Freud only saw society in the superego but not history; his view was narrow. His ego depends on a superego that represents society but not history.[916] He ignores that at the beginning of history very few could say *I* because *I* did not exist; it was community. The present capacity for all to say *I* represents the forward march of history.

The return of the repressed matriarchy, expressed in Bachofen, Lafitau and Morgan, followed by so many others from different disciplines, has been successfully kept at bay by a patriarchal academia. The available traits of matriarchy cannot be placed together as archeologists do to reconstruct the whole. Feminist input is gradually and rather independently changing this picture. The history of matriarchal Right has been silenced, repressed, disavowed, but it is coming in its most positive form when we most need it in the form of constructive proposals for future alternatives for humanity, particularly a return to a different form of economy, and a society without reified hierarchy.

We need to complete our human history and we cannot do it without our history of origins. Marx said: "We know only a single science, the science of history. One can look at history from two sides and divide it into the history of nature and the history of men. The two sides are, however, inseparable; the history of nature and the history of men are dependent on each other so long as men exist. The history of nature, called natural science, does not concern us here; but we will have to examine the history of men, since almost the whole ideology amounts either to a distorted conception of this history or to a complete abstraction from it. Ideology is itself only one of the aspects of this history."[917] A history without beginnings cannot guide humanity to its future; here is where the pronounce-

---

916 Freud, S. (1949). *The Ego and the Id.* Trans. James Strachey. The Hogarth Press Ltd. London, (Orig. Pub. 1923).

917 Marx, K. (1845). "The Illusions of German Ideology." In: *The German Ideology.* Part I: Feuerbach. Opposition of the Materialist and Idealist Outlook. A. Idealism and Materialism. (Written: 1845-6). Online in MIA. Accessed from <https://www.marxists.org/archive/marx/works/1845/german-ideology/ch01a.htm> on 2015-06-17.

ment "there is no alternative" makes sense. We cannot see the alternative because we have not been able to see the beginning. The snake needs to bite its tail to make itself whole.

2.9.2.13 Self and Language

Following the leads of G.H. Mead I propose that communicative language in humans must have its roots in the cry of the infant that creates the reflexivity necessary for consciousness, and inherent in the simultaneous communication with others and myself. When the infant cries she not only begs others but at the same time hears herself and catches a glimpse of herself in the act. In this sense the cry is the material ground of the duality of consciousness, the fact that all communication is reflexive in the sense that it always involves other and me as addressees. This is one of the first sensory phenomena at birth, the first communicative act that has the social function of coercing the other by communicating distress and urgency, and concurrently apprehending itself in the first social act. The elements of this act are biologically wired and exquisitely self-tuned. The pitch of the newborn's cry is intensely coercive. The first cry arouses the other and primes the self. I thus propose that the infant not only cries but, by hearing herself cry, establishes the foundations of her self and its mirroring quality. Hearing here becomes a primary human sense along with proprioception and sudden temperature change that make the world appear hostile. Proprioception had been already rather uniformly turned on in the vaginal canal with the extreme muscular force applied upon all parts of the body. Sudden temperature change is the impact of a new cold aerobic environment that contrasts with the uniform warmth of the uterus. Breathing and hearing are the first reflex arcs.

The duality of emitting and receiving sound makes possible the monist duality of consciousness and of the self G. H. Mead: "There would not be a call for assistance if there was not a tendency to respond to the cry of distress. It is such significant symbols, in the sense of a sub-set of social stimuli initiating a cooperative response, that do in a certain sense constitute our mind, provided that not only the symbol but also the responses are in our own nature. What the human being has succeeded in doing is in organizing the response to a certain symbol which is a part of the social act, so that he takes the attitude of the other person who cooperates with him. It is that which gives him a mind...The sentinel of a herd is that member of the herd which is more sensitive to odor or sound than the others. At the approach of danger, he starts to run earlier than the others, who then follow along, in virtue of a herding tendency to run together. There is a social stimulus, a gesture, if you like, to which the other forms respond. The first form gets the odor earlier and starts to run, and its starting to run is a stimulus to the others to run also. It is all external; there is no mental process involved. The sentinel does not regard itself as the individual who is to give a signal; it just runs at a certain moment and so starts the others to run. But with a mind, the animal that gives the signal also takes the attitude of the others who respond to it. He knows what his signal means. A man who calls 'fire' would be able to call out in himself the reaction he calls out in the other. In so far as the man can take the attitude of the other-his attitude of response to fire, his sense of terror-that response to his own cry is something that makes of his conduct a mental affair, as over against the conduct of the others.."[918] That is how close the self is to language, the expression of a consciousness stemming from animal instinct.

Consciousness thus started with language and can only be communicated through language.

---

918 G.H. Mead (1934). "Mind as the Individual Importation of the Social Process." From George Herbert Mead, Mind, Self, and Society from the Standpoint of a Social Behaviorist. (Edited by Charles W. Morris). Section 24. Chicago: University of Chicago Press. P. 190. Accessed from <https://www.brocku.ca/MeadProject/Mead/pubs2/mindself/Mead_1934_24.html> on 2015-11-29.

2.9.3 THE EVOLUTION OF MORALITY AND THE MORALITY OF EVOLUTION

> "Thus, for example, in Hegel's philosophy of law, civil law superseded equals morality, morality superseded equals the family, the family superseded equals civil society, civil society superseded equals the state, the state superseded equals world history. In the actual world civil law, morality, the family, civil society, the state, etc., remain in existence, only they have become moments – states of the existence and being of man – which have no validity in isolation, but dissolve and engender one another, etc. They have become moments of motion."

Marx[919]

2.9.3.1 Supersession and Moment

Following the Hegelian method as Marx did, morality is not to be seen as an abstract concept that remains so throughout, as it seems, the same always present and always violated. If we follow the evolution of morality and its moments, we will arrive at an understanding of the morality of evolution. The mechanism of this process according to Hegel is supersession, the mechanism of negation that conserves, and that operates in three steps, thesis, antithesis and synthesis. Each step does not annihilate the previous one but builds upon it the synthesis being the richer. This conserving negation is the driver of motion that transforms everything in reality, and conse-

---

919 Marx, K (1959). "Critique of Hegel's Philosophy in General." In: *Economic and Philosophic Manuscripts of 1844*. Trans: Martin Mulligan, (Written: Between April and August 1844; First Published: 1932). Moscow, USSR. Progress Publishers. Online in MIA. Accessed from <https://www.marxists.org/archive/marx/works/1844/manuscripts/hegel.htm> on 2015-12-20.

quently in consciousness. The cosmos is the result of transformation and so are consciousness, morality and the self.

The conceptualization of negation as supersession is not an invention but a discovery. It is possible in the mind because it is a reflection of the natural phenomenon. A seed is superseded, negated and conserved, in a plant, and a plant likewise in its flowers or fruits that in turn produce a new plant. This is the natural cycle of organisms and perhaps even of the universe. The thermodynamic law of conservation of energy, that postulates in a closed system no energy can be created or destroyed, but only transformed, is an application of the Hegelian axiom of supersession.

In Hegel's philosophy for example, Self-conscious God became embodied in unconscious nature, Spirit objectified, and It recovered itself in the Hegelian philosophy of capitalist Prussia. Within the same model, the succeeding schools of philosophy in history are no capricious events, random ideas of individuals, but part of a dialogical process. Each step syllogistically supersedes the previous one. Hegel was thus the first evolutionist, and it is in this manner that we ought to approach the historical phenomenon of morality.

Natural *sense* in physical and chemical processes is superseded by more complex forms of *coherent reciprocity*, such as biological fitness in organisms. The supersession of coherence arrives at consciousness and that of the latter at human *self-consciousness.* These processes are based on a superseding dialectic, the struggle of those steps as opposites that produces motion.

In this huge process that encompasses the continuous motion of everything, there are punctuations, similar to those proposed by Eldridge and Gould as punctuated equilibrium in biology, and earlier by Engels, as qualitative jumps. "For Hegel, only the whole is true. Every stage or phase or moment is partial, and therefore partially untrue. Hegel's grand idea is 'totality,' which preserves within it each of the ideas or stages that it has overcome or subsumed. Overcoming or subsuming is a developmental process made up of 'moments' (stages or phases). The totality is the product of that process which preserves all of its 'moments' as elements in a structure, rather than as stages or phases."[920] For Marx: "The *übergreifendes Moment* [overriding factor] of this complex is, of course, the supersession of alienation in social practice itself. Since, however, alienated social practice is already integrated, in an 'inverted' and alienated form, with 'abstractly material' science and speculative philosophy, the actual transcendence of alienation in social practice is inconceivable without superseding at the same time the alienations of the theoretical fields as well. Thus Marx conceives the actual process of *Aufhebung* as a dialectical interchange between these two poles – the theoretical and the practical – in the course of their reciprocal integration."[921]

That we hear today of scientific talk about the beginning of an anthropocene age,[922] means there may be natural evidence that the self-consciousness' struggle with nature has reached a new level of significance; an eonic moment. It is not simply theory but has the deepest repercussions for all life.

2.9.3.2 Some of the Early Moments of the Syllogism of Morality

In the present view morality, as we think of it today, could not have existed in the earliest matriarchal society. The reason is that since society was one natural protoplasm, without rules except collaborative self-survival, there was no individual person, no private property, and no government. The economy was based on giving and sharing inspired by maternal instinctual disposition. Morality

---

920 Spencer, L., and Krauze A. (2006). *Hegel for Beginners*. Totality. London. Icon Books, P. 14. Online in MIA. Accessed from <https://www.marxists.org/reference/archive/hegel/help/easy.htm> on 2017-05-01.

921 Meszaros, I. (1970). *Marx's Theory of Alienation*. 3. Conceptual Structure of Marx's Theory of Alienation. 2. Conceptual Framework of Marx's Theory of Alienation. Online in MIA. Accessed from <https://www.marxists.org/archive/meszaros/works/alien/meszaro3.htm> on 2017-05-01.

922 Carrington, D. (2016). "How the domestic chicken rose to define the Anthropocene." The Guardian. Wednesday 31 August 2016 04.46 EDT. Accessed from <https://www.theguardian.com/environment/2016/aug/31/domestic-chicken-anthropocene-humanity-influenced-epoch> on 2016-08-31.

became necessary with the reorganization of society after the implementation of patriarchal second-order inversions.

In contrast, not so different from today was the Spartan morality that trained boys for war through scarce feeding, and, although condemning stealing, condoned boys stealing food. Stealing was not punished as such, since in this case it was considered resourcefulness, but for being caught, considered lack of cleverness.[923] This is when food had been converted into private property, one of the inversions of patriarchy.

The historical syllogism of morality, its moments, means the whole process of how the range of a natural property, *i.e.* going from useful to harmful, successfully became virtue *vs.* vice, sensual *vs,* painful, good *vs.* bad, moral *vs.* corrupt, fit *vs.* unfit, tenable *vs.* untenable, sustainable *vs.* indefensible, *etc.* Emphasis is placed on notions that are relevant to the historical context.

The fact that linguistically ethics originally meant habit or custom,[924] corroborates the original human status of natural morality. That being the case, what is characteristic of mothers is their altruistic tendency, the opposite of selfishness, which makes it possible to place the survival of the other if not first, at least on equal footing with that of the self. There is altruism in males also but their overriding tendency is to fight and to take..

What then challenged and superseded what would have been consensual habit into a prescriptive, institutionalized ethics reiteratively challenged and apparently redefined throughout history? Why challenge the natural syllogism that appeared habitual and consensual? Logically, the answer is the need to rationalize, to make non-natural appear natural. This could only have happened with a shift from the habitual universality of customs to the class virtues

---

923 Bradley P. (2014). *The Ancient World Transformed. Societies, Personalities and Historical Periods from Egypt, Greece and Rome.* Chapter 3. Cambridge University Press. Port Melbourne. Australia. P. 85.

924 Wikipedia. "Ethics." Accessed from <https://en.wikipedia.org/wiki/Ethics> on 2017-04-26.

of Plato.

The introduction of conflicting individual and particular social interests challenged communal habit. There was no need for institutionalized ethics during the epoch of matriarchy for a society that was organized around the collaborative universal fulfillment of needs, within natural conditions, predominantly in a familiar, gentile environment. Morality was still natural, meaning the morality evolution had handed the species in female selection. Natural variation was transformed into inequality and consequently survival of the fittest. As new superstructure, this becomes the ground for individualistic reasoning. The previous incipient morality that made it possible to think about equality was subverted along with the subversion of the social order and the installation of patriarchy.

An externally prescribed guide to moral choice only became necessary with the division of society into classes with different interests to defend, different forms of life based on property. This started with patriarchy and slavery, only about ten thousand years ago. In this short period of time compared to the eons of evolution and the millennia of maternal leadership, what was considered good was for the first time not universal in practice. This is clearly illustrated in the moral works of Plato, in particular. For the first time, ethics is institutionalized according to the needs of a ruling class, virtue's taking on a hierarchical form, different virtues for different social strata. In moral theory, what was convenient for the ruling patriarch became good for the rest of society. The Sophists discovered in logic all sorts of spinning stratagems to rationalize the forcefully imposed objectification of human subjects for the first time in history.

To invert real class division, Xenophanes (ca. 570-ca.478 BCE) proclaimed one unifying God, the anthropomorph at the top of hierarchy of being. "One god greatest among gods and men"[925] means new patriarchal individuality, hierarchy and privilege. The individ-

---

925 Lesher, J., (2017) "Xenophanes", The Stanford Encyclopedia of Philosophy (Fall 2014 Edition), Edward N. Zalta (ed.), URL = <https://plato.stanford.edu/archives/fall2014/entries/xenophanes/>.

ual anthropomorph is a perfect ruler and therefore the repository of virtue to be emulated by all independent of social class. Matriarchal goddesses that had been the representation of nature and its generosity earlier, are replaced by idealistically inflated abstract gods. Still some sophists, particularly Protagoras (c.485-415 BCE), supported the contrasting view that free man instead was the moral measure; free man is a class within a class.

Socrates (469–399 BC) emphasized *knowledge*, an exclusive property of the ruling class, as the way to happiness. Plato (429?-347 B.C.E.) is more concerned about *social justice*, injustice resulting in unhappiness. Ethics became with him prescriptive and normative according to class conditions. The social virtues were wisdom for rulers, guardians, or king-philosophers, courage for the regulatory if not repressive middle class of military and civil servants, and austerity for the rest, the productive rabble. Aristotle (384-322 B.C.E.) placed a momentous landmark by emphasizing *self-realization*, making real the human potential. Morality in Aristotle is always located, for a particular virtue, within the two extremes of virtue and its opposite, vice, not clingy, for example, not detached, but optimally friendly. The Stoics carried the Aristotelian notion in the direction of *asceticism,* self-mastery, and the Epicureans saw things similarly, although their emphasis was not on abstinence but on measured *self-satisfaction* that has prompted their being considered hedonists.

The Middle Ages was religious alienation based on Plato, emphasizing a sinful human nature sustainable through contrition, confession, and penance, a view promoted by Christianity. The standards for good behavior and self-regulation was external, impoverished individuals' being dependent on the religious system. Spinoza (1632-1677 CE) argued on the other hand that *nature*, being one; with God, is ethical. Body and mind are one and opposing philosophies had been victims of limited perspectives. The ambiguity of one two-faced Being created confusion, as did his two types of reasoning, sensory and scientific. But Spinoza was the prophet

606

of modernity. His vision opens ways to understanding the nature of the other side of the person, the self with all its psychological implications.

2.9.3.3 The More Influential Recent Moments: Kant and Hegel

Kant's (1724-1804) belief was that morality is part of rationality and therefore endowed to all rational beings. He then enshrines the notion of *duty* which is highly prescriptive, almost militaristic and narcissist. Behind it is the individual commanded only by himself to set an example for others out of his good will. The Categorical Imperative is an universal edict on how to behave morally that is obviously ignored by large sections of society. But it only repeats the matriarchal Golden Rule in various iterations. "A person is a subject who is capable of having his actions imputed to him. Moral personality is, therefore, nothing but the freedom of a rational being under moral laws; and it is to be distinguished from psychological freedom as the mere faculty by which we become conscious of ourselves in different states of the identity of our existence. Hence it follows that a person is properly subject to no other laws than those he lays down for himself, either alone or in conjunction with others. A thing is what is incapable of being the subject of imputation. Every object of the free activity of the will, which is itself void of freedom, is therefore called a thing. Right or wrong applies, as a general quality, to an act, in so far as it is in accordance with duty or contrary to duty, no matter what may be the subject or origin of the duty itself. An act that is contrary to duty is called a transgression. An unintentional transgression of a duty, which is, nevertheless, imputable to a person, is called a mere fault or culpa. An intentional transgression -that is, an act accompanied with the consciousness that it is a transgression- constitutes a crime. Whatever is juridically in accordance with external laws is said to be just; and whatever is not juridically in accordance with external laws is unjust."[926] All the

---

926 Kant, I. (1785). *General Introduction to the Metaphysic of Morals.* IV. General Preliminary Conceptions Defined and Explained. (Philosophia practica universalis).

pirouetting is necessary to actualize the class imperative. "In conjunction with others" means class, behind which is individualistic ideology, elected "representatives" legislating for all. The same general abstraction is expressed by utilitarians but opposed to duty: "the greatest *happiness* for the greatest number,"[927] happiness generally meaning property.

Hegel contributed the notion of relativity, that morality and ethics are *cultural* products the first applying to the individual in the family and the second in civil society. "The idea of freedom... the good become alive and actualized in self-conscious action... the foundation of self-consciousness... and the end which actuates its effort... the concept of freedom developed into the existing world... the nature of self-consciousness,"[928] are his descriptions of ethical life. Marx then replaced "the idea of freedom" with "praxis," that is freedom applied. Acting self-consciously, that is acting humanely and truthfully, it is for Hegel and Marx inherently ethical. Saying that self-consciousness is the epitome of humanity is the same as saying that being fully human is conducting an ethical life. The difference is that in Hegel this remains ideal. Goodness inherent in nature becomes alive, self-conscious, and manifest in ethical life for Hegel who picks up the monistic thread from Spinoza but remains slanted to idealism. Human means being recognized as such and this happens in a necessarily hierarchical social structure of master and slave in civil society. Paradoxically, "The family, as the immediate

---

Trans: W. Hastie. Source: Steve Palmquist's web site. Online in MIA. Accessed from <https://www.marxists.org/reference/subject/ethics/kant/morals/ch03.htm> on 2015-11-22.

927 Bentham, J. (1907). *An Introduction to the Principles of Morals and Legislation.* Chapter 1: The Principle of Utility. London, New York and Toronto. Clarendon Press. Online in LibertyFund.org. Accessed from <http://oll.libertyfund.org/titles/bentham-an-introduction-to-the-principles-of-morals-and-legislation> on 2017-04-27.

928 Hegel, G.W.F. (1897). *Philosophy of* Right. Section 3. Ethical Life. § 142. The 1897 Dyde translation with some modifications is used for the Preface & the Introduction and the Knox translation for the remainder of Hegel's Philosophy of Right, which was first published in 1821, and is an extended version of Objective Spirit from the Encyclopedia, and a continuation of Hegel's early writings on political economy. Online in MIA. Accessed from <https://www.marxists.org/reference/archive/hegel/works/pr/prmorali.htm> on 2015-12-19.

substantiality of mind, is specifically characterized by love, which is mind's feeling of its own unity. Hence in a family, one's frame of mind is to have self-consciousness of one's individuality within this unity as the absolute essence of oneself, with the result that one is in it not as an independent person but as a member." As we can see this description of the family is matriarchal. Furthermore: "Love means in general terms the consciousness of my unity with another, so that I am not in selfish isolation but win my self-consciousness only as the renunciation of my independence and through knowing myself as the unity of myself with another and of the other with me."[929] For Hegel, the ethical life is the truly human life based on unity, not split but integrated with the other. This enters into contradiction with his political stand, as it does with that of other philosophers, particularly idealists.

Even if Hegel may have been hostile to the concept of natural evolution, [930]his whole opus is a syllogistic theory of evolution from God to nature to man to God, a theodicy. "A building is not finished when its foundation is laid; and just as little, is the attainment of a general notion of a whole the whole itself. When we want to see an oak, we are not satisfied to be shown an acorn instead. In the same way science, the crowning glory of a spiritual world, is not found complete in its initial stages."[931] But paradoxically the foundation of Hegel's whole edifice is the idea. However, the Hegelian dialectic reminds us that there can be no superstructure without its dialectical base, from which it emerges to make a whole. Marx made the metaphor even compelling to us: there can be no productive thinking in an empty stomach.[932]

929 Hegel, G.W.F. (1897). *Philosophy of* Right. Section 3. Ethical Life. §158. Ibid.
930 Houlgate, S. (2005). "Hegel and Evolution." In: *An Introduction to Hegel, Freedom, Truth and History.* Blackwell, pp. 173-4. Online in MIA. Accessed from <https://www.marxists.org/reference/archive/hegel/help/houlgate1.htm> on 2015-12-20.
931 Hegel, G.W.F. (1807). *Phenomenology of Mind.* Preface: On Scientific Knowledge. 3. Present Position of the Spirit.§12.From Harper Torchbooks' edition of the Phenomenology (1807), from University of Idaho, Department of Philosophy by Jean McIntire. Online in MIA, Hegel by Hypertext. Accessed from <https://www.marxists.org/reference/archive/hegel/works/ph/phprefac.htm> on 2015-12-12.
932 Frederick Engels' Speech at the Grave of Karl Marx. Highgate Cemetery, London.

Hegel in his own way tells us what Darwin did, that everything is a result of a connected process of motion and relations. As far as morality is concerned, we can apply the notion and derive it from the supersessions of natural *sense* by reciprocal *coherence, fitness* in the organismic world, to *usefulness* in animals and *virtue* in humans. These are the successive forms of presentation of the same evolutionary phenomenon. Consciousness comes from natural sense properly apprehended by humans.

Hegel's Philosophy of Right is foremost concerned with morality and ethics applied within the parameters of the patriarchal perspective. It starts with property. Although the family is the cradle of morality the state is the ethical culmination. The state is the legitimacy of life in civil society. That the *Philosophy of Right* starts from property, human objectification, leads logically to the problem of alienations, the ground of right.

2.9.3.4 Morality of Darwin (1809-1882)

By bringing *evolution* to its historical moment, with his concept of natural selection Darwin shifted the ground of morality from the metaphysical realm of theology to the scientific one of natural science. The morality of animals is based on utilitarian fitness that can be traced back to natural sense. Selection implies sense. The morality of humans is different precisely by what Darwin found puzzling and difficult to solve: instinctual altruism. Altruism converts selection from fit individual phenomenon, to collective, group instinct. "Any animal whatever, endowed with well-marked social instincts, would inevitably acquire a moral sense or conscience, as soon as its intellectual powers had become as well developed as in man."[933]

March 17, 1883. Online in MIA. Accessed from <https://www.marxists.org/archive/marx/works/1883/death/burial.htm> on 2015-12-19.

933 Darwin, C. (1874). *The Descent Of Man, And Selection In Relation To Sex*. Chapter IV. Comparison Of The Mental Powers Of Man And The Lower Animals. P.98. Second Edition. London: John Murray. Darwin Online. Accessed from <http://darwin-online.org.uk/content/frameset?keywords=become%20in%20animal%20intellectual%20powers%20a%20or%20conscience%20developed%20well%20inev-

Sociality is inseparable from morality.

Darwin attests to the fact that the human animal is no exception to evolution; it is part of it in its sexuated form that requires two opposite instincts. He grounds man on equal footing with the rest of nature and other social species, and he also finds that human's highest distinctive species attribute, morality, has its roots in the universal process that also produced the altruistic characteristics of other species. Like Hegel, Darwin places morality as the zenith of consciousness, of intellectual power. Morality is the steering wheel of the human species.

The social instinct of Darwin produces the reciprocal benefit of cooperation to produce group rather than individual fitness. The apparent cost in self-reproductive fitness is balanced by quality of collective reproduction and maintenance.[934] Darwin did not see that in capitalism the benefits of altruism are not realized, but remain pre-human in their class one-sidedness. This is where we have parted with the morality of evolution. Workers contribute to enlarge capital as ants do with their queen, a phenomenon moral in the latter but immoral in the former, qualified as *sapiens*. In capitalism the necessary reciprocity inherent in human altruistic parity is lost.

The difference between insects and humans is that the latter can alter the balance of the instinctual disposition of the species through mediations. By suppressing female will, as Hegel would say, by depriving women of their freedom, the instinctual disposition of males has come to express itself unconstrained, resulting in war and disparity. The mechanisms of natural selection have been corrupted by human-mediated reification.

It is important to observe here that the central factor in evolution is not fitness but selection, the intelligence part. The usual academic

itably%20social%20soon%20whatever%20any%20sense%20had%20instincts%20 endowed%20moral%20would%20man%20its%20marked%20acquire%20with%20 as&pageseq=121&itemID=F944&viewtype=text> on 2015-12-12.

934 Okasha, S. (2013). "Biological Altruism." Stanford Encyclopedia of Philosophy. Online. Accessed from <http://plato.stanford.edu/entries/altruism-biological/> on 2015-12-19.

presentation of the matter however, including Darwin's view, ideologically places the fighting male as natural agent and the selecting female as incidental. This is a serious if apparently subliminal ideological twist.

Historical and exclusively human alienation, the human introduction of spurious material and conscious mediations, has corrupted the evolutionary morality of the species. Money has become in humans the burdensome peacock's tail as a result of the serious error of substituting quality for quantity.[935]

2.9.3.5 Morality in Marx (1818-1883)

The morality of Marx is in *praxis,* a type of practice guided by conscious theory. Marx converges with Aristotle and with Karen Horney in the notion that, not in theory but in this type of practice resides the path to *self-realization.* A way of life is ethical when what you do makes you progressively more human, more of a moral person. Up until Marx morality was stated in terms of what people "should" do; it remained abstract, implying that people in fact do differently. This reflects the premise of capitalism based on leading a split life: "Don't do what I do but what I tell you to do." In this moral climate the self becomes split, alienated from its human quality, and this is why repression is necessary, politically and psychologically. The presupposition of Kant, Hegel, and others is the Hobbesian and Malthusian belief that humans are competitive, meaning that left to their own they produce war against each other. This premise is convenient for capitalist repression, since capitalism is a constant war of all against all. Marx adopts the opposite premise, Rousseau's, that humans are born as good as nature, and that their competitive drive, typical to other species, is neutralized by an overriding balance resulting from the play of two opposite instinctual dispositions. It is

---

935 Callaway, E. (2011). "Size doesn't always matter for peacocks. Peahens don't necessarily choose the males with the biggest tails — but small tails are right out." Published online, 18 April 2011. Nature. Accessed from <http://www.nature.com/news/2011/110418/full/news.2011.245.html> on 2015-12-20.

the historical repression of the female instinctual disposition that ends up in the expression of an unbalanced aggression. Marx asks himself what would be required for society to be returned to its original balance, and based on the scientific study of the regularities of history he finds that such a society would be one of sexual parity and substantial economical equality. In a society of substantial equality, meaning one in which people's needs would be cooperatively fulfilled for all, there would be no need for ethical guidelines because that society would be inherently ethical.

The need to economically use life to improve adaptation is an imperative humans share with all other species. The difference is that humans have the unique instruments of self-representation, consciousness, and subjectivity that makes them active mediatory agents, and language to make cooperation possible. These instruments are designed to make possible the best form of economy, construction with minimal destruction. War inverts these terms.

Human constructive production does not have to be based so much on destruction and slow morphological change as adaptation required in other species. The human body has remained the same for two hundred thousand years but its mind has substantially transformed the world. And yet, the difference between what is possible, as compared to how we operate in terms of a moral species, in terms of species' quality of life, is still so considerable and, alarmingly nowhere present in the political agenda.

That we remain bound by material imperatives does not mean we cannot be substantially free. Freedom is also dialectical. Unfortunately freedom, the essence of morality, is commonly misunderstood. Instead of being the knowledge of necessity as it was for Marx precisely on the basis of our material imperatives, it is ideologically understood as the capacity of a class of individuals to take advantage of the weaknesses of others. This is politically translated into deeper and deeper alienation from species-being; the universality of the species is lost. That we are alienated means we do not live, we do not behave, as humans. This is the reason morality, unlike for any other philosopher, for Marx means social transformation in practice. This is a radical departure from traditional conceptions of morality that has led some to falsely believe that Marx is against morality.

Capitalism makes us see the world with a reifying lens that distorts our reality. The spurious need for having money substitutes the central and uniquely human need for self-realization: being human, moral in our relation to nature and to each other as we fulfill material imperatives and the historical needs we have created. The reciprocal use of both hands and brain that makes our species unique, continues to define us, as class structure dictates. And yet, there is a wide class gap according to how we use one or the other endowment. The competitive division of labor typically makes all individuals slaves of knowing well, in skill or in theory, only a very small segment of reality. This is necessary if we are to succeed in the competitive society of specialization. At the end we are all idiot savants, victims of the fragmentation of our particularized reality that once was universal. Those who benefit from capital also control spiritual production and distribution, being exclusively able to hire others not only to materially produce for them but, also to produce the ideology necessary to maintain reification. This is how science, the universal endowment, remains alien to most of humanity, particularly in its compartmentalized form of super-specialization. The result is a very different experience of the world, a narrow class experience alien to the species' design, irreconcilable, and therefore war-engendering.

Marx believed that balanced material-spiritual labor develops the balance of the human mind. Unfortunately, manual labor has come to be despised because the form it has taken does not contribute to pride and self-realization, but makes labor aversive instead of being the fulfillment of self-expression. This begins with the capitalist alienation of the product of labor for profitable exchange. The uppermost imperative of capital is to grow for itself and in the process enslave humans. The capitalist ethical syllogism imposes the framework of individualistic interests upon the natural universality of the species. The result is at least two classes that contend through ideologies, the ruling class having the advantage of means that is translated into further alienating education and media in defense of the *status quo*. The result is the representative forms of government typically based on broken promises and elections, which alternate seemingly opposite views that in fact hide class interests made unconscious through distraction.

Alienation blurs the fact that life and psychology industry and psychology are not separate but one and the same. "We see how the history of industry and the established objective existence of industry are the open book of man's essential powers, the perceptibly existing human psychology. Hitherto this was not conceived in its connection with man's essential being, but only in an external relation of utility, because, moving in the realm of estrangement, people could only think of man's general mode of being -religion or history in its abstract-general character as politics, art, literature, etc.- as the reality of man's essential powers and man's species-activity. We have before us the objectified essential powers of man in the form of sensuous, alien, useful objects, in the form of estrangement, displayed in ordinary material industry (which can be conceived either as a part of that general movement, or that movement can be conceived as a particular part of industry, since all human activity hitherto has been labour – that is, industry – activity estranged from itself)." He continues: "A psychology for which this book, the part of history existing in the most perceptible and accessible form, remains a closed book, cannot become a genuine, comprehensive and real science. What indeed are we to think of a science which airily abstracts from this large part of human labour and which fails to feel its own incompleteness, while such a wealth of human endeavor, unfolded before it, means nothing more to it than, perhaps, what can be expressed in one word –'need,' "vulgar need?"[936] This paragraph

936 Marx, K. (1959). *Economic & Philosophic Manuscripts of 1844*. Third Manuscript. "Private Property and Communism." (4). Trans: Martin Mulligan. Moscow: Progress Publishers. (Written: Between April and August 1844; First Published: 1932). Online in MIA. Accessed from <https://www.marxists.org/archive/marx/works/1844/manuscripts/comm.htm> on 2015-07-02.

summarizes Marx's critique of intrapsychic psychology that colludes with political economy to hide the fact that we objectify our life in labor, transcend ourselves in selfobjects, the product of our labor, and that finally our selfobject is alienated from us as private property, taking with it our power. Our power has been reified: the power of commodity-market-corporation-money is our zero-sum powerlessness.

Our psychology is objectified, meaning that ideas are made into useful ways and things we produce for life and survival and pleasure. Our morality is equally objectified in the particular way we relate to each other: hierarchically in capitalism. Here how we relate to each other is through exchange wherein the other has what one needs and vice versa thus far being equal. Behind this simple transaction, however, a commodity transaction, Marx saw hidden the whole history of capitalism, of production, circulation, consumption and accumulation, capital as a historical form of human relation. The peculiarity of this unique phase of history is that it has disempowered the subject humanity to empower the thing, capital. Habit makes this alienated relation look natural, but it is far from it.

In opposition to this was the matriarchal morality of giving when in any case everything was communal. Mothers could give because they had the privilege of being attuned to the needs of their gens or family. Each distributed according to need and that precedent does not sound like a bad idea to consider for a society of the future. Even after they were demoted and silenced by their sons historically, mothers have been able to substantially maintain that type of morality in families. Mothers have, in this fashion, behaved subversively even through the patriarchalization of the family. I repeat from Hegel: "The family, as the immediate substantiality of mind, is specifically characterized by love, which is mind's feeling of its own unity. Hence in a family, one's frame of mind is to have self-consciousness of one's individuality within this unity as the absolute essence of oneself, with the result that one is in it not as an independent person but as a member."[937] This is how Hegel saw morality as a family virtue of unity required to produce "mind."

It has taken some ten thousand years of patriarchal rule to get us to the crossroads we are in. Our morality was radically changed by patriarchy and its product competitive civil society, the cure for which is the state as mediator. The external events, internally represented, form the structure of the mind, the self's being the equivalent of the external state, the regulator. From slavery to feudalism to wage labor, we have made strides, including full self-representation. The present paradox is that although capitalism badly requires ethics, it keeps them shelved in abstraction. The practice of morality that would lead to self-realization, praxis, and a new society, is possible only in very few individuals who are willing to pay the price of moral satisfaction. As soon as a collectivity, a group or nation, tries to move in that direction, an inexorable amount of force is applied against it, in one or several of the forms of war.

2.9.3.6 Vygotsky (1896-1934) as an application of Marx's Morality in Education

Capitalist education is based on the model of capitalism: accumulation of knowledge, a great deal of it unnecessary, provided in a competitive fashion, costly and wasteful. Some educators[938] have been critical of this approach and some have proposed alternative models. One of them, outstandingly, is Lev Vygotsky, who did his developmental research using the model of education. Education is giving, even though capitalism has transformed it into another commodity like everything else. Giving is the mode of the original society, the matriarchal paradigm, and Vygotsky's theory, inspired

---

937 Hegel, G.W.F. (1897). *The Philosophy of Right*. Third Part. Ethical Life. § 158. Trans: Dyde and Knox.(Orig. Pub. 1821). Online in MIA. Accessed from <https://www.marxists.org/reference/archive/hegel/works/pr/prfamily.htm> on 2015-12-13.

938 Freire, P. (2005). Pedagogy Of The Oppressed. 30th. Anniversary Edition. Trans. Myra Bergman Ramos. With an Introduction by Donaldo Macedo. New York and London. Continuum. Accessed from <https://libcom.org/files/Freire/PedagogyoftheOppresed.pdf> on 2014-10-05.

by Marx's moral stand, has offered in psychology the alternative matriarchal perspective to Hegel's master-slave paradigm of human development. Hegel's stand was competitive, adultomorphic and patriarchal; Vygotsky's is collaborative, developmental and matriarchal; they are opposites.

Vygotsky tell us that "Without question, the foundation of moral feelings has to be sought in the instinctive sense of sympathy for another person, in social instincts, and in much else besides. As it comes into contact with every imaginable datum, concept, and phenomenon in the process of growth, these innate reactions turn into those conditional forms of behavior we refer to collectively as moral behavior. Hence the general conclusion that moral behavior is a form of behavior which is amenable to education through the social environment in exactly the same way as is everything else."[939] There is no morality in fact for Vygotsky, there is only moral behavior, part of which is moral consciousness. "Moral education should be dissolved entirely imperceptibly into all those general modes of behavior that may be established and regulated by the social environment."[940]

Remember that the Hegelian paradigm was hierarchical and highly exploitative based on slavery that paradoxically ends up in equality. The Vygotskian paradigm is prototypically hierarchical in the other direction, giving with the intent of equalizing. This is why it is presented as educational in nature, not primarily economic or therapeutic; the educator, like a mother, gives. Collaboration is here the essence, solidarity, and, unlike the prevalent model, the developmental relation is always considered to be reciprocal. The mother intuitively knows what her child is going to be ready for and it is within that zone of prospective readiness that the mother taps the

---

939 Vygotsky, L. (1992). "The Nature of Ethics from the Psychological Point of View." Educational Psychology. Chapter 12: Ethical Behavior. Trans: Robert Silverman. Florida. St. Lucie Press. Online in MIA. Accessed from <https://www.marxists.org/archive/vygotsky/works/1926/educational-psychology/ch12.htm> on 2015-07-01.

940 Vygotsky, L. (1992). "The Nature of Ethics from the Psychological Point of View." Ibid.

intelligence of her child. It is the same with the educator, teacher, mentor, friend or collaborator; there is always a zone where throwing the seeds will result in growth. That area where the seeds of education can flower is called the zone of proximal development, the zone where development is ready to catch up with learning. "What, then, is defined by the zone of proximal development, as determined through problems that children cannot solve independently but only with assistance? The zone of proximal development defines those functions that have not yet matured but are in the process of maturation, functions that will mature tomorrow but are currently in an embryonic state. These functions could be termed the buds or flowers of development rather than the 'fruits' of development. The actual developmental level characterizes mental development retrospectively, while the zone of proximal development characterizes mental development prospectively."[941]

Furthermore: "To summarize, the most essential feature of our hypothesis is the notion that developmental processes do not coincide with learning processes. Rather, the developmental process lags behind the learning process; this sequence then results in zones of proximal development. Our analysis alters the traditional view that at the moment a child assimilates the meaning of a word, or masters an operation such as addition or written language, her developmental processes are basically completed. In fact, they have only just begun at that moment. The major consequence of analyzing the educational process in this manner is to show that the initial mastery of, for example, the four arithmetic operations provides the basis for the subsequent development of a variety of highly complex internal processes in children's thinking."[942]

I consider Vygotsky's developmental theory the alternative to

---

941 Vygotsky, L. S. (1978). Mind in society: The development of higher psychological processes. Chapter 6 Interaction between learning and development (79-91). Cambridge, MA: Harvard University Press. Accessed from <http://www.cles.mlc.edu.tw/~cerntcu/099-curriculum/Edu_Psy/EP_03_New.pdf> on 2014-09-28.
942 Vygotsky, L. S. (1978). Mind in society: The development of higher psychological processes. Chapter 6 Interaction between learning and development (79-91). Ibid.

Hegel's master-slave paradigm. We don't learn from development; we develop learning.

2.9.3.7 Horney's Morality of Evolution

In her deconstruction of Freud, Karen Horney (1885-1952) substituted the notion of superego morality, a representation of social norms, with that of "morality of evolution." We must remember that in general Horney substituted instinct for culture as the causative factor of neurosis. If in Freud the problem was lack of resolution of the dialectic nature-culture *à la* Hobbes, for Horney it is the Rousseauian cultural divergence from the morality of evolution that is the problem. In other words, instinctual disposition and culture are not equal magnitudes in that the former is constituted by irreversible compelling material imperatives, while the latter is determined by reversible incidental historical mediations. The first is necessary, the second contingent in its form.

Horney's notion of morality acknowledges the sense of the evolutionary process as the legitimate base of the superstructure consciousness, ideology in patriarchy. Humanity is not an exception to evolutionary determination even if we have managed to significantly exit the narrowness of the law of natural selection. Horney uses the Hegelian metaphor: if an acorn is designed to, under appropriate circumstances, become an oak tree, that is its moral sense. Along the same lines, if the design of human beings is to become growingly human, through the mutual constraint of two opposite instinctual dispositions, they cannot possibly be fully human when they have obliterated the expression of one of the two dispositions, the female one of altruism. If the acorn needs soil and water to grow, it cannot possibly grow on soil alone.

Unfortunately the self, although universal in humans, does not correspond to its natural design, because it has been historically tampered with. Idealized, the self does not really express the being of its carrier. The self is idealized, culturally and starting in the family environment, along three basic value dimensions. One dimension goes from self-assertion to aggression, a second from bonding to clinging, and the third from freedom to detachment. These three ingredients, variously titrated, are the stuff of all human relations and constitute the personality of the individual as well as of cultural groups that also tend to idealization along the same parameters. The self is the manager of the consciousness that produces personality, and collectively the culture.

"Lastly, the problem of morality is again different when we believe that inherent in man are evolutionary constructive forces, which urge him to realize his given potentialities. This belief does not mean that man is essentially good —which would presuppose a given knowledge of what is good or bad. It means that man, by his very nature and of his own accord, strives toward self-realization, and that his set of values stems from such striving. Apparently he cannot, for example, develop his full human potentialities unless he is truthful to himself; unless he is active and productive; unless he relates himself to others in the spirit of mutuality. Apparently he cannot grow if he indulges in a "dark idolatry of self " (Shelley) and consistently attributes all his own shortcomings to the deficiencies of others. He can grow, in the true sense, only if he assumes responsibility for himself."[943] Horney's approach to morality, as it concerns evolution, was quite different from Freud's.

Marx and Engels in the *German Ideology* agree with Horney: "Hitherto men have constantly made up for themselves false conceptions about themselves, about what they are and what they ought to be. They have arranged their relationships according to their ideas of God, of normal man, etc. The phantoms of their brains have got out of their hands. They, the creators, have bowed down before their creations. Let us liberate them from the chimeras, the ideas, dogmas, imaginary beings under the yoke of which they are pining away. Let us revolt against the rule of thoughts. Let us teach men, says one, to exchange these imaginations for thoughts which correspond to

---

943 Horney, K. (1950) *Neurosis and Human* Growth. New York. Norton. P. 15.

the essence of man; says the second, to take up a critical attitude to them; says the third, to knock them out of their heads; and existing reality will collapse."[944]

By splitting society into opposite antagonistic classes, patriarchy split consciousness which in turn split the self. Split consciousness is ideology and a split self is narcissistically idealized, falsely presented with a surplus of inflation. The individual self is the representation of the state that, in a society without a need for ethics would have no function because there would be no repression or need to mediate opposing segments.

GRAPH OF SELF-CONSCIOUSNESS

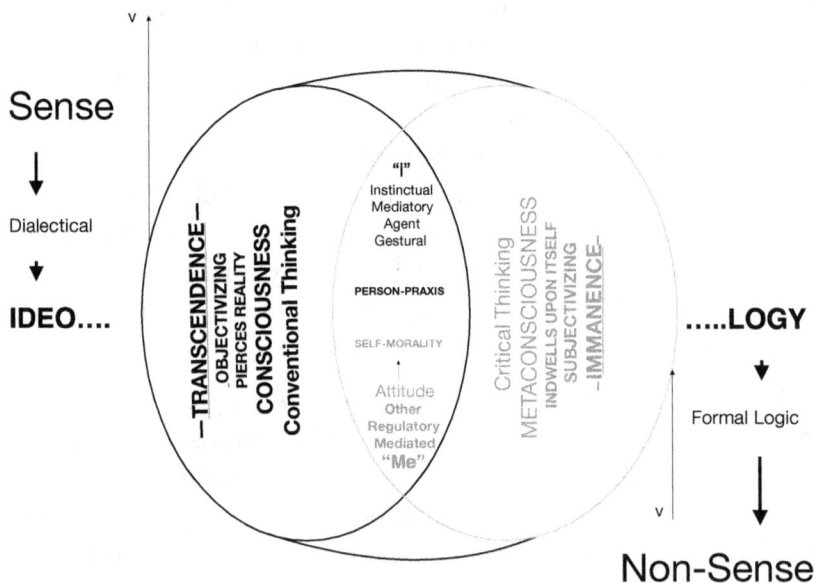

944 Marx, K. Engels, F. (1932). *The German* Ideology. Critique of Modern German Philosophy According to Its Representatives Feuerbach, B. Bauer and Stirner, and of German Socialism According to Its Various Prophets. Preface. (Written: Fall 1845 to mid-1846); Preface: from Marx-Engels Collected Works, Volume 5. Online in MIA. Accessed from <https://www.marxists.org/archive/marx/works/1845/german-ideology/> on 2015-07-06.

Explanation of the Graph: The first sphere and its characteristics are in boldface represent Consciousness. The second sphere, non-bold, is metaconsciousness. The two spheres are intersected, split by ideology that creates competing forms and destroys the prior unity. This is the result of the patriarchal trauma of war on the species. Ideology transforms natural sense into non-sense in part by transforming original dialectical logic into formal logic. The horizontal relationship of the spheres is their natural relation; their vertical relation manifests in their overlap, the self, is historical, resulting from the trauma. Transcendence is the capacity to objectivize piercing or penetrating reality. It results in consciousness, conventional thinking. The critical thinking of metaconsciousness indwells upon itself purely subjectively and results in immanence. This is a dialectical set of interconnected opposites.

The self is represented by the intersection of the two ovals. The *I* is the instinctual mediatory agent, the gesture of Mead. The *me* is the opposite, mediated regulatory other, in Mead's the more basic attitude. The person is the external practical presentation to others while the Self is the internal representation.

EPILOGUE - WHY WAR?

In his correspondence with Einstein,[945] Freud was aware that *might* is a natural category and referred to *violence* instead, the morally corrupted, historical transformation of power. If we agree that historical transformations, unlike natural phenomena, are reversible, there is much more room for hope than what Freud pessimistically offered in his answer to Einstein: "Conflicts of interest between man and man are resolved, in principle, by the recourse to violence. It is the same in the animal kingdom, from which man cannot claim exclusion." This literally applies to male problem-solving and alone leaves not much room for hope. But Freud himself adds: "nevertheless, men are also prone to conflicts of opinion, touching, on occasion, the loftiest peaks of abstract thought, which seem to call for settlement by quite another method." Here Freud is referring to reason, the other method derived from feminine altruism, the method of women. After all, it was women who successfully implemented the original revolution of culture without a drop of combat blood. Reasoning, leading to dialogue and compromise, is a derivative of feminine natural selection based on the altruistic maternal instinct that produces empathy and solidarity. Females of the species are the ones naturally biased to carry this instinctual disposition, to intelligently select. Here I see the stark opposition between two polar instinctual dispositions, male and female, violent and peaceful, that must constrain each other to achieve a balance in the midst of constantly changing natural and historical conditions predictable only by reason.

I propose that Freud could have parsed out the two opposite instinctual dispositions, along the natural divide of sex, had he not been blinded by patriarchal misogyny and individualistic ideology.

---

945 Einstein, A, and Freud, S. (1931-2)."The Einstein-Freud Correspondence." Online in Arizona State University. Accessed from <www.public.asu.edu/~jmlynch/273/documents/FreudEinstein.pdf> on 2016-11-07

With the exception of the legendary Amazons, war has always been the exclusive business of men. In the present work I venture into the evolutionary field and analyze history from its origins to support the proposition that, even though men and women are endowed with, and can cultivate either one or both instinctual dispositions, the never-to-be-infringed-upon natural design is for a *reciprocal balance* of their opposite sexual biases. This entails the recognition of the two separate and opposite instincts Freud recognized, Eros and Thanatos, each embodied in the female and male of the species respectively. This inter- and intra-subjective equilibrium is possible only in humans that can mediate. It is achieved culturally, dialectically, by reshaping the mindset, the natural infrastructure or instinctual disposition inhered in each individual sex. This perspective totally changes Freud's view of the inevitability of war, which among other things, contradicts his own theory of sublimation.

Besides being the clearest manifestation of the raw male instinctual disposition, organized war as such is exclusively a human phenomenon. Although ants collectively storm termites' colonies and slave-making ants raid others to steel their brood and enslave them, these remain instinctual actions that do not fulfill the conscious characteristics of a planned war.[946] Although chimps raid neighboring communities to annex their territory, human war differs in that it is intentional, anticipated in the individual and collective mind along with its consequences, before it is implemented. War is of a different magnitude, and consciously rationalized as moral, peace-seeking, preventive, humanitarian, *etc.*, and furthermore it has grown to be socially professionalized and prestigiously institutionalized in our age influencing other social institutions as important as government and the economy.[947] Most crucially, in animals might may be used to destroy other species but in humans war became an intra-

---

946 Langley, L. (2016). "Do animals go to war?" National Geographic News. Question of the week Jan. 30. Accessed from <http://news.nationalgeographic.com/2016/01/160130-animals-insects-ants-war-chimpanzees-science/> on 2016-11-04.

947 O'Hanlon, M.E. (2010) The Science of War: Defense Budgeting, Military Technology, Logistics, and Combat Outcomes. Princeton, N.J., Princeton University Press.

species phenomenon. Other species lack alternative capacities such as reason, dialogue, negotiation and compromise, not to mention the unique human capacity to fight about, even if not always, legitimate abstract moral ideas. The enormous waste of war, not only in monetary, developmental and emotional terms, but in biological and economic terms, is incalculable. The waste of costly youth and healthy life to resolve material or ideological differences makes no ecological, biological, evolutionary or, most important, moral sense, unless one adopts the unsustainable Malthusian standpoint that there is excess humanity that must be wasted. Even if that were the case, the problem would be solvable through proper planning. From the point of view of biological economy it does not make sense to reiteratively send costly youth to their death while fiercely arguing about the morality of comparatively economic and morally justifiable abortion.

Given appropriate environmental conditions, the compromise of a dynamic dual instinctual structure in humans becomes manifest in intelligence and moral habit, both forcefully overriden by war at present. Peace would entail dispositional mutual constraints to achieve an expressive balance constructively responsive to changing natural condition and to also changing appropriate historical circumstances. That humans are not directly governed by irrepressible instinct is the reason Freud introduced the notion of *drive* that, following Briffault, I instead call here *instinctual disposition*, instinct that, modified by cultural learning into *habit*, still conserves its basic bias. The animal expression of aggression, triggered by discrete environmental stimuli, in humans must be symbolically mediated and morally rationalized in advance.

Instinctual aggressive behavior originates in the phylogenetically oldest parts of the brain indicating its prior evolutionary existence. It is however dually regulated through its interplay with subcortical structures such as amygdala and hypothalamus where emotions originate, and further through the prefrontal cognitive centers where the final fine tuning of response behavior takes place as learned habitual behavior.[948] This is the *universal* biological infrastructure of humans modified by *particular* cultural experiences in each individual. Culture is the result of all the historical mediations introduced by all prior generations of problem-solving humans. Paradoxically, technological gains achieved today largely in a military context only serve to create artificial scarcity for the majority through massive destruction that ultimately affects all involved.

The instinctual disposition to aggression in the individual is further mediated by a hormonal marker differently titrated in males and females of the species. This is *testosterone* that also regulates bone and muscle mass as well as bodily distribution of fatty reserves.[949] Ontogenetically testosterone determines a *sexual dimorphism* that starts with the brain. Behaviorally, testosterone increases anger, aggression, competitiveness and dominance, and, in humans, levels of testosterone are typically more than five times higher in males than in females.[950] This only in part explains the increased tendency to violence in males, because culture ultimately mediates genetic and hormonal expression. I quote from *Psychology Today*: "In almost every society men are the ones who are overwhelmingly involved in wars, in all kinds of intergroup aggressions and intra-group homicide; they mobilize themselves in armies of violent fans, in criminal gangs, in bands of thugs, etc. These observations are as old as the world and have allowed us to create a clear distinction between male and female sexes regarding their predisposition to violence. Wars are a biosocial product of men and a field for male's manifestation."[951] The same is true of crime and cruelty, closely linked to masculini-

948 Batrinos, M.L. (2012) "Testosterone and Aggressive Behavior in Man." International Journal of Endocrinology Metabolism. Summer; 10(3): 563–568. Accessed from <https://www.ncbi.nlm.nih.gov/pmc/articles/PMC3693622/> on 2016-11=10.

949 Finkelstein, J.S, Lee, H., et al. (2013). "Gonadal Steroids and Body Composition, Strength, and Sexual Function in Men." Online in New England Journal of Medicine. Accessed from <http://www.nejm.org/doi/full/10.1056/NEJMoa1206168#t=article> on 2016-11-10.

950 Burtis CA, Ashwood ER, Bruns DE (2012). Tietz Textbook of Clinical Chemistry and Molecular Diagnostics. (5th ed.). Elsevier Health Sciences. p. 1975.

951 Goldstein J. (2001). War and gender: How Gender Shapes the War System and Vice Versa. Cambridge: Cambridge University Press.

ty.[952] What must be pointed out here is that the failure to rein in the instinctual expression of men has a historical determination. It came to be used politically by males' forcefully usurping the evolutionary role of females as strategists and ushers of the species. In the first political coup of history, sons, perhaps even with the partial acquiescence of their mothers, substituted for matriarchy, the natural form of human governance, patriarchy, the inversion of all previous, naturally designed forms of mother right, first-order mediations introduced by mothers in the form of culture.

For the instinctual infrastructure of violence to come to expression, the environmental cultural superstructure must provide facilitating circumstances. Culture must provide appropriate conditions which it does mainly through rational and moral justification. This is why war is often declared in the name of peace and freedom and humanitarian reasons. It is well documented however that through the news, entertainment, and children's games, our culture desensitizes children to violence very early, making it appear just another way of problem-solving and success. This rationalized desensitization equally affects all males and females.[953]

Applied psychoanalysis is arguably uniquely qualified to explain the phenomenon of war both from an instinctual as well as from a moral vantage point. We must start by properly reframing Einstein's question: Why the cultural habit of war over alternative compromise solutions based on dialogue, reason, and mediation? The psychoanalytic method applied to history listens with special attention to repressive sequences. *Slavery* stands out in the manifest narrative and behind it is the ominous *patriarchal coup* that originated it, the memory of which is fiercely repressed even in academia. *Communal substantial equality,* the rule during *matriarchy,* is not documented

952 Furtuna, D. (2014)."Homo Aggressivus. Male Aggression. Why are men more violent? Online in Psychology Today. Accessed from <https://www.psychologytoday.com/blog/homo-aggressivus/201409/male-aggression> on 2016-11-07.

953 Krahé, B., Möller, I., et al. (2011). "Desensitization to Media Violence: Links With Habitual Media Violence Exposure, Aggressive Cognitions, and Aggressive Behavior." J Pers Soc Psychol. Apr; 100(4): 630–646. Accessed from <https://www.ncbi.nlm.nih.gov/pmc/articles/PMC4522002/> on 2017-05-05.

in hieroglyphs or scrolls because it existed prior to them. It is deeply immersed in the earliest unconscious of humanity and recoverable only through the method of archeology that places fragmentary and circumstantial proof, often mythical, together into a whole. As we have seen, attempts to do this have been repeatedly rejected by mainstream patriarchal academia.

The earliest period of humanity, is the analogue of infancy and early childhood. Descriptions of it since Lewis Morgan and Johann Bachofen confirm our irrepressible animal nature, misrepresented as polymorphous and perverse. Similarly, the historical *trauma* of the patriarchal coup that unseated mothers and placed the control of history in the hands of fathers is inverted in Sophocles' *Oedipus Rex*. Bachofen already pointed out that Aeschylus' Oresteia is the pivotal myth representing the filial matricide that transitioned to patriarchy. This we can fathom only if we don't neglect the history of the earliest origins of humanity and substitute them with a simplistic, voluntaristic history of marriage. The reason myths are important is that they are anthropology before the written word. They show us where and how historical morality traumatically departed from the morality of evolution, where our self-imposed slavery started. Here is where women were converted into annoying Erinyes without much transcendence except for their nagging, Pandora's being their prototype. At a glance we can easily note that all historical developments pursuant to the traumatic event have been geared to the restoration of gender parity and substantial equality that must go hand-in-hand. This would constitute the real abolition of slavery. Today we are told that slavery does not exist, that we are free in a democracy because we use words differently. We are not told that wage labor is the last form of slavery, and that slavery is constant class war waged in subliminal legal and political ways besides military war.

Behind the fact that the pre-emptive *defense* from the return of the repressed, *slavery,* still prevails most visibly in the compromised form of wage-labor (the invisible patriarchal tax on all forms of labor), we find the masculine *fear of substantial equality*. This is a guilty fear of feminine retaliation based on the projection that women, if in power, will respond in kind, thus conjuring the image of the dreaded archaic and ominous *castrating mother*. Alive in the collective unconscious, and based on the historical memory of mother's saying "No!", thus inventing lawfulness and deeply hurting narcissism, since the repressed always comes home to roost, the history of patriarchy is one of struggle and compromise. The limit of that historical process, cyclic return of the repressed-struggle-compromise, is expressed today in the uppermost cultural form of *globalized financial capitalism*, the name of the historical moment we live *per* the economist. Two observations lead to the conclusion that it is not only the limit of capitalism but that of patriarchy: first, the Thatcher-Reagan motto *"there is no alternative,"* that in fact reflects the understandable conscious pessimism; the second is *globalization* that goes with it and that has reached the end of the process of capitalist expansion.

Financial capital is the material objectification of male narcissism, and globalization a univocal symbol of the opposite, of compelling universality that will sooner or later translate into the return of substantial equality of the members of the species. A pervasively idealized narcissistic ruling class produces its own reflection in economic inflation, idle, parasitic and non-productive finance. "Hedge funds," "futures," "options," "derivatives," are the hot air that inflates gambling in the financial economy. The model of betting on the future with borrowed capital is unsustainable. It is anticipatory imagination sophistically overriding a lawful reality. The important conclusion to be drawn here is that there is a relation of *reciprocal determination* between market and ideology, and that such dialectical interaction has a pathoplastic effect on personality and self.

Looking carefully, we can see analogues in the economy of civil society, its ideology, as well as in individual and group psychology and psychopathology. The pandemic of pathological narcissism is not an accident; in both individual and upper class character pathology it is reciprocally determinative of finance economy and parasitic idleness. They all appear natural because they are explainable only through their own logic. The universal scoptophilic surveillance of citizens, the *governmental panopticon,* is a logical derivative of the system coupled with the highly protected *governmental secrecy* that is intended to block the perception of the reality of corruption. This is what makes entertainment, such as reality television and the media depiction of imaginary corrupt governments parallel with the real ones, mesmerizing, imagination and reality having lost their boundary as we all lose the sense of reality through alienation. Since the capitalist system is corrupt in its premise of the few arbitrarily *taxing* all, the standards to morally judge corruption have to be set upon corruption itself. Morality then regresses to the stage where it means not being caught red-handed.

Consciousness has no choice but to ideologically reflect the reality of social life, of our relations with ourselves and nature, and our modes of producing our lives daily, today within the structures of the prevailing capitalist model. We use ideology because it is the only way to reflect our social reality. Psychoanalysis, confronted with the results of this perversion of consciousness has limited itself to the interpretation of the narrow biographical unconscious, leaving consciousness intact. In this fashion it can at best help individuals adapt to the same environment that is causing their alienation, because there is no analysis of the iceberg of ideology. Although Freud's theory made inroads particularly with his dynamic notions of repression and defense, his unfortunate resort to metapsychology and explanatory entelechies is mystifying: it reproduces the current myth. A new psychoanalysis is needed then, that uncovers the whole structure of our social relations based on reification, ideology, and unnatural verticality and hierarchy. It is time to stop analyzing political activism as an Oedipal failure, reducing legitimate political activity to psychological myth. This of course would require a whole reexamination of the parameters of psychoanalytic treatment and its pretended neutrality, because today's neutrality is the implicit endorsement of the corrupt system in a mystifying therapeutic collusion. This will be no easy task, I recognize.

Thus, our two hundred thousand year-old patient misnamed *Homo sapiens* suffers from a serious ailment that was already diagnosed by Hegel and Marx, in psychoanalysis by Sigmund Freud but more explicitly by Karen Horney and Erich Fromm among others: alienation. Homo excludes half of the species, and automatically disavows its qualifier "wise." Alienation is here self-misperception, the illusion that particularity can substitute for universality. At its origin, alienation started with the estranging universality of religious collective projection of the idealized self as God. Alienation evolved historically to mean more specifically reification, self-perception in the estranged social product universalized as money. Its pathological nature becomes manifest in the split of social class that common sense denominates as haves and have-nots, or one versus ninety-nine percent. The antagonism (incapacity to resolve itself logically through historical attempts at compromise) leads to the warring consequences. Individually, it also manifest in the split of the self that Horney saw as self-contempt behind self-idealization that substitutes for the normal dialectic of the real self, compromising *I* and *me*, being the latter universality, the carrier of the interests of the species. Needless to say, reification is a universally disempowering and impoverishing process for the species.

Initial religious alienation was a necessary form, consciousness perceiving itself through infantile, magical eyes. It had to lean on natural, totemic hybridization. Animism had to be the first self-perception of a blossoming human consciousness. Today's alienation in contrast is not the result of naïveté but of corruption, although it may use religion as its shield. It is guided not by necessity but by the artificiality of greed. The whole patriarchal history has been a struggle of consciousness trying to re-appropriate itself for itself in its universal nature, although all attempts have resulted in meager and often reversed compromise. Class wars have often wrested compromises that, in their reversibility, further kindle class war.

A hypertrophic patriarchal *I* has been able to pare its counterpart, *me*, to express unilateral agency, ultimately at the cost of morality, their balance. All that has been learned by all generations of active humans materially and spiritually accrues to what illusively looks like the earned benefit of a few. Among other results, division of labor has become *compartmentalization*. Brilliant super-specialization, expertise in minute segments of reality, has rendered us ignorant of the forest for the hyper-perception of the tree. We have lost vision of totalities for their parts. A partial effect of this phenomenon is the loss of the capacity to identify the aggressor amongst ourselves.

To summarize, our patient the species was born in the Middle Paleolithic, a new bifurcation of the genus *homo* with the unique capacity to mediate, to make nature *appear* human. Structured sexually for reproduction, although with a female default and strategic bias, in a bloodless revolution females invented culture as the self-producing tool of the species. This required having already advanced from an initially nomadic to a relatively sedentary life based on agriculture and domestication of animals, self included. A cultural infancy and early childhood allowed her to introduce essential first-order mediations of humans such as: self-governance in gentes clans and tribes; a gift-and-need-fulfillment economy; solidarily substantive equality; symbolic communication; and social institutions. The latter included division of labor, communal living, lawfulness, and religion as the repository of morality, its higher form of consciousness. A patriarchal political coup initiated by her sons not only unseated her but symbolically transformed her into a de-transcendentalized slave, objectified and muzzled. Subsequent patriarchal rule based on an alternative civil society and a state created to mediate between new, antagonistic class formations, resulted in male hegemony, economy based on accumulation and exchange, social hierarchy, and an inversion of all previous mediations through second-order, patriarchal ones. Slavery was instituted, subordinating wider segments of society to the patriarchs. The rest is well-known, written history. With slavery came reification, slaves as productive machines, that would extend rather universally.

The species' current age is *global financial capitalism*, encompassing capitalism in turn having been preceded by feudalism and slavery during the last ten thousand years or so. The different stadial names cover the same class struggle, wherein a small minority, mainly male, substantially appropriates the social labor of all including previous generations. In present financial capitalism those same few individuals gamble with the resources produced by all and presently risk the survival of the species as a consequence of crossing natural red lines. This has totally destroyed the equilibrium that nature consists of, to which humans are no exception, and which is about to name a new eon as *anthropocene*. The species has become victim of an alienating inner class struggle that has split it into antagonistic, instead of the original dialectical, sex opposites, unable to compromise. Today this process, entrenched in patriarchal capitalism looks like a malignancy.

The species' center of gravity has shifted to patriarchs, thus leading to the two related problems of slavery and its current expression, capitalism. This is the basic central conflict, war being waged materially and ideologically between classes. It is also the war between ideologies, the most universal being the closer to consciousness. Each individual reflects this struggle in its self, its idealized and despised selves. The real self that Horney spoke about will be possible only through freedom from ideology,

Designed to reflect a social and historical reality, consciousness cannot escape assuming the form of the reality it reflects. This reflects the central, basic conflict of the species, its battle to reappropriate its own design, the manifest battle between ideology and good sense. As ideology has pervaded the patriarchal family and all forms of civil society, foremost the state, we can only fight ideology with ideology. The measure of a progressive ideology, of its closeness to consciousness is its universality: the more universally inclusive the benefits of a particular ideology, the closer it comes to consciousness. Consciousness is possible only in a society structured totally differently, with universal prevalence over particularity that means substantive equality and real sexual parity. This view is not incompatible but complementary to that of political economy, which sees socialism as the society of the future based on substantive equality.

The same way consciousness irremediably must reflect actual, not ideal, social reality as its natural content, the self must reflect current social governance. This is a most important conclusion, logical if we consider that self is only the organizer of a given consciousness. From this perspective all individual selves are corrupted to the extent that, to survive and thrive culturally, they must not only assimilate but successfully accommodate and express the structure of their alienating culture. Here we see in the self the same class split we saw in the species, and in its consciousness. A split self leads to alienation, self-idealization in a form that is analogic to species split and ideological corruption. The mother of all repression is the trauma inflicted upon the species by patriarchy in slavery and female submission. Fortunately, mothers and women, and then the ninety-nine percent, although largely deprived of their transcendence by repression, have been able to conserve intact their immanence, the basic capacity to reflect reality that is connected to natural good sense. The current battle of consciousness is between corrupted ideology and good sense, the evolutionary endowment of each individual here seen as aimed to achieve a balance between two opposite but equal instinctual dispositions.

Having looked at history with the psychoanalytic lens, in this volume I have presented an alternative to mainstream history that includes what I consider the form of the origins of society as matriarchal. History is then divided into three epochs, matriarchal, patriarchal, and the society of the future, a real compromise of the two. The evidence for the existence of matriarchy is first of all evolutionary, otherwise reconstructible only through a method similar to the one of forensics and archeology, by putting pieces together. I see no better theoretical alternative. The degree of academic repression of the theory of matriarchy in patriarchal academia reinforces the fact that the knowledge of the legitimacy of the theory is countered by the bad faith of its repression. In a world still based on a pre-human ethos of force, it appears natural that men would have always led the species and invented culture. We have enough scientific evidence however, I believe, to propose as axiomatic that evolutionarily females are biased to select as males are to fight, that such a basic characteristic makes the female the strategist of the species and therefore its first usher, that the transition to male hegemony was historical not natural, that it is likely that the original forms of social organization besides matriarchal were communal, and that patriarchy has brought imbalance by repression through unconstrained expression of the male instinctual disposition. That this artificial imbalance has lead to dominance and hierarchy, and thus being our situation of constant war a, historical phenomenon alien to the morality of evolution, is a logical conclusion and reason for hope.

The present work aims at starting the discussion about psycho-analysis' being the science not of the unconscious, but of consciousness and therefore inclusive of ideology, morality's being the highest expression of consciousness. The search started as a reflection on consciousness, but it soon realized that consciousness includes everything and that therefore it had to start with natural history and continue with human history evolutionarily as much as possible. Here it found that there had been an unnatural and traumatic historical shift from matriarchy, the natural design, to patriarchy, its current detour. The question of the post-traumatic effect on consciousness and the self then becomes inevitable and an attempt has been made to answer it. Finally, it is humbly realized that posing the question is just the beginning of an holistic, scientific quest.

GLOSSARY

In parenthesis after the time the word is first used and original meaning (mostly from the Online Dictionary of Etymology); also an opposite (Opp.) concept in the present context to emphasize the dialectical approach. Also in parenthesis are names of relevant authors to pursue. Words in italics are defined in the glossary.

ACT: (late 14c., a thing done. Opp. *inhibition, repression*). *Self*-originated human motion. Acts usually maintain life-processes by the *selection* of stimuli based on *need*. Through its selective acts an organism reciprocally creates its environment. A human *act* has various stages such as *attitude*, impulse, *selection*, manipulation or *mediation*, and consummation. The basic unit of a *social act* is the *gesture*. Significant or symbolic gestures make possible human *thought*, communication, and the intentional initiation of actions (G.H. Mead). Unit of life of the physical *subject* mediated by psychic reflection orienting the *subject* in the objective world. (Leontiev).

ACTIVITY: (1,400 active or secular life. Opp. *inertia*). Collaborative pursuit of social ends (Leontiev). The result of motion, the mechanical property of *matter*, being organically internalized in animals to become purposeful *self*-government. Humans' willful *activity* driven by consciousness, characteristic of subjects, that leads to *praxis*. In psychology they are units of life mediated by psychic reflection. A system with its own *structure*, transitions, transformations, and development (Leontiev). Alienated, social *activity* of *capitalism*, produced by *culture* (Marx, Horney). Socialist *philosophy* takes *activity* as the basic substance of its *philosophy*, rather than *matter* and motion, which are the substances of a mechanical view of the world.

ADAPTATION: (c. 1600, action of something fitting something else. Opp. *poorness of fit*). Survival through reciprocal change (Dar-

637

win).The history of Nature's technology. Before Darwin, cooperation: the vegetable kingdom supplying nutriment to the animal kingdom and conversely the animal kingdom supplying plants with carbonic acid and manure. Natural processes are characterized by adaptive traits, specific functional roles in the life of an organism (Marx). *Self-consciousness*, becoming aware of one's *self* by seeing one's *self* through the eyes of another *self-* is the most idiosyncratic adaptive human trait leading to both struggle for and dependence on *recognition* (Hegel).

AGENCY: (1650s, active operation. Opp. *other-directedness*). The capacity to, consciously, meaningfully and purposefully, *self*-initiate *I activity*. *Agency* results from the proper balance of opposites in consciousness, from *self*-regulation. Human *existence* is social *activity* and the form of I *activity* is determined by *culture*. Through *agency* I build myself, on top of what others initially made of *me* (Sartre), socially, in the context of necessary *recognition* (Hegel), to arrive at *praxis* (Marx).

ALIENATION: (late-XIVc., transfer of ownership. Opp. *self-realization*). Diversion from the norm. The type of relation that separates the worker from the product of her of his *labor,* precluding him from its use and enjoyment, beside the *self-recognition* in it as *self-objectification,* resulting in human *self*-estrangement (Marx). Detour from the evolutionary design of being morally human. Ideologically altered *self*-representation stemming from hierarchical subjection, coercion and mystification, resulting in the idealized corruption of the real *self* (Horney). Ideal anthropomorphic *god* opposed to humanity (Feuerbach). A tool to perpetuate human *slavery.*

ATTITUDE: (1660s, disposition, posture. Opp. *symbolic gesture*). *Unconscious* conveyance. What a *subject* reverberationally conveys, intersubjectively, in her or his demeanor. Attitudes as part of *character* and *personality* precede acts. Emotions are objectified and manifested primarily through attitudes (GH Mead). Non-verbal communication.

BASE: (early 14c., bottom, foundation, pedestal. Opp. *super-*

structure). On the metaphor of a building, the part of society that comprises the forces and relations of production —employer–employee work conditions, the technical division of labor, and property relations— into which individuals, largely unconsciously, enter towards the collective production of their lives. These relations dialectically, not mechanically, determine society's superstructural relationships such as ideas, values, institutions and ideologies (Marx). There can be no *superstructure* without *base* (or infrastructure) and for that *reason* the *base*, in the last instance, determines the *superstructure*. In other words, the life of man depends in the last resort upon how s/he obtains bread and butter. The *character* of a community varies according to whether it depends for its sustenance upon agriculture, commerce, industry or war. The environment, changed by humans, creates new orders of influence which moulds the entire order of society. Ideas and ideals are *subject* to the determining influence of those conditions. The conceptions, the notions, the prejudices, the standards of judgment and of conduct, the literature, the *philosophy*, the *morality* of the community, are shaped and colored by the nature of the established ruling interests which the material conditions have determined (Marx).

BEHAVIOR: (early-XVc., to have or bear oneself in a *particular* way, comport. Opp. inner experience). Outward expression or *objectification* of consciousness in practice. In animals, teleological instinctually driven practical adaptation reciprocally driven by the environment. *Self*-expression that can be understood only in terms of the *behavior* of the whole social group of which the *individual* is a member, the result of an *attitude*, and an impulse seeking expression and selecting a stimulus that it reciprocally seeks (G.H. Mead).

BEING: (1300, condition, state, circumstances; presence, fact of existing. Opp. *essence*, alienated having). What appears, what objective *logic* is concerned with (Hegel). As one totality, the manifold of material and social conditions, including *matter* and consciousness (Marx). *Being* is qualified as in itself before consciousness and for itself after it. Marx speaks of *species being* referring to the universality of humans. Human *being* is *social being*.

BECOMING: (VIc. BCE., Heraclitus said that nothing in this world is constant except change and *becoming*. Opp. *Parmenides' unchanging reality*, stillness). *Being* always active, always changing. *Social being*. We are what we build on top of what they built (Sartre).

CAPITALISM: (1611, a grant of land from the king. Opp. *socialism*). A historical mode of production and upon it a form of social relations (Marx). Third and last economic and political system in *patriarchy*, after *slavery* and feudalism, based on the planned maintenance of artificial scarcity through wasteful accumulation of wealth by a minority of individuals. The goal of production in *capitalism* is not direct use and *need* fulfillment but exchange and accumulation of profit. Economical phenomena are for the most part controlled unconsciously by the *market* that comprehends the total exchange of commodities.

CHARACTER: (mid-14c., *symbol* marked or branded on the body. Opp. *temperament, personality*). In humans the objectified history of attitudes currently manifest in the *individual*'s *behavior* as a set of organized habits. Set of attitudes of a *person* the concern *psychoanalysis*.

CIVIL SOCIETY: (late 14c., relating to civil law or life; pertaining to the internal affairs of a *state*. Opp. family, *state*). A *self*-sufficient association of individuals, governed patriarchally, in what is a *particular* form of pseudo-universality imposed through the interests of the rulers seen as those of all. It includes and overrides the family. The group is governed through a *state* framed according to the needs and interests of the rulers, reflected in a legal constitution and the *state*'s monopoly of the use of violence. In capitalism, its moral motto is from each according to capacity; to each according to previous accumulation.

CIVILIZATION: (1704, law which makes a criminal process civil. Also, advanced condition of society. Opp. *savagery, barba-*

rism). The third period of human history characterized by strict patriarchal rule after matriarchal savagery and transitional barbarism. The encompassing historical process of acculturation from *slavery* to capitalism (Morgan).

COGNITION: (mid-15c., ability to comprehend. Opp. *emotion*). The sphere of consciousness that deals with the representation of *reality*, external and internal to itself. It produces understanding through the senses and reasoning, symbols, ideas, *thought*, knowledge, experience, and so forth.

COMMONSENSE: (14c., originally the power of mentally uniting the impressions conveyed by the five physical senses, thus ordinary understanding. Opp. *foolish or insane*). The diffuse, uncoordinated features of a general form of *thought* common to a *particular* period and a *particular* popular environment. It contains a healthy nucleus of *good sense* which deserves to be made more unitary and coherent (Gramsci).

COLLABORATION: (late 14c., work together. Opp. *competition*). In development the mutual creation of *zones of proximal development* by subjects, where their intellects and affects are fused in a unified whole, facilitating the pursuit of a goal. Dialectically inherent in nature, *collaboration* is the prevailing original mode of human relations in gentes, before *civil society* displaced the preference to *competition*. Partners who succeed in constructing such a joint system benefit from their reciprocal sensitivity to the *sense* and *meaning* of each other's *language* (Vygotsky).

COMPETITION: (1610s a contest for something. Opp. *collaboration*). Characteristic of the patriarchal rule as *collaboration* was for the matriarchal. Social preference for domination and hierarchy in human relations. War of all against all (Hobbes). The way to increased fitness towards natural *selection* (Malthus, Darwin). The operational opposite of *collaboration* (Marx).

CONDENSATION: (c. 1600, *becoming* more dense. Opp. *displacement, sublimation*). Combination and amalgamation. With symbolization and *displacement,* a basic mechanism of the *un-conscious* processes (Freud). *Condensation,* and *displacement,* are equivalent to metaphor and metonymy in *language* (Lacan).

CONSCIOUSNESS: (1630 internal knowledge. Opp. *language, unconscious*). The result of social activity (Hegel). The condition for all forms of *thought* that must ultimately be defined in terms of it. Accrued reasoned symbolic representation based on historical experience. A relationship, social experience of experience. Simultaneous social contact with oneself and another *object.* Reflection of *reality* in a social context that historically defines it. The human condition of a socialized *subject* capable of operating with internalized forms or images of *reality.* Mechanically it starts as reflection; dialectically it becomes active and reciprocal, reverberational between subjects. The adaptive instrument of anticipation. Through its negative power we can posit *nothingness* and imagine. In *patriarchy* always class *consciousness* constructed by social practice that when from in-itself becomes for-itself, it leads to *praxis* and liberation (Marx).

CULTURE: (mid-15c., the tilling of land. Opp. *civilization*). The *particular* way a group of humans transforms *reality* for survival through objectified historical mediations. Society's *self* representation as an objectified extension of memory. Humanely transformed nature. Cumulative expression of *self* mediations. A *particular* society's *self* representation, form of *consciousness.*

DESIRE: (mid-14c., *sense* of lust). In Hegel *need* for *recognition* in socialization. Human transformation of *need* resulting from the transformation of demand (Freud).

DIALECTIC: (12c., originally synonymous with *logic.* Opp. *formal, mechanical logic*). The original ancient Greek *logic* rescued and refined by Hegel as a *logic* of motion and *activity.* Motion, activity and development result from the struggle of opposites, merging contradictions in a *synthesis.* Everything is inherently contradictory, the truth and the essential nature of things.

DISPLACEMENT: (1810 change in position. Opp. *condensation*). *Unconscious* basic mechanism (Freud) analogue of metonymy in *language* (Lacan).

DRIVE: (1690s., urge to go forward. Opp. *instinct*). Tendency, impulse, transformed *instinct* with a bodily source, a magnitude, an aim and an *object* (Freud). *Instinctual disposition* or proclivity (Briffault).

ECONOMY: (1530s, household management. Opp. *carelessness*). The management of needs and resources. Economics is the *science* which deals with the objective quasi-natural laws and processes governing the production of commodities, their values and money (M.I.A.). It began as the study of scarcity and, ideologically, became the technique of sustaining artificial scarcity. Political *economy* is a term first used by Rousseau to designate the *economy* of a nation or *state*. As a study of capital, was refined by Marx.

EGO: (1714, as a term in metaphysics for the *self*. Opp. *me*). Reified as an explanatory entelechy following the old metaphysical model of the *soul*, the *ego* was mistakenly seen originally as the *self* rather than its mere component, the *I*.

EMOTION: (1570s, a (social) moving, stirring, agitation. Opp: *cognition*). An inner instinctive internal proto-*language* of animals that warns of changes in surrounding conditions prompting appropriate actions. Opposed to cognitions that can misrepresent, emotions are always legitimate. Thus their importance in the analysis of *attitude* and the *unconscious*. Humans learn to repress emotions for political expediency, thus reinforcing the *idealization* and *alienation* of their selves.

ENSEMBLE OF THE SOCIAL RELATIONS: (1845, the human *essence*. Opp. *It*). Marx used this term to refer to what Feuerbach had called *species being*. In the present theory the historical *structure* referred to by Marx is the *me* part of the *self*. It is the whole of the social relations that have materially formed cultures since the transition from apehood to arrive at the present conscious *individual* bound to a *particular* family tree and cultural sequence, like everyone else.

ESSENCE: (1650s, basic element of anything. Opp. *existence*). The truth of *being* after it has been penetrated by *consciousness* to expose the sequence of its phenomenological presentations. (Hegel).

EVOLUTION: (1620s, opening of what was rolled up. Opp. *creationism*). The process of development and history of the cosmos on the model of Darwin's findings on natural *selection* about live species.

EXISTENCE: (late 14c., *reality*, to stand out. Opp. *essence*). The quality of the real. How an *object* appears phenomenologically (Hegel). *Social being* in humans.

EXOGAMY: (1865, outside marriage. Opp: *endogamy*). Rule that prohibits sexual intercourse with partners of the same moiety of the *gens*; It similarly prohibits eating your own produce and hunt (Knight).

FORM: (c. 1200, semblance, image, likeness. Opp. *substance*). The semblance of *matter* internalized as *consciousness*. The dialectical influence of environment is exercised over the *form*, and the *adaptation* of the *form* results from the influences of the environment in natural *selection*. Spencer conceived of the central nervous system as *being* continually played upon by stimuli which set up certain paths, so that it was the environment which was fashioning the *form* (GH Mead). The internalization of forms by the nervous system leads to *thought* and *consciousness*.

FREE ASSOCIATION: (1892, elimination of censoring in expression. Opp: *repression*). First was the political phenomenon of free expression. Then came the method Freud used after hypnosis to discover the repressed in the unconscious coming back as symptoms. Freud encouraged patients to say everything coming to *mind* no *matter* how incorrect, offensive or absurd.

FUNCTION: (1530s, proper work or purpose; power of acting

in a specific proper way. Opp. *structure*). Teleological *activity* adequate to a *particular structure*.

GENS: (1847, tribe, clan, house of families having a name and certain religious rites in common and a presumed common origin. Opp. *civil society*). The first organized social group in ancient society, consisting of very extended matrilineal families. *Gens* has the primary signification of kin; signifying to beget, it implies an immediate common descent of the members. A *gens*, therefore, was a body of consanguines descended from the same common ancestor, distinguished by a gentile name, and bound together by blood. It evolved to include a moiety, half of such descendants in a dual organization for *exogamy*. Where descent is in the female line, as it was universally in the archaic period, the *gens* is composed of a female ancestor and her children, together with the children of her female descendants in perpetuity. The same with male *gentes*. The family name amongst ourselves is a survival of the gentile organization with descent in the male line. (Morgan).

GESTURE: (early 15c., manner of carrying the body. Opp. *attitude*), Unit of subjective communication, the basic mechanism of the social process of social animals. Animals communicate through gestures and humans also converse unconsciously through gestures. Advanced symbolic communication requires significant gestures processed by *consciousness*. *Language*, the expression of *consciousness*, is communication through significant gestures, and communication through nonsignificant gestures is *unconscious*. *Gesture* makes possible the appropriate responses of subjects to one another's *behavior*. Within any given *social act* a balance is negotiated gesturally, between the actions of one organism involved and the actions of another. Vygotsky's *zone of proximal development* is unconsciously intuited and negotiated gesturally. In the field of operation of gestures, human *consciousness* has risen and developed through the process of the symbolization of experience. The specialization of the human animal within this field of the gesture has been responsible, ultimately, for the origin and growth of human society and knowledge, with all the control over nature and over the human environment which *science* makes possible (G.H. Mead).

GOD: (supreme *being*, deity. Opp. *matter*, *devil*). A *universal* concept coming from ancient religious cultures, its universality being a puzzle to anthropologists. *God* is the species-specific human projection of a perfect guiding moral anthropomorph. *Morality* is the uppermost human attribute of consciousness, a replica of the *sense* of nature (Feuerbach). *God*, as an idealized leader that originally was a Goddess (Bachofen), is the result of the psychological projection of a perfect human to be emulated. Morally the opposite of a *God* is a demon, an incarnation of evil. For many, perhaps most people, *God* remains a repository of *morality*.

GOOD SENSE: (1726 sound practical judgment. Opp. *commonsense, sophistication*). Sound judgment often instinctive or unlearned and therefore more in sync with the evolutionary process. *Good sense* is *instinctual disposition*, adhering to the *morality* of *evolution* and influenced by forms of explanation such as *science*. It is ideologically perverted into commonsense (Gramsci).

HABIT: (mid-15c., customary, belonging to one's inherent disposition. Opp. *instinct*). Learned stereotypical *behavior* similar to and derived from *instinct*.

HOMO SAPIENS: (1802 the genus of human beings. Opp. *brute*). William Turton's translation of Linnaeus, coined in Modern Latin: man that is wise. Used in logical and scholastic writing for human *being*. A term that would deserve revision since, as we know it is not homo but *femina* that started culture, and no *particular* wisdom but *universal* mediatory conscious *activity* that qualifies the species.

I: (12 C., a shortening of Old English ic, the first *person* singular nominative pronoun. Opp. *accusative and dative me*). *Ego* or *subject*. What appears phenomenologically from the expression of the *self* after having negotiated an outcome, proper to present conditions, with its dialectical objective *self*-counterpart mediated by *me*.

The active and observable part of the *self* that objectifies.

IDEA: (late 14c., archetype, concept of a thing in the *mind* of God. Opp. *symbol*). A thought. The *meaning* aspect of symbols. (GH Mead.).

IDEOLOGY: (1796, *science* of ideas. Opp. *consciousness*). Consciousness corrupted by lack of universality, serving only the *particular* interests of an exclusionary group. Ideas pseudo-logically spun in a class society. In *patriarchy* it defines *reality* according to the interests of the ruling class. *Ideology* started necessarily as *religion* but as such it was universal, a necessary form of *alienation* when *consciousness* and *morality* were archaic and underdeveloped. *Ideology* is inherently an inescapable false *form* of *consciousness*. True *consciousness* is geared to serve the universality of the species. *Ideology* can only be fought with universalizing, inclusionary *ideology*.

IDEALIZATION: (1786, making ideal what is real. Opp: *actualization, realization*). The use of imagination to alter the representation of the *reality* of the *self*; converts real *self* into the idealized *self* of the neurotic. (Horney).

INDIVIDUAL: (c. 1600 single *object* or thing. Opp. *universal, particular*). Singular. Distinct from *particular*: individuality is the third stage (moment) of the Concept in Hegel's triad of *universal – particular – individual*. Historically the *individual* emerges from the *particular culture* within the *universal* of the species. In other words, the *individual* emerges from the universal through the *particular*.

INERTIA: (1713, that property of *matter* by virtue of which it retains its state of rest or of uniform rectilinear motion so long as no foreign cause changes that state. Opp. motion, *activity*). A state of repose or stillness that exists in nature only phenomenologically, in appearance, and relative to motion. The concept is metaphorically applied to objects that, to the senses, do not appear to move. In this *sense*, the concept has been applied to the accretion of past human history and its effect (Sartre).

INHIBITION: (late 14c., formal prohibition; interdiction of legal proceedings by authority. Opp. *act*). Blocked expression, temporary suspension, *repression*.

INSTINCT: (mid-15c., animal faculty of intuitive *perception*). A natural complex of mediated reflexes arranged in a specific way with an adaptive purpose, and genomically encoded for expression in a nervous system. Part of the good-*sense* of nature. *Instinct* is built-in in animals to satisfy basic natural necessities, and its characteristic is to be stereotypically bound as a response to a specific stimulus. For Darwin *instinct* is animal *intelligence*, the precursor of human *intelligence* in the design of natural *selection*. In humans *instinct* is mediated to become *intelligence* and habit.

INSTINCTUAL DISPOSITION: (1931, modified *instinct*). *Instinct* transformed by *culture,* human *mediation* and through learning, into *habit* (Briffault). *Instinctual disposition* conserves the proclivity or tendency, what Freud called *drive*. In natural *selection*, it is opposite in males and females; females select and males fight to be selected (Darwin).

INTELLIGENCE: (c. 1400, faculty of understanding, comprehension. Opp. brute) Behaviorally applied practical *consciousness.* The *particular form consciousness* takes when it is practically deployed in problem solving. The *intelligence* concept of Binet follows the capitalist mode of accumulation and individualistic *ideology*; it is quantitative. The *intelligence* concept of Vygotsky follows a relational *ideology*; it is cooperative, qualitative and *intersubjective*. *Intelligence* and knowledge are deployed in the process of behavior.

INTERPERSONAL: (1911, *behavior* between people in an encounter. Opp. *intrapsychic*). The relation between two persons. Psychoanalytically the shift from an intrapsychic perspective, typical of Freud, to a relational view that, more dialectically, became *intersubjective* (H.S, Sullivan).

INTERSUBJECTIVE: (1883, existing between conscious minds. Opp. *solipsistic*). The reverberating phenomenon of reciprocally *self*-correcting attitudes and gestures conforming the material process of *interpersonal* communication in social relationships.

IT: (1923, *unconscious.* Opp. *superego*). Symptomatic manifestation of *repression* (Groddeck). In Freud's theory what was not accessible to *consciousness* besides the repository of *repression* (Id). The instinctual *object* upon which the *self* stands.

LABOR: (c. 1300, a task, a project. Opp. *idleness*). The prototype of human *activity* geared to *need* fulfillment typified in human reproduction at birth. *Self*-expression through *objectification*. The necessary condition for effecting exchange of *matter* between man and nature for survival. The everlasting nature-imposed condition of human *existence*, and therefore independent of every social phase of that *existence*, or rather common to every such phase (Marx).

LANGUAGE: (late 13c., words, what is said, conversation, talk. Opp. *meaninglessness, silence*). The bulk of human expression starting with meaningful attitudes, gestures and their *objectification*. *Language* is manifest in all historical human objectifications such as art, institutions, languages and *speech*.

LOGIC: (mid-14c., branch of *philosophy* that treats of forms of thinking, *science* of distinction of true from false reasoning. Opp. *irrationality*). The study of forms of *thought* used in reasoning, social practice and history. The first type was dialectical used by the Pre-Socratics. Then came the formal *logic* of Aristotle, used mostly by Idealists that gave precedence to the Platonic forms over their *reality*. Hegel brought back the dialectical *logic* that was also adopted by Marx and his followers.

MARKET: (early 12c., a meeting at a fixed time for buying and selling livestock and provisions. Opp. *barter*). By analogy, a virtual social space where products are sold and prices agreed in a way approximating the "ideal" conditions of the ancient marketplace. An institution in which the needs of people are met by the product of the labor of other people in a network of exchange relations connecting everyone to everyone else. The metaphor for commodity exchange, a *displacement* from exploitative production that enhances human *alienation*.

MASTER-SLAVE PARADIGM: (1807, Hegel's theory of humanization by recogntion. Opp. *zone of proximal development paradigm*). A parable used by Hegel to illustrate the birth and development of human *consciousness* and *self* in the process of humanization. *It* represents the exploitative patriarchal paradigm.

MATTER: (early 14c., physical substance generally. Opp. *energy*). Denoting all that exists outside of and independently of *thought* – objective *reality*. A philosophical category form Marx the most fundamental.

MATRIARCHY: (1881, family or tribe headed by a mother. Opp. *patriarchy*). The first form of social organization implemented by mothers. *Matriarchy* provided leadership during the transition from the animal to the human stage of *evolution*, and from *evolution* to history. Evolutionarily it starts in the last bifurcation in the hominin branch; historically the first epoch, the first chapter of human history in old anthropology called savagery. It started with a revolution through which females of the species, for the first time, implemented solidarity towards their liberation, as a class, from natural randomness and male sexual oppression. *Matriarchy* was communist as there was no private property, it was non-hierarchical, internally peaceful and collaborative, and a gift rather than exchange-based *economy*.

ME: (? Old English *me* (dative), *me*, mec (accusative); oblique cases of *I*. Opp. *I*). The other, internally objectified part of the *self* besides the *I*. It represents inherited *culture*, tradition, what Marx called the *ensemble of the social relations* and G.H. Mead considered socialization after William James. *Me* is the compounded social *object*.

MEANING: (c. 1300, *sense*, import, intent. Opp. *meaningless*). The form of gestures that intersubjectively conveys the form of objects or processes. The significant ingredient of reverberating social communication. For Vygotsky social *sense*, one of the zones of *sense*, the most stable and precise zone, the product of the word or *gesture*. Meaning arises and lies within the field of the relation between the *gesture* of a given human organism and the subsequent *behavior* of this organism as indicated to another human organism by that *gesture*. Meaning is implicit, if not always explicit, in the relationship among the various phases of the *social act* to which it refers, and out of which it develops. Its development is symbolic in humans.

MEDIATION: (Late XIV C., a division in the middle). An intermediary necessarily act between heterogeneous terms, *i.e.*, human labor between nature and humans or language between subjects' consciousness. *Existence* or definition of a thing contingent on the revelation of its relation to another thing. The properties of things are revealed in their interconnection with other things. A mirror mediates a thing and its image through its property of reflection. Knowledge of *reality* is mediated by past experience, by reflective capacity, *reason,* and memory. The central thesis of Marxist psychology is that all human *activity* is mediated by artifacts such as words, money, tools, other people or organizations, institutions, *etc. Reification* displaces power from human *activity* to the resulting artifact. The mediating *subject,* if unconsciously, is irremediably involved in the labor process, in the ownership of the means of production, in the historical development of the forces of production, in the *state* and political leadership, and in the form of *social consciousness.* Legally *mediation* is used to denote conflict-solving, and in Hegel the syllogism is *mediation* of any two terms by the third. *Mediation* also connotes introduction of an alteration within a natural gap such as between stimulus and response in Pavlov's conditioning, or in Freud's defense.

MIND: (Late 12c., memory, remembrance, state of *being* remembered; *thought*, purpose; conscious *mind*, intellect, intention. Opp. brute). In this book the term is used metaphorically as the container of *consciousness*. *Mind* is the twofold nature of human beings as a species: the explicit individuality of *consciousness* and will, and the universality that knows and wills what is substantive. *Mind* is what it does, behavior, and its history is its own *act*, its *act being* to make itself the *object* of its own consciousness objectified as *mind* (Hegel). *Mind* arises and develops in a social process, through communication by a conversation of meaningful gestures. Reflexiveness, the turning-back of the experience of the *individual* upon himself, allows the social process to be brought into the experience of the individuals involved in it. Each individuals takes the attitude of the other toward himself, allowing him to empathically modify the process of the social act. Reflexiveness is the essential condition, within the social process, for the development of *mind* (Mead).

MIRRORING: (1590s reflecting. Opp. *ignoring*). Subjective acknowledging and mimicking the other. Important mechanism in the creation of *self*-identity starting from other-identity. Mirror neurons have been identified in apes and human's frontal cortex. The first humanizing mirror of humans is the mothering one, as has been documented by neurobiology (Schore). A relevant quote from Marx: "It is with man as with commodities. Since he comes into the world neither with a looking glass in his hand, nor as a Fichtean philosopher, to whom '*I* am *I*' is sufficient, man first sees and recognizes himself in other men. Peter only establishes his own identity as a man by first comparing himself with Paul as *being* of like kind. And thereby Paul, just as he stands in his Pauline personality, becomes to Peter the type of the genus homo." (Marx, *Das Kapital*. Ch.1, Footnote 19).

MORALITY: (Late XIV C., manner, *character*. Opp. *immorality*). Essential set of principles in humans, concerning the distinction between right and wrong or good and bad *behavior*. How a *person* acts in relation to their rights and the ethics of her or his society. *Morality* of individuals is fundamentally based on the kind of society they live and the class position in that society that they occupy. Moral incontinence was a term used by the Greek philosophers as opposite of *morality*, today psychopathy or sociopathy. Based on the fact that *evolution* selects, Karen Horney proposed a *morality of evolution*. Non-evolutionary applied *morality* has led to *civilization*.

MORALITY OF *EVOLUTION*: (1950, natural right and wrong. Opp. *ideological morality*). Objective *morality*, a guide for human *morality* in secular society. *Evolution* selected the human species to demonstrate increasing solidarity and inclusive universality, moral by design. In other words, progressively human.

MYTH: (1818 *speech*, *thought*, story, *myth*, anything delivered by word of mouth. Opp. *philosophy*, *science*). Precursor of *religion*, philosophy and *science* as explanatory model. It remains an ingredient of those explanations used to fill gaps in understanding, or purposefully to mystify.

NEED: (before 900, necessity, compulsion, duty; hardship, distress; errand, business. Opp. *nonessential*). Necessity is what naturally has to be, necessarily, as it is. *Need* has the connotation of historicity and can be spurious in that it can be based on unnecessary mediations introduced by humans as in advertising that creates needs. The felt lag that prompts human *activity* is always a mixture, natural and social, and determined by sexual dual *instinctual disposition*.

NOTHINGNESS: (1630s nonexistence. Opp. *thing*). The immediate, indeterminate notion of being (Hegel). The absence of *being* experienced by humans as a constant state of incompleteness vis à vis *God* (Sartre). The experience of *morality* particularly hindered in patriarchal society by *being's* having been replaced by having.

OBJECT: (late 14c., tangible thing, something perceived or presented to the senses. Opp. *Subject*). A physical entity devoid of *self*-representation. In itself, not for itself, unknowable for Kant and other idealists including Lacan.

OBJECTIFICATION: (1860, noun of action from objectify. Opp: *recognition*). The process whereby human beings materially externalize themselves onto external *reality* through *labor*. Human expressive power attributed to objects. *Objectification* of women is the attempt at lack of *recognition* of their *subjectivity*.

PARTICULAR: (late 14 C., a part or section of a whole. Opp: *universal, individual*). A member of a class defined by properties. The *particular* can be seen as individual or universal sharing of both. Distinct from *individual*: particularity is the second stage (moment) of the Concept in Hegel's triadic syllogism of *universal – particular – individual*.

PATRIARCHY: (1560s, system of society or government by fathers or elder males of the community. Opp. *matriarchy*). The age in history that started with the enslavement of mothers and the shift of social governance to hierarchically organized males. It comprises loosely the last ten-thousand years of *civilization*. American anthropologist Evelyn Reed has uniquely proposed an intermediate phase of fratriarchy, when a sort of brotherhood prevailed.

PERCEPTION: (late 14c., receiving, collection. Opp: sensation, *thought*). Immediate whole experience of the object acknowledged by the senses. *Perception* is neither the passive awareness of an *object* nor a bundle of sensations mechanically united, but rather one kind of action. A "telescoped" *act* in which there is immediate experience of what would result should we go through a series of movements. Ice looks cold because it would produce certain effects were we to go toward it and touch it. The imagery of the past fuses with the excitation of the present and objects that have been organized are thus perceived (G.H. Mead).

PERSON: (early 13 C human *being*; originally mask, false face. Opp. *self, role*). The *self* objectified to be perceived by other. The external version of the *self*, as *language* is the external version of *consciousness*. What *self* presents to others based on the negotiation between what *self* is and what others expect from a *role* (Sartre), therefore subject to idealized transformation (Horney). Historically the concept *person* preceded that of *self*.

PERSONALITY: (late 14c., "quality or fact of *being* a *person*. Opp: *selfhood*). Man's idiosyncratic appearance derived from nature and mediated by attitudes and habits learned culturally. Personal acting is always determined within a society with expectations. The ongoing social process with its prescribed habits, customs, *language*, and institutions is a demanding pre-existent organization into which every child is born to be shaped by it.

PHILOSOPHY: (c. 1300, knowledge, body of knowledge. Opp: *myth, science*). Mode of cultural explanation that followed *myth* and *religion* and preceded *science*. Hegel saw it as representing a dialogical chain of epochs with philosophers as interlocutors.

PHRATRY: (1833, a kinship group forming a subdivision of a Greek phyle, the largest political subdivision among the ancient Athenians. Opp: *phyle*). Second to the *gens*, the *phratry*, an assemblage of related *gentes* united in a higher association for certain common objectives as a sort of brotherhood.

PRAXIS: (1580's, practice, exercise, action). The synchronicity of *consciousness* with social *activity*. The term is also used to designate the application of theories to practice; but theories may represent corrupt *ideology,* in which *sense* it is not true praxis in the Marxist *sense*, practice guided by *consciousness*. Conscious, not ideological, human *activity*.

PROGRESS: (late 14c., a going on, action of walking forward. Opp: *stagnation, regression*). The increase of the power of life to control the conditions of its *activity*, and the consequent extension of their scope and of that power (Briffault).

PSYCHOANALYSIS: (1806, the analysis of the *mind*. Opp: *hypnotism, behaviorism*). A school of psychology based on the study of *unconscious* phenomena. The *unconscious* as an entity contains the product of *self-repression*. The notion was challenged by Sartre on ontological grounds and replaced by bad faith. Ideologically conscious agents have bad faith, which in the oppressed may be *unconscious* (de Beauvoir).

REALITY: (1540s, quality of having *existence*. Opp. *fantasy*). What exists independent of *consciousness*. Nature from which *con-*

sciousness has developed as a property achieved during *evolution,* for human *adaptation. Reality* is culturally defined, and therefore *subject* to the distortions of *ideology.*

REASON: (early 14c., to question someone, also to challenge. Opp. *understanding*) Discursive thought. A quality of *thought* that operates between feeling and reaction. A *adaptation* of the organism to the most general and fundamental *character* of man's external environment (Briffault). The ultimate purpose of *reason* is to comprehend total unity, break down false or limited distinctions, and resolve conflicts. In so far as *reason* reveals contradictions in the products of the understanding, it is dialectical; in so far as it resolves these contradictions in higher unities, it is speculative (Hegel).

RECOGNITION: (mid-15c., knowledge of an event or incident; understanding. Opp: *ignoring*). The fundamental *need* humans must fulfill through mirroring, *recognition* by another human, in order to become human. *Recognition* is what, in humans, idiosyncratically fulfills *desire*, the foundation of *subjectivity* (Hegel).

REFLEX: (1877 involuntary nerve stimulation. Opp: *instinct*). Here the neurological response to an environmental stimulus. The precursor of more complex *instinct* and of humanly mediated *instinctual disposition.*

REIFICATION: (1846). A form of *alienation* in which the power of *subjectivity* is projected into a material *object*, typically money, machine or fetish (Lukacs).

RELIGION: (c. 1200, state of life bound by monastic vows, also conduct indicating a belief in a divine power. Opp: *secularism*). A form of alienated consciousness. The first form of culture based on projective animism. Form of *social consciousness* in which natural forces are conceived as "supernatural" forms and which constitutes a systematic and dogmatic doctrine supported by an organization.

REPRESSION: (late 14c., to check, restrain. Opp: *free association*). Voids content from *consciousness*. Psychological *sense* is from 1908). A universal defense mechanism in *psychoanalysis*, it ensures that what is unacceptable to the conscious *mind*, politically incorrect, which would arouse anxiety if recalled, is prevented from entering into it (Freud).

ROLE: (early 17th c., the roll of paper on which the actor's part was written. Opp. *person*). The specific part played by a *person* in a social organization. Universal social form of classification of the members of a society.

SCIENCE: (mid-14c., what is known, knowledge, acquired by study; information. Opp: *philosophy*, *religion*). The best and most recent form of explanation, based on observation, proof and experiment. Preceded by *philosophy*, based on reasoning, in turn preceded by *religion* and *myth* based on belief.

SELECTION: (1837, applied to the methodical actions of breeders: Opp: *randomness*). The mechanism Darwin proposed for the direction of nature in growingly complex species: natural selection. It is the dialectical, reciprocal interaction between an organism and its *particular* environment.

SELF: (Old English, one's own *person*. For Locke that which feels, acts, or thinks. Opp: *object*). The internal *self*-representation of a *person*. The *self* has two component parts, *I* or *self-agency* or individual *subject*, and *me*, or internalized *culture* or *object* (GH Mead). The *self* healthily aims at *self*-realization, becoming more human, under optimal circumstances, that is if uncontaminated by repression and *ideology* (Horney). The *self* is the *structure* that characterizes a *subject* and that constantly totalizes consciousness in practice by updating all present conditions.

SELF-CONSCIOUSNESS: (1680s, aware of one's action, a word of the English Enlightenment, Locke was using it by 1690. Opp: *alienation*). *Consciousness* of *consciousness* (Hegel). In the human *subject* exclusively, the evolutionary capacity of *consciousness* extended to the representation of itself in the *act* of *consciousness*. Meta-*consciousness*. *Self-consciousness* transforms *activity* into *agency*, protagonism and *praxis* (Marx).

SELF-IDEALIZATION: (1786, make ideal, consider as ideal. Opp: *self-realization*) Karen Horney's culture-determined detour from *being* and human potential, to alienated actualization. Historically *civilization* idealized itself in philosophical idealism since the Greek philosophers mainly Plato until Bacon and Spinoza.

SELF-REALIZATION: (1839 action of making real. Opp. *self-idealization*). The position (closest to the attainment) of a state of *being* fully human (Horney), that is acting through a *praxis* guided by *consciousness* as opposed to *ideology* (Marx). This follows the design of *evolution* that characterizes humans as morally conscious (Horney), and the cultural project of a full, totalized, universal humanity (Marx). The *self* is never fully realized; it follows an asymptotic nearness, always getting closer but never attaining perfection as new needs appear. Shared universality with all others, and *universal* empathy.

SENSE: (c. 1400, faculty of *perception, meaning*, import, interpretation. Opp: *nonsense*). The direction of nature. *Individual meaning*, effect of a reasoned image of reality. *Good sense* conserves its evolutionary direction; *commonsense* is usually contaminated by *ideology* (Gramsci).

SLAVERY: (1550s, severe toil, hard work, drudgery. Opp. *freedom, selfhood*). The stage of history that came after primitive communism and *matriarchy*. *Slavery* deprived women, prisoners of war, children, and workers of their most basic rights including the right to life and the right to control one's own body and participate in a social contract. Slave's rights became the rights of the slave-owner. *Slavery* is also, the first stage of *patriarchy*. Although hidden under more sophisticated forms, *slavery* is still extant under the form of *wage labor*. The end of *slavery* will be with a society based on substantive equality in the fulfillment of needs and no exploitation of human by human.

SOCIAL BEING: (1859, *essence* of humans. Opp: *abstract being*). *Being* necessarily connected to others of its species or class. It is not the *consciousness* (Lynnaeus' sapiens) of humans that specifically determines their *being*; on the contrary, their *social being* produces and determines their *consciousness*. Humans are social foremost through their cooperative labor (Marx).

SOCIAL CONSCIOUSNESS: (1630s -1870, the internal knowledge of friendly gathering. Opp: *social alienation*). Representations through which different spheres of society are reproduced. They can be broken down into economic, scientific, moral, legal, political, religious, *etc.* According to Marx and Engels the economic *structure* of society which essentially determines social processes does not exist in the economic *social consciousness*; it is *unconscious*. Formal accrual of mankind's social experience and social practice that does not perish with the death of *individuals*. It is handed down from one generation to the next by a process in which it is not created afresh, but modified (Leontiev).

SOCIALISM: (1789, society organized as a national workshop (Talleyrand). Opp. *capitalism*). The only scientifically proposed future stage of history (Marx and Engels) to follow *capitalism* and *patriarchy*, organized in such a manner that any *individual*, man or woman, truly finds at birth, and continues through their life to have, equal access to the means for their human development. In it exploitation would be impossible, and long-standing human *alienation* would begin its correction in a political climate of dialogue, *collaboration* and the elimination of social domination and verticality. A society based on the *universal* fulfillment of needs.

SOUL: (Old English, a substantial entity believed to be that in each *person* which lives, feels, thinks and wills. Opp. *inanimate*) The predecessor of psyche or *consciousness* in metaphysical *philosophy*. Connexion with God. The reader who finds any comfort in the *idea* of the *Soul*, William James states, is perfectly free to continue to believe in it; for our reasonings have not established the non-*existence* of the *Soul*; they have only proved its superfluity for scientific purposes.

SPECIES BEING: (XIV C. A class of *existence*. Opp. *asocial being*). Term used by Feuerbach to refer to the *ensemble of the so-*

cial relations (Marx).

SPEECH: (Old English, *act* of speaking, formal utterance; *language*: Opp. *language*). Vocal *gesture* produced through the manipulation of air passing through the laryngeal, nasopharyngeal, and buccal organs. It is *behavior* specialized in carrying *meaning*, and the *meaning* is a result of the social effects of the *speech*. The importance of the vocal *gesture* is that the one who stimulates another, since he hears his own voice, stimulates himself at the same time. The *self*-stimulation makes possible *self*-response and this response is influenced by the response of the other. The result is the ability to take the *role* of the other which becomes sometimes empathic introspection but, what is even more important, leads the *self* to take the *attitude* of the other to himself, thus *becoming* an *object* to himself, with all that this implies (GH Mead).

STATE: (c. 1300, political organization of a country, supreme civil power, government, Opp: family, *civil society*). Civil governance. To an organized collectivity, the equivalent of the *self*. The *mind* of a nation, lawfully permeating all relationships and *consciousness* of its citizens. The constitution of any given nation depends on the *character* and development of its *self-consciousness*. Here its subjective freedom is rooted, the actuality of its constitution. Hence every nation has the constitution appropriate to it and suitable for it (Marx).

STRUCTURE: (mid-15c., action or process of building or construction. Opp. *function*). The ensemble of relations that constitute an *object*.

SUBJECT: (early 14c., *person* under control or dominion of another, specifically a government or ruler. Opp: *object*). Today *self*-controlled. In humans the result of internalization of control by the *self* through collective identification with the state. The knowing *subject* is not the *individual* but society, and *self*-control is replica of government. The *individual subject* represents the manner of *existence* of the social *subject*.

SUBJECTIVITY: (1803, characteristic of one who is submissive or obedient. Opp: *objectivity*). The evolutionary capacity to mediate, related to *consciousness, agency, personhood, reality,* and *truth,* exclusive of humans. The capacity to *self*-regulate, submit to oneself, related to conscious experiences, *self,* perspective, feelings, beliefs, and desires. *Subjectivity* is the result of the evolutionary internalization of external forms, images, of objects and their properties and relations, including the *self* as *object.*

SUBLATION: (1899s, assimilate a prior entity into a present one. Opp: *destruction*). From German aufheben to transcend or to supersede without annihilating. Literally aufheben meant "to pocket," as when you pocket others' product and they continue to work for you. Sublate, supersede, and transcend have a similar connotation contrary to "abolish." *Sublation* carries the connotation of inclusion of the old within the new (MIA Encyclopedia).

SUBLIMATION: (Late XIVC refinement. Opp. *regression, inhibition, condensation*). *Psychoanalysis* borrowed the term from chemistry where it means phase transition, or a change in a state of *matter,* just like melting, freezing, and evaporation. Change from a solid to a gas form without passing through a liquid phase. *Civilization* a result of instinctual *sublimation* (Freud). *Consciousness* a result of *reflex* conditioning (Pavlov).

SUPEREGO: (1924, part of the psyche which controls the impulses of the id. OPP it, *ego*). The internalization of societal rules (Freud). *Ensemble of the social relations* (Marx). *Me* (G.H. Mead).

SUPERSTRUCTURE: (1640s, built on top of something else. Opp: *base, infrastructure*). The forms of *consciousness, culture* and *self*-governance humans produce and reconstruct according to their level of development and the mode of production and reproduction of their material lives. Although reciprocal and therefore relatively autonomous, this *superstructure* is in the last instance determined by its *base,* because it cannot exist without it.

SYMBOL: (early 15c., creed, summary, religious belief, token, mark. Opp: *image*). Something that represents or stands for something else. The vehicle for a meaningful *idea* other than itself. Symbolic gestures, shared, constitute the *mind* (G.H. Mead).

TEMPERAMENT: (late 14c., proportioned mixture of elements. Opp: *character, personality*). Inborn set of *activity* characteristics of a *person* and their fit to the social environment.

THOUGHT: (Old English, process of thinking, a *thought*; compassion, to conceive of in the *mind*, to consider. Opp: action) The social activity of *consciousness* that semiotically mediates action in humans. Evolutionarily *thought* and *consciousness* were co-created by organism and environment, through the introduction of tools. Mediating activity is instrumental and its human paradigm is *language* (Vygotsky). Temporary productive *inhibition* of *reflex* arc or instinctual action. The *mirroring* reciprocal response of two persons' *becoming* a stimulus to control their action as they share the *meaning* of each other's *act* in their own experience. In order for *thought* to exist there must be symbols, vocal gestures generally, which arouse in the *individual* himself the response that he is calling out in the other, and such that from the point of view of that response he is able to direct his later conduct. It involves not only communication in the *sense* in which birds and animals communicate with each other, but also an arousal in the *individual* himself of the response which he is calling out in the other *individual*, a taking of the *role* of the other, a tendency to *act* as the other *person* acts. One participates in the same process the other *person* is carrying out and controls his action with reference to that participation. It is that which constitutes the *meaning* of an *object*, namely, the common response in one's *self* as well as in the other *person*, which becomes, in turn, a stimulus to one's *self* (GH Mead).

TOTALIZATION: (1590s, proceeding towards the whole of something. Opp: *fragmentation, alienation, totalitarian.*). The processes by which randomness is finally understood through its connection to a larger explanatory whole to achieve completeness and unified closure (Hegel).

UNCONSCIOUS: (1712, unaware, not marked by conscious *thought*. Opp: *conscious*). What has been psychologically repressed for safety or political correctness (Freud). What unawares spills out intersubjectively in the conversation of attitudes (GH Mead). *Totalization* taking place beyond the totalizing agent (Meszaros). Collectively, man's lack of *consciousness* particularly of his authorship of history. Real social processes, economic relationships, that do not exist in the economic *social consciousness* (Marx).

UNIVERSAL: (late 14c., pertaining to the whole of something specified; occurring everywhere). The social class for which, at a given point in history, *self*-interested action coincides with the needs of humanity as a whole (Marx). Non-*particular*. The stages (moments) of the Concept in are the *universal*, that develops into the *particular*, that develops into the *individual*. The *universal* constitutes the *essence* of a thing; when a thing is fully developed (actual), the *universal* is concrete. *Thought* is exclusively concerned with universals. The *universal* is also the theoretical expression of the *particular* and the of *individual*, an expression of the law of their *existence* (Hegel). Our laws of *thought* are the abstractions of social intercourse. Our whole process of abstract *thought*, technique and method is essentially social. The organization of the social act answers to what we call the *universal*. Functionally it is the *universal*. (GH Mead)

VALUE: (c. 1300, price equal to the intrinsic worth of a thing. Opp. *price*). Worth or usefulness. Utility of an *object* based on *attitude* of a *subject* (GH Mead). Ultimately, whatsoever promotes the efficiency of the expansion of life's control (Briffault). Economically use *value* and exchange *value* (Marx), are parameters of social *existence* in *matriarchy* and *patriarchy* respectively.

WAGE LABOR: (c. 1300s. A mode of production in *capitalism*. Opp. *capital*). The form of economic relation in *capitalism*, in which laborers sell their capacity to work, their *labor* force essential for human survival and human *self*-expression, as a commodity like any other. *Wage labor* requires a social *structure* with opposite clas-

ses, one that has no other way of surviving, because the other appropriates the socially produced means of production as their private
property. The wage worker is alienated from her/his own labor, his
human *objectification* (Marx) or selfobject. Conditions such as the
price and amount of *wage labor* are set by the *market* and through a
contract. *Wage labor* is the last remnant of *slavery*.

ZONE OF PROXIMAL DEVELOPMENT PARADIGM: (1930,
Vygotsky's theory of human development. Opp. *Hegel's master-slave paradigm*). The area, in the *intersubjective* relationship,
where most optimally the better adapted or more skillful *subject* can
constructive influence the lesser adapted, learning *subject*. This is
considered in this book the prototype of human development from
a matriarchal standpoint. The paradigm of human *collaboration* opposite to the master-slave metaphor of Hegel.

www.ingramcontent.com/pod-product-compliance
Lightning Source LLC
Chambersburg PA
CBHW060301030426
42336CB00011B/900